D1106011

Retracing Our Steps

Studies in Documents From the American Past, Vol. 2

MYRON A. MARTY

H. THEODORE FINKELSTON

Florissant Valley Community College
St. Louis, Missouri

Canfield Press

San Francisco
A Department of Harper & Row, Publishers, Inc.
New York · Evanston · London

About the Cover

"Wells, Fargo and Company's Stage and Express Routes 1867" by Maverick, Stephan & Co., New York. The map is reproduced from the collection of Wells Fargo Bank History Room, San Francisco, California.

Cover and Interior Book Design by Gracia A. Alkema

RETRACING OUR STEPS: STUDIES IN DOCUMENTS FROM THE AMERICAN PAST, Vol. 2

Copyright © 1972 by Myron A. Marty and H. Theodore Finkelston

Printed in the United States of America. All rights reserved. No part of this book may be used or reproduced in any manner whatsoever without written permission except in the case of brief quotations embodied in critical articles and reviews. For information address Harper & Row, Publishers, Inc., 49 East 33rd Street, New York, N.Y. 10016.

International Standard Book Number: 0–06–385436–8

Library of Congress Catalog Card Number: 76–170130

Contents

13. The Cold War: Containing Communism

14. McCarthyism

15. Out of Their Place: Voices of Protest in the 1960s

Preface

How a nation looks at the future depends to a great extent on how it looks at the past. In 1801 President Thomas Jefferson could regard the nation's brief history with satisfaction, and his inaugural address reflected his confidence in the future of the young republic. Today, however, as the country approaches its 200th birthday in the 1970s, national confidence is threatened by uncertainty and apprehension. Now is the time, perhaps more than ever, for a new look at the past.

Jefferson himself invited a retracing of the past in uncertain times. In his inaugural address, he outlined what he believed to be essential principles of government, including such things as "equal and exact justice to all men," "peace, commerce, and honest friendship with all nations, entangling alliances with none," "a jealous care of the right of election by the people," "freedom of religion; freedom of the press; and freedom of person under the protection of habeas corpus." He then asserted:

> These principles form the bright constellation which has gone before us and guided our steps through an age of revolution and reformation. The wisdom of our sages and blood of our heroes have been devoted to their attainment. They should be the creed of our political faith, the text of civic instruction, the touchstone by which to try the services of those we trust; and should we wander from them in moments of error or of alarm, let us hasten to retrace our steps and to regain the road which alone leads to peace, liberty, and safety.

Our aim in this book is to assist students in retracing some of the important steps of the American past. If they conclude that the nation has wandered from the principles Jefferson held so dear, they may be encouraged to help the country "regain the road," or perhaps motivated to redefine the principles in light of historical developments and present circumstances.

The text is edited on the premise that retracing the past is done best through an in-depth study of selected topics. The real value, as well as the real excitement, in studying history comes from digging in here and there to discover what is below the surface. This is most rewarding when documents from primary sources provide the focus of study.

This volume is comprised of seventeen self-contained chapters, each built around a single topic or theme. They are purposely narrow in scope. Our goal has been to select specific issues and ideas from the story of America's development and to retrace them through appropriate documents. Since the documents we have chosen represent only a small portion of those available, students and instructors should exercise caution in drawing conclusions or making judgements on the basis of material included in this text.

Each chapter is organized around a core document. The chapter introduction sets the stage for the core document and presents the theme of the chapter. It has not been our practice to recount factual information generally presented in basic history textbooks or lectures. The introduction to the core document provides information concerning its author, context, purpose or function, and perhaps an appropriate comment about its organization. To help students analyze the source materials, specific points to note are suggested in the document introductions. Difficult or confusing matters have explanatory footnotes. Following the core documents are several questions designed to promote a better understanding of the documents and to provide starters for class discussion. We have tried to phrase the questions so that there is no one answer; in other words, they are open-ended questions. Also included in each chapter is a cluster of related, shorter documents. The brief introductions to these readings include a question or two that help to illustrate the relationship. We have tried to keep each chapter to a manageable length so that supplementary books, especially paperbacks, may also be used. Each chapter concludes with a suggested list of such books.

The nature of this volume's organization permits a selective use of topics. Neither continuity nor understanding of the textual material will be sacrificed if the instructor decides to skip certain chapters, and selection within chapters is also possible. For example, cluster documents may be assigned to the entire class or used for individual assignments. They may be omitted if time does not allow an examination of all the material during a given semester or quarter.

The documents are presented as they appeared originally or in authoritative scholarly editions except for occasional paragraphing. In editing the documents it has been necessary at times to delete sentences or even entire paragraphs. Standard use of ellipses indicates minor omissions, and line spaces within a document indicate the deletion of complete paragraphs.

In presenting this work we express our appreciation to our students and colleagues for the stimulation they have provided us and to Gracia Alkema of Canfield Press for her invaluable editorial guidance. We are also indebted to the library staffs at Florissant Valley Community College (Sidney Reedy was particularly helpful), Washington University, and St. Louis University. The encouragement and assistance we received from our wives, Shirley Marty and Karen Finkelston, is immeasurable. They join us in the hope that teachers and students will find this volume to be an effective, flexible teaching instrument—a worthy supplement to their ingenuity.

Myron A. Marty

H. Theodore Finkelston

1. Jim-Crowism in the Making

The war aims of the Union during the Civil War progressed through three roughly identifiable stages. In the first stage, lasting more than a year after the firing on Fort Sumter in April 1861, the aim—as stated by President Lincoln —was simply to restore the Union. This implied the continued acceptance of the institution of slavery.

For military and diplomatic reasons, emancipation of slaves became an expressed aim in September 1862 with the announcement of the impending Emancipation Proclamation, and thus a second stage emerged.

As the war neared its conclusion, the radical wing in the Republican Party formulated a third aim: civil equality for the freedmen. In the face of Northern indifference, well-organized Southern intransigence, the illiteracy, inexperience, and poverty of the freedmen themselves, and the frailty of the Republican Party in the South, the Radicals succeeded in making civil equality a national issue for a decade after the war ended.

Early efforts to provide immediate assistance to the freedmen and to establish a long-range program to insure them a viable place in the economy were meager and short-lived. But a remarkable set of laws was enacted to protect the freed slaves from falling back into servitude, either in the old or in some new form. Between 1866 and 1875, eleven acts and three constitutional amendments became law.

The supporters of these laws and amendments believed that civil equality could be promoted through such measures. But as the promise of the black

1

vote diminished, concern for the welfare of the freedmen lessened, and the Radicals lost their grip on national power. The civil rights laws either fell into disuse or were overturned in the courts, and a new set of laws, referred to as "Jim-Crow" laws, developed for the purpose of promoting civil *inequality*.[1]

Successful court challenges to these Jim-Crow laws and enactment of new civil rights laws in the past two decades (a "Second Reconstruction") has awakened interest in the civil rights laws of the First Reconstruction. This chapter is concerned chiefly with the Supreme Court decision in 1883, which marked a turning point in efforts to promote civil equality by law and made Jim-Crowism possible.

Core Document

On the Civil Rights Cases: A Speech by Frederick Douglass at Lincoln Hall

In 1875 Congress passed the last civil rights bill until 1957, when another mild one was enacted. By the time the 1875 bill was passed, the courts had already begun to question the validity of such laws. Between 1871 and 1875 more than 3,000 criminal cases under these laws were handled in federal courts in the South, with only about twenty percent leading to conviction.

It was therefore no surprise when the Supreme Court ruled in 1883 that the key provisions of the 1875 act were unconstitutional. Nevertheless, it was a major blow to the blacks, who had placed their hopes in the federal government working in their behalf. Without knowing the details of either the act or the decision, it is possible to gain an appreciation of their disappointment in the following speech by Frederick Douglass.

Douglass was born a slave around 1817. He escaped from slavery in 1838 and soon became an able orator, journalist, and author in the abolitionist cause. During the war he played a key role in recruiting black troops for the Union army. As a loyal Republican following the war, he served as marshall and recorder of deeds of the District of Columbia and as minister resident and consul general to Haiti. He died in 1895.

In writing about the 1883 Supreme Court decision in his Life and Times, *Douglass noted that the "colored men in the capital of the nation where the deed was done were quick to perceive its disastrous significance." In the helpless horror of the moment, he said, they called upon him and others to express their*

---

[1]The name "Jim Crow" derived from an act by an entertainer who based it on an anonymous song called *Jim Crow*.
Frederick Douglass, *Life and Times of Frederick Douglass* (Boston: DeWolfe and Fisk Co., 1892), pp. 654–69.

grief and indignation. This they did in Lincoln Hall, which was "packed by an audience of all colors." About 2,000 persons were present and about as many more could not get in.

In studying Douglass' speech, pay attention to:
- *the depth of the emotions he expressed.*
- *signs of oratorical restraint.*
- *actions he advocated.*
- *the larger historical context into which he put the decision.*
- *the arguments he raised against the validity of the decision.*
- *his ideas on balance and separation of powers and on the "object and intention" of laws.*
- *the distinction drawn between civil rights and social rights.*

OCTOBER 22, 1883

I have only a few words to say to you this evening. . . . It may be, after all, that the hour calls more loudly for silence than for speech. Later on in this discussion, when we shall have before us the full text of the Supreme Court and the dissenting opinion of Judge Harlan, who must have weighty reasons for separating from his associates and incurring thereby, as he must, an amount of criticism from which even the bravest man might shrink, we may be in a better frame of mind, better supplied with facts, and better prepared to speak calmly, correctly, and wisely than now. The temptation at this time is to speak more from feeling than reason, more from impulse than reflection.

We have been, as a class, grievously wounded, wounded in the house of our friends, and this wound is too deep and too painful for ordinary and measured speech.

> When a deed is done for freedom,
> Through the broad earth's aching breast
> Runs a thrill of joy prophetic,
> Trembling on from East to West.

But when a deed is done for slavery, caste, and oppression, and a blow is struck at human progress, whether so intended or not, the heart of humanity sickens in sorrow and writhes in pain. It makes us feel as if some one were stamping upon the graves of our mothers, or desecrating our sacred temples. Only base men and oppressors can rejoice in a triumph of injustice over the weak and defenseless, for weakness ought itself to protect from assaults of pride, prejudice, and power.

The cause which has brought us here tonight is neither common nor trivial. Few events in our national history have surpassed it in magnitude, importance and significance. It has swept over the land like a cyclone, leaving moral desolation in its track. This decision belongs with a class of judicial and legislative wrongs by which we have been oppressed.

We feel it as we felt years ago the furious attempt to force the accursed system of slavery upon the soil of Kansas—as we felt the enactment of the Fugitive Slave Bill, the repeal of the Missouri Compromise, and the Dred Scott decision. I look upon it as one more shocking development of that moral weakness in high places which has attended the conflict between the spirit of liberty and the spirit of slavery, and I venture to predict that it will be so regarded by aftercoming generations. Far down the ages, when men shall wish to inform themselves as to the real state of liberty, law, religion, and civilization in the United States at this juncture of our history, they will overhaul the proceedings of the Supreme Court, and read this strange decision declaring the Civil Rights Bill unconstitutional and void.

From this more than from many volumes they will learn how far we had advanced, in this year of grace, from the barbarism of slavery toward civilization and the rights of man.

Fellow-citizens! Among the great evils which now stalk abroad in our land, the one, I think, which most threatens to undermine and destroy the foundations of our free institutions in this country is the great and apparently increasing want of respect entertained for those to whom are committed the responsibility and the duty of administering our government. On this point I think all good men must agree, and against the evil I trust you feel the deepest repugnance, and that we will, neither here nor elsewhere, give it the least breath of sympathy or encouragement. We should never forget, whatever may be the incidental mistakes or misconduct of rulers, that government is better than anarchy, and that patient reform is better than violent revolution.

But while I would increase this feeling and give it the emphasis of a voice from heaven, it must not be allowed to interfere with free speech, honest expression of opinion, and fair criticism. To give up this would be to give up progress, and to consign the nation to moral stagnation, putrefaction, and death.

In the matter of respect for dignitaries, it should, however, never be forgotten that duties are reciprocal, and that while the people should frown down every manifestation of levity and contempt for those in power, it is the duty of the possessors of power so to use it as to deserve and insure respect and reverence.

To come a little nearer to the case now before us. The Supreme Court of the United States, in the exercise of its high and vast constitutional power, has suddenly and unexpectedly decided that the law intended to secure to colored people the civil rights guaranteed to them by the following provision of the Constitution of the United States, is unconstitutional and void. Here it is:

"No state," says the Fourteenth Amendment, "shall make or enforce any law which shall abridge the privileges or immunities of citizens of the United States; nor shall any state deprive any person of life, liberty, or property, without due process of the law; or deny any person within its jurisdiction the equal protection of the laws."

Now, when a bill has been discussed for weeks and months and even years, in the press and on the platform, in Congress and out of Congress; when it has been calmly debated by the clearest heads and the most skillful and learned lawyers in the land; when every argument against it has been over and over again carefully considered and fairly answered; when its constitutionality has been especially discussed, pro and con; when it has passed the United States House of Representatives and has been solemnly enacted by the United States Senate (perhaps the most imposing legislative body in the world); when such a bill has been submitted to the cabinet of the nation, composed of the ablest men in the land; when it has passed under the scrutinizing eye of the Attorney-General of the United States; when the Executive of the Nation has given to it his name and formal approval; when it has taken its place upon the statute-book and has remained there for nearly a decade, and the country has largely assented to it, you will agree with me that the reasons for declaring such a law unconstitutional and void should be strong, irresistible and absolutely conclusive.

Inasmuch as the law in question is a law in favor of liberty and justice, it ought to have had the benefit of any doubt which could arise as to its strict constitutionality. This, I believe, will be the view taken of it, not only by laymen like myself, but by eminent lawyers as well.

All men who have given any thought to the machinery, structure, and practical operation of our government, must have recognized the importance of absolute harmony between its various departments and their respective powers and duties. They must have seen clearly the mischievous tendency and danger to the body politic of any antagonisms between any of its various branches. . . .

Now let me say here, before I go on a step or two further in this discussion, that if any man has come here tonight with his breast heaving with passion, his heart flooding with acrimony, and wishing and expecting to hear violent denunciation of the Supreme Court on account of this decision, he has mistaken the object of this meeting and the character of the men by whom it is called.

We neither come to bury Caesar nor to praise him. The Supreme Court is the autocratic point in our government. No monarch in Europe has a power more absolute over the laws, lives, and liberties of his people than that court has over our laws, lives, and liberties. Its judges live, and ought to live, an eagle's flight beyond the reach of fear or favor, praise or blame, profit or loss. No vulgar prejudice should touch the members of that court anywhere. Their decisions should come down to us like the calm, clear light of infinite justice. We should be able to think of them and to speak of them with profoundest respect for their wisdom and deepest reverence for their virtue, for what his Holiness the Pope is to the Roman Catholic Church, the Supreme Court is to the American State. Its members are men, to be sure, and may not, like the Pope, claim infallibility, and they are not infallible, but they are the supreme law-giving power of the nation, and their decisions are law until changed by that court.

What will be said here tonight will be spoken, I trust, more in sorrow than in anger—more in a tone of regret than in bitterness and reproach, and more to promote sound views than to find bad motives for unsound views.

We cannot, however, overlook the fact that though not so intended, this decision has inflicted a heavy calamity upon seven millions of the people of this country, and left them naked and defenseless against the action of a malignant, vulgar, and pitiless prejudice from which the Constitution plainly intended to shield them.

It presents the United States before the world as a nation utterly destitute of power to protect the constitutional rights of its own citizens upon its own soil.

It can claim service and allegiance, loyalty and life from them, but it cannot protect them against the most palpable violation of the rights of human nature, rights to secure which governments are established. It can tax their bread and tax their blood, but it has no protecting power for their persons. Its national power extends only to the District of Columbia and the territories— to where the people have no votes, and to where the land has no people. All else is subject to the states. In the name of common sense, I ask what right have we to call ourselves a nation, in view of this decision and of this utter destitution of power? . . .

Today our Republic sits as a queen among the nations of the earth. Peace is within her walls and plenteousness within her palaces, but he is bolder and a far more hopeful man than I am who will affirm that this peace and prosperity will always last. History repeats itself. What has happened once may happen again.

The Negro, in the Revolution, fought for us and with us. In the war of 1812 General Jackson, at New Orleans, found it necessary to call upon the colored people to assist in its defense against England. Abraham Lincoln found it necessary to call upon the Negro to defend the Union against rebellion. In all cases the Negro responded gallantly.

Our legislators, our presidents, and our judges should have a care, lest, by forcing these people outside of law, they destroy that love of country which in the day of trouble is needful to the nation's defense.

I am not here in this presence to discuss the constitutionality or the unconstitutionality of this decision of the Supreme Court. The decision may or may not be constitutional. That is a question for lawyers and not for laymen, and there are lawyers on this platform as learned, able, and eloquent as any who have appeared in this case before the Supreme Court, or as any in the land. To these I leave the exposition of the Constitution, but I claim the right to remark upon a strange and glaring inconsistency of this decision with former decisions, where the rules of law apply. It is a new departure, entirely out of the line of precedents and decisions of the Supreme Court at other times and in other directions where the rights of colored men were concerned. It has utterly ignored and rejected the force and application of the object and intention of the adoption of the Fourteenth Amendment. It has made no account whatever of the intention and purpose of Congress and the President in putting the Civil Rights Bill upon the statute-book of the nation. It has seen fit in this case, affecting a weak and much persecuted people, to be guided by the narrowest and most restricted rules of legal interpretation. It has viewed both the Constitution and the law with a strict regard to their letter, but without any generous recognition and application of their broad and liberal spirit. Upon those narrow principles the decision is logical and legal, of course. But what I complain of, and what every lover of liberty in the United States has a right to complain of, is this sudden and causeless reversal of all the great rules of legal interpretation by which this court was once governed in the construction of the Constitution and of laws respecting colored people.

In the dark days of slavery this court on all occasions gave the greatest importance to intention as a guide to interpretation. The object and intention of the law, it was said, must prevail. Everything in favor of slavery and against the Negro was settled by this object and intention rule. We were over and over again referred to what the framers meant, and plain language itself was sacrificed and perverted from its natural and obvious meaning that the so affirmed intention of these framers might be positively asserted and given the force of law. When we said in behalf of the Negro that the Constitution of the United States was intended to establish justice and to secure the blessings of liberty to ourselves and our posterity, we were told that the words said so, but that that was obviously not its intention—that it was intended to apply only to white people, and that the intention must govern.

When we came to the clause of the Constitution which declares that the immigration or importation of such persons as any of the states may see fit to admit shall not be prohibited, and the friends of liberty declared that this provision of the Constitution did not describe the slave-trade, they were told that while its language applied not to the slaves but to persons, still the object and intention of that clause of the Constitution was plainly to protect the slave-trade, and that that intention was the law and must prevail. When we came to that clause of the Constitution which declares that "No person held to labor or service in one state under the laws thereof, escaping into another, shall in consequence of any law or regulation therein be discharged from such labor or service, but shall be delivered upon claim of the party to whom such labor or service may be due," we insisted that it neither described nor applied to slaves—that it applied only to persons owing service and labor—that slaves did not and could not owe service and labor—that this clause of the Constitution said nothing of slaves or of the masters of slaves—that it was silent as to slave states or free states—that it was simply a provision to enforce a contract and not to force any man into slavery, for the slave could not owe service or make a contract.

We affirmed that it gave no warrant for what was called "The Fugutive Slave Bill," and we contended that the bill was therefore unconstitutional, but our arguments were laughed to scorn by that court and by all the courts of the Country. We were told that the intention of the Constitution was to enable masters to recapture slaves, and that the law of '93 and the Fugitive Slave Law of 1850 were constitutional, binding not only on the state but upon each citizen of the state.

Fellow-citizens! While slavery was the base line of American society, while it ruled the church and state, while it was the interpreter of our law and the exponent of our religion, it admitted no quibbling, no narrow rules of legal or scriptural interpretations of the Bible or of the Constitution. It sternly demanded its pound of flesh, no matter how the scale turned or how much blood was shed in the taking of it. It was enough for it to be able to show the intention to get all it asked in the courts or out of the courts. But now slavery is abolished. Its reign was long, dark, and bloody. Liberty is now the base line of the Republic. Liberty has supplanted slavery, but I fear it has not supplanted the spirit or power of slavery. Where slavery was strong, liberty is now weak.

Oh, for a Supreme Court of the United States which shall be as true to the claims of humanity as the Supreme Court formerly was to the demands of slavery! When that day comes, as come it will, a Civil Rights Bill will not be declared unconstitutional and void, in utter and flagrant disregard of the objects and intentions of the national legislature by which it was enacted and of the rights plainly secured by the Constitution.

This decision of the Supreme Court admits that the Fourteenth Amendment is a prohibition on the states. It admits that a state shall not abridge the privileges or immunities of citizens of the United States, but commits the seeming absurdity of allowing the people of a state to do what it prohibits the state itself from doing.

It used to be thought that the whole was more than a part, that the greater included the less, and that what was unconstitutional for a state to do was equally unconstitutional for an individual member of a state to do. What is a state, in the absence of the people who compose it? Land, air, and water. That is all. Land and water do not discriminate. All are equal before them. This law was made for people. As individuals, the people of the State of South Carolina may stamp out the rights of the Negro wherever they please, so long as they do so as a state, and this absurd conclusion is to be called a law. All the parts can violate the Constitution, but the whole cannot. It is not the act itself, according to this decision, that is unconstitutional. The unconstitutionality of the case depends wholly upon the party committing the act. If the state commits it, the act is wrong; if the citizen of the state commits it, the act is right.

O consistency, thou art indeed a jewel! What does it matter to a colored citizen that a state may not insult and outrage him, if the citizen of the state may? The effect upon him is the same, and it was just this effect that the framers of the Fourteenth Amendment plainly intended by that article to prevent.

It was the act, not the instrument—it was the murder, not the pistol or dagger—which was prohibited. It meant to protect the newly enfranchised citizen from injustice and wrong, not merely from a state, but from the individual members of a state. It meant to give the protection to which his citizenship, his loyalty, his allegiance, and his services entitled him, and this meaning and this purpose and this intention are now declared by the Supreme Court of the United States to be unconstitutional and void.

I say again, fellow-citizens, Oh, for a Supreme Court which shall be as true, as vigilant, as active and exacting in maintaining laws enacted for the protection of human rights, as in other days was that court for the destruction of human rights!

It is said that this decision will make no difference in the treatment of colored people—that the Civil Rights Bill was a dead letter and could not be enforced. There may be some truth in all this, but it is not the whole truth. That bill, like all advance legislation, was a banner on the outer wall of American liberty, a noble moral standard uplifted for the education of the American people. There are tongues in trees, sermons in stones, and books in the running brooks. This law, though dead, did speak. It expressed the sentiment of justice and fair play common to every honest heart. Its voice was against popular prejudice and meanness. It appealed to all the noble and patriotic instincts of the American people. It told the American people that they were all equal before the law—that they belonged to a common country and were equal citizens. The Supreme Court has hauled down this broad and glorious flag of liberty in open day and before all the people, and has thereby given joy to the heart of every man in the land who wishes to deny to others the rights he claims for himself. It is a concession to race pride, selfishness, and meanness, and will be received with joy by every upholder of caste in the land, and for this I deplore and denounce this decision.

It is a frequent and favorite device of an indefensible cause to misstate and pervert the views of those who advocate a good cause, and I have never seen this device more generally resorted to than in the case of the late decision on the Civil Rights Bill. When we dissent from the opinion of the Supreme Court and give the reasons why we think the opinion unsound, we are straightway charged in the papers with denouncing the court itself, and thus put in the attitude of bad citizens. Now, I utterly deny that there has ever been any denunciation of the Supreme Court by the speakers on this platform, and I defy any man to point out one sentence or one syllable of any speech of mine in denunciation of that Court.

Another illustration of this tendency to put opponents in a false position is seen in the persistent effort to stigmatize the Civil Rights Bill as a Social Rights Bill. Now, where under the whole heavens, outside of the United States, could any such perversion of truth have any chance of success? No man in Europe would ever dream that because he has a right to ride on a railway, or stop at a hotel, he therefore has the right to enter into social relations with anybody. No one has a right to speak to another without that other's permission. Social equality and civil equality rest upon an entirely different basis, and well enough the American people know it; yet, in order to inflame a popular prejudice, respectable papers like the *New York Times* and the *Chicago Tribune* persist in describing the Civil Rights Bill as a Social Rights Bill.

When a colored man is in the same room or in the same carriage with white people, as a servant, there is no talk of social equality, but if he is there as a man and a gentleman, he is an offense. What makes the difference? It is not color, for his color is unchanged. The whole essence of the thing is in its purpose to degrade and stamp out the liberties of the race. It is the old spirit of slavery and nothing else. To say that because a man rides in the same car with another he is therefore socially equal is one of the wildest absurdities.

When I was in England, some years ago, I rode upon highways, byways, steamboats, stagecoaches, and omnibuses. I was in the House of Commons, in the House of Lords, in the British Museum, in the Coliseum, in the National Gallery, everywhere—sleeping in rooms where lords and dukes had slept—sitting at tables where lords and dukes [had sat]. I hardly think that some of our Democratic circumstances made me socially the equal of these lords and dukes. I hardly think that some of our Democratic friends would be regarded among those lords as their equals. If riding in the same car makes one equal, I think that the little poodle dog I saw one day sitting in the lap of a lady was made equal by riding in the same car with her. Equality, social equality, is a matter between individuals. It is a reciprocal understanding. I do not think that when I ride with an educated, polished rascal he is thereby made my equal, or that when I ride with a numbskull it makes him my equal. Social equality does not necessarily follow from civil equality, and yet for the purpose of a hell-black and damning prejudice, our papers still insist that the Civil Rights Bill is a bill to establish social equality.

If it is a bill for social equality, so is the Declaration of Independence, which declares that all men have equal rights; so is the Sermon on the Mount; so is the golden rule that commands us to do to others as we would that others should do to us; so is the teaching of the Apostle that of one blood God has made all nations to dwell on the face of the earth; so is the Constitution of the United States, and so are the laws and customs of every civilized country in the world; for nowhere, outside of the United States, is any man denied civil rights on account of his color.

Discussion Starters

1. How important should "object and intention" be in determining constitutionality of laws?

2. How valid was Douglass' claim that "object and intention" had historically been used to the black man's disadvantage?

3. Evaluate the distinction Douglass drew between social equality and civil equality. How important is this distinction today?

4. To what extent was Douglass correct when he asserted that even a dead law on the books has some value? In this light, what damage was done by this decision?

5. What arguments by Douglass might be used in promoting civil equality by law today?

Related Documents

I. *"Civil Rights Cases"*

The Supreme Court decision discussed by Frederick Douglass was rendered on October 15, 1883. The court had considered five cases on appeal from various circuit courts in which blacks had been denied some accommodation or other privilege because of their color. By an 8 to 1 majority the court held the first two sections of the 1875 Civil Rights Act to be unconstitutional.

In the excerpts from the decision given here, identify the key judgments of the court. Explain why Douglass and other blacks had or did not have reasons to despair over this decision.

Mr. Justice Bradley delivered the opinion of the court. After stating the facts in the above language he continued:

It is obvious that the primary and important question in all the cases is the constitutionality of the law: for if the law is unconstitutional none of the prosecutions can stand.

The sections of the law referred to provide as follows:

"SEC. 1. That all persons within the jurisdiction of the United States shall be entitled to the full and equal enjoyment of the accommodations, advantages, facilities, and privileges of inns, public conveyances on land or water, theatres, and other places of public amusement; subject only to the conditions and limitations established by law, and applicable alike to citizens of every race and color, regardless of any previous condition of servitude.

"SEC. 2. That any person who shall violate the foregoing section by denying to any citizen, except for reasons by law applicable to citizens of every race and color, and regardless of any previous condition of servitude, the full enjoyment of any of the accommodations, advantages, facilities, or privileges in said section enumerated, or by aiding or inciting such denial, shall for every such offence forfeit and pay the sum of five hundred dollars to the person aggrieved therby, to be recovered in an action of debt, with full costs; and shall also, for every such offence, be deemed guilty of a misdemeanor, and, upon conviction thereof, shall be fined not less than five hundred nor more than one thousand dollars, or shall be imprisoned not less than thirty days nor more than one year. . . .

Are these sections constitutional? The first section, which is the principal one, cannot be fairly understood without attending to the last clause, which qualifies the preceding part.

The essence of the law is, not to declare broadly that all persons shall be entitled to the full and equal enjoyment of the accommodations, advantages, facilities, and privileges of inns, public conveyances, and theatres; but that such

109 *U.S. Reports*, pp. 8–11, 13–14, 20, 24–25.

enjoyment shall not be subject to any conditions applicable only to citizens of
a particular race or color, or who had been in a previous condition of servitude. . . .

Has Congress constitutional power to make such a law? Of course, no one
will contend that the power to pass it was contained in the Constitution before
the adoption of the last three amendments. The power is sought, first, in the
Fourteenth Amendment, and the views and arguments of distinguished Senators, advanced whilst the law was under consideration, claiming authority to
pass it by virtue of that amendment, are the principal arguments adduced in
favor of the power. . . .

The first section of the Fourteenth Amendment (which is the one relied
on), after declaring who shall be citizens of the United States, and of the several
States, is prohibitory in its character, and prohibitory upon the States. It
declares that:

"No State shall make or enforce any law which shall abridge the privileges
or immunities of citizens of the United States; nor shall any State deprive any
person of life, liberty, or property without due process of law; nor deny to any
person within its jurisdiction the equal protection of the laws."

It is State action of a particular character that is prohibited. Individual
invasion of individual rights is not the subject-matter of the amendment. It has
a deeper and broader scope. It nullifies and makes void all State legislation,
and State action of every kind, which impairs the privileges and immunities
of citizens of the United States, or which injures them in life, liberty or
property without due process of law, or which denies to any of them the equal
protection of the laws. It not only does this, but, . . . the last section of the
amendment invests Congress with power to enforce it by appropriate legislation. To enforce what? To enforce the prohibition. To adopt appropriate
legislation for correcting the effects of such prohibited State laws and State
acts, and thus to render them effectually null, void, and innocuous. This is
the legislative power conferred upon Congress, and this is the whole of
it. . . .

And so in the present case, until some State law has been passed, or some
State action through its officers or agents has been taken, adverse to the rights
of citizens sought to be protected by the Fourteenth Amendment, no legislation of the United States under said amendment, nor any proceeding under
such legislation, can be called into activity: for the prohibitions of the amendment are against State laws and acts done under State authority. . . .

An inspection of the law shows that it makes no reference whatever to
any supposed or apprehended violation of the Fourteenth Amendment on the
part of the States. It is not predicated on any such view. It proceeds *ex directo*
to declare that certain acts committed by individuals shall be deemed offences,
and shall be prosecuted and punished by proceedings in the courts of the
United States. . . .

If this legislation is appropriate for enforcing the prohibitions of the
amendment, it is difficult to see where it is to stop. Why may not Congress with

equal show of authority enact a code of laws for the enforcement and vindication of all rights of life, liberty, and property? . . .

But the power of Congress to adopt direct and primary, as distinguished from corrective legislation, on the subject in hand, is sought, in the second place from the Thirteenth Amendment, which abolishes slavery. . . .

This amendment, as well as the Fourteenth, is undoubtedly self-executing without any ancillary legislation, so far as its terms are applicable to any existing state of circumstances. By its own unaided force and effect it abolished slavery, and established universal freedom. . . .

It is true, that slavery cannot exist without law, any more than property in lands and goods can exist without law: and, therefore, the Thirteenth Amendment may be regarded as nullifying all State laws which establish or uphold slavery. But it has a reflex character also, establishing and decreeing universal civil and political freedom throughout the United States; and it is assumed, that the power vested in Congress to enforce the article by appropriate legislation, clothes Congress with power to pass all laws necessary and proper for abolishing all badges and incidents of slavery in the United States: and upon this assumption it is claimed, that this is sufficient authority for declaring by law that all persons shall have equal accommodations and privileges in all inns, public conveyances, and places of amusement; the argument being, that the denial of such equal accommodations and privileges is, in itself, a subjection to a species of servitude within the meaning of the amendment. . . .

Now, conceding, for the sake of the argument, that the admission to an inn, a public conveyance, or a place of public amusement, on equal terms with all other citizens, is the right of every man and all classes of men, is it any more than one of those rights which the states by the Fourteenth Amendment are forbidden to deny to any person? And is the Constitution violated until the denial of the right has some State sanction or authority? Can the act of a mere individual, the owner of the inn, the public conveyance or place of amusement, refusing the accommodation, be justly regarded as imposing any badge of slavery or servitude upon the applicant, or only as inflicting an ordinary civil injury, properly cognizable by the laws of the State, and presumably subject to redress by those laws until the contrary appears?

After giving to these questions all the consideration which their importance demands, we are forced to the conclusion that such an act of refusal has nothing to do with slavery or involuntary servitude, and that if it is violative of any right of the party, his redress is to be sought under the laws of the State; or if those laws are adverse to his rights and do not protect him, his remedy will be found in the corrective legislation which Congress has adopted, or may adopt, for counteracting the effect of State laws, or State action, prohibited by the Fourteenth Amendment. It would be running the slavery argument into the ground to make it apply to every act of discrimination which a person may see fit to make as to the guests he will entertain, or as to the people he will take into his coach or cab or car, or admit to his concert or theatre, or deal with in other matters of intercourse or business. . . .

When a man has emerged from slavery, and by the aid of beneficent legislation has shaken off the inseparable concomitants of that state, there must be some stage in the progress of his elevation when he takes the rank of a mere citizen, and ceases to be the special favorite of the laws, and when his rights as a citizen, or a man, are to be protected in the ordinary modes by which other men's rights are protected. There were thousands of free colored people in this country before the abolition of slavery, enjoying all the essential rights of life, liberty and property the same as white citizens; yet no one, at that time, thought that it was any invasion of his personal status as a freeman because he was not admitted to all the privileges enjoyed by white citizens, or because he was subjected to discriminations in the enjoyment of accommodations in inns, public conveyances and places of amusement. Mere discriminations on account of race or color were not regarded as badges of slavery. If, since that time, the enjoyment of equal rights in all these respects has become established by constitutional enactment, it is not by force of the Thirteenth Amendment (which merely abolishes slavery), but by force of the Thirteenth and Fifteenth Amendments.

On the whole we are of opinion, that no countenance of authority for the passage of the law in question can be found in either the Thirteenth or Fourteenth Amendment of the Constitution; and no other ground of authority for its passage being suggested, it must necessarily be declared void, at least so far as its operation in the several States is concerned.

II. *"Civil Rights Cases"—A Dissenting Opinion*

In his lengthy dissent, Justice John Marshall Harlan cited numerous precedents to contradict the majority opinion. On the basis of the brief portions included here, try to determine how his views of both law and precedent differed from those of his fellow justices. Where did they agree with Douglass' views?

Mr. Justice Harlan dissenting.

The opinion in these cases proceeds, it seems to me, upon grounds entirely too narrow and artificial. I cannot resist the conclusion that the substance and spirit of the recent amendments of the Constitution have been sacrificed by a subtle and ingenious verbal criticism. "It is not the words of the law but the internal sense of it that makes the law: the letter of the law is the body; the sense and reason of the law is the soul." Constitutional provisions, adopted in the interest of liberty, and for the purpose of securing, through national legislation, if need be, rights inhering in a state of freedom, and belonging to American citizenship, have been so construed as to defeat the ends the people desired to accomplish, which they attempted to accomplish, and which they supposed they had accomplished by changes in their fundamental law. By this I do not mean that the determination of these cases should have been materially controlled by considerations of mere expediency or policy. I mean only, in this form, to express an earnest conviction that the court has departed from the familiar rule requiring, in the interpretation of constitutional provisions, that full effect be given to the intent with which they were adopted. . . .

My brethren say, that when a man has emerged from slavery, and by the aid of beneficent legislation has shaken off the inseparable concomitants of that state, there must be some stage in the progress of his elevation when he takes the rank of a mere citizen, and ceases to be the special favorite of the laws, and when his rights as a citizen, or a man, are to be protected in the ordinary modes by which other men's rights are protected. It is, I submit, scarcely just to say that the colored race has been the special favorite of the laws. The statute of 1875, now adjudged to be unconstitutional, is for the benefit of citizens of every race and color. What the nation, through Congress, has sought to accomplish in reference to that race, is—what had already been done in every State of the Union for the white race—to secure and protect rights belonging to them as freemen and citizens; nothing more. It was not deemed enough "to help the feeble up, but to support him after." The one underlying purpose of congressional legislation has been to enable the black race to take the rank of mere citizens. The difficulty has been to compel a recognition of the legal right of the black race to take the rank of citizens, and to secure the enjoyment of privileges belonging, under the law, to them as a component part of the people for whose welfare and happiness government is ordained. . . . If the constitutional amendments be enforced, according to the intent with which, as I conceive, they were adopted, there cannot be, in this republic, any class of human beings in practical subjection to another class, with power in the latter to dole out to the former just such privileges as they may choose to grant. The supreme law of the land has decreed that no authority shall be exercised in this country upon the basis of discrimination, in respect of civil rights, against freemen and citizens because of their race, color, or previous condition of servitude. To that decree—for the due enforcement of which, by appropriate legislation, Congress has been invested with express power—every one must bow, whatever may have been, or whatever now are, his individual views as to the wisdom or policy, either of the recent changes in the fundamental law, or of the legislation which has been enacted to give them effect.

For the reasons stated I feel constrained to withhold my assent to the opinion of the court.

III. Editorials

THE NATION

*That the constitutionality of the Civil Rights Act was widely challenged is
apparent in the general approval given the Supreme Court's decision. One of the
magazines that regarded it as unconstitutional was* The Nation, *a weekly
founded in 1865 with the blessing of William Lloyd Garrison as the successor
to* The Liberator. *Although Wendell Phillips Garrison, William's son, was an
editor of* The Nation, *its editorial policy after 1870 called for time and education rather than laws as the means of achieving equality.*

Included here is an editorial from The Nation *at the time of the passage
of the Civil Rights Act and another at the time of the Supreme Court's voiding
of that act. How do you account for the differences between* The Nation's *and
Douglass' appraisal of the act and of the effect of the Court's decision?*

MARCH 4, 1875

Congress has at last passed the Civil-Rights Bill, and the President has signed
it. The bill, as passed, does not enforce mixed schools, and only secures negroes
equal rights in public conveyances, inns, theatres, and other places of amusement. While the bill was on its passage in the Senate, Mr. Tipton of Nebraska
moved to insert the word "churches" after the word "theatres," including the
former under the head of places of amusement—a suggestion which of course
brought down the galleries, though it really is not much more amusing than
the bill itself. The negroes of the South, being mainly occupied in tilling the
soil, or in labor of some kind, are not as a rule in the habit of travelling much
from place to place; and when they do go from time to time to some local
court-house or county-seat for a holiday, they are apt to move in crowds on
foot, or in wagons not subject to the jurisdiction of Congress. They do not
frequent hotels much, for similar reasons, and the number of theatres and
opera-houses in the South is not so great as to warrant the expectation of a
great advance of the race through the influence of the drama and music.
Indeed, it is a harmless bill, and does not seem to have had much effect on
public opinion in the South. The chief objection to it is its entire unconstitutionality, which Mr. Carpenter showed, much to the consternation of the
Radical Republicans, in an able and convincing speech.

OCTOBER 18, 1883

The calm with which the country receives the news that the leading sections
of the celebrated Civil-Rights Act of 1875 have been pronounced unconstitutional by the Supreme Court, shows how completely the extravagant expectations as well as the fierce passions of the war have died out. The Act was forced

The Nation, March 4, 1875, and October 18, 1883.

through Congress as the crowning measure of the plan of reconstructing the South on which the Republican party entered at the close of the war, and under the influence of that feeling of omnipotence with regard to the South which was the natural and unavoidable result of the prolonged exercise of the war power, and which survived the war for fully fifteen years. Some of the ablest lawyers in both houses saw its unconstitutionality clearly enough, and pointed it out; but some voted for it as a useful piece of party work, which might do good and could not possibly do any harm. . . .

The reason why the Fourteenth Amendment had not given Congress power to legislate directly in defence of the social rights of the negroes in the several States was plain enough, too. It was that the Republican party, when the amendment was adopted in 1868, was occupied solely with the defence of the ordinary civil rights of the freedmen against hostile or reactionary State legislation. It was, in short, due to the fear that slavery might be succeeded, for the colored people, by a carefully prepared condition of legal inferiority, and against this the men who abolished slavery determined to guard. An amendment providing for the admission of negroes to hotels and theatres and public conveyances would not have been adopted, because the notion that the social equality of the colored people could be hastened by legislation sprang up later,when they had come more distinctly into view as citizens and property-holders, theatre-goers and travellers; but it never was strong enough to procure either the adoption of a Constitutional amendment or the passage of an act which anybody expected to be enforced. The Civil-Rights Act was really rather an admonition, or statement of moral obligation, than a legal command. Probably nine-tenths of those who voted for it knew very well that whenever it came before the Supreme Court it would be torn to pieces.

Any one who has forgotten, or is not old enough to remember, the arguments which were made to do duty in the service of the bill when it was before Congress, will find an interesting summary of them in the comments of Mr. Greener, the colored lawyer, on the late decision of the Court, in the *Evening Post* of Tuesday. As a reminiscence of ways of thinking about constitutional questions which have almost wholly passed away, they are interesting reading. It will be seen that there is very little flavor even of legality about them. They are almost all based on moral considerations with which courts of law under our system have little or nothing to do. The decision is wrong because it is likely to annoy and inconvenience the colored race. It is wrong because it disregards, in disobedience to the Constitution, certain primeval natural rights brought over here by the first settlers; because it may lead to Catholic bishops or Jewish rabbis being expelled from railroad cars; because it raises inconvenient questions of social equality; and because, coming just after the Ohio election, "it can scarcely be construed as anything else than a covert and insidious blow at the institutions of the Republican party."

What the Court had decided, we need hardly say, is simply that the Fourteenth Amendment does not authorize Congress to protect the civil rights of colored people within the States against anything but hostile State legislation; or, in other words, that the powers of Congress are defined by the

Constitution, and not by considerations of humanity, or even general utility, or by the opinions or wishes of prominent politicians. Consequently, nearly all that the arguments originally produced in support of the Act, as well as those of Mr. Greener now against the Court's interpretation of it, really prove is, that the division of powers made by the Constitution between the States and the Union is not a proper one, and that the framers might have made a far better Government than the one they did make, if they had only tried.

IV. News Report

THE NEW YORK TRIBUNE

Among the many newspapers reporting on the Supreme Court's decision was The New York Tribune. In reading the following article, keep in mind that the sentiments expressed by Justice Donohue and the hotel manager were fairly representative of the public's general reaction: that the Civil Rights Act was unconstitutional. What kind of rebuttal might Frederick Douglass have offered to the statement that, "If a colored person behaves himself, nobody will trouble him or think about him"?

OCTOBER 17, 1883

Justice Donohue, of the Supreme Court [of New York], was asked by a *Tribune* reporter yesterday what he thought of the decision of the United States Supreme Court declaring the Civil Rights bill unconstitutional. In reply he said: "I think that it shows that we are getting back to our constitutional moorings. . . . The difficulty in this whole matter is due to the fact that there has been too much agitation over the color line. Leave the colored people alone and they will take care of themselves as other people do. The matter will take care of itself on a common-sense basis. . . . If a colored person behaves himself, nobody will trouble him or think about him. Let him alone, just as you would anybody else who attends to his business. . . . I have had darkey clients and got along with them as I did with other clients."

"Do you think that this decision will leave the negro at the mercy of those who dislike him, especially in the South?"

"Not at all. There is not the least danger of it. He will have his rights, as everybody else has. Nobody would turn him out of a theatre or of a street-car any more than before. His status before the law will be essentially unchanged." . . .

Several managers of hotels who were asked for their views regarding the decision thought that it would have little effect on their interests, though it might save them from an occasional suit for damages. Mr. Wetherbee of the

Windsor, said that colored people never trouble him and he was never sued by them. "They usually are too sensible to go where they are not wanted," said he, "and they prefer hotels where they are sure to be welcome—usually a cheap class of house."

V. Editorial

THE ST. LOUIS REPUBLICAN

As in the preceding news report, this editorial from The St. Louis Republican *expresses the belief that there had been way too much agitation by colored leaders over supposed prejudice. How valid were such observations? Speculate on how Douglass might have answered these arguments.*

OCTOBER 24, 1883

Probably the most effective answer to the outcry of the colored leaders against the recent civil rights decision is to be found in their own statement of their complaint. Fred Douglass says the decision "has inflicted a heavy calamity upon seven millions of colored people, and left them naked and defenceless against the action of malignant, vulgar and pitiless prejudice." Seven millions is an extravagant estimate of the negro population of the country, and Mr. Douglass evidently imagines that the more negroes there are in the land the greater is the "calamity" which the decision brings upon them. If they were seventy millions the grievance would be augmented ten-fold. But to ordinary eyes a race seven millions strong ought to be able to take care of itself without the aid of special laws, noisy meetings and hulabaloos. If, with such vast numbers—double the population of the colonies in the struggle with Great Britain in the Revolution—it is not able to take care of itself without perpetually bringing its complaints before the public, the suspicion is strong that it lacks the fibre by which alone rights can be first conquered, and afterwards maintained. . . .

If the colored people want to enjoy the rights and privileges which the civil rights act never did secure to them, and which the present decision does not deprive them of, they will have to go about the task in some other way than by violent speeches, in which they plead their own helplessness and proclaim their own inferiority.

The St. Louis Republican, October 24, 1883.

VI. Civil Right Not Social Choice

GEORGE WASHINGTON CABLE

Many of the opponents of civil rights legislation, in addition to affirming its unconstitutionality, tried to argue that civil equality was identical with social equality and could not be promoted by laws. George Washington Cable, a white native Southerner (who moved to New England in 1884) and a champion of the freedmen's rights, attempted to discuss this matter in practical terms.

Analyze and evaluate his arguments and determine how well they support those of Frederick Douglass.

Let us then make our conception of the right and wrong of this matter unmistakable. Social relations, one will say, are sacred. True, but civil rights are sacred, also. Hence social relations must not impose upon civil rights nor civil rights impose upon social relations. We must have peace. But for peace to be stable we must have justice. Therefore, for peace, we must find that boundary line between social relations and civil rights, from which the one has no warrant ever to push the other; and, for justice, this boundary must remain ever faithfully the same, no matter whose the social relations are on one side or whose the civil rights are on the other.

Suppose a case. Mr. A. takes a lady, not of his own family, to a concert. Neither one is moved by compulsion or any assertion of right on the part of the other. They have chosen each other's company. Their relation is social. It could not exist without mutual agreement. They are strangers in that city, however, and as they sit in the thronged auditorium and look around them, not one other soul in that house, so far as they can discern, has any social relation with them. But see, now, how impregnable the social relation is. That pair, outnumbered a thousand to one, need not yield a pennyweight of social interchange with any third person unless they so choose. Nothing else in human life is so amply sufficient to protect itself as are social relations. Provided one thing—that the law will protect every one impartially in his civil rights, one of the foremost of which is that both men and laws shall let us alone to our personal social preferences. If any person, no matter who or what he is, insists on obtruding himself upon this pair in the concert-hall he can only succeed in getting himself put out. Why? Because he is trying to turn his civil right-to-be-there into a social passport. And even if he make no personal advances, but his behavior or personal condition is so bad as to obtrude itself offensively upon others, the case is the same; the mistake and its consequences are his. But, on the other hand, should Mr. A. and his companion demand the expulsion of this third person when he had made no advances and had encroached no more on their liberty than they had on his, demanding it simply on the ground that he was their social or intellectual inferior or probably had

George Washington Cable, *The Silent South* (New York: Charles Scribner's Sons, 1885), pp. 57–63.

relatives who were, then the error, no matter who or what he is, would be not his, but theirs, and it would be the equally ungenteel error of trying to turn their social choice into a civil right; and it would be simply increasing the error and its offensiveness, for them to suggest that he be given an equally comfortable place elsewhere in the house providing it must indicate his inferiority. There is nothing comfortable in ignominy, nor is it any evidence of high mind for one stranger to put it upon another.

Now, the principles of this case are not disturbed by any multiplication of the number of persons concerned, or by reading for concert-hall either theatre or steamboat or railway station or coach or lecture-hall or street car or public library, or by supposing the social pair to be English, Turk, Jap, Cherokee, Ethiopian, Mexican, or "American." But note the fact that, even so, Mr. A. and his companion's social relations are, under these rulings, as safe from invasion as they were before; nay, even safer, inasmuch as the true distinction is made publicly clearer, between the social and the civil relations. Mr. A. is just as free to decline every sort of unwelcome social advance, much or little, as ever he was; and as to his own house or estate may eject any one from it, not of his own family or a legal tenant, and give no other reason than that it suits him to do so. Do you not see it now, gentlemen of the other side? Is there anything new in it? Is it not as old as truth itself? Honestly, have you not known it all along? Is it not actually the part of good breeding to know it? You cannot say no. Then why have you charged us with proposing "to break down every distinction between the races," and "to insist on their intermingling in all places and in all relations," when in fact we have not proposed to disturb any distinction between the races which nature has made, or molest any private or personal relation in life, whatever? Why have you charged us with "moving to forbid all further assortment of the races," when the utmost we have done is to condemn an *arbitrary* assortment of the races, crude and unreasonable, by the stronger race without the consent of the weaker, and in places and relations where no one, exalted or lowly, has any right to dictate to another because of the class he belongs to? We but turn your own words to our use when we say this battery of charges "is as false as it is infamous." But let that go.

Having made it plain that the question has nothing to do with social relations, we see that it is, and is only, a question of *indiscriminative civil rights.* This is what "The Freedman's Case in Equity" advocates from beginning to end, not as a choice which a *race* may either claim or disclaim, but as every citizen's individual yet impersonal right until he personally waives or forfeits it. The issue, we repeat, is not met at all by the assertion that "Neither race wants it." There is one thing that neither race wants, but even this is not because either of them is one race or another, but simply because they are members of a civilized human community. It is that thing of which our Southern white people have so long had such an absurd fear; neither race, or in other words nobody, wants to see the civil rewards of decency in dress and behavior usurped by the common herd of clowns and ragamuffins. But there is another thing that the colored race certainly does want: the freedom for those of the race who can to earn the indiscriminative and unchallenged *civil* —*not social*—rights of gentility by the simple act of being genteel. This is what we insist the best intelligence of the South is willing—in the interest of right, and therefore of both races—to accord. But the best intelligence is not the majority, and the majority, leaning not upon the equities, but the traditional sentiments of the situation, charge us with "theory" and "sentiment" and give us their word for it that "Neither race wants it." . . .

Would our friends on the other side of the discussion say they mean only, concerning these indiscriminative civil rights, "Neither race wants them *now*"? This would but make bad worse. For two new things have happened to the colored race in these twenty years; first, a natural and spontaneous assortment has taken place within the race itself along scales of virtue and intelligence, knowledge and manners; so that by no small fraction of their number the wrong of treating the whole race alike is more acutely felt than ever it was before; and, second, a long, bitter experience has taught them that "equal accommodations, but separate" means, generally, accommodations of a conspicuously ignominious inferiority. Are these people opposed to an arrangement that would give them instant release from organized and legalized incivility?—For that is what a race distinction in civil relations is when it ignores intelligence and decorum.

For Further Reading

Political questions related to civil rights are given thorough treatment in *Farewell to the Bloody Shirt: Northern Republicans and the Southern Negro, 1877–1893** (1962), by Stanley P. Hirshon, and *Republicans Face the Southern Question: The New Departure Years* (1959), by Vincent P. DeSantis. Legal questions are treated or touched upon in Stanley I. Kutler, *Judicial Power and Reconstruction Politics* (1968); Morroe Berger, *Equality by Statute: The Revolution in Civil Rights* (1967); and in *Discrimination and the Law* (1965), edited by Vern Countryman.

Frederick Douglass' *Life and Times** (1892; reprinted in 1962) is perhaps the best source about him. *Frederick Douglass** (1968), edited by Benjamin Quarles, contains his writings as well as commentaries by his contemporaries and current historians.

General accounts of the Reconstruction years are given in John Hope Franklin's *Reconstruction After the Civil War** (1961), and Kenneth M. Stampp's *The Era of Reconstruction* (1965).

The role of blacks is considered in *The Negro in Reconstruction** (1969), by Robert Cruden; *The Negro in American Life and Thought: The Nadir, 1877–1901* (1954), by Rayford Logan; and *Negro Thought in American, 1880–1915* (1963), by August Meier. Three volumes by C. Vann Woodward are also pertinent: *Origins of the New South, 1877–1913* (1951), *Reunion and Reaction:*

*Paperbound edition available.

The Compromise of 1877 and the End of Reconstruction (1956), and *The Strange Career of Jim Crow** (1966). The status of blacks in individual states is dealt with in Frenise Logan, *The Negro in North Carolina, 1876–1894* (1964); George B. Tindall, *South Carolina Negroes, 1877–1900* (1952); Joel Williamson, *After Slavery: The Negro in South Carolina During Reconstruction, 1861–1877** (1965); and Charles E. Wynes, *Race Relations in Virginia, 1870–1902* (1961).

Primary sources are available in the *Documentary History of Reconstruction* (1906–1907; reprinted in 1966), edited by Walter L. Fleming. Problems books include *Reconstruction** (1967), edited by Staughton Lynd, and *Reconstruction: A Tragic Era?** (1968), edited by Seth M. Scheiner.

*Paperbound edition available.

2. The American West

When the first white men settled on the Atlantic Coast of North America, they were immediately fascinated by what lay to the interior of their newly claimed lands. Lured by its promise of game, wealth, and more land, the more adventuresome were not long in moving there.

During the seventeenth and eighteenth centuries, as the frontier of exploration, exploitation, and settlement edged persistently westward, there was territory enough east of the Mississippi River. In 1803, however, President Thomas Jefferson was able to extend the domain of the United States by the purchase of the Louisiana Territory. This acquisition doubled the size of the United States and opened up a vast new area for further westward movement. Given this stimulus, the push westward continued beyond the Louisiana Territory into the areas of Texas and Oregon, and with the conclusion of the Mexican War, the United States added California and the Southwest to the national domain. The lure of the West reached epidemic proportions after the discovery of gold near Sacramento, California, in 1848. Most of the settlers and adventurers, in moving to the Far West, simply traveled through the Great Plains and mountainous regions of the central portion of the United States without paying them much heed.

The discovery of gold in Nevada and Colorado (1859), Idaho (1860–66), Arizona (1862), Montana (1862–64), and Wyoming (1867) prompted settlement of the mountainous regions of the West, but the settlement of the high plains, referred to as the Great American Desert, had to await the transcontinental railroad. The completion of the Union Pacific in 1869 and the later addition of its feeder lines meant that transportation was available to bring produce from the eastern regions of the plains to the urban markets, but what could be produced in the semiarid regions west of the 98th meridian? Raising cattle provided one possibility, and with the extension of the railroads into the high plains this became a profitable venture. The introduction of the barbed wire fence by those who were trying to farm the treeless plains hastened the end of the open range, although it was the unusually severe winters of 1885 and 1886 that dealt the death blow to the long drive phase of the cattle business. As farmers became more numerous in the region, they introduced new techniques of dry farming and deep plowing, and they enjoyed prosperity during most of the 1870s and early 1880s. After reaching a peak in the mid-1880s, their prosperity was rapidly destroyed by a long drought that began in 1887.

The subduing of the West took a tremendous amount of back-breaking work, and the threat of failure or death was ever-present. Among the hazards faced by the miners, cattlemen, and farmers were deserts, treacherous rivers, blizzards, droughts, and disease. Beyond this, they had to cope with the Indian tribes that occupied the areas these new exploiters or settlers desired. Some of the Indian tribes tried to cooperate, others tried to resist the encroachment of the white man upon their ancestral lands, but whether they cooperated or resisted, these once proud and independent people were eventually subdued and confined to those portions of the land that had no value to the white man. This was accomplished through a series of wars fought from the 1860s to the 1890s in which the new Americans' superiority in numbers and technology proved to be more than the Indians could match.

Despite the difficult climate and the hostility of Indians, the Great Plains were populated fairly rapidly. Taking note of this, in a statement that later became famous, the Superintendent of the Census reported in 1890: "Up to and including 1880 the country had a frontier of settlement, but at present the unsettled area has been so broken into by isolated bodies of settlement that there can hardly be said to be a frontier line. In the discussion of its extent, its westward movement, etc., it can not, therefore, any longer have a place in the census reports."

The Western frontier stage of American history was thus officially closed. This did not mean that men would no longer move to the West, or talk about and write about the frontier, but it did mean that Americans faced the task of developing what was already known or explored; they had reached the continental limits of the national domain.

Core Document

An Englishman Looks at Western America

JAMES BRYCE

The United States has been visited by many foreign observers during its national life. Many of these travelers, after returning to their native countries, wrote of their experiences while in America. During the last quarter of the nineteenth century one such traveler was the Englishman James Bryce, a noted scholar, educational leader, Member of Parliament, and world traveler. He became so intrigued by the United States that he visited it four times between 1870 and 1890. After his third visit in 1883 he decided to write an account of his experiences and to analyze the political system of the United States. His work was published in 1888 as The American Commonwealth. *The book gained immediate popularity and has become recognized as not only one of the best descriptions of the United States in the late nineteenth century, but also as one of the best analyses of the constitutional theory and the political realities of the American system.*

James Bryce did not confine his travels to any particular area of the United States. As he journeyed through the general geographic sections of the country he tried to describe their peculiarities and to identify the role each section played in the overall development of an American character. While reading his account of the West note what he believed to be:

- *the type of people who moved to the West.*
- *the style of life of the Westerner.*
- *the degree of materialism of the western American.*
- *the use of natural resources by the Westerner.*
- *the Westerner's concern for the future.*

Western America is one of the most interesting subjects of study the modern world has seen. There has been nothing in the past resembling its growth, and probably there will be nothing in the future. A vast territory, wonderfully rich in natural resources of many kinds; a temperate and healthy climate fit for European labor; a soil generally, and in many places marvellously, fertile; in some regions mountains full of minerals, in others trackless forests where every tree is over two hundred feet high; and the whole of this virtually unoccupied territory thrown open to a vigorous race, with all the appliances and contrivances of modern science at its command,—these are phenomena absolutely without precedent in history, and which cannot recur elsewhere, because our planet contains no such other favoured tract of country.

James Bryce, *The American Commonwealth* (New York: Macmillan, 1914), II, pp. 891–901.

The Spaniards and Portuguese settled in tropical countries, which soon enervated them. They carried with them the poison of slavery; their colonists were separated, some by long land journeys, and all by still longer voyages, from the centres of civilization. But the railway and the telegraph follow the Western American. The Greeks of the sixth and seventh centuries before Christ, who planted themselves all around the coasts of the Mediterranean, had always enemies, and often powerful enemies, to overcome before they could found even their trading-stations on the coast, much less occupy the lands of the interior. In Western America the presence of the Indians has done no more than give a touch of romance or a spice of danger to the exploration of some regions, such as Western Dakota and Arizona, while over the rest of the country the unhappy aborigines have slunk silently away, scarcely even complaining of the robbery of lands and the violation of plighted faith. Nature and time seem to have conspired to make the development of the Mississippi basin and the Pacific slope the swiftest, easiest, completest achievement in the whole record of the civilizing progress of mankind since the founder of the Egyptian monarchy gathered the tribes of the Nile under one government.

The details of this development and the statistics that illustrate it have been too often set forth to need re-statement here. It is of the character and temper of the men who have conducted it that I wish to speak, a matter which has received less attention, but is essential to a just conception of the Americans of to-day. For the West is the most American part of America; that is to say, the part where those features which distinguish America from Europe come out in the strongest relief. What Europe is to Asia, what England is to the rest of Europe, what America is to England, that the Western States are to the Atlantic States, the heat and pressure and hurry of life always growing as we follow the path of the sun. In Eastern America there are still quiet spots, in the valleys of the Alleghanies, for instance, in nooks of old New England, in university towns like Princeton or Amherst, Ithaca or Ann Arbor. In the West there are none. All is bustle, motion, and struggle, most of course among the native Americans, yet even the immigrant from the secluded valleys of Thuringia, or the shores of some Norwegian fjord, learns the ways almost as readily as the tongue of the country, and is soon swept into the whirlpool.

It is the most enterprising and unsettled Americans that come West; and when they have left their old haunts, broken their old ties, resigned the comforts and pleasures of their former homes, they are resolved to obtain the wealth and success for which they have come. They throw themselves into work with a feverish yet sustained intensity. They rise early, they work all day, they have few pleasures, few opportunities for relaxation. I remember in the young city of Seattle on Puget Sound to have found business in full swing at seven o'clock A.M.: the shops open, the streets full of people. Everything is speculative, land (or, as it is usually called, "real estate") most so, the value of lots of ground rising or falling perhaps two or three hundred per cent in the year. No one has any fixed occupation; he is a storekeeper to-day, a ranchman to-morrow, a miner next week. I once found the waiters in the chief hotel at

Denver, in Colorado, saving their autumn and winter wages to start off in the spring "prospecting" for silver "claims" in the mountains. Few men stay in one of the newer cities more than a few weeks or months; to have been there a whole year is to be an old inhabitant, an oracle if you have succeeded, a by-word if you have not, for to prosper in the West you must be able to turn your hand to anything, and seize the chance to-day which every one else will have seen to-morrow. This venturesome and shifting life strengthens the reckless and heedless habits of the people. Everyone thinks so much of gaining that he thinks little of spending, and in the general dearness of commodities, food (in the agricultural districts) excepted, it seems not worth while to care about small sums. In California for many years no coin lower than a ten-cent piece . . . was in circulation; and even in 1881, though most articles of food were abundant, nothing was sold at a lower price than five cents. The most striking alternations of fortune, the great *coups* which fascinate men and make them play for all or nothing, are of course commoner in mining regions than elsewhere. But money is everywhere so valuable for the purposes of speculative investment, whether in land, live stock, or trade, as to fetch very high interest. At Walla Walla (in what was then the Territory of Washington) I found in 1881 that the interest on debts secured on good safe mortgages was at the rate of fourteen per cent per annum, of course payable monthly.

The carelessness is public as well as private. Tree stumps were left standing in the streets of a large and flourishing town like Leadville, because the municipal authorities cannot be at the trouble of cutting or burning them. Swamps were left undrained in the suburbs of a populous city like Portland, which every autumn were breeding malarial fevers; and the risk of accidents to be followed by actions does not prevent the railways from pushing on their lines along loosely heaped embankments, and over curved trestle bridges which seem as if they could not stand a high wind or the passage of a heavy train.

This mixture of science and rudeness is one of a series of singular contrasts which runs through the West, not less conspicuous in the minds of the people than in their surroundings. They value strong government, and have a remarkable faculty for organizing some kind of government, but they are tolerant of lawlessness which does not directly attack their own interest. Horse-stealing and insults to women are the two unpardonable offenses; all others are often suffered to go unpunished. I was in a considerable Western city, with a population of 70,000 people, some years ago, when the leading newspaper of the place, commenting on one of the train robberies that had been frequent in the State, observed that so long as the brigands had confined themselves to robbing the railway companies and the express companies of property for whose loss the companies must answer, no one had greatly cared, seeing that these companies themselves robbed the public; but now that private citizens seemed in danger of losing their personal baggage and money, the prosperity of the city might be compromised, and something ought to be done—a sentiment delivered with all gravity, as the rest of the article showed. Brigandage tends to disappear when the country becomes populous, though there are places in comparatively old States like Illinois and Missouri where the railways are still unsafe. But the same heedlessness suffers other evils to take root, evils likely to prove permanent, including some refinements of political roguery which it is strange to find amid the simple life of forests and prairies.

Another such contrast is presented by the tendency of this shrewd and educated people to relapse into the oldest and most childish forms of superstition. Fortune-telling, clairvoyance, attempts to pry by the help of "mediums" into the book of fate, are so common in parts of the West that the newspapers devote a special column, headed "astrologers," to the advertisements of these wizards and pythonesses. I have counted in one issue of a San Francisco newspaper as many as eighteen such advertisements, six of which were of simple fortune-tellers, like those who used to beguile the peasant girls of Devonshire. In fact, the profession of a soothsayer or astrologer is a recognized one in California now, as it was in the Greece of Homer. Possibly the prevalence of mining speculation, possibly the existence of a large mass of ignorant immigrants from Europe, may help to account for the phenomenon, which, as California is deemed an exceptionally unreligious State, illustrates the famous saying that the less faith the more superstition.

All the passionate eagerness, all the strenuous effort of the Westerners is directed towards the material development of the country. To open the greatest number of mines and extract the greatest quantity of ore, to scatter cattle over a thousand hills, to turn the flower-spangled prairies of the North-west into wheat-fields, to cover the sunny slopes of the South-west with vines and olives: this is the end and aim of their lives, this is their daily and nightly thought. . . .

The passion is so absorbing, and so covers the horizon of public as well as private life that it almost ceases to be selfish—it takes from its very vastness a tinge of ideality. To have an immense production of exchangeable commodities, to force from nature the most she can be made to yield, and send it east and west by the cheapest routes to the dearest markets, making one's city a centre of trade, and raising the price of its real estate—this, which might not have seemed a glorious consummation to Isaiah or Plato, is preached by Western newspapers as a kind of religion. It is not really, or at least it is not wholly, sordid. These people are intoxicated by the majestic scale of the nature in which their lot is cast, enormous mineral deposits, boundless prairies, forests which, even squandered—wickedly squandered—as they now are, will supply timber to the United States for centuries; a soil which, with the rudest cultivation, yields the most abundant crops, a populous continent for their market. They see all round them railways being built, telegraph wires laid, steamboat lines across the Pacific projected, cities springing up in the solitudes, and settlers making the wilderness to blossom like the rose. Their imagination revels in these sights and signs of progress, and they gild their own struggles for fortune with the belief that they are the missionaries of civilization and the instruments of Providence in the greatest work the world has seen. The following extract from a newspaper published at Tacoma in Washington (then a Territory) expresses with frank simplicity the conception of greatness and happiness which is uppermost in the Far West; and what may seem a touch of conscious humour is, if humour it be, none the less an expression of sincere conviction.

WHY WE SHOULD BE HAPPY

"Because we are practically at the head of navigation on Puget Sound. Tacoma is the place where all the surplus products of the south and of the east, that are exported by way of the Sound, must be laden on board the vessels that are to carry them to the four corners of the world. We should be happy because being at the head of navigation on Puget Sound, and the shipping point for the south and east, the centre from which shall radiate lines of commerce to every point on the circumference of the earth, we are also nearer by many miles than any other town on Puget Sound to that pass in the Cascade mountains through which the Cascade division of the Northern Pacific railroad will be built in the near future; not only nearer to the Stampede pass, but easily assessible from there by a railroad line of gentle grade, which is more than can be said of any town to the north of us.

"We should be happy for these reasons and because we are connected by rail with Portland on the Willamette, with St. Paul, Chicago, and New York; because being thus connected we are in daily communication with the social, political, and financial centres of the western hemisphere; because all the people of the south and of the east who visit these shores must first visit New Tacoma; because from here will be distributed to the people of the north-west all that shall be brought across the continent on the cars, and from here shall be distributed to merchants all over the United States the cargoes of ships returning here from every foreign port to load with wheat, coal, and lumber. We should be and we are happy because New Tacoma is the Pacific coast terminus of a transcontinental line of railroad. Because this is the only place on the whole Pacific coast north of San Francisco where through freight from New York can be loaded on ship directly from the cars in which it came from the Atlantic side.

"Other reasons why we should be happy are, that New Tacoma is in the centre of a country where fruits and flowers, vegetables and grain, grow in almost endless variety; that we are surrounded with everything beautiful in nature, that we have scenery suited to every mood, and that there are opportunities here for the fullest development of talents of every kind. We have youth, good health, and opportunity. What more could be asked?"

If happiness is thus procurable, the Great West ought to be happy. But there is often a malignant influence at work to destroy happiness in the shape of a neighbouring city, which is making progress as swift or swifter, and threatens to eclipse its competitors. The rivalry between these Western towns is intense and extends to everything. It is sometimes dignified by an unselfish devotion to the greatness of the city which a man has seen grow with his own growth from infancy to a vigorous manhood. Citizens of Chicago are prouder of Chicago than a Londoner, in the days of Elizabeth, was proud of London. They show you the splendid parks and handsome avenues with as much pleasure as a European noble shows his castle and his pictures: they think little of offering hundreds of thousands of dollars to beautify the city or enrich it with a library or an art gallery. In other men this laudable corporate pride is stimulated, not only by the love of competition which lies deep in the American as it does in the English breast, but also by personal interest, for the prosperity of the individual is inseparable from that of the town. As its fortunes rise or fall, so will his corner lots or the profits of his store. It is not all towns that succeed. Some after reaching a certain point stand still, receiving few accessions; at other times, after a year or two of bloom, a town wilts and withers; trade declines; enterprising citizens depart, leaving only the shiftless and impecunious behind; the saloons are closed, the shanties fall to ruin, in a few years nothing but heaps of straw and broken wood, with a few brick houses awaiting the next blizzard to overthrow them, are left on the surface of the prairie. Thus Tacoma is harassed by the pretensions of the even more eager and enterprising Seattle; thus the greater cities of St. Paul and Minneapolis have striven for many a year for the title of Capital of the North-west. In 1870 St. Paul was already a substantial city, and Minneapolis just beginning to be known as the possessor of immense water advantages from its position on the Mississippi at the Falls of St. Anthony. In 1883, though St. Paul contained some 135,000 inhabitants, Minneapolis with 165,000 had distanced her in the race, and had become, having in the process destroyed the beauty of her Falls, the greatest flour-milling centre in America. The newspapers of each of such competing cities keep up a constant war upon the other; and everything is done by municipal bodies and individual citizens to make the world believe that their city is advancing and all its neighbours standing still. Prosperity is largely a matter of advertising, for an afflux of settlers makes prosperity, and advertising, which can take many forms, attracts settlers. Many a place has lived upon its "boom" until it found something more solid to live on; and to a stranger who asked in a small Far Western town how such a city could keep up four newspapers, it was well answered that it took four newspapers to keep up such a city.

Confidence goes a long way towards success. And the confidence of these Westerners is superb. I happened in 1883 to be at the city of Bismarck in Dakota when this young settlement was laying the corner-stone of its Capitol, intended to contain the halls of the legislature and other State offices of Dakota when that flourishing Territory should have become a State, or perhaps, for they spoke even then of dividing it, two States. The town was then only some five years old, and may have had six or seven thousand inhabitants. It was gaily decorated for the occasion, and had collected many distinguished guests—General U. S. Grant, several governors of neighbouring States and Territories, railroad potentates, and others. By far the most remarkable figure was that of Sitting Bull, the famous Sioux chief, who had surprised and slain a detachment of the American army some years before. Among the speeches made, in one of which it was proved that as Bismarck was the centre of Dakota, Dakota the centre of the United States, and the Untied States the centre of the world, Bismarck was destined to "be the metropolitan hearth of the world's civilization," there came a short but pithy discourse from this grim old warrior, in which he told us, through an interpreter, that the Great Spirit moved him to shake hands with everybody. However, the feature of the ceremonial which struck us Europeans most was the spot chosen for the Capitol. It was not in the city, nor even on the skirts of the city; it was nearly a mile off, on the top of a hill in the brown and dusty prairie. "Why here?" we asked. "Is it because you mean to enclose the building in a public park?" "By no means; the Capitol is intended to be in the centre of the city; it is in this direction that the city is to grow." It is the same everywhere, from the Mississippi to the Pacific. Men seem to live in the future rather than in the present: not that they fail to work while it is called to-day, but that they see the country not merely as it is, but as it will be, twenty, fifty, a hundred years hence, when the seedlings shall have grown to forest trees.

This constant reaching forward to and grasping at the future does not so much express itself in words, for they are not a loquacious people, as in the air of ceaseless haste and stress which pervades the West. . . . Time seems too short for what they have to do, and the result always to come short of their desire. One feels as if caught and whirled along in a foaming stream, chafing against its banks, such is the passion of these men to accomplish in their own life-times what in the past it took centuries to effect. Sometimes in a moment of pause, for even the visitor finds himself infected by the all-pervading eagerness, one is inclined to ask them: "Gentlemen, why in heaven's name this haste? You have time enough. No enemy threatens you. No volcano will rise from beneath you. Ages and ages lie before you. Why sacrifice the present to the future, fancying that you will be happier when your fields teem with wealth and your cities with people? In Europe we have cities wealthier and more populous than yours, and we are not happy. You dream of your posterity; but your posterity will look back to yours as the golden age, and envy those who first burst into this silent splendid nature, who first lifted up their axes upon these tall trees and lined these waters with busy wharves. Why, then, seek to complete in a few decades what the other nations of the world took thousands of years over in the older continents? Why do things rudely and ill which need to be done well, seeing that the welfare of your descendants may turn upon them? Why, in your hurry to subdue and utilize nature, squander her splendid gifts? Why allow the noxious weeds of Eastern politics to take root in your new soil, when by a little effort you might keep it pure? Why hasten the advent of that threatening day when the vacant spaces of the continent shall all have been filled, and the poverty or discontent of the older States shall find no outlet? You have opportunities such as mankind has never had before, and may never have again. Your work is great and noble: it is done for a future longer and vaster than our imagination can embrace. Why not make its outlines and beginnings worthy of these destinies the thought of which gilds your hopes and elevates your purposes?"

Being once suddenly called upon to "offer a few remarks" to a Western legislature, and having on the spur of the moment nothing better to offer, I tendered some such observations as these, seasoned, of course, with the compliments to the soil, climate, and "location" reasonably expected from a visitor. They were received in good part, as indeed no people can be more kindly than the Western Americans; but it was surprising to hear several members who afterwards conversed with me remark that the political point of view—the fact that they were the founders of new commonwealths, and responsible to posterity for the foundations they laid, a point of view so trite and obvious to a European visitor that he pauses before expressing it—had not crossed their minds. If they spoke truly,—as no doubt they did,—there was in their words a further evidence of the predominance of material efforts and interests over all others, even over those political instincts which are deemed so essential a part of the American character. The arrangements of his government lie in the dim background of the picture which fills the Western eye. In the foreground he sees ploughs and sawmills, ore-crushers and railway locomotives. These so absorb his thoughts as to leave little time for constitutions and legislation; and when constitutions and legislation are thought of, it is as means for better securing the benefits of the earth and of trade to the producer, and preventing the greedy corporation from intercepting their fruits.

Politically, and perhaps socially also, this haste and excitement, this absorption in the development of the material resources of the country, are unfortunate. As a town built in a hurry is seldom well built, so a society will be the sounder in health for not having grown too swiftly. Doubtless much of the scum will be cleared away from the surface when the liquid settles and cools down. Lawlessness and lynch law will disappear; saloons and gambling-houses will not prosper in a well-conducted population; schools will improve and universites grow out of the raw colleges which one already finds even in the newer Territories. Nevertheless the bad habits of professional politics, as one sees them on the Atlantic coast, are not unknown in these communities; and the unrestfulness, the passion for speculation, the feverish eagerness for quick and showy results, may so soak into the texture of the popular mind as to colour it for centuries to come. These are the shadows which to the eye of the traveller seem to fall across the glowing landscape of the Great West.

Discussion Starters

1. How does James Bryce's description of the fate of the Indian tribes and their place in the settlement of the West compare with the traditional description of the Indian barrier and its destruction by the new Americans?

2. Bryce wrote in the 1880s that the West was the most American part of America, and he enumerated the general characteristics of the Western American. Measured according to these characteristics, how does the American of the 1970s compare with the Western American of Bryce's day? In what ways have the characteristics of the West become the characteristics of all Americans?

3. Evaluate, in the context of the 1970s, Bryce's belief that the Westerner's concern for the future and his haste in trying to build a new society is not a blessing, but a failure of character. If he was right, what defects in our society might be attributed to the haste of the past?

4. In reading Bryce's assessment of the American West, what preconceptions and assumptions of America did he apparently make before he began his travels? In what ways would such prior beliefs affect the validity of his evaulation of America?

Related Documents

I. Life on the Trail: A Texas Herd Moves Northward

ANDY ADAMS

The discovery of gold in California and later in the mountain states of the West helped to populate those areas. The demand for beef products in the rapidly industrializing East promoted the expansion of the cattle industry into the trans-Mississippi West, especially the high plains, after the Civil War. Open ranges for grazing, lack of settlement, and the extension of railroads into this region encouraged large-scale cattle operations and the long drive phase of the industry's development. With the long drive came the cowboy, and with the cowboy came the romance and myths that created one of the most prevalent of American folk traditions. Many books have been written about the cowboy and his life on the trail, but one of the best is Andy Adams' The Log of a Cowboy.

Andy Adams, *The Log of a Cowboy* (Boston: Houghton Mifflin, 1903), pp. 56–69.

Although a fictionalized account, Adams drew heavily from his own experiences as a cowboy and his Log *seems to be one of the most reliable accounts of life on the long drive.*

How do Andy Adams and his friends personify the characteristics James Bryce enumerated in The American Commonwealth?

. . . There was no regular trail through the lower counties, so we simply kept to the open country. Spring had advanced until the prairies were swarded with grass and flowers, while water, though scarcer, was to be had at least once daily. We passed to the west of San Antonio—an outfitting point which all herds touched in passing northward—and Flood and our cook took the wagon and went in for supplies. But the outfit with the herd kept on, now launched on a broad, well-defined trail, in places seventy-five yards wide, where all local trails blent into the one common pathway, known in those days as the Old Western Trail. It is not in the province of this narrative to deal with the cause or origin of this cattle trail, though it marked the passage of many hundred thousand cattle which preceded our Circle Dots, and was destined to afford an outlet to several millions more to follow. The trail proper consisted of many scores of irregular cow paths, united into one broad passageway, narrowing and widening as conditions permitted, yet ever leading northward. After a few years of continued use, it became as well defined as the course of a river. . . .

. . . The first week after leaving San Antonio, our foreman scouted in quest of water a full day in advance of the herd. One evening he returned to us with the news that we were in for a dry drive, for after passing the next chain of lakes it was sixty miles to the next water, and reports regarding the water supply even after crossing this arid stretch were very conflicting.

"While I know every foot of this trail through here," said the foreman, "there's several things that look scaly. There are only five herds ahead of us, and the first three went through the old route, but the last two, after passing Indian Lakes, for some reason or other turned and went westward. These last herds may be stock cattle, pushing out west to new ranges; but I don't like the outlook. It would take me two days to ride across and back, and by that time we could be two thirds of the way through. I've made this drive before without a drop of water on the way, and wouldn't dread it now, if there was any certainty of water at the other end. I reckon there's nothing to do but tackle her; but isn't this a hell of a country? I've ridden fifty miles to-day and never saw a soul."

The Indian Lakes, some seven in number, were natural reservoirs with rocky bottoms, and about a mile apart. We watered at ten o'clock the next day, and by night camped fifteen miles on our way. There was plenty of good grazing for the cattle and horses, and no trouble was experienced the first night. McCann had filled an extra twenty gallon keg for this trip. Water was too precious an article to be lavish with, so we shook the dust from our clothing and went unwashed. This was no serious deprivation, and no one could be critical of another, for we were all equally dusty and dirty. The next morning by daybreak the cattle were thrown off the bed ground and started grazing before the sun could dry out what little moisture the grass had absorbed during the night. The heat of the past week had been very oppressive, and in order to avoid it as much as possible, we made late and early drives. Before the wagon passed the herd during the morning drive, what few canteens we had were filled with water for the men. The *remuda*[1] was kept with the herd, and four changes of mounts were made during the day, in order not to exhaust any one horse. . . .

After the fourth change of horses was made, Honeyman pushed on ahead with the saddle stock and overtook the wagon. Under Flood's orders he was to tie up all the night horses, for if the cattle could be induced to graze, we would not bed them down before ten that night, and all hands would be required with the herd. McCann had instructions to make camp on the divide, which was known to be twenty-five miles from our camp of the night before, or forty miles from the Indian Lakes. As we expected, the cattle grazed willingly after nightfall, and with a fair moon, we allowed them to scatter freely while grazing forward. The beacon of McCann's fire on the divide was in sight over an hour before the herd grazed up to camp, all hands remaining to bed the thirsty cattle. The herd was given triple the amount of space usually required for bedding, and even then for nearly an hour scarcely half of them lay down.

We were handling the cattle as humanely as possible under the circumstances. The guards for the night were doubled, six men on the first half and the same on the latter, Bob Blades being detailed to assist Honeyman in night-herding the saddle horses. If any of us got more than an hour's sleep that night, he was lucky. Flood, McCann, and the horse wranglers did not even try to rest. To those of us who could find time to eat, our cook kept open house. Our foreman knew that a well-fed man can stand an incredible amount of hardship, and appreciated the fact that on the trail a good cook is a valuable asset. Our outfit therefore was cheerful to a man, and jokes and songs helped to while away the weary hours of the night.

The second guard, under Flood, pushed the cattle off their beds an hour before dawn, and before they were relieved had urged the herd more than five miles on the third day's drive over this waterless mesa. In spite of our economy of water, after breakfast on this third morning there was scarcely enough left to fill the canteens for the day. In view of this, we could promise ourselves no midday meal—except a can of tomatoes to the man; so the wagon was ordered to drive through to the expected water ahead, while the saddle horses were held available as on the day before for frequent changing of mounts. The day turned out to be one of torrid heat, and before the middle of the forenoon, the cattle

[1] *Editors' note:* A string of extra horses.

lolled their tongues in despair, while their sullen lowing surged through from rear to lead and back again in piteous yet ominous appeal. The only relief we could offer was to travel them slowly, as they spurned every opportunity offered them either to graze or to lie down.

It was nearly noon when we reached the last divide, and sighted the scattering timber of the expected watercourse. The enforced order of the day before—to hold the herd in a walk and prevent exertion and heating—now required four men in the lead, while the rear followed over a mile behind, dogged and sullen. Near the middle of the afternoon, McCann returned on one of his mules with the word that it was a question if there was water enough to water even the horse stock. . . .

The outlook was anything but encouraging. Flood and Forrest scouted the creek up and down for ten miles in a fruitless search for water. The outfit held the herd back until the twilight of evening, when Flood returned and confirmed McCann's report. It was twenty miles yet to the next water ahead, and if the horse stock could only be watered thoroughly, Flood was determined to make the attempt to nurse the herd through to water. McCann was digging an extra well, and he expressed the belief that by hollowing out a number of holes, enough water could be secured for the saddle stock. . . .

Holding the herd this third night required all hands. Only a few men at a time were allowed to go into camp and eat, for the herd refused even to lie down. What few cattle attempted to rest were prevented by the more restless ones. By spells they would mill, until riders were sent through the herd at a break-neck pace to break up the groups. During these milling efforts of the herd, we drifted over a mile from camp; but by the light of moon and stars and the number of riders, scattering was prevented. . . .

Good cloudy weather would have saved us, but in its stead was a sultry morning without a breath of air, which bespoke another day of sizzling heat. We had not been on the trail over two hours before the heat became almost unbearable to man and beast. Had it not been for the condition of the herd, all might yet have gone well; but over three days had now elapsed without water for the cattle, and they became feverish and ungovernable. The lead cattle turned back several times, wandering aimlessly in any direction, and it was with considerable difficulty that the herd could be held on the trail. The rear overtook the lead, and the cattle gradually lost all semblance of a trail herd. Our horses were fresh, however, and after about two hours' work, we once more got the herd strung out in trailing fashion; but before a mile had been covered, the leaders again turned, and the cattle congregated into a mass of unmanageable animals, milling and lowing in their fever and thirst. The milling only intensified their sufferings from the heat, and the outfit split and quartered them again and again, in the hope that this unfortunate outbreak might be checked. No sooner was the milling stopped than they would surge hither and yon, sometimes half a mile, as ungovernable as the waves of an ocean. After wasting several hours in this manner, they finally turned back over the trail, and the utmost efforts of every man in the outfit failed to check them. We threw our ropes in their faces, and when this failed, we resorted to shooting; but in defiance of the fusillade and the smoke they walked sullenly through the line of horsemen across their front. Six-shooters were discharged so close to the leaders' faces as to singe their hair, yet, under a noonday sun, they disregarded this and every other device to turn them, and passed wholly out of our control. In a number of instances wild steers deliberately walked against our horses, and then for the first time a fact dawned on us that chilled the marrow in our bones,—*the herd was going blind.*

The bones of men and animals that lie bleaching along the trails abundantly testify that this was not the first instance in which the plain had baffled the determination of man. It was now evident that nothing short of water would stop the herd, and we rode aside and let them pass. As the outfit turned back to the wagon, our foreman seemed dazed by the sudden and unexpected turn of affairs, but rallied and met the emergency.

"There's but one thing left to do," said he, as we rode along, "and that is to hurry the outfit back to Indian Lakes. The herd will travel day and night, and instinct can be depended on to carry them to the only water they know. It's too late to be of any use now, but it's plain why those last two herds turned off at the lakes; some one had gone back and warned them of the very thing we've met. We must beat them to the lakes, for water is the only thing that will check them now. It's a good thing that they are strong, and five or six days without water will hardly kill any. It was no vague statement of the man who said if he owned hell and Texas, he'd rent Texas and live in hell, for if this isn't Billy hell, I'd like to know what you call it."

We spent an hour watering the horses from the wells of our camp of the night before, and about two o'clock started back over the trail for Indian Lakes. We overtook the abandoned herd during the afternoon. They were strung out nearly five miles in length, and were walking about a three-mile gait. . . .

It was fortunate for us that there were no range cattle at these lakes, and we had only to cover a front of about six miles to catch the drifting herd. It was nearly noon the next day before the cattle began to arrive at the water holes in squads of from twenty to fifty. Pitiful objects as they were, it was a novelty to see them reach the water and slack their thirst. Wading out into the lakes until their sides were half covered, they would stand and low in a soft moaning voice, often for half an hour before attempting to drink. Contrary to our expectation, they drank very little at first, but stood in the water for hours. After coming out, they would lie down and rest for hours longer, and then drink again before attempting to graze, their thirst overpowering hunger. . . .

By early evening, the rear guard of our outfit returned and reported the tail end of the herd some twenty miles behind when they left them. During the day not over a thousand head reached the lakes, and towards evening we put these under herd and easily held them during the night. All four of the men who constituted the rear guard were sent back the next morning to prod up the rear again, and during the night at least a thousand more came into the lakes, which held them better than a hundred men. With the recovery of the cattle our hopes grew, and with the gradual accessions to the herd, confidence was again completely restored. . . .

II. *Buffalo Bill Wins the Title of Champion Hunter of the Plains*

WILLIAM F. CODY

Among the major obstacles faced by railroad builders as they extended their lines across the vast distances of the West were the Indians and the buffalo herds. To men of the twentieth century it may seem strange that buffaloes posed a problem, but the roaming herds threatened the safety and the schedules of the trains and provided the Indians with food and materials with which to continue to resist the white man. The buffaloes were in the way, and, like the Indian, they were destroyed for the sake of progress.

When the Kansas Pacific Railroad extended its tracks into the high plains, it hired men to kill buffaloes for food for the rail-laying crews and to provide safety for the trains. One of these men was William F. Cody, or, as he was popularly known in the late 1860s, "Buffalo Bill." In the following article Buffalo Bill described his winning the title of champion buffalo hunter of the plains in a match with Billy Comstock, another hunter and scout.

In what ways does Cody's account illustrate James Bryce's conclusions about the character of the western American?

It was arranged that I should shoot a match with him, and the preliminaries were easily and satisfactorily arranged. We were to hunt one day of eight hours, beginning at eight o'clock in the morning. The wager was five hundred dollars a side, and the man who should kill the greater number of buffaloes from horseback was to be declared the winner. Incidentally my title of "Buffalo Bill" was at stake.

The hunt took place twenty miles east of Sheridan. It had been well advertised, and there was a big "gallery." An excursion party, whose members came chiefly from St. Louis and numbered nearly a hundred ladies and gentlemen, came on a special train to view the sport. Among them was my wife and my little daughter Arta, who had come to visit me for a time.

From *An Autobiography of Buffalo Bill* by Colonel W. F. Cody. Copyright 1920 by Cosmopolitan Book Corporation. Copyright 1948 by William J. Garlow, Frederick H. Garlow and Jane Garlow Mallehan. Reprinted by permission of Holt, Rinehart and Winston, Inc.

Buffaloes were plentiful. It had been agreed that we should go into the herd at the same time and make our "runs," each man killing as many animals as possible. A referee followed each of us, horseback, keeping well out of sight of the buffaloes, so as not to frighten them until the time came for us to dash into the herd. They were permitted to approach closely enough to see what was going on.

For the first "run" we were fortunate in getting good ground. Comstock was mounted on his favorite horse. I rode old Brigham. I felt confident that I had the advantage in two things: first, I had the best buffalo horse in the country; second, I was using what was known at the time as a needle-gun, a breech-loading Springfield rifle, caliber .50. This was "Lucretia," the weapon of which I have already told you. Comstock's Henry rifle, though it could fire more rapidly than mine, did not, I felt certain, carry powder and lead enough to equal my weapon in execution.

When the time came to go into the herd, Comstock and I dashed forward, followed by the referees. The animals separated. Comstock took the left bunch, I the right. My great forte in killing buffaloes was to get them circling by riding my horse at the head of the herd and shooting their leaders. Thus the brutes behind were crowded to the left, so that they were soon going round and round.

This particular morning the animals were very accommodating. I soon had them running in a beautiful circle. I dropped them thick and fast till I had killed thirty-eight, which finished my "run."

Comstock began shooting at the rear of the buffaloes he was chasing, and they kept on in a straight line. He succeeded in killing twenty-three, but they were scattered over a distance of three miles. The animals I had shot lay close together.

Our St. Louis friends set out champagne when the result of the first run was announced. It proved a good drink on a Kansas prairie, and a buffalo hunter proved an excellent man to dispose of it.

While we were resting we espied another herd approaching. It was a small drove, but we prepared to make it serve our purpose. The buffaloes were cows and calves, quicker in their movements than the bulls. We charged in among them, and I got eighteen to Comstock's fourteen.

Again the spectators approached, and once more the champagne went round. After a luncheon we resumed the hunt. Three miles distant we saw another herd. I was so far ahead of my competitor now that I thought I could afford to give an exhibition of my skill. Leaving my saddle and bridle behind, I rode, with my competitor, to windward of the buffaloes.

I soon had thirteen down, the last one of which I had driven close to the wagons where the ladies were watching the contest. It frightened some of the tender creatures to see a buffalo coming at full speed directly toward them, but I dropped him in his tracks before he had got within fifty yards of the wagon. This finished my "run" with a score of sixty-nine buffaloes for the day. Comstock had killed forty-six.

It was now late in the afternoon. Comstock and his backers gave up the idea of beating me. The referee declared me the winner of the match, and the champion buffalo hunter of the Plains.

On our return to camp we brought with us the best bits of meat, as well as the biggest and best buffalo heads. The heads I always turned over to the company, which found a very good use for them. They were mounted in the finest possible manner and sent to the principal cities along the road, as well as to the railroad centers of the country. Here they were prominently placed at the leading hotels and in the stations, where they made an excellent advertisement for the road. Today they attract the attention of travelers almost everywhere. Often, while touring the country, I see one of them, and feel reasonably certain that I brought down the animal it once ornamented. Many a wild and exciting hunt is thus called to my mind.

III. *"We Want Peace and Love"*

CHIEF RED CLOUD

The fate of the American Indian at the hands of the white man is one of the great tragedies of American history. As occupants of the areas desired by the new Americans, the Indians were simply in the way. Treaties were written and sworn to by both sides, only to be undermined almost immediately by the increasing numbers of miners, cattlemen, and farmers who were looking for new opportunities and a fresh start. When the Indian tribes realized that the treaties did not effectively guarantee their ancestral lands, they turned to warfare to keep the invaders out. From 1862 to 1890 there were half a dozen wars between the United States and the western Indian tribes. The wars were characterized by a savagery that created bitterness and hatred on both sides. The mutually uncompromising positions that soon developed could only be settled, it seemed, by further resort to arms.

In different sections of the West various Indian tribes resisted courageously for more than three decades, but the eventual outcome of the struggle was apparent to both sides by the late 1870s. Those Indians who recognized the realities of the situation knew that nothing could stop the onslaught of the new Americans. If the Indians continued their resistance they were destroyed, but when they cooperated they were defrauded, starved, and penned up in reservations. There was no way out for the tribes, no effective recourse for their grievances, so they suffered the fate of a conquered people. Because most of the new Americans saw the Indian as a savage who had stood in the way of progress, their expressions of regret did not soften their conviction that it was necessary that the Indian tribes be removed from the desirable areas.

Red Cloud was Chief of the Oglala Sioux during the sixties and seventies. While visiting the East to present his views to President Ulysses S. Grant, he was asked to address the Indian Peace Commission at the Cooper Institute in New

New York Times, June 17, 1870.

York City. How does the following speech by Chief Red Cloud call into question the traditional view of the savage red man? How might Red Cloud have responded to James Bryce's assertion that the presence of the Indians in the West had added a certain spice to the movement of the new Americans into the West?

JUNE 17, 1870

THE GREAT CHIEF

Red Cloud Meets His White Brethren at Cooper Institute

A "Big Talk" There in the Interests of Peace

VAST GATHERING OF PALE FACES

Speeches by the Indian Chieftains and Their White Advocates

The Wrongs of the Past and Redress for the Future

My Brothers and my Friends who are before me today: God Almighty has made us all, and He is here to hear what I have to say to you today. The Great Spirit made us both. He gave us lands and He gave you lands. You came here and we received you as brothers. When the Almighty made you, He made you all white and clothed you. When He made us, He made us with red skins and poor. When you first came we were very many and you were few. Now you are many and we are few. You do not know who appears before you to speak. He is a representative of the original American race, the first people of this continent. We are good, and not bad. The reports which you get about us are all on one side. You hear of us only as murderers and thieves. We are not so. If we had more lands to give to you we would give them, but we have no more. We are driven into a very little island, and we want you, our dear friends, to help us with the Government of the United States. The Great Spirit made us poor and ignorant. He made you rich and wise and skillful in things which we know nothing about. The good Father made you to eat tame game and us to eat wild game. Ask anyone who has gone through to California. They will tell you we have treated them well. You have children. We, too, have children, and we wish to bring them up well. We ask you to help us do it. At the mouth of Horse Creek, in 1852, the Great Father made a treaty with us. We agreed to let him pass through our territory unharmed for fifty-five years. We kept our word. We committed no murders, no depredations, until the troops came there. When the troops were sent there trouble and disturbance arose. Since that time there have been various goods sent from time to time to us, but only once did they reach us, and soon the Great Father took away the only good man he had sent us, Colonel Fitzpatrick. The Great Father said we must go to farming, and some of our men went to farming near Fort Laramie, and were treated very badly indeed. We came to Washington to see our Great Father that peace might be continued. The Great Father that made us both wishes peace to be kept; we want to keep peace. Will you help us? In 1868 men came out and brought papers. We could not read them, and they did not tell us truly what was in them. We thought the treaty was to remove the forts, and that we should then cease from fighting. But they wanted to sent us traders on to Missouri. We did not want to go on to Missouri, but wanted traders where we were. When I reached Washington the Great Father explained to me what the treaty was, and showed me that the interpreters had deceived me. All I want is right and justice. I have tried to get from the Great Father what is right and just. I have not altogether succeeded. I want you to help me to get what is right and just. I represent the whole Sioux nation, and they are bound by what I say. I am no SPOTTED TAIL,[1] to say one thing one day and be bought for a pin the next. Look at me. I am poor and naked, but I am the Chief of the nation. We do not want riches, but we want to train our children right. Riches would do us no good. We could not take them with us to the other world. We do not want riches, we want peace and love.

The riches that we have in this world, Secretary Cox[2] said truly, we cannot take with us to the next world. Then I wish to know why Commissioners are sent out to us who do nothing but rob us and get the riches of this world away from us? I was brought up among the traders, and those who came out there in the early times treated me well and I had a good time with them. They taught us to wear clothes and to use tobacco and ammunition. But, by and by, the Great Father sent out a different kind of men; men who cheated and drank whiskey; men who were so bad that the Great Father could not keep them at home and so sent them out here. I have sent a great many words to the Great Father but they never reached him. They were drowned on the way, and I was afraid the words I spoke lately to the Great Father would not reach you, so I came to speak to you myself; and now I am going away to my home. I want to have men sent out to my people whom we know and can trust. I am glad I have come here. You belong in the East and I belong in the West, and I am glad I have come here and that we could understand one another. I am very much obliged to you for listening to me. I go home this afternoon. I hope you will think of what I have said to you. I bid you all an affectionate farewell.

---

[1] *Editors' note:* Chief of the Brutes Sioux and sometime rival of Red Cloud.
[2] *Editors' note:* Secretary of the Interior Jacob D. Cox.

IV. Life on the Plains: A Sod-House Farmer Stakes His Claim

HOWARD RUEDE

The trans-Mississippi West went through many stages of settlement during the last half of the nineteenth century, but the final stage for most areas came with the arrival of the farmer and his fences and cultivated fields. The farmers came chiefly from the older eastern states, but many European immigrants also came to settle and cultivate the wilderness. These pioneer farmers led lives filled with monotonous physical labor and suffering. There was no romance in working from sunup to sundown day after day, week after week, year after year on a plot of land miles from neighbors and towns, nourishing the hope of someday having a prosperous farm. But work they did, and they contributed immeasurably to the final settlement of the West.

Howard Ruede migrated to Kansas from Pennsylvania in 1877 in the hope of establishing a farm. As he struggled to establish himself on the frontier he wrote of his experiences to his family back in Pennsylvania. How do the attitudes expressed in the following letters compare with James Bryce's attitude toward the western style of life and the concept of future he found among the people he encountered in the West?

MARCH 22, 1877

. . . We got home about noon, and between 2 and 3 we three started for Squire Walrond's office to make application for land. We took out homesteads directly. We might have "filed" on the land, and that filing would have been good for 30 months, at the end of which time (or before) we could have bought the land or put a homestead on it. As it is, we must live on it five years. The first two years we live "off and on"—that is, we must sleep on it once in a while and make some improvements on it within 6 months, or it will be forfeited. It is to be our home, but we can hire out by the day or month as we like. A man here has three rights—homestead, filing and timber filing. By taking land under the first he must live on it five years, and at the end of five years of actual residence can "prove up" and get a deed. The second right I explained above. The timber filing requires a man to break 10 acres the first year, which he must plant with trees 12 feet apart the second year, besides breaking an additional 10 acres. The third year he must plant these 10, and break 20, which must be planted the fourth year. Then he is entitled to an additional 160 acres. It is a hard thing to live up to the law on a timber filing because young trees are hard to get, and when you have them, the question is whether they will grow. The application and affidavit cost us $16—50 cents cheaper than if we had gone at separate times. If we had gone to the land office at Kirwin it would have cost but $15 but then we would have had the expenses to and from Kirwin, besides our meals there. We were recommended by Mr. Schweitzer to go to Walrond.

Howard Ruede, *Sod-House Days,* ed. John Ise (New York: Columbia University Press, 1937), pp. 19–20, 30–33, 91–92.

MARCH 28, 1877

AT SNYDER'S, KILL CREEK, KANSAS

Noah staked two of the corners of my claim this morning, before he went out
to herd the cattle and Jim and I followed him, looking for a place to make our
dugout. We found a spot about ¾ mile from Snyders house where a patch of
wild sunflowers had killed the grass. Here we began to dig, and by noon had
made some progress. We laid off the ground 10 × 14 feet, and we'll have to
dig it about 6 feet deep. Just before dinner I wished myself back home, and
would have started for Osborne, but Jim persuaded me to stay. After dinner
we went back to the hole and in about two hours had dug about half of it to
the depth of two feet. And then we were stopped by a shower coming up, which
bid fair to keep on till night, but did not, though the clouds hung very low.
We went back to the house, and Snyder fixed the handle to our ax. My dugout
is at the head of the prettiest draw on my claim, and if the clouds clear off we
will have it finished by the middle of next week. This afternoon Bevvy Neusch-
wanger rode up to see Mrs. Snyder and while they were talking we made off
and put in a little more work on the claim. Talk about hard work will you?
Just try digging in the ground out here two feet from the surface—oh, I should
have written 6 inches from the surface. The ground is packed just as hard
as could be, and it is no fun to pick and shovel it. It is damp as far as we
have gone down (some 27 inches) and sticky as putty. Sometimes we can
throw out lumps as big as your head. About 3 o'clock we had a little
shower and then we quit work and went back to the house. We wanted a
little instruction about putting the handle into the axe, and Snyder offered
to do it for us, for which we were glad enough and by the time it was
dark, the axe was fixed. Now our possessions consist of an axe, shovel and
tincup, besides our clothing.

The prairie chickens are about as pretty a bird as you will come across.
They are about as big as a half-grown barnyard fowl, and are not much shyer.
The folks say they become more numerous as the land is broken up. The law
forbids a man shooting them on any claim but his own, but if a poor fellow
shoots a couple on somebody else's claim for food, no one thinks of having him
up for it. The folks here all talk German more than English, but they can all
get along, even if they cannot use the latter tongue very fluently. I talk English
altogether and they may talk what they please.

MARCH 29, 1877

AT SNYDER'S, KILL CREEK, KANSAS

The people here don't go to church—they "go to meeting." Services are held
in private houses. The various denominations are not exclusive, and everybody

is welcome to the services whether he is the particular faith of the preacher or not. A Roman Catholic and a Hardshell Baptist, or a Methodist are on just as friendly terms as though both had precisely the same creed and observed the same forms in their worship. A visiting preacher, no matter of what denomination, is always sure of an audience in proportion to the size of the house in which he has been invited to hold the service, and often the room is full and others unable to get into the house stand by the door and windows to catch what they can of the sermon.

At whatever house the services are held all the people present are expected to stay for dinner, which follows the sermon. . . . The dinner is usually substantial and palatable. It seems to be thought no imposition for fifty or more people to take dinner at a place, and even sometimes people take offense if you attend meeting and leave without partaking of their hospitality. In some cases those who attend meeting arrive the night before, coming ten to fifteen miles to hear preaching by a minister of their own denomination. This is especially true of the Dunkards, who have a small organization east of Osborne.

JUNE 4, 1877

The people who live in sod houses, and, in fact, all who live under a dirt roof, are pestered with swarms or bed bugs. . . . The vermin were not brought here by the immigrants; they grew on the trees along the river and creeks before the first settlers arrived. The bugs infest the log and sod chicken coops, too, in countless thousands, or, if you wish to measure them in a spoon, you can gather them up in that way from between the sods in the wall. I have heard chicken raisers complain that their fowls are killed by the bugs getting into their ears. Whether or not that is the cause of the fowls dying, the bugs are blamed. Where the sod houses are plastered the bed bugs are not such a nuisance.

You don't have to keep a dog in order to have plenty of fleas, for they are natives too and do their best to drive out the intruding settlers. Just have a dirt floor and you have fleas, sure. They seem to spring from the dust of the earth. Coal oil and water are sometimes used to sprinkle the floor, but that abates the pest only for a short time, and oil costs 35 cents a gallon. People who have board floors are not bothered so much with these fleas.

Another nuisance here is what people call "Kansas itch," which attacks nearly everybody within a short time after arrival here; few are immune. Not all are affected alike; some scratch a few days, other are affected for months. It is not contagious—at least not all who come in contact with those suffering with it take the disease. There is only one way in which a sufferer can get relief —scratching; and that aggravates the itching and sometimes produces raw sore spots. But those are easier to heal than it is to get the disease out of your system. Change of water is sometimes given as the cause; bed bugs and fleas are sometimes blamed, but it seems as if the itch has to run its course in every case. It disappears as mysteriously as it came.

For Further Reading

Hundreds of books have been written on the different aspects of the westward expansion of the United States in the nineteenth century. Introductions to the vast amount of material produced by the research going into these books can be found in general accounts of the period such as Ray Allen Billington's *America's Frontier Heritage**(1966) and *Westward Expansion* (1967), John C. Parrish's *The Persistence of the Westward Movement* (1943), Robert E. Riegel and Robert G. Athearn's *America Moves West* (1971), Henry Nash Smith's *Virgin Land**(1950), and Louis B. Wright's *Culture on the Moving Frontier** (1955).

Each of these historians has, in some measure, been influenced by Frederick Jackson Turner's thesis on the role of the frontier in American history; therefore, Turner's "Significance of the Frontier in American History" in *Frontier & Section**(1961) is a must in order to understand the historiography of western America. Turner's thesis is central to Merle Curti's *The Making of an American Community**(1959) and is further explained in Wilbur R. Jacobs' *The Historical World of Frederick Jackson Turner* (1968). Since there is considerable controversy over the validity of the "frontier thesis," one should also consult *The Frontier Thesis: Valid Interpretation of American History?**(1966) by Ray Allen Billington.

The mining phase of western development is described in *Gold Rush Diary* (1967), edited by Thomas D. Clark, and *Mining Frontiers of the Far West: 1848–1880** (1963), by Rodman W. Paul. As for the opening of the West, or, as some historians have labeled it, the "transportation frontier," consult W. Turrentine Jackson's *Wagon Roads West* (1965), Robert E. Riegel's *The Story of the Western Railroads** (1926; reprinted in 1964), and Oscar O. Winther's *The Transportation Frontier* (1964).

The story of the cowboy and the cattleman has received great attention in the last fifty years, the most notable works being Edward E. Dale's *The Range Cattle Industry* (1930), Robert R. Dykstra's *The Cattle Towns* (1968), Joe B. Frantz and Julian E. Choate, Jr., *The American Cowboy: The Myth and the Reality* (1955), Wayne Gard's *The Chisholm Trail* (1954), Ernest S. Osgood's *The Day of the Cattlemen** (1929; reprinted but n.d.), Louis Pelzer's *The Cattlemen's Frontier* (1936; reprinted in 1969), and Floyd B. Streeter's *Prairie Trails and Cow Towns* (1936; reprinted in 1963). Special consideration has been given to a heretofore neglected topic in western history in *The Negro Cowboys* (1965), by Philip Durham and Everett L. Jones. Other aspects of western development are found in Henry D. and Frances T. McCallum's *The Wire That Fenced the West* (1965) and Charles W. Towne and Edward N. Wentworth's *Shepherd's Empire* (1945).

The Indian tribes have received increasing recognition in the last twenty years. The current list of books includes: Robert K. Andrist, *The Long Death** (1964); William Brandon, *The American Heritage Book of Indians* (1961); Dee

*Paperbound edition available.

Brown, *Bury My Heart At Wounded Knee* (1971); Henry E. Fritz, *The Movement for Indian Assimilation, 1860–1890* (1963); William T. Hagan, *American Indians** (1962); Helen Hunt Jackson, *A Century of Dishonor* (1881; reprinted but n.d.); and Loring B. Priest, *Uncle Sam's Stepchildren* (1969). More selective topics are described in Stan Hoig's *The Sand Creek Massacre* (1961), E. Adamson Hoebel's *The Cheyennes** (1966), Alvin M. Josephy, Jr., *The Nez Percé Indians and the Opening of the Northwest* (1965); and C. M. Oehler's *The Great Sioux Uprising* (1959). The effect of the destruction of the buffalo on the Plains Indians is described in Wayne Gard's *The Great Buffalo Hunt** (1959).

The settlement of the Great Plains receives detailed attention in *The Sod House Frontier* (1937; reprinted in 1954), by Everett Dick, *The Farmer's Frontier* (1966), by Gilbert C. Fite, and *The Great Plains* (1931; reprinted in 1957), by Walter P. Webb. The problems of land disposal and government land policies are described in Roy M. Robbins' *Our Landed Heritage** (1942).

Collections of documents relating to the West include Martin Ridge and Ray Allen Billington, eds., *America's Frontier Story: A Documentary History of Westward Expansion** (1969).

*Paperbound edition available.

3. The Perils of the City

"Those who labor in the earth," wrote Jefferson in 1784, "are the chosen people of God, if ever he had a chosen people. . . . The mobs of great cities add just so much to the support of pure government, as sores do to the strength of the human body." A century later the laborers of the earth, chosen of God or not, were abandoning the countryside to join the mobs of great cities. In the last decades of the nineteenth century the Jeffersonian ideal was still alive in theory, but in fact agrarianism as the American way of life had had its day. Instead, urbanization and industrialization, partners in progress, had become the driving forces in America's development.

Measured in almost any terms—extended boundaries, changed land-scapes, rising populations—the growth of cities in the United States in the years of rapid industrialization is striking. Urban statistics reveal a dramatic story: In 1910 the urban population (that is, the population of cities of 2,500 and larger) was seven times greater than it had been in 1860. In the same period the number of cities of 100,000 or more increased from 9 to 50, and those in the 10,000 to 25,000 range increased from 58 to 369.

The reasons for this rapid urbanization are not mysterious. As industry was added to commerce, employment opportunities in cities attracted many who sought to better themselves. Some came from farms and small towns, where high birth rates produced populations larger than could be easily sustained and where opportunities seemed limited. Vast numbers also came to the cities from foreign countries. The foreign-born population of Chicago in 1890, for example, almost equaled Chicago's *entire* population a decade earlier. Both immigration and migration, furthermore, were encouraged by promotional efforts of cities, and these in turn were stimulated by intercity rivalries. In addition, population shifts were facilitated by important developments in transportation, particularly the establishment of a vast railroad network.

The growing pains of cities were severe. Besides making economic adjustments, a growing city had to develop technological capabilities for handling concentrated and congested populations. Housing, sewage and garbage disposal, traffic, and fire protection all taxed the resources of cities to their limits. Housing was also a social problem, as were the rapid increases in vice and crime and the rising demands for health services. Beyond this, cities were hindered in their response to pressing problems by corruption in their governments, although the hindrance was probably not as great as was once assumed.

Yet these problems—economic, technological, social, and political—were all in some way manageable. In the eyes of many, the greater problems presented by the rise of the city were ethical problems, for the city seemed to put traditional American ideals and values in peril. These ethical problems raised by the growth of cities are the central concern of this chapter.

Core Document

Perils—The City

JOSIAH STRONG

Among those in the 1880s who were alert to the perils posed by the city was Josiah Strong, a Congregational clergyman and mission society secretary. When Strong was commissioned by the American Home Missionary Society to update the society's Our Country—*which had first been published in periodical form in 1841 and revised several times since—he saw his task as a large one. In 1885 he produced an entirely new work, one that was far more than a mere missionary pamphlet. Yet the tone and thrust of Strong's* Our Country *reflect his missionary zeal and outlook.*

Strong wrote from an establishment position. To him America had a predetermined task: God would use it as the instrument for the world's redemption. To be true to this task America had to stay on course, to hold together, to meet the challenges and overcome the perils it faced. The perils were dealt with

Josiah Strong, *Our Country* (New York: Baker and Taylor, rev. ed., 1891), pp. 171–74, 176–86.

specifically: immigration, Romanism, attacks on religion in the public schools by the Roman Catholic hierarchy and secularists, Mormonism, intemperance, wealth, and the city. The city, in Strong's view, was the real testing ground of American democracy and Protestant Christianity, and he was anxious to see it survive the test.

The response to Our Country *was sensational. Statistics, scientific evidence, and biblical references were blended in such a way that its theme was widely regarded as plausible, and it dealt with matters of concern to large numbers of Americans. Strong immediately became a celebrity. Not yet forty years of age when the first edition appeared, 175,000 copies were sold during his lifetime. Yet Strong's fame does not rest on this book alone; for more than three decades after its publication he was one of Protestantism's foremost spokesmen and a leader in the social gospel movement.*

In reading this chapter from Our Country, *note Strong's beliefs concerning:*

- *specific forces in the city that made it a serious menace to America.*
- *institutions that, had they been effective and sufficient, might have turned back the perilous forces.*
- *the hope for the future of cities.*
- *the importance of cities in the future of America.*
- *the time in the development of the city when American institutions would meet their real test.*

The city is the nerve center of our civilization. It is also the storm center. The fact, therefore, that it is growing much more rapidly than the whole population is full of significance. In 1790 one-thirtieth of the population of the United States lived in cities of 8,000 inhabitants and over; in 1800, one twenty-fifth; in 1810, and also in 1820, one-twentieth; in 1830, one-sixteenth; in 1840, one-twelfth; in 1850, one-eighth; in 1860, one-sixth; in 1870, a little over one-fifth; and in 1880, 22.5 per cent, or nearly one-fourth. From 1790 to 1880 the whole population increased twelve fold, the urban population eighty-six fold. From 1830 to 1880 the whole population increased a little less than four fold, the urban population thirteen fold. From 1870 to 1880 the whole population increased thirty per cent, the urban population forty per cent. During the half century preceding 1880, population in the city increased more than four times as rapidly as that of the village and country. In 1800 there were only six cities in the United States which had a population of 8,000 or more. In 1880 there were 286, and in 1890, 437.

The city has become a serious menace to our civilization, because in it, excepting Mormonism, each of the dangers we have discussed [in earlier chapters] is enhanced, and all are focalized. It has a peculiar attraction for the immigrant. Our fifty principal cities in 1880 contained 39.3 per cent of our entire German population, and 45.8 per cent of the Irish. Our ten larger cities at that time contained only nine per cent of the entire population, but 23 per cent of the foreign. While a little less than one-third of the population of the

United States was foreign by birth or parentage, sixty-two per cent of the population of Cincinnati was foreign, eighty-three per cent of Cleveland, sixty-three per cent of Boston, eighty per cent of New York, and ninety-one per cent of Chicago. A census of Massachusetts, taken in 1885, showed that in 65 towns and cities of the state 65.1 per cent of the population was foreign by birth or parentage.

Because our cities are so largely foreign, Romanism [Catholicism] finds in them its chief strength.

For the same reason the saloon, together with the intemperance and the liquor power which it represents, is multiplied in the city. East of the Mississippi there was, in 1880, one saloon to every 438 of the population; in Boston, one to every 329; in Cleveland, one to every 192; in Chicago, one to every 179; in New York, one to every 171; in Cincinnati, one to every 124. Of course the demoralizing and pauperizing power of the saloons and their debauching influence in politics increase with their numerical strength.

It is the city where wealth is massed; and here are the tangible evidences of it piled many stories high. Here the sway of Mammon is widest, and his worship the most constant and eager. Here are luxuries gathered—everything that dazzles the eye, or tempts the appetite; here is the most extravagant expenditure. Here, also, is the *congestion* of wealth the severest. Dives and Lazarus are brought face to face; here, in sharp contrast, are the *ennui* of surfeit and the desperation of starvation. The rich are richer, and the poor are poorer, in the city than elsewhere; and, as a rule, the greater the city, the greater are the riches of the rich and the poverty of the poor. Not only does the proportion of the poor increase with the growth of the city, but their condition becomes more wretched. The poor of a city of 8,000 inhabitants are well off compared with many in New York; and there are hardly such depths of woe, such utter and heart-wringing wretchedness in New York as in London. . . .

Socialism centers in the city, and the materials of its growth are multiplied with the growth of the city. Here is heaped the social dynamite; here roughs, gamblers, thieves, robbers, lawless and desperate men of all sorts, congregate; men who are ready on any pretext to raise riots for the purpose of destruction and plunder; here gather foreigners and wage-workers who are especially susceptible to socialist arguments; here skepticism and irreligion abound; here inequality is the greatest and most obvious, and the contrast between opulence and penury the most striking; here is suffering the sorest. As the greatest wickedness in the world is to be found not among the cannibals of some far-off coast, but in Christian lands where the light of truth is diffused and rejected, so the utmost depth of wretchedness exists not among savages who have few wants, but in great cities, where, in the presence of plenty and of every luxury men starve. Let a man become the owner of a home, and he is much less susceptible to socialistic propagandism. But real estate is so high in the city that it is almost impossible for a wage-worker to become a householder. . . .

Said a New York Supreme Judge, a few years ago: "There is a large class—I was about to say a majority—of the population of New York and Brooklyn, who just live, and to whom rearing of two or more children means inevitably a boy for the penitentiary, and a girl for the brothel." "When an English Judge tells us, as Mr. Justice Wills did the other day, that there were any number of parents who would kill their children for a few pounds' insurance money, we can form some idea of the horrors of the existence into which many of the children of this highly favored land are ushered at their birth." Under such conditions smolder the volcanic fires of a deep discontent.

We have seen how the dangerous elements of our civilization are each multiplied and all concentered in the city. Do we find there the conservative forces of society equally numerous and strong? Here are the tainted spots in the body-politic; where is the salt? In 1890 there was in the United States one Protestant church organization to every 438 of the population. Including all Protestant churches, together with missions, there was in Boston one church to every 1778 of the population, and in St. Louis, one to 2662; not including missions, there was in Cincinnati one Protestant church to every 2195; in Buffalo, one to 2650; in Chicago, one to 3601. The average city church is larger than the average country church, but allowing for this fact we may say that the city, where the forces of evil are massed, and where the need of Christian influence is peculiarly great, is from one-half to one-quarter as well supplied with churches as the nation at large. And church accommodations in the city are growing more inadequate every year. Including all Protestant churches, Chicago had in 1836 one church to every 1042 of the population; in 1851, one to every 1577; in 1860, one to 1820; in 1870, one to 2433; in 1880, one to 3062; and in 1890, one to 3601. . . . So far as I have made investigations, there is a general tendency, with variations, in the growth of urban population to outrun church provision. It is true that church buildings are larger now than they used to be, but after recognizing this fact, it is evident that church provision is becoming more and more inadequate to the needs of the city.

In Chicago, "There is a certain district of which a careful examination has been made; and in that district, out of a population of 50,000, there are 20,000 under twenty years of age, and there are Sunday-school accommodations for less than 2,000; that is, over 18,000 of the children and youth are compelled to go without the gospel of Jesus Christ, because the Christian churches are asleep. Mr. Gates says: 'What wonder that the police arrested last year 7,200 boys and girls for various petty crimes? The devil cares for them. There are 261 saloons and dago shops, three theaters and other vile places, and the Christian church offers Sunday-school accommodation to only 2,000!' " The writer has found similar destitution in the large cities of Ohio. And the statistics given above indicate that in the large cities generally, it is common to find extensive districts nearly or quite destitute of the gospel. In the Fourth and Seventh wards of New York City there are 70,000 people, and seven Protestant churches and chapels, or one place of worship to every 10,000 of the population. In the Tenth ward there is a population of 47,000 and two churches and chapels. South of Fourteenth Street there was in 1880 a population of 541,726, for whom there were 109 Protestant churches and missions, or about one to every 5000 souls. In 1890, according to the police census, there was in the same quarter a population of 596,878, an increase of 50,000 people, while of churches and missions there was an increase of *one.* . . .

If moral and religious influences are peculiarly weak at the point where our social explosives are gathered, what of city government? Are its strength and purity so exceptional as to insure the effective control of these dangerous elements? In the light of notorious facts, the question sounds satirical. It is commonly acknowledged that the government of large cities in the United States is a failure. "In all the great American cities there is to-day as clearly defined a ruling class as in the most aristocratic countries in the world. Its members carry wards in their pockets, make up the slates for nominating conventions, distribute offices as they bargain together, and—though they toil not, neither do they spin—wear the best of raiment and spend money lavishly. They are men of power, whose favor the ambitious must court, and whose vengeance he must avoid. Who are these men? The wise, the good, the learned —men who have earned the confidence of their fellow-citizens by the purity of their lives, the splendor of their talents, their probity in public trusts, their deep study of the problems of government? No; they are gamblers, saloon-keepers, pugilists, or worse, who have made a trade of controlling votes and of buying and selling offices and official acts." It has come to this, that holding a municipal office in a large city almost impeaches a man's character. Known integrity and competency hopelessly incapacitate a man for any office in the gift of a city rabble. In a certain western city, the administration of the mayor had convinced good citizens that he gave constant aid and comfort to gamblers, thieves, saloon-keepers and all the worst elements of society. He became a candidate for a second term. The prominent men and press of both parties and the ministry of all denominations united in a Citizens' League to defeat him; but he was triumphantly returned to office by the "lewd fellows of the baser sort." And again, after a desperate struggle on the part of the better elements to defeat him, he was re-elected to a third term of office.

Popular government in the city is degenerating into government by a "boss." During his visit to this country, Herbert Spencer said: "You retain the forms of freedom; but so far as I can gather, there has been a considerable loss of the substance. It is true that those who rule you do not do it by means of retainers armed with swords; but they do it through regiments of men armed with voting papers, who obey the word of command as loyally as did the dependents of the old feudal nobles, and who thus enable their leaders to override the general will, and make the community submit to their exactions as effectually as their prototypes of old. Manifestly those who framed your Constitution never dreamed that twenty thousand citizens would go to the polls led by a 'boss.' "

As a rule, our largest cities are the worst governed. It is natural, therefore, to infer that, as our cities grow larger and more dangerous, the government will become more corrupt, and control will pass more completely into the hands of those who themselves most need to be controlled. If we would appreciate the significance of these facts and tendencies, we must bear in mind that the disproportionate growth of the city is undoubtedly to continue, and the number of great cities to be largely increased. The extraordinary growth of urban population during this century has not been at all peculiar to the United States. It is a characteristic of nineteenth century civilization. And this growth of the city is taking place not only in England and Germany, where the increase of population is rapid, but also in France, where population is practically stationary, and even in Ireland where it is declining. This strong tendency toward the city is the result chiefly of agricultural machinery, of manufactures and railway communication, and their influence will, of course, continue. If the growth of the city in the United States has been so rapid during this century, while many millions of acres were being settled, what may be expected when the settlement of the West has been completed? The rise in the value of land, when once the agricultural lands have all been occupied and population has become dense, will stimulate yet more the growth of the city; for the man of small means will be unable to command a farm, and the town will become his only alternative. When the public lands are all taken, immigration, though it will be considerably restricted thereby, will continue, and will crowd the cities more and more.

This country will undoubtedly have a population of several hundred millions, for the simple reason that it is capable of sustaining that number. And it looks as if the larger proportion of it would be urban. There can be no indefinite increase of our agricultural population. Its growth must needs be slow after the farms are all taken, and it is necessarily limited; but the cities may go on doubling and doubling again. Even if the growth of population should be very greatly and unexpectedly retarded, there are many now living who will see 150,000,000 inhabitants in the United States, and more than a quarter of that number living in cities of 8,000 and upward. And the city of the future will be more crowded than that of to-day, because the elevator makes it possible to build, as it were, one city above another. Thus is our civilization multiplying and focalizing the elements of anarchy and destruction. Nearly forty years ago De Tocqueville wrote: "I look upon the size of certain American cities, and especially upon the nature of their population, as a real danger which threatens the security of the democratic republics of the New World." That danger grows more real and imminent every year.

And this peril . . . peculiarly threatens the West. The time will doubtless come when a majority of the great cities of the country will be west of the Mississippi. This will result naturally from the greater eventual population of the West; but, in addition to this fact, what has been pointed out must not be forgotten, that agriculture will occupy a much smaller place *relatively* in the industries of the West than in those of the East, because a much smaller proportion of the land is arable. The vast region of the Rocky Mountains will be inhabited chiefly by a mining and manufacturing population, and such populations live in cities.

1. In gathering up the results of the foregoing discussion of these several perils, it should be remarked that to preserve republican institutions requires

a *higher average* intelligence and virtue among large populations than among small. The government of 5,000,000 people was a simple thing compared with the government of 50,000,000; and the government of 50,000,000 is a simple thing compared with that of 500,000,000. There are many men who can conduct a small business successfully, who are utterly incapable of managing large interests. In the latter there are multiplied relations whose harmony must be preserved. A mistake is farther reaching. It has, as it were, a longer leverage. This is equally true of the business of government. The man of only average ability and intelligence discharges creditably the duties of mayor in his little town; but he would fail utterly at the head of the state or the nation. If the people are to govern, they must grow more intelligent as the population and the complications of government increase. And a higher morality is even more essential. As civilization increases, as society becomes more complex, as labor-saving machinery is multiplied and the division of labor becomes more minute, the individual becomes more fractional and dependent. Every savage possesses all the knowledge of his tribe. Throw him upon his own resources, and he is self-sufficient. A civilized man in like circumstances would perish. The savage is independent. Civilize him, and he becomes dependent; the more civilized, the more dependent. And, as men become more dependent on each other, they should be able to rely more implicitly on each other. More complicated and multiplied relations require a more delicate conscience and a stronger sense of justice. And any failure in character or conduct under such conditions is farther reaching and more disastrous in its results.

Is our progress in morals and intelligence at all comparable to the growth of population? The nation's illiteracy has not been discussed, because it is not one of the perils which peculiarly threaten the West; but any one who would calculate our political horoscope must allow it great influence in connection with the baleful stars which are in the ascendant. But the danger which arises from the corruption of popular morals is much greater. The republics of Greece and Rome, and, if I mistake not, all the republics that have ever lived and died, were more intelligent at the end than at the beginning; but growing intelligence could not compensate decaying morals. What, then, is our moral progress? Are popular morals as sound as they were twenty years ago? There is, perhaps, no better index of general morality than Sabbath observance; and everybody knows there has been a great increase of Sabbath desecration in twenty years. We have seen that we are now using as a beverage 29 per cent more of alcohol per caput than we were fifty years ago. Says Dr. S. W. Dike: "It is safe to say that divorce has been doubled, in proportion to marriages or population, in most of the Northern States within thirty years. Present figures indicate a still greater increase." And President Woolsey, speaking of the United States, said in 1883: "On the whole, there can be little, if any, question that the ratio of divorces to marriages or to population exceeds that of any country in the Christian world." While the population increased thirty per cent from 1870 to 1880, the number of criminals in the United States increased 82.33 per cent. It looks very much as if existing tendencies were in the direction of the dead-line of vice. Excepting Mormonism, all the perils which have been discussed seem to be increasing more rapidly than the population. *Are popular morals likely to improve under their increasing influence?*

2. The fundamental idea of popular government is the distribution of power. It has been the struggle of liberty for ages to wrest power from the hands of one or the few, and lodge it in the hands of the many. We have seen, in the foregoing discussion, that centralized power is rapidly growing. The "boss" makes his bargain, and sells his ten thousand or fifty thousand voters as if they were so many cattle. Centralized wealth is centralized power; and the capitalist and corporation find many ways to control votes. The liquor power controls thousands of votes in every considerable city. The president of the Mormon Church casts, say, sixty thousand votes. The Jesuits, it is said, are all under the command of one man in Washington. The Roman Catholic vote is more or less perfectly controlled by the priests. That means that the Pope can dictate some hundreds of thousands of votes in the United States. Is there anything un-republican in all this? And we must remember that, if present tendencies continue, these figures will be greatly multiplied in the future. And not only is this immense power lodged in the hand of one man, which in itself is perilous, but it is wielded without the slightest reference to any policy or principle of government, solely in the interests of a church or a business, or for personal ends.

The result of a national election may depend on a single state; the vote of that state may depend on a single city; the vote of that city may depend on a "boss," or a capitalist, or a corporation; or the election may be decided, and the policy of the government may be reversed, by the socialist, or liquor, or Roman Catholic or immigrant vote.

It matters not by what name we call the man who wields this centralized power—whether king, czar, pope, president, capitalist, or boss. Just so far as it is absolute and irresponsible, it is dangerous.

3. These several dangerous elements are singularly netted together, and serve to strengthen each other. It is not necessary to prove that any *one* of them is likely to destroy our national life, in order to show that it is imperiled. A man may die of wounds no one of which is fatal. No sober-minded man can look fairly at the facts, and doubt that *together* these perils constitute an array which will seriously endanger our free institutions, if the tendencies which have been pointed out continue; and especially is this true in view of the fact that these perils peculiarly confront the West, where our defense is weakest.

These dangerous elements are now working, and will continue to work, incalculable harm and loss—moral, intellectual, social, pecuniary. But the supreme peril, which will certainly come unless there is found for existing tendencies some effectual check, and must probably be faced by many now living, will arise, when, the conditions having been fully prepared, some great industrial or other crisis precipitates an open struggle between the destructive and the conservative elements of society. As civilization advances, and society becomes more highly organized, commercial transactions will be more complex and immense. As a result, all business relations and industries will be more sensitive. Commercial distress in any great business center will the more surely create wide-spread disaster. Under such conditions, industrial paralysis is likely to occur from time to time, more general and more prostrating than any heretofore known. When such a commercial crisis has closed factories by the ten thousand, and wage-workers have been thrown out of employment by the million; when the public lands, which hitherto at such times have afforded relief, are all exhausted; when our urban population has been multiplied several fold, and our Cincinnatis have become Chicagos, our Chicagos New Yorks, and our New Yorks Londons; when class antipathies are deepened; when socialistic organizations, armed and drilled, are in every city, and the ignorant and vicious power of crowded populations has fully found itself; when the corruption of city governments is grown apace; when crops fail, or some gigantic "corner" doubles the price of bread; with starvation in the home; with idle workmen gathered, sullen and desperate, in the saloons; with unprotected wealth at hand; with the tremendous forces of chemistry within easy reach; then, with *the opportunity, the means, the fit agents, the motive, the temptation to destroy, all brought into evil conjunction,* THEN will come the real test of our institutions, then will appear whether we are capable of self-government.

Discussion Starters

1. Which of the perils of the city identified by Strong have been overcome or eliminated? Which have become greater? Which were exaggerated in importance by Strong?

2. Assuming Strong's analysis of urban perils to be accurate and his implied prescriptions for countering these perils to be sound, what specific plans of action might city dwellers have adopted to improve their condition? What problems would each of these plans have faced?

3. What remains of Strong's analysis when the religious emphasis is stripped away? How would a nonreligious urban analyst have supplemented or expanded these remains?

4. Although Strong deplored the decline in number and influence of churches, he made little effort to account for it. How would you account for it?

5. Evaluate the prophetic character of Strong's work by relating the dire conditions he foresaw for cities with actual conditions as they exist today. Based on this evaluation, speculate on what conclusions Strong would draw about our capacity for self-government if he were around to see the testing of his prophecy.

Related Documents

I. "When a Girl Leaves Her Home at Eighteen . . ."

THEODORE DREISER

When Theodore Dreiser moved to Chicago in the 1880s from a small town in Indiana, the big city made a profound impression on him. Living and working in the city, together with his reading and study, led him to the conclusion that man's fate was largely determined by forces over which he had little control. In his first novel, Sister Carrie, *completed in 1900, Dreiser seems to have recalled his own initial impressions of the city. Included here are two short sections from the opening chapter of this novel. Note how Dreiser set the stage for later developments in Sister Carrie's life; eventually she became a married man's mistress, and as she achieved success as an actress he degenerated into abject poverty and suicide.*

Evaluate Dreiser's assertion that as Sister Carrie settled in the city, unless she fell into "saving hands" she would assume the "cosmopolitan standard of virtue" and become worse. Under these circumstances, how might anyone survive in the city? Given his Protestant bias, how would Josiah Strong have been likely to respond to a philosophy like Dreiser's?

When Caroline Meeber boarded the afternoon train for Chicago, her total outfit consisted of a small trunk, a cheap imitation alligator-skin satchel, a small lunch in a paper box, and a yellow leather snap purse, containing her ticket, a scrap of paper with her sister's address in Van Buren Street, and four dollars in money. It was in August, 1889. She was eighteen years of age, bright, timid, and full of the illusions of ignorance and youth. Whatever touch of regret at parting characterised her thoughts, it was certainly not for advantages now being given up. A gush of tears at her mother's farewell kiss, a touch in her throat when the cars clacked by the flour mill where her father worked by the day, a pathetic sigh as the familiar green environs of the village passed in review, and the threads which bound her so lightly to girlhood and home were irretrievably broken.

To be sure there was always the next station, where one might descend and return. There was the great city, bound more closely by these very trains which came up daily. Columbia City was not so very far away, even once she was in Chicago. What, pray, is a few hours—a few hundred miles? She looked at the little slip bearing her sister's address and wondered. She gazed at the green landscape, now passing in swift review, until her swifter thoughts re-

Theodore Dreiser, *Sister Carrie* (New York: World Publishing Co., 1900), pp. 1–3, 8–9.

placed its impression with vague conjectures of what Chicago might be.

When a girl leaves her home at eighteen, she does one of two things. Either she falls into saving hands and becomes better, or she rapidly assumes the cosmopolitan standard of virtue and becomes worse. Of an intermediate balance, under the circumstances, there is no possibility. The city has its cunning wiles, no less than the infinitely smaller and more human tempter. There are large forces which allure with all the soulfulness of expression possible in the most cultured human. The gleam of a thousand lights is often as effective as the persuasive light in a wooing and fascinating eye. Half the undoing of the unsophisticated and natural mind is accomplished by forces wholly superhuman. A blare of sound, a roar of life, a vast array of human hives, appeal to the astonished senses in equivocal terms. Without a counsellor at hand to whisper cautious interpretation, what falsehoods may not these things breathe into the unguarded ear! Unrecognised for what they are, their beauty, like music, too often relaxes, then weakens, then perverts the simpler human perceptions.

Caroline, or Sister Carrie, as she had been half affectionately termed by the family, was possessed of a mind rudimentary in its power of observation and analysis. Self-interest with her was high, but not strong. It was, nevertheless, her guiding characteristic. Warm with the fancies of youth, pretty with the insipid prettiness of the formative period, possessed of a figure promising eventual shapeliness and an eye alight with certain native intelligence, she was a fair example of the middle American class—two generations removed from the emigrant. Books were beyond her interest—knowledge a sealed book. In the intuitive graces she was still crude. She could scarcely toss her head gracefully. Her hands were almost ineffectual. The feet, though small, were set flatly. And yet she was interested in her charms, quick to understand the keener pleasures of life, ambitious to gain in material things. A half-equipped little knight she was, venturing to reconnoitre the mysterious city and dreaming wild dreams of some vague, far-off supremacy, which should make it prey and subject—the proper penitent, grovelling at a woman's slipper. . . .

They were nearing Chicago. Signs were everywhere numerous. Trains flashed by them. Across wide stretches of flat, open prairie they could see lines of telegraph poles stalking across the fields toward the great city. Far away were indications of suburban towns, some big smoke-stacks towering high in the air.

Frequently there were two-story frame houses standing out in the open fields, without fence or trees, lone outposts of the approaching army of homes.

To the child, the genius with imagination, or the wholly untravelled, the approach to a great city for the first time is a wonderful thing. Particularly if it be evening—that mystic period between the glare and gloom of the world when life is changing from one sphere or condition to another. Ah, the promise of the night. What does it not hold for the weary! What old illusion of hope is not here forever repeated! Says the soul of the toiler to itself, "I shall soon be free. I shall be in the ways and the hosts of the merry. The streets, the lamps, the lighted chamber set for dining, are for me. The theatre, the halls, the

parties, the ways of rest and the paths of song—these are mine in the night."
Though all humanity be still enclosed in the shops, the thrill runs abroad. It
is in the air. The dullest feel something which they may not always express
or describe. It is the lifting of the burden of toil.

II. Chicago: A Real City

RUDYARD KIPLING

*Rudyard Kipling, the English writer, visited Chicago around 1890 on his return
to England from India by way of Japan and the United States. His impressions
of the various places he visited, including Chicago, were recorded in a series of
letters that were later published in* From Sea to Sea.

*As seen by Kipling in the following paragraphs, what were the ethical perils
posed by Chicago? What were Chicago's good points? Speculate on the reaction
Josiah Strong might have had to Kipling's account of his experiences, particularly his visit to the church.*

I have struck a city,—a real city,—and they call it Chicago. The other places
do not count. San Francisco was a pleasure-resort as well as a city, and Salt
Lake was a phenomenon. This place is the first American city I have encountered. It holds rather more than a million people with bodies, and stands on
the same sort of soil as Calcutta. Having seen it, I urgently desire never to see
it again. It is inhabited by savages. Its water is the water of the Hughli, and
its air is dirt. Also it says that it is the 'boss' town of America.

I do not believe that it has anything to do with this country. They told
me to go to the Palmer House, which is a gilded and mirrored rabbit-warren,
and there I found a huge hall of tessellated marble, crammed with people
talking about money and spitting about everywhere. Other barbarians charged
in and out of this inferno with letters and telegrams in their hands, and yet
others shouted at each other. A man who had drunk quite as much as was good
for him told me that this was 'the finest hotel in the finest city on God
Almighty's earth.' By the way, when an American wishes to indicate the next
county or State he says, 'God A'mighty's earth.' This prevents discussion and
flatters his vanity.

Then I went out into the streets, which are long and flat and without end.
And verily it is not a good thing to live in the East for any length of time. Your
ideas grow to clash with those held by every right-thinking white man. I looked
down interminable vistas flanked with nine, ten, and fifteen storied houses, and
crowded with men and women, and the show impressed me with a great
horror. Except in London—and I have forgotten what London is like—I had
never seen so many white people together, and never such a collection of
miserables. There was no colour in the street and no beauty—only a maze of

Rudyard Kipling, *From Sea to Sea* (London: Macmillan, 1904), II, pp. 151–57.

wire-ropes overhead and dirty stone flagging underfoot. A cab-driver volunteered to show me the glory of the town for so much an hour, and with him I wandered far. He conceived that all this turmoil and squash was a thing to be reverently admired; that it was good to huddle men together in fifteen layers, one atop of the other, and to dig holes in the ground for offices. He said that Chicago was a live town, and that all the creatures hurrying by me were engaged in business. That is to say, they were trying to make some money, that they might not die through lack of food to put into their bellies. He took me to canals, black as ink, and filled with untold abominations, and bade me watch the stream of traffic across the bridges. He then took me into a saloon, and, while I drank, made me note that the floor was covered with coins sunk into cement. A Hottentot would not have been guilty of this sort of barbarism. The coins made an effect pretty enough, but the man who put them there had no thought to beauty, and therefore he was a savage. Then my cab-driver showed me business-blocks, gay with signs and studded with fantastic and absurd advertisements of goods, and looking down the long street so adorned it was as though each vender stood at his door howling: 'For the sake of money, employ or buy of *me* and me only!' Have you ever seen a crowd at our famine-relief distributions? You know then how men leap into the air, stretching out their arms above the crowd in the hope of being seen; while the women dolorously slap the stomachs of their children and whimper. I had sooner watch famine-relief than the white man engaged in what he calls legitimate competition. The one I understand. The other makes me ill. And the cabman said that these things were the proof of progress; and by that I knew he had been reading his newspaper, as every intelligent American should. The papers tell their readers in language fitted to their comprehension that the snarling together of telegraph wires, the heaving up of houses, and the making of money is progress. . . .

Sunday brought me the queerest experience of all—a revelation of barbarism complete. I found a place that was officially described as a church. It was a circus really, but that the worshippers did not know. There were flowers all about the building, which was fitted up with plush and stained oak and much luxury, including twisted brass candlesticks of severest Gothic design. To these things, and a congregation of savages, entered suddenly a wonderful man completely in the confidence of their God, whom he treated colloquially and exploited very much as a newspaper reporter would exploit a foreign potentate. But, unlike the newspaper reporter, he never allowed his listeners to forget that he and not He was the centre of attraction. With a voice of silver and with imagery borrowed from the auction-room, he built up for his hearers a heaven on the lines of the Palmer House (but with all the gilding real gold and all the plate-glass diamond) and set in the centre of it a loud-voiced, argumentative, and very shrewd creation that he called God. One sentence at this point caught my delighted ear. It was *apropos* of some question of the Judgment Day and ran: 'No! I tell you God doesn't do business that way.' He was giving them a deity whom they could comprehend, in a gold and jewel heaven in which they could take a natural interest. He interlarded his performance with the slang of the streets, the counter, and the Exchange, and he said that religion ought to enter into daily life. Consequently I presume he introduced it *as* daily life—his own and the life of his friends.

Then I escaped before the blessing, desiring no benediction at such hands. But the persons who listened seemed to enjoy themselves, and I understood that I had met with a popular preacher. Later on when I had perused the sermons of a gentleman called Talmage and some others, I perceived that I had been listening to a very mild specimen. Yet that man, with his brutal gold and silver idols, his hands-in-pocket, cigar-in-mouth, and hat-on-the-back-of-the-head style of dealing with the sacred vessels would count himself spiritually quite competent to send a mission to convert the Indians. All that Sunday I listened to people who said that the mere fact of spiking down strips of iron to wood and getting a steam and iron thing to run along them was progress. That the telephone was progress, and the network of wires overhead was progress. They repeated their statements again and again. One of them took me to their city hall and board of trade works and pointed it out with pride. It was very ugly, but very big, and the streets in front of it were narrow and unclean. When I saw the faces of the men who did business in that building I felt that there had been a mistake in their billeting.

III. *Color Prejudice in Philadelphia*

W. E. B. DU BOIS

Included among the migrants to the city in the last decades of the nineteenth century were large numbers of blacks. The magnitude of the black migration is sometimes obscured by the awareness that in 1890 more than ninety percent of America's black population was still concentrated in the South and that the urban black population, particularly in the North, was relatively small. When one recognizes the extent of the black migration, he can appreciate the strains it put on the institutions of the black communities from which they migrated as well as on those of the communities, both black and white, that received them.

The role and plight of blacks in Philadelphia was the subject of a study conducted from 1896 to 1898 by W. E. B. Du Bois, a brilliant young scholar who had recently received a Ph.D. degree from Harvard. As a result of this study, Du Bois produced a massive report entitled The Philadelphia Negro. *The report is thorough and well balanced, yet it suggests some of the themes that later led Du Bois into some heated and protracted controversies. It provoked a generally favorable response in part, no doubt, because of Du Bois' willingness to criticize blacks as well as whites.*

If whites had taken the report seriously and resolved to improve the condi-

W. E. B. Du Bois, *The Philadelphia Negro* (Philadelphia: University of Pennsylvania, 1899), pp. 322–25, 353–55.

tion of blacks, what steps might they have taken? Josiah Strong's Our Country *showed no concern at all for blacks. Considering the circumstances of blacks in cities, as reported by Du Bois in the excerpts included here, and the ethical problems posed by these conditions, how might you account for such an omission?*

Incidentally throughout this study the prejudice against the Negro has been again and again mentioned. It is time now to reduce this somewhat indefinite term to something tangible. Everybody speaks of the matter, everybody knows that it exists, but in just what form it shows itself or how influential it is few agree. In the Negro's mind, color prejudice in Philadelphia is that widespread feeling of dislike for his blood, which keeps him and his children out of decent employment, from certain public conveniences and amusements, from hiring houses in many sections, and in general, from being recognized as a man. Negroes regard this prejudice as the chief cause of their present unfortunate condition. On the other hand most white people are quite unconscious of any such powerful and vindictive feeling; they regard color prejudice as the easily explicable feeling that intimate social intercourse with a lower race is not only undesirable but impracticable if our present standards of culture are to be maintained; and although they are aware that some people feel the aversion more intensely than others, they cannot see how such a feeling has much influence on the real situation, or alters the social condition of the mass of Negroes.

As a matter of fact, color prejudice in this city is something between these two extreme views: it is not to-day responsible for all, or perhaps the greater part of the Negro problems, or of the disabilities under which the race labors; on the other hand it is a far more powerful social force than most Philadelphians realize. The practical results of the attitude of most of the inhabitants of Philadelphia toward persons of Negro descent are as follows:

1. As to getting work:

No matter how well trained a Negro may be, or how fitted for work of any kind, he cannot in the ordinary course of competition hope to be much more than a menial servant.

He cannot get clerical or supervisory work to do save in exceptional cases.

He cannot teach save in a few of the remaining Negro schools.

He cannot become a mechanic except for small transient jobs, and cannot join a trades union.

A Negro woman has but three careers open to her in this city: domestic service, sewing, or married life.

2. As to keeping work:

The Negro suffers in competition more severely than white men.

Change in fashion is causing him to be replaced by whites in the better paid positions of domestic service.

Whim and accident will cause him to lose a hard-earned place more quickly than the same things would affect a white man.

Being few in number compared with the whites the crime or carelessness of a few of his race is easily imputed to all, and the reputation of the good, industrious and reliable suffer thereby.

Because Negro workmen may not often work side by side with white workmen, the individual black workman is rated not by his own efficiency, but by the efficiency of a whole group of black fellow workmen which may often be low.

Because of these difficulties which virtually increase competition in his case, he is forced to take lower wages for the same work than white workmen.

3. As to entering new lines of work:

Men are used to seeing Negroes in inferior positions; when, therefore, by any chance a Negro gets in a better position, most men immediately conclude that he is not fitted for it, even before he has a chance to show his fitness.

If, therefore, he set up a store, men will not patronize him.

If he is put into public position men will complain.

If he gain a position in the commercial world, men will quietly secure his dismissal or see that a white man succeeds him.

4. As to his expenditure:

The comparative smallness of the patronage of the Negro, and the dislike of other customers makes it usual to increase the charges or difficulties in certain directions in which a Negro must spend money.

He must pay more house-rent for worse houses than most white people pay.

He is sometimes liable to insult or reluctant service in some restaurants, hotels and stores, at public resorts, theatres and places of recreation; and at nearly all barber-shops.

5. As to his children:

The Negro finds it extremely difficult to rear children in such an atmosphere and not have them either cringing or impudent: if he impresses upon them patience with their lot, they may grow up satisfied with their condition; if he inspires them with ambition to rise, they may grow to despise their own people, hate the whites and become embittered with the world.

His children are discriminated against, often in public schools.

They are advised when seeking employment to become waiters and maids.

They are liable to species of insult and temptation peculiarly trying to children.

6. As to social intercourse:

In all walks of life the Negro is liable to meet some objection to his presence or some discourteous treatment; and the ties of friendship or memory seldom are strong enough to hold across the color line.

If an invitation is issued to the public for any occasion, the Negro can never know whether he would be welcomed or not; if he goes he is liable to have his feelings hurt and get into unpleasant altercation; if he stays away, he is blamed for indifference.

If he meet a lifelong white friend on the street, he is in a dilemma; if he does not greet the friend he is put down as boorish and impolite; if he does greet the friend he is liable to be flatly snubbed.

If by chance he is introduced to a white woman or man, he expects to be ignored on the next meeting, and usually is.

White friends may call on him, but he is scarcely expected to call on them, save for strictly business matters.

If he gain the affections of a white woman and marry her he may invariably expect that slurs will be thrown on her reputation and on his, and that both his and her race will shun their company.

When he dies he cannot be buried beside white corpses.

7. The result:

Any one of these things happening now and then would not be remarkable or call for especial comment; but when one group of people suffer all these little differences of treatment and discriminations and insults continually, the result is either discouragement, or bitterness, or over-sensitiveness, or recklessness. And a people feeling thus cannot do their best. . . .

It is high time that the best conscience of Philadelphia awakened to her duty; her Negro citizens are here to remain; they can be made good citizens or burdens to the community; if we want them to be sources of wealth and power and not of poverty and weakness then they must be given employment according to their ability and encouraged to train that ability and increase their talents by the hope of reasonable reward. To educate boys and girls and then refuse them work is to train loafers and rogues.

From another point of view it could be argued with much cogency that the cause of economic stress, and consequently of crime, was the recent inconsiderate rush of Negroes into cities; and that the unpleasant results of this migration, while deplorable, will nevertheless serve to check the movement of Negroes to cities and keep them in the country where their chance for economic development is widest. This argument loses much of its point from the fact that it is the better class of educated Philadelphia-born Negroes who have the most difficulty in obtaining employment. The new immigrant fresh from the South is much more apt to obtain work suitable for him than the black boy born here and trained in efficiency. Nevertheless it is undoubtedly true that the recent migration has both directly and indirectly increased crime and competition. How is this movement to be checked? Much can be done by correcting misrepresentations as to the opportunities of city life made by designing employment bureaus and thoughtless persons; a more strict surveillance of criminals might prevent the influx of undesirable elements. Such efforts, however, would not touch the main stream of immigration. Back of that stream is the world-wide desire to rise in the world, to escape the choking narrowness of the plantation, and the lawless repression of the village, in the South. It is a search for better opportunities of living, and as such it must be discouraged and repressed with great care and delicacy, if at all. The real movement of reform is the raising of economic standards and increase of economic opportunity in the South. Mere land and climate without law and order, capital and skill, will not develop a country. When Negroes in the South have a larger opportunity to work, accumulate property, be protected in life and limb, and encourage pride and self-respect in their children, there will be a diminution in the stream of immigrants to Northern cities. At the same time if those cities practice industrial exclusion against these immigrants to such an extent that they are forced to become paupers, loafers and criminals, they can scarcely complain of conditions in the South. Northern cities should not, of course, seek to encourage and invite a poor quality of labor, with low standards of life and morals. The standards of wages and respectability should be kept up; but when a man reaches those standards in skill, efficiency and decency no question of color should, in a civilized community, debar him from an equal chance with his peers in earning a living.

IV. *The Growth of Cities*

ADNA F. WEBER

The growth of cities was frequently viewed with fear and suspicion because of the problems it created. It should not be assumed, however, that the promise of cities was totally overlooked. In 1899 Adna F. Weber, a young social scientist, published a significant study, The Growth of Cities, *in which he examined both the causes and benefits of urban growth. Although he did not ignore the perils posed by cities, he was more concerned with the desirable aspects of their growth. The following excerpt contains Weber's conclusions on the social benefits of urbanization.*

Note how his ideas reflect a Social Darwinist, survival-of-the-fittest outlook. Which points in his conclusion would most likely be acceptable to Josiah Strong? Which would be unacceptable?

What, if any, are the benefits secured to the entire social body in compensation for these evil effects of concentration of population upon the life of the non-urban population? And is there no advantage to the villages themselves?

Economically, as we have learned, the concentration of large masses of people upon small areas at once multiplies human wants and furnishes the means of their satisfaction; and the benefits are communicated to the surrounding country, which finds in the cities a market for its production and a stimulus to the diversification of the same.

Socially, the influence of the cities is similarly exerted in favor of liberal and progressive thought. The variety of occupation, interests and opinions in the city produces an intellectual friction, which leads to a broader and freer

Adna F. Weber, *The Growth of Cities* (Ithaca, N.Y.: Cornell University Press, 1963; originally published in 1899), pp. 439–43.

judgment and a great inclination to and appreciation of new thoughts, manners, and ideals. City life may not have produced genius, but it has brought thinkers into touch with one another, and has stimulated the divine impulse to originate by sympathy or antagonism. As the seat of political power, as the nursery of the arts and sciences, as the center of industry and commerce, the city represents the highest achievements of political, intellectual and industrial life. The rural population is not merely conservative; it is full of error and prejudice; it receives what enlightenment it possesses from the city. Nor is the small city free from the same reproach; while it performs the useful function of an intermediary between the progressiveness, liberalism, radicalism of the great city, and the conservatism, bigotry, of the country, it is the chief seat of the pseudo-bourgeois Philistine. . . . The contrast between city and rural populations and civilizations is as clearly marked in the United States as in any other modern country; the North represents one, the South the other. While not denying the many admirable traits of Southern character, we cannot overlook the prevalence of prejudice and provincialism which has cut off the South from participation in the lofty patriotism and national feeling existent in other parts of the United States. Americans of the present generation are destined to see this provincialism vanish before the powerful influences of large cities, which the introduction of manufactures and commerce on a large scale will in a short time produce. The South will be brought into contact with the current of world-thought. To the negro race justice will at length be accorded, and a stronger feeling of fraternity toward the North will grow up, strengthening the bonds of patriotism.

It is emphatically true that the growth of cities not only increases a nation's economic power and energy, but quickens the national pulse. In the present age, the influence of the cities is not perhaps so strong in the direction of the noblest thought and culture, because the present age is essentially materialistic. But there is some reason for believing that Materialism is gradually giving way before Humanitarianism, and we may hope in time to see the great cities exercise as noble a domination in the world of thought as was maintained by the Athens of Pericles and Aeschylus, by the Rome of Lucretius and Juvenal, by the Florence of Michel Angelo, by the London of Elizabeth, and by the Paris of the second half of the seventeenth century.

It is at least ground for encouragement that the leading nations of the modern world are those which have the largest city populations. That cities are both cause and consequence of a high *Cultur* can hardly be doubted.

But the highest social service performed by the cities will not be realized until we have made clear to ourselves their function in the process of natural selection.

The city is the spectroscope of society; it analyzes and sifts the population, separating and classifying the diverse elements. The entire progress of civilization is a process of differentiation, and the city is the greatest differentiator. The mediocrity of the country is transformed by the city into the highest talent or the lowest criminal. Genius is often born in the country, but it is brought to light and developed by the city. On the other hand, the opportunities of the city work just as powerfully in the opposite direction upon the countrymen of an ignoble cast; the boy thief of the village becomes the daring bank robber of the metropolis.

Taking this view of the cities as the central instruments of the process of differentiation, we shall be able to reconcile the differences of those who regard the cities as "ulcers on the body politic" (Jefferson) and those who place them at the apex of civilization. The fact that the cities make the opinions, fashions and ideals of mankind, rests upon the vastness of opportunity that they afford. But it is clear that opportunity to do good and become great involves opportunity to accomplish evil, that is, temptation. Compare the devices against burglary in an advanced country with those in a more backward country; the Yale lock of America with the ponderous keys and old-fashioned locks, that almost any one can pick with a button-hook, in Germany. Compare the wonderfully complicated equipment against burglars in a metropolitan bank with the ordinary safes and vaults of a country bank. A progressive or dynamic civilization implies the good and bad alike. The cities, as the foci of progress, inevitably contain both good and bad.

V. Tenement Living in New York

JACOB RIIS

How bad were living conditions in the cities? Did city residents face perils other than the moral and ethical ones discussed by Strong? Some answers to these questions are provided in Jacob Riis' vivid account of tenement living in New York City. Riis, a Danish immigrant, was a newspaper reporter whose How the Other Half Lives *attracted wide attention and gave him a reputation as a social reformer. His book is primarily a collection of stories about tenements; few suggestions for solving tenement problems are offered.*

How can one account for the fact that Strong's concerns for the city do not seem to have included such conditions as those described by Riis? What conclusions might one draw about the role of the church in solving social problems at the turn of the century?

. . . When the summer heats come with their suffering they have meaning more terrible than words can tell. Come over here. Step carefully over this baby— it is a baby, spite of its rags and dirt—under these iron bridges called fire- escapes, but loaded down, despite the incessant watchfulness of the firemen, with broken household goods, with wash-tubs and barrels, over which no man could climb from a fire. This gap between dingy brick-walls is the yard. That strip of smoke-colored sky up there is the heaven of these people. Do you

Jacob Riis, *How the Other Half Lives* (New York: Charles Scribner's Sons, 1906), pp. 44–47.

wonder the name does not attract them to the churches? That baby's parents live in the rear tenement here. She is at least as clean as the steps we are now climbing. There are plenty of houses with half a hundred such in. The tenement is much like the one in front we just left, only fouler, closer, darker—we will not say more cheerless. The word is a mockery. A hundred thousand people lived in rear tenements in New York last year. Here is a room neater than the rest. The woman, a stout matron with hard lines of care in her face, is at the wash-tub. "I try to keep the childer clean," she says, apologetically, but with a hopeless glance around. The spice of hot soapsuds is added to the air already tainted with the smell of boiling cabbage, of rags and uncleanliness all about. It makes an overpowering compound. It is Thursday, but patched linen is hung upon the pulley-line from the window. There is no Monday cleaning in the tenements. It is wash-day all the week round, for a change of clothing is scarce among the poor. They are poverty's honest badge, these perennial lines of rags hung out to dry, those that are not the washerwoman's professional shingle. The true line to be drawn between pauperism and honest poverty is the clothes-line. With it begins the effort to be clean that is the first and the best evidence of a desire to be honest.

What sort of an answer, think you, would come from these tenements to the question "Is life worth living?" were they heard at all in the discussion? It may be that this, cut from the last report but one of the Association for the Improvement of the Condition of the Poor, a long name for a weary task, has a suggestion of it: "In the depth of winter the attention of the Association was called to a Protestant family living in a garret in a miserable tenement in Cherry Street. The family's condition was most deplorable. The man, his wife, and three small children shivering in one room through the roof of which the pitiless winds of winter whistled. The room was almost barren of furniture; the parents slept on the floor, the elder children in boxes, and the baby was swung in an old shawl attached to the rafters by cords by way of a hammock. The father, a seaman, had been obliged to give up that calling because he was in consumption, and was unable to provide either bread or fire for his little ones."

Perhaps this may be put down as an exceptional case, but one that came to my notice some months ago in a Seventh Ward tenement was typical enough to escape that reproach. There were nine in the family, husband, wife, an aged grandmother, and six children; honest, hard-working Germans, scrupulously neat, but poor. All nine lived in two rooms, one about ten feet square that served as parlor, bedroom, and eating-room, the other a small hall-room made into a kitchen. The rent was seven dollars and a half a month, more than a week's wages for the husband and father, who was the only bread-winner in the family. That day the mother had thrown herself out of the window, and was carried up from the street dead. She was "discouraged," said some of the other women from the tenement, who had come in to look after the children while a messenger carried the news to the father at the shop. They went stolidly about their task, although they were evidently not without feeling for the dead woman. No doubt she was wrong in not taking life philosophically, as did the four families a city missionary found housekeeping in the four corners of one room. They got along well enough together until one of the families took a boarder and made trouble. Philosophy, according to my optimistic friend, naturally inhabits the tenements. The people who live there come to look upon death in a different way from the rest of us—do not take it as hard. He has never found time to explain how the fact fits into his general theory that life is not unbearable in the tenements. Unhappily for the philosophy of the slums, it is too apt to be of the kind that readily recognizes the saloon, always handy, as the refuge from every trouble, and shapes its practice according to the discovery.

For Further Reading

These volumes provide a general background for the material in this chapter: Charles N. Glaab and A. Theodore Brown, *A History of Urban America** (1967); Constance McL. Green, *The Rise of Urban America** (1965); Blake McKelvey, *The Urbanization of America, 1860–1915** (1963); and Arthur M. Schlesinger, Sr., *The Rise of the City, 1878–1898** (1933).

Three collections of documents containing selections from this period are: Charles N. Glaab, ed., *The American City: A Documentary History** (1963); Wilson Smith, ed., *Cities of Our Past and Present** (1964); and Anselm Strauss, ed., *The American City: A Sourcebook of Urban Imagery* (1968). *American Urban History: An Interpretive Reader with Commentaries** (1969), edited by Alexander B. Callow, includes a number of excellent essays.

As the percentage of blacks in cities has increased in recent decades there has been a greater interest in studying the early days of black migration. Books on this subject include *Harlem: The Making of a Ghetto. Negro New York, 1890–1930** (1966), by Gilbert Osofsky; *Negro Mecca: A History of the Negro in New York City, 1865–1920** (1965), by Seth M. Scheiner; and *Black Chicago: The Making of a Negro Ghetto, 1890–1920** (1967), by Allan H. Spear.

Appropriate problems books are *The Challenge of the City, 1860–1910** (1968), edited by Lyle W. Dorsett, and *The City in American History** (1969), edited by Blake McKelvey.

*Paperbound edition available.

4. "...When the People Come In"

The story of the industrialization of the United States in the last decades of the nineteenth century can be told from two points of view. One view would emphasize the rapidity of industrial expansion, the remarkable production figures of such commodities as oil and steel, the spreading of the railroad network, and the shrewdness and power of the entrepreneurs and the huge fortunes they amassed. The other would stress the impact of industrialization on the people who made it possible, the urban laborers and farmers.

By the 1890s, the lot of industrial workers and farmers was not a happy one. It would be difficult, even if one told the story from the first viewpoint, to ignore the conditions industrialization and its parallel forces had created for them. The urban laborer was beset by uncertainty of employment, low wages, long hours, and unsafe or unsanitary working conditions. Farmers were principally victims of low prices for their products and high prices for the things they had to buy.

A natural course for industrial laborers lay in the formation of unions, but legal barriers, unsympathetic public opinion, and unfavorable government attitudes made this difficult, Furthermore, big business could be expected to employ all its resources in resisting unionizing efforts. In the eighties and nineties every major industrial union was broken or severely weakened by the combined action of big business and government. Only the American Federation of Labor, representing skilled craftsmen, escaped a crippling setback during those years.

The farmers, too, attempted collective action, although their organizations were more political and less directly coercive than labor unions. In the sixties and seventies the main farm organization was the Grange. In addition to bringing farmers together for social and educational purposes, the Grangers worked rather effectively at securing legislation to curb the grossest abuses of railroads. In the 1880s various Farmers' Alliances emerged, and by the 1890s many farmers were ready to shed their political affiliations and to establish their own political party, the People's (or Populist) party.

There were in the People's party and in various labor unions persons who envisioned a yet more effective step to be taken by farmers and industrial workers: Think of the power they would hold if they could unite! Might not a farm-labor alliance bring real power to the people? Could not such an alliance promote real reform, perhaps even revolution?

Core Document

The Revolution Is Here

HENRY DEMAREST LLOYD

The formation of the People's party in 1891–92 provided the impetus for seriously considering the idea of farmers and urban laborers working together to promote their mutual welfare. The depression of 1893 aggravated the plight of both industrial workers and farmers, and gave the idea greater currency. To implement it, leaders, spokesmen, and organizers were needed. For the most part, they did not emerge from the ranks of either laborers or farmers. Instead, these roles were filled by professional men, with politicians ready to contribute if they saw gain for themselves as a possibility.

The best known and perhaps most eloquent promoter of the idea of alliance was Henry Demarest Lloyd. By nature Lloyd was an intellectual and by profession a journalist, but his calling was that of social reformer and political activist. Whatever his motives—and they may have been to unite the industrial workers and farmers under the Populist banner and lead them gradually to acceptance of socialism—Lloyd worked with all his energies and resources to bring industrial workers into the People's party. Because he was sympathetic to the basic ideals of populism, particularly its resistance to monopolistic power of big busi-

Chester McArthur Destler, *American Radicalism, 1865–1901: Essays and Documents* (New London, Conn.: Connecticut College, 1946), pp. 213–21.

ness and its leaning in the direction of collectivism, he could work zealously without compromising his own principles.

The story of alliances and coalitions among farmers and industrial workers is not easy to tell, largely because of differences in their priorities of concern and factionalism within each group. It is impossible to trace here the organizational aspects of alliance building; they are simply too complex and confusing. Our concern here is limited to the matter of shaping an ideology around which farmers and industrial workers could not only unite, but that would rally them to eager pursuit of a reformed society in which each group would receive its due.

Lloyd's activity was concentrated in Illinois, particularly in Chicago. Severe economic distress and bitter discontent growing out of the depression of 1893 prompted both farmers and laborers to think in terms more ideological than was their custom. The Pullman strike and its aftermath deepened their ideological inclinations, and by the late summer of 1894 their misery caused them to work politically in ways that would otherwise have been unlikely. As the 1894 election approached, a working alliance, even if only a temporary one, appeared to be within reach. The high point in the People's party campaign in Chicago came on October 6, 1894, with a party meeting at Central Music Hall. Presiding was Clarence Darrow, the noted lawyer; Henry Demarest Lloyd was a main speaker.

Lloyd's speech, an effort to provide the ideological rallying point for the alliance, is the core document in this chapter. Although the campaign ended in total failure for the Populists, this speech stands as an expression of their highest ideals and goals. In studying it, note:

- *the tone of impatience and urgency.*
- *references to emerging parties with parallel interests in Europe.*
- *attempts to draw upon experiences in American history for support.*
- *denunciations of the wealthy and their role in American politics.*
- *the descriptions of the revolution that had already come and the counter-revolution Lloyd hoped for.*
- *the emphasis on collectivism and the benefits to be derived from it.*

OCTOBER 6, 1894

All our parties are Reform parties. The democracy has been lowering the tariff ever since the government was established. They have done so well that their rates are higher in 1894 than they were in 1842. The republicans have been "saving the union" for thirty years, and the tramp, tramp, tramp, of a million men on the march still sounds through the country—the tramp of the tramp. The appearance at the polls of a new party, which was not known in 1888, and in 1892, in its first presidential campaign, cast over 1,000,000 votes, is a hint that a new conception of reform is shaping itself in the minds of our fellow citizens. They want reform that will reform, and they want it now. Reform that is reform, and reform in our time, not in our great-grandchildren's, is what the people need and what they mean to have.

Lafayette said in 1791 that it would take twenty years to bring freedom to France; in two years feudalism was dead. Our great Emerson said in 1859

—within four years of the emancipation proclamation—"We shall not live to see slavery abolished." Jefferson, the young delegate in the house of burgesses of Virginia, in one year abolished entail, and primogeniture, and the whole fabric of aristocracy, in that colony. The patricians pleaded for delay, for compromise. "Let our oldest sons inherit by law at least a double portion." "Not unless they can do twice as much work and eat twice as much as their younger brothers," was the reply of this first great social democrat, and he finished his reform at the same session at which he began it.

No great idea is ever lost. The greatest of human ideas is democracy. It has often disappeared, but it has never been lost. We have democratized religion, and the humblest men have equal rights with all others to find the Almighty within themselves, without the intervention of a privileged class. We have nearly finished democratizing kings, and we are now about to democratize the millionaire. Under absolutism the people mend their fortunes by insurrection. Under popular government they start a new party. All over the world, wherever popular government exists with its provisions for peaceful revolution instead of violent revolution, the people are forming new parties— in England, France, Germany, Australia, as well as in this country. This is the great political fact of our times. Some of these, like the distinctively working-men's parties, are class movements. They are the natural and inevitable reaction from class movements against the workingmen. These parties all have practically the same object—to democratize the millionaire, and, as Jefferson did when he democratized the provincial patricians of Virginia, to do it as nearly as possible at one sitting.

The Evils of Concentrated Wealth

A broad view of the reforms demanded by the new parties rising in Europe and America and Australia shows the substance of them all to be the same. There is nothing, Lowell says, that men prize so much as some kind of privilege, even though it be only the place of chief mourner at a funeral. In all the great industries a few men are building themselves up into the chief places, not as mourners themselves, but to make their fellow citizens mourners. The millions produce wealth; only the tens have it. There is the root of the whole matter. The first and last political issue of our time is with its concentrated wealth. Not with wealth, but with its concentration. "Far-seeing men," says James Russell Lowell, "count the increasing power of wealth and its combinations as one of the chief dangers with which the institutions of the United States are threatened in the not distant future." This concentration of wealth is but another name for the contraction of currency,[1] the twin miseries of monopoly and pauperism, the tyranny of corporations, the corruption of the government, the depopulation of the country, the congestion of the cities, and

[1]*Editors' note:* A reduction in the quantity of money in circulation. Populists blamed their price difficulties on scarcity of money. Free coinage of silver, they believed, would alleviate their problem.

the host of ills which now form the staple theme of our novelists and magazinists, and the speeches of the new-party orators.

Those faithful watchers who are sounding these alarms are ridiculed as calamity howlers. When strong, shrewd, grasping, covetous men devote themselves to creating calamities, fortunate are the people who are awakened by faithful calamity howlers. Noah was a calamity howler, and the bones of the men who laughed at him have helped to make the phosphate beds out of which fertilizers are now dug for the market. It was a calamity howler who said, "Sweet are the uses of adversity," and another averred that "Man was born to trouble, as the sparks fly upward." There are thirty-two paragraphs in the Declaration of Independence; twenty-nine of the thirty-two are calamity howls about the wrongs and miseries of America under British rule.

The contraction of the currency is a terrible thing, but there is another as terrible—the contraction of commodities and work by stoppage of production, lockout, the dismantling of competitive works, the suppression of patents, and other games of business. The institutions of America were founded to rest on the love of the people for their country; we have a new cement now to hold society together—injunctions and contempt of court.

And we see materializing out of the shadows of our great counting-rooms a new system of government—government by campaign contribution. The people maintain their national, state, city, and local governments at a cost of $1,000,000,000 a year; but the trusts, and armor-plate contractors, and the whisky ring, and the subsidized steamship companies, and the street and other railways, buy the privilege of running these governments to enrich themselves, to send troublesome leaders of the people to jail, to keep themselves out of jail. By campaign contributions of a few millions is thus bought away from the people the government which cost the people $1,000,000,000 a year. There are many marvels of cheapness in the market, but the greatest counter bargains in modern business are such as the sugar trust got when, by contributing a few hundred thousand dollars to both parties, it bought the right to tax the people untold millions a year.

The Coming Revolution Is Here

We talk about the coming revolution and hope it will be peaceful. The revolution has come. This use of the government of all for the enrichment and aggrandizement of a few is a revolution. It is a revolution which has created the railroad millionaires of this country. To maintain the highways is one of the sacredest functions of a government. Railroads are possible only by the exercise of the still more sacred governmental power of eminent domain, which when citizens will not sell the right of way takes their property through the forms of law by force—none the less by force because the money value is paid. These sovereign powers of the highway and of eminent domain have been given by you and me, all of us, to our government, to be used only for the common and equal benefit of all. Given by all to be used for all, it is a revolution to have made them the perquisite of a few. Only a revolution could have made possible in the speech of a free people such a phrase as a railroad king.

It is a revolution which has given the best parts of the streets that belong to all the people to street-railway syndicates, and gas companies, and telephone companies, and power companies. It is a revolution which has created national-bank millionaires, and bond millionaires, and tariff millionaires, and land-grant millionaires, out of the powers you and I delegated to the government of the United States for the equal good of every citizen. The inter-state commerce act was passed to put into prison the railroad managers who used their highway power to rob the people, to ruin the merchants and manufacturers whose business they wanted to give to favored shippers. The anti-trust law was passed to put into prison the men who make commerce a conspiracy, to compel the people every day to pay a ransom for their lives. It is a revolution which is using these inter-state commerce and anti-trust laws to prosecute the employes of the railways for exercising their inalienable rights as free men to unite for defense against intolerable wrong.[2] It is a revolution which lets the presidents, and managers, and owners of the railroads and trusts, go free of all punishment for the crimes they are committing; which sends out no process against any of the corporations or corporation men in the American Railway Association, while it uses all the powers of the attorney-general of the United States to prosecute, and, if possible, to send to prison, the members of the American Railway Union. It is a revolution which is putting the attorneys of corporations into ermine on the bench to be attorneys still.

It is a revolution by which great combinations, using competition to destroy competition, have monopolized entire markets, and as the sole sellers of goods make the people buy dear, and as the sole purchasers of labor make the people sell themselves cheap. The last and deepest and greatest revolution of all is that by which the mines, machinery, factories, currency, land, entrusted to private hands as private property, only as a stewardship, to warm, feed, clothe, serve mankind, are used to make men cold, hungry, naked, and destitute. Coal mines shut down to make coal scarce, mills shut down to make goods scarce, currency used to deprive people of the means of exchange, and the railways used to hinder transportation.

Counter Revolution of the People

This is the revolution that has come. With local variation it is world-wide, and against it the people are rising world-wide in peaceful counter revolutions, in people's parties. It begins now to be seen generally what a few have been pointing out from the beginning, that the workingmen in organizing to defend themselves have been only pioneers. The power which denied them a fair share of their production was the same power which is now attacking the consumer, the farmer, and even the fellow capitalist. In organizing against modern capi-

[2] *Editors' note:* Antitrust laws, in particular, were used to prevent organization or growth of labor unions.

talism the workingmen set the example which all the people are now driven by self-preservation to follow. The trades union of the workingmen was the precursor of the farmers' alliance, the grange, and the people's party.

Chicago to-day leads the van in this great forward movement. Here the workingmen, capitalists, single-taxers,[3] and socialists have come together to join forces with each other and with the farmers, as has been done in no other city. Its meetings are attended here by thousands, as you see to-night. It is the most wonderful outburst of popular hope and enthusiasm in the recent politics of this country. Chicago thus leads in numbers and in enthusiasm and promises of success, because it has led in boldness and sincerity and thoroughness of reform doctrine. The workingmen of Chicago at the Springfield conference, which was the fountainhead of this tidal wave, stood firm as a rock for the principle without which the industrial liberties of the people can never be established—the principle that they have the right at their option to own and operate collectively any or all of the means of production, distribution, and exchange. They already own some; they have the right to own as many more as they want. This is the mother principle of the government we already have, and it covers the whole brood of government railroads, telegraphs, telephones, banks, lands, street railways, all the municipalizations and nationalizations in which everywhere the people are giving utterance to their belief that they are the only proper and the only competent administrators of the wealth which they create.

The Declaration of Independence of 1776 declared that the people felt themselves able to manage for themselves the government, all of whose powers sprang from them. This declaration of 1894 is the proclamation of the next step in independence. The people have done so well that they will move forward again and manage for themselves some more departments of the commonwealth all of whose powers spring from them. The democratization of government, the democratization of collective industry—they are parts of one great upward emancipation. The American idea, says Emerson, is emancipation. The co-operative commonwealth is the legitimate offspring and lawful successor of the republic. Our liberties and our wealth are from the people and by the people and both must be for the people. Wealth, like government, is the product of the co-operation of all, and, like government, must be the property of all its creators, not of a privileged few alone. The principles of liberty, equality, union, which rule in the industries we call government must rule in all industries. Government exists only by the consent of the governed. Business, property, capital, are also governments and must also rest on the consent of the governed. This assertion of the inherent and inalienable right, and ability, of the people to own and operate, at their option, any or all of the wealth they create, is the fundamental, irrepressible, and uncompromisable

[3] *Editors' note:* Supporters of the single-tax idea of Henry George, the author of *Progress and Poverty*. It is interesting to note that efforts to unite farmers and laborers were severely undercut by George.

keynote of the crisis, and with this trumpet note you can lead the people through any sacrifice to certain victory.

Things the People Have Learned

Jefferson, one of his biographers tells us, was one of the most successful politicians of his time because he kept his ear close to the bosom of the people. If we will do the same we will hear the great heart of the common people beating the world over with this new hope of coming to own their means of production and the fruit of their labor, and so for the first time in history owning themselves. The people always think quicker and straighter than the philosophers, because while the philosopher simply meditates the people suffer. The people here to-night have learned in their marketing, in their cut wages, in their lockouts and search for employment, in the prices they pay for sugar, and coal, and matches, and meat, and hundreds of other things, that all the other reforms—of the tariff, the banks, the land system, the railroads, and the currency—would leave them still the slaves of syndicates which hold the necessaries of life and means of production in absolute right as private property, beyond the reach of all these reforms, and with wealth which puts them beyond competition. Herein is the inner citadel of monopoly and "plank 10" is the battering-ram which will bring down its walls.[4]

This cardinal principle, to which every candidate of the people's party of Cook county who seeks the support of the workingmen must subscribe, has been adopted in substance by the party in New York. The party in Connecticut in their last platform show themselves ready for it. It will without doubt be adopted overwhelmingly by the next national convention of the people's party, and under the banner of this principle—which is as big as the crisis—the party will move into the presidency, perhaps as soon as 1896. It is not to the parties that have produced the pandemonium of intermittent panic which is called trade and industry that the people can look for relief. To vote for them is to vote for more panics, more pandemoniums. Both these parties have done good work, but their good work is done. The republican party took the black man off the auction block of the slave power, but it has put the white man on the auction block of the money power, to be sold to the lowest bidder under the iron hammer of monopoly. The democratic party for a hundred years has been the pull-back against the centralization in American politics, standing for the individual against the community, the town against the state, and the state against the nation. But in one hour here last July it sacrificed the honorable devotion of a century to its great principle and surrendered both the rights of states and the rights of man to the centralized corporate despotism to which the presidency of the United States was then abdicated.[5]

[4] *Editors' note:* "Plank 10" in the party platform was socialist in origin. As modified by Lloyd in an effort at compromise within the party, it urged voting for "those candidates of the People's Party who will pledge themselves to the principle of collective ownership by the people of all such means of production and distribution as the people elect to operate for the commonwealth."
[5] *Editors' note:* A reference to federal intervention in the Pullman strike.

There ought to be two first-class political funerals in this country in 1896, and if we do our duty the corpses will be ready on time. "Are you going to the funeral of Benedict Arnold?" one of his neighbors asked another. "No, but I approve of it." We will not go to the republican and democratic funerals, but we approve of them. There is a party that the people can trust because in the face of overwhelming odds, without distinguished leaders, money, office, or prestige, it has raised the standard of a principle to save the people. The continual refrain of Mommsen, the great historian of Rome, is that its liberties and prosperity were lost because its reformers were only half reformers, and none of its statesmen would strike at the root of its evils. By that mistake we must profit.

It is a fact of political history that no new party was ever false to the cause for which it was formed. If the people's party as organized in Cook county is supported by the country, and the people get the control of their industries as of the governments, the abolition of monopoly will as surely follow as the abolition of slavery followed the entrance of Abraham Lincoln into the white house in 1861. Then we will have the judges and the injunctions, the president and the house of representatives. There will be no senate; we will have the referendum, and the senate will go out when the people come in. The same constitution that could take the property of unwilling citizens for the railroads for rights of way can take the railroads, willing or unwilling, to be the nation's property when the people come in. Then the national debt, instead of representing the waste of war, will represent the railroads and other productive works owned by the people and worth more, as in Australia, than the bonds issued for them. The same constitution that could demonetize silver can remonetize it, or demonetize gold for a better money than either. The honest dollar will come in when the people come in, for it will not be a dollar that can be made scarce, to produce panics, and throw millions of men out of work, and compel the borrower to pay two where he received only one.

Women Must Vote Now

Women will vote, and some day we will have a woman president when the people come in. The post office will carry your telegrams and your parcels as well as your letters, and will be the people's bank for savings, and their life and accident insurance company, as it is elsewhere already. Every dark place in our cities will be brilliant with electricity, made by the municipalities for themselves. Working men and women will ride for 3 cents and school children for 2½ cents, as in Toronto, on street-car lines owned by the municipalities, and paying by their profits a large part of the cost of government now falling on the tax-payer. When the people come in, political corruption, boss rule, and boodle will go out, because these spring mainly from the intrigues and briberies of syndicates to get hold of public functions for their private profit. We will have a real civil service, the inevitable and logical result of the demands of the people's party, founded, as true civil-service reform must be, on a system of public education which shall give every child of the republic the opportunity to fit himself for the public service. The same constitution which granted empires of public lands to create the Pacific railroad kings will find land for workingmen's homes and land for co-operative colonies of the unemployed.

There will soon be no unemployed when the people come in. They will have no shoemakers locked out or shoe factories shut down while there is a foot unshod, and all the mills and mines and factories the needs of the people require the people will keep going. Every man who works will get a living and every man who gets a living shall work, when the people come in. These are some of the things the people's party of Cook county means. At the coming election let every man and woman vote—for the women must vote through the men until they vote themselves—let every man and woman vote for those, and only for those, who accept this grand principle of the liberation of the people by themselves. Let this platform get a popular indorsement at the polls next November that will advertise to the world that the people have at last risen in their might, not to rest until another great emancipation has been added to the glorious record of the liberties achieved by mankind.

Discussion Starters

1. What are the implications of Lloyd's expressed desire to "democratize the millionaire"? What measures would have been necessary, in view of the millionaire's hold on government, to achieve this?

2. Assuming that Lloyd's description of the revolution that had already come was accurate, how feasible was his proposed "counter revolution of the people"? What might some alternative counterrevolutions have called for? What were some options besides the cooperative or collective commonwealth?

3. An effective alliance of farmers and laborers would require that the interests of both groups be served. How effectively did Lloyd represent the concerns of each group? To what extent might he be charged with putting his own ideology above their needs?

4. Before the turn of the century Lloyd became bitterly disillusioned with the Populist party and turned avowedly socialist. The party itself failed to survive. Speculate on why farmers and laborers, then and since, have not bought the idea of having "the people come in" in the sense that Lloyd envisioned it. What conditions would be necessary to make them receptive to the idea in the future?

Related Documents

I. Preamble: National People's Party Platform

The first national platform of the People's party was adopted in Omaha in July 1892. It was drafted principally by the dynamic Populist orator and agitator from Minnesota, Ignatius Donnelly. In 1892 the Populist party represented agrarian interests almost exclusively, although it did assert that "the interests of rural and civic labor are the same; their enemies are identical." It also expressed cordial sympathy for the efforts of organized workingmen to shorten the hours of labor and it specifically supported the Knights of Labor in one of its showdown cases.

The platform evoked enthusiastic support from the convention delegates and was adopted with "cheers and yells which rose like a tornado from four thousand throats and raged without cessation for thirty-four minutes," convincing at least one reporter that "there was something at the back of all this turmoil more than the failure of crops or the scarcity of ready cash."

What was at back of it was expressed clearly in the preamble to the platform, included here, which was as long as the platform itself. In reading it, identify similarities and differences between it and the speech by Lloyd. What in these paragraphs would be likely to attract favorable attention from industrial workers?

JULY 4, 1892

Assembled upon the 116th anniversary of the Declaration of Independence, the People's Party of America, in their first national convention, invoking upon their action the blessing of Almighty God, put forth in the name and on behalf of the people of this country, the following preamble and declaration of principles:

Preamble

The conditions which surround us best justify our co-operation; we meet in the midst of a nation brought to the verge of moral, political, and material ruin. Corruption dominates the ballot-box, the Legislatures, the Congress, and touches even the ermine of the bench. The people are demoralized; most of the States have been compelled to isolate the voters at the polling places to prevent universal intimidation and bribery. The newspapers are largely subsidized or muzzled, public opinion silenced, business prostrated, homes covered with mortgages, labor impoverished, and the land concentrating in the hands of capitalists. The urban workmen are denied the right to organize for self-

The World Almanac (New York, 1893), pp. 83–84.

protection, imported pauperized labor beats down their wages, a hireling standing army, unrecognized by our laws, is established to shoot them down, and they are rapidly degenerating into European conditions. The fruits of the toil of millions are boldly stolen to build up colossal fortunes for a few, unprecedented in the history of mankind; and the possessors of those, in turn, despite the Republic and endanger liberty. From the same prolific womb of governmental injustice we breed the two great classes—tramps and millionaires.

The national power to create money is appropriated to enrich bondholders; a vast public debt payable in legal tender currency has been funded into gold-bearing bonds, thereby adding millions to the burdens of the people.

Silver, which has been accepted as coin since the dawn of history, has been demonetized to add to the purchasing power of gold by decreasing the value of all forms of property as well as human labor, and the supply of currency is purposely abridged to fatten usurers, bankrupt enterprise, and enslave industry. A vast conspiracy against mankind has been organized on two continents, and it is rapidly taking possession of the world. If not met and overthrown at once it forebodes terrible social convulsions, the destruction of civilization, or the establishment of an absolute despotism.

We have witnessed for more than a quarter of a century the struggles of the two great political parties for power and plunder, while grievous wrongs have been inflicted upon the suffering people. We charge that the controlling influences dominating both these parties have permitted the existing dreadful conditions to develop without serious effort to prevent or restrain them. Neither do they now promise us any substantial reform. They have agreed together to ignore, in the coming campaign, every issue but one. They propose to drown the outcries of a plundered people with the uproar of a sham battle over the tariff, so that capitalists, corporations, national banks, rings, trusts, watered stock, the demonetization of silver and the oppressions of the usurers may all be lost sight of. They propose to sacrifice our homes, lives, and children on the altar of mammon; to destroy the multitude in order to secure corruption funds from the millionaires.

Assembled on the anniversary of the birthday of the nation, and filled with the spirit of the grand general and chief who established our independence, we seek to restore the government of the Republic to the hands of "the plain people," with which class it originated. We assert our purposes to be identical with the purposes of the National Constitution; to form a more perfect union and establish justice, insure domestic tranquillity, provide for the common defence, promote the general welfare, and secure the blessings of liberty for ourselves and our posterity.

We declare that this Republic can only endure as a free government while built upon the love of the whole people for each other and for the nation; that it cannot be pinned together by bayonets; that the civil war is over, and that every passion and resentment which grew out of it must die with it, and that we must be in fact, as we are in name, one united brotherhood of free men.

Our country finds itself confronted by conditions for which there is no precedent in the history of the world; our annual agricultural productions amount to billions of dollars in value, which must, within a few weeks or months, be exchanged for billions of dollars' worth of commodities consumed in their production; the existing currency supply is wholly inadequate to make this exchange; the results are falling prices, the formation of combines and rings, the impoverishment of the producing class. We pledge ourselves that if given power we will labor to correct these evils by wise and reasonable legislation, in accordance with the terms of our platform.

We believe that the power of government—in other words, of the people —should be expanded (as in the case of the postal service) as rapidly and as far as the good sense of an intelligent people and the teachings of experience shall justify, to the end that oppression, injustice, and poverty shall eventually cease in the land.

While our sympathies as a party of reform are naturally upon the side of every proposition which will tend to make men intelligent, virtuous, and temperate, we nevertheless regard these questions, important as they are, as secondary to the great issues now pressing for solution, and upon which not only our individual prosperity but the very existence of free institutions depend; and we ask all men to first help us to determine whether we are to have a republic to administer before we differ as to the conditions upon which it is to be administered, believing that the forces of reform this day organized will never cease to move forward until every wrong is remedied and equal rights and equal privileges securely established for all the men and women of this country.

II. Organized Labor in the Campaign

SAMUEL GOMPERS

Vital to the success of an alliance between industrial workers and the People's party was the support of key labor leaders. Such support was sought in 1892, the first year in which the People's party ran candidates. Daniel DeLeon, who dominated the Socialist Labor party, coldly rejected Populist overtures. Samuel Gompers, head of the American Federation of Labor, was also unsympathetic. His reasons for opposing organized labor's participation in the People's party were summarized in an article in the North American Review, *excerpts from which are given here.*

Identify and evaluate Gompers' principal arguments. What in his general philosophy, as reflected here, would compel him to oppose the approach advocated in the speech by Lloyd?

North American Review, August 1892, pp. 92–93, 95–96.

AUGUST 1892

The members of the organizations affiliated with the Federation will no doubt, in a large measure, as citizens, vote for the candidate of the party of their own political predilections. But the number is ever on the increase who disenthral themselves from partisan voting and exercise their franchise to reward or chastise those parties and candidates, that deserve either their friendship or resentment. With us it is not a question of parties or men; it is a question of measures.

That there exists a feeling of dissatisfaction with, and bitter antagonism to, both the Republican and Democratic parties is not to be gainsaid. Broken promises to labor, insincere, halfhearted support and even antagonism of legislation in the interest of the toilers on the one hand, and the alacrity and devotion with which the interests of the corporations and the wealth-possessing class are nurtured, protected and advanced on the other, have had their effect, and the result is that many toilers have forever severed their connection with the old parties. That the number will continue to grow larger year by year I have not the slightest doubt. To me this party defection of the wageworkers is one of the signs of the dawn of a healthier public opinion, a sturdier manhood and independence, and a promise to maintain the liberties that the people now enjoy, as well as to ever struggle on to attain that happy goal towards which, throughout its entire history, the human family have been perpetually pushing forward.

But in leaving the old parties, to whom, to what shall former Democratic or Republican workmen turn? To the People's Party? Are such changes and improvements promised there that the workers can with any degree of assurance throw in their political fortunes with that party? Of course, acting upon the principle "of all evils choose the least," they will more generally coöperate with the People's Party than with any similar party heretofore gracing the Presidential political arena.

As a matter of fact, however, to support the People's Party under the belief that it is a *labor* party is to act under misapprehension. It is not and cannot, in the nature of its make-up, be a labor party, or even one in which the wageworkers will find their haven. Composed, as the People's Party is, mainly of *employing* farmers without any regard to the interests of the *employed* farmers of the country districts or the mechanics and laborers of the industrial centres, there must of necessity be a divergence of purposes, methods, and interests.

In speaking thus frankly of the composition of the People's Party there is no desire to belittle the efforts of its members, or even to withhold the sympathy due them in their agitation to remedy the wrongs which they suffer from corporate power and avarice; on the contrary, the fullest measure of sympathy and all possible encouragement should and will be given them; for they are doing excellent work in directing public attention to the dangers which threaten the body politic of the republic. But, returning to the consideration of the entire coöperation or amalgamation of the wage-workers' organizations with the People's Party, I am persuaded that all who are more than superficial observers, or who are keen students of the past struggles of the proletariat of all countries, will with one accord unite in declaring the union impossible, because it is unnatural. Let me add that, before there can be any hope of the unification of labor's forces of the field, farm, factory, and workshop, the people who work on and in them for wages must be organized to protect *their* interests against those who pay them wages for that work. . . .

As time goes on we discern that the organized workingmen place less reliance upon the help offered by others, and it is a spark upon the altar of progress that they have learned to more firmly depend upon their own efforts to secure those changes and improvements which are theirs by right.

Of course it must not be imagined that we have no interest in the political affairs of our country; on the contrary, we believe that it is our mission to gather the vast numbers of the wealth-producers, agricultural, industrial, and commercial, into a grand army of organized labor, and, by our struggles for improved conditions and emancipation, instil into the minds of the workers a keener appreciation of their true position in society and of their economic, political and social duties and rights as citizens and workers. Every advantage gained in the economic condition of the wage-workers must necessarily have its political and social effect, not only upon themselves but upon the whole people. Hence for the present, at least, nearly all our efforts are concentrated upon the field as indicated above. . . .

Whatever has been gained for the toilers in our country has been the achievement of the trades-unions, and it would be most unwise, not to say anything harsher, to abandon the organization, position and methods of past success to fly "to others we know not of." More than half of the battle of labor has already been won. No really intelligent man to-day disputes the claims of labor. The stage of ridicule is happily past; the era of reason has taken its place; and what is now needed is the means and the power to enforce our claim. To that end we are marshalling our forces, and we will demonstrate to the world that the demands and struggles of the toiling masses, while ostensibly and immediately concerned with their own improvement and emancipation, will develop the possibilities, grandeur and true nobility of the human family.

Having mapped out our course, the members of the American Federation of Labor can look on the coming Presidential campaign with a degree of equanimity not often attained by the average citizen. The excitement and turmoil, criminations and recriminations will not rend our organization asunder, as it has done so many others; and during it all, and when the blare of trumpets has died away, and the "spell-binders" have received their rewards, the American Federation of Labor will still be found plodding along, doing noble battle in the struggle for the uplifting of the toiling masses.

III. Address of Protest

JACOB S. COXEY

Efforts to unite farmers and laborers took place on the practical as well as the ideological level. In 1894 a number of tramping industrial armies, mainly unemployed workers, moved toward Washington, D.C., to petition the government for redress of their grievances. The most famous of these was the "Army of the Commonweal of Christ," led by "General" Jacob S. Coxey of Massilon, Ohio.

Although he was a businessman, Coxey's ideas paralleled those of the Populists; Lloyd, in fact, suggested him as a presidential candidate of the Populist party in 1896. Specifically, Coxey's plan called for a program of public works to be financed by fiat money (that is, money printed by the government and backed only by its word), as was used in the Civil War.

Washington was thoroughly prepared for Coxey's Army. Every move was watched with fear, despite the pathetic condition of his men. Coxey was not permitted to deliver his address; instead, along with others, he was roughed up by the police and arrested for stepping on the grass.

Considering the reception Coxey's Army received, and in the light of the moderateness of his address and the minimal threat that he posed, how realistic was Lloyd's prediction of what would happen "when the people come in"? On May 1, 1944, Coxey stood on Capitol Hill and delivered the address he intended to give fifty years before. What conclusions might one draw about change in the American system from the fact that the contents of the speech did not seem irrelevant in 1944?

MAY 1, 1894

The Constitution of the United States guarantees to all citizens the right to peaceably assemble and petition for redress of grievances, and furthermore declares that the right of free speech shall not be abridged.

We stand here to-day to test these guaranties of our Constitution. We choose this place of assemblage because it is the property of the people, and if it be true that the right of the people to peacefully assemble upon their own premises and utter their petitions has been abridged by the passage of laws in direct violation of the Constitution, we are here to draw the eyes of the entire nation to this shameful fact. Here rather than at any other spot upon the continent it is fitting that we should come to mourn over our dead liberties and by our protest arouse the imperiled nation to such action as shall rescue the Constitution and resurrect our liberties.

Upon these steps where we stand has been spread a carpet for the royal

Congressional Record, May 9, 1894, p. 4512.

feet of a foreign princess, the cost of whose lavish entertainment was taken from the public Treasury without the consent or the approval of the people. Up these steps the lobbyists of trusts and corporations have passed unchallenged on their way to committee rooms, access to which we, the representatives of the toiling wealth-producers, have been denied. We stand here to-day in behalf of millions of toilers whose petitions have been buried in committee rooms, whose prayers have been unresponded to, and whose opportunities for honest, remunerative, productive labor have been taken from them by unjust legislation, which protects idlers, speculators, and gamblers: we come to remind the Congress here assembled of the declaration of a United States Senator, "that for a quarter of a century the rich have been growing richer, the poor poorer, and that by the close of the present century the middle class will have disappeared as the struggle for existence becomes fierce and relentless."

We stand here to remind Congress of its promise of returning prosperity should the Sherman act be repealed. We stand here to declare by our march of over 400 miles through difficulties and distress, a march unstained by even the slightest act which would bring the blush of shame to any, that we are law-abiding citizens, and as men our actions speak louder than words. We are here to petition for legislation which will furnish employment for every man able and willing to work; for legislation which will bring universal prosperity and emancipate our beloved country from financial bondage to the descendants of King George. We have come to the only source which is competent to aid the people in their day of dire distress. We are here to tell our Representatives, who hold their seats by grace of our ballots, that the struggle for existence has become too fierce and relentless. We come and throw up our defenseless hands, and say, help, or we and our loved ones must perish. We are engaged in a bitter and cruel war with the enemies of all mankind—a war with hunger, wretchedness, and despair, and we ask Congress to heed our petitions and issue for the nation's good a sufficient volume of the same kind of money which carried the country through one awful war and saved the life of the nation.

In the name of justice, through whose impartial administration only the present civilization can be maintained and perpetuated, by the powers of the Constitution of our country upon which the liberties of the people must depend, and in the name of the commonweal of Christ, whose representatives we are, we enter a most solemn and earnest protest against this unnecessary and cruel usurpation and tyranny, and this enforced subjugation of the rights and privileges of American citizenship. We have assembled here in violation of no just laws to enjoy the privileges of every American citizen. We are now under the shadow of the Capitol of this great nation, and in the presence of our national legislators are refused that dearly bought privilege, and by force of arbitrary power prevented from carrying out the desire of our hearts which is plainly granted under the great magna-charta of our national liberties.

We have come here through toil and weary marches, through storms and tempests, over mountains, and amid the trials of poverty and distress, to lay our grievances at the doors of our National Legislature and ask them in the name of Him whose banners we bear, in the name of Him who plead for the poor and the oppressed, that they should heed the voice of despair and distress that is now coming up from every section of our country, that they should consider the conditions of the starving unemployed of our land, and enact such laws as will give them employment, bring happier conditions to the people, and the smile of contentment to our citizens.

Coming as we do with peace and good will to men, we shall submit to these laws, unjust as they are, and obey this mandate of authority of might which overrides and outrages the law of right. In doing so, we appeal to every peace-loving citizen, every liberty-loving man or woman, every one in whose breast the fires of patriotism and love of country have not died out, to assist us in our efforts toward better laws and general benefits.

IV. The Menace of Coxeyism

THOMAS BYRNES

Coxey's Army struck real fear into the hearts of many Americans. Included here are excerpts from an article by Thomas Byrnes, superintendent of the New York Police Department. His remarks represent a "law and order" position that was widely shared. Speculate on how Lloyd, Coxey, and leaders in the People's party might have responded to his arguments.

JUNE 1894

It is apparent that the men who form the "Industrial" armies now marching to Washington are unable to influence legislation in the legitimate way, by securing enough votes to elect their representatives. This is plain, because were they so able, they would at once avail themselves of their political strength. They represent the smallest sort of a minority, and, not content to submit to the majority, they propose to get what they want by intimidating Congress.

The men who compose these so-called armies are, so far as I can learn, what are ordinarily called tramps. That is, they are men who do not earn and have not earned a living and supported themselves. They have banded together, a menace to the communities in which they were, and they propose to demand that Congress pass certain laws. Their avowed object is to assemble in front of the Capitol in Washington, and there, by their presence and numbers, to so intimidate the Congress of the United States as to force that body to pass certain laws dictated by them. Think of it for a moment: these idle, useless dregs of humanity—too lazy to work, too miserably inefficient to earn a living—intend to "demand" that Congress shall pass laws at their dictation. "Demand," that is the word they use in their so-called proclamations. Two thousand, three thousand, five thousand tramps—whatever their number may be—"demand" when they speak to the government of the greatest country on earth! No wonder the people laugh. . . .

The hard times in this country during the past year have enormously increased the number of the unemployed. More than this, there has been a spread of socialistic doctrines to an extent that I have never seen before in an equal space of time. Men have preached the theory that the government is bound to support them. Finding that the great majority of the people, who are industrious and self-supporting, will not vote for any such measure, this small minority, which would live, and does live for the most part, on the earnings of others, has resorted to this army movement, and is on its way to demand legislation. It is easily understood that a tramp, to whom all places are alike, would find a pleasurable excitement in such a march. He is supported as he walks, which is all he cares for, and from being the most despised object in the community—the beggar for broken food—he suddenly finds a certain dignity and interest attaching themselves to him when he joins one of these armies.

When there are enough of him, he shows his natural laziness and his contempt for law by seizing on railroad trains and riding in place of walking. To him, the army movement is a vast picnic.

It is claimed the sympathy of the law-abiding and self-supporting population of the States, for the movement, has been shown by the gifts of food and the help afforded. I have read the published accounts carefully, and I have noticed in every case that help, in whatever form, has been given to get the men to move away. The farmers are not to be blamed. They know from bitter experience what it means to have tramps in the neighborhood, they are powerless to defend themselves, and naturally they do anything to get rid of such unwelcome visitors. I would do the same were I in their place. There is a standing order on the Central Pacific Railroad forbidding conductors of freight trains to put off tramps. Why? Simply because there are hundreds of miles of wooden snowsheds on the roads, and when the tramps are put off they set these on fire. It is cheaper to carry them on the trains. It was cheaper for the farmers to feed the Coxeyites and haul them along the road than to have them stay. No doubt if the farmers could feed and transport the seventeen-year locusts and the army-worms, they would with pleasure. So they have fed and transported these army-worms.

I think this movement is the most dangerous this country has seen since the Civil War. Our Government rests on the submission of the minority to the will of the majority, and this army movement is nothing more than that the minority of the minority appeals to force and intimidation to secure the legislation it wants. It is an outrage that this army of tramps and socialists, officered by self-constituted "Generals," "Colonels," and the like, should be permitted to march through the States with the avowed intention of intimidating Congress. The movement is illegal, un-American, and a disgrace, and it should have been stopped long ago.

I am told there is no law which may be appealed to. If this be true, the Congress is in session, and a law should be passed at once, making all such movements impossible for the future. The evil this will do is to be found in the spread of the Socialistic doctrine that the majority may be ruled by the minority. This doctrine crops up whenever there is a dispute between employers and employed. The ground is taken that men who have real or supposed grievances are above the law, the law in this country being the expression of the will of the majority of the voters; and that they have a right to act in a way forbidden by law.

If this thing is ever successfully carried out, then the United States will fall into a chaos in which mobs will be fighting mobs everywhere. There is a legal method defined by the Constitution, of securing legislation in Congress, and this is by electing a majority of Congressmen. Any other method of influencing Congress is illegal and should be stopped. Intimidation of Congress by the presence of a body of armed men is Rebellion pure and simple, and should be stamped out just as the great Rebellion was in 1861.

V. Populism and the Republic: An Editorial

Populist party successes in various parts of the country were always met with a measure of alarm by those who represented a more conservative perspective. This editorial appeared in Harper's Weekly *following an election in Georgia in which the Populist vote had been sizable. Determine whether it really comes to grips with the issues raised by the Populists, especially those contained in the speech by Lloyd. Speculate on how a good Populist might have responded to this editorial.*

OCTOBER 20, 1894

The astonishingly large vote cast by the Populists in Georgia has alarmed a good many people who forget the history of the rise and fall of political and economic heresies in this country. In every period which suggests a fatal crisis to the naturally lively American imagination the best preventive of panic is a little serious reflection on our political history. There have been few Presidential terms in which the alarmists of one party or the other have not predicted the annihilation of democratic institutions. The government has been on the verge of destruction from monarchists, from Jacobins, from Irish immigration, from greenbackers, and now from Populists. And yet there has never a heresy arisen whose advocates have not been scattered like chaff before the wind

Harper's Weekly, October 20, 1894, pp. 986–87.

whenever a serious and earnest crusade was entered upon by the advocates of reason and common sense.

It is as true to-day as it was at the time when the Jeffersonian Republican was patronizing a French tailor, and the Hamiltonian Federalist was wearing English clothes, that honest common-sense is the best "vote-catcher" in this country. In our own day we have seen the republic preserve its life against the slave power in arms, and many of us have helped to give the quietus to sectionalism, to grangerism, and to greenbackism. . . .

All these false doctrines being overcome, there is every reason why men who have had experience in American politics should cease to fly into a panic at the uprising of every movement which inexperience may be justified in mistaking for a fatality.

It is true that the danger of Populism is not to be underrated, and it is, on the whole, better to be too much than too little afraid of it. But Populism is merely a new symptom of an old trouble. Perhaps it is the most serious symptom that has yet appeared. At the same time it does not threaten the country with any such danger as will excuse a panic. A little resolute common-sense will dissipate it; but the sooner it is dissipated the better for the country and for those who have been misled into joining in the movement. In the effort to defeat the Populists it will be found that the restoration of prosperity is a most potent, probably the most potent, ally of reason, for every such agitation as this is intensified by hard times.

Populism is the expression of the discontent of the unthrifty. It does not matter what it demands, whether free coinage, or paper money, or government loans to the farmers on their crops, or government ownership of railroads, the cause of Populism is the feeling of those who have little money that the government ought to help them to more. This feeling has been intensified and embittered by certain acts of Federal government which have seemed to the discontented to evince an undue care for those already rich. Even when the acts of the government were dictated by wisdom and partiotism . . . they have nevertheless aroused the anger of those who have been compelled to pay taxes and who have had very little to pay them with. The chief cause of Populism in its present phase has been that fruitful breeder of trusts and monopolies, the protective tariff. More than anything else, it has been an object-lesson of evil import to those who are forced to contend with arduous circumstances for a slender living. It has bred the habit of mind which looks to the government as a distributer of bounties. It has made paternalism popular. It has been the source of much of the socialism of those who do not realize that protection itself is the fruit and flower of socialism. Finally it has culminated in a wide-spread movement, which is strongest in those parts of the country which, consciously or unconsciously, have suffered most from high tariff taxes. The condition which is illustrated by the recent election in Georgia is essentially a struggle of the communism of poverty against the communism of wealth.

Such a struggle is largely sectional. The opposition to it must be against its latest phase. If it is for free silver, or for flat money, or for State ownership of railroads, or for legislation which will enable one party to a labor contract to violate it without the consent of the other—whatever is the movement's particular mode of expression—it is of course against that that the war must be waged. At present, . . . the probability is that Populism and its allies will make a strong effort in behalf of flat money, and flat money is the direct fruit of paternalism. The political parties, as at present constituted, are not to be depended on in such a contest. The republican party is a Populist party in Kansas, and the Democratic party is Populist in Georgia. The Republicans help the professed Populists in Alabama, while the Democrats do the same in the Northwest. Some day perhaps the two parties will divide on the currency question, but that day has not yet arrived.

In the mean time it is the duty of all who have the interests of the country at heart in those States where sound views prevail to see that they are represented in Congress by men who not only share those views, but who are also able to advance and defend them. Something more than mere votes is needed. There is no cure for an economic or political heresy like debate. Therefore the more debaters we have in Congress for sound principles, the sooner will the prevailing miasma of Populism be dissipated. . . . By the very nature of its constitution a republic is prone to deviate from scientific economic methods, and those who, knowing better, do not help to keep the government headed in the right direction are simply subordinating the public welfare to their own greed. It is certain that no Congressman will be sent to Washington from a district governed by Populistic ignorance who is not in sympathy with the prejudices of his constituents. A people who are given over to a heresy are always possessed of a fanatical enthusiasm and intolerance. It behooves those who have saner views to be equally determined. Populism does not endanger the existence of the republic, but in it are the potentialities of obstructed progress, of commercial disaster, of individual distress and ruin. The sooner and more thoroughly it is met and enlightened, in whatever form it appears, the better for every man who lives by his own industry, for the country, and for civilization itself.

For Further Reading

*American Radicalism, 1865–1901: Essays and Documents** (1946, 1966), by Chester McArthur Destler, is the volume most directly related to this chapter; it provided the core document.

The most comprehensive study of the Populist movement was done by John D. Hicks in *The Populist Revolt** (1931, 1961). Recent volumes treating aspects of Populism are O. Gene Clanton's *Kansas Populism: Ideas and Men* (1969), Robert F. Durden's *The Climax of Populism** (1965), and Norman Pollack's *The Populist Response to Industrialism** (1962). *The Age of Reform:*

*Paperbound edition available.

From Bryan to FDR* (1955), by Richard Hofstadter, offers an interesting but controversial interpretation of Populism.

Documents from the Populist era can be found in *The Populist Mind** (1967), edited by Norman Pollack, and in *The Populist Reader** (1966), edited by George Brown Tindall.

The discontent giving rise to Populism is treated in Carlton Beals' *The Great Revolt and Its Leaders* (1968) and in Donald L. McMurry's *Coxey's Army: A Study of the Industrial Army Movement of 1894** (1968; originally published in 1929).

These are problems books: Raymond J. Cunningham, ed., *The Populists in Historical Perspective** (1968); Theodore Saloutos, ed., *Populism: Reaction or Reform?** (1968); and Irwin Unger, ed., *Populism: Nostalgic or Progressive?** (1964).

*Paperbound edition available.

5. American Expansionism: A Question of "True" Patriotism

In the last decades of the nineteenth century the United States was preoccupied with the development of its abundant resources and the industrialization of its economy. This preoccupation allowed little time or energy for the nation to imitate the efforts of the Western European countries in acquiring colonial empires. The continental limits of the national domain had been reached and there was little enthusiasm to extend the American flag beyond those limits. This does not mean that there was a complete absence of American "imperialism." It does mean, however, that public apathy to colonial projects and congressional reluctance to use public funds to support overseas adventures restrained the ambitions of those who were interested in expansion.

Thus, when Secretary of State William H. Seward acquired Alaska from Russia in 1867 at the bargain price of $7,200,000, he was ridiculed in the press and in Congress for his "folly." President Ulysses S. Grant had an interest in the acquisition of the Dominican Republic during the 1870s, but his intentions, although serious, did not have sufficient support to be translated into policy. During the late 1880s, Secretary of State James G. Blaine tried to bring about closer ties with Latin America through the development of a Pan-American Conference, but his "America first" attitude crippled the project from the very beginning. In the Pacific, though, Blaine was able to secure part of Samoa for use by the U.S. Navy in 1889, and his concern for American security led to closer ties with the Hawaiian Islands, which were ruled by a native monarchy supported by American missionaries and planters. Seward, Grant, and Blaine were the exceptions in a nation that was isolated and at peace and not interested in the acquisition of a colonial empire. This anti-imperialist attitude continued into the 1890s, as was amply illustrated by the negative reaction of Congress and the Cleveland administration to an American-supported revolution in Hawaii in 1893 and the unsuccessful bids by the new Hawaiian government for annexation by the United States in 1894 and 1897.

The indifference toward the acquisition of colonies on the part of the government and the majority of the American people changed dramatically when the American battleship *Maine* was blown up while on a courtesy visit to the Spanish city of Havana, Cuba, on February 15, 1898. The native Cubans had been fighting for freedom for many years and the American public, agitated by the press, had been sympathetic to their cause. When the news arrived that 260 Americans had lost their lives in the disaster, the press immediately demanded retribution. President William McKinley finally agreed and on April 11, 1898, he asked Congress for troops to be used in Cuba to punish the Spanish for their alleged attack on the *Maine* and to free the Cuban people from Spanish domination.

Spain tried to forestall war, but after the American declaration of intervention the Madrid government responded with a declaration of war against the United States. The American victory came with greater ease than even the most enthusiastic of the imperialists could have imagined. The American republic won the war and gained an empire; the next question was what to do with the new territories.

Core Document

The Policy of Imperialism

CARL SCHURZ

The Spanish-American War ended with a preliminary agreement between the two belligerents on August 12, 1898. The provisions of the agreement included a Spanish declaration of intent to free and evacuate Cuba at once and to turn Puerto Rico and an island in the Pacific over to the United States. The question of the ownership of the Philippines, where United States naval forces under

Frederic Bancroft, ed., *Speeches, Correspondence and Political Papers of Carl Schurz* (New York: G. P. Putnam's, 1913), VI, pp. 78–79, 91–92, 97–110, 112, 114–20.

Commodore George Dewey had defeated a Spanish fleet on May 1, 1898, was left unanswered. The people of the Philippines, like the Cubans, had fought a series of insurrections against the Spanish authorities during the 1890s. Emilio Aguinaldo, the leader of the Philippine rebels, had met with several American officials before Dewey sailed from Hong Kong to Manila, and had been promised arms and ammunition by the United States if he would return to the islands and aid the American cause. Aguinaldo agreed, the aid was given, and the rebels were successful in taking over most of the inland areas of the islands. Meanwhile, the Americans blockaded Manila and on August 13, 1898, American military units seized the city from the Spanish.

On February 6, 1899, a peace treaty with Spain was ratified by the Senate. It provided for the ceding to the United States of Puerto Rico, Guam, and the Philippines. The cession of the first two offered little difficulty, but in the Philippines Aguinaldo and his rebels realized that they had not gained their independence, but had simply changed masters. Their rebellion against their new master, the United States, aroused a sense of determination among some Americans and of indignation among others. The imperialists called for the destruction of the rebels at all costs, while the anti-imperialists condemned with equal intensity the annexation of the Philippines by the United States.

One of the best known of the anti-imperialists was Carl Schurz, who, as a hunted revolutionary in his native Germany, had emigrated as a political refugee to the United States in 1852 at the age of twenty-three. Through his powers of leadership and oratory he quickly rose to prominence in American politics. Joining the Republican party in 1856, he campaigned against slavery and later for the election of Abraham Lincoln. During the Civil War Schurz achieved the rank of general in the Union Army and commanded troops at Chancellorsville and Gettysburg. A confidant of President Lincoln, Schurz favored Lincoln's plan for reconstruction of the South and in 1869 was elected to the United States Senate by the Missouri legislature.

Schurz became the leader of the liberal element in the Republican party in the 1870s, and in 1877 he was appointed Secretary of the Interior by President Rutherford B. Hayes. Throughout the 1870s and 1880s he wrote numerous articles for the newspapers and magazines and became a staff writer for Harper's Weekly *in 1892. His connection with* Harper's *ended in 1898 when he refused to support the "hawks" in the coming war with Spain. Schurz was one of the leading opponents of the Spanish-American War and of the annexation of territories from Spain once the war ended. The following speech, made to the Anti-Imperialist League in Chicago in 1899, is one of the clearest arguments against American imperialism to appear during the period of the Spanish-American War and its aftermath.*

In reading Schurz's speech give close attention to what he believed to be:
- *the immorality of the American presence in the Philippines.*
- *the McKinley administration's policy toward the Philippines.*
- *the constitutional issues brought about by the insurrection in the Philippines.*

- *the dangerous precedents set by the McKinley administration in making war upon the Filipinos.*
- *the effect an immediate armistice or cease-fire would have upon America and the world.*
- *the commercial considerations affecting the annexation of the Philippines.*
- *the reaction of the Filipinos to American rule.*
- *the various types of American imperialists.*
- *true patriotism.*

OCTOBER 17, 1899

We all know that the popular mind is much disturbed by the Philippine war, and that, however highly we admire the bravery of our soldiers, nobody professes to be proud of the war itself. There are few Americans who do not frankly admit their regret that this war should ever have happened. I think I risk nothing when I say that it is not merely the bungling conduct of military operations, but a serious trouble of conscience, that disturbs the American heart about this war, and that this trouble of conscience will not be allayed by a more successful military campaign, just as fifty years ago the trouble of conscience about slavery could not be allayed by any compromise.

Many people now, as the slavery compromisers did then, try to ease their minds by saying: "Well, we are in it, and now we must do the best we can." In spite of the obvious futility of this cry in some respects, I will accept it with the one proviso, that we make an honest effort to ascertain what really is *the best* we can do. . . .

Let us recapitulate. We go to war with Spain in behalf of an oppressed colony of hers. We solemnly proclaim this to be a war—not of conquest—God forbid!—but of liberation and humanity. We invade the Spanish colony of the Philippines, destroy the Spanish fleet, and invite the coöperation of the Filipino insurgents against Spain. We accept their effective aid as allies, all the while permitting them to believe that, in case of victory, they will be free and independent. By active fighting they get control of a large part of the interior country, from which Spain is virtually ousted. When we have captured Manila and have no further use for our Filipino allies, our President directs that, behind their backs, a treaty be made with Spain transferring their country to us; and even before that treaty is ratified, he tells them that, in place of the Spaniards, they must accept us as their masters, and that if they do not, they will be compelled by force of arms. They refuse, and we shoot them down; and, as President McKinley said at Pittsburgh, we shall continue to shoot them down "without useless parley." . . .

I am far from meaning to picture the Phillipine Islanders as paragons of virtue and gentle conduct. But I challenge the imperialists to show me any instances of bloody disturbance or other savagery among them sufficient to create any necessity for our armed interference to "restore order" or to "save them from anarchy." I ask and demand an answer: Is it not true that, even if there has been such a disorderly tendency, it would have required a long time for it to kill one-tenth as many human beings as we have killed and to cause one-tenth as much devastation as we have caused by our assaults upon them? Is it not true that, instead of being obliged to "restore order," we have carried riot and death and desolation into peaceful communities whose only offense was not that they did not maintain order and safety among themselves, but that they refused to accept us as their rulers? And here is the rub.

In the vocabulary of our imperialists "order" means, above all, submission to their will. Any other kind of order, be it ever so peaceful and safe, must be suppressed with a bloody hand. This "order" is the kind that has been demanded by the despot since the world had a history. Its language has already become dangerously familiar to us—a familiarity which cannot cease too soon.

From all these points of view, therefore, the Philippine war was as unnecessary as it is unjust. A wanton, wicked and abominable war—so it is called by untold thousands of American citizens, and so it is at heart felt to be, I have no doubt, by an immense majority of the American people. Aye, as such it is cursed by many of our very soldiers whom our Government orders to shoot down innocent people. And who will deny that this war would certainly have been avoided had the President remained true to the National pledge that the war against Spain should be a war of liberation and humanity and not of conquest? Can there be any doubt that, if the assurance had honestly been given and carried out, we might have had, for the mere asking, all the coaling-stations, and facilities for commercial and industrial enterprise, and freedom for the establishment of schools and churches we might reasonably desire? And what have we now? After eight months of slaughter and devastation, squandered treasure and shame, an indefinite prospect of more and more slaughter, devastation, squandered treasure and shame.

But, we are asked, since we have to deal with a situation not as it might have been, but as it is, what do we propose to do now? We may fairly turn about and say, since not we, but you, have got the country into this frightful mess, what have you to propose? Well, and what is the answer? "No useless parley! More soldiers! More guns! More blood! More devastation! Kill, kill, kill! And when we have killed enough, so that further resistance stops, then we shall see." Translated from smooth phrase into plain English, this is the program. Let us examine it with candor and coolness.

What is the ultimate purpose of this policy? To be perfectly fair, I will assume that the true spirit of American imperialism is represented not by the extremists who want to subjugate the Philippine Islanders at any cost and then exploit the islands to the best advantage of the conquerors, but by the more humane persons who say that we must establish our sovereignty over them to make them happy, to prepare them for self-government, and even recognize their right to complete independence as soon as they show themselves fit for it.

Let me ask these well-meaning citizens a simple question. If you think that the American people may ultimately consent to the independence of those islanders as a matter of right and good policy, why do you insist upon killing them now? You answer: Because they refuse to recognize our sovereignty. Why do they so refuse? Because they think themselves entitled to independence, and are willing to fight and die for it. But if you insist upon continuing to shoot them down for this reason, does not that mean that you want to kill them for demanding the identical thing which you yourself think that you may ultimately find it just and proper to grant them? Would not every drop of blood shed in such a guilty sport cry to Heaven? For you must not forget that establishing our sovereignty in the Philippines means the going on with the work of slaughter and devastation to the grim end, and nobody can tell where that end will be. To kill men in a just war and in obedience to imperative necessity is one thing. To kill men for demanding what you yourself may ultimately have to approve, is another. How can such killing adopted as a policy be countenanced by a man of conscience and humane feelings? And yet, such killing without useless parley is the policy proposed to us.

We are told that we must trust President McKinley and his advisers to bring us out "all right." I should be glad to be able to do so; but I cannot forget that they have got us in all wrong. And here we have to consider a point of immense importance, which I solemnly urge upon the attention of the American people.

It is one of the fundamental principles of our system of democratic government that only the Congress has the power to declare war. What does this signify? That a declaration of war, the initiation of an armed conflict between this Nation and some other Power—the most solemn and responsible act a nation can perform, involving as it does the lives and fortunes of an uncounted number of human beings—shall not be at the discretion of the Executive branch of the Government, but shall depend upon the authority of the legislative representatives of the people—in other words, that, as much as the machinery of government may make such a thing possible, the deliberate will of the people Constitutionally expressed shall determine the awful question of peace or war. . . .

We are now engaged in a war with the Filipinos. You may quibble about it as you will, call it by whatever name you will—it *is* a war; and a war of conquest on our part at that—a war of barefaced, cynical conquest. Now, I ask any fairminded man whether the President, before beginning that war, or while carrying it on, has ever taken any proper steps to get from the Congress, the representatives of the people, any proper authority for making that war. He issued his famous "benevolent assimilation" order, directing the Army to bring the whole Philippine archipelago as promptly as possible under the military government of the United States, on December 21, 1898, while Congress was in session, and before the treaty with Spain, transferring her shadowy sovereignty over the islands, had acquired any force of law by the assent of the Senate. That was substantially a declaration of war against the Filipinos asserting their independence. He took this step of his own motion. To be sure, he has constantly been telling us that "the whole subject is with Congress," and that "Congress shall direct." But when did he, while Congress was in session, lay a full statement before that body and ask its direction? Why did he not, before he proclaimed that the slaughter must go on without useless parley, call Congress together to consult the popular will in Constitutional form? Why, even in these days, while "swinging around the circle," the President and his Secretaries are speaking of the principal thing, the permanent annexation of the Philippines, not as a question still to be determined, but as a thing done—concluded by the Executive, implying that Congress will have simply to regulate the details.

Now you may bring ever so many arguments to show that the President had *technically* a right to act as he did, and your reasoning may be ever so plausible—yet the great fact remains that the President did not seek and obtain authority from Congress as to the war to be made, and the policy to be pursued, and that he acted upon his own motion. And this autocratic conduct is vastly aggravated by the other fact that in this democratic Republic, the government of which should be that of an intelligent and well-informed public opinion, a censorship of news has been instituted, which is purposely and systematically seeking to keep the American people in ignorance of the true state of things at the seat of war, and by all sorts of deceitful tricks to deprive them of the knowledge required for the formation of a correct judgment. And this censorship was practised not only in Manila, but directly by the Administration in Washington. Here is a specimen performance revealed by a member of Congress in a public speech; the War Department gave out a despatch from Manila, as follows: "Volunteers willing to remain." The Congressman went to the War Department and asked for the original, which read: "Volunteers unwilling to reënlist, but willing to remain until transports arrive." You will admit that such distortion of official news is a downright swindle upon the people. Does not this give strong color to the charge of the war correspondents that the news is systematically and confessedly so doctored by the oficials that it may "help the Administration"?

Those are, therefore, by no means wrong who call this "the President's war." And a war so brought about and so conducted the American people are asked to approve and encourage, simply because "we are in it"—that is, because the President of his own motion has got us into it. Have you considered what this means?

Every man of public experience knows how powerful and seductive precedent is as an argument in the interpretation of laws and of constitutional provisions, or in justification of governmental practices. When a thing, no matter how questionable, has once been done by the government, and approved, or even acquiesced in, by the people, that act will surely be used as a justification of its being done again. In nothing is the authority of precedent more dangerous than in defending usurpations of governmental power. . . .

We cannot expect all our future Presidents to be models of public virtue and wisdom, as George Washington was. Imagine now in the Presidential office a man well-meaning but, it may be, short-sighted and pliable, and under the influence of so-called "friends" who are greedy and reckless speculators, and who would not scruple to push him into warlike complications in order to get great opportunities for profit; or a man of that inordinate ambition which intoxicates the mind and befogs the conscience; or a man of extreme partisan spirit, who honestly believes the victory of his party to be necessary for the salvation of the universe, and may think that a foreign broil would serve the chances of his party; or a man of an uncontrollable combativeness of temperament which might run away with his sense of responsibility—and that we shall have such men in the Presidential chair is by no means unlikely with our loose way of selecting candidates for the Presidency. Imagine, then, a future President belonging to either of these classes to have before him the precedent of Mr. McKinley's management of the Philippine business, sanctioned by the approval or only the acquiescence of the people, and to feel himself permitted —nay, even encouraged—to say to himself that, as this precedent shows, he may plunge the country into warlike conflicts of his own motion, without asking leave of Congress, with only some legal technicalities to cover his usurpation, or, even without such, and that he may, by a machinery of deception called a war-censorship, keep the people in the dark about what is going on; and that into however bad a mess he may have got the country, he may count upon the people, as soon as a drop of blood has been shed, to uphold the usurpation and to cry down everybody who opposes it as a "traitor," and all this because "we are in it"! Can you conceive a more baneful precedent, a more prolific source of danger to the peace and security of the country? Can any sane man deny that it will be all the more prolific of evil if in this way we drift into a foreign policy full of temptation for dangerous adventure?

I say, therefore, that, if we have the future of the Republic at heart, we must not only not uphold the Administration in its course, because "we are in it," but just because we are in it, have been got into it in such a way, the American people should stamp the Administration's proceedings with a verdict of disapproval so clear and emphatic, and "get out of it" in such a fashion, that this will be a solemn warning to future Presidents instead of a seductive precedent.

What, then, to accomplish this end is to be done? Of course, we, as we are here, can only advise. But by calling forth expressions of the popular will by various means of public demonstration, and, if need be, at the polls, we can make that advice so strong that those in power will hardly disregard it. We have often been taunted with having no positive policy to propose. But such a policy has more than once been proposed and I can only repeat it.

In the first place, let it be well understood that those are egregiously mistaken who think that if by a strong military effort the Philippine war be stopped, everything will be right and no more question about it. No, the

American trouble of conscience will not be appeased, and the question will be as big and virulent as ever, unless the close of the war be promptly followed by an assurance to the islanders of their freedom and independence, which assurance, if given now, would surely end the war without more fighting.

We propose, therefore, that it be given now. Let there be at once an armistice between our forces and the Filipinos. . . .

Those who talk so much about "fitting a people for self-government" often forget that no people were ever made "fit" for self-government by being kept in the leading-strings of a foreign Power. You learn to walk by doing your own crawling and stumbling. Self-government is learned only by exercising it upon one's own responsibility. Of course there will be mistakes, and troubles and disorders. We have had and now have these, too—at the beginning our persecution of the Tories, our flounderings before the Constitution was formed, our Shays's rebellion, our whisky war and various failures and disturbances—among them a civil war that cost us a loss of life and treasure horrible to think of, and the murder of two Presidents. But who will say that on account of these things some foreign Power should have kept the American people in leading-strings to teach them to govern themselves? . . .

Now, what objection is there to the policy dictated by our fundamental principles and our good faith? I hear the angry cry: "What? Surrender to Aguinaldo? Will not the world ridicule and despise us for such a confession of our incompetency to deal with so feeble a foe? What will become of our prestige?" No, we shall not surrender to Aguinaldo. In giving up a criminal aggression, we shall surrender only to our own consciences, to our own sense of right and justice, to our own understanding of our own true interests and to the vital principles of our own Republic. Nobody will laugh at us whose good opinion we have reason to cherish. . . .

The true friends of this Republic . . . all over the world, who are now grieving to see us go astray, will rejoice, and their hearts will be uplifted with new confidence in our honesty, in our wisdom and in the virtue of democratic institutions when they behold the American people throwing aside all the puerilities of false pride, and returning to the path of their true duty. The world knows how strong we are. It knows full well that if the American people chose to put forth their strength, they could quickly overcome a foe infinitely more powerful than the Filipinos, and that, if we, possessing the strength of the giant, do not use the giant's strength against this feeble foe, it is from the noblest of motives—our love of liberty, our sense of justice and our respect for the rights of others—the respect of the strong for the rights of the weak. The moral prestige which, in fact, we have lost, will be restored, while our prestige of physical prowess and power will certainly not be lessened by showing that we have not only soldiers, guns, ships and money, but also a conscience. . . .

There are some American citizens who take of this question a purely commercial view. I declare I am ardently in favor of the greatest possible expansion of our trade, and I am happy to say that, according to official statistics, our foreign commerce, in spite of all hindrances raised against it, is now expanding tremendously, owing to the simple rule that the nation offering the best goods at proportionately the lowest prices will have the markets. It will have them without armies, without war fleets, without bloody conquests, without colonies. I confess I am not in sympathy with those, if there be such men among us, who would sacrifice our National honor and the high ideals of the Republic, and who would inflict upon our people the burdens and the demoralizing influences of militarism for a mere matter of dollars and cents. They are among the most dangerous enemies of the public welfare. But as to the annexation of the Philippines, I will, for argument's sake, adopt even their point of view for a moment and ask: Will it pay?

Now, it may well be that the annexation of the Philippines would pay a speculative syndicate of wealthy capitalists, without at the same time paying the American people at large. As to people of our race, tropical countries like the Philippines may be fields of profit for rich men who can hire others to work for them, but not for those who have to work for themselves. Taking a general view of the Philippines as a commercial market for us, I need not again argue against the barbarous notion that in order to have a profitable trade with a country we must own it. If that were true, we should never have had any foreign commerce at all. Neither need I prove that it is very bad policy, when you wish to build up a profitable trade, to ruin your customer first, as you would ruin the Philippines by a protracted war. It is equally needless to show to any well-informed person that the profits of the trade with the islands themselves can never amount to the cost of making and maintaining the conquest of the Philippines. . . .

It is useless to say that the subjugated Philippine Islanders will become our friends if we give them good government. However good that government may be, it will, to them, be foreign rule, and foreign rule especially hateful when begun by broken faith, cemented by streams of innocent blood and erected upon the ruins of devastated homes. The American will be and remain to them more a foreigner, an unsympathetic foreigner, than the Spaniard ever was. Let us indulge in no delusion about this. People of our race are but too much inclined to have little tenderness for the rights of what we regard as inferior races, especially those of darker skin. . . .

Although I have by no means exhausted this vast subject, discussing only a few phases of it, I have said enough, I think, to show that this policy of conquest is, from the point of view of public morals, in truth "criminal aggression"—made doubly criminal by the treacherous character of it; and that from the point of view of material interest it is a blunder—a criminal blunder, and a blundering crime. I have addressed myself to your reason by sober argument, without any appeal to prejudice or passion. Might we not ask our opponents to answer these arguments, if they can, with equally sober reasoning, instead of merely assailing us with their wild cries of "treason" and "lack of patriotism," and what not? Or do they really feel their cause to be so weak that they depend for its support on their assortment of inarticulate shouts and nebulous phrases?

Here are our "manifest destiny" men who tell us that, whether it be right or not, we must take and keep the Philippines because "destiny" so wills it. . . . The cry of destiny is most vociferously put forward by those who want to do a wicked thing and to shift the responsibility. The destiny of a free people lies in its intelligent will and its moral strength. When it pleads destiny, it pleads "the baby act." Nay, worse; the cry of destiny is apt to be the refuge of evil intent and of moral cowardice.

Here are our "burden" men, who piously turn up their eyes and tell us, with a melancholy sigh, that all this conquest business may be very irksome, but that a mysterious Providence has put it as a "burden" upon us, which, however sorrowfully, we must bear; that this burden consists in our duty to take care of the poor people of the Philippines; and that in order to take proper care of them we must exercise sovereignty over them; and that if they refuse to accept our sovereignty, we must—alas! alas!—kill them, which makes the burden very solemn and sad. . . .

Next there are our "flag" men, who insist that we must kill the Filipinos fighting for their independence to protect the honor of the stars and stripes. I agree that the honor of our flag sorely needs protection. We have to protect it against desecration by those who are making it an emblem of that hypocrisy which seeks to cover a war of conquest and subjugation with a cloak of humanity and religion; an emblem of that greed which would treat a matter involving our National honor, the integrity of our institutions and the peace and character of the Republic as a mere question of dollars and cents; an emblem of that vulgar lust of war and conquest which recklessly tramples upon right and justice and all our higher ideals; an emblem of the imperialistic ambitions which mock the noblest part of our history and stamp the greatest National heroes of our past as hypocrites or fools. These are the dangers threatening the honor of our flag, against which it needs protection, and that protection we are striving to give it.

Now, a last word to those of our fellow-citizens who feel and recognize as we do that the Philippine war of subjugation is wrong and cruel, and that we ought to recognize the independence of those people, but who insist that, having begun that war, we must continue it until the submission of the Filipinos is complete. I detest, but I can understand, the Jingo whose moral sense is obscured by intoxicating dreams of wild adventure and conquest, and to whom bloodshed and devastation have become a reckless sport. I detest even more, but still I can understand, the cruel logic of those to whom everything is a matter of dollars and cents and whose greed of gain will walk coolly over slaughtered populations. But I must confess I cannot understand the reasoning of those who have moral sense enough to recognize that this war is criminal aggression—who must say to themselves that every drop of blood shed in it by friend or foe is blood wantonly and wickedly shed, and that every act of devastation is barbarous cruelty inflicted upon an innocent people—but who still maintain that we must go on killing, and devastating, and driving our brave soldiers into a fight which they themselves are cursing, because we have once begun it. This I cannot understand. Do they not consider that in such a war, which they themselves condemn as wanton and iniquitous, the more complete our success, the greater will be our disgrace? . . .

I know the imperialists will say that I have been pleading here for Aguinaldo and his Filipinos against our Republic. No—not for the Filipinos merely, although as one of those who have grown gray in the struggle for free and honest government, I would never be ashamed to plead for the cause of freedom and independence, even when its banner is carried by dusky and feeble hands. But I am pleading for more. I am pleading for the cause of American honor and self-respect, American interests, American democracy—aye, for the cause of the American people against an administration of our public affairs which has wantonly plunged this country into an iniquitous war; which has disgraced the Republic by a scandalous breach of faith to a people struggling for their freedom whom we had used as allies; which has been systematically seeking to deceive and mislead the public mind by the manufacture of false news; which has struck at the very foundation of our Constitutional government by an Executive usurpation of the war-power; which makes sport of the great principles and high ideals that have been and should ever remain the guiding star of our course; and which, unless stopped in time, will transform this government of the people, for the people and by the people into an imperial government cynically calling itself republican—a government in which the noisy worship of arrogant might will drown the voice of right; which will impose upon the people a burdensome and demoralizing militarism, and which will be driven into a policy of wild and rapacious adventure by the unscrupulous greed of the exploiter—a policy always fatal to democracy.

I plead the cause of the American people against all this, and I here declare my profound conviction that if this administration of our affairs were submitted for judgment to a popular vote on a clear issue, it would be condemned by an overwhelming majority.

I confidently trust that the American people will prove themselves too clear-headed not to appreciate the vital difference between the expansion of the Republic and its free institutions over contiguous territory and kindred populations, which we all gladly welcome if accomplished peaceably and honorably—and imperialism which reaches out for distant lands to be ruled as subject provinces; too intelligent not to perceive that our very first step on the road of imperialism has been a betrayal of the fundamental principles of democracy, followed by disaster and disgrace; too enlightened not to understand that a monarchy may do such things and still remain a strong monarchy, while a democracy cannot do them and still remain a democracy; too wise not to detect the false pride or the dangerous ambitions or the selfish schemes which so often hide themselves under that deceptive cry of mock patriotism: "Our country, right or wrong!" They will not fail to recognize that our dignity, our free institutions and the peace and welfare of this and coming generations of Americans will be secure only as we cling to the watchword of *true* patriotism: "Our country—when right to be kept right; when wrong to be put right."

Discussion Starters

1. What constitutional questions did Schurz see in the way the executive department was carrying out the war in the Philippines?

2. Evaluate Schurz's concern over the future of the American presidency if Americans continued to approve of the policy of the President simply because "we are in it"?

3. How did Schurz answer those who argued that the war involved the honor of the United States and that signing an armistice with the Filipinos would be to surrender the prestige of the United States before the nations of the world? In what ways could his answer be interpreted as "un-American"?

4. How valid are Schurz's arguments that the proposed annexation of the Philippines would not be a financial success for the vast majority of the American people?

5. Evaluate Schurz's contention that the cry of manifest destiny by the American imperialists was simply a ruse to hide evil intentions and a symbol of moral cowardice.

6. How would Schurz's brand of dissent, regarded by him as "true patriotism," be received today? Consider his declaration: "Our country—when right to be kept right; when wrong to be put right." What might a true patriot do to put America right?

Related Documents

I. The Future in Relation to American Naval Power

ALFRED T. MAHAN

One of the most influential proponents of American expansion during the 1890s and after the Spanish-American War was Captain Alfred T. Mahan of the U. S. Navy. In 1890 he published The Influence of Sea Power upon History, 1660–1783 *and in 1892* The Influence of Sea Power upon the French Revolution and Empire, 1793–1812. *The two works were greeted with enthusiasm in the United States and Europe, especially by the "Big Navy" men of both areas. Mahan's ideas were of primary significance in the arguments of the American imperialists in their fight for overseas expansion.*

In the following article Captain Mahan discusses the role of American naval power and how it might affect the future status of the United States in world politics. How do the ideas in this article compare with Carl Schurz's argument that American expansion would destroy American power?

1898

That the United States Navy within the last dozen years should have been recast almost wholly, upon more modern lines, is not, in itself alone, a fact that should cause comment, or give rise to questions about its future career or sphere of action. . . .

The conditions which now constitute the political situation of the United States, relative to the world at large, are fundamentally different from those that obtained at the beginning of the century. It is not a mere question of greater growth, of bigger size. It is not only that we are larger, stronger, have, as it were, reached our majority, and are able to go out into the world. That alone would be a difference of degree, not of kind. The great difference between the past and the present is that we then, as regards close contact with the power of the chief nations of the world, were really in a state of political isolation which no longer exists. This arose from our geographical position—reinforced by the slowness and uncertainty of the existing means of intercommunication—and yet more from the grave preoccupation of foreign statesmen with questions of unprecedented and ominous importance upon the continent of Europe. A policy of isolation was for us then practicable,—though even then only partially. It was expedient, also, because we were weak, and in order to allow the individuality of the nation time to accentuate itself. Save the questions

Alfred T. Mahan, *The Interest of America in Sea Power, Present and Future* (Boston: Little, Brown, 1898), pp. 137, 146–49, 157–60, 170–72.

connected with the navigation of the Mississippi, collision with other peoples was only likely to arise, and actually did arise, from going beyond our own borders in search of trade. The reasons now evoked by some against our political action outside our own borders might have been used then with equal appositeness against our commercial enterprises. Let us stay at home, or we shall get into trouble. . . .

. . . But would it be more prudent now to ignore the fact that we are no longer —however much we may regret it—in a position of insignificance or isolation, political or geographical, in any way resembling the times of Jefferson, and that from the changed conditions may result to us a dilemma similar to that which confronted him and his supporters? Not only have we grown,—that is a detail, —but the face of the world is changed, economically and politically. The sea, now as always the great means of communication between nations, is traversed with a rapidity and a certainty that have minimized distances. Events which under former conditions would have been distant and of small concern, now happen at our doors and closely affect us. Proximity, as has been noted, is a fruitful source of political friction, but proximity is the characteristic of the age. The world has grown smaller. Positions formerly distant have become to us of vital importance from their nearness. But, while distances have short-ened, they remain for us water distances, and, however short, for political influence they must be traversed in the last resort by a navy, the indispensable instrument by which, when emergencies arise, the nation can project its power beyond its own shore-line. . . .

For national security, the correlative of a national principle firmly held and distinctly avowed is, not only the will, but the power to enforce it. The clear expression of national purpose, accompanied by evident and adequate means to carry it into effect, is the surest safeguard against war, provided always that the national contention is maintained with a candid and courteous consideration of the rights and susceptibilities of other states. On the other hand, no condition is more hazardous than that of a dormant popular feeling, liable to be roused into action by a moment of passion, such as that which swept over the North when the flag was fired upon at Sumter, but behind which lies no organized power for action. It is on the score of due preparation for such an ultimate contingency that nations, and especially free nations, are most often deficient. Yet, if wanting in definiteness of foresight and persistency of action, owing to the inevitable frequency of change in the governments that represent them, democracies seem in compensation to be gifted with an instinct, the result perhaps of the free and rapid interchange of thought by which they are characterized, that intuitively and unconsciously assimilates political truths, and prepares in part for political action before the time for action has come. That the mass of United States citizens do not realize understandingly that the nation has vital political inter-ests beyond the sea is probably true; still more likely is it that they are not tracing any connection between them and the reconstruction of the navy. Yet the interests exist, and the navy is growing; and in the latter fact is the best surety that no breach of peace will ensue from the maintenance of the former.

It is, not, then, the indication of a formal political purpose, far less of anything like a threat, that is, from my point of view, to be recognized in the recent development of the navy. Nations, as a rule, do not move with the foresight and the fixed plan which distinguish a very few individuals of the human race. They do not practise on the pistol-range before sending a challenge; if they did, wars would be fewer, as is proved by the present long-continued armed peace in Europe. Gradually and imperceptibly the popular feeling, which underlies most lasting national movements, is aroused and swayed by incidents, often trivial, but of the same general type, whose recurrence gradually moulds public opinion and evokes national action, until at last there issues that settled public conviction which alone, in a free state, deserves the name of national policy. What the origin of those particular events whose interaction establishes a strong political current in a particular direction, it is perhaps unprofitable to inquire. Some will see in the chain of cause and effect only a chapter of accidents, presenting an interesting philosophical study, and nothing more; others, equally persuaded that nations do not effectively shape their mission in the world, will find in them the ordering of a Divine ruler, who does not permit the individual or the nation to escape its due share of the world's burdens. But, however explained, it is a common experience of history that in the gradual ripening of events there comes often suddenly and unexpectedly the emergency, the call for action, to maintain the nation's contention. That there is an increased disposition on the part of civilized countries to deal with such cases by ordinary diplomatic discussion and mutual concession can be gratefully acknowledged; but that such dispositions are not always sufficient to reach a peaceable solution is equally an indisputable teaching of the recent past. Popular emotion, once fairly roused, sweeps away the barriers of calm deliberation, and is deaf to the voice of reason. That the consideration of relative power enters for much in the diplomatic settlement of international difficulties is also certain, just as that it goes for much in the ordering of individual careers. "Can," as well as "will," plays a large share in the decisions of life. . . .

That we shall seek to secure the peaceable solution of each difficulty as it arises is attested by our whole history, and by the disposition of our people; but to do so, whatever the steps taken in any particular case, will bring us into new political relations and may entail serious disputes with other states. In maintaining the justest policy, the most reasonable influence, one of the political elements, long dominant, and still one of the most essential, is military strength—in the broad sense of the word "military," which includes naval as well—not merely potential, which our own is, but organized and developed, which our own as yet is not. We wisely quote Washington's warning against entangling alliances, but too readily forget his teaching about preparation for war. The progress of the world from age to age, in its ever-changing manifestations, is a great political drama, possessing a unity, doubtless, in its general development, but in which, as act follows act, one situation alone can engage, at one time, the attention of the actors. Of this drama war is simply a violent and tumultuous political incident. A navy, therefore, whose primary sphere of action is war, is, in the last analysis and from the least misleading point of view, a political factor of the utmost importance in international affairs, one more often deterrent than irritant. It is in that light, according to the conditions of the age and of the nation, that it asks and deserves the appreciation of the state, and that it should be developed in proportion to the reasonable possibilities of the political future.

II. Distant Possession—The Parting of the Ways

ANDREW CARNEGIE

The anti-imperialist forces contained men and women from a great variety of backgrounds. There were authors, politicians, reformers, and philosophers, but one of the most widely read and respected of the anti-imperialists was the millionaire steel mill owner Andrew Carnegie. Carnegie's life was a rags-to-riches story that was used as an example of what hard work, prudence, and organization could accomplish in the American environment. The general belief in the business community at the end of the Spanish-American War was that new territories and colonies would benefit America, but Carnegie warned against overseas expansion.

How does Carnegie's article on expansion supplement the arguments found in Schurz's speech, and how does it answer the contention of the imperialists that expansion would benefit the economy of the United States?

AUGUST 1898

In considering the issue now before us, the agitator, the demagogue, has no part. Not feeling, not passion, but deliberate judgment alone should have place. The question should be calmly weighed; it is not a matter of party, nor of class; for the fundamental interest of every citizen is a common interest, that which is best for the poorest being best for the richest. Let us, therefore, reason together and be well assured, before we change our position, that we are making no plunge into an abyss. . . .

To reduce it to the concrete, the question is: Shall we attempt to establish ourselves as a power in the Far East and possess the Philippines for glory? The glory we already have, in Dewey's victory overcoming the power of Spain in a manner which adds one more to the many laurels of the American navy, which, from its infancy till now, has divided the laurels with Britain upon the sea. The Philippines have about seven and a half millions of people, composed of races bitterly hostile to one another, alien races, ignorant of our language

North American Review, August 1898, pp. 240–48.

and institutions. Americans cannot be grown there. The islands have been exploited for the benefit of Spain, against whom they have twice rebelled, like the Cubans; but even Spain has received little pecuniary benefit from them. The estimated revenue of the Philippines in 1894–95 was £2,715,980, the expenditure being £2,656,026, leaving a net result of about $300,000. The United States could obtain even this trifling sum from the inhabitants only by oppressing them as Spain has done. But, if we take the Philippines, we shall be forced to govern them as generously as Britain governs her dependencies, which means that they will yield us nothing, and probably be a source of annual expense. Certainly, they will be a grievous drain upon revenue if we consider the enormous army and navy which we shall be forced to maintain upon their account. . . .

It has hitherto been the glorious mission of the Republic to establish upon secure foundations Trimphant Democracy, and the world now understands government of the people for the people and by the people. Tires the Republic so soon of its mission that it must, perforce, discard it to undertake the impossible task of establishing Triumphant Despotism, the rule of the foreigner over the people, and must the millions of the Philippines who have been asserting their God-given right to govern themselves, be the first victims of Americans, whose proudest boast is that they conquered independence for themselves? . . .

It is the parting of the ways. We have a continent to populate and develop; there are only 23 persons to the square mile in the United States. England has 370, Belgium 571, Germany 250. A tithe of the cost of maintaining our sway over the Philippines would improve our internal waterways; deepen our harbors; build the Nicaraguan Canal; construct a waterway to the ocean from the Great Lakes; an inland canal along the Atlantic seaboard; a canal across Florida, saving 800 miles distance between New York and New Orleans; connect Lake Michigan with the Mississippi; deepen all the harbors upon the lakes; build a canal from Lake Erie to the Allegheny River; slackwater through movable dams the entire length of the Ohio River to Cairo; thoroughly improve the Lower and Upper Mississippi, and all our seaboard harbors. All these enterprises would be as nothing in cost in comparison to the sums required for the experiment of possessing the Philippine Islands, 7,000 miles from our shores. If the object be to render our Republic powerful among nations, can there be any doubt as to which policy is the better? To be more powerful at home is the surest way to be more powerful abroad. To-day the Republic stands the friend of all nations, the ally of none; she has no ambitious designs upon the territory of any power upon another continent; she crosses none of their ambitious designs, evokes no jealousy of the bitter sort, inspires no fears; she is not one of them, scrambling for "possessions;" she stands apart, pursuing her own great mission, and teaching all nations by example. Let her become a power annexing foreign territory, and all is changed in a moment. . . .

Whether the United States maintain its present unique position of safety or forfeit it through acquiring foreign possessions, is to be decided by its action in regard to the Philippines; for, fortunately, the independence of Cuba is assured, for this the Republic has proclaimed to the world that she has drawn the sword. But why should the less than two millions of Cuba receive national existence and the seven and a half millions of the Philippines be denied it? The United States, thus far in their history, have no page reciting self-sacrifice made for others; all their gains have been for themselves. This void is now to be grandly filled. The page which recites the resolve of the Republic to rid her neighbor Cuba from the foreign "possessor" will grow brighter with the passing centuries, which may dim many pages now deemed illustrious. Should the coming American be able to point to Cuba and the Philippines rescued from foreign domination and enjoying independence won for them by his country and given to them without money and without price, he will find no citizen of any other land able to claim for his country services so disinterested and so noble. . . .

From every point of view we are forced to the conclusion that the past policy of the Republic is her true policy for the future; for safety, for peace, for happiness, for progress, for wealth, for power—for all that makes a nation blessed.

III. The Republic That Never Retreats

ALBERT J. BEVERIDGE

Albert J. Beveridge served as United States Senator from Indiana from 1899 to 1911. During his two terms in the Senate he gained fame for his jingoistic "America first" attitude and his role in progressive legislation. Beveridge supported the expansion of America overseas and his gifts of oratory made him a popular speaker in imperialist circles. His role in publicizing and connecting expansion with patriotism played an influential role in the public acceptance of the peace treaty with Spain and the acquisition of the Philippines.

In what ways can one reconcile the patriotism of Senator Beveridge with that of Carl Schurz?

FEBRUARY 15, 1899

Mr. President and Gentlemen:—The Republic never retreats. Why should it retreat? The Republic is the highest form of civilization, and civilization must advance. The Republic's young men are the most virile and unwasted in the world, and they pant for enterprise worthy of their power. The Republic's

Ashley H. Thorndike, ed., *Modern Eloquence* (New York: Modern Eloquence Corporation, 1923), I, pp. 116–18.

preparation has been the self-discipline of a century, and that preparedness has found its task. The Republic's opportunity is as noble as its strength, and that opportunity is here. The Republic's duty is as sacred as its opportunity is real, and Americans never desert their duty.

The Republic could not retreat if it would. Whatever its destiny it must proceed. For the American Republic is a part of the movement of a race—the most masterful race of history—and race movements are not to be stayed by the hand of man. They are mighty answers to divine commands. . . .

The dominant notes in American history have thus far been self-government and internal improvements. But these were not ends; they were means. They were modes of preparation. The dominant notes in American life henceforth will be, not only self-government and internal development, but also administration and world improvement. . . .

The Philippines are ours forever. Let faint hearts anoint their fears with the thought that some day American administration and American duty there may end. But they never will end. England's occupation of Egypt was to be temporary; but events, which are the commands of God, are making it permanent. And now God has given us this Pacific empire for civilized administration. The first office of the administration is order. Order must be established throughout the archipelago.

Rebellion against the authority of the flag must be crushed without delay, for hesitation encourages revolt, and without anger, for the turbulent children know not what they do. And then civilization must be organized, administered and maintained. Law and justice must rule where savages, tyranny and caprice have rioted. The people must be taught the art of orderly and continuous industry.

The frail of faith declare that those peoples are not fitted for citizenship. It is not proposed to make them citizens. Those who see disaster in every forward step of the republic prophesy that cheap labor from the Philippines will overrun our country and starve our workingmen. But the Javanese have not so overrun Holland. New Zealand's Malays, Australia's bushmen, Africa's Kaffirs, Zulus and Hottentots, and India's millions of surplus labor have not so overrun England.

Those who measure duty by dollars cry out at the expense. When did America ever count the cost of righteousness? And, besides, this Republic must have a mighty navy in any event. And new markets secured, new enterprises opened, new resources in timber, mines and products of the tropics acquired, and the vitalization of all our industries which will follow, will pay back a thousandfold all the government spends in discharging the highest duty to which the Republic may be called.

The blood already shed is but a drop to that which would flow if America should desert its post in the Pacific. And the blood already spilled was poured out upon the altar of the world's regeneration. Manila is as noble as Omdurman, and both are holier than Jericho. Retreat from the Philippines on any pretext would be the master cowardice of history. It would be the betrayal of a trust as sacred as humanity. It would be a crime against Christian civilization, and would mark the beginning of the decadence of our race. And so, thank God, the Republic never retreats.

Imperialism is not the word for our vast work. Imperialism, as used by the opposers of national greatness, means oppression, and we oppress not. Imperialism, as used by the opposers of national destiny, means monarchy, and the days of monarchy are spent. Imperialism, as used by the opposers of national progress, is a word to frighten the faint of heart, and so is powerless with the fearless American people.

The Republic never retreats. Its flag is the only flag that has never known defeat. Where that flag leads we follow, for we know that the hand that bears it onward is the unseen hand of God. We follow the flag and independence is ours. We follow the flag and nationality is ours. We follow the flag and oceans are ruled. We follow the flag, and in Occident and Orient tyranny falls and barbarism is subdued.

We followed the flag at Trenton and Valley Forge, at Saratoga and upon the crimson seas, at Buena Vista and Chapultepec, at Gettysburg and Mission ridge, at Santiago and Manila, and everywhere and always it means larger liberty, noble opportunity, and greater human happiness; for everywhere and always it means the blessings of the greater Republic. And so God leads, we follow the flag, and the Republic never retreats.

IV. Senator Ben Tillman Explains the White Man's Burden

BENJAMIN TILLMAN

In the fight on the Senate floor to ratify or reject the peace treaty with Spain, one of the most outspoken opponents of the treaty was Senator Benjamin Tillman of South Carolina. A prominent figure of the time, he championed, in the extreme, the states' rights philosophy of the South. In foreign affairs he supported naval expansion and the declaration of war with Spain, but he bitterly fought the annexation of Hawaii and the Philippines. Although Senator Tillman may represent the more controversial side of the anti-imperialist forces, his arguments against expansion were not without support by many Americans.

How does Tillman's emotionalism compare with that found in the speech by Schurz? What, if any, are the similarities in their arguments?

Congressional Record, February 7, 1899, pp. 1531–32.

FEBRUARY 7, 1899

I wish now to present for the consideration of Senators, and especially of those Senators who stand committed here to a proposition that they are opposed to expansion and are opposed to annexation, but desire to ratify the treaty in order to close the condition of war with Spain and then address themselves to what shall be done in the Philippine Islands afterwards—I say I wish to address to those Senators some remarks in regard to what appears to me our plain and bounden duty at this time, our duty not only to them, but more especially to ourselves. . . .

As though coming at the most opportune time possible, you might say, just before the treaty reached the Senate, or about the time it was sent to us, there appeared in one of our magazines a poem by Rudyard Kipling, the greatest poet of England at this time. Mr. President, this poem, unique, and in some places difficult to understand, is to my mind a prophecy. I do not imagine that in the history of human events any poet has ever felt inspired so clearly to portray our danger and our duty. It is called "The White Man's Burden." With the permission of Senators I will read a stanza, and I beg them to listen to it, for it is well worth their attention. This man has lived in the Indies. In fact he is a citizen of the world, and has been all over it, and knows whereof he speaks.

> *Take up the White Man's burden—*
> *Send forth the best ye breed—*
> *Go, bind your sons to exile,*
> *To serve your captive's need;*
> *To wait, in heavy harness,*
> *On fluttered folk and wild—*
> *Your new-caught sullen peoples,*
> *Half devil and half child.*

Mr. President. I will pause here. I intend to read more, but I wish to call attention to a fact which may have escaped the attention of Senators thus far, that with five exceptions every man in this Chamber who has had to do with the colored race in this country voted against the ratification of the treaty. It was not because we are Democrats, but because we understand and realize what it is to have two races side by side that can not mix or mingle without deterioration and injury to both and the ultimate destruction of the civilization of the higher. We of the South have borne this white man's burden of a colored race in our midst since their emancipation and before.

It was a burden upon our manhood and our ideas of liberty before they were emancipated. It is still a burden, although they have been granted the franchise. . . . Why do we as a people want to incorporate into our citizenship ten millions more of different or of differing races, three or four of them?

But, Mr. President, we have not incorporated them yet, and let us see what this English poet has to say about it, and what he thinks.

> *Take up the White Man's burden—*
> *No iron rule of kinds,*
> *But toil of serf and sweeper—*
> *The tale of common things.*
> *The ports ye shall not enter,*
> *The roads ye shall not tread,*
> *Go, make them with your living*
> *And mark them with your dead.*

Ah, if we have no other consideration, if no feeling of humanity, no love of our fellows, no regard for others' rights, if nothing but our self-interest shall actuate us in this crisis, let me say to you that if we go madly on in the direction of crushing the Philippines into subjection and submission we will do so at the cost of many, many thousands of the flower of American youth. There are 10,000,000 of these people some of them fairly well civilized, and running to the other extreme of naked savages, who are reported in our press dispatches as having stood out in the open and fired their bows and arrows, not flinching from the storm of shot and shell thrown into their midst by the American soldiers last Sunday.

The report of the battle claims that we lost only 75 killed and a hundred and odd wounded; but the first skirmish has carried with it what anguish, what desolation, to homes in a dozen States! How many more victims are we to offer up on this altar of Mammon or national greed? When those regiments march back, if they return with decimated ranks, as they are bound to come, if we have to send thousands and tens of thousands of reenforcements there to press onward until we have subdued those ten millions, at whose door will lie these lives—their blood shed for what? An idea. If a man fires upon the American flag, shoot the last man and kill him, no matter how many Americans have to be shot to do it.

The city of Manila is surrounded by swamps and marshes, I am told. A few miles back lie the woods and jungles and mountains. These people are used to the climate. They know how to get about, and if they mean to have their liberties, as they appear to do, at what sacrifice will the American domination be placed over them? Here is another verse of Kipling. I have fallen in love with this man. He tells us what we will reap:

> *Take up the White Man's burden,*
> *And reap his old reward—*
> *The blame of those ye better,*
> *The hate of those ye guard—*
> *The cry of hosts ye humor*
> *(Ah, slowly!) toward the light—*

> *"Why brought ye us from bondage,*
> *Our loved Egyptian night?"*

Those peoples are not suited to our institutions. They are not ready for liberty as we understand it. They do not want it. Why are we bent on forcing upon them a civilization not suited to them and which only means in their view degradation and a loss of self-respect, which is worse than the loss of life itself? . . .

Mr. President, I yield to no man in loyalty to the sentiment, "my country, may it ever be right, but right or wrong, my country." But, oh, my God! when I think how dishonorable the prosecution of the war promises to be to us as a people, how little justification for it we have, even to ourselves, I would that you, my brother Senators on this floor, would pass a resolution which could bring about immediately a cessation of hostilities and a condition which might give the Philippine people the same right to bless us as Cuba will possess, and command for us the admiration and respect of the civilized and pagan world!

V. Mr. Dooley Speaks Out on Expansion

FINLEY PETER DUNNE

In 1893 Finley Peter Dunne began a newspaper column in the Chicago Evening Post *under the by-line of "Mr. Dooley." Dunne's Mr. Dooley was an old-fashioned Irishman who had settled in Chicago before it had become a great metropolis, and as the city grew Mr. Dooley commented on its politics, society, and values. The column gained a nationwide audience during the Spanish-American War as Mr. Dooley extended his comments to the principal personalities in the war, the battles, the corrupt practices of the war contractors, and the newly acquired colonies.*

How do Mr. Dooley's arguments on the acquisition of the Philippines differ from those of Carl Schurz? Just which side was Mr. Dooley on?

"Whin we plant what Hogan calls th' starry banner iv Freedom in th' Ph'lippeens," said Mr. Dooley, "an' give th' sacred blessin' iv liberty to the poor, down-trodden people iv thim unfortunate isles—damn thim!—we'll larn thim a lesson."

"Sure," said Mr. Hennessy, sadly, "we have a thing or two to larn our-silves."

"But it isn't f'r thim to larn us," said Mr. Dooley. "'Tis not f'r thim

"Expansion" is reprinted by permission of Charles Scribner's Sons from *Mr. Dooley at His Best* by Finley Peter Dunne, edited by Elmer Ellis. Copyright 1938 Charles Scribner's Sons; renewal copyright © 1966.

wretched an' degraded crathers, without a mind or a shirt iv their own, f'r to give lessons in politeness an' liberty to a nation that mannyfacthers more dhressed beef than anny other imperyal nation in th' wurruld. We say to thim: 'Naygurs,' we say, 'poor, dissolute, uncovered wretches,' says we, 'whin th' crool hand iv Spain forged man'cles f'r ye'er limbs, as Hogan says, who was it crossed th' say an' shtruck off th' comealongs? We did—by dad, we did. An' now, ye mis'rable, childish-minded apes, we propose f'r to larn ye th' uses iv liberty. In ivry city in this unfair land we will erect schoolhouses an' packin' houses an' houses iv correction; an' we'll larn ye our language, because 'tis aisier to larn ye ours than to larn oursilves yours. An' we'll give ye clothes, if ye pay f'r thim; an', if ye don't ye can go without. An', whin ye're hungry, ye can go to th' morgue—we mane th' resth'rant—an' ate a good square meal iv ar-rmy beef. . . .

"But, glory be, 'tis more like a rasslin' match than a father's embrace. Up gets this little monkey iv an Aggynaldoo, an' says he, 'Not for us,' he says. 'We thank ye kindly; but we believe,' he says, 'in pathronizin' home industhries,' he says. 'An',' he says, 'I have on hand,' he says, 'an' f'r sale,' he says, 'a very superyor brand iv home-made liberty, like ye'er mother used to make,' he says. ''Tis a long way fr'm ye'er plant to here,' he says, 'an' be th' time a cargo iv liberty,' he says, 'got out here an' was handled be th' middlemen,' he says, 'it might spoil,' he says. 'We don't want anny col' storage or embalmed liberty,' he says. 'What we want an' what th' ol' reliable house iv Aggynaldoo,' he says, 'supplies to th' thrade,' he says, 'is fr-resh liberty r-right off th' far-rm,' he says. 'I can't do annything with ye'er proposition,' he says. 'I can't give up,' he says, 'th' rights f'r which f'r five years I've fought an' bled ivry wan I cud reach,' he says. 'Onless,' he says, 'ye'd feel like buyin' out th' whole business,' he says. 'I'm a pathrite,' he says; 'but I'm no bigot,' he says.

"An' there it stands, Hinnissy, with th' indulgent parent kneelin' on th' stomach iv his adopted child, while a dillygation fr'm Boston bastes him with an umbrella. There it stands, an' how will it come out I dinnaw. I'm not much iv an expansionist mesilf. F'r th' las' tin years I've been tryin' to decide whether 'twud be good policy an' thrue to me thraditions to make this here bar two or three feet longer, an manny's th' night I've laid awake tryin' to puzzle it out. But I don't know what to do with th' Philippeens anny more thin I did las' summer, befure I heerd tell iv thim. We can't give thim to anny wan without makin' th' wan that gets thim feel th' way Doherty felt to Clancy whin Clancy med a frindly call an' give Doherty's childher th' measles. We can't sell thim, we can't ate thim, an' we can't throw thim into th' alley whin no wan is lookin'. An' 'twud be a disgrace f'r to lave befure we've pounded these frindless an' ongrateful people into insinsibility. So I suppose, Hinnissy, we'll have to stay an' do th' best we can, an' lave Andhrew Carnegie secede fr'm th' Union. They'se wan consolation; an' that is, if th' American people can govern thimsilves, they can govern annything that walks."

"'Twill cost a power iv money," said Mr. Hennessy, the prudent.

"Expand, ixpind," said Mr. Dooley. "That's a joke, an' I med it."

For Further Reading

The process of overseas expansion by the United States during the late nineteenth century has come under close scrutiny by American historians in the twentieth century. The general histories of the period include Foster R. Dulles' *Prelude to World Power: American Diplomatic History, 1860–1900* (1965), Walter La Feber's *The New Empire** (1963), Ernest K. May, *Imperial Democracy* (1961), Frederick Merk's *Manifest Destiny and Mission in American History** (1963), J. W. Pratt's two excellent works, *America's Colonial Experiment* (1950) and *Expansionists of 1898** (1936; 1964), and William A. Williams' controversial *The Tragedy of American Diplomacy** (1962).

Studies of some of the leading personalities of the era are H. K. Beale's *Theodore Roosevelt and the Rise of America to World Power** (1956), Margaret Leech's *In the Days of McKinley* (1959), William E. Livezey's *Mahan on Sea Power* (1947), and H. Wayne Morgan's *William McKinley and His America* (1963).

The Spanish-American War from the Spanish point of view has been covered in Orestes Ferrara's *The Last Spanish War* (1937), while the most notable recent work on the war is Frank Freidel's *The Splendid Little War** (1958). The acquisition of colonies as a consequence of the war and their impact upon America are considered in: G. A. Grunder and William E. Livezey, *The Philippines and the United States* (1951); Sylvester K. Stevens, *American Expansion in Hawaii, 1842–1898* (1945; 1968); and Leon Wolff, *Little Brown Brother* (1961). The development of an ideology of imperialism in America has been well covered in Richard Hofstadter's *Social Darwinism in American Thought** (1959), while the anti-imperial view is found in R. L. Beisner's *Twelve Against Empire: The Anti-Imperialists** (1968), and in E. Berkeley Tompkins' *Anti-imperialism in the United States* (1970). Walter Millis has also concerned himself with the development of imperialism in his *The Martial Spirit* (1931).

A problems book on the era is *American Imperialism in 1898** (1965), edited by Theodore P. Greene, while Henry F. Graff's *American Imperialism and the Philippine Insurrection** (1969) contains the edited comments of the leading American participants before the Senate Committee on the Philippines in 1902.

*Paperbound edition available.

6. *Socialist Sentiment in the Progressive Era*

The years between the Spanish War and World War I were characterized by a variety of reform efforts. These efforts have traditionally been interpreted as progressive attempts to correct social, economic, and political injustices in American society. In the 1950s this interpretation was challenged by historians, who concluded that such reforms as actually developed grew out of the desire of persons in the middle class to regain the status they believed they were losing as both business and labor organizations increased in size and influence. Still more recent analyses assert that whatever changes took place were inspired, not by progressive attitudes, but by the desires of big business to attain stability, predictability, and security in their operations, or of upper-class leaders to protect their special interests.

In all these interpretations "progressives" are regarded as essentially conservative opponents of radical change in the American system. Despite the generally conservative character of the progressive movement, however, there were some advocates of radical change, and at times their sentiments were selectively absorbed by others. Most radicals called themselves socialists. Some were strongly ideological, claiming to be scientific in their analysis of society. Socialists of this type generally considered socialism to be a form of communism described in Marxist-Leninist theory or perhaps a first step toward such communism. Most representative of this type was Daniel De Leon, the head of the Socialist Labor party. His ideological orthodoxy eventually required him to vigorously oppose cooperation with nonsocialist labor groups such as the American Federation of Labor.

Other socialists emphasized political activities in more conventional, less revolutionary terms. Through participation in organized political parties, these socialists hoped to reshape American society along lines that would reduce economic competition and bring about collective ownership of the larger means of production. Eugene V. Debs, who founded the Socialist Party of America in 1901, perhaps best represents this type of socialist. He was his party's presidential candidate in 1904, 1908, 1912, and 1920. In his final campaign, conducted while he was in prison, he polled almost a million votes.

In this chapter no attempt is made to untangle the web of confusion growing out of the political and ideological differences between various types of socialists. Rather, the focus is on the widely shared feeling that socialism in some form would lead in an evolutionary way to the elimination of social injustice. Sharing this feeling, sometimes in only vague terms, were romantic or angry idealists, Christian Social Gospelers, literary radicals, social malcontents, alienated immigrants, sincere reformers, socially conscious millionaires, embittered workers, old-line Populists, and even some semiauthentic Marxists.

In focusing on socialist sentiment, this chapter considers chiefly the impact it had on progressivism and on the failure of the socialist appeal to attract a more enthusiastic response, especially in view of the deplorable conditions prevailing in many areas of American life.

Core Document

The Conversion of Jurgis

UPTON SINCLAIR

If an advocate of socialism was to win converts, he had to describe in convincing terms the worst aspects of American life under the existing system. The writer who did this with the greatest impact during the progressive years was Upton Sinclair. The Jungle, Sinclair's account of working and living conditions in Chicago, particularly in Packingtown, quickly became a best seller and caused a national sensation. It brought a clamor for meat inspection and other food and drug laws. Sinclair was even invited to the White House for a discussion with President Theodore Roosevelt. Despite all this, Sinclair was disappointed: he had aimed, he said, at the public's heart and by accident he hit it in the stomach.

Perhaps the reason for Sinclair's misplaced punch lay in the very effective-

Upton Sinclair, *The Jungle* (New York: The Jungle Publishing Co., 1905), pp. 368–78.

ness with which he told his story. The contemporary reader of The Jungle *was introduced, among other things, to the unsanitary conditions in the packing-houses, the abusive labor practices and ruthless policies of the trusts, and to fraudulent real estate dealings and corrupt politics in Chicago. He saw the Lithuanian immigrant Jurgis, the leading character in the story, lose his health, his job, his pride, and his family. Jurgis' possessions were always meager, but he lost them too. When all hope was gone, Jurgis, looking only for a place to sit down, wandered into a meeting where a socialist speaker delivered an impassioned address. He was stirred to learn more. The core document in this chapter describes what he learned about socialism and where he learned it.*

In the context of the book the speech and its effect on Jurgis were anti-climactic. The reader was emotionally spent by the time Sinclair made his appeal for socialistic solutions. Yet, in the context of Sinclair's life and outlook, it is easy to see why he presented the appeal as he did. Sinclair was active in the affairs of the Socialist Party of America. The speech Jurgis heard, Sinclair wrote later, was one the author himself had delivered at a mass meeting in Chicago in support of Debs' presidential candidacy.

In reading this chapter from The Jungle, *note how Sinclair described:*
- *the emotional effect of the speech on Jurgis.*
- *the conditions the competitive wage system imposed on Jurgis' host.*
- *the characteristics of the competitive wage system.*
- *the purpose, strategy, and character of the Socialist party.*
- *the principles of socialism.*
- *the applicability of the socialist solution to Jurgis' problems.*

The man had gone back to a seat upon the platform, and Jurgis realized that his speech was over. The applause continued for several minutes, and then some one started a song, and the crowd took it up, and the place shook with it. Jurgis had never heard it, and he could not make out the words, but the wild and wonderful spirit of it seized upon him—it was the "Marseillaise!" As stanza after stanza of it thundered forth, he sat with his hands clasped, trembling in every nerve. He had never been so stirred in his life—it was a miracle that had been wrought in him. He could not think at all, he was stunned; yet he knew that in the mighty upheaval that had taken place in his soul, a new man had been born. He had been torn out of the jaws of destruction, he had been delivered from the thraldom of despair; the whole world had been changed for him—he was free, he was free! Even if he were to suffer as he had before, even if he were to beg and starve, nothing would be the same to him; he would understand it, and bear it. He would no longer be the sport of circumstances, he would be a man, with a will and a purpose; he would have something to fight for, something to die for, if need be! Here were men who would show him and help him; and he would have friends and allies, he would dwell in the sight of justice, and walk arm in arm with power.

The audience subsided again, and Jurgis sat back. The chairman of the meeting came forward and began to speak. His voice sounded thin and futile after the other's, and to Jurgis it seemed a profanation. Why should any one else speak, after that miraculous man—why should they not all sit in silence? The chairman was explaining that a collection would now be taken up to defray the expenses of the meeting, and for the benefit of the campaign fund of the party. Jurgis heard; but he had not a penny to give, and so his thoughts went elsewhere again.

He kept his eyes fixed on the orator, who sat in an armchair, his head leaning on his hand and his attitude indicating exhaustion. But suddenly he stood up again, and Jurgis heard the chairman of the meeting saying that the speaker would now answer any questions which the audience might care to put to him. The man came forward, and some one—a woman—arose and asked about some opinion the speaker had expressed concerning Tolstoy. Jurgis had never heard of Tolstoy, and did not care anything about him. Why should any one want to ask such questions, after an address like that? The thing was not to talk, but to do; the thing was to get hold of others and rouse them, to organize them and prepare for the fight!

But still the discussion went on, in ordinary conversational tones, and it brought Jurgis back to the everyday world. A few minutes ago he had felt like seizing the hand of the beautiful lady by his side, and kissing it; he had felt like flinging his arms about the neck of the man on the other side of him. And now he began to realize again that he was a "hobo," that he was ragged and dirty, and smelt bad, and had no place to sleep that night!

And so, at last, when the meeting broke up, and the audience started to leave, poor Jurgis was in an agony of uncertainty. He had not thought of leaving—he had thought that the vision must last forever, that he had found comrades and brothers. But now he would go out, and the thing would fade away, and he would never be able to find it again! He sat in his seat, frightened and wondering; but others in the same row wanted to get out, and so he had to stand up and move along. As he was swept down the aisle he looked from one person to another, wistfully; they were all excitedly discussing the address —but there was nobody who offered to discuss it with him. He was near enough to the door to feel the night air, when desperation seized him. He knew nothing at all about that speech he had heard, not even the name of the orator; and he was to go away—no, no, it was preposterous, he must speak to some one; he must find that man himself and tell him. He would not despise him, tramp as he was!

So he stepped into an empty row of seats and watched, and when the crowd had thinned out, he started toward the platform. The speaker was gone; but there was a stage door that stood open, with people passing in and out, and no one on guard. Jurgis summoned up his courage and went in, and down a hallway, and to the door of a room where many people were crowded. No one paid any attention to him, and he pushed in, and in a corner he saw the man he sought. The orator sat in a chair, with his shoulders sunk together and his eyes half closed; his face was ghastly pale, almost greenish in hue, and one arm lay limp at his side. A big man with spectacles on stood near him, and kept pushing back the crowd, saying, "Stand away a little, please; can't you see the comrade is worn out?"

So Jurgis stood watching, while five or ten minutes passed. Now and then the man would look up, and address a word or two to those who were near him; and, at last, on one of these occasions, his glance rested on Jurgis. There seemed to be a slight hint of inquiry about it, and a sudden impulse seized the other. He stepped forward.

"I wanted to thank you, sir!" he began, in breathless haste. "I could not go away without telling you how much—how glad I am I heard you. I—I didn't know anything about it all—"

The big man with the spectacles, who had moved away, came back at this moment. "The comrade is too tired to talk to any one—" he began; but the other held up his hand.

"Wait," he said. "He has something to say to me." And then he looked into Jurgis' face. "You want to know more about Socialism?" he asked.

Jurgis started. "I—I—" he stammered. "Is it Socialism? I didn't know. I want to know about what you spoke of—I want to help. I have been through all that."

"Where do you live?" asked the other.

"I have no home," said Jurgis, "I am out of work."

"You are a foreigner, are you not?"

"Lithuanian, sir."

The man thought for a moment, and then turned to his friend. "Who is there, Walters?" he asked. "There is Ostrinski—but he is a Pole—"

"Ostrinski speaks Lithuanian," said the other.

"All right, then; would you mind seeing if he has gone yet?"

The other started away, and the speaker looked at Jurgis again. He had deep, black eyes, and a face full of gentleness and pain. "You must excuse me, comrade," he said. "I am just tired out—I have spoken every day for the last month. I will introduce you to some one who will be able to help you as well as I could—"

The messenger had had to go no further than the door; he came back, followed by a man whom he introduced to Jurgis as "Comrade Ostrinski." Comrade Ostrinski was a little man, scarcely up to Jurgis' shoulder, wizened and wrinkled, very ugly, and slightly lame. He had on a long-tailed black coat, worn green at the seams and the buttonholes; his eyes must have been weak, for he wore green spectacles that gave him a grotesque appearance. But his hand-clasp was hearty, and he spoke in Lithuanian, which warmed Jurgis to him.

"You want to know about Socialism?" he said. "Surely. Let us go out and take a stroll, where we can be quiet and talk some."

And so Jurgis bade farewell to the master wizard, and went out. Ostrinski asked where he lived, offering to walk in that direction; and so he had to explain once more that he was without a home. At the other's request he told his story; how he had come to America, and what had happened to him in the stockyards, and how his family had been broken up, and how he had become a wanderer. So much the little man heard, and then he pressed Jurgis' arm tightly. "You have been through the mill, comrade!" he said. "We will make a fighter out of you!"

Then Ostrinski in turn explained his circumstances. He would have asked Jurgis to his home—but he had only two rooms, and had no bed to offer. He would have given up his own bed, but his wife was ill. Later on, when he understood that otherwise Jurgis would have to sleep in a hallway, he offered him his kitchen floor, a chance which the other was only too glad to accept. "Perhaps tomorrow we can do better," said Ostrinski. "We try not to let a comrade starve."

Ostrinski's home was in the Ghetto district, where he had two rooms in the basement of a tenement. There was a baby crying as they entered, and he closed the door leading into the bedroom. He had three young children, he explained, and a baby had just come. He drew up two chairs near the kitchen stove, adding that Jurgis must excuse the disorder of the place, since at such a time one's domestic arrangements were upset. Half of the kitchen was given up to a workbench, which was piled with clothing, and Ostrinski explained that he was a "pants finisher." He brought great bundles of clothing here to his home, where he and his wife worked on them. He made a living at it, but it was getting harder all the time, because his eyes were failing. What would come when they gave out he could not tell; there had been no saving anything —a man could barely keep alive by twelve or fourteen hours' work a day. The finishing of pants did not take much skill, and anybody could learn it, and so the pay was forever getting less. That was the competitive wage system; and if Jurgis wanted to understand what Socialism was, it was there he had best begin. The workers were dependent upon a job to exist from day to day, and so they bid against each other, and no man could get more than the lowest man would consent to work for. And thus the mass of the people were always in a life-and-death struggle with poverty. That was "competition," so far as it concerned the wage-earner, the man who had only his labor to sell; to those on top, the exploiters, it appeared very differently, of course—there were few of them, and they could combine and dominate, and their power would be unbreakable. And so all over the world two classes were forming, with an unbridged chasm between them,—the capitalist class, with its enormous fortunes, and the proletariat, bound into slavery by unseen chains. The latter were a thousand to one in numbers, but they were ignorant and helpless, and they would remain at the mercy of their exploiters until they were organized—until they had become "class conscious." It was a slow and weary process, but it would go on—it was like the movement of a glacier, once it was started it could never be stopped. Every Socialist did his share, and lived upon the vision of the "good time coming,"—when the working class should go to the polls and seize the powers of government, and put an end to private property in the means of production. No matter how poor a man was, or how much he suffered, he could never be really unhappy while he knew of that future; even if he did not live to see it himself, his children would, and, to a Socialist, the victory of his class was his victory. Also he had always the progress to encourage him; here in Chicago, for instance, the movement was growing by leaps and bounds. Chicago was the industrial center of the country, and nowhere else were the unions so strong; but their organizations did the workers little good, for the employers were organized, also; and so the strikes generally failed, and as fast as the unions were broken up the men were coming over to the Socialists.

Ostrinski explained the organization of the party, the machinery by which the proletariat was educating itself. There were "locals" in every big city and town, and they were being organized rapidly in the smaller places; a local had anywhere from six to a thousand members, and there were fourteen hundred of them in all, with a total of about twenty-five thousand members, who paid dues to support the organization. "Local Cook County," as the city organization was called, had eighty branch locals, and it alone was spending several thousand dollars in the campaign. It published a weekly in English, and one each in Bohemian and German; also there was a monthly published in Chicago, and a co-operative publishing house, that issued a million and a half of Socialist books and pamphlets every year. All this was the growth of the last few years—there had been almost nothing of it when Ostrinski first came to Chicago.

Ostrinski was a Pole, about fifty years of age. He had lived in Silesia, a member of a despised and persecuted race, and had taken part in the proletarian movement in the early seventies, when Bismarck, having conquered France, had turned his policy of blood and iron upon the "International." Ostrinski himself had twice been in jail, but he had been young then, and had not cared. He had had more of his share of the fight, though, for just when Socialism had broken all its barriers and become the great political force of the empire, he had come to America, and begun all over again. In America every one had laughed at the mere idea of Socialism then—in America all men were free. As if political liberty made wage slavery any the more tolerable! said Ostrinski.

The little tailor sat tilted back in his stiff kitchen chair, with his feet stretched out upon the empty stove, and speaking in low whispers, so as not to waken those in the next room. To Jurgis he seemed a scarcely less wonderful person than the speaker at the meeting; he was poor, the lowest of the low, hunger-driven and miserable—and yet how much he knew, how much he had dared and achieved, what a hero he had been! There were others like him, too —thousands like him, and all of them workingmen! That all this wonderful machinery of progress had been created by his fellows—Jurgis could not believe it, it seemed too good to be true.

That was always the way, said Ostrinski; when a man was first converted to Socialism he was like a crazy person—he could not understand how others could fail to see it, and he expected to convert all the world the first week. After a while he would realize how hard a task it was; and then it would be fortunate that other new hands kept coming, to save him from settling down into a rut. Just now Jurgis would have plenty of chance to vent his excitement, for a presidential campaign was on, and everybody was talking politics. Ostrinski would take him to the next meeting of the branch local, and introduce him, and he might join the party. The dues were five cents a week, but any one who could not afford this might be excused from paying. The Socialist party was a really democratic political organization—it was controlled absolutely by its own membership, and had no bosses. All of these things Ostrinski explained, as also the principles of the party. You might say that there was really but one Socialist principle—that of "no compromise," which was the essence of the proletarian movement all over the world. When a Socialist was elected to office he voted with old party legislators for any measure that was likely to be of help to the working class, but he never forgot that these concessions, whatever they might be, were trifles compared with the great purpose—the organizing of the working class for the revolution. So far, the rule in America had been that one Socialist made another Socialist once every two years; and if they should maintain the same rate they would carry the country in 1912—though not all of them expected to succeed as quickly as that.

The Socialists were organized in every civilized nation; it was an international political party, said Ostrinski, the greatest the world had ever known. It numbered thirty millions of adherents, and it cast eight million votes. It had started its first newspaper in Japan, and elected its first deputy in Argentina; in France it named members of cabinets, and in Italy and Australia it held the balance of power and turned out ministries. In Germany, where its vote was more than a third of the total vote of the empire, all other parties and powers had united to fight it. It would not do, Ostrinski explained, for the proletariat of one nation to achieve the victory, for that nation would be crushed by the military power of the others; and so the Socialist movement was a world movement, an organization of all mankind to establish liberty and fraternity. It was the new religion of humanity—or you might say it was the fulfillment of the old religion, since it implied but the literal application of all the teachings of Christ.

Until long after midnight Jurgis sat lost in the conversation of his new acquaintance. It was a most wonderful experience to him—an almost supernatural experience. It was like encountering an inhabitant of the fourth dimension of space, a being who was free from all one's own limitations. For four years, now, Jurgis had been wandering and blundering in the depths of a wilderness; and here, suddenly, a hand reached down and seized him, and lifted him out of it, and set him upon a mountaintop, from which he could survey it all,—could see the paths from which he had wandered, the morasses into which he had stumbled, the hiding places of the beasts of prey that had fallen upon him. There were his Packingtown experiences, for instance—what was there about Packingtown that Ostrinski could not explain! To Jurgis the packers had been equivalent to fate; Ostrinski showed him that they were the Beef Trust. They were a gigantic combination of capital, which had crushed all opposition, and overthrown the laws of the land, and was preying upon the people. Jurgis recollected how, when he had first come to Packingtown, he had stood and watched the hog-killing, and thought how cruel and savage it was, and come away congratulating himself that he was not a hog; now his new acquaintance showed him that hog was just what he had been—one of the packers' hogs. What they wanted from a hog was all the profits that could be got out of him; and that was what they wanted from the workingman, and also that was what they wanted from the public. What the hog thought of it, and what he suffered, were not considered; and no more was it with labor, and no more with the purchaser of meat. That was true everywhere in the world, but it was especially true in Packingtown; there seemed to be something about the work of slaughtering that tended to ruthlessness and ferocity—it was literally the fact that in the methods of the packers a hundred human lives did not balance a penny of profit. When Jurgis had made himself familiar with the Socialist literature, as he would very quickly, he would get glimpses of the Beef Trust from all sorts of aspects, and he would find it everywhere the same; it was the incarnation of blind and insensate Greed. It was a monster devouring with a thousand mouths, trampling with a thousand hoofs; it was the Great Butcher—it was the spirit of Capitalism made flesh. Upon the ocean of commerce it sailed as a pirate ship; it had hoisted the black flag and declared war upon civilization. Bribery and corruption were its every-day methods. In Chicago the city government was simply one of its branch offices; it stole billions of gallons of city water openly, it dictated to the courts the sentences of disorderly strikers, it forbade the mayor to enforce the building laws against it. In the national capital it had power to prevent inspection of its product, and to falsify government reports; it violated the rebate laws, and when an investigation was threatened it burned its books and sent its criminal agents out of the country. In the commercial world it was a Juggernaut car; it wiped out thousands of businesses every year, it drove men to madness and suicide. It had forced the price of cattle so low as to destroy the stock-raising industry, an occupation upon which whole states existed; it had ruined thousands of butchers who had refused to handle its products. It divided the country into districts, and fixed the price of meat in all of them; and it owned all the refrigerator cars, and levied an enormous tribute upon all poultry and eggs and fruit and vegetables. With the millions of dollars a week that poured in upon it, it was reaching out for the control of other interests, railroads and trolley lines, gas and electric light franchises—it already owned the leather and the grain business of the country. The people were tremendously stirred up over its encroachments, but nobody had any remedy to suggest; it was the task of Socialists to teach and organize them, and prepare them for the time when they were to seize the huge machine called the Beef Trust, and use it to produce food for human beings and not to heap up fortunes for a band of pirates. It was long after midnight when Jurgis lay down upon the floor of Ostrinski's kitchen; and yet it was an hour before he could get to sleep, for the glory of that joyful vision of the people of Packingtown marching in and taking possession of the Union Stockyards!

Discussion Starters

1. Identify aspects of this chapter that relate to concerns of "progressives." Then compare the solutions the progressives offered with those given by Sinclair. How realistic were Sinclair's solutions? How desirable were they?

2. Identify factors in the larger scene in America that would tend to reduce the appeal of Sinclair's solution (e.g., the rags-to-riches notion, the optimism supposedly created by the frontier, the fear of an "alien" ideology, the willingness of labor unions to accept their niche in the capitalist system, and so on). Ultimately, which was of greater importance in defeating Sinclair's proposals: these factors or the power held by the established interests? What evidence supports your conclusion?

3. How valid is the assertion that the influence of socialist sentiment, despite its failure to gain widespread support, was significant in its impact on American society? Which reforms of the progressive years might be attributable to socialist pressures?

4. Evaluate the claim made by some in the United States today that we in fact are living under socialism and that therefore Sinclair's ideas have become part of the existing order.

Related Documents

I. How I Became a Socialist

JACK LONDON

In 1905, before the publication of The Jungle, *Upton Sinclair called together a number of socialists in New York to organize the Intercollegiate Socialist Society.* [1] *The purpose of the new organization was to foster an interest in and*

---

[1] *Editors' note:* The Intercollegiate Socialist Society changed its name after World War I to the League for Industrial Democracy. In the 1960s the Students for a Democratic Society (SDS) had its origin in the youth section of the League for Industrial Democracy, from which it was eventually expelled.

Jack London, *War of the Classes* (New York: Macmillan, 1905) pp. 267–75, 277–789 *understanding of socialism in college and university circles. The first president of the society was Jack London; Sinclair was chosen as a vice president.*

Although London is better known as a writer of fiction, he also merits recognition for his contribution to socialist causes. His participation in party activities was erratic, but his pen was always powerful and he was widely in demand as a speaker. His literary works, many of them infused with socialist sentiment, achieved great popularity abroad, particularly in the Soviet Union, even though he met death at his own hand the year before the Bolshevik Revolution of 1917.

Great numbers of men undoubtedly held comparable attitudes and suffered experiences similar to those described by London in this essay. How can it be explained that more of them were not led to similar conversions? Respond to the suggestion that London was attracted to socialism because socialism is adverse to hard work. Compare the conversion of London with that of Jurgis in Sinclair's novel.

It is quite fair to say that I became a Socialist in a fashion somewhat similar to the way in which the Teutonic pagans became Christians—it was hammered into me. Not only was I not looking for Socialism at the time of my conversion, but I was fighting it. I was very young and callow, did not know much of anything, and though I had never even heard of a school called "Individualism," I sang the paean of the strong with all my heart.

This was because I was strong myself. By strong I mean that I had good health and hard muscles, both of which possessions are easily accounted for. I had lived my childhood on California ranches, my boyhood hustling newspapers on the streets of a healthy Western city, and my youth on the ozone-laden waters of San Francisco Bay and the Pacific Ocean. I loved life in the open, and I toiled in the open, at the hardest kinds of work. Learning no trade, but drifting along from job to job, I looked on the world and called it good, every bit of it. Let me repeat, this optimism was because I was healthy and strong, bothered with neither aches nor weaknesses, never turned down by the boss because I did not look fit, able always to get a job at shovelling coal, sailorizing, or manual labor of some sort.

And because of all this, exulting in my young life, able to hold my own at work or fight, I was a rampant individualist. It was very natural. I was a winner. Wherefore I called the game, as I saw it played, or thought I saw it played, a very proper game for MEN. To be a MAN was to write man in large capitals on my heart. To adventure like a man, and fight like a man, and do a man's work (even for a boy's pay)—these were things that reached right in and gripped hold of me as no other thing could. And I looked ahead into long vistas of a hazy and interminable future, into which, playing what I conceived to be MAN'S game, I should continue to travel with unfailing health, without accidents, and with muscles ever vigorous. As I say, this future was interminable. I could see myself only raging through life without end like one of Nietzsche's *blond beasts,* lustfully roving and conquering by sheer superiority and strength.

As for the unfortunates, the sick, and ailing, and old, and maimed, I must confess I hardly thought of them at all, save that I vaguely felt that they, barring accidents, could be as good as I if they wanted to real hard, and could work just as well. Accidents? Well, they represented FATE, also spelled out in capitals, and there was no getting around FATE. Napoleon had had an accident at Waterloo, but that did not dampen my desire to be another and later Napoleon. Further, the optimism bred of a stomach which could digest scrap iron and a body which flourished on hardships did not permit me to consider accidents as even remotely related to my glorious personality.

I hope I have made it clear that I was proud to be one of Nature's strong-armed noblemen. The dignity of labor was to me the most impressive thing in the world. Without having read Carlyle, or Kipling, I formulated a gospel of work which puts theirs in the shade. Work was everything. It was sanctification and salvation. The pride I took in a hard day's work well done would be inconceivable to you. It is almost inconceivable to me as I look back upon it. I was as faithful a wage slave as ever capitalist exploited. To shirk or malinger on the man who paid me my wages was a sin, first, against myself, and second, against him. I considered it a crime second only to treason and just about as bad.

In short, my joyous individualism was dominated by the orthodox bourgeois ethics. I read the bourgeois papers, listened to the bourgeois preachers, and shouted at the sonorous platitudes of the bourgeois politicians. And I doubt not, if other events had not changed my career, that I should have evolved into a professional strike-breaker, (one of President Eliot's [of Harvard University] American heroes), and had my head and my earning power irrevocably smashed by a club in the hands of some militant trades-unionist.

Just about this time, returning from a seven months' voyage before the mast, and just turned eighteen, I took it into my head to go tramping. On rods and blind baggages I fought my way from the open West, where men bucked big and the job hunted the man, to the congested labor centres of the East, where men were small potatoes and hunted the job for all they were worth. And on this new *blond-beast* adventure I found myself looking upon life from a new and totally different angle. I had dropped down from the proletariat into what sociologists love to call the "submerged tenth," and I was startled to discover the way in which that submerged tenth was recruited.

I found there all sorts of men, many of whom had once been as good as myself and just as *blond-beastly;* sailor-men, soldier-men, labor-men, all wrenched and distorted and twisted out of shape by toil and hardship and accident, and cast adrift by their masters like so many old horses. I battered on the drag and slammed back gates with them, or shivered with them in box cars and city parks, listening the while to life-histories which began under auspices as fair as mine, with digestions and bodies equal to and better than mine, and which ended there before my eyes in the shambles at the bottom of the Social Pit.

And as I listened my brain began to work. The woman of the streets and the man of the gutter drew very close to me. I saw the picture of the Social Pit as vividly as though it were a concrete thing, and at the bottom of the Pit

I saw them, myself above them, not far, and hanging on to the slippery wall by main strength and sweat. And I confess a terror seized me. What when my strength failed? when I should be unable to work shoulder to shoulder with the strong men who were as yet babes unborn? And there and then I swore a great oath. It ran something like this: *All my days I have worked hard with my body, and according to the number of days I have worked, by just that much am I nearer the bottom of the Pit. I shall climb out of the Pit, but not by the muscles of my body shall I climb out. I shall do no more hard work, and may God strike me dead if I do another day's hard work with my body more than I absolutely have to do.* And I have been busy ever since running away from hard work. . . .

To return to my conversion. I think it is apparent that my rampant individualism was pretty effectively hammered out of me, and something else as effectively hammered in. But, just as I had been an individualist without knowing it, I was now a Socialist without knowing it, withal, an unscientific one. I had been reborn, but not renamed, and I was running around to find out what manner of thing I was. I ran back to California and opened the books. I do not remember which ones I opened first. It is an unimportant detail anyway. I was already It, whatever It was, and by aid of the books I discovered that It was a Socialist. Since that day I have opened many books, but no economic argument, no lucid demonstration of the logic and inevitableness of Socialism affects me as profoundly and convincingly as I was affected on the day when I first saw the walls of the Social Pit rise around me and felt myself slipping down, down, into the shambles at the bottom.

II. A Propaganda of Socialism: An Editorial

The Nation

The Nation *responded editorially to the news that Sinclair, London, and others had formed the Intercollegiate Socialist Society. Evaluate the editorial's analysis of socialism and its prognosis concerning the future acceptability of socialism in the United States. Speculate on how Sinclair, through Jurgis, might have answered this editorial.*

OCTOBER 5, 1905

A new society has been formed to propagate the doctrines of collectivism, particularly in American colleges. Its list of members includes some names well known in literature and philanthropy. They are the names of native Americans, not of naturalized citizens, who have gathered about them some two hundred souls zealous for the realization of their ideal. It is not necessary

The Nation, October 5, 1905, pp. 272–73.

to take such persons too seriously. Were their plan to be adopted, they would probably be among the first to chafe under the new conditions of life and government. They belong to that class of reformers of whom Voltaire said: "Ils défendent les ragoûts dont ils ne mangent pas."[1]

It is rather remarkable that educated Americans should be sanguine as to the success of Socialism here. In Europe there is indeed a tendency to regard the United States as the Mecca, if not the home, of the Socialist; but most Americans know better. Socialism is exotic here; and here less than anywhere else should its missionaries be successful. As understood on the Continent of Europe, and as expounded by European writers, it exaggerates the idea of equality, but opposes more or less consciously the idea of liberty. Fortunately, the organization of society and of the state is the effect, not the cause, of national sentiment; and individual liberty is conserved not so much by a particular form of government as by harmony between the popular will and the statute law. In so far as popular sentiment in the United States is native, and in the best sense patriotic, it is hostile to the despotic spirit of the proposed collectivism.

This may explain why the Socialistic orators who before every election are vociferous in East Side halls and on street corners, are so often men (and women, too) who know almost as little about the language as they do about the political institutions of this nation. The Socialism which comes as an emigrant from France, Germany, and Russia, seeking hospitality and asylum, finds a welcome chiefly from those who have confounded the idea of equality with that of liberty. The hope of the Socialist in this country is not to gain proselytes among those who are American by birth and tradition, but among the masses of those who, having come here as immigrants, are not yet rid of their hereditary misconception of freedom. In European, especially in Latin, countries the idea of equality has usually been uppermost in the minds of revolutionists, while the sentiment in favor of liberty has been comparatively feeble. . . .

But the programme of the Socialist is even more threatening than the rise of a plutocracy. If its ideal is to be realized, there must be a dictatorship as absolute as that of an Oriental despot. The intelligent Socialist must care very little for individual liberty, and, considering the economic conditions to which he looks hopefully forward, he must care even less for the arts and sciences. It is difficult to see upon what utilitarian principle such a future should be preferred even to the sad abuses of our present civilization. In the Socialist Utopia, the workmen will have the State as their taskmaster—not the State as an abstraction, but in the person of an overseer who will drive them as if they were slaves or criminals. With the loss of personal initiative, there will come also a loss of comfort and repose. The well-meaning enthusiasts who would

[1] *Editors' note:* Translated freely, this means "They are mixing a brew of which they would not themselves partake."

thus gain equality at the price of liberty, may enjoy the prospect of eating this ragout; but it requires little knowledge of human nature to be convinced that even the most oppressed worker in a factory, or delver at the bottom of a mine, would soon long to regain his previous condition of servitude, if only he might be his own master.

There is an atheistic Socialism, and there is a Socialism grafted upon the teachings of the New Testament in the hope that where logic failed to convince, conscience might lead. This form of collectivism has not made much progress among men of science, but it has become a favorite theory of those who are called "workers"—by which name are designated those who for religious or moral reasons are engaged in philanthropic pursuits. Christian Socialism, which plays some part in the politics of European nations, particularly of Austria, has obtained some vogue in our theological seminaries and university settlements, and has led to a vague idea that the church of the future will be identical with the community. . . .

It is not probable that Socialism of any kind will make many converts among our younger university men, even those who have tasted the joys of collectivism under an athletic director at the training-table. With its contraband literature and its visions of the future, Socialism has been singularly attractive to students in some of the foreign universities; but this may have been as a species of amusement, just as college sporting men of a former generation delighted to transgress the statute which forbade the keeping of "a gun, dog, horse, or any other explosive weapon."

III. Means Toward the End!

VICTOR L. BERGER

Victor L. Berger was one of the few socialists ever to serve in the United States Congress (1911–13, 1923–29). As a representative from Wisconsin, his political strength lay in the Milwaukee area. His early career as a journalist gave him a platform for expressing his socialist ideas; when he moved into party activities he was regarded as a reformist or moderate socialist.

Evaluate Berger's interpretation of history and his plan for conversion to socialism as they are outlined here. How compatible are his ideas with Sinclair's?

The fact is being recognized more and more by scientists that our civilization is in a constant flow, like a river the current of which is ever changing. Yet one of the greatest obstacles with which Socialists have to contend is the notion that whatever is, must be the immutable order of nature. Because the wage system has prevailed as far back as any one can remember, people fancy that this system constitutes the necessary condition for civilized society. Social-

Victor L. Berger, *Broadsides* (Milwaukee: Social-Democratic Pub. Co., 1912), pp. 30–34.

Democrats say this is a fundamental error, and history proves it.

The present state of things grew out of feudalism and serfdom, which followed a system of master and slave.

In the ancient states there was no wage system, there was slavery. The master was the absolute lord of the persons of his slaves, of the soil, and of the instruments of labor, which then were crude and simple.

Serfdom constitutes the next great stage. The lords of the soil were the dominant class, but the workers of the soil were personally free, although attached to the soil where they were born. Now this second stage, although far below our civilization, was at any rate much above chattel slavery.

But the progress of mankind demanded another step, and that was capitalism. This was unknown during the former periods of the world—which had wealth but not capital. This third stage of the development of our race has given occasion for the rise of a class of exploiters unknown to any of the former civilizations. Our plutocracy, our industrial, commercial and moneyed aristocracy are now the masters of all production in all civilized countries on whose good will, or rather, upon whose profits, the laboring people of the world depend for a living.

And all these evils are heightened by cut-throat competition, which not only forces wage-workers into a struggle to see who shall live and who shall starve, but which also compels the employers to pay as little for their labor as possible.

But the laborers are by no means the only sufferers. The small employers and the small merchants are just as much victims of that cruel kind of competition as the wage-workers. This fierce competition lessens the profit on each article, and that must be compensated for by greater numbers of them being produced and sold; that is, the cheaper the goods, the more capital is required.

Precisely then, for the same reason that the mechanic with his own shop and working on his own account has disappeared in the struggle between hand-work and machine-work, for the same reason the small employers with their little machinery, their small capital, and their little stock of goods are being driven from the fields by the trusts.

Our social order or rather social disorder may fitly be compared to a ladder of which the middle rounds are being torn away one by one. And this absorption of the smaller fortunes by the large ones is much hastened by the industrial crises, called "panics," which make their appearance every fifteen or twenty years.

The principle involved in "trusts" is the principle of co-operation instead of competition—but it is the co-operation of capitalists only, not the co-operation of the people. The object of a "trust" is greater regularity of production, steadiness of price and a uniform system of credit. It is the shadow of Socialism and it is used for the benefit of a few capitalists, instead of the nation.

And if this goes on, and according to all natural consequences it must go on, for all the great capital wants to be invested, then in a very short time we shall find most of our industries conducted by "trusts" from the Atlantic to the Pacific.

But these phenomena have also another meaning. They bring before the public mind the question whether we are to have organized capital or organized production? For it is perfectly evident that we must in the future have organized business action of some sort. Shall we have it for the capitalists only, or for the whole people?

In other words the "trusts" prepare the public mind for Socialism.

If our "statesmen" were less blind to the logic of events which are pushing us with railroad speed toward a total and abrupt revolution, they might bring about a state of Socialism gradually and peaceably by a series of measures, each consistently developing itself out of the previous ones. They might begin from two poles of society.

Thus, it is now proposed, even by very conservative people, to take the telegraph system and the railroads and the mines of our country under government control and own them like our postoffice department.

Suppose this measure is realized, as it is sure to be in the near future.

Then do likewise with our express business, our steam and sailing vessels and our mines, and thus onward.

Absorb the Standard Oil Company, the steel trust and every other trust, and one great enterprise after another as quickly as possible.

And so from the other pole.

Why could not cities begin by taking under their control and operating their gas works, and electric light, railway and telephone plants? And why should they not operate their bakeries and drug stores? Let cities furnish to their citizens fuel in winter and ice in summer.

For are these things not just as essential to public health as water?

Then let them also furnish all the milk, flour and meat needed. For the millers of the country have a trust now and a few big packers furnish the meat to the butchers. Yes, and let the city take charge of the liquor traffic, so that Milwaukee would have more reading rooms and fewer drinking places—we have 2,600 saloons at present.

And furthermore, let the city furnish all the school books and at least one meal a day, free of charge, to all the children, not only the poor, and clothes to such as are needy.

I do not say, nor even think, that the social question will be solved in this manner. Our people are neither wise nor peaceable enough to do it. And some of our Socialists are just about as lunatic in that respect as are some capitalists. But it seems to me that would be the most practical way to solve the social question for a practical people.

IV. Individualism: A Wise Alternative to Socialism

CHARLES JOHNSTON

Writing in the North American Review *in 1907, Charles Johnston cited James J. Hill, the railroad magnate, as an indirect critic of socialism. Referring to a speech in which Hill pointed to the need to look ahead and to be wise in the use of natural resources, Johnston emphasized that of four great resources, the sea was of little use, and the forests and the mines were being used up. Only the soil remained, and the prosperity of the future depended on its wise use. In his view, turning to socialism would only aggravate the problem of insuring adequate resources for the future.*

Evaluate Johnston's rejection of the socialist solution to the pressing problems of the day. How could individualism, based on the soil, have reached into the lives of such persons as Jurgis? How might Sinclair have responded to the ideas in this article?

JANUARY 18, 1907

. . . Our salvation lies in a wise use of the soil, our greatest inheritance, and "the mother of humanity." If not another acre were to be redeemed from the wilderness, if the soil were treated kindly and intelligently, if industry were distributed duly, and popular attention were concentrated upon the best possible utilization of our one unfailing national resource, there would be produced all necessary food for more than six hundred million people. Now, as ever, . . . to the nation and the race, as to the individual, Nature, the unrelenting task-mistress of the centuries, holds out in one hand her horn of plenty and in the other her scourge. This country has brought itself within the reach of the thong, while grasping at the satisfaction of present appetite, and forgetting the primal relation between the earth and man. The pathway to prosperity is still open. The divinity of the earthy life at heart is kind. Under her rule there are work and abundant reward for all, but these must be won in her designated way and in no other. Her pointing finger, that has never varied since man came upon the earth, shows the old and only way to safety and honor. Upon the readiness with which this is understood, the sober dignity with which a whole nation rises to the winning of its broad and permanent prosperity, will depend the individual well-being of this and many generations. Largely by this method will posterity, our fit and righteous judge, determine whether what issues from the crucible of this twentieth century is a bit of rejected dross to be cast aside, or a drop of golden metal to shine forever upon the rosary of the years.

North American Review, January 18, 1907, pp. 173–74.

The eloquence of this and its truth are undeniable. What seems to me quite as noteworthy is its bearing on Socialism. . . . Socialism perceives the same symptoms: our overcrowded cities, the wretched surroundings of so many of our poor, the growing pressure of privation. And Socialism declares that these evils are the fruit of Capitalism. To gain redemption, we must give back to the people the great resources of Nature. The people must own the coal, the iron, the land. Then all will be well. Now, the essence of the matter is this: the argument we have just followed shows conclusively that the nationalization of coal and iron would be the merest palliative, useless within two generations; while, as to the land, we have, in fact, distributed it to the people to a degree never seen in human history. Within the memory of men still living, half a continent has been given to the people, for the mere asking. Yet the misuse of this splendid gift has been deplorable, and threatens to be disastrous. What the people need is not more land, but the wisdom and temperance to use wisely what they already have, and of which they till only a fraction, and that so badly, that its value, instead of rising, steadily falls. There is a boundless demand for labor in our fields, but the people, flowing into this country at the rate of a million a year, cling to our cities and our tenements, and refuse to go to the land. We want, not Socialism, but a wise Individualism. Individual honesty in dealing with nature, individual providence in building for the future of the soil, individual sacrifice in refraining from an immediate gain for the sake of those who shall come after us. The whole of human experience shows that individual ownership of the soil, with individual love of the soil, such as the peasants of France and Ireland have, is the true way to increase our treasure. The ills Socialism deplores do not rest on Capitalism at all. They rest on moral deficiencies in vast numbers of individuals, ourselves included, and deficiences well within our power to cure.

V. Where We Can Work with Socialists

THEODORE ROOSEVELT

Theodore Roosevelt was President at the time that Sinclair wrote The Jungle. *Although they differed ideologically, they were friends, and Sinclair was a guest of Roosevelt at the White House not long after* The Jungle *was published. Immediately upon leaving office in 1909, Roosevelt became a contributing editor to* The Outlook. *His first contribution was a series of two articles on socialism; excerpts from the second article are included here.*

Evaluate his interpretation of the role socialism could play in improving the quality of American life. Where does he differ from Sinclair?

The Outlook, March 27, 1909, pp. 662–64.

MARCH 27, 1909

It is true that the doctrines of communistic Socialism, if consistently followed, mean the ultimate annihilation of civilization. Yet the converse is also true. Ruin faces us if we decline steadily to try to reshape our whole civilization in accordance with the law of service and if we permit ourselves to be misled by any empirical or academic consideration into refusing to exert the common power of the community where only collective action can do what individualism has left undone, or can remedy the wrongs done by an unrestricted and ill-regulated individualism. There is any amount of evil in our social and industrial conditions of today, and unless we recognize this fact and try resolutely to do what we can to remedy the evil, we run great risk of seeing men in their misery turn to the false teachers whose doctrines would indeed lead them to greater misery, but who do at least recognize the fact that they are now miserable. At the present time there are scores of laws in the interest of labor—laws putting a stop to child labor, decreasing the hours of labor where they are excessive, putting a stop to unsanitary crowding and living, securing employers' liability, doing away with unhealthy conditions in various trades, and the like—which should be passed by the National and the various State Legislatures; and those who wish to do effective work against Socialism would do well to turn their energies into securing the enactment of these laws.

Moreover, we should always remember that Socialism is both a wide and a loose term, and that the self-styled Socialists are of many and utterly different types. If we should study only the professed apostles of radical Socialism, of what these men themselves like to call "scientific Socialism," or if we should study only what active leaders of Socialism in this country have usually done, or read only the papers in which they have usually expressed themselves, we would gain an utterly wrong impression of very many men who call themselves Socialists. There are many peculiarly high-minded men and women who like to speak of themselves as Socialists, whose attitude, conscious or unconscious, is really merely an indignant recognition of the evil of present conditions and an ardent wish to remedy it, and whose Socialism is really only an advanced form of liberalism. Many of these men and women in actual fact take a large part in the advancement of moral ideas, and in practice wholly repudiate the purely materialistic, and therefore sordid, doctrines of those Socialists whose creed really is in sharp antagonism to every principle of public and domestic morality, who war on private property with a bitterness but little greater than that with which they war against the institutions of the home and the family, and against every form of religion, Catholic or Protestant. The Socialists of this moral type may in practice be very good citizens indeed, with whom we can at many points co-operate. They are often joined temporarily with what are called the "opportunist Socialists"—those who may advocate an impossible and highly undesirable Utopia as a matter of abstract faith, but who in practice try to secure the adoption only of some given principle which will do away with some phase of existing wrong. With these two groups of Socialists it is often possible for all far-sighted men to join heartily in the effort to secure a given reform or do away with a given abuse. Probably, in practice, wherever and whenever Socialists of these two types are able to form themselves into a party, they will disappoint both their own expectations and the fears of others by acting very much like other parties, like other aggregations of men; and it will be safe to adopt whatever they advance that is wise, and to reject whatever they advance that is foolish, just as we have to do as regards countless other groups who on one issue or set of issues come together to strive for a change in the political or social conditions of the world we live in. The important thing is generally the next step. We ought not to take it unless we are sure that it is advisable; but we should not hesitate to take it when once we are sure; and we can safely join with others who also wish to take it, without bothering our heads overmuch as to any somewhat fantastic theories they may have concerning, say, the two hundredth step, which is not yet in sight.

There are many schemes proposed which their enemies, and a few of their friends, are pleased to call Socialistic, or which are indorsed and favored by men who call themselves Socialists, but which are entitled each to be considered on its merits with regard only to the practical advantage which each would confer. Every public man, every reformer, is bound to refuse to dismiss these schemes with the shallow statement that they are "Socialistic;" for such an attitude is one of mere mischievous dogmatism. . . . Let each proposition be treated on its own merits, soberly and cautiously, but without any of that rigidity of mind which fears all reform. . . .

Socialism strives to remedy what is evil alike in domestic and in economic life, and its tendency is to insist that the economic remedy is all-sufficient in every case. We should all join in the effort to do away with the evil; but we should refuse to have anything to do with remedies which are either absurd or mischievous, for such, of course, would merely aggravate the present suffering. The first thing to recognize is that, while economic reform is often vital, it is never all-sufficient. The moral reform, the change of character—in which law can sometimes play a large, but never the largest, part—is the most necessary of all. . . .

So with our industrial system. In many respects the wage system can be bettered; but screaming about "wage slavery" is largely absurd; at this moment, for instance, I am a "wage slave" of The Outlook. Under certain conditions and in certain cases the co-operative system can to a greater or less degree be substituted with advantage for, or, more often, can be used to supplement, the wage system; but only on condition of recognizing the widely different needs occasioned by different conditions, which needs are so diverse that they must sometimes be met in totally different ways.

We should do everything that can be done, by law or otherwise, to keep the avenues of occupation, of employment, of work, of interest, so open that there shall be, so far as it is humanly possible to achieve it, a measurable equality of opportunity; an equality of opportunity for each man to show the stuff that is in him. When it comes to reward, let each man, within the limits set by a sound and far-sighted morality, get what, by his energy, intelligence, thrift, courage, he is able to get, with the opportunity open. We must set our faces against privilege; just as much against the kind of privilege which would let the shiftless and lazy laborer take what his brother has earned as against the privilege which allows the huge capitalist to take toll to which he is not entitled. We stand for equality of opportunity, but not for equality of reward unless there is also equality of service. If the service is equal, let the reward be equal; but let the reward depend on the service; and, mankind being composed as it is, there will be inequality of service for a long time to come, no matter how great the equality of opportunity may be; and just so long as there is inequality of service it is eminently desirable that there should be inequality of reward.

For Further Reading

These volumes, to a greater or lesser extent, deal with socialism in the progressive era: Albert Fried, ed., *Socialism in America: A Documentary History* (1970); David Herreshoff, *American Disciples of Marx: From the Age of Jackson to the Progressive Era* (1967); Ira Kipnis, *The American Socialist Movement, 1897–1917* (1952, 1968); H. Wayne Morgan, ed., *American Socialism, 1900–1960** (1964); Howard H. Quint, *The Forging of American Socialism: Origins of the Modern Movement** (1953, 1964); and James Weinstein, *The Decline of Socialism in America, 1912–1925** (1967). More specific is an essay by Kenneth McNaught, "Socialism and the Progressives: Was Failure Inevitable?" in *Dissent: Explorations in the History of American Radicalism** (1968), edited by Alfred Young.

    Socialism and American Life, 2 vols. (1952), edited by Donald D. Egbert and Stow Persons, contains excellent essays and an extensive bibliography.

    Of the many books on the progressive era, only three are mentioned here: Richard Hofstadter, *The Age of Reform: From Bryan to FDR** (1955), provides the standard "status" interpretation of progressivism; Gabriel Kolko, *The Triumph of Conservatism: A Reinterpretation of American History, 1900–1916** (1967), offers a revisionist viewpoint; and Carl Rezek, ed., *The Progressives** (1967), is a collection of primary sources.

    Problems books are *Progressivism: The Critical Issues** (1971), edited by David M. Kennedy, and *The Progressive Era: Liberal Renaissance or Liberal Failure** (1963), edited by Arthur Mann.

**Paperbound edition available.

7. *"Why Should Women Vote?"*

The woman's rights movement in the United States traces its origins to the Woman's Rights Convention held at Seneca Falls, New York, in July 1848. Under the leadership of Elizabeth Cady Stanton and Lucretia Mott, this convention produced a Declaration of Sentiments, signed by a hundred men and women, that served as a foundation and rallying point for the movement for the next seventy-two years.

Many of the women who came into the movement were abolitionists, and experience in that crusade helped them to organize for the struggle to gain their own rights. One of the key issues at Seneca Falls and in all later conventions was the enfranchisement of women. In the 1850s the extension of the vote seemed to be a possibility, but the outbreak of the Civil War pushed the issue into the background and leaders of the movement, including such new leaders as Susan B. Anthony, concerned themselves with the war effort. But after the Civil War Stanton and Anthony again campaigned for the woman's vote, only to be frustrated by the adoption of the Fourteenth Amendment with the exclusive term "male" inserted to designate the new voters.

The woman's movement met some successes, however, as various states and territories began to allow women to vote in school and municipal elections. In 1890 Wyoming was admitted to the Union with full suffrage for both sexes; in 1893 Colorado and in 1896 Idaho and Utah extended suffrage to their women. But winning the vote on a state-by-state basis was a slow, frustrating, and usually unsuccessful process. The state legislatures were ordinarily controlled by antisuffrage elements, and even if they were willing to submit to the voters amendments granting suffrage, the women usually met defeat at the hands of a tradition-bound electorate of male voters. Out of the forty-one state campaigns conducted from 1869 to 1916, there were only nine victories. Such a record led many women in the movement to look at the precedent of the Fourteenth and later Fifteenth amendments, which prohibited racial discrimination in voting, and to conclude that an amendment was their only hope for obtaining the right to vote.

Pursuing this hope, the "Anthony Amendment" was drafted: "The right of citizens of the United States to vote shall not be denied or abridged by the United States or by any state on account of sex." Forty-two years after its first introduction in Congress by Senator Sargent of California in 1878 it became the Nineteenth Amendment to the Constitution. Although equal rights for women involves much more than the simple right to vote, voting was certainly a critical first step. As such, it provides the theme of this chapter.

Core Document

Why the Federal Amendment?

CARRIE CHAPMAN CATT

The attempt to bring about the acceptance of woman's suffrage required American women to organize politically. In the early years the two most important organizations were the American Woman Suffrage Association and the National Woman Suffrage Association. The former concerned itself with working for the passage of state amendments, while the latter, led by Susan B. Anthony and Elizabeth Cady Stanton, committed itself to gaining the vote for women primarily through a federal amendment. In 1890 these two organizations united to form the National American Woman Suffrage Association. The advent of the Progressive Era, with its emphasis upon reform, helped to increase the public's awareness of the cause of woman's suffrage and to bring more women into the movement.

From 1890 until 1916 the National Association concerned itself on both the state and federal levels, attempting always to convince the American people of the wisdom and justice of woman's suffrage. In 1915 Carrie Chapman Catt, who

Carrie Chapman Catt, *Woman Suffrage by Federal Constitutional Amendment* (New York: National Woman Suffrage Pub. Co., 1917), pp. 1–11, 69–74, 80–81, 86–91.

had been president of the National Association from 1900 to 1902, was again chosen to lead the organization. She evolved a plan by which the federal amendment was to be the key to the emanicipation of women. To convince the men in Congress of the justice of her cause and to inform the American public of the reasons for the move to bring about a federal amendment, Mrs. Catt, along with dozens of other suffragists, wrote articles, made speeches, and lobbied in Congress.

In the following article Mrs. Catt explains why women were seeking a federal amendment and answers some of the objections to such an amendment. In reading the article pay close attention to her:

- *seven points justifying the federal amendment process to gain woman's suffrage.*
- *response to the states' rights objection to a federal amendment.*
- *answer to the argument that all women should wait until all women wanted the vote.*
- *interpretation of "government by the people."*
- *contention that woman's suffrage would increase the moral vote and improve voting procedures.*

WHY THE FEDERAL AMENDMENT?

Woman Suffrage is coming—no intelligent person in the United States or in the world will deny that fact. The most an intelligent opponent expects to accomplish is to postpone its establishment as long as possible. When it will come and how it will come are still open questions. Woman Suffrage by Federal Amendment is supported by seven main reasons. These main reasons are evaded or avoided; they are not answered.

I. Keeping Pace With Other Countries Demands It.

Suffrage for men and suffrage for women in other lands, with few and minor exceptions, has been granted by parliamentary act and not by referenda. By such enactment the women of Australia were granted full suffrage in Federal elections by the Federal Parliament (1902), and each State or Province granted full suffrage in all other elections by act of their Provincial Parliaments. By such enactment the Isle of Man, New Zealand, Finland, Norway, Iceland and Denmark gave equal suffrage in all elections to women. By such process the Parliaments of Manitoba, Saskatchewan and Alberta gave full provincial suffrage to their women in 1916. British Columbia referred the question to the voters in 1916, but the Provincial Parliament had already extended all suffrage rights except the parliamentary vote, and both political parties lent their aid in the referendum which consequently gave a majority in every precinct on the home vote and a majority of the soldier vote was returned from Europe later. By parliamentary act all other Canadian Provinces, the Provinces of South Africa, the countries of Sweden and Great Britain have extended far more voting privileges than any woman citizen of the United States east of the

Missouri River (except those of Illinois) has received. To the women of Belise (British Honduras), the cities of Rangoon (Burmah), Bombay (India), the Province of Baroda (India), the Province of Voralberg (Austria), and Laibach (Austria) the same statement applies. In Bohemia, Russia and various Provinces of Austria and Germany, the principle of representation is recognized by the grant to property-holding women of a vote by proxy. The suffragists of France reported just before the war broke out that the French Parliament was pledged to extend universal municipal suffrage to women. Men and women of high repute say the full suffrage is certain to be extended by the British Parliamant to the women of England, Scotland, Ireland and Wales soon after the close of the war and already these women have all suffrage rights except the vote for Parliamentary members. These facts are strange since it was the United States which first established general suffrage for men upon the two principles that "taxation without representation is tyranny" and that governments to be just should "derive their consent from the governed." The unanswerable logic of these two principles is responsible for the extension of suffrage to men and women the world over. In the United States, however, women are still taxed with "representation" and still live under a government to which they have given no "consent." IT IS OBVIOUSLY UNFAIR TO SUBJECT WOMEN OF THIS COUNTRY—WHICH BOASTS THAT IT IS THE LEADER IN THE MOVEMENT TOWARD UNIVERSAL SUFFRAGE—TO A LONGER, HARDER, MORE DIFFICULT PROCESS THAN HAS BEEN IMPOSED BY OTHER NATIONS UPON MEN OR WOMEN. American constitutions of the nation and the states have closed the door to the simple processes by which men and women of other countries have been enfranchised. An amendment to our Federal Constitution is the nearest approach to them. To deny the benefits of this method to the women of this country is to put upon them a PENALTY FOR BEING AMERICANS.

2. Equal Rights Demands It.

Men of this country have been enfranchised by various extensions of the voting privilege but IN NO SINGLE INSTANCE were they compelled to appeal to an electorate containing groups of recently naturalized and even unnaturalized foreigners, Indians, Negroes, large numbers of illiterates, ne'-er-do-wells, and drunken loafers. The Jews, denied the vote in all our colonies, and the Catholics, denied the vote in most of them, received their franchise through the revolutionary constitutions which removed all religious qualifications for the vote in a manner consistent with the self-respect of all. The property qualifications for the vote which were established in every colony and continued in the early state constitutions were usually removed by a referendum but the question obviously went to an electorate limited to property-holders only. The largest number of voters to which such an amendment was referred was that of New York. Had every man voted who was qualified to do so, the electorate would not have exceeded 200,000 and probably not more than 150,000.

The next extensions of the vote to men were made to certain tribes of

Indians by act of Congress; and to the Negro by amendment to the Federal Constitution.

At least three-fourths of the present electors secured their votes through direct naturalization or that of their forefathers. Congress determines conditions of citizenship and state constitutions fix qualifications of voters. In no instance has the foreign immigrant been forced to plead with a vast electorate for his vote. The suffrage has been "thrust upon him" without effort or even request on his part. National and State constitutions not only close to women the comparatively easy processes by which the vote was extended to men and women of other countries but also those processes by which the vote was secured to men of our own land. The simplest method now possible is by amendment of the Federal Constitution. To deny the privilege of that method to women is a discrimination against them so unjust and insufferable that no fair-minded man North or South, East or West, can logically share in the denial.

3. Relief from Unjust Constitutional Obstructions Demands It.

The constitutions of many states have provided for amendments by such difficult processes that they either have never been amended or have not been amended when the subject is in the least controversial. Their provisions not infrequently are utilized by opponents of a cause to delay action for years. A present case illustrates. Newspapers in Kentucky which have opposed woman suffrage, and still do so, have started a campaign (December, 1916) to submit a woman suffrage amendment to voters with the announced intention of securing its defeat at the polls in order to remove it from politics for five years as the same question cannot be again submitted for that length of time.

There are state constitutions so impossible of amendment that women of those states can only secure enfranchisement through Federal action and fair play demands the submission of a Federal constitutional amendment.

4. Protection from Inadequate Election Laws Demands It.

The election laws of all states make inadequate provision for safeguarding the vote on constitutional amendments. Since election laws do not protect suffrage referenda, suffragists justly demand the method prescribed by our national constitution to appeal their case from male voters at large to the higher court of Congress and the Legislatures.

5. Equal Status of Men and Women Voters Demands It.

Until the adoption of the Fourteenth Amendment the National Constitution did not discriminate against women but in Section 2 of that amendment provision was made whereby a penalty may be directed against any state which denies the right to vote to its *male inhabitants* possessed of the necessary qualifications as prescribed by nation and state. If the entire 48 states should severally enfranchise women their political status would still be inferior to that of men, since no provision for national protection in their right to vote would exist.

The women of eleven states are said to vote on equal terms with men. As a matter of fact they do not, since they not only lose their vote whenever they change their residence to any one of the 37 other states (except Illinois, where they lose only a portion of their privileges), but they enjoy no national protection in their right to vote. Women justly demand "Equal Rights for All and Special Privileges for None." Amendment to the National Constitution alone can give them an equal status. Equality of rights can never be secured through state by state enfranchisement.

6. National Significance of Question Demands It.

Woman suffrage in every other country is a National question. With eleven American states and nearly half the territory of the civilized world already won; with the statement of the press still unchallenged that women voters were "the balance of power" which decided the last presidential election, the movement has reached a position of national significance in the United States. Any policy which seeks to shift responsibility or to procrastinate action, is, to use the mildest phraseology, unworthy of the Congress in whose charge the making of American political history reposes.

7. Treatment of Question Demands Intelligence.

The handicaps of a popular vote upon a question of human liberty which must be described in technical language will be clear to all who think. It is probable that at least a fourth of the voters in West Virginia, one of the recent suffrage campaign states, could not define the following words intelligently: constitution, amendment, franchise, suffrage, majority, plurality. It is probable they would succeed even less well at an attempt to give an account of the Declaration of Independence, the Revolution, Taxation without Representation, the will of the majority, popular government. Such men might make a fairly intelligent choice of men for local offices because their minds are trained to deal with persons and concrete things. They could decide between Mr. Wilson and Mr. Hughes with some discrimination, but would have slight if any knowledge of the platforms upon which either stood. A referendum in many of our states, means to defer woman suffrage until the most ignorant, most narrow-minded, most un-American, are ready for it. The removal of the question to the higher court of the Congress and the Legislatures of the several states means that it will be established when the intelligent, Americanized, progressive people of the country are ready for it. . . .

OBJECTIONS TO THE FEDERAL AMENDMENT

STATES RIGHTS. THIS OBJECTION IS URGED BY ALL OPPONENTS OF WOMAN SUFFRAGE, BUT IS EITHER A BARRICADE TO DEFEND THEMSELVES FROM THE NECESSITY OF EXPOSING THE FACT THAT THEY HAVE NO REASONS, OR IS A PLAY TO POSTPONE WOMAN SUFFRAGE AS LONG AS POSSIBLE. BY A FEW IT IS URGED CONSCIENTIOUSLY AND WITH CONVICTION.

That there are many problems whose treatment belongs so appropriately to state governments that any infringement of that right by the Federal Government would be an act of tyranny, no American will question. But assuredly woman suffrage is not one of these. One by one classes of men have been granted the vote until women are the only remaining unenfranchised class. States have set up various restrictive qualifications so that criminality, idiocy, insanity, pauperism, drunkenness, foreign birth are accepted as ordinary causes of disfranchisement. Yet not one of these conditions is common to all the states. The foreigner votes on his first papers in eight states and a five years' residence will usually secure his naturalization and a consequent vote in any state. The criminal, idiot and insane are not denied a vote in several states, and in most a large class of ignorant un-American men with no comprehension of our problems, our history, or ideals, are conspicuous voters on election day. Millions of new voters have entered our country and without the expenditure of time, money, or service have received the vote since the pending Federal Amendment was first introduced.

For two generations groups of women have given their lives and their fortunes to secure the vote for their sex and hundreds of thousands of other women are now giving all the time at their command. No class of men in our own or any other country has made one-tenth the effort nor sacrificed one-tenth as much for the vote. The long delay, the double dealing, the broken faith of political parties, the insult of disfranchisement of the qualified in a land which freely gives the vote to the unqualified, combines to produce as insufferable a tyranny as any modern nation has perpetuated upon a class of its citizens. The souls of women which should be warm with patriotic love of their country are growing bitter over the inexplicable wrong their country is doing them. Hands and heads that should be busy with other problems of our nation are withheld that they may get the tools with which to work. Purses that should be open to many causes are emptied into suffrage coffers until this monumental injustice shall be wiped away. Woman suffrage is a question of righting a nation-wide injustice, of establishing a phase of unquestioned human liberty and of carrying out a proposition to which our nation is pledged; it therefore transcends all considerations of states rights. This objection comes chiefly from Southern Democrats, who claim that it is a form of oppression for three-fourths of the states to foist upon one-fourth measures of which the minority of states do not approve. Yet the provision for so amending the Constitution was adopted by the states and has stood unchallenged in the Constitution for more than a century. If it be unfair, undemocratic or even unsatisfactory, it is curious that no movement to change the provision has ever developed. The Constitution has been twice amended recently and it is interesting to note that it happened under a Democratic Administration. More, the child labor and eight-hour bills, while not constitutional amendments, are subject to the same plea that no state shall have laws imposed upon it without its consent. Both measures were introduced by Southern Democrats. The pending Federal Prohibition Amendment was also introduced by a Southern Democrat and is supported by many others. Upon consideration of these facts, it would seem that "states rights" is either a theory to be invoked whenever necessary to conceal an unreasoning hostility to a measure or that those who advance it are guilty of extremely muddy thinking.

The Constitution of the United States as now amended provides that no male citizen subject to state qualifications shall be denied the vote by any state. Were all the state constitutions amended so as to enfranchise women, the word male would still stand in the National Constitution. Men and women would still be unequal, since the National Constitution can impose a penalty upon a state which denies the vote to men, but none upon the state which discriminates against women. A woman comes from Montana to represent that state in Congress. The State of Montana has done its utmost to remove her political disabilities, yet should she cross the border of her state and live in North Dakota, she loses all that Montana gave her. Not so the male voter. Enfranchised in one state, he is enfranchised in all (subject to difference of qualification only). The women of this nation will never be content with less protection in their right to vote than is given to men and there is no other possible way to secure that protection except through amendment to the National Constitution. No single state, nor the forty-eight collectively, can grant that protection except through the Federal Constitution.

As granting to half the population of our country the right of consent to their own government, whose expenses they help to pay, is a question of fundamental human liberty, Congress and the legislatures should be proud to act and to add one more immortal chapter to America's history of freedom. . . .

WOMEN DO NOT WANT TO VOTE AND HENCE IT IS UNFAIR TO THRUST THE VOTE UPON THEM BY FEDERAL AMENDMENT.

We have two classes of voters in the United States, young men who automatically become voters at twenty-one, and naturalized citizens. No one among them has ever been asked whether he wishes the vote. It was "thrust upon them" all as a privilege which each would use or not as he desired. To extend the suffrage to those who do not desire it is no hardship, since only those who wish the privilege will use it. On the other hand, it becomes an intolerable oppression to deny it to those who want it. The vote is permissive, not obligatory. It imposes no definite responsibility; it extends a liberty. That there are women who do not want the vote is true, but the well-known large number of qualified men who do not use the vote, indicates that the desire to have someone else assume the responsibility of public service is not confined to women. It is an easy excuse to say "wait until all the women want it," but it is a poor rule which doesn't work both ways. Had it been necessary for members of Congress to wait until all men wanted the vote before they had one for themselves, we should be living in an unconstitutional monarchy. More, had it been necessary for women to wait until all women approved of college or even public school education for girls, property rights, the right of free speech, or any one of the many liberties now enjoyed by women, but formerly denied them, the iniquities of the old common law would still measure the privileges of women, and high schools and colleges would still close their doors to women. . . .

Political Expediency. The South professes to fear the increased Negro vote; the North, the increased Foreign vote; the rich, the increased labor vote; the conservative, the increased illiterate vote. The Republicans since the recent presidential election fear the increased Democratic vote; the Democrats fear the woman voters' support was only temporary. The "wet" fears the increased dry vote; the "dry" the increased controlled wet vote. Certain very numerous elements fear the increased Catholic vote and still others the increased Jewish vote. The Orthodox Protestant and Catholic fear the increased free-thinking vote and the free-thinkers are decidedly afraid of the increased church vote. Labor fears the increased influence of the capitalistic class, and capitalists, especially of the manufacturing group, are extremely disturbed at the prospect of votes being extended to their women employees. Certain groups fear the increased Socialist vote and certain Socialists fear the "lady vote." Party men fear women voters will have no party consciousness and prove so independent as to disintegrate the party. Radical or progressive elements fear that women will be "stand-pat" partisans. Ballot reformers fear the increased corrupt vote and corruptionists fear the increased reform vote. Militarists are much alarmed lest women increase the peace vote and, despite the fact that the press of the country has poured forth increasing evidence that the women of every belligerent country have borne their full share of the war burden with such unexpected skill and ability that the authorities have been lavish in acknowledgment, seem certain that women of the United States will prove the exception to the world's rule and show the white feather if war threatens.

Ridiculous as this list of objections may appear, each is supported earnestly by a considerable group, and collectively they furnish the basis of opposition to woman suffrage in and out of Congress.

The answer to one is the answer to all.

Government by "the people" is expedient or it is not. If it is expedient, then obviously *all* the people must be included. If it is not expedient, the simplest logic leads to the conclusion that the classes to be deprived of the franchise should be determined by their qualities of unfitness for the vote. If education, intelligence, grasp of public questions, patriotism, willingness and ability to give public service, respect of law, are selected as fair qualifications for those to be entrusted with the vote and the opposite as the qualities of those to be denied the vote, it follows that men and women will be included in the classes adjudged fit to vote, and also in those adjudged unfit to vote. Meanwhile the system which admits the unworthy to the vote provided they are men, and shuts out the worthy provided they are women, is so unjust and illogical that its perpetuation is a sad reflection upon American thinking.

The clear thinker will arrive at the conclusion that women must be included in the electorate if our country wishes to be consistent with the principles it boasts as fundamental. The shortest method to secure this enfranchisement is the quickest method to extricate our country from the absurdity of its present position. . . .

Woman suffrage would increase the *moral* vote. Only one out of every twenty criminals are women. Women constitute a minority of drunkards and petty misdemeanants, and in all the factors that tend to handicap the progress of society women form a minority; whereas in churches, schools and all organizations working for the uplift of humanity, women are a majority. In all American states and countries that have adopted equal suffrage the vote of the disreputable woman is practically negligible, the slum wards of cities invariably having the lightest woman vote and the respectable residence wards the heaviest. Woman suffrage would increase the number of *native born voters* as for every 100 foreign white women immigrants coming to this country there are 129 men, while among Asiatic immigrants the men outnumber the women two to one, according to the Census of 1910.

Woman suffrage would help to *correct election procedure.* In all states where women vote, the polling booths have been moved into homes, church parlors, school houses or other similar respectable places. Women serve as election officials and the subduing influence of woman's presence elsewhere has had its effect upon the elections. Women greatly increase the number of competent persons who can be drawn upon as election officials. No class of persons in the nation is so well trained as school teachers for this work. The presence of women as voters and officials would in itself eliminate certain types of irregularity and go a long way toward establishing a higher standard of election procedure. Woman suffrage cannot possibly make political conditions worse, since all the elements which combine to produce those conditions are less conspicuous among women than men. On the other hand the introduction of a new class possessing a very large number of persons who would unwillingly tolerate some of the conditions now prevailing offers evidence that a powerful influence for better things would come with the woman's vote.

Discussion Starters

1. Evaluate the argument that in removing the question of woman suffrage from the local to the national level the National Association was ignoring the basic tenet of American democracy, that of allowing local populations to decide for themselves what would be best for them.

2. Evaluate Mrs. Catt's arguments that the extension of the franchise to women was a political expediency and would increase the native American vote, as well as produce higher standards of election procedures.

3. Considering the role of women in American society today, how correct

was Mrs. Catt's suggestion that the vote for women was their key to complete emancipation?

4. In what ways did the movement for woman's suffrage compare with the other reform movements of the Progressive Era?

5. Account for the fact that ideas such as those presented by Carrie Chapman Catt, which today seem plausible and acceptable, could at one time be regarded as radical and provoke hostile reaction.

Related Documents

I. *Declaration of Sentiments*

WOMAN'S RIGHTS CONVENTION

The first Woman's Rights Convention was held in Seneca Falls, New York, in the summer of 1848. Called by Elizabeth Cady Stanton, with the support of several other women, it was the formal beginning of the movement in the United States. But the convention was the culmination of various private meetings and years of frustration on the part of some concerned women in America. During the nineteenth century women had begun to play a larger role in the political life of the nation through their work in abolitionism, the temperance movement, and the peace crusade. Such activities led them to seek changes in the system that blocked their program. Change could be effected, they believed, only at the polls, so the vote was essential to bring about reform and to release women from the subordinate role they had played in American society. How does the Declaration, *which was approved by the convention, anticipate Mrs. Catt's arguments sixty-nine years later for the enfranchisement of women?*

JULY 19, 1848

When, in the course of human events, it becomes necessary for one portion of the family of man to assume among the people of the earth a position different from that which they have hitherto occupied, but one to which the laws of nature and of nature's God entitle them, a decent respect to the opinions of mankind requires that they should declare the causes that impel them to such a course.

Elizabeth Cady Stanton, Susan B. Anthony, and Matilda J. Gage, eds., *History of Woman Suffrage* (Rochester: Charles Mann, 1889), I, pp. 70–71.

We hold these truths to be self-evident: that all men and women are created equal; that they are endowed by their Creator with certain inalienable rights; that among these are life, liberty, and the pursuit of happiness; that to secure these rights governments are instituted, deriving their just powers from the consent of the governed. Whenever any form of government becomes destructive of these ends, it is the right of those who suffer from it to refuse allegiance to it, and to insist upon the institution of a new government, laying its foundation on such principles, and organizing its powers in such form, as to them shall seem most likely to effect their safety and happiness. Prudence, indeed, will dictate that governments long established should not be changed for light and transient causes; and accordingly all experience hath shown that mankind are more disposed to suffer, while evils are sufferable, than to right themselves by abolishing the forms to which they were accustomed. But when a long train of abuses and usurpations, pursuing invariably the same object envinces a design to reduce them under absolute despotism, it is their duty to throw off such government, and to provide new guards for their future security. Such has been the patient sufferance of the women under this government, and such is now the necessity which constrains them to demand the equal station to which they are entitled.

The history of mankind is a history of repeated injuries and usurpations on the part of man toward woman, having in direct object the establishment of an absolute tyranny over her. To prove this, let facts be submitted to a candid world.

He has never permitted her to exercise her inalienable right to the elective franchise.

He has compelled her to submit to laws, in the formation of which she had no voice.

He has withheld from her rights which are given to the most ignorant and degraded men—both natives and foreigners.

Having deprived her of this first right of a citizen, the elective franchise, thereby leaving her without representation in the halls of legislation, he has oppressed her on all sides.

He has made her, if married, in the eye of the law, civilly dead.

He has taken from her all right in property, even to the wages she earns.

He has made her, morally, an irresponsible being, as she can commit many crimes with impunity, provided they be done in the presence of her husband. In the covenant of marriage, she is compelled to promise obedience to her husband, he becoming, to all intents and purposes, her master—the law giving him power to deprive her of her liberty, and to administer chastisement.

He has so framed the laws of divorce, as to what shall be the proper causes, and in case of separation, to whom the guardianship of the children shall be given, as to be wholly regardless of the happiness of women—the law, in all cases, going upon a false supposition of the supremacy of man, and giving all power into his hands.

After depriving her of all rights as a married woman, if single, and the owner of property, he has taxed her to support a government which recognizes her only when her property can be made profitable to it.

He has monopolized nearly all the profitable employments, and from those she is permitted to follow, she receives but a scanty remuneration. He closes against her all the avenues to wealth and distinction which he considers most honorable to himself. As a teacher of theology, medicine, or law, she is not known.

He has denied her the facilities for obtaining a thorough education, all colleges being closed against her.

He allows her in Church, as well as State, but a subordinate position, claiming Apostolic authority for her exclusion from the ministry, and, with some exceptions, from any public participation in the affairs of the Church.

He has created a false public sentiment by giving to the world a different code of morals for men and women, by which moral delinquencies which exclude women from society, are not only tolerated, but deemed of little account in man.

He has usurped the prerogative of Jehovah himself, claiming it as his right to assign for her a sphere of action, when that belongs to her conscience and to her God.

He has endeavored, in every way that he could, to destroy her confidence in her own powers, to lessen her self-respect, and to make her willing to lead a dependent and abject life.

Now, in view of this entire disfranchisement of one-half the people of this country, their social and religious degradation—in view of the unjust laws above mentioned, and because women do feel themselves aggrieved, oppressed, and fraudulently deprived of their most sacred rights, we insist that they have immediate admission to all the rights and privileges which belong to them as citizens of the United States.

In entering upon the great work before us, we anticipate no small amount of misconception, misrepresentation, and ridicule; but we shall use every instrumentality within our power to effect our object. We shall employ agents, circulate tracts, petition the State and National legislatures, and endeavor to enlist the pulpit and the press in our behalf. We hope this Convention will be followed by a series of Conventions embracing every part of the country.

II. The Constitutionality of the "Anthony Amendment"

FRANK BRANDEGEE

When the "Anthony Amendment" was reported favorably out of a Senate committee in September 1917 and a House committee in January 1918, it appeared

Congressional Record, June 27, 1918, pp. 8348–49.

*that a real showdown would be fought in the Sixty-fifth Congress of the United
States. On January 10, 1918, the House passed the amendment and sent it to
the Senate. The struggle in the House had been long and hard, but the coming
struggle in the Senate seemed to suggest an even more difficult time. The
supporters of suffrage for women in the Senate faced an uphill battle, for the
opposition included senators such as Henry Cabot Lodge of Massachusetts,
Thomas Martin of Virginia, James Reed of Missouri, and Frank Brandegee of
Connecticut. It took over a year before the amendment came to a vote, and when
it did on February 10, 1919, it was defeated by one vote. Later, during a special
session of the Sixty-sixth Congress, the House again passed the amendment and
on June 4, 1919, the necessary two-thirds vote was obtained in the Senate.*

*Throughout the struggle Senator Brandegee worked to defeat the measure.
Speaking for the opposition, Brandegee concerned himself with the constitutional questions of the amendment. How does Senator Brandegee's interpretation of the Constitution and the rights of Congress conflict with Mrs. Catt's
assertion that Congress must pass a federal amendment giving women the vote?*

JUNE 27, 1918

I think the Constitution of the United States was designed to be a broad charter
defining the character of our Government. It divided the powers of Government into three parts—the legislative, the judicial, and the executive—and in
broad outline it indicated the kind of government we were to have as a nation;
but the Constitution was framed by delegates from the several States, and they
carefully reserved to the States all the rights that they had not specifically
delegated to the National Government or which were not necessarily implied
from the specifically delegated powers. I do not think the Constitution was
designed to be a criminal code nor a set of local ordinances nor a book of
statutes. I do not think it was intended that we should put into the Constitution
of the United States, at the behest of the legislatures of three-fourths of the
States, without any submission whatever to the people of the States, provisions
as to what we should eat and what we should drink and when we should go
to bed and what should be our local customs in our home communities.

I think the framers of the Constitution were a very wise and learned set
of men of great experience, and they intended to formulate the frame and kind
of government that should exist in this country. They never intended, in my
opinion, that Congress should attempt to say at what age a child shall work
in Louisiana or in Mississippi, or whether or not the people of California shall
raise grapes or shall make them into wine after they have raised them, or that
three-quarters of the States should say that nothing produced by negro labor
in the South should ever come north of Mason and Dixon's line. I do not think
that they intended, when they made the Constitution of the United States,
defining and limiting the powers of the National Government, to deprive the
people in their respective home communities of the right of local self-government and home rule. To talk that way now may sound like an old fogy; it may

be that the Congress now thinks that wherever there appears an insistent and persistent vocalization for a cause or a propaganda, Congress has no duty in the premises except to yield to it and pass the thing on to the legislatures of the States. That is not my view of our duty, Mr. President.

If I recall the language of the Constitution, it is in substance this: That whenever two-thirds of the Senate and two-thirds of the House of Representatives of the Congress think the United States Constitution should be amended, they shall pass a resolution to that effect and submit it to the legislatures of the several States—whenever two-thirds of each branch of Congress thinks it is *necessary* they shall submit it to the legislatures of the several States. I do not think this is *necessary,* and I have some doubt as to whether some gentlemen who are inclined to vote for this thing think it is *necessary.* I say that because I have heard Senators express in ordinary cloakroom conversation their notion that whenever there was a persistent demand for a thing they would vote to submit it to the several States.

Mr. President, the framers of the Constitution thought the people of this country would send to Congress men who had ideas of their own and did their own thinking; they did not think we were simply to be a funnel to pass on to the States whatever some newspaper or some propaganda should agitate sufficiently strenuously and sufficiently loudly. They intended the Constitution to be of such fundamental character that it could not be amended, except when the Congress thought it was *necessary* and the legislatures of three-quarters of the States thought it was *necessary.* . . .

What do the proponents of this constitutional amendment say? They all try to utilize the war as a reason why they should have the privilege of voting. They call it a right. Of course it is not a right. They know that just as well as we do. Every court in the country has decided, wherever the question has been presented, that the suffrage was not a right but was a privilege conferred by the Government. There is no more reason in morals or nature why sex should constitute a natural right to the suffrage than there is why a boy 15 years old should not vote. The Government says he can not vote until he is 21. There is no inherent right whatever about it. The only question is the honest, sane judgment of the men in charge of the government of the United States and of the several States as to what is best for the Government of the United States and for the States in this matter.

I am not discussing the question of suffrage. I admit freely that each State can and ought to decide that question for itself, as the President of the United States himself said, and as both political platforms say. I am perfectly willing that each State should decide it for itself, and they are the proper tribunals to decide it, for they know their own local conditions; but we are asked here to use the Constitution of the United States as an instrument, by the vote not of the people but of the legislatures of three-quarters of the States, to impose this thing upon the other quarter of the States, whether they want it or not. Now, is that democracy? Is that home rule? Is that local self-government? Why, it can not be so, Mr. President. As the Supreme Court said in the child-labor case, such a theory is utterly subversive of every notion of democracy upon which this Government was founded and upon which the Constitution was founded.

III. Why Should Women Vote?

ALICE STONE BLACKWELL

To answer the various arguments against women concerning themselves with politics and suffrage, the National American Woman Suffrage Association published the "Blue Book." This publication contained the history of the movement and reasons why women should vote.

One article in the "Blue Book" was written by Alice Stone Blackwell, the daughter of Lucy Stone, who had been a leader in the movement during the latter part of the nineteenth century. Miss Blackwell had served as editor of the Woman's Journal *and was one of the foremost propagandists for the movement. How does her article compare with Mrs. Catt's in justifying the case for woman's suffrage?*

1917

Why Should Women Vote?

The reasons why women should vote are the same as the reasons why men should vote—the same as the reasons for having a republic rather than a monarchy. It is fair and right that the people who must obey the laws should have a voice in choosing the law-makers, and that those who must pay the taxes should have a voice as to the amount of the tax, and the way in which the money shall be spent.

Roughly stated, the fundamental principle of a republic is this: In deciding what is to be done, we take everybody's opinion, and then go according to the wish of the majority. As we cannot suit everybody, we do what will suit the greatest number. That seems to be, on the whole, the fairest way. A vote is simply a written expression of opinion.

In thus taking a vote to get at the wish of the majority, certain classes of persons are passed over, whose opinions for one reason or another are thought not to be worth counting. In most of our states, these classes are children, aliens, idiots, lunatics, criminals and women. There are good and obvious reasons for making all these exceptions but the last. Of course no account ought to be taken of the opinions of children, insane persons, or criminals. Is there any equally good reason why no account should be taken of the opinions of women? Let us consider the reasons commonly given, and see if they are sound.

Frances M. Björkman and Annie G. Porritt, eds., *The Blue Book* (New York: National Woman Suffrage Pub. Co., 1917), pp. 144–46, 169–70, 185–86, 188–89.

Are Women Represented?

Women are represented already by their husbands, fathers and brothers.

This so-called representation bears no proportion to numbers. Here is a man who has a wife, widowed mother, four or five unmarried sisters, and half a dozen unmarried daughters. His vote represents himself and all these women, and it counts one; while the vote of his bachelor neighbor next door, without a female relative in the world, counts for just as much. Since the object of taking a vote is to get at the wish of the majority, it is clear that the only fair and accurate way is for each grown person to have one vote, and cast it to represent himself or herself.

American men are the best in the world, and if it were possible for any men to represent women, through kindness and good will to them, American men would do it. But a man is by nature too different from a woman to be able to represent her. The two creatures are unlike. Whatever his good will, he cannot fully put himself in a woman's place, and look at things exactly from her point of view. To say this is no more a reflection upon his mental or moral ability than it would be a reflection upon his musical ability to say that he cannot sing both soprano and bass. Unless men and women should ever become alike (which would be regrettable and monotonous), women must either go unrepresented or represent themselves. . . .

Too Emotional

Women are too emotional and sentimental to be trusted with the ballot.

Mrs. E. T. Brown, at a meeting of the Georgia State Federation of Women's Clubs, read a paper, in which she said:

"You tell us that women are not fitted for dealing with the problems of government, being too visionary and too much controlled by sentiment.

"Now it is very true of women that they are largely controlled by sentiment, and, as a matter of fact, men are largely controlled by sentiment also, in spite of their protesting blushes. Was it logic that swept like a wave over this country and sent our army to protect the Cubans when their suffering grew too intense to be endured even in the hearing? Is it shrewd business calculation that sends thousands of dollars out of this country to feed a starving people during the ever-recurring famines in unhappy India? Was it hard common sense that sent thousands of American soldiers into what looked like the death-trap of China in the almost baseless hope of rescuing a few hundred American citizens? Do not men like Washington, Lincoln, Jefferson and Lee live in the hearts of American men, not alone for what they did, but still more for what they dreamed of? The man who is not controlled by sentiment betrays his friends, sells his vote, is a traitor to his country, or wrecks himself, body and soul, with immoralities; for nothing but sentiment prevents any of these things. The sense of honor is pure sentiment. The sentiment of loyalty is the only thing that makes truth and honesty desirable, or a vote a non-salable commodity.

"Government would be a poor affair without sentiment, and is not likely to be damaged by a slightly increased supply." . . .

Would Unsex Women

It will turn women into men.

The differences between men and women are natural; they are not the result of disfranchisement. The fact that all men have equal rights before the law does not wipe out natural differences of character and temperament between man and man. Why should it wipe out the natural differences between men and women? The women of England, Scotland, Canada, Yucatan, Ireland, Australia, New Zealand, the Scandinavian countries and our own equal suffrage States are not perceptibly different in looks or manners from women elsewhere, although they have been voting for years. . . .

Suffrage and Feminism

Suffrage is a branch of Feminism and Feminism includes free love.

Feminism merely means the general movement for woman's rights. The word is used in this sense in England and Europe, and is coming into use in America. There is no more authority for saying that Feminism means free love than that the woman's rights movement means free love—an accusation often made against it without warrant. Mrs. Beatrice Forbes Robertson Hale (a strong opponent of free love) says in her book, "What Women Want":

"Feminism is that part of the progress of democratic freedom which applies to women. It is a century-old struggle conducted by large groups of people in different parts of the world to bring about the removal of all artificial barriers to the physical, mental, moral and economic development of the female half of the race."

In this sense the woman suffrage movement, of course, is a part of it.

Suffrage and Marriage

Suffragists and Feminists are the enemies of marriage and the home.

The National American Woman Suffrage Association at its annual convention in Washington in December, 1915, passed the following resolution by a unanimous vote:

"That we believe the home is the foundation of the State; we believe in the sanctity of the marriage relation; and, furthermore, we believe that woman's ballot will strengthen the power of the home, and sustain the dignity and sacredness of marriage; and we denounce as a gross slander the charges made by opponents of equal suffrage that its advocates as a class entertain opinions to the contrary." . . .

IV. A Senatorial Response to Militancy

The suffrage movement was dominated by the National American Woman Suffrage Association. In 1913 an activist faction developed in the organization under the leadership of Alice Paul, who became acquainted with militancy while studying in England and taking part in the drive for the vote by English women. Once back in the United States she became chairman of the National Association's Congressional Committee, and to concentrate upon the passage of a federal amendment she organized the Congressional Union. The C.U. later broke with the national organization and became the Woman's party.

It was the aim of Miss Paul and her followers to demonstrate through parades, and later, acts of civil disobedience, the injustice of the government in not permitting women to vote. They opposed President Wilson and the Democratic party in the 1916 election because they felt Wilson and the Democrats had not done enough to further the aims of the suffragists. When Wilson and his party were returned to office and nothing was done immediately about woman's suffrage, the Woman's party began to picket the White House. This picketing eventually led to disturbances caused by angry antisuffragists, but the militants were held responsible and many were sentenced to jail terms ranging from six days to six months.

The militancy of these women focused attention on the issue, and when they went on hunger strikes in the workhouses and jails, and in turn were force-fed by the jail officials, they became martyrs for the cause. But martyrs or not, the Senate was quick to denounce their actions and several sympathetic senators disassociated themselves from the violence that surrounded them.

In the following debates Senator James Reed of Missouri condemns the actions of the militants. How does his position concerning the rights of the Woman's party to express its discontent foreshadow later arguments against the use of militancy by any group to bring about reforms in American society?

AUGUST 8, 1918

Mr. McKELLAR. Mr. President, several days ago there occurred here in the city what seems to me was an unseemly protest on the part of the organization known as the National Woman's Party. In this protest, published on their banners and exhibited in one of our parks, it is said:

> We protest against the continued disfranchisement of American women, for which the President of the United States is responsible.
> We deplore the weakness of the President in permitting the Senate to line itself with the Prussian Reichstag by denying democracy to the people.

Congressional Record, August 8, 1918, pp. 9211, 9213–14.

Mr. President, this criticism of the President is so unfair and unjust and untrue that I think it ought to be condemned by everyone. I am, as everyone knows, a strong advocate of woman suffrage. I voted for the national amendment while I was a Member of the House. I believe in it thoroughly. I am going to vote for it again when it comes up in the Senate. This kind of criticism coming from any body of our women seems to me to be very hurtful, indeed, to the cause of suffrage. It is an uncalled-for and wanton insult to the man who is doing more for the suffrage amendment than perhaps anyone else in this country. . . .

Mr. SMOOT. If the Senator will permit me just a word——

Mr. McKELLAR. Of course.

Mr. SMOOT. Mr. President, I, like the Senator from Tennessee, am heartily in favor of woman suffrage and have so expressed myself many times on the floor of the Senate, but I really can not approve of many of the demonstrations made in the past or the one made day before yesterday by the members of the National Woman's Party. I think the Senator in making the request is magnifying this unfortunate occurrence. I do not believe Tuesday's demonstration would have taken place if the papers would ignore such actions. I believe, with the Senator from Colorado (Mr. THOMAS), that the principal object of these demonstrations is to get publicity. I want to say to those good women that they are not advancing the cause of woman suffrage one iota, but in my opinion such actions as have taken place in the past have proven positively harmful.

I have tried to harmonize their actions with their seeming desire for early action on the resolution, and from my point of view it seems to me that there can be but one of two conclusions: Either the securing of the object referred to by the Senator from Colorado or they are not prepared for the passage of the resolution for some unknown reason.

I hope, Mr. President, these un-American demonstrations will cease, for the American people are not convinced of the righteousness of any cause by any such actions. I am ready at any time to do all in my power to bring the suffrage resolution to a vote in the Senate, and I also say that I do not believe that such actions as have taken place in the past will gain one single, solitary vote, and, if I am to judge, they will affect adversely the final result. I mean any action which will bring an early vote and a successful vote for the resolution. . . .

Mr. REED. Mr. President, "here endeth the first lesson." What a singular thing it is to find two advocates of a cause praying that the newspapers will not mention the conduct of the leaders of the cause! . . .

There are some things we expect of the women that are not demanded of men, and, thank God, they have performed those duties through all the ages with a fidelity and devotion that is sublime beyond description. But they are the duties of the women. They have kept the home. There are some women today who think that that is an ignoble calling. Just in proportion as there are such women the demonstration is the more complete that those women at least never ought to be permitted to vote. The woman who thinks that the keeping of the home is beneath her and beneath her sex is not fit to vote and is not fit for anything else. It is the noblest attribute of humanity. The mothers who bore us are today the highest ideals of our souls.

There are some differences between men and women that were ordained by the Almighty and that all the cranks and agitators of earth can never remove. This is true whether the agitator appears in the form of a petticoat virago whose conduct is such that the friends of woman suffrage beg that the newspapers will no longer mention it, or whether the agitator belongs to that type of male or female who thinks that all the world must be revolutionized; everything turned upside down; that thinks all change means progress. . . .

I wonder who are the leaders of this movement! If you want me to name the real leaders of it, I will say this: For some five or six or seven or eight or nine years, perhaps even longer than that, there has been a general state of unrest throughout the world. It has manifested itself in this country and in other lands. . . .

The demands of the agitators have varied in degree, but fundamentally their purpose was to undermine the confidence of the people in law, in courts, and in government. The vile fruitage of that sort of teaching has been manifested in many places.

I recently read a pronunciamento of the Socialist Party, and I intend to pay more particular attention to it in the near future. It is enough to say that their real doctrines, if they were carried into effect, would dismantle the United States Navy, dissolve the United States Army, and leave us with Germany at our throats, as the action of the Bolsheviki left Russia with Germany her master.

This bolshevism of Russia exists in our own country and in England—in every country under a different name. Fundamentally it is a warfare upon the precepts of civilization, on property rights, on government of law, upon the orderly course of justice. The propaganda basically denounces the existing order and demands a change in everything that is.

Because of that undertow, the woman-suffrage movement has gained its great force. People who have been taught to distrust all that is are willing to accept any change that is offered. So they say women should vote. If you ask them what wrongs women have suffered and you can get a concrete statement of the wrong, you can invariably demonstrate that the wrong does not exist or that it is not the result of a refusal of the right to vote.

If you ask them what reforms they propose to work, they are likely to point to the glorious laws of certain suffrage States. But you can invariably point to nonsuffrage States that have adopted the same reforms years before they were adopted in the suffrage States. If you ask them what particular thing they propose to do, the only answer you get, in the long run, is that "they propose to vote," and when you ask them what they propose to do with that vote they answer that "they propose to vote."

When you ask them, then, why they are not willing to go into the various States and ask the people of those States to amend their constitution or their laws giving them the right to vote in that particular State, what is their answer? They answer that they do not want to go to that much trouble. The cold truth of the matter is they very well understand that unless they can force suffrage upon the States the majority of whose people do not want suffrage they will not obtain the right to vote in certain States.

For Further Reading

The history of woman's suffrage in the United States can be found in Carrie Chapman Catt and Nettie Rogers Shuler's *Woman Suffrage and Politics* (1926); Eleanor Flexner's *Century of Struggle: The Woman's Rights Movement in the United States* (1959); Aileen S. Kraditor's *The Ideas of the Woman Suffrage Movement: 1890–1920* (1965); and the six-volume *History of Woman Suffrage* (1881–1922), edited at different times by Elizabeth Cady Stanton, Susan B. Anthony, Matilda J. Gage, and Ida H. Harper. Quite pertinent to the movement are William L. O'Neill's *Everyone Was Brave** (1971) and *The Woman Movement** (1971).

Biographies of the leading women in the movement are: Jane Adams, *A Centennial Reader* (1960); Katharine Anthony, *Susan B. Anthony: Her Personal History and Her Era* (1954); Elinor Rice Hays, *Morning Star: A Biography of Lucy Stone* (1961); Alma Lutz, *Created Equal: Elizabeth Cady Stanton* (1940); Mary Gray Peck, *Carrie Chapman Catt* (1944); and Theodore Stanton and Harriet Stanton Blatch, *Elizabeth Cady Stanton* (1922). An excellent autobiography is Maud Wood Park's *Front Door Lobby* (1960).

The history of the militant Constitutional Union and Woman's party is enthusiastically portrayed in Inez Haynes Irwin's *The Story of the Woman's Party* (1921) and Doris Stevens' *Jailed for Freedom* (1920).

*Paperbound edition available.

8. Neutrality: What Is the Price of Peace?

On January 22, 1917, President Woodrow Wilson declared in a speech before a joint session of Congress that the European powers must accept "peace without victory" and bring to a close the terrible war that had been raging in Europe since 1914. Seventy-eight days later, on April 6, the Congress passed a resolution declaring war on the German Imperial Government. President Wilson, whose followers had campaigned for his reelection in 1916 on the slogan "He kept us out of the war," felt compelled to state in his war message on April 2: "the day has come when America is privileged to spend her blood and might for the principles that gave her birth and happiness and the peace which she has treasured."

The President believed the war had been thrust upon America by the criminal actions of the German government. In May 1915 the Germans had sunk the *Lusitania*, with the loss of 128 American lives. They later pledged to discontinue such actions, but with the sinking of the *Sussex* (March 1916) they resumed their submarine warfare. When the United States threatened to sever diplomatic relations the Germans renewed their promise to restrict submarine warfare (the "Sussex Pledge," May 1916), but by January 1917 the Germans were becoming desperate to break the British blockade of German ports. On January 31 Germany broke its pledge and began sinking all ships on sight within a prescribed war zone. The American response was to sever diplomatic relations with the German government. With the disclosure of the famous Zimmermann Note (February) and a successful revolution against the Czarist government in Russia (March), Wilson became convinced that the war in Europe was a life-and-death struggle of the democracies against the autocracies, and the Americans had to choose sides. On April 6, 1917, the United States entered the war "to make the world itself at last free."

Core Documents

"The Right Is More Precious Than Peace. . . ."

WOODROW WILSON

President Wilson's anguished conclusion that the United States had to enter the war had been reached by late March 1917. He had tried since 1914, by offers of mediation and by following an official policy of neutrality, to either end the war or at least keep the United States out of it, but his policies and his offers failed. In reading Wilson's speech note why he believed:

- *American neutrality had failed.*
- *armed neutrality was impracticable.*
- *the United States could not overlook the most recent violations of its neutrality.*
- *America was fighting the German government, not the German people.*
- *the fate of western civilization demanded American participation in the war.*

APRIL 2, 1917

I have called the Congress into extraordinary session because there are serious, very serious, choices of policy to be made, and made immediately, which it was neither right nor constitutionally permissible that I should assume the responsibility of making.

On the third of February last I officially laid before you the extraordinary announcement of the Imperial German Government that on and after the first day of February it was its purpose to put aside all restraints of law or of humanity and use its submarines to sink every vessel that sought to approach either the ports of Great Britain and Ireland or the western coasts of Europe or any of the ports controlled by the enemies of Germany within the Mediterranean. That had seemed to be the object of the German submarine warfare

Woodrow Wilson, *Public Papers*, ed. Ray S. Baker and William E. Dodd (New York: Harper's, 1925–27), III, pp. 6–16.

earlier in the war, but since April of last year the Imperial Government had somewhat restrained the commanders of its undersea craft in conformity with its promise then given to us that passenger boats should not be sunk and that due warning would be given to all other vessels which its submarines might seek to destroy, when no resistance was offered or escape attempted, and care taken that their crews were given at least a fair chance to save their lives in their open boats. The precautions taken were meager and haphazard enough, as was proved in distressing instance after instance in the progress of the cruel and unmanly business, but a certain degree of restraint was observed. The new policy has swept every restriction aside. Vessels of every kind, whatever their flag, their character, their cargo, their destination, their errand, have been ruthlessly sent to the bottom without warning and without thought of help or mercy for those on board, the vessels of friendly neutrals along with those of belligerents. Even hospital ships and ships carrying relief to the sorely bereaved and stricken people of Belgium, though the latter were provided with safe conduct through the proscribed areas by the German Government itself and were distinguished by unmistakable marks of identity, have been sunk with the same reckless lack of compassion or of principle.

I was for a little while unable to believe that such things would in fact be done by any government that had hitherto subscribed to the humane practices of civilized nations. International law had its origin in the attempt to set up some law which would be respected and observed upon the seas, where no nation had right of dominion and where lay the free highways of the world. By painful stage after stage has that law been built up, with meager enough results, indeed, after all was accomplished that could be accomplished, but always with a clear view, at least, of what the heart and conscience of mankind demanded. This minimum of right the German Government has swept aside under the plea of retaliation and necessity and because it had no weapons which it could use at sea except these which it is impossible to employ as it is employing them without throwing to the winds all scruples of humanity or of respect for the understandings that were supposed to underlie the inter-course of the world. I am not now thinking of the loss of property involved, immense and serious as that is, but only of the wanton and wholesale destruc-tion of the lives of non-combatants, men, women, and children, engaged in pursuits which have always, even in the darkest periods of modern history, been deemed innocent and legitimate. Property can be paid for; the lives of peaceful and innocent people cannot be. The present German submarine war-fare against commerce is a warfare against mankind.

It is a war against all nations. American ships have been sunk, American lives taken, in ways which it has stirred us very deeply to learn of, but the ships and people of other neutral and friendly nations have been sunk and over-whelmed in the waters in the same way. There has been no discrimination. The challenge is to all mankind. Each nation must decide for itself how it will meet it. The choice we make for ourselves must be made with a moderation of counsel and a temperateness of judgment befitting our character and our motives as a nation. We must put excited feeling away. Our motive will not be revenge or the victorious assertion of the physical might of the nation, but only the vindication of right, of human right, of which we are only a single champion.

When I addressed the Congress on the twenty-sixth of February last I thought that it would suffice to assert our neutral rights with arms, our right to use the seas against unlawful interference, our right to keep our people safe against unlawful violence. But armed neutrality, it now appears, is impracticable. Because submarines are in effect outlaws when used as the German submarines have been used against merchant shipping, it is impossible to defend ships against their attacks as the law of nations has assumed that merchantmen would defend themselves against privateers or cruisers, visible craft giving chase upon the open sea. It is common prudence in such circumstances, grim necessity indeed, to endeavor to destroy them before they have shown their own intention. They must be dealt with upon sight, if dealt with at all. The German Government denies the right of neutrals to use arms at all within the areas of the sea which it has proscribed, even in the defense of rights which no modern publicist has ever before questioned their right to defend. The intimation is conveyed that the armed guards which we have placed on our merchant ships will be treated as beyond the pale of law and subject to be dealt with as pirates would be. Armed neutrality is ineffectual enough at best; in such circumstances and in the face of such pretensions it is worse than ineffectual: it is likely only to produce what it was meant to prevent; it is practically certain to draw us into the war without either the rights or the effectiveness of belligerents. There is one choice we cannot make, we are incapable of making: we will not choose the path of submission and suffer the most sacred rights of our Nation and our people to be ignored or violated. The wrongs against which we now array ourselves are no common wrongs; they cut to the very roots of human life.

With a profound sense of the solemn and even tragical character of the step I am taking and of the grave responsibilities which it involves, but in unhesitating obedience to what I deem my constitutional duty, I advise that the Congress declare the recent course of the Imperial German Government to be in fact nothing less than war against the government and people of the United States; that it formally accept the status of belligerent which has thus been thrust upon it; and that it take immediate steps not only to put the country in a more thorough state of defense but also to exert all its power and employ all its resources to bring the Government of the German Empire to terms and end the war.

What this will involve is clear. It will involve the utmost practicable coöperation in counsel and action with the governments now at war with Germany, and, as incident to that, the extension to those governments of the most liberal financial credits, in order that our resources may so far as possible be added to theirs. . . .

We have no quarrel with the German people. We have no feelings towards them but one of sympathy and friendship. It was not upon their impulse that their government acted in entering this war. It was not with their previous knowledge or approval. It was a war determined upon as wars used to be determined upon in the old, unhappy days when peoples were nowhere consulted by their rulers and wars were provoked and waged in the interest of dynasties or of little groups of ambitious men who were accustomed to use their fellow men as pawns and tools. Self-governed nations do not fill their neighbor states with spies or set the course of intrigue to bring about some critical posture of affairs which will give them an opportunity to strike and make conquest. Such designs can be successfully worked out only under cover and where no one has the right to ask questions. Cunningly contrived plans of deception or aggression, carried, it may be, from generation to generation, can be worked out and kept from the light only within the privacy of courts or behind the carefully guarded confidences of a narrow and privileged class. They are happily impossible where public opinion commands and insists upon full information concerning all the nation's affairs.

A steadfast concert for peace can never be maintained except by a partnership of democratic nations. No autocratic government could be trusted to keep faith within it or observe its covenants. It must be a league of honor, a partnership of opinion. Intrigue would eat its vitals away; the plottings of inner circles who could plan what they would and render account to no one would be a corruption seated at its very heart. Only free peoples can hold their purpose and their honor steady to a common end and prefer the interests of mankind to any narrow interest of their own.

Does not every American feel that assurance has been added to our hope for the future peace of the world by the wonderful and heartening things that have been happening within the last few weeks in Russia? Russia was known by those who knew it best to have been always in fact democratic at heart, in all the vital habits of her thought, in all the intimate relationships of her people that spoke their natural instinct, their habitual attitude towards life. The autocracy that crowned the summit of her political structure, long as it had stood and terrible as was the reality of its power, was not in fact Russian in origin, character, or purpose; and now it has been shaken off and the great, generous Russian people have been added in all their naïve majesty and might to the forces that are fighting for freedom in the world, for justice, and for peace. Here is a fit partner for a League of Honor.

One of the things that has served to convince us that the Prussian autocracy was not and could never be our friend is that from the very outset of the present war it has filled our unsuspecting communities and even our offices of government with spies and set criminal intrigues everywhere afoot against our national unity of counsel, our peace within and without, our industries and our commerce. Indeed, it is now evident that its spies were here even before the war began; and it is unhappily not a matter of conjecture but a fact proved in our courts of justice that the intrigues which have more than once come perilously near to disturbing the peace and dislocating the industries of the country have been carried on at the instigation, with the support, and even under the personal direction of official agents of the Imperial Government accredited to the Government of the United States. Even in checking these things and trying to extirpate them we have sought to put the most generous interpretation possible upon them because we knew that their source lay not in any hostile feeling or purpose of the German people towards us (who were no doubt as ignorant of them as we ourselves were), but only in the selfish designs of a Government that did what it pleased and told its people nothing. But they have played their part in serving to convince us at last that that Government entertains no real friendship for us and means to act against our peace and security at its convenience. That it means to stir up enemies against us at our very doors the intercepted note to the German Minister at Mexico City is eloquent evidence.

We are accepting this challenge of hostile purpose because we know that in such a Government, following such methods, we can never have a friend; and that in the presence of its organized power, always lying in wait to accomplish we know not what purpose, there can be no assured security for the democratic Governments of the world. We are now about to accept gage of battle with this natural foe to liberty and shall, if necessary, spend the whole force of the Nation to check and nullify its pretensions and its power. We are glad, now that we see the facts with no veil of false pretense about them, to fight thus for the ultimate peace of the world and for the liberation of its peoples, the German peoples included: for the rights of nations great and small and the privilege of men everywhere to choose their way of life and of obedience. The world must be made safe for democracy. Its peace must be planted upon the tested foundations of political liberty. We have no selfish ends to serve. We desire no conquest, no dominion. We seek no indemnities for ourselves, no material compensation for the sacrifices we shall freely make. We are but one of the champions of the rights of mankind. We shall be satisfied when those rights have been made as secure as the faith and the freedom of nations can make them.

Just because we fight without rancor and without selfish object, seeking nothing for ourselves but what we shall wish to share with all free peoples, we shall, I feel confident, conduct our operations as belligerents without passion and ourselves observe with proud punctilio the principles of right and of fair play we profess to be fighting for. . . .

It will be all the easier for us to conduct ourselves as belligerents in a high spirit of right and fairness because we act without animus, not in enmity towards a people or with the desire to bring any injury or disadvantage upon them, but only in armed opposition to an irresponsible government which has thrown aside all considerations of humanity and of right and is running amuck. We are, let me say again, the sincere friends of the German people, and shall desire nothing so much as the early reëstablishment of intimate relations of mutual advantage between us,—however hard it may be for them, for the time being, to believe that this is spoken from our hearts. We have borne with their present Government through all these bitter months because of that friendship, —exercising a patience and forbearance which would otherwise have been impossible. We shall, happily, still have an opportunity to prove that friendship in our daily attitude and actions towards the millions of men and women of German birth and native sympathy who live amongst us and share our life, and we shall be proud to prove it towards all who are in fact loyal to their neighbors and to the Government in the hour of test. They are, most of them, as true and loyal Americans as if they had never known any other fealty or allegiance. They will be prompt to stand with us in rebuking and restraining the few who may be of a different mind and purpose. If there should be disloyalty, it will be dealt with with a firm hand of stern repression; but, if it lifts its head at all, it will lift it only here and there and without countenance except from a lawless and malignant few.

It is a distressing and oppressive duty, Gentlemen of the Congress, which I have performed in thus addressing you. There are, it may be, many months of fiery trial and sacrifice ahead of us. It is a fearful thing to lead this great peaceful people into war, into the most terrible and disastrous of all wars, civilization itself seeming to be in the balance. But the right is more precious than peace, and we shall fight for the things which we have always carried nearest our hearts,—for democracy, for the right of those who submit to authority to have a voice in their own Governments, for the rights and liberties of small nations, for a universal dominion of right by such a concert of free peoples as shall bring peace and safety to all nations and make the world itself at last free. To such a task we can dedicate our lives and our fortunes, everything that we are and everything that we have, with the pride of those who know that the day has come when America is privileged to spend her blood and her might for the principles that gave her birth and happiness and the peace which she has treasured. God helping her, she can do no other.

Senator La Follette Condemns President Wilson's Request for War

ROBERT M. LA FOLLETTE

Although President Wilson quickly won the support of Congress and the nation, prominent dissenters challenged his position. Perhaps the most eloquent leader of the opposition was Robert M. La Follette, who had been one of the first progressive leaders of national stature in the Republican party. Born in a log cabin, he had become to many of his followers the "Lincoln from Wisconsin." He served in the House of Representatives from 1885 to 1891 and was elected

Congressional Record, April 4, 1917, pp. 225–28.

governor of Wisconsin in 1901. During his governorship La Follette successfully brought about a program of tax reform, regulation of railroads, and provisions for more direct legislative processes. In 1905 he was elected to the first of his three senatorial terms.

As the end of his first term approached he organized the progressive wing of the Republican party into the National Progressive Republican League. The League worked with other progressive groups for such reforms as the direct election of senators and direct primaries. When the European war broke out in 1914, La Follette argued against American participation because he believed it would only benefit the rich of Wall Street. He was hostile to the British cause and early in 1917 filibustered in the Senate against the arming of American merchant ships. The following speech was delivered by La Follette on April 4, 1917, during the debate over the presidential request for a declaration of war against Germany.

In studying La Follette's speech note what he believed to be:
- *the role of the loyal opposition in Congress.*
- *the groups that would be most harmed by participation in the war.*
- *his best arguments against Wilson's request for a declaration of war.*
- *the German position on neutrality.*
- *the character of Britain and her policies.*
- *Wilson's failure to be neutral.*

APRIL 4, 1917

Mr. President, let me make another suggestion. It is this: That a minority in one Congress—mayhap a small minority in one Congress—protesting, exercising the rights which the Constitution confers upon a minority, may really be representing the majority opinion of the country, and if, exercising the right that the Constitution gives them, they succeed in defeating for the time being the will of the majority, they are but carrying out what was in the mind of the framers of the Constitution; that you may have from time to time in a legislative body a majority in numbers that really does not represent the principle of democracy; and that if the question could be deferred and carried to the people it would be found that a minority was the real representative of public opinion. So, Mr. President, it was that they wrote into the Constitution that a President—that one man—may put his judgment against the will of a majority not only in one branch of the Congress but in both branches of the Congress; that he may defeat the measure that they have agreed upon and may set his one single judgment above the majority judgment of the Congress. That seems, when you look at it nakedly, to be in violation of the principle that the majority shall rule; and so it is. Why is that power given? It is one of those checks provided by the wisdom of the fathers to prevent the majority from abusing the power that they chance to have, when they do not reflect the real judgment, the opinion, the will of the majority of the people that constitute the sovereign power of the democracy.

The poor, sir, who are the ones called upon to rot in the trenches, have no organized power, have no press to voice their will upon this question of peace or war; but, oh, Mr. President, at some time they will be heard. I hope and I believe they will be heard in an orderly and a peaceful way. I think they may be heard from before long. I think, sir, if we take this step, when the people to-day who are staggering under the burden of supporting families at the present prices of the necessities of life find those prices multiplied, when they are raised a hundred per cent, or 200 percent, as they will be quickly, aye, sir, when beyond that those who pay taxes come to have their taxes doubled and again doubled to pay the interest, on the nontaxable bonds held by Morgan and his combinations, which have been issued to meet this war, there will come an awakening; they will have their day and they will be heard. It will be as certain and as inevitable as the return of the tides, and as resistless, too. . . .

In his address of April 2 the President says:

> Since April of last year the Imperial Government had somewhat re-strained the commands of its undersea craft in conformity with its prom-ise then given to us that passenger boats should not be sunk, and that due warning would be given to all other vessels which its submarines might seek to destroy when no resistance was offered or escape at-tempted, and care taken that their crews were given at least a fair chance to save their lives in their open boats.

Beside that statement I wish to place exactly what the German Govern-ment did say:

> The German Government, moreover, is prepared to do its utmost to confine the operations of war for the rest of its duration to the fighting forces of the belligerents, thereby also insuring the freedom of the seas, a principle upon which the German Government believes now as before, to be in agreement with the Government of the United States.
> The German Government guided by this idea, notifies, the Govern-ment of the United States that the German naval forces have received the following orders: In accordance with the general principles of visit and search and destruction of merchant vessels recognized by interna-tional law, such vessels, both within and without the area declared as naval war zone, shall not be sunk without warning and without saving human lives, unless these ships attempt to escape or offer resistance.
> But neutrals cannot expect that Germany, forced to fight for her existence, shall, for the sake of neutral interest, restrict the use of an effective weapon if her enemy is permitted to continue to apply at will methods of warfare violating the rules of international law. Such a de-mand would be incompatible with the character of neutrality, and the German Government is convinced that the Government of the United States does not think of making such a demand, knowing that the Gov-

ernment of the United States has repeatedly declared that it is determined to restore the principle of the freedom of the seas, from whatever quarter it is violated.

Accordingly the German Government is confident that in consequence of the new orders issued to its naval forces, the Government of the United States will now also consider all impediments removed which may have been in the way of a mutual cooperation toward the restoration of the freedom of the seas during the war, as suggested in the note of July 23, 1915, and it does not doubt that the Government of the United States will now demand and insist that the British Government shall forthwith observe the rules of international law universally recognized before the war as they are laid down in the notes presented by the Government of the United States to the British Government on December 28, 1914, and November 5, 1915. Should the steps taken by the Government of the United States not attain the object it desires, to have the laws of humanity followed by all belligerent nations, the German Government would then be facing a new situation, in which it must reserve itself complete liberty of decision. (May 4, 1916).

It must be perfectly apparent therefore that the promise, so called, of the German Government was conditioned upon England's being brought to obedience of international law in her naval warfare. Since no one contends that England was brought to conduct her naval operations in accordance with international law, and even the poor protests our Government has lodged against her show that she has not done so, was it quite fair to lay before the country a statement which implies that Germany had made an unconditional promise which she has dishonorably violated?

This is a time of all times when the public mind should be calm, not inflamed; when accuracy of statement is vitally essential to presenting the issues to the Congress and to the people of the country.

In his message of April 2 the President says:

I was for a little while unable to believe that such things (referring to German submarine methods of warfare) would in fact be done by any Government that had heretofore subscribed to the humane practices of civilized nations. International law had its origin in the attempt to set up some law which would be respected and observed upon the sea, where no nation had right of dominion and where lay the free highways of the world. By painful stage after stage has that law been built up with meager enough results indeed, after all was accomplished that could be accomplished, but always with a clear view at least of what the heart and conscience of mankind demanded.

The recognition by the President that Germany had always heretofore subscribed to the humane practices of civilized nations is a most important statement. Does it not suggest a question as to why it is that Germany has departed from those practices in the present war? What the President had so admirably stated about international law and the painful stage by which it has been builded up is absolutely true. But in this connection would it not be well to say also that it was England, not Germany, who refused to obey the declaration of London, which represented the most humane ideas and was the best statement of the rules of international law as applied to naval warfare? Keep that in mind. Would it not have been fair to say, and to keep in mind, that Germany offered to abide by those principles and England refused: that in response to our request Germany offered to cease absolutely from the use of submarines in what we characterized an unlawful manner if England would cease from equally palpable and cruel violations of international law in her conduct of naval warfare?

The President in his message of April 2 says:

The present German warfare against commerce is a warfare against mankind. It is a war against all nations.

Again referring to Germany's warfare he says:

There has been no discrimination. The challenge is to all mankind.

Is it not a little peculiar that if Germany's warfare is against all nations the United States is the only nation that regards it necessary to declare war on that account? If it is true, as the President says, that "there has been no discrimination," that Germany has treated every neutral as she has treated us, is it not peculiar that no other of the great nations of the earth seem to regard Germany's conduct in this war as a cause for entering into it? Are we the only nation jealous of our rights? Are we the only nation insisting upon the protection of our citizens? Does not the strict neutrality maintained on the part of all the other nations of the earth suggest that possibly there is a reason for their action, and that that reason is that Germany's conduct under the circumstances does not merit from any nation which is determined to preserve its neutrality a declaration of war?

Norway, Sweden, the Netherlands, Switzerland, Denmark, Spain and all the great Republics of South America are quite as interested in this subject as we are, yet they have refused to join with us in a combination against Germany. I venture to suggest also that the nations named, and probably others, have somewhat better right to be heard than we, for by refusing to sell war material and munitions to any of the belligerents they have placed themselves in a position where the suspicion which attaches to us a desire for war profits can not attach them. . . .

In his message of April 2, the President said:

> We have no quarrel with the German people—it was not upon their
> impulse that their Government acted in entering this war; it was not with
> their previous knowledge or approval.

Again he says:

> We are, let me say again, sincere friends of the German people and shall
> desire nothing so much as the early reestablishment of infinite relations
> of mutual advantage between us.

At least the German people, then, are not outlaws. What is the thing the
President asks us to do to these German people of whom he speaks so highly
and whose sincere friend he declares us to be?

Here is what he declares we shall do in this war. We shall undertake he
says—

> The utmost practicable cooperation in council and action with the Gov-
> ernment now at war with Germany, and as an incident to that, the
> extension to the Governments of the most liberal financial credits in
> order that our resources may, so far as possible, be added to theirs.

"Practicable cooperation!" Practicable cooperation with England and her
allies in starving to death the old men and women, the children, the sick and
the maimed of Germany. The thing we are asked to do is the thing I have
stated. It is idle to talk of a war upon a government only. We are leagued in
this war, or it is the President's proposition that we shall be leagued, with the
hereditary enemies of Germany. Any war with Germany, or any other country
for that matter, would be bad enough, but there are not words strong enough
to voice my protest against the proposed combination with the ententé allies.
When we cooperate with those Governments we endorse their methods, we
indorse the violations of international law by Great Britian, we indorse the
shameful methods of warfare against which we have again and again protested
in this war; we indorse her purpose to wreak upon the German people the
animosities which for years her people have been taught to cherish against
Germany; finally when the end comes, whatever it may be, we find ourselves
in cooperation with our ally, Great Britain, and if we can not resist now the
pressure she is exerting to carry us into the war, how can we hope to resist,
then, the thousandfold greater pressure she will exert to bend us to her purposes and compel compliance with her demands? . . .

Just a word of comment more upon one of the points in the President's
address. He says that this is a war "for the things which we have always carried

nearest to our hearts—for democracy, for the right of those who submit to authority to have a voice in their own government." In many places throughout the address is this exalted sentiment given expression.

It is a sentiment peculiarly calculated to appeal to American hearts and, when accompanied by acts consistent with it, is certain to receive our support; but in this same connection, and strangely enough, the President says that we have become convinced that the German Government as it now exists— "Prussian autocracy" he calls it—can never again maintain friendly relations with us. His expression is that "Prussian autocracy was not and could never be our friend," and repeatedly throughout the address the suggestion is made that if the German people would overturn their Government it would probably be the way to peace. So true is this that the dispatches from London all hailed the message of the President as sounding the death knell of Germany's Government.

But the President proposes alliance with Great Britain, which however liberty-loving its people, is a hereditary monarchy, with a hereditary ruler, with a hereditary House of Lords, with a hereditary landed system, with a limited and restricted suffrage for one class and a multiplied suffrage power for another, and with grinding industrial conditions for all the wageworkers. The President has not suggested that we make our support of Great Britain conditional to her granting home rule to Ireland, or Egypt, or India. We rejoice in the establishment of a democracy in Russia, but it will hardly be contended that if Russia was still an autocratic Government we would not be asked to enter this alliance with her just the same. Italy and lesser powers of Europe, Japan in the Orient; in fact, all of the countries with whom we are to enter into alliance, except France and newly revolutionized Russia, are still of the old order—and it will be generally conceded that no one of them has done as much for its people in the solution of municipal problems and in securing social and industrial reforms as Germany.

Is it not a remarkable democracy which leagues itself with allies already far overmatching in strength of the German nation and holds out to such beleaguered nation the hope of peace only at the price of giving up their Government? I am not talking now of the merits or demerits of any government, but I am speaking of a profession of democracy that is linked in action with the most brutal and domineering use of autocratic power. Are the people of this country being so well represented in this war movement that we need to go abroad to give other people control of their governments? Will the President and the supporters of this war bill submit it to a vote of the people before the declaration of war goes into effect? Until we are willing to do that, it illy becomes us to offer as an excuse for our entry into the war the unsupported claim that this war was forced upon the German people by their Government "without their previous knowledge or approval."

Who has registered the knowledge or approval of the American people of the course this Congress is called upon to take in declaring war upon

Germany? Submit the question to the people, you who support it. You who support it dare not do it, for you know that by a vote of more than ten to one the American people as a body would register their declaration against it.

Discussion Starters

1.   Evaluate Senator La Follette's response to President Wilson's concept of moral diplomacy. What evidence did he present to support his criticism of the President's policies?

2.   How valid was La Follette's suggestion that, as a minority voice in Congress, he spoke for a national majority in opposing the war? In what ways have similar situations existed since?

3.   How did President Wilson's explanation for going to war against Germany try to anticipate and answer the arguments voiced two days later by La Follette?

4.   What role should moral judgments play in making foreign policy decisions? What dangers grow out of ignoring moral judgments? What of making too much of them?

Related Documents

I. German Memorandum on Submarine Warfare

In retaliation for the blockade thrown up by Great Britain to prevent war material from neutral sources from reaching Germany, the German government issued in February 1915 a declaration dealing with their use of submarine warfare. What were the likely motives of the German government in issuing this declaration? How do the arguments for submarine warfare used by the German government support or detract from Wilson's and La Follette's assessment of the situation in 1917?

FEBRUARY 4, 1915

Since the beginning of the present war Great Britain has carried on a mercantile warfare against Germany in a way that defies all the principles of interna-

U. S. Department of State, *Papers Relating to the Foreign Relations of the United States, Supplement, 1915* (Washington, D.C.: Government Printing Office, 1928), pp. 96–97.

tional law. It is true the British government has announced in a number of decrees the London declaration concerning naval warfare to be binding on its naval forces, but in reality she has renounced the declaration in its most important particulars, although her own delegates at the London Conference on Naval Warfare had recognized its conclusions to be valid as international law.

The British Government has put a number of articles in the list of contraband which are not or at most only indirectly useful for military purposes and therefore according to the London declaration as well as according to the universally recognized rules of international law may not be designated as contraband. She has further actually abolished the distinction between absolute and relative contraband, inasmuch as she has subjected to capture all articles of relative contraband intended for Germany without reference to the harbor in which they are to be unloaded or to the hostile or peaceful use to which they are to be put.

She does not even hesitate to violate the Paris declaration, as her naval forces have seized on neutral ships German property that was not contraband, in violation of her own desires concerning the London declaration she has further through her naval forces taken from neutral ships numerous Germans liable to military service and has made of them prisoners of war. Finally she has declared the entire North Sea to be an area of war, and if she has not made impossible the passage of neutral shipping through the sea between Scotland and Norway, has rendered it so difficult and so dangerous, that she has to a certain extent effected a blockade of neutral coasts and neutral ports in violation of all international law.

All these measures have the obvious purpose through the illegal paralyzation of legitimate neutral commerce not only to strike at the German military strength, but also at the economic life of Germany and finally through starvation doom the entire population of Germany to destruction.

The neutral powers have generally acquiesced in the steps taken by the English Government, especially they have not succeeded in inducing the British Government to restore the German individuals and property seized in violation of international law. In certain directions they have also aided the British measures, which are irreconcilable with the freedom of the sea, in that they have obviously under the pressure of England hindered by export and transit embargoes the transit of wares for peaceful purposes to Germany. The German Government has in vain called the attention of neutral powers to the fact, that it must face the question of whether it can longer persevere in its hitherto strict observance of the rules of the London declaration, if Great Britain were to continue its course, and the neutral powers were to continue to acquiesce in these violations of neutrality to the detriment of Germany; for her violations of international law Great Britain pleads the vital interest of belligerents as sufficient excuse for every method of warfare. Germany must now appeal to these same vital interests to its regret. It therefore sees itself forced to military measures aimed at England in retaliation against the English procedure. Just as England has designated the area between Scotland and Norway as an area of war, so Germany now declares all the waters surrounding Great Britain and Ireland including the entire English Channel as an area of war, and thus will proceed against the shipping of the enemy.

For this purpose beginning February 18, 1915, it will endeavor to destroy every enemy merchant ship that is found in this area of war without its always being possible to avert the peril, that thus threatens persons and cargoes. Neutrals are therefore warned against further entrusting crews, passengers and wares to such ships. Their attention is tialso called to the fact, that it is advisable for their ships to avoid entering this area, for even though the German naval forces have instructions to avoid violence to neutral ships in so far as they are recognizable, in view of the misuse of neutral flags ordered by the British Government and the contingencies of naval warfare their becoming victims of torpedoes directed against enemy ships cannot always be avoided; at the same time it is specifically noted that shipping north of Shetland Islands in the eastern area of the North Sea and in a strip of at least thirty sea miles in the width along the Netherlands coast is not imperiled. The German Government gives such early notice of these measures, that hostile as well as neutral ships may have time accordingly to adapt their plans for landing at ports in this area of war and may expect that the neutral powers will show no less consideration for the vital interests of Germany than for those of England and will aid in keeping their citizens and the property of the latter from this area. This is the more to be expected, as it must be to the interest of the neutral powers to see this destructive war end as soon as possible.

II. War by Assassination: An Editorial

Germany's use of submarines to blockade Great Britain in 1915 led to one of the most infamous episodes of World War I. On May 7, 1915, the giant Cunard liner Lusitania *was torpedoed by a German submarine, which had an immediate adverse effect on German-American relations. But of possibly more importance, it brought home to the Americans the British-inspired conception of the inhuman Huns, trampling innocent lives beneath their hobnailed boots and drowning women and children with their torpedoes. The effect of the* Lusitania *incident on American public opinion did much to create a pro-British attitude among many Americans.*

The following editorial from the New York Times *is one example of the reaction of the press to the sinking of the* Lusitania. *How does this assessment of German war aims compare with President Wilson's and Senator La Follette's views of German policy?*

New York Times, May 8, 1915. © 1915 by The New York Times Company. Reprinted by permission.

MAY 8, 1915

From the Department of State there must go to the Imperial Government at Berlin a demand that the Germans shall no longer make war like savages drunk with blood, that they shall cease to seek the attainment of their ends by the assassination of non-combatants and neutrals. In the history of wars there is no single deed comparable in its inhumanity and its horror to the destruction, without warning, by German torpedoes of the great steamship Lusitania, with more than 1,800 souls on board and among them more than 100 Americans. Our demand must be made, and it will be heeded unless Germany in her madness would have it understood that she is at war with the whole civilized world. For many hours yesterday the hope was cherished that the passengers and crew of the ship had been saved, but later it was made certain that there had been an appalling loss of life and then there was here full realization of the extreme seriousness of this latest act of barbarity and of its effect upon our relations to the war. It will stir the American people as they have not been stirred since the destruction of the Maine in the harbor of Havana, and Government and people will be united in the resolve that Germany must be called upon to bring her practices into conformity with the usages of civilized warfare.

Germany has wantonly and without provocation sent to their death a large, though as yet unknown, number of Americans. The American passengers aboard the Lusitania were going about their lawful concerns, they were entirely within their right, for no effective and lawfully established blockade annulled their privilege to take passage for England aboard a British ship. Had such a blockade been established even, it would have been a monstrous crime for a German submarine to send the ship to the bottom without warning and without affording an opportunity to save the lives of the ship's company. The commander of the German submarine had a right to destroy the Lusitania, an enemy ship, since it is obvious that he could not with safety have attempted to take her as a prize to a German port, but it has always been the law of war at sea that the passengers and crew of a ship stopped or seized must be taken off before she is sunk. The loss of so great a number of passengers and crew of the Lusitania shows that this humane rule was ruthlessly disregarded by the German Captain. It is an act, therefore, which falls clearly within the scope and intent of our solemn admonition to Germany.

It was on Feb. 10 that our Ambassador at Berlin was instructed to say to the German Government that we could not assent to the policy embodied in its declaration of a war zone about the British Isles and to request that Government "to consider before action is taken the critical situation in respect to the relations between this country and Germany which might arise were the German naval forces . . . to destroy any merchant vessel of the United States or cause the death of American citizens." We further warned Germany that it would be difficult for this Government to view such acts in any other light than as an indefensible violation of neutral rights. . . .

Germany has disregarded that warning. The series of acts . . . which now reaches its culmination in the sending to their death by dastardly assassin methods of a large number of American passengers on the Lusitania. It is a matter of the gravest import for Germany that in this case there can be no disclaimer of responsibility.

The evidence of deliberation, of an intent to destroy this particular ship, is too nearly conclusive to be ignored. Upon the very day the Lusitania sailed the Imperial German Embassy at Washington caused to be published in the newspapers of the country an advertisement warning travelers that ships flying the flag of Great Britain were liable to destruction in the waters about the British Isles and that passengers "sailing in the war zone on ships of Great Britain or her allies do so at their own risk." There were no other warnings. They were not heeded by the passengers who sailed on the Lusitania simply because it was impossible for them to believe that a great civilized nation like Germany would wantonly destroy a merchant ship carrying only peaceable non-combatants. We have learned much about Germany since the war began, much that has shocked the world's sense of humanity, but this frightful deed was held to be within the domain of the incredible until it was perpetrated. It transcends in atrocity anything our Government could have apprehended at the time it issued its warnings.

Now as a necessary sequence of our note of Feb. 10 there must be a further communication to the German Government, and it must be something more than a protest. We must demand that Germany shall not continue to make war on us. We may present the demand with reasonable confidence that Germany will pay heed to it. She has done herself irreparable harm by her procedures in the war, beginning with the devastation of Belgium, and it is harm in its latest dreadful instance without any compensating gain. The Germans cannot advance their cause by forcing the world to perceive and admit that they are a people apart, that they are bent upon making war by methods and practices which civilized nations have long since renounced and condemned and by exhibiting a degree of brutality which is commonly associated with maddness. It is not to be believed that either the German Government or the German people are wholly mad, and the notice we are compelled to take of the destruction of the Lusitania will, we hope, serve to recall them to sense and reason.

They cannot fail to understand the effect this deed will have upon public sentiment in the United States. While there may have been some among us who, up to this moment, were inclined to hold a suspended judgment as to the justifications and procedures of Germany, now the American people will be of one mind. We are proverbially a people not easily aroused to passion, there will now be little of that. The American people will feel that it is their duty to be calm, because the occasion is too serious for indulgence in vain excitement. And happily there is at the head of the nation a man of proved strength and the habitual soberness of his judgment, will resist all promptings to unreasonable or hasty action. But he knows the people who have put him at the head of the nation, he will instinctively know and understand the feeling that pervades the country today, and he will respond to it by taking the firm, wise course which justice, right, and honor demand.

III. An American Company Protests the British Blacklist

THE EDWARD MAURER COMPANY

In December 1915 the British government issued a list of "suspected" neutral ships and companies that were thought to be trading with Germany. This list, with subsequent additions, became known as the "blacklist" and was used by the British to prevent all suspect trading with Germany.

In the following selection the Edward Maurer Company petitioned the Secretary of State for relief from the blacklist of the British government. What were the principles behind the arguments set forth by the Maurer Company? How do these arguments relate to the positions taken by Wilson and La Follette in April 1917?

THE EDWARD MAURER COMPANY, INC., TO THE SECRETARY OF STATE

NEW YORK, *May 3, 1916.*

DEAR SIR: We beg to call your attention to the [action of] various steamship lines for South America in blacklisting a number of large import houses in Montevideo because they are of German origin, which interferes very seriously with our export business. We enclose herewith a circular sent out by the Lamport & Holt Line, advising shippers that hereafter all names must be given and intimating that any house which may be unacceptable to the British Government will be blacklisted.

We have done business for over 40 years with the house of Ernest Quincke, Montevideo, exporting for them large quantities of agricultural and hardware implements, and we now find that the name of this house seems to be on the black list and none of the steamship lines will accept freight for them.

We had a contract with the Houston Line for the steamer *Helenus* sailing on the 13th of May, but they just notified us that they would not receive the freight for this firm. We understand that the Barber Line also, which is an American concern and sending neutral steamers to South America, is in the same combination and refuses to accept freight for this house.

U.S. Department of State, *Papers Relating to the Foreign Relations of the United States, Supplement, 1916* (Washington, D.C.: Government Printing Office, 1929), pp. 383–85.

We always thought that any steamship line touching at this port was a common carrier and, as such, was obliged to accept freight for any consignee except naturally for belligerent countries.

It appears to us that if anything is a "combination in restraint of trade" it is this action of all steamship lines to a certain port in neutral South American countries by which certain old established houses are boycotted and shippers here are prevented from executing orders, and we certainly think there should be relief afforded by the authorities. There must be some way of forcing common carriers that make use of the facilities of this port to take freight for all neutrals in South American countries, and we would thank you to let us know whether we shall seek relief through the courts here in bringing suit against the steamship lines under the Sherman anti-trust law.

Our business has been greatly interfered with by the British Government holding up all our cables and cables sent to us from Java, where we have been buying in the past a large quantity of rubber, but which has now entirely stopped as our correspondents advise us that the British censor has intercepted all cables and will not allow any from us to get through or theirs to come to us. This is a serious loss to us, and as there seems to be no warrant for such interference, we also would like to know what remedy there is for relief.

Another unwarranted interference in our import business with Venezuela is that recently all shippers have been notified in Ciudad Bolivar that all freight passing through for transshipment to Trinidad must be consigned in New York to houses acceptable to the British Government and be consigned to the British Consul, New York. Meanwhile certain houses have also been mentioned as being on the black list, so that business houses in Venezuela are prevented from shipping their goods to New York except with the consent and permission of the British Government.

We can understand why the British Government should interfere with trade with neutral countries in Europe, but when it comes to such interference with South American countries, who have for years been shipping their produce and obtaining their goods from New York, it seems an unwarranted interference with our trade and from which merchants in the United States should be able to obtain relief.

IV. "We Covet Peace, and Shall Preserve It at Any Cost But the Loss of Honor"

WOODROW WILSON

From 1914 to 1917, as the neutralists in Congress became more and more concerned with the American position toward the war, they looked for some way to prevent situations from arising that might bring the United States into the war.

Woodrow Wilson, "Letter to Senator Stone," *Current History,* April 1916, pp. 16–17.

One plan, introduced in Congress as the Gore-McLemore Resolution, would have forbidden American citizens from traveling on any armed ship of any type, passenger or otherwise, of a belligerent. President Wilson believed, however, that such interference by the government in the freedom of its citizens was not in keeping with American democratic ideals. In a letter to Senator William Stone of Missouri he also explained why he believed such a resolution was inconsistent with international law.

What were Wilson's arguments against such restrictions? Why would La Follette agree, but at the same time disagree, with the arguments found in this letter?

APRIL 1916

My Dear Senator: . . .I shall do everything in my power to keep the United States out of war. I think the country will feel no uneasiness about my course in that respect. Through many anxious months I have striven for that object, amidst difficulties more manifold than can have been apparent upon the surface, and so far I have succeeded. I do not doubt that I shall continue to succeed. The course which the Central European Powers have announced their intention of following in the future with regard to undersea warfare seems for the moment to threaten insuperable obstacles, but its apparent meaning is so manifestly inconsistent with explicit assurances recently given us by those powers with regard to their treatment of merchant vessels on the high seas that I must believe that explanations will presently ensue which will put a different aspect upon it. We have had no reason to question their good faith or their fidelity to their promises in the past, and I for one feel confident that we shall have none in the future.

But in any event our duty is clear. No nation, no group of nations, has the right while war is in progress to alter or disregard the principles which all nations have agreed upon in mitigation of the horrors and sufferings of war; and if the clear rights of American citizens should ever unhappily be abridged or denied by any such action we should, it seems to me, have in honor no choice as to what our own course should be.

For my own part, I cannot consent to any abridgment of the rights of American citizens in any respect. The honor and self-respect of the nation are involved. We covet peace, and shall preserve it at any cost but the loss of honor. To forbid our people to exercise their rights for fear we might be called upon to vindicate them would be a deep humiliation indeed. It would be an implicit, all but an explicit, acquiescence in the violation of the rights of mankind everywhere, and of whatever nation or allegiance. It would be a deliberate abdication of our hitherto proud position as spokesmen, even amidst the turmoil of war, for the law and the right. It would make everything this Government has attempted, and everything that it has achieved during this terrible struggle of nations, meaningless and futile.

It is important to reflect that if in this instance we allowed expedience to take the place of principle the door would inevitably be opened to still further concessions. Once accept a single abatement of right, and many other humiliations would certain follow, and the whole fine fabric of international law might crumble under our hands piece by piece. What we are contending for in this matter is of the very essence of the things that have made America a sovereign nation. She cannot yield them without conceding her own impotency as a nation, and making virtual surrender of her independent position among the nations of the world.

I am speaking, my dear Senator, in deep solemnity, without heat, with a clear consciousness of the high responsibilities of my office, and as your sincere and devoted friend. If we should unhappily differ, we shall differ as friends; but where issues so momentous as these are involved we must, just because we are friends, speak our minds without reservation. Faithfully yours,

WOODROW WILSON

V. *War for Justice and Liberty: An Editorial*

The public response to President Wilson's war speech of April 2, 1917, was one of excited patriotism and national determination. The vast majority of the members of Congress and the congressional gallery had cheered the President when he finished his speech, and the cheering continued from the crowds that lined Pennsylvania Avenue as the President rode back to the White House. The reaction from the heartland of the nation was not much different, as is seen in the following editorial from Joseph Pulitzer's St. Louis Post-Dispatch.

Note how this editorial uses Wilson's arguments for war to assure the German population of St. Louis that it was their war as well as the war of Americans of other national origins.

APRIL 3, 1917

The justice of our cause and our high purpose in undertaking war with Germany are set forth with clarity and force in the President's war message.

Indicting the Imperial German Government for violation of our rights, for faithlessness and crimes against civilization and humanity, the President expressed sympathy and good will for the German people. We have no quarrel with the German people, but we have a deadly feud with the treacherous and inhuman German autocracy.

Our purpose is neither gain nor glory, but the defense and establishment of the rights of mankind against aggression and the peace and security of the

St. Louis Post-Dispatch, April 3, 1917.

free peoples of the world against imperial will to conquer. We are fighting for justice, liberty and equitable peace.

All Americans of all origins can join heartily in this warfare. Americans of German origin can with clear conscience and sound heart support the United States in this effort to punish and overthrow the imperial autocracy which oppresses and deceives the German people and misdirects their power. In doing this they are not fighting to crush Germany, but to free Germany. . . .

The democracies of the world are fighting together to wipe brutal and bloody autocracy from the face of the earth, that the earth may be a fit habitation for all men.

For Further Reading

The politics of American neutrality and Woodrow Wilson's decision to bring America into World War I has been the concern of many historians since the end of the war in 1918. Of the many books written on these subjects the most notable are: Karl E. Birnbaum, *Peace Moves and U–Boat Warfare* (1958); John M. Blum, *Woodrow Wilson and the Politics of Morality** (1956); Edward H. Buehrig, *Woodrow Wilson and the Balance of Power* (1955); N. Gordon Levin, Jr., *Woodrow Wilson and World Politics* (1968); Arthur S. Link's three excellent volumes, *Wilson: The Struggle for Neutrality, 1914–1915* (1960), *Wilson: Confusions and Crises, 1915–1916* (1964), and *Wilson: Campaigns for Progressivism and Peace, 1916–1917* (1965); Ernest R. May, *The World War and American Isolation, 1914–1917** (1959); Arno J. Mayer, *The Political Origins of the New Diplomacy** (1959); Walter Millis, *Road to War: America, 1914–1917* (1935); Harley Notter, *The Origins of the Foreign Policy of Woodrow Wilson (1937; reprinted in 1965); Robert E. Osgood, Ideals and Self-Interest in America's Foreign Relations* (1953); Daniel M. Smith, *The Great Departure: The United States and World War I** (1965); and Samuel R. Spencer, Jr., *Decision for War, 1917** (1953; reprinted in 1968).

An account of the American participation in the war can be found in S. L. A. Marshall's *World War I** (1964), while domestic opposition to the war is covered in Horace C. Peterson and Gilbert C. Fite's *Opponents of War, 1917–1918** (1968) and H. N. Scheiber's *The Wilson Administration and Civil Liberties, 1917–1920* (1960).

The use of propaganda by the British to gain American support is described in Horace C. Peterson's *Propaganda for War* (1939; reprinted in 1968), while Anglo-American relationships are amply covered in *The Great Rapprochement: England and the United States, 1895–1914* (1968), by Bradford Perkins. The British involvement with Wilson's decision to go to war is clearly documented in Barbara Tuchman's *The Zimmermann Telegram** (1958).

*Paperbound edition available.

The role of William Jennings Bryan and Robert Lansing in the politics of neutrality and the coming of the war are examined in *An Uncertain Tradition: American Secretaries of State in the Twentieth Century* * (1961), edited by Norman A. Graebner.

Problems books concerned with American involvement in World War I are: Herbert J. Bass, ed., *American's Entry Into World War I* * (1964); Warren I. Cohen, ed., *Intervention, 1917: Why America Fought* * (1966); and Daniel M. Smith, ed., *American Intervention, 1917* * (1966).

*Paperbound edition available.

9. *"One-Hundred–Per Cent Americanism"*

When William Joseph Simmons and a handful of his followers revived the Ku Klux Klan at Stony Mountain near Atlanta, Georgia, late in 1915, they had only a name and some fading memories to build on. They could hardly have imagined that within a decade their organization would extend into every state in the union and enlist a membership in the millions. Nor, through its first several years as a struggling secret fraternal order, could they have dreamed of the extent of the political power and influence their organization would soon achieve.

Yet despite its unpromising beginnings, by 1921 the Klan had gained sufficient notoriety to find itself the target of a full-scale exposé by the New York *World* and eighteen other leading newspapers. A congressional investigation followed. Both the newspaper series and the investigation, because of the interest they generated, boosted the Klan's membership and support rather than damaging it. Its power was on the rise until 1924 or 1925, and not until 1928 was it clear that the Klan as an organization had been turned back.

The Ku Klux Klan in the 1920s was many things, so its successes were built on a number of foundations. First, as a secret fraternal order in a nation of joiners, an initial measure of success was assured. Second, as a business venture it promised dividends to its organizers on all levels. In 1920 recruitment of members was placed in the hands of professional promoters who turned the selling of memberships into a profitable enterprise. The Klan's national leaders (in fact, they were its owners) derived great personal wealth from it. Third, as a political machine, backing causes and candidates and trying to get Klan members to vote as a bloc, it enlarged its following by supporting those who endorsed it and threatening those who opposed it.

Most important to the Klan's success, however, was its ability to play on the shared anxieties of the American people. The propaganda machine of World War I had explicitly taught them to hate what was not American, and the disillusionment growing out of the war and tensions of the troubled twenties prevented many of them from forgetting the lesson. If scapegoats were needed, the Klan found them: Catholics, Jews, immigrants, blacks, radicals, evolutionists, intellectuals, modernist theologians, bootleggers, prostitutes, gamblers, criminals, and other assorted types. If a positive program was called for, the Klan claimed to offer it: law and order, maintenance of old moral standards, better public schools, and fundamentalist Protestantism. And in the 1920s, the decade of such phenomena as prohibition, immigration restriction, and the Scopes trial, many Americans were looking for scapegoats and trying to prove their Americanism.

It is not surprising, then, that so many people turned to the Klan as a way of expressing their attitudes and beliefs. Nor is it surprising that the issue of the Klan itself became so important, virtually paralyzing political processes in some cities and states. Even national politics were affected: The Democratic National Convention of 1924, for example, split so severely over the Klan issue that 103 ballots were required to nominate a presidential candidate.

The heart of the controversy surrounding the Klan was this: The Klan attempted to define "one-hundred–per cent Americanism," and not all Americans were willing to accept its definition. The questions raised by the controversy are of continuing interest.

Core Document

The Klan's Fight for Americanism

HIRAM WESLEY EVANS

The secrecy of the Ku Klux Klan covered only its rituals, handbooks, membership lists, political maneuvering, and night-riding activities of bullying and violence. What it stood for was discussed freely by its leaders and by many of

Reprinted from *The North American Review*, March 1926 (pp. 49, 51–55, 57–62), by permission of the University of Northern Iowa.

its members. (Many others in its membership no doubt had only vague knowledge of the Klan's purposes, having joined out of expediency or coercion.)

The most articulate national spokesman of the Klan at the height of its power was Imperial Wizard Hiram Wesley Evans. After wresting the leadership from Simmons in 1922, Evans enjoyed unchallenged domination of the Klan until the last several years before his retirement in 1939.

In 1926, even though the Klan was past its peak, the North American Review *invited Evans to present the case for his organization. Excerpts from his lengthy article provide the core document for this chapter. In analyzing Evans' point of view, note:*

- *who he claimed as friend and who as foe.*
- *his faith in instincts and emotions.*
- *the ingredients of his "Americanism."*
- *the limitations he imposed on traditional American ideals.*
- *specific actions he recommended.*
- *his admission of Klan faults.*
- *justifications he offered for an attitude of intolerance.*
- *his outright rejection of a pluralist America.*
- *his hope for the future.*

MARCH 1926

We are a movement of the plain people, very weak in the matter of culture, intellectual support, and trained leadership. We are demanding, and we expect to win, a return of power into the hands of the everyday, not highly cultured, not overly intellectualized, but entirely unspoiled and not de-Americanized, average citizen of the old stock. Our members and leaders are all of this class —the opposition of the intellectuals and liberals who held the leadership, betrayed Americanism, and from whom we expect to wrest control, is almost automatic. . . .

Our critics have accused us of being merely a "protest movement", of being frightened; they say we fear alien competition, are in a panic because we cannot hold our own against the foreigners. That is partly true. We are a protest movement—protesting against being robbed. We are afraid of competition with peoples who would destroy our standard of living. We are suffering in many ways, we have been betrayed by our trusted leaders, we are half beaten already. But we are not frightened nor in a panic. We have merely awakened to the fact that we must fight for our own. We are going to fight—and win!

The Klan does not believe that the fact that it is emotional and instinctive, rather than coldly intellectual, is a weakness. All action comes from emotion, rather than from ratiocination. Our emotions and the instincts on which they are based have been bred into us for thousands of years; far longer than reason has had a place in the human brain. They are the many-times distilled product of experience; they still operate much more surely and promptly than reason can. For centuries those who obeyed them have lived and carried on the race; those in whom they were weak, or who failed to obey, have died. They are the foundations of our American civilization, even more than our great historic documents; they can be trusted where the fine-haired reasoning of the denatured intellectuals cannot.

Thus the Klan goes back to the American racial instincts, and to the common sense which is their first product, as the basis of its beliefs and methods. The fundamentals of our thought are convictions, not mere opinions. We are pleased that modern research is finding scientific backing for these convictions. We do not need them ourselves; we know that we are right in the same sense that a good Christian knows that he has been saved and that Christ lives—a thing which the intellectual can never understand. These convictions are no more to be argued about than is our love for our children; we are merely willing to state them for the enlightenment and conversion of others.

There are three of these great racial instincts, vital elements in both the historic and the present attempts to build an America which shall fulfill the aspirations and justify the heroism of the men who made the nation. These are the instincts of loyalty to the white race, to the traditions of America, and to the spirit of Protestantism, which has been an essential part of Americanism ever since the days of Roanoke and Plymouth Rock. They are condensed into the Klan slogan: "Native, white, Protestant supremacy."

First in the Klansman's mind is patriotism—America for Americans. He believes religiously that a betrayal of Americanism or the American race is treason to the most sacred of trusts, a trust from his fathers and a trust from God. He believes, too, that Americanism can only be achieved if the pioneer stock is kept pure. There is more than race pride in this. Mongrelization has been proven bad. It is only between closely related stocks of the same race that interbreeding has improved men; the kind of interbreeding that went on in the early days of America between English, Dutch, German, Hugenot, Irish and Scotch.

Racial integrity is a very definite thing to the Klansman. It means even more than good citizenship, for a man may be in all ways a good citizen and yet a poor American, unless he has racial understanding of Americanism, and instinctive loyalty to it. It is in no way a reflection on any man to say that he is un-American; it is merely a statement that he is not one of us. It is often not even wise to try to make an American of the best of aliens. What he is may be spoiled without his becoming American. The races and stocks of men are as distinct as breeds of animals, and every boy knows that if one tries to train a bulldog to herd sheep, he has in the end neither a good bulldog nor a good collie.

Americanism, to the Klansman, is a thing of the spirit, a purpose and a point of view, that can only come through instinctive racial understanding. It has, to be sure, certain defined principles, but he does not believe that many aliens understand those principles, even when they use our words in talking about them. Democracy is one, fairdealing, impartial justice, equal opportunity, religious liberty, independence, self-reliance, courage, endurance, acceptance of individual responsibility as well as individual rewards for effort, willingness to sacrifice for the good of his family, his nation and his race before anything else but God, dependence on enlightened conscience for guidance, the right to unhampered development—these are fundamental. But within the bounds they fix there must be the utmost freedom, tolerance, liberalism. In short, the Klansman believes in the greatest possible diversity and individualism within the limits of the American spirit. But he believes also that few aliens can understand that spirit, that fewer try to, and that there must be resistance, intolerance even, toward anything that threatens it, or the fundamental national unity based upon it.

The second word in the Klansman's trilogy is "white". The white race must be supreme, not only in America but in the world. This is equally undebatable, except on the ground that the races might live together, each with full regard for the rights and interests of others, and that those rights and interests would never conflict. Such an idea, of course, is absurd; the colored races today, such as Japan, are clamoring not for equality but for their supremacy. The whole history of the world, on its broader lines, has been one of race conflicts, wars, subjugation or extinction. This is not pretty, and certainly disagrees with the maudlin theories of cosmopolitanism, but it is truth. The world has been so made that each race must fight for its life, must conquer, accept slavery or die. The Klansman believes that the whites will not become slaves, and he does not intend to die before his time.

Moreover, the future of progress and civilization depends on the continued supremacy of the white race. The forward movement of the world for centuries has come entirely from it. Other races each had its chance and either failed or stuck fast, while white civilization shows no sign of having reached its limit. Until the whites falter, or some colored civilization has a miracle of awakening, there is not a single colored stock that can claim even equality with the white; much less supremacy.

The third of the Klan principles is that Protestantism must be supreme; that Rome shall not rule America. The Klansman believes this not merely because he is a Protestant, nor even because the Colonies that are now our nation were settled for the purpose of wresting America from the control of Rome and establishing a land of free conscience. He believes it also because Protestantism is an essential part of Americanism; without it America could never have been created and without it she cannot go forward. Roman rule would kill it.

Protestantism contains more than religion. It is the expression in religion of the same spirit of independence, self-reliance and freedom which are the highest achievements of the Nordic race. It sprang into being automatically at the time of the great "upsurgence" of strength in the Nordic peoples that opened the spurt of civilization in the fifteenth century. It has been a distinctly

Nordic religion, and it has been through this religion that the Nordics have found strength to take leadership of all whites and the supremacy of the earth. Its destruction is the deepest purpose of all other peoples, as that would mean the end of Nordic rule.

It is the only religion that permits the unhampered individual development and the unhampered conscience and action which were necessary in the settling of America. Our pioneers were all Protestants, except for an occasional Irishman—Protestants by nature if not by religion—for though French and Spanish dared and explored and showed great heroism, they made little of the land their own. America was Protestant from birth.

She must remain Protestant, if the Nordic stock is to finish its destiny. We of the old stock Americans could not work—and the work is mostly ours to do, if the record of the past proves anything—if we become priest-ridden, if we had to submit our consciences and limit our activities and suppress our thoughts at the command of any man, much less of a man sitting upon Seven Hills thousands of miles away. This we will not permit. Rome shall not rule us. Protestantism must be supreme.

Let it be clear what is meant by "supremacy". It is nothing more than power of control, under just laws. It is not imperialism, far less is it autocracy or even aristocracy of a race or stock of men. What it does mean is that we insist on our inherited right to insure our own safety, individually and as a race, to secure the future of our children, to maintain and develop our racial heritage in our own, white, Protestant, American way, without interference. . . .

One of the Klan's chief interests is in education. We believe that it is the duty of government to insure to every child opportunity to develop its natural abilities to their utmost. We wish to go to the very limit in the improvement of the public schools; so far that there will be no excuse except snobbery for the private schools.

Further, the Klan wishes to restore the Bible to the school, not only because it is part of the world's great heritage in literature and philosophy and has profoundly influenced all white civilization, but because it is the basis on which all Christian religions are built, and to which they must look for their authority. The Klan believes in the right of each child to pass for itself on the ultimate authority behind the creed he is asked to adopt; it believes in preserving to all children their right to religious volition, to full freedom of choice. This is impossible if they are barred from the Bible. We oppose any means by which any priesthood keeps its hold on power by suppressing, hiding or garbling the fundamental Christian revelation.

This is one of the reasons for the Klan's objection to parochial schools of any church. They very readily become mere agencies of propaganda. Another reason is that in many the teaching is in the hands of aliens, who cannot possibly understand Americanism or train Americans to citizenship. In many, even, the textbooks have been so perverted that Americanism is falsified, distorted and betrayed. The Klan would like to see all such schools closed. If they cannot be abolished, the Klan aims to bring them under control of the State, so as to eliminate these evils, insure religious volition, and enforce the teaching of true Americanism.

This, then, is the mental attitude, the purpose and the plan of the Klan today, and it is against this position of ours, and against nothing else, that charges of bigotry, narrowness, intolerance and prejudice can fairly be brought. Charges made on other grounds need not be discussed, but we of the Klan are prepared to admit that some of these charges are at least partly justified.

This does not mean merely that there are "bigots and fanatics" among us. There certainly are; we are weeding them out, but we have some left, and others will join in spite of our utmost care. The fault is serious but not fatal. Every such movement has them, as Roosevelt found when he dubbed the similar nuisances in his own movement "the lunatic fringe".

Nor does this mean, either, an admission of the charges of those who deny to Americans the right—which every alien claims and uses—to speak his mind freely and criticize things about him. Jews or Catholics are lavish with their caustic criticism of anything American. Nothing is immune; our great men, our historic struggles and sacrifices, our customs and personal traits, our "Puritan consciences"—all have been scarified without mercy. Yet the least criticism of these same vitriolic critics or of their people brings howls of "anti-Semitic" or "anti-Catholic". We of the Klan pay no attention to those who argue with epithets only. They thereby admit their weakness. And we are still waiting for some one to try to answer us with facts and reasons.

Aside from these things, however, we of the Klan admit that we are intolerant and narrow in a certain sense. We do not think our intolerance is so serious as that of our enemies. It is not an intolerance that tries to prevent free speech or free assembly. The Klan has never broken up a meeting, nor tried to drive a speaker to cover, nor started a riot, nor attacked a procession or parade, nor murdered men for belonging to the Knights of Columbus or the B'nai B'rith.

And we deny that either bigotry or prejudice enters into our intolerance or our narrowness. We are intolerant of everything that strikes at the foundations of our race, our country or our freedom of worship. We are narrowly opposed to the use of anything alien—race, loyalty to any foreign power or to any religion whatever—as a means to win political power. We are prejudiced against any attempt to use the privileges and opportunities which aliens hold only through our generosity as levers to force us to change our civilization, to wrest from us control of our own country, to exploit us for the benefit of any foreign power—religious or secular—and especially to use America as a tool or cat's-paw for the advantage of any side in the hatreds and quarrels of the Old World. This is our intolerance; based on the sound instincts which have saved us many times from the follies of the intellectuals. We admit it. More and worse, we are proud of it.

But this is all of our intolerance. We do not wish harm to any man, even to those we fight. We have no desire to abuse, enslave, exploit, or deny any legal, political or social right to any man of any religion, race or color. We grant them full freedom—except freedom to destroy our own freedom and ourselves. In many ways we honor and respect them. Every race has many fine and admirable traits, each has made notable achievements. There is much for us to learn from each of them. But we do insist that we may learn what we choose, and what will best fit the peculiar genius of our own race, rather than have them choose our lessons for us, and then ram them down our throats.

The attitude of the Klan toward outsiders is derived logically from these beliefs. From all Americans except the racial and spiritual expatriates we expect eventual support. Of the expatriates nothing can be hoped. They are men without a country and proud of it.

The Negro, the Klan considers a special duty and problem of the white American. He is among us through no wish of his; we owe it to him and to ourselves to give him full protection and opportunity. But his limitations are evident; we will not permit him to gain sufficient power to control our civilization. Neither will we delude him with promises of social equality which we know can never be realized. The Klan looks forward to the day when the Negro problem will have been solved on some much saner basis than miscegenation, and when every State will enforce laws making any sex relations between a white and a colored person a crime.

For the alien in general we have sympathy, opportunity, justice, but no permanent welcome unless he becomes truly American. It is our duty to see that he has every chance for this, and we shall be glad to accept him if he does. We hold no rancor against him; his race, instincts, training, mentality and whole outlook of life are usually widely different from ours. We cannot blame him if he adheres to them and attempts to convert us to them, even by force. But we must see that he can never succeed.

The Jew is a more complex problem. His abilities are great, he contributes much to any country where he lives. This is particularly true of the Western Jew, those of the stocks we have known so long. Their separation from us is more religious than racial. When freed from persecution these Jews have shown a tendency to disintegrate and amalgamate. We may hope that shortly, in the free atmosphere of America, Jews of this class will cease to be a problem. Quite different are the Eastern Jews of recent immigration, the Jews known as the Askhenasim. It is interesting to note that anthropologists now tell us that these are not true Jews, but only Judaized Mongols—Chazars. These, unlike the true Hebrew, show a divergence from the American type so great that there seems little hope of their assimilation.

The most menacing and most difficult problem facing America today is this of the permanently unassimilable alien. The only solution so far offered is that of Dr. Eliot, president emeritus of Harvard. After admitting that the melting pot has failed—thus supporting the primary position of the Klan!— he adds that there is no hope of creating here a single, homogeneous race-stock of the kind necessary for national unity. He then suggests that, instead, there shall be a congeries of diverse peoples, living together in sweet harmony, and all working for the good of all and of the nation! This solution is on a par with the optimism which foisted the melting pot on us. Diverse races never have lived together in such harmony; race antipathies are too deep and strong. If such a state were possible, the nation would be too disunited for progress. One race always ruled, one always must, and there will be struggle and reprisals till the mastery is established—and bitterness afterwards. And, speaking for us Americans, we have come to realize that if all this could possibly be done, still within a few years we should be supplanted by the "mere force of breeding" of the low standard peoples. We intend to see that the American stock remains supreme.

This is a problem which must shortly engage the best American minds. We can neither expel, exterminate nor enslave these low-standard aliens, yet their continued presence on the present basis means our doom. Those who know the American character know that if the problem is not soon solved by wisdom, it will be solved by one of those cataclysmic outbursts which have so often disgraced—and saved!—the race. Our attempt to find a sane solution is one of the best justifications of the Klan's existence.

Toward the Catholic as an individual the Klan has no "attitude" whatever. His religion is none of our business. But toward the Catholic Church as a political organization, and toward the individual Catholic who serves it as such, we have a definite intolerance. We are intolerant of the refusal of the Roman Church to accept equality in a democracy, and resent its attempts to use clerical power in our politics. We resent, too, the subservience of members who follow clerical commands in politics. We are intolerant, also, of the efforts of the Roman Church to prevent the assimilation of immigrant members. We demand that in politics and in education the Roman Church abandon its clutching after special and un-American privileges, and that it become content to depend for its strength on the truth of its teachings and the spiritual power of its leaders. Further than this we ask nothing. We admit that this is intolerant; we deny that it is either bigoted or unjust.

The Klan today, because of the position it has come to fill, is by far the strongest movement recorded for the defense and fulfillment of Americanism. It has a membership of millions, the support of millions more. If there be any truth in the statement that the voice of the people is the voice of God, then we hold a Divine commission. . . .

The future of the Klan we believe in, though it is still in the hands of God and of our own abilities and consecration as individuals and as a race. Previous movements of the kind have been short-lived, killed by internal jealousies and personal ambitions, and partly, too, by partial accomplishment of their purposes. If the Klan falls away from its mission, or fails in it, perhaps even if it succeeds—certainly whenever the time comes that it is not doing needed work —it will become a mere derelict, without purpose or force. If it fulfills its mission, its future power and service are beyond calculation so long as America has any part of her destiny unfulfilled. Meantime we of the Klan will continue, as best we know and as best we can, the crusade for Americanism to which we have been providentially called.

Discussion Starters

1. Identify and evaluate the major premises on which Evans' arguments rest.

2. "Superpatriots" who espouse "one-hundred–per cent Americanism" run the risk of sacrificing cherished American ideals by attempting to impose on others their "love it or leave it" versions of Americanism. Identify ideals that Evans seemed willing to sacrifice to achieve his goals. Evaluate the importance of these ideals in the American system.

3. According to one interpretation, various conditions contributed to the decline of the Klan: its internal splits and financial chaos, the opposition of the press and of churches, public revulsion at the talk and use of violence, and the failure of some of its prophesies to be realized. This suggests that disapproval of the Klan's ideology was not a major cause in its decline, and that its ideology perhaps persisted after its collapse. Evaluate this interpretation. Identify Klan ideals that might readily find popular appeal today.

4. Assuming that it would be a good idea to reach national consensus in defining "one-hundred–per cent Americanism," who should have the responsibility for drafting the definition and how should they proceed?

Related Documents

I. What Is Wrong With the Klan?: An Editorial

The Ku Klux Klan was a major political issue in 1924. The Democratic National Convention was left in a shambles by a controversy over whether the Klan should be specifically identified in its platform as an undesirable organization. The attempt to identify it by name was defeated by the barest of margins, and the two main contenders for the nomination, Alfred E. Smith and William G. McAdoo (who had Klan backing), were deadlocked through more than 100 ballots. Finally a third candidate, John W. Davis, was nominated on the 103rd ballot.

Why all the furor? Before the issue was raised in the convention, it was the

The Nation, June 18, 1924, p. 698.

topic of an editorial in The Nation, *a weekly magazine of news and opinion. Respond to* The Nation's *condemnation of Klannishness. Which aspects of the Klan emphasized by* The Nation *were ignored by Evans in his article?*

JUNE 18, 1924

The New York *World*, which has been waging a vigorous campaign against the Klan, has conducted an interesting poll of Democrats and Republicans on the question whether the political conventions should go on record against "all groups, open or secret, which attempt to take the law into their own hands;" against prejudice or discrimination on account of race, color, or creed; and, specifically, against the Ku Klux Klan. The answers are various; most of the politicians declare in vague, general terms against race prejudice but prefer to avoid mention of the word "Klan." The most pithy comes from the Republican national committeeman from Oklahoma, Jim A. Harris. "All this hullabaloo about the Klan and the anti-Klan," says Mr. Harris, "reminds me of a statement once made by Josh Billings: 'Thur hez bin a heep sed consarnin' the wether, but nuthin' hes ever bin dun about it yet.' "

There has been too much said about the Klan, and too little done about Klannishness. The organization is not as important as its spirit. As the Klan has spread through the North and entered politics it has acquired an increasing restraint without changing its inner nature. The atrocities with which the early history of the Klan was punctuated seem to have been declining while the bitter, intolerant spirit of the Klan has been spreading. To kill the organization today would mean little if its spirit persisted.

Klannishness is not confined to the Klan. At Hicksville, Long Island, the Knights of Columbus were in charge this year of the Memorial Day exercises. As it happened, the three sons of Hicksville who had died in the World War were all Catholics. When the paraders reached the monument they found a wreath at its base, marked "K. K. K.," and were unwilling to leave it there. A fist fight followed, in which the wreath was stamped on and destroyed. The incident is trifling, but it marked another triumph for Klannishness. The wreath may have been intended as an insult, but a decent respect for the dead men and for the inclusiveness of their country would have let it lie untouched. There are good men in the Klan, although it can hardly be said that there are tolerant men; but they will never be converted to a decent respect for their fellow-countrymen if these others adopt the Klan's own intolerance.

To assume that all Klansmen are reprobates is to adopt the habit of mind exemplified in the ridiculous campaign posters distributed by the Klan in Indiana, reading:

> Every criminal, every gambler, every thug, every libertine, every girl-ruiner, every home-wrecker, every wife-beater, every dope-peddler, every moonshiner, every crooked politician, every pagan Papist priest,

every shyster lawyer, every K. of C., every white slaver, every brothel madam, every Rome-controlled newspaper, every black-spider—is fighting the Klan. Think it over. Which side are you on?

Well, we are on the side of those who fight Klannishness, although sometimes the fight against the Klan seems to borrow its evils. We are against those who assume that every Catholic is bad, or that every Klansman is bad; that every Jew is an outcast, or that every Gentile has a right to be called a Christian; that every Jap should be barred from the land or that every American is better than any foreigner. It will certainly help if the Klan is forced into the open —made to unmask, and to act, when it acts, publicly. . . . The Klan has invented no new crimes. Anti-Catholic sentiment is an old story in American political life; it had its greatest success in the fifties and was active again in the nineties. The Klan has revived an old intolerance, which will still be an evil when the passions now stirred by the three K's have been forgotten. The fight against the Klan will make most headway when it abandons personalities and vague principles. The worst sample of Klannishness in recent American history was the immigration law, and with that, as far as we know, the Ku Klux Klan had nothing to do.

II. The Shape of Fear

W. E. B. DU BOIS

The ideology of the Klan was frequently subjected to critical analysis, and four such analyses appeared in The North American Review *in the issue following the one containing Evans' article. These criticisms were written without a direct knowledge of what Evans had written, but at least three of them responded pointedly to his position. An excerpt from the article by W. E. B. Du Bois, the noted black leader, is presented here.*

Compare Du Bois' interpretation of the motivation of the Klan with that offered by Evans. Speculate on how the Klan would attempt to answer Du Bois' arguments, particularly his assertion that "the American of English descent is not holding his own physically or spiritually in this country."

JUNE 1926

What is there after all, of truth back of what the Klan attacks? And perhaps first what does the Klan attack? I will not stop to argue this. I simply quote from their own blank application for membership seven of their twenty questions: "7.—Were your parents born in the United States of America?" "8.— Are you a Gentile or Jew?" "9.—Are you of the white race or of a colored

Reprinted from *The North American Review*, June 1926 (pp. 300–3), by permission of the University of Northern Iowa.

race?" "13.—Do you believe in White Supremacy?" "15.—What is your religious faith?" "17.—Of what religious faith are your parents?" "20.—Do you owe ANY KIND of allegiance to any foreign nation, government, institution, sect, people, ruler or person?"

Here then is clearly the groundwork for opposition to the foreign-born, the Jew, the colored races and the Catholic Church. I am not the one to defend Catholic or Jew. The Catholic Church and modern European civilization are largely synonymous and to attack the one is to accuse the other. For the alleged followers of Jesus Christ and worshipers of the Old Testament to revile Hebrew culture is too impudent for words. But in this crazy combination of hates fathered by the Ku Klux Klan (and so illogical that in any intelligent country it would be laughed out of court), is included the American Negro. What is the indictment against him? He was a slave. He is ignorant. He is poor. He has the stigmata of poverty and ignorance—that is crime. He laughs and sings and dances. He is black. He isn't all black. The very statement of such a bill of indictment is like accusing ashes of fire. The real arraignment of the Negro is the fear that white America with its present machinery is not going to be able to keep black folk down. They are achieving equality with startling swiftness. Neither caricature nor contempt, rape of women or insult of children, murder or burning at the stake, have succeeded in daunting this extraordinary group.

Against it open reasoning and arguments has been employed but it has failed to convince even those who employed it. This was followed by propaganda; and the propaganda of emphasizing "race", "racial" characteristics, "racial" inferiority, is a propaganda which according to all modern scientific dicta is unreliable and untrue. Yet these terms flourish and these things are taught in school and college; they appear in books and lectures and they are used because of what men want them to accomplish, namely, the continual fear and hate of black folk instead of that natural rebound of sympathy and admiration which their work in a half century deserves.

But as I have said, even this propaganda has not been successful. What next then? Next comes the Ku Klux Klan. Next comes the leadership of mob and perpetration of outrage by forces, secret, hidden and underground. And the danger and shame are not in the movement itself, so much as in the wide tolerance and sympathy which its methods evoke among educated and decent Americans. These people see in the Ku Klux Klan a way of doing and saying that which they themselves are ashamed to do and say. Go into any western town from Pittsburgh to Kansas City: "The Klan? Silly—*but!*—You see these Catholics, rich, powerful, silent, organized. Got all the foreigners corraled— I don't *know.* And Jews—the Jews own the country. They are trying to rule the world. They are too smart, pushing, impudent. And *niggers!* And that isn't all. Dagoes, Japs; and then *Russia!* I tell you we gotta *do* something. The Klan?—silly, of course—*but*—."

Thus the Ku Klux Klan is doing a job which the American people, or certainly a considerable portion of them, want done; and they want it done because as a nation they have fear of the Jew, the immigrant, the Negro. They realize that the American of English descent is not holding his own physically or spiritually in this country; that America survives and flourishes because of the alien immigrant with his strong arm, his simple life, his faith and hope, his song, his art, his religion. They realize that no group in the United States is working harder to push themselves forward and upward than the Negroes; and over all this rises the Shape of Fear.

The worst aspect of all this is that when we resort to the underground method it involves a conscious surrender of Truth. It must base itself upon lies. One of the greatest difficulties in estimating the power and spread of the Ku Klux Klan is that its members are evidently sworn to lie. They are ordered to deny their membership in the Klan; they are ordered to deny their participation in certain of its deeds; they are ordered above all to keep at least partially secret its real objects and desires. Now the lie has often been used to advance human culture, but it is an extremely dangerous weapon, and surely we have lived beyond the need of it today. . . .

Without doubt, of all the dangerous weapons that civilized man has attempted to use in order to advance human culture the secret mass lie is the most dangerous and the most apt to prove a boomerang. This is the real thing that we are to fear in the Ku Klux Klan. We need not fear its logic. It has no logic. Whatever there is of truth in its hatred of three groups of Americans can be discussed openly and fearlessly by civilized men. If Negroes are ignorant underbidders of labor, unhealthy and lazy aspirants to undeserved equality there are plain and well-known social restraints and remedies. First, to improve the condition of Negroes so far as it is improvable; secondly, to teach them the reason behind the objections to their rise so far as there are reasons; and above all to examine thoroughly and honestly what the real questions at issue are. If the hierarchy of the Catholic church is in any way threatening democracy in America there is a chance for perfectly open and honest investigation and conference between this young democracy and that old and honorable government of the spirit of men. If the Jew in self-defense against age-long persecution has closed his fist against the world there is more than a chance to clasp that human hand. In fine, unless we are willing to give up human civilization in order to preserve civilization we cannot for a moment contemplate turning to secret, underground methods as a cure for anything; and the appearance of such a movement is not a case where we stop to ask whether the movement in itself has at present laudable objects or not. It does not make any difference what the Ku Klux Klan is fighting for or against. Its method is wrong and dangerous and uncivilized, and those who oppose it, whether they be its victims like the Jews, Catholics and Negroes, or those who are lauded as its moral sponsors like the white Southerners, the American Legion and the "Anglo-Saxons", it is the duty of all these people to join together in solemn phalanx against the method which is an eternal menace to human culture.

III. Oath of Allegiance to the Ku Klux Klan

In order to become a Klansman a person was required to swear an oath of allegiance to the organization and its leaders. Henry Peck Fry, an ex-Klansman who provided much of the information used by the New York World *in its exposé of the Klan, criticized the oath on three main grounds: (1) It bound men to obey unconditionally laws they knew nothing about and laws that might be enacted in the future, and to follow blindly an organization that was largely a one-man affair. (2) It placed allegiance to the Ku Klux Klan ahead of allegiance to the government of the United States. (3) Its last paragraph was illegal in that it condoned mob rule and the use of methods in carrying out its views that were contrary to the basic laws of the land.*

Read the oath in the light of these criticisms. Why would they be regarded as unjustified by true Klansmen, such as Evans?

SECTION I.—OBEDIENCE.

"I, . . . —————, In the presence of God and Man most solemnly pledge, promise and swear unconditionally, that I will faithfully obey the constitution and laws and will willingly conform to all regulations, usages and requirements of the Knights of the Ku Klux Klan which do now exist or which may hereafter be enacted, and will render at all times loyal respect and steadfast support to the Imperial Authority of the same, and will heartily heed all official mandates, decrees, edicts, rulings and instructions of the Imperial Wizard thereof. I will yield prompt response to all summonses, I having knowledge of same, Providence alone preventing.

SECTION II.—SECRECY.

"I most solemnly swear that I will forever keep sacredly secret the signs, words and grip and any and all other matters and knowledge of the Knights of the Ku Klux Klan regarding which a most rigid secrecy must be maintained, which may at any time be communicated to me, and will never divulge same nor even cause same to be divulged to any person in the whole world unless I know positively that such person is a member of this Order in good and regular standing and not even then unless it be for the best interest of this Order.

"I most sacredly vow and most positively swear that I will never yield to bribe, flattery, threats, passion, punishment, persecution, persuasion nor any enticements whatever coming from or offered by any person or persons, male or female, for the purpose of obtaining from me a secret or secret information

The Outlook, January 2, 1924, p. 21. Included in connection with an article on the Klan in a series by Stanley Frost. The text of the oath as printed for Klan use contained asterisks in place of the name of the Klan and of certain other identifying words. In this text these have been filled in, and the directions as to action have been omitted where they are obvious.

of the Knights of the Ku Klux Klan. I will die rather than divulge same, so help me God. AMEN!"

(The candidate then waits till the Exalted Cyclops and his Klan have decided whether to admit him. If this is done, he is taken into the Klavern, and the oath continues:—)

SECTION III.—FIDELITY.

"I, . . . _____, Before God and in the presence of these mysterious Klansmen, on my sacred honor do most solemnly and sincerely pledge, promise and swear that I will diligently guard and faithfully foster every interest of the Knights of the Ku Klux Klan and will maintain its social caste and dignity.

"I swear I will never recommend any person for membership in this Order whose mind is unsound or whose reputation I know to be bad or whose character is doubtful or whose loyalty to our country is in any way questionable.

"I swear that I will pay promptly all just and legal demands made upon me to defray the expenses of my Klan and this Order when same are due or called for.

"I swear that I will protect the property of the Knights of the Ku Klux Klan of any nature whatsoever and if any should be intrusted to my keeping I will properly keep or rightly use same and will freely and promptly surrender same on official demand or if I am ever banished from or voluntarily discontinue my membership in this Order.

"I swear that I will most determinedly maintain peace and harmony in all the deliberations of the gatherings or assemblies of the Invisible Empire and of any subordinate jurisdiction or Klan thereof.

"I swear that I will most strenuously discourage selfishness and selfish political ambition on the part of myself or any Klansman.

"I swear that I will never allow personal friendship, blood or family relationship, nor personal, political or professional prejudice, malice nor illwill to influence me in casting my vote for the election or rejection of any applicant for membership in this Order, God being my helper.

AMEN

SECTION IV.—KLANNISHNESS.

"I, . . . _____, Most solemnly pledge, promise and swear that I will never slander, defraud, deceive or in any manner wrong the Knights of the Ku Klux Klan, a Klansman nor a Klansman's family, nor will I suffer the same to be done if I can prevent it.

"I swear that I will be faithful in defending and protecting the home, reputation and physical and business interest of a Klansman and that of a Klansman's family.

"I swear that I will at any time, without hesitating, go to the assistance or rescue of a Klansman in any way, at his call I will answer. I will be truly Klannish toward Klansmen in all things honorable.

"I swear that I will never allow any animosity, friction nor illwill to arise and remain between myself and a Klansman, but will be constant in my efforts to promote real Klannishness among the members of this Order.

"I swear that I will keep secure to myself the secret of a Klansman when same is committed to me in the sacred bond of Klansmanship, the crime of violating THIS solemn oath, treason against the United States of America, rape, and malicious murder alone excepted.

"I most solemnly assert and affirm that to the government of the United States of America and any State thereof of which I may become a resident, I sacredly swear an unqualified allegiance above any other and every kind of government in the whole world. I here and now pledge my life, my property, my vote, and my sacred honor to uphold its flag, its constitution and constitutional laws and will protect, defend and enforce same unto death.

"I most Solemnly Promise and Swear That I will always, at all Times and in all places, Help, aid and assist, The duly Constituted officers of The law in The proper performance of Their Legal Duties.

"I swear that I will most zealously and valiantly shield and preserve by any and all justifiable means and methods the sacred constitutional rights and privileges of free public schools, free speech, free press, separation of church and state, liberty, white supremacy, just laws, and the pursuit of happiness against any encroachment of any nature by any person or persons, political party or parties, religious sect or people, native, naturalized or foreign, of any race, color, creed, lineage or tongue whatsoever.

"All to which I have sworn by THIS oath I will seal with my blood, be Thou my witness, Almighty God,

AMEN!"

IV. Concerning Klan Psychology

JOHN MOFFAT MECKLIN

A contemporary scholarly critique of the Klan was given by a Dartmouth College sociologist, John Moffat Mecklin. To him, the Klan's crude insistence on like-mindedness was a consequence of shallow and superficial thinking and a desire for superficial conformity. These, in turn, grew out of thoughtless reliance on mental stereotypes.

What is left of Evans' article after it is stripped of the mental stereotypes referred to by Mecklin? In the light of Mecklin's ideas, evaluate the depth of conformity required by Evans' "one-hundred–per cent Americanism."

John Moffat Mecklin, *The Ku Klux Klan: A Study of the American Mind* (New York: Harcourt, Brace, 1924; reprinted New York: Russell & Russell, 1963), pp. 109–13, 115–20.

One finds on every page of Klan literature an insistent, imperative, and even intolerant demand for like-mindedness. It is, of course, the beliefs and traditions of the old native American stock that are to provide the basis for this like-mindedness. The Catholic is free to entertain his own ideas in religion but he must feel, think, and act in terms of pure and unadulterated Americanism. The foreign-born member of the community is tolerated only on the presupposition that he learns the American tongue, adopts the American dress and conventionalities, in a word assimilates as quickly and thoroughly as possible the traditions of the old American stock. The eternal quarrel of the Klan with the Jew and the Negro is that mental and physical differences seem to have conspired to place them in groups entirely to themselves so that it becomes to all intents and purposes impossible for them to attain with anything like completeness this like-mindedness synonymous with one hundred percent Americanism. The Negro is granted a place in American society only upon his willingness to accept a subordinate position, for one hundred percent Americanism means white supremacy. The Jew is tolerated largely because native Americanism can not help itself. The Jew is disliked because of the amazing tenacity with which he resists absolute Americanization, a dislike that is not unmingled with fear; the Negro is disliked because he is considered essentially an alien and unassimilable element in society.

Back of the Klan's insistence upon like-mindedness there is, to be sure, a measure of democratic common sense. If there is to be any sort of effective and intelligent social coöperation a measure of agreement upon fundamentals is necessary. Within the social order, to be sure, there will always be group and class differences. These differences may be made a most valuable means of cultivating a vigorous and enlightened citizenship. It is a peculiarity of human thinking that truth is far more apt to emerge where we discuss our differences than where we emphasize our agreements. It is only when these differences cut so deeply that they threaten the integrity of the social tissue that they become dangerous. To play the game of citizenship successfully there must be a punctilious regard for the "rules of the game" that all contestants have agreed to observe. The Klan belongs to the crop of patriotic organizations that sprang up during and after the war and have for their general object the preservation of that measure of like-mindedness which was felt to be absolutely necessary not only for the prosecution of the immediate task of winning the war but also for coping successfully with the welter of problems created by the war. To this extent the Klan undoubtedly represents the natural reaction of conservative Americans against the perils of revolutionary and un-American ideas. It is a militant attempt to secure team-work in national life.

Back of the Klan's crude insistence upon like-mindedness, however, there is much shallow and superficial thinking. To the average Klansman what appears on the surface of things to be alike is alike, what appears unlike is unlike. The accident of a black skin is made an excuse for debarring from the charmed circles of one hundred percent Americanism a man who may be, in spite of his Negro blood, intensely, intelligently, and patriotically American.

On the other hand, a man with the external earmarks of the old American stock is accepted uncritically as a one hundred percent American. All the Klan asks is a superficial conformity. For the average Klansman, apparently, one hundred percent Americanism is often identified with the crude and unreasoned emotional enthusiasms that are excited by external symbols such as the flag, the soldier's uniform, or the words of the Declaration of Independence. There is reason to believe that, just as the primitive savage creates for himself a grotesque image of his enemy, sticks his dagger into it, and imagines that he has thereby done his enemy to death, so many members of the Klan create a mental image of the Pope that in actual reality bears little or no resemblance to that reverend gentleman, and then proceed to belabor this mental fiction with fierce un-Christian invectives. A child whipping its contumacious dolly is hardly more irrational.

The mental attitudes emphasized by the Klan under the labels of one hundred percent Americanism, anti-Catholicism, and the like, consist for the most part of a set of external and factitious mental symbols that often have little or no correspondence with reality. The Klansman, like the mass of average Americans, lives and moves in a world of mental stereotypes. . . .

Men and women act upon the assumption that these mental symbols or artifacts by which they picture to themselves the world actually correspond with the utmost fidelity to reality. That is to say, they identify their ideas of men and things with the absolute truth as to men and things. . . . They act upon the assumption that these mental pictures actually correspond to the ultimate facts. They conclude that the Roman Catholic Church is subversive of all true Americanism and hostile to the national educational ideal. Acting upon this assumption, they bring pressure to bear upon their legislatures, as in Oregon, to eliminate the Catholic parochial schools. These mental pictures have all the practical implications in conduct, therefore, of actual reality. The seriousness with which men take their mental pictures, the bewildering fashion in which these mental pictures vary from group to group and the appalling difficulty we meet when we try to reconcile all these various mental pictures or seek to bring them into some sort of harmony with the actual facts, all combine to give us some insight into the exasperating difficulties that beset the problem of rational social control. The problem of the Klan is the problem of stubborn, uncritical mental stereotypes. . . .

Much might be said in defense of stereotypes as part of our mental furniture. They are useful in that they are economical. Each stereotype may be looked upon as coin current, struck out of the crude ore of social experience. We use these stereotypes because they spare us the trouble of going through all the experience of the past that is crystallized and condensed into a mental stereotype. Think of all the mental wear and tear the average man is saved by the mental stereotypes struck out for him in radical, socialist, atheist, Bolshevist, higher criticism, evolution, white supremacy, democracy, the divinity of

Jesus, purity of womanhood, free speech, or one hundred percent Americanism. These stereotypes are passively assimilated by the child in the home, the
church, the school, the community. They literally close down upon the child's
budding mental life and shape it as the molds shape the potter's clay. . . .

Since we must have stereotypes and since they are a manifest source of
danger to the integrity of our mental lives it would appear that the only wise
course is to use our stereotypes with the constant realization of the fact that
they are after all merely mental pictures. This would imply more or less of a
critical attitude towards the pictures we carry around in our heads about men
and things. It would emancipate us from the tyranny of the stereotyped attitudes that we inherit in religion, politics, business, and morals. As an inevitable
result of this critical attitude men would be inclined to be more tolerant of
those who differ with them. For, after all, differences between Catholic and
Protestant, native American and foreigner, laborer and capitalist, resolve
themselves back into stereotypes that are indigenous to each group or class and
which the member of that class has absorbed under the conviction that they
are ultimate and absolute truth. If we approach our stereotypes in this critical
and tolerant attitude their use will be found to be thoroughly justifiable and
even indispensable. But our stereotypes should at all times be our mental
servants and never our intellectual tyrants. The man who surrenders abjectly
to the mental stereotypes of his church, party, business, community, nation,
or race permits himself to be branded like a sheep and should realize that in
time like a sheep he will either be sheared or slaughtered.

V. Alma Mater, K.K.K.

*In 1923 the Ku Klux Klan tried to purchase Valparaiso University, a financially
pressed institution in northern Indiana, where the Klan was strong. The grand
plan called for it to become National University, a place where Klan ideals could
be perpetuated. For various reasons the attempt failed and the Klan never took
possession, but the episode still evoked a response in the press. Through the years,
much of the criticism of the Klan was heavy-handed, but the university venture
prompted a more satirical response, and a writer in* The New Republic *looked
a dozen years into the future and speculated on the university's character.*

*Though the article is satirical, it reveals many sharp criticisms of the Klan.
Which implicit criticisms in this article are justified if Evans' article states the
true position and purpose of the Klan? Speculate on how Evans might have
responded to this article.*

SEPTEMBER 5, 1923

It is a warm spring afternoon in 1935. On the campus all is quiet, save for one
far corner where a group of Seniors hangs the Dean to a lamp-post as a protest

The New Republic, September 5, 1923, p. 36.

against probation. Too early in the day for incandescent lamps to light the fiery cross above Mob Hall. Scarcely a sign of life in this square of close-cropped turf, speckled with bright patches where the sun shines through the elm trees. Over near Memorial Arch stands a group of Sophomores. From the red tassels on their hoods, the giant keys that hang around their shoulders on hemp rope, one might guess that they are able students. Phi Beta Ku Klux Kappa men.

Not that they are exceptional in this respect. Old Dr. Borebright, Dean of the College of Arts and Fetters, who got his start in the more conservative universities of the East, hustling from the faculty whichever colleagues dared to disagree with him in principles of economics, used often to remark that nowhere in the country could there be found a student body more intent upon the acquisition of true knowledge. And Dr. Borebright ought to know. For his are two of the stiffest courses in the whole curriculum. *Applied Psychology*, 3: Waving the Flag and Bullying the Jury. *Modern Philosophical Systems*, 2: the Protocols of Zion.

Grant that the institution has its rowdies. No college can escape them. There are young bucks at Valparaiso who persist in spending evenings at the movies, instead of patrolling the town for Knights of Columbus meetings large enough to be worth breaking up. No discipline seems to touch them. And of course, too, there is the inevitable distraction of an athletic system that claims more than its due share of student interest. Harvard and Yale know what that means. But in certain respects Valparaiso is more fortunate than its fellows. The whole student body participates in contests on cinder path and diamond. Certain events, to be sure, are reserved for individual competition. The Running Gauntlet, for example—and the Standing Tar and Feather. But at the psychological moment the entire college throws itself into the game. It is a tradition, at Valparaiso, to mob the referee just before the last race or final inning, no matter what the score, and throw him from the cupola of Law and Order Chapel.

Surprising, on the whole, how rapidly traditions of this sort take on stature even in the youngest of collegiate institutions. Is it Columbia that decrees round button caps for Freshmen—Princeton that bans smoking on the village streets? Valparaiso has its own unwritten laws of college custom. It would be a bold yearling who would dare to lynch a professor within two blocks of the Dining Hall, or light a fire in a synagogue on any day but Friday. Such flouting of time-honored custom would handicap a man in his pursuit of prestige, spoil his chances for election to much-prized fraternities like Delta Kappa Kleagle. Old Dr. Caldwell, Registrar of the University since its founding, is never tired of the story of Brother Aldwich, '27. Freshmen banquets listen to that story every year. Here was a man who worked his way through college—he drove the motor van in which "Undesirables" were spirited across the county border—yet rose through sheer observance of collegiate custom to the rank of Cyclops on Commencement Day. Not only that. For all his lowly start, his classmates made him Chairman of the Junior Riot.

Quiet enough today, this sun-patched square of campus underneath the elms. A snatch of song from trellised windows—a group of Kleagles gathered on the Fence. But there are often days when life flows briskly through the veins of Valparaiso. Once a year, at graduation time, come alumni from a thousand points to light the flaming cross. Parades, reunions, costumes. Class of '25 goes down the street behind its Cyclops, arrayed as Minute Men of '76. Class of '29 as Spartans at Thermopylae. Class of '32 as Native-Born White Protestant Americans.

All picturesque enough; noise, color and excitement. Yet these are not the days old Klansmen cherish. It is another picture they love best. . . . The quiet campus gleams beneath an Indian moon. Over the tree-tops glows the fire of some lynching party late in coming home.

> *My country Ku Klux Klan,*
> *Down with the Vatican,*
> *Of thee I sing—*

A lonely voice is chanting Valparaiso's Alma Mater:

> *Land where the mob is boss,*
> *Land of the rope and toss,*
> *On every flaming cross*
> *Let freedom swing.*

VI. *H. L. Mencken on the Klan*

Few issues or institutions escaped the acid-filled pen of the columnist and critic H. L. Mencken. His caustic commentaries were uncomfortably pointed. This brief paragraph (by-lined also by George Nathan) suggests that the Klan was really in the mainstream of American life and thought. How valid are his observations? At what point does it underscore the arguments offered by Evans?

MARCH 1923

Not a single solitary sound reason has yet been advanced for putting the Ku Klux Klan out of business. If the Klan is against the Jews, so are half of the good hotels of the Republic and three-quarters of the good clubs. If the Klan is against the foreign-born or the hyphenated citizen, so is the National Institute of Arts and Letters. If the Klan is against the Negro, so are all of the States south of the Mason-Dixon line. If the Klan is for damnation and persecution, so is the Methodist Church. If the Klan is bent upon political control, so are the American Legion and Tammany Hall. If the Klan wears grotesque uniforms, so do the Knights of Pythias and the Mystic Shriners. If the Klan holds

Smart Set, March 1923, p. 49.

its meetings in the dead of night, so do the Elks. If the Klan conducts its business in secret, so do all college Greek letter fraternities and the Department of State. If the Klan holds idiotic parades in the public streets, so do the police, the letter-carriers and firemen. If the Klan's officers bear ridiculous names, so do the officers of the Lambs' Club. If the Klan uses the mails for shaking down suckers, so does the Red Cross. If the Klan constitutes itself a censor of private morals, so does the Congress of the United States. If the Klan lynches a Moor for raping someone's daughter, so would you or I.

For Further Reading

Three interesting books pertaining to the Ku Klux Klan in this era are: *The Ku Klux Klan in the Southwest** (1966), by Charles C. Alexander; *Hooded Americanism: The First Century of the Ku Klux Klan** (1965), by David M. Chalmers; and *The Ku Klux Klan in the City** (1967), by Kenneth T. Jackson. Less valuable, but still worth consulting, is *The Ku Klux Klan in American Politics* (1962), by Arnold Rice. A good look at the original Klan is given by Allen W. Trelease in *White Terror: The Ku Klux Klan Conspiracy and Southern Reconstruction* (1971).

Several volumes on the Klan written during the period considered in this chapter have been reprinted. They are: *The Modern Ku Klux Klan* (1922, 1969), by Henry Peck Fry, and *The Ku Klux Klan: A Study of the American Mind* (1924, 1963), by John Moffatt Mecklin. The volume by Fry is an elaboration of the exposé of the Klan in the New York *World* referred to in this chapter.

The Klan cannot be understood apart from the context in which it flourished. These volumes on the 1920s are valuable in gaining an understanding of that context: Frederick Lewis Allen, *Only Yesterday** (1931, 1957); John Braeman, Robert H. Bremner, and David Brody, eds., *Change and Continuity in Twentieth Century America: The 1920s* (1968) (see especially the essay by Robert Moats Miller, pp. 215–53); Paul Carter, *The Twenties in America** (1968); and William E. Leuchtenberg, *The Perils of Prosperity, 1914–1932** (1958). Milton Plesur's *The 1920's: Problems and Paradoxes** (1969) is a good collection of interpretive articles, and *The Twenties: Fords, Flappers, and Fanatics** (1963), edited by George E. Mowry, contains primary source documents.

Anti-Democratic Trends in the Twentieth Century* (1969), edited by Roland L. DeLorme and Raymond G. McInnis, shows how the Klan relates to other similar movements.

*Paperbound edition available.

10. The New Deal: A Social Role for the Government

Although the United States had been shaped out of a mercantile tradition, the national government in its early years assumed a generally passive role in economic and social matters. During the nineteenth and early twentieth centuries its involvement was limited to subsidizing business through such devices as protective tariffs and land grants, curbing the most grotesque business abuses, and, in a rather haphazard way, controlling and manipulating the currency.

During the presidency of Franklin D. Roosevelt, in response to the Great Depression then gripping the nation, the national government assumed a markedly greater responsibility in promoting such social goals as economic growth, security, and stability. The passive or negative role of government yielded to a more active, positive role. While becoming more vigorous as subsidizer, regulator, and money manager, the government also became planner, welfare insurer, and guarantor of national prosperity.

Roosevelt's New Deal has been praised by those who believe that as a peaceful revolution it saved a social and economic system from imminent destruction without doing major damage to the system itself. Critics from the Left have tended to regard it as merely a patchwork job on a system that needed major repairs or overhauling. They believe that it concentrated too much on method without bringing much-needed reforms, and that the changes it brought were palliative rather than substantive. In their view, Roosevelt

217

merely continued to move the government in a direction set during the Hoover administration. On the other hand, critics from the Right have considered the New Deal as based on an alien ideology, destructive of American values and goals, and a threat to the survival of the "American way of life."

What has been done during the New Deal and in the years since will not be undone. A look at the debate surrounding the New Deal is nevertheless helpful in finding an answer to the continuing question: What are the limits of responsibility of the national government in the pursuit of social goals?

Core Documents

Bold, Persistent Experimentation: An Address at Oglethorpe University

FRANKLIN D. ROOSEVELT

Franklin Roosevelt has been called an experimenter and a pragmatist. In a systematic sense he was neither; he was rather a nonideological political activist. He believed in trying various approaches in order to solve the multitude of problems that the nation faced during his administration. Because he worked in the political arena he had to rely on persuasion, pressure, and organization to achieve his goals.

The first core document is an address drafted by Ernest K. Lindley, one of the small group of advisers known as the Brain Trust. In this address, delivered at Oglethorpe University in Georgia, Roosevelt gave the fullest and most advanced expression of what he deemed to be the proper role of government in promoting social goals. The address was given before Roosevelt received the nomination as the Democratic party's presidential candidate, and some close observers suggest that political exigencies prompted a retreat from this position as his prospect of wielding power came closer to realization.

In reading this address, note particularly:
- *efforts to identify with the "have nots" rather than the "haves."*
- *direct or implied criticism of the American economic system or of the way it worked.*
- *references to theories on the causes of the Depression.*
- *Roosevelt's specific hopes and goals.*
- *the context of the references to "planning."*

Samuel I. Rosenman, ed., *The Public Papers and Addresses of Franklin D. Roosevelt* (New York: Random House, 1938), I, pp. 639–47.

MAY 22, 1932

For me, as for you, this is a day of honorable attainment. For the honor conferred upon me I am deeply grateful, and I felicitate you upon yours, even though I cannot share with you that greater satisfaction which comes from a laurel worked for and won. For many of you, doubtless, this mark of distinction which you have received today has meant greater sacrifice by your parents or by yourselves, than you anticipated when you matriculated almost four years ago. The year 1928 does not seem far in the past, but since that time, as all of us are aware, the world about us has experienced significant changes. Four years ago, if you heard and believed the tidings of the time, you could expect to take your place in a society well supplied with material things and could look forward to the not too distant time when you would be living in your own homes, each (if you believed the politicians) with a two-car garage; and, without great effort, would be providing yourselves and your families with all the necessities and amenities of life, and perhaps in addition, assure by your savings their security and your own in the future. Indeed, if you were observant, you would have seen that many of your elders had discovered a still easier road to material success. They had found that once they had accumulated a few dollars they needed only to put them in the proper place and then sit back and read in comfort the hieroglyphics called stock quotations which proclaimed that their wealth was mounting miraculously without any work or effort on their part. Many who were called and who are still pleased to call themselves the leaders of finance celebrated and assured us of an eternal future for this easy-chair mode of living. And to the stimulation of belief in this dazzling chimera were lent not only the voices of some of our public men in high office, but their influence and the material aid of the very instruments of Government which they controlled.

How sadly different is the picture which we see around us today! If only the mirage had vanished, we should not complain, for we should all be better off. But with it have vanished, not only the easy gains of speculation, but much of the savings of thrifty and prudent men and women, put by for their old age and for the education of their children. With these savings has gone, among millions of our fellow citizens, that sense of security to which they have rightly felt they are entitled in a land abundantly endowed with natural resources and with productive facilities to convert them into the necessities of life for all our population. More calamitous still, there has vanished with the expectation of future security the certainty of today's bread and clothing and shelter.

Some of you—I hope not many—are wondering today how and where you will be able to earn your living a few weeks or a few months hence. Much has been written about the hope of youth. I prefer to emphasize another quality. I hope that you who have spent four years in an institution whose fundamental purpose, I take it, is to train us to pursue truths relentlessly and to look at them courageously, will face the unfortunate state of the world about you with greater clarity of vision than many of your elders.

As you have viewed this world of which you are about to become a more active part, I have no doubt that you have been impressed by its chaos, its lack of plan. Perhaps some of you have used stronger language. And stronger language is justified. Even had you been graduating, instead of matriculating, in these rose-colored days of 1928, you would, I believe, have perceived this condition. For beneath all the happy optimism of those days there existed lack of plan and a great waste.

This failure to measure true values and to look ahead extended to almost every industry, every profession, every walk of life. Take, for example, the vocation of higher education itself.

If you had been intending to enter the profession of teaching, you would have found that the universities, the colleges, the normal schools of our country were turning out annually far more trained teachers than the schools of the country could possibly use or absorb. You and I know that the number of teachers needed in the Nation is a relatively stable figure, little affected by the depression and capable of fairly accurate estimate in advance with due consideration for our increase in population. And yet, we have continued to add teaching courses, to accept every young man or young woman in those courses without any thought or regard for the law of supply and demand. In the State of New York alone, for example, there are at least seven thousand qualified teachers who are out of work, unable to earn a livelihood in their chosen profession just because nobody had the wit or the forethought to tell them in their younger days that the profession of teaching was gravely oversupplied.

Take, again, the profession of the law. Our common sense tells us that we have too many lawyers and that thousands of them, thoroughly trained, are either eking out a bare existence or being compelled to work with their hands, or are turning to some other business in order to keep themselves from becoming objects of charity. The universities, the bar, the courts themselves have done little to bring this situation to the knowledge of young men who are considering entering any one of our multitude of law schools. Here again foresight and planning have been notable for their complete absence.

In the same way we cannot review carefully the history of our industrial advance without being struck with its haphazardness, the gigantic waste with which it has been accomplished, the superfluous duplication of productive facilities, the continual scrapping of still useful equipment, the tremendous mortality in industrial and commercial undertakings, the thousands of dead-end trails into which enterprise has been lured, the profligate waste of natural resources. Much of this waste is the inevitable by-product of progress in a society which values individual endeavor and which is susceptible to the changing tastes and customs of the people of which it is composed. But much of it, I believe, could have been prevented by greater foresight and by a larger measure of social planning. Such controlling and directive forces as have been developed in recent years reside to a dangerous degree in groups having special interests in our economic order, interests which do not coincide with the interests of the Nation as a whole. I believe that the recent course of our history has demonstrated that, while we may utilize their expert knowledge of certain problems and the special facilities with which they are familiar, we cannot allow our economic life to be controlled by that small group of men whose chief outlook upon the social welfare is tinctured by the fact that they can make huge profits from the lending of money and the marketing of securities—an outlook which deserves the adjectives "selfish" and "opportunist."

You have been struck, I know, by the tragic irony of our economic situation today. We have not been brought to our present state by any natural calamity—by drought or floods or earthquakes or by the destruction of our productive machine or our man power. Indeed, we have a superabundance of raw materials, a more than ample supply of equipment for manufacturing these materials into the goods which we need, and transportation and commercial facilities for making them available to all who need them. But raw materials stand unused, factories stand idle, railroad traffic continues to dwindle, merchants sell less and less, while millions of able-bodied men and women, in dire need, are clamoring for the opportunity to work. This is the awful paradox with which we are confronted, a stinging rebuke that challenges our power to operate the economic machine which we have created.

We are presented with a multitude of views as to how we may again set into motion that economic machine. Some hold to the theory that the periodic slowing down of our economic machine is one of its inherent peculiarities— a peculiarity which we must grin, if we can, and bear because if we attempt to tamper with it we shall cause even worse ailments. According to this theory, as I see it, if we grin and bear long enough, the economic machine will eventually begin to pick up speed and in the course of an indefinite number of years will again attain that maximum number of revolutions which signifies what we have been wont to miscall prosperity, but which, alas, is but a last ostentatious twirl of the economic machine before it again succumbs to that mysterious impulse to slow down again. This attitude toward our economic machine requires not only greater stoicism, but greater faith in immutable economic law and less faith in the ability of man to control what he has created than I, for one, have. Whatever elements of truth lie in it, it is an invitation to sit back and do nothing; and all of us are suffering today, I believe, because this comfortable theory was too thoroughly implanted in the minds of some of our leaders, both in finance and in public affairs.

Other students of economics trace our present difficulties to the ravages of the World War and its bequest of unsolved political and economic and financial problems. Still others trace our difficulties to defects in the world's monetary systems. Whether it be an original cause, an accentuating cause, or an effect, the drastic change in the value of our monetary unit in terms of the commodities is a problem which we must meet straightforwardly. It is self-evident that we must either restore commodities to a level approximating their dollar value of several years ago or else that we must continue the destructive process of reducing, through defaults or through deliberate writing down, obligations assumed at a higher price level.

Possibly because of the urgency and complexity of this phase of our problem some of our economic thinkers have been occupied with it to the exclusion of other phases of as great importance.

Of these other phases, that which seems most important to me in the long run is the problem of controlling by adequate planning the creation and distribution of those products which our vast economic machine is capable of yielding. It is true that capital, whether public or private, is needed in the creation of new enterprise and that such capital gives employment.

But think carefully of the vast sums of capital or credit which in the past decade have been devoted to unjustified enterprises—to the development of unessentials and to the multiplying of many products far beyond the capacity of the Nation to absorb. It is the same story as the thoughtless turning out of too many school teachers and too many lawyers.

Here again, in the field of industry and business many of those whose primary solicitude is confined to the welfare of what they call capital have failed to read the lessons of the past few years and have been moved less by calm analysis of the needs of the Nation as a whole than by a blind determination to preserve their own special stakes in the economic order. I do not mean to intimate that we have come to the end of this period of expansion. We shall continue to need capital for the production of newly-invented devices, for the replacement of equipment worn out or rendered obsolete by our technical progress; we need better housing in many of our cities and we still need in many parts of the country more good roads, canals, parks and other improvements.

But it seems to me probable that our physical economic plant will not expand in the future at the same rate at which it has expanded in the past. We may build more factories, but the fact remains that we have enough now to supply all of our domestic needs, and more, if they are used. With these factories we can now make more shoes, more textiles, more steel, more radios, more automobiles, more of almost everything than we can use.

No, our basic trouble was not an insufficiency of capital. It was an insufficient distribution of buying power coupled with an oversufficient speculation in production. While wages rose in many of our industries, they did not as a whole rise proportionately to the reward to capital, and at the same time the purchasing power of other great groups of our population was permitted to shrink. We accumulated such a superabundance of capital that our great bankers were vying with each other, some of them employing questionable methods, in their efforts to lend this capital at home and abroad.

I believe that we are at the threshold of a fundamental change in our popular economic thought, that in the future we are going to think less about the producer and more about the consumer. Do what we may have to do to inject life into our ailing economic order, we cannot make it endure for long unless we can bring about a wiser, more equitable distribution of the national income.

It is well within the inventive capacity of man, who has built up this great social and economic machine capable of satisfying the wants of all, to insure that all who are willing and able to work receive from it at least the necessities of life. In such a system, the reward for a day's work will have to be greater, on the average, than it has been, and the reward to capital, especially capital which is speculative, will have to be less. But I believe that after the experience of the last three years, the average citizen would rather receive a smaller return upon his savings in return for greater security for the principal, than experience for a moment the thrill or the prospect of being a millionaire only to find the next moment that his fortune, actual or expected, has withered in his hand because the economic machine has again broken down.

It is toward that objective that we must move if we are to profit by our recent experiences. Probably few will disagree that the goal is desirable. Yet many, of faint heart, fearful of change, sitting tightly on the roof-tops in the flood, will sternly resist striking out for it, lest they fail to attain it. Even among those who are ready to attempt the journey there will be violent differences of opinion as to how it should be made. So complex, so widely distributed over our whole society are the problems which confront us that men and women of common aim do not agree upon the method of attacking them. Such disagreement leads to doing nothing, to drifting. Agreement may come too late.

Let us not confuse objectives with methods. Too many so-called leaders of the Nation fail to see the forest because of the trees. Too many of them fail to recognize the vital necessity of planning for definite objectives. True leadership calls for the setting forth of the objectives and the rallying of public opinion in support of these objectives.

Do not confuse objectives with methods. When the Nation becomes substantially united in favor of planning the broad objectives of civilization, then true leadership must unite thought behind definite methods.

The country needs and, unless I mistake its temper, the country demands bold, persistent experimentation. It is common sense to take a method and try it: If it fails, admit it frankly and try another. But above all, try something. The millions who are in want will not stand by silently forever while the things to satisfy their needs are within easy reach.

We need enthusiasm, imagination and the ability to face facts, even unpleasant ones, bravely. We need to correct, by drastic means if necessary, the faults in our economic system from which we now suffer. We need the courage of the young. Yours is not the task of making your way in the world, but the task of remaking the world which you will find before you. May every one of us be granted the courage, the faith and the vision to give the best that is in us to that remaking!

The Golden Rule in Government: An Extemporaneous Speech at Vassar College

FRANKLIN D. ROOSEVELT

The second core document is an excerpt from an extemporaneous speech given by Roosevelt at Vassar College in 1933, after he had become President. It reveals his approach to questions concerning the proper role of government in social and economic questions. Note:

- *the simple, common-sense quality of Roosevelt's style.*
- *references to local, state, and national responsibility in social and economic affairs.*
- *points of consistency or inconsistency between this and the previous speech.*

AUGUST 26, 1933

Here and there, in spots that are altogether too rare, there is a town or a city or a county or even a State that has, through the interest of its own citizenship, become conscious of the fact that under the old order the social, economic or political life of the community was drifting down hill either through lack of action or through adherence to old rules promulgated to fit conditions of a bygone age.

In such cases, aroused citizens have chosen new public servants or have changed the form of conducting their local affairs to the advantage of the community, without destroying the principles of self-government that are inherent in our American civilization.

You and I know that history in this State and elsewhere gives us many local examples of that. In a sense, this arousing of people's interest is what has occurred throughout the country in this year 1933; and it has made itself felt in the national capital.

I think it is the first time in our history that the Nation as a whole, regardless of party, has approved such drastic changes in the methods and forms of the functions of government without destroying the basic principles.

Perhaps I can best illustrate the change that I am talking about by putting it this way—that we have been extending to our national life the old principle of the local community, the principle that no individual, man, woman or child, has a right to do things that hurt his neighbors.

And this being neighbors' day, I think we can properly emphasize that word.

Many centuries ago, as you know, it was the principle of the old English common law—nearly 1,000 years ago, and its development has been constant

Samuel I. Rosenman, ed., *The Public Papers and Addresses of Franklin D. Roosevelt* (New York: Random House, 1938), II, pp. 339–42.

and consistent—to be fair to one's neighbors and not do things that hurt them.

In the old days, when there were only agricultural communities, it was unfair, for example, to our neighbors to allow our cattle to roam on our neighbors' land. We were told we had to fence in our cattle.

And then when we got into great cities it became unfair to maintain, let us say, a pigsty on Main and Market Streets.

As this principle was extended, it became unfair to our neighbors if we —any individual or association of individuals—sought to make unfair profits from monopolies in things that everybody had to use, such as gas and electric lights and railroad tickets and freight rates and things of that kind.

Still later on, it became uniformly accepted throughout the country, almost, that it was not fair to our neighbors to let anybody hire their children when they were little bits of things, when they ought to be at school, and especially that it was unfair to hire them at pitiful wages and with long hours of work.

Many years ago we went even further in saying that the Government— State Government or national Government—would have the right to impose increasing taxes on increasing profits because of a simple principle that very large profits were made at the expense of neighbors and, therefore, should at least to some extent be used through taxes for the benefit of the neighbors.

Now the extension of the idea of not hurting our neighbors is recognized today as no infringement on the guarantee of personal liberty—personal liberty to the individual.

For example, it is no more a restriction to tell a man that he must pay adequate wages than it is to tell that man that he must not hire child labor, or that he must not maintain a nuisance against his neighbors.

I think it is within this understanding of the deeper purposes of things today that the National Recovery Act we have heard so much about is proceeding, and that that Act is being accepted by the people of the country with the understanding of what it is all about.

Of course, it is true that your Government in Washington hopes that the building up of wages that are too low, that are starvation wages, and the shortening of hours of work, hours that are too long, in every part of the Union, will result in a greater distribution of income and wages and will thereby increase the number of people in this country that can be employed.

It is true that we in Washington are seeking definitely to increase the purchasing power of the average American citizen and, therefore, of the Nation as a whole.

It is also true, I think, that we are definitely succeeding in this purpose and that the down-hill drift of America has definitely turned, and has become the upward surge of America.

Now, my friends, that is a matter of dollars and cents. But it is also true that the people, through government, are insisting as a permanent part of American life—not just for one year or two years—that individuals and associations of individuals shall cease doing many things that have been hurting their neighbors in bygone days.

We are engaged today, as you know—not just the Government in Washington, but groups of citizens everywhere—in reviewing all kinds of human relationships, and in making these reviews we are asking an old question in a new form. We are saying, "Is this practice, is this custom, something which is being done at the expense of the many?"

And the many are the neighbors. In a national sense the many, the neighbors, are the people of the United States as a whole.

Nationally, we must think of them as a whole and not just by sections or by States.

We cannot give special consideration to the people of the North if, in so doing, it will not result in good to the people of the South or the West.

We cannot give special privileges to those who farm one particular crop if the giving makes things more difficult for those who farm some other crop.

We cannot single out one industry at the expense of others.

The national Government must, of course, think in national terms, but your responsibility, your interest in national Government ought not to stop there. The greater part of government, as it affects your daily lives and mine, is your local government.

The opportunity in this field of local government for improvement, for a betterment that will be felt in your lives, is just as great as it is in Washington.

Discussion Starters

1. How valid are the reasons given by Roosevelt to justify national economic planning? What additional reasons might be offered today?

2. What legal or constitutional basis is there for the sort of government activity Roosevelt advocated? How adequately did he deal with problems of legality and constitutionality? What might be inferred from this about Roosevelt's approach to the presidency?

3. What is there of either radicalism or conservatism in these two speeches?

4. What are the limits of responsibility of the national government in the pursuit of social goals?

5. What arguments for and against a larger role for the national government might be offered in the 1970s?

Related Documents

I. The Social Economics of the New Deal

ADOLF A. BERLE, JR.

During his campaign, and later during his presidency, Roosevelt surrounded himself with two groups of advisers. The politicians had the responsibility of building and operating the political organization. The thinkers, known as the Brain Trust, provided Roosevelt with a program, or at least with a rationale for the program he himself shaped. An example of such a rationale is found in this excerpt from an essay in The New York Times *by Adolf Berle, a member of the Brain Trust. Note how he attempts to provide a theory to justify national planning. What arguments would an opponent of Roosevelt use in attacking Berle's essay?*

OCTOBER 29, 1933

There is no mystery about the economics of the New Deal. For several generations, governments ran their affairs on the theory that natural economic forces balance themselves out. The law of supply and demand would regulate prices. When there was too little supply, the price would go up, and this would automatically increase the supply. When there was too much, the price would go down, and this would automatically decrease the supply. The efficient producer would succeed, the inefficient would fail, and this would keep the productive capacity of the country about in line with the needs for consumption. When credit was needed, bankers would supply it; when too much credit had been extended, there was a period of general inflation cutting down the debt. All this was comprehended in the governmental theory of the time which was really based on the classical economics of Adam Smith.

A tremendous force came into the world in the middle of the nineteenth century. It is usually tied up with what is called the industrial revolution and the advent of large-scale production. But we know now that the actual forces released ran further than that. The power and force of organization had come into economics. Originally this collected around great investments of capital in huge plants, such as railroads, steel companies and the like. But as the economic machinery adapted itself to the idea of great organizations to run these plants, it became possible to have great organizations only partly dependent upon such plants.

This has led to a revision in some of our economic thinking. No longer

The New York Times Magazine, October 29, 1933, p. 4. © 1933 by the New York Times Company. Reprinted by permission. The complete essay is included in William E. Leuchtenberg, *The New Deal* (Columbia: University of South Carolina Press, 1968), pp. 34–42.

can we rely on the economics of balance to take care of human needs. The effect of organization will distort and delay the forces leading to a balance to a degree as yet unmeasured. A falling price does not mean a falling supply under an agricultural system plus a credit system so organized that when the price went down every one tried to produce more wheat, or more cotton or more sugar in order to get out of debt. A big inefficient plant does not shut down because it cannot make a profit. It reorganizes, cuts its debt to nothing, and goes right on. Then it has no interest charges to pay, and only a small investment. It can accordingly undersell a more efficient producer, and drive him into bankruptcy, too. And this is repeated all through the industry.

Only after the entire industry has been bankrupted, do inefficient plants actually begin to go out of business. This process may take fifteen or twenty years, during which time the capital, the labor, the customers, and the industry generally, suffer from the effects of a disorganized and unsound condition.

The old economic forces still work and they do produce a balance after a while. But they take so long to do it and they crush so many men in the process that the strain on the social system becomes intolerable. Leaving economic forces to work themselves out as they now stand will produce an economic balance, but in the course of it you may have half of the entire country begging in the streets or starving to death.

The New Deal may be said to be merely a recognition of the fact that human beings cannot indefinitely be sacrificed by millions to the operation of economic forces accentuated by this factor of organization. Further, the mere process of organization which could create the economic mechanism can be invoked to prevent the shocking toll on life and health and happiness which readjustment under modern conditions demands.

Whatever the outcome, President Roosevelt will live in history as a great President only if for this one fact. He not only appreciated the situation, but had the courage to grapple with the cardinal economic problem of modern life. And he did so not in the spirit of hatred manifested by the red revolutionary or the black Fascist abroad, but in the typical American spirit of great generosity and great recognition that individual life and individual homes are the precious possessions; all else is merely machinery for the attainment of a full life.

II. The Dangerous Road for Democracy

HERBERT HOOVER

Perhaps Roosevelt's most persistent antagonist was his predecessor in the White House, Herbert Hoover. In speech after speech, Hoover attacked Roosevelt's principles, policies, and program. In this selection Hoover presents a wholesale

Herbert Hoover, *Addresses Upon the American Road, 1933–1938* (New York: Charles Scribner's Sons, 1938), pp. 349–53. Reprinted by permission of the Herbert Hoover Foundation, Inc.

indictment of economic planning as practiced by the Roosevelt administration.
Note how both his arguments and his style contrast with Roosevelt's. How valid
is his charge that under Roosevelt the United States was imperiled by authoritar-
ian bureaucracy, alien ideology, and potential dictatorship, and that all these
things caused or at least aggravated the Depression?

And now let us examine the dangerous road we have been travelling.

It would startle this country if our people had a detailed list of the powers
over their daily life they have surrendered to the President and his bureaucracy. More and more we have submitted to authoritarian action. A large part
of these powers are invisible. But they weave together and expand within a
bureaucracy. And bear in mind, power is just as powerful through subsidies
and favor of political jobs as it is by coercion and jail.

And the sheep's clothing of these powers is that righteous phrase, Planned
Economy. The Communists first invented it. The Fascists adopted it. It still
serves to fool the people. It carries the illusion that it means forward-looking.
But its reality is the wolf of bureaucratic power. And it bites the flock.

Never before except in a dictatorship have such powers been given to the
head of a state. And the craving of bureaucracy for more power is never
satisfied. Failure does not stop their dreams; it only multiplies their alibis.

If these are not at least the infant steps along the dangerous road that
European democracies took, then they are an astonishing parallel.

We also have had credit and currency manipulation, pump priming and
spending with huge deficits. We have had huge increase of taxes, government
restriction of production, government price fixing. We have had artifically
increased prices and genuinely stifled consumption. And these manipulations
are shot through with dictation and threat. They are accompanied by forays
of the government into competition with private enterprise. But why recite all
the creeping collectivism?

This country was definitely on the way to recovery in 1932 with all the
rest of the world. These manipulations beginning in 1933 at first retarded us.
Then they produced an artificial and distorted appearance of recovery claimed
in 1936–37. Like all shots in the arm, a lovely time was had by all. Except for
some 5,000,000 men who never got jobs. Then the President and submanagers
concluded the dose of stimulants must have been too big. They gave us an-
tidotes. They reduced bank reserves to curtail credit. They sterilized gold to
reduce credit. They publicly denounced prices. They denounced and threatened business. They proposed more measures in control of wages, hours, and
farmers. But if this were not sufficient to confuse and scare the people they
prepared for more powers by attempting to manipulate the Supreme Court.
And out of it all, we have got this depression. . . .

But let me give you a word of comfort. It is true that we have been
following that dangerous road for democracy that led to disaster in Europe.
But those countries were young in freedom and weak in their fidelities to
liberty. They were economically lean from the war. We are tough in our

fidelities. We still have some economic fat on our national body. We still have powers of resistance. We have great powers of recovery right now.

And let me add that there should be improvement from this immediate situation no matter what the government does—but it will not be real recovery with full or permanent employment if we continue down this dangerous road. And we are not going to go down that road without a lot more fighting free speech.

But what does the New Deal propose to do about this depression of theirs?

They propose that we travel further down this dangerous road. More bureaucratic dictation to business, more inflation, more pump-priming, more Planned Economy. We are to have more budget deficits, new inflations, more increase in national debts, more taxes for the future. We put the pea of $1,400,000,000 of gold under the other shell. These new actions may produce another shot in the arm.

There is in these proposals a hopeless confusion of cause and effect. You do not get employment out of an economy scarcity. You do not prime the pump to any purpose by taking money out of the pockets of the taxpayer and giving it to the consumer. They are the same person. Men borrow to expand their businesses, not because money is cheap but because they have confidence in the future. The Nation gets no richer by increasing its debts. Truly you can mortgage your house and go on a spree. It does not add to your productivity and you may lose your house.

The constructive action today is to change the national direction and get off this dangerous road. That would allay fear and re-establish confidence in the future. That would release the enormous reserves of private enterprise in place of a trickle of government money. That would take men back to their jobs tomorrow and permanently.

In order that the government may give real proof that it has abandoned this road dangerous to democracy, we need to get down out of cloudy objectives. We need to take some practical steps. This cannot be done by encouraging words. It must be proved by definite acts that re-establish faith. Faith that ours is going to continue as a system of free men and private enterprise.

III. Better Days Are Coming

B. C. FORBES

The business community generally shared the idea that the policies of the New Deal impeded or even prevented economic recovery. B. C. Forbes, editor and publisher of Forbes Magazine, *gave eloquent expression to this point of view.*

Reprinted with permission from the June 1935 *Reader's Digest* (pp. 13–15). Condensed from *Liberty,* April 20, 1935. Copyright 1935 by Liberty Pub. Corp. Copyright 1935 and 1962 by the Reader's Digest Assn., Inc.

How convincing is his analysis of the situation? Which points in Roosevelt's speeches in the core documents would he particularly attack? If Forbes' view was correct, why was Roosevelt able to maintain such strong popular support?

JUNE 1935

Not since the Civil War has America been so ripe and ready for a business boom.
Never before have so many individuals and families gone so long without things needed or desired. Never before has the equipment in American factories been so in need of renovation or replacement. Never before have homes throughout the land needed so much modernization and improvement. Never before have so many new homes been keenly wanted. Never before have so many farm buildings needed repainting and repairing. Never before have so many farms needed new implements, machinery, tools. Never before have so many families been anxious to purchase up-to-date automobiles to replace the cars of ancient vintage that clutter up our highways. Never before have so many housewives been eager for refrigerators, washing machines, radios, vacuum cleaners, modern ranges and cooking utensils.

Then consider the demand for air-conditioning, which promises to rival in its growth and employment-giving even the automotive industry. And before long television may sweep the country, affording new employment to vast numbers.

It is one thing to need these things, to want them; but unless we can obtain the wherewithal to buy them, what's the use? *Happily, Americans do have the wherewithal to gratify enough of their desires to bring about a boom in business and in employment.*

"Oh, yeah!" you may reply. "Don't you know that there are more families living on public relief today than at any time in the nation's history?"

True. But these facts and figures are also true:

The total savings deposits of the people of this country have been increasing at the rate of more than $2,000,000 *every day* for many months. Despite the drain of five painfully lean years, our savings deposits amount to $22,-000,000,000, a reduction of only 21 percent from the peak reached during the wild 1928–29 boom. So colossal are the unprecedented excess bank reserves that more than $28,000,000,000 of new credit could be granted without resorting to currency inflation.

Never before was America so ideally prepared to finance business and employment expansion. Not only so, but a veritable Niagara of gold has been deluging this country from other parts of the world. In ten recent weeks fully $350,000,000 of foreign gold poured into America.

Our banking laws and regulations are such that each $100 of gold can theoretically be made the basis for granting $1000 of credit. This means that recent importations of gold alone are sufficient to finance almost the entire four billion dollars Congress recently allocated to President Roosevelt for work-giving purposes.

So clogged up with money is America today that funds are being rented out in Wall Street at interest rates so low as to be unbelievable among those not familiar with the facts. Never before did lendable money go a-begging at such easy terms.

Thus every material and financial ingredient for greater prosperity than ever is now assuredly at hand. All that is lacking is confidence—confidence among industrial leaders, among investors, among business men, among employers—that Washington won't upset things, but will instead cooperate wholeheartedly in encouraging the return of a much greater volume of employment. I am hopeful that it has already become clear to Washington that genuine prosperity cannot be achieved by politicians alone, but that business, industry, employers, investors, consumers must all take part.

President Roosevelt intimated six months ago that he had awakened to a realization that in order to expedite revival of trade the government must seek and win the cooperation of the fillers of pay envelopes. It had become evident that the administration, single-handedly, could not create prosperity no matter how much money it might collect from taxpayers and spend on "made" work, in doles, or for other purposes. President Roosevelt began calling into council men of mature business experience. Hopefulness arose. Men of affairs started to exercise a greater measure of courage and aggression.

Unfortunately, this promising forward movement suffered a jolt when President Roosevelt announced that he hoped to see the government establish all over the country public-utility experiments similar to the Tennessee Valley Authority, to compete with existing companies. Other uncertainties have since injected themselves, including Washington's decision to spend billions on construction and other projects to give work to unemployed. Business and industry are apprehensive lest such a vast program interfere with private enterprise and also pile up such a public debt that a balanced budget within the reasonably near future may be impossible and crushingly heavy taxes inescapable.

No mortal can foretell at this moment *when* the one missing ingredient —confidence—will be supplied. But this much can be said with emphatic certainty: Sooner or later America will regain confidence and will proceed to resume normal spending and normal living.

When this time comes, we shall reach heights of prosperity beyond anything enjoyed in 1928–29 or in any earlier period of our history.

IV. But I, Too, Hate Roosevelt

ROBERT HALE

Opposition to Roosevelt quickly made Roosevelt-hating something of a national pastime. Journalist Marquis Childs analyzed the phenomenon in an article in Harper's, "They Hate Roosevelt." Portions of a response to this article by a Roosevelt-hater are presented here. What does this response reveal about the writer? Speculate on how this writer would have responded to the Roosevelt speeches included in this chapter.

AUGUST 1936

For the past twenty years I have earned money in a modest way, paid my taxes, and spent less than I have earned. It is true that I am always sure where my next meal is coming from, but I never have been and am not now sure about next year's meals. At this happily elusive moment I happen to be stupendously insolvent, a condition from which I perceive no immediate hope of escape. I can assure any apologist of the New Deal that, so far as I am aware, I don't know anyone with a present income of fifty thousand dollars a year. Nevertheless, I hate Roosevelt. Definitively, articulately, vociferously, I hate Roosevelt. My hatred is no "crumb of emotion dropped from the tables of the rich." On the contrary, it is the spontaneous dictate of my own reason.

Why do I hate the President of the United States and why do I wish to go into print about it while it is still possible for an avowed President-hater to go at large? It was Mr. Marquis Childs who prompted me to that inquiry, and if Mr. Childs' article in the May HARPER'S can stimulate the Roosevelt-haters to give testimonials as to the nature and quality of their aversion, he will have done a pious work, because our testimony is certain to be of value, either objectively as evidencing something abut Mr. Roosevelt, or subjectively as evidencing something about what Mr. Childs evidently regards as a *psychopathia politica*. But Mr. Childs and the whole breed of contemners of the American Liberty League and other organized forms of dissent mistakenly believe the alleged malady to be confined to the very rich, "the two percent." Or at least they believe that it exhibits its most virulent symptoms only among the very rich, and I am out to say in a nice way that it ain't so.

Let me attempt an analysis of the "phenomenon which social historians of the future will very likely record with perplexity if not with astonishment." If any social historian of the future is perplexed or astonished at anybody's hating Franklin Roosevelt he will be perplexed and astonished because General Sherman was not popular in Georgia and because Mussolini has not gone over big in Addis Ababa. He certainly will never understand why Germany

Copyright © 1936, by Minneapolis Star and Tribune Co., Inc. Reprinted from the August 1936 issue of *Harper's* Magazine.

has never taken to the Treaty of Versailles, or why Jews feel antipathy toward their Führer. . . .

Now then, let us see if there is not indeed some unifying principle that may offer a clear and indeed a rational explanation for us Roosevelt haters. And it may assist my approach to the subject to observe that I hate Mr. Childs' article for much the same cause that I hate Roosevelt—for it shallow falseness. The semi-fictitious characters whom Mr. Childs sketched in his article as characteristic Roosevelt haters—my very own fellow Roosevelt haters—old Jerry Skeane's widow, James Hamilton, Mr. and Mrs. Joshua Thornberry— are all very rich; and there is implicit in Mr. Childs' article as in the Presidential utterances a sneer at these highly privileged. It seems to be assumed that their alleged fatuities are in some way the result of their social and economic advantages. Now I should like to find out straight from the White House, or from one of its duly authorized spokesmen, or failing that, from Mr. Childs himself, what our attitude ought to be toward Mrs. Jerry Skeane; and if I could get a straight authoritative answer to that simple question my ardor as a Roosevelt hater, while it might not vanish, would cool perceptibly, for the plain reason that an answer to that question might set at rest the apprehensions that now reasonably beset us.

But here in the foreground of our vision stands, mark you, old Jerry Skeane's widow who has not done a lick of work since she married, very rich, with servants galore, a country seat outside of Philadelphia, a private car in which to take her grandchildren to Florida, and a living standard that bespeaks an annual income (doubtless net after taxes) of fifty thousand dollars.

Is Mrs. Skeane as a social phenomenon enviable or deplorable? Should the objective of our social and economic efforts be forcibly to destroy the Mrs. Skeanes, or to create more of them, or simply to let them languish in public derision and contempt? Mrs. Skeane is not sure of the President's answer. I am not sure of the President's answer, the Russian leaders who have made some very intelligent and penetrating comments on our President do not know the answer. We know the Soviet answer. Mrs. Skeane is bourgeoise. She must go. She will be lucky if she saves her skin. We know the American answer down anyway to 1932. It was that Mrs. Skeane was a thoroughly enviable lady and we all hoped we could do as well for our beloved relicts.

Mrs. Skeane suspects that President Roosevelt is against her and all her kind; and, faith, she has reason. His advocacy of higher inheritance taxes is obviously against her as a social phenomenon. His devaluation of the dollar obliges her to hedge her investments against inflation and, while she may do this successfully, she properly regards devaluation as a hostile move. Her investment counsel has advised her that if she owns the bonds of a public utility within striking range of TVA she must consider selling them, perhaps at a serious loss. If she has the securities of a holding company she is well aware that she may see them undergo something closely approaching confiscation. She knows that the pending bill on corporate taxation advocated by the President with virtually no support either in the business or the academic world menaces the prudent conduct of the affairs of the Skeane Company whose stock she has retained. She knows that the burdens of the Federal Social Security Act may put it out of business, thereby creating anything but security for the ten thousand men and women it employs. And she knows that if the Presidential policy of getting the country into debt is allowed to go on it will result either in repudiation (equivalent to inflation) or in stupendous taxation which is certainly going to strike the rich first.

In short, she is convinced, as even Mr. Childs admits, that she is being butchered to make a Roman holiday in the name of recovery. Under the circumstances she cannot be tremendously exhilarated because her General Motors yields her more and her United States Steel has tripled in value. If she and her friends are to be butchered as a social and economic class, she remains comparatively indifferent to the fact that circumstances beyond her control, and equally beyond the President's, make her slightly more prosperous before the butchery. It is too much like the delicious meal that is vouchsafed to a tenant of the death house just before he is strapped into the electric chair. Incidentally, she doesn't think that she has Warden Roosevelt to thank for the delicious meal.

I repeat that Mrs. Skeane, who as a secretary was smart enough to marry her rich boss, is amply smart enough to know that, whatever the stock market does today, every implication of the New Deal is against her. And yet the President of the United States does not avow himself as her enemy or align himself *nominally* with a political party that has ever advocated her destruction as a social phenomenon. And so perfectly naturally, although to the perplexity of Mr. Childs, "a great many liberals and certainly all radicals, complain that President Roosevelt's chief mission has been to save the fortunes of the very rich." In other words, they complain that Mrs. Skeane, though under the closest surveillance, has not yet reached the electric chair. . . .

It is a mistake to suppose that the rich are always dumb. Occasionally they aren't. Like myself, Mrs. Skeane listened to the President of the United States addressing his Congress on January 4, 1935 regarding the state of the Nation, and heard him say: "In spite of our efforts and in spite of our talk, we have not weeded out the overprivileged, and we have not effectively lifted up the underprivileged." Mrs. Skeane is amply clever enough to understand that she is overprivileged and is on the list for weeding out; but she would like to know how. Is it going to be a "purge" à la Nazi, or is she going to be liquidated like a Kulak? Or is it to be a gradual seeping away of the investments which ensure her present amenities of life?

Those are the queries that bother Mrs. Skeane. But my quandary is a little different. I want to know which list I am on. Am I, with my industry and my debts, destined for the lifting-up process, or am I, because I have earned more than the minimum necessary for my survival, on the weeding-out list? The President's lists may be as complicated as those of that humane Mikado of W. S. Gilbert. I can see a line of functionaries in the Treasury Department with blue pencils poised in air above a stack of income tax returns. Here will fall the WO to designate those to be weeded out, and there the LU for those who must be lifted up. Or perhaps anyone who is rich enough to have to file an income tax return will fall automatically on the WO list. . . .

That consciousness that as a social and economic class we, who have lived or tried to live in any part on money saved, are being liquidated is the tie that binds Roosevelt haters whether they have a million a year or twenty dollars a week and fifty dollars in the savings bank. Whether or not we are negligible at the polls or too stupid to see the point, as the New Deal strategists believe, I cannot say. But to the social historian of the future in his perplexity if not astonishment, I pass this along as the key to the phenomenon of an aversion which is no more obscure than our aversion to dying.

V. Folklore of Capitalism

THURMAN ARNOLD

Thurman Arnold, who later served in the Justice Department during the Roosevelt administration, here offers a description and analysis of the antipathy to Roosevelt. How valid is Arnold's suggestion that the minds that opposed the New Deal were trapped in outmoded thinking. How far would such minds have been moved by the words of Roosevelt in the core documents of this chapter?

In the spring of 1936 the writer heard a group of bankers, businessmen, lawyers, and professors, typical of the learned and conservative thinkers of the time, discussing a crisis in the affairs of the bankrupt New York, New Haven, and Hartford Railroad—once the backbone of New England, the support of its institutions and its worthy widows and orphans. They were expressing indignation that a bureaucratic Interstate Commerce Commission, operating from Washington, had decreed that passenger rates be cut almost in half. Every man there would directly benefit from the lower rate. None were stockholders. Yet all were convinced that the reduction in rate should be opposed by all conservative citizens and they were very unhappy about this new outrage committed by a government bent on destroying private business by interfering with the free judgment of its managers.

This sincere indignation and gloom had its roots not in selfishness nor the pursuit of the profit of the moment, but in pure idealism. These men, though they owned no stock, were willing to forego the advantage of lower fares to save the railroad from the consequences of economic sin. They took a long-range view and decided that in the nature of things the benefits of the lower

Thurman W. Arnold, *The Folklore of Capitalism* (New Haven, Conn.: Yale University Press, 1938), pp. 48–51.

rates would be only temporary, because they had been lowered in violation of the great principle that government should not interfere with business. Some sort of catastrophe was bound to result from such an action. The writer tried to get the picture of the impending catastrophe in clearer detail. Did the gentlemen think that, under the new rates, trains would stop running and maroon them in the City of Elms? It appeared that no one quite believed this. The collapse which they feared was more nebulous. Trains would keep on running, but with a sinister change in the character of the service. Under government influence, it would become as unpleasant as the income taxes were unpleasant. And in the background was an even more nebulous fear. The Government would, under such conditions, have to take over the railroad, thus ushering in bureaucracy and regimentation. Trains would run, but there would be no pleasure in riding on them any more.

There was also the thought that investors would suffer. This was difficult to put into concrete terms because investors already had suffered. The railroad was bankrupt. Most of the gentlemen present had once owned stock, but had sold it before it had reached its present low. Of course, they wanted the stock to go up again, along with everything else, provided, of course, that the Government did not put it up by "artificial" means, which would be inflation.

The point was raised as to whether the Interstate Commerce Commission was right in believing that the road would actually be more prosperous under the lower rates. This possibility was dismissed as absurd. Government commissions were always theoretical. This was a tenet of pure faith about which one did not even argue.

In addition to faith, there were figures. One gentleman present had the statistical data on *why* the railroad would suffer. In order to take care of the increased traffic, new trains would have to be added, new brakemen and conductors hired, more money put into permanent equipment. All such expenditures would, of course, reflect advantageously on the economic life of New Haven, remove persons from relief rolls, stimulate the heavy goods industries, and so on. This, however, was argued to be unsound. Since it was done in violation of sound principle it would damage business confidence, and actually result in less capital goods expenditures, in spite of the fact that it appeared to the superficial observer to be creating more. And besides, where was the money coming from? This worry was also somewhat astonishing, because it appeared that the railroad actually could obtain the necessary funds for the present needed improvements. However, the answer to that was that posterity would have to pay through the nose.

And so the discussion ended on a note of vague worry. No one was happy over the fact that he could travel cheaper. No one was pleased that employment would increase, or that the heavy industries would be stimulated by the reduction of rates. Out of pure mystical idealism, these men were opposing every selfish interest both of themselves and the community, because the scheme went counter to the folklore to which they were accustomed. And since it went counter to that folklore, the same fears resulted from every other current scheme which violated traditional attitudes, whether it was relief, housing, railroad rates, or the Securities Exchange Act. Anything which could be called governmental interference in business necessarily created bureaucracy, regimentation, inflation and put burdens on posterity.

All this discussion was backed by much learning and theory. Yet it was easy to see its emotional source. These men pictured the railroad corporation as a big man who had once been a personal friend of theirs. They were willing to undergo financial sacrifice in order to prevent injustice being done to that big man. The personality of the corporation was so real to them that it was impossible to analyze the concept into terms of selfish interest. Does one think of personal gain when a member of one's family is insulted? With that emotional beginning, the balance of the discussion flowed out of the learned myths of the time, and ended where all the economic arguments of the time ended, in a parade of future horrors. The thinking was as primitive and naïve as all such thinking must be when it is divorced from practical issues and involved in prevailing taboos. As to the merits of the rate reduction from a practical point of view, neither the writer, nor any member of the group, knew anything. Yet such was the faith of these men in the formula they recited, that they felt that knowledge of details was completely unnecessary in having a positive and unchangeable opinion.

The way of thinking illustrated by the above incident is a stereotype. Its pattern is the same to whatever problems it is applied. It starts by reducing a situation, infinitely complicated by human and political factors, to a simple parable which illustrates fundamental and immutable principles. It ends by proving that the sacrifice of present advantage is necessary in order to protect everything we hold most dear. All such discussions end with arguments based on freedom, the home, tyranny, bureaucracy, and so on. All lead into a verbal crusade to protect our system of government. In this way certainty of opinion is possible for people who know nothing whatever about the actual situation. They feel they do not have to know the details. They know the principles.

For Further Reading

General surveys of the New Deal include several shorter volumes: William E. Leuchtenberg, *Franklin Roosevelt and the New Deal, 1932–1940** (1963); and Broadus Mitchell, *Depression Decade: From New Era Through New Deal, 1929–1941** (1947, 1969). More detailed is the multivolume study by Arthur M. Schlesinger, Jr., *The Crisis of the Old Order** (1957), *The Coming of the New Deal** (1959), and *The Politics of Upheaval** (1960). A short critical essay is provided by Paul Conkin in *The New Deal** (1967).

Franklin Roosevelt has been the subject of numerous biographies, and works by James M. Burns, Frank Freidel, Dexter Perkins, Frances Perkins, Edgar E. Robinson, and Rexford Tugwell might be consulted. In addition, the

*Paperbound edition available.

monographs on specialized topics pertaining to the New Deal are too numerous to mention here, but are worth seeking out.

*The New Deal and the American People** (1964), edited by Frank Freidel, and *The New Deal: A Documentary History** (1968), edited by William E. Leuchtenberg, contain primary source material.

*The New Deal: Analysis and Interpretation** (1969), edited by Alonzo Hamby, *The New Deal: Doctrines and Democracy** (1966), edited by Bernard Sternsher, and *New Deal Thought** (1966), edited by Howard Zinn, are anthologies of interpretations.

These are appropriate problems books: Otis L. Graham, Jr., ed., *The New Deal: The Critical Issues** (1971); Edwin C. Rozwenc, ed., *The New Deal: Revolution or Evolution** (1959); and Morton Keller, ed., *The New Deal: What Was It?** (1963).

*Paperbound edition available.

11. World War II: Intervention or America First?

The United States was not going to be the policeman of the world. That was the foreign policy commitment of America in the 1920s and 1930s. As President, Warren G. Harding stated at the beginning of the era, "We will accept no responsibility except as our own conscience and judgment may determine." Harding's rhetoric was applauded by an America that had not forgotten the horrors of World War I. Americans were determined never again to become involved in another such holocaust.

This attitude, popularly labeled isolationism, did not totally block American interest in foreign affairs, but it did prohibit any American intervention to maintain peace in the world. Since the United States was the nation most capable of intervention, its commitment to isolationism weakened the possibility that the western democracies and the League of Nations might resist aggression. Such a stance by the United States in the twenties was greatly reinforced in the thirties by the Great Depression. The Depression sapped the energy and the will of the nation to be active in world affairs, and made direct intervention virtually impossible.

American withdrawal from active responsibility in international crises was first demonstrated by events in China. In September 1931 the Japanese invaded Manchuria. Although the United States deplored the invasion, as did the League of Nations (of which America was not a member), no affirmative action was taken to help Chiang Kai-shek's forces protect the Chinese borders.

But the crisis in Asia was soon overshadowed by events in Europe.

In 1933 Adolf Hitler became Chancellor of Germany and nine months later withdrew Germany from the League of Nations. Benito Mussolini, dictator of Italy, ordered the invasion of Ethiopia in 1935, and although the League condemned Italy, no action was taken to intervene on behalf of the hapless Ethiopians. In 1936 the Spanish Civil War began, and Hitler marched German troops into the Rhineland. Through all of this President Roosevelt made numerous statements criticizing the actions of the aggressor nations, but, along with the majority of Americans, he considered intervention out of the question.

Five years later the United States entered a worldwide war to preserve western civilization from destruction at the hands of the totalitarian regimes of Germany, Italy, and Japan. The dilemma over such active American responsibility in international affairs has been the subject of much discussion. Although the opponents of intervention failed to keep the United States out of the war, their point of view has continued to influence a segment of American opinion to the present day.

Core Documents

"Quarantine the Aggressor"

FRANKLIN D. ROOSEVELT

Franklin Roosevelt was elected President in the midst of the greatest depression in American history. While his primary concern was with domestic issues, his administration did not turn its back on foreign affairs. In his first inaugural address he proposed a "good neighbor" policy toward Latin America that disavowed intervention of the United States in the internal affairs of her southern neighbors. Such a policy was symptomatic of the attitude of the American government: It did not wish to divorce the nation from foreign interest, just from foreign entanglements.

While America was becoming a "good neighbor" in Latin America, Europe was starting down the road of crisis and China was falling under the pressure of Japanese aggression. But sentiment in the United States continued to build against any intervention in these troubled areas. The attitude against involvement and potential war was strengthened by Senator Gerald P. Nye's investigation in 1934 of the munitions industry's role in World War I. The investigation,

Samuel I. Rosenman, ed., *The Public Papers and Addresses of Franklin D. Roosevelt* (New York: Macmillan, 1941), VI, pp. 407–11.

if one believed Nye—and many did—demonstrated unusual influence on the part of the arms makers and some Wall Street interests in bringing the United States into the war. Nye's condemnation of the "merchants of death" was applauded by the American public, and many resolved never again to let the young men of the nation face death in a foreign war.

The public support of the isolationists and the developing crisis in Europe and Asia were key factors in the passage of the Neutrality Acts of the mid-thirties. These acts were intended to guarantee nonintervention on the part of the United States in foreign troubles. But the Italian invasion of Ethiopia (1935), the outbreak of the Spanish Civil War (1936), and the Japanese invasion of China (1937) set Roosevelt's administration upon a new course in foreign policy. Public opinion to the contrary, the President became convinced that the aggressors did indeed threaten the peace of the United States and he began efforts to bring the American public to accept a more active role for their country in world affairs. Although such a role was full of peril, the President believed that collective security could effectively "quarantine" the aggressor nations.

On October 5, 1937, in a speech in Chicago, Roosevelt assessed the international situation. Note what he believed to be:

- *the condition of the international situation.*
- *the threat to America.*
- *the role that the "peace-loving nations" must play in the world.*
- *the need to maintain international morality.*
- *the future condition of mankind if the aggressors were not stopped.*
- *the way to accomplish an end to aggression and keep the United States out of war.*

OCTOBER 5, 1937

I am glad to come once again to Chicago. . . .

On my trip across the continent and back I have been shown many evidences of the result of commonsense cooperation between municipalities and the Federal Government, and I have been greeted by tens of thousands of Americans who have told me in every look and word that their material and spiritual well-being has made great strides forward in the past few years.

And yet, as I have seen with my own eyes the prosperous farms, the thriving factories and the busy railroads—as I have seen the happiness and security and peace which covers our wide land—almost inevitably I have been compelled to contrast our peace with very different scenes being enacted in other parts of the world.

It is because the people of the United States under modern conditions must, for the sake of their own future, give thought to the rest of the world, that I, as the responsible executive head of the nation, have chosen this great inland city . . . to speak to you on a subject of definite national importance.

The political situation in the world, which of late has been growing progressively worse, is such as to cause grave concern and anxiety to all the peoples and nations who wish to live in peace and amity with their neighbors.

Some nine years ago the hopes of mankind for a continuing era of international peace were raised to great heights when more than sixty nations solemnly pledged themselves not to resort to arms in furtherance of their national aims and policies. The high aspirations expressed in the Briand-Kellogg Peace Pact[1] and the hopes for peace thus raised have of late given way to a haunting fear of calamity.

The present reign of terror and international lawlessness began a few years ago. It began through unjustified interference in the internal affairs of other nations or the invasion of alien territory in violation of treaties, and has now reached a stage where the very foundations of civilization are seriously threatened.

The landmarks and traditions which have marked the progress of civilization toward a condition of law, order and justice are being wiped away.

Without a declaration of war and without warning or justification of any kind, civilians, including women and children, are being ruthlessly murdered with bombs from the air.

In times of so-called peace, ships are being attacked and sunk by submarines without cause or notice. Nations are fomenting and taking sides in civil warfare in nations that have never done them any harm. Nations claiming freedom for themselves deny it to others.

Innocent peoples and nations are being cruelly sacrificed to a greed for power and supremacy which is devoid of all sense of justice and humane consideration.

To paraphrase a recent author: "Perhaps we foresee a time when men, exultant in the technique of homicide, will rage so hotly over the world that every precious thing will be in danger, every book and picture and harmony, every treasure garnered through two millenniums, the small, the delicate, the defenseless—all will be lost or wrecked or utterly destroyed."

If those things come to pass in other parts of the world, let no one imagine that America will escape, that it may expect mercy, that this Western Hemisphere will not be attacked and that it will continue tranquilly and peacefully to carry on the ethics and the arts of civilization.

If those days come, "there will be no safety by arms, no help from authority, no answer in science. The storm will rage till every flower of culture is trampled and all human beings are leveled in a vast chaos."

If those days are not to come to pass—if we are to have a world in which we can breathe freely and live in amity without fear—the peace-loving nations must make a concerted effort to uphold laws and principles on which alone peace can rest secure.

The peace-loving nations must make a concerted effort in opposition to those violations of treaties and those ignorings of humane instincts which

[1]*Editors' note:* A pact signed by 65 nations of the world in 1928 renouncing war as an instrument of national policy.

today are creating a state of international anarchy and instability from which there is no escape through mere isolation or neutrality.

Those who cherish their freedom and recognize and respect the equal right of their neighbors to be free and live in peace must work together for the triumph of law and moral principles in order that peace, justice and confidence may prevail in the world.

There must be a return to a belief in the pledged word, in the value of a signed treaty. There must be recognition of the fact that national morality is as vital as private morality.

A Bishop wrote me the other day:

"It seems to me that something greatly needs to be said in behalf of ordinary humanity against the present practice of carrying the horrors of war to helpless civilians, especially women and children.

"It may be that such a protest might be regarded by many, who claim to be realists, as futile, but may it not be that the heart of mankind is so filled with horror at the present needless suffering that that force could be mobilized in sufficient volume to lessen such cruelty in the days ahead?

"Even though it may take twenty years, which God forbid, for civilization to make effective its corporate protest against this barbarism, surely strong voices may hasten the day."

There is a solidarity and interdependence about the modern world, both technically and morally, which makes it impossible for any nation completely to isolate itself from economic and political upheavals in the rest of the world, especially when such upheavals appear to be spreading and not declining.

There can be no stability or peace either within nations or between nations except under laws and moral standards adhered to by all. International anarchy destroys every foundation for peace. It jeopardizes either the immediate or the future security of every nation, large or small.

It is, therefore, a matter of vital interest and concern to the people of the United States that the sanctity of international treaties and the maintenance of international morality be restored.

The overwhelming majority of the peoples and nations of the world today want to live in peace.

They seek the removal of barriers against trade.

They want to exert themselves in industry, in agriculture and in business, that they may increase their wealth through the production of wealth-producing goods, rather than striving to produce military planes and bombs and machine guns and cannon for the destruction of human lives and useful property.

In those nations of the world which seem to be piling armament on armament for purposes of aggression, and those other nations which fear acts of aggression against them and their security, a very high proportion of the national income is being spent directly for armaments. It runs from 30 to as high as 50 per cent.

The proportion that we in the United States spend is far less—11 or 12 per cent.

How happy we are that the circumstances of the moment permit us to put our money into bridges and boulevards, dams and reforestation, the conservation of our soil and many other kinds of useful works, rather than into huge standing armies and vast supplies of implements of war.

I am compelled and you are compelled, nevertheless, to look ahead. The peace, the freedom and the security of 90 per cent of the population of the world is being jeopardized by the remaining 10 per cent who are threatening a breakdown of all international order and law.

Surely the 90 per cent who want to live in peace under law and in accordance with moral standards that have received almost universal acceptance through the centuries, can and must find some way to make their will prevail.

The situation is definitely of universal concern. The questions involved relate not merely to violations of specific provisions of particular treaties; they are questions of war and of peace, of international law, and especially of principles of humanity. It is true that they involve definite violations of agreements, and especially of the Covenant of the League of Nations, the Briand-Kellogg Pact and the Nine-Power Treaty. But they also involve problems of world economy, world security and world humanity.

It is true that the moral consciousness of the world must recognize the importance of removing injustices and well-founded grievances; but at the same time it must be aroused to the cardinal necessity of honoring sanctity of treaties, of respecting the rights and liberties of others and of putting an end to acts of international aggression.

It seems to be unfortunately true that the epidemic of world lawlessness is spreading.

When an epidemic of physical disease starts to spread, the community approves and joins in a quarantine of the patients in order to protect the health of the community against the spread of the disease.

It is my determination to pursue a policy of peace and to adopt every practicable measure to avoid involvement in war.

It ought to be inconceivable that in this modern era, and in the face of experience, any nation could be so foolish and ruthless as to run the risk of plunging the whole world into war by invading and violating, in contravention of solemn treaties, the territory of other nations that have done them no real harm and which are too weak to protect themselves adequately. Yet the peace of the world and the welfare and security of every nation is today being threatened by that very thing.

No nation which refuses to exercise forbearance and to respect the freedom and rights of others can long remain strong and retain the confidence and respect of other nations. No nation ever loses its dignity or good standing by conciliating its differences, and by exercising great patience with, and consideration for, the rights of other nations.

War is a contagion, whether it be declared or undeclared. It can engulf states and peoples remote from the original scene of hostilities. We are determined to keep out of war, yet we cannot insure ourselves against the disastrous effects of war and the dangers of involvement. We are adopting such measures as will minimize our risk of involvement, but we cannot have complete protection in a world of disorder in which confidence and security have broken down.

If civilization is to survive, the principles of the Prince of Peace must be restored. Shattered trust between nations must be revived.

Most important of all, the will for peace on the part of peace-loving nations must express itself to the end that nations that may be tempted to violate their agreements and the rights of others will desist from such a cause. There must be positive endeavors to preserve peace.

America hates war. America hopes for peace. Therefore, America actively engages in the search for peace.

The Arsenal of Democracy

FRANKLIN D. ROOSEVELT

In the years following the "Quarantine the Aggressor" speech President Roosevelt developed a more active role for the United States in international affairs. This role became increasingly partial toward England and France as the totalitarian nations continued to press for more concessions. The Munich Conference in 1938 temporarily stabilized the situation in Europe, but the stability was shattered by the Nazi-Soviet Non-Aggression Pact and the subsequent invasion of Poland in September 1939.

With war declared in Europe, Roosevelt decided to aid the Allies by requesting and receiving from Congress the repeal of those parts of the Neutrality Acts that prevented arms from being sent to any nation at war. Therefore, after November 1939, the Allies were able to buy munitions from the United States on a cash-and-carry basis. There quickly followed the famous "destroyer deal" with Great Britain, the fall of France, and the British air victory of the Battle of Britain.

Then, with the Allies pushed to the limit and Britain standing alone against the Axis powers, Roosevelt decided that the United States had to aid as quickly and as fully as possible Britain's struggle against totalitarianism. Thus was born the concept of Lend-Lease that the President explained to the American people in a radio "fireside chat."

In the following talk take note of Roosevelt's:
- *avowed purpose as President of the United States.*
- *concern over the crisis that confronted America.*

Samuel I. Rosenman, ed., *The Public Papers and Addresses of Franklin D. Roosevelt* (New York: Macmillan, 1941), IX, pp. 633–44.

- *evaluation of the Axis menace.*
- *concept of the role of the Monroe Doctrine in the crisis.*
- *assessment of the vulnerability of the United States.*
- *view of what happened to nations that trusted Hitler.*
- *warning of foreign agents trying to divide America.*
- *assertion that it was impossible to appease Hitler.*
- *belief that his policies would not lead to war.*
- *determination that the United States must be the "arsenal of democracy."*

DECEMBER 29, 1940

My Friends: This is not a fireside chat on war. It is a talk on national security; because the nub of the whole purpose of your President is to keep you now, and your children later, and your grandchildren much later, out of a last-ditch war for the preservation of American independence and all the things that American independence means to you and to me and to ours.

Tonight, in the presence of a world crisis, my mind goes back eight years to a night in the midst of a domestic crisis. It was a time when the wheels of American industry were grinding to a full stop, when the whole banking system of our country had ceased to function.

I well remember that while I sat in my study in the White House, preparing to talk with the people of the United States, I had before my eyes the picture of all those Americans with whom I was talking. I saw the workmen in the mills, the mines, the factories; the girl behind the counter; the small shopkeeper; the farmer doing his Spring plowing; the widows and the old men wondering about their life's savings.

I tried to convey to the great mass of American people what the banking crisis meant to them in their daily lives.

Tonight I want to do the same thing, with the same people, in this new crisis which faces America.

We met the issue of 1933 with courage and realism. We face this new crisis —this new threat to the security of our nation—with the same courage and realism.

Never before since Jamestown and Plymouth Rock has our American civilization been in such danger as now.

For on Sept. 27, 1940—this year—by an agreement signed in Berlin, three powerful nations, two in Europe and one in Asia, joined themselves together in the threat that if the United States of America interfered with or blocked the expansion program of these three nations—a program aimed at world control—they would unite in ultimate action against the United States.

The Nazi masters of Germany have made it clear that they intend not only to dominate all life and thought in their own country, but also to enslave the whole of Europe, and then to use the resources of Europe to dominate the rest of the world.

It was only three weeks ago that their leader stated this: "There are two worlds that stand opposed to each other." And then in defiant reply to his opponents he said this: "Others are correct when they say: 'With this world we cannot ever reconcile ourselves.' * * * I can beat any other power in the world." So said the leader of the Nazis.

In other words, the Axis not merely admits but the Axis proclaims that there can be no ultimate peace between their philosophy—their philosophy of government—and our philosophy of government.

In view of the nature of this undeniable threat, it can be asserted, properly and categorically, that the United States has no right or reason to encourage talk of peace until the day shall come when there is a clear intention on the part of the aggressor nations to abandon all thought of dominating or conquering the world.

At this moment the forces of the States that are leagued against all peoples who live in freedom are being held away from our shores. The Germans and the Italians are being blocked on the other side of the Atlantic by the British and by the Greeks, and by thousands of soldiers and sailors who were able to escape from subjugated countries. In Asia the Japanese are being engaged by the Chinese nation in another great defense.

In the Pacific Ocean is our fleet.

Some of our people like to believe that wars in Europe and in Asia are of no concern to us. But it is a matter of most vital concern to us that European and Asiatic war-makers should not gain control of the oceans which lead to this hemisphere.

One hundred and seventeen years ago the Monroe Doctrine was conceived by our government as a measure of defense in the face of a threat against this hemisphere by an alliance in Continental Europe. Thereafter, we stood guard in the Atlantic, with the British as neighbors. There was no treaty. There was no "unwritten agreement."

And yet there was the feeling, proven correct by history, that we as neighbors could settle any disputes in peaceful fashion. And the fact is that during the whole of this time the Western Hemisphere has remained free from aggression from Europe or from Asia.

Does any one seriously believe that we need to fear attack anywhere in the Americas while a free Britain remains our most powerful naval neighbor in the Atlantic? And does any one seriously believe, on the other hand, that we could rest easy if the Axis powers were our neighbors there?

If Great Britain goes down, the Axis powers will control the Continents of Europe, Asia, Africa, Australasia, and the high seas—and they will be in a position to bring enormous military and naval resources against this hemisphere. It is no exaggeration to say that all of us in all the Americas would be living at the point of a gun—a gun loaded with explosive bullets, economic as well as military.

We should enter upon a new and terrible era in which the whole world, our hemisphere included, would be run by threats of brute force. And to survive in such a world, we would have to convert ourselves permanently into a militaristic power on the basis of war economy.

Some of us like to believe that even if Britain falls, we are still safe, because of the broad expanse of the Atlantic and of the Pacific.

But the width of those oceans is not what it was in the days of clipper ships. At one point between Africa and Brazil the distance is less than it is from Washington to Denver, Colo., five hours for the latest type of bomber. And at the north end of the Pacific Ocean, America and Asia almost touch each other.

Why, even today we have planes that could fly from the British Isles to New England and back again without refueling. And remember that the range of the modern bomber is ever being increased.

During the past week many people in all parts of the nation have told me what they wanted me to say tonight. Almost all of them expressed a courageous desire to hear the plain truth about the gravity of the situation. One telegram, however, expressed the attitude of the small minority who want to see no evil and hear no evil, even though they know in their hearts that evil exists. That telegram begged me not to tell again of the ease with which our American cities could be bombed by any hostile power which had gained bases in this Western Hemisphere. The gist of that telegram was: "Please, Mr. President, don't frighten us by telling us the facts."

Frankly and definitely there is danger ahead—danger against which we must prepare. But we well know that we cannot escape danger, or the fear of danger, by crawling into bed and pulling the covers over our heads.

Some nations of Europe were bound by solemn non-intervention pacts with Germany. Other nations were assured by Germany that they need never fear invasion. Non-intervention pact or not, the fact remains that they were attacked, overrun, thrown into modern slavery at an hour's notice or even without any notice at all.

As an exiled leader of one of these nations said to me the other day, "the notice was a minus quantity. It was given to my government two hours after German troops had poured into my country in a hundred places." The fate of these nations tells us what it means to live at the point of a Nazi gun.

The Nazis have justified such actions by various pious frauds. One of these frauds is the claim that they are occupying a nation for the purpose of "restoring order." Another is that they are occupying or controlling a nation on the excuse that they are "protecting it" against the aggression of somebody else.

For example, Germany has said that she was occupying Belgium to save the Belgians from the British. Would she then hesitate to say to any South American country: "We are occupying you to protect you from aggression by the United States"?

Belgium today is being used as an invasion base against Britain, now fighting for its life. And any South American country, in Nazi hands, would always constitute a jumping off place for German attack on any one of the other republics of this hemisphere. . . .

Their secret emissaries are active in our own and in neighboring countries. They seek to stir up suspicion and dissension, to cause internal strife. They try to turn capital against labor, and vice versa. They try to reawaken long slumbering racial and religious enmities which should have no place in this country. They are active in every group that promotes intolerance. They exploit for their own ends our own natural abhorrence of war.

These trouble-breeders have but one purpose. It is to divide our people, to divide them into hostile groups and to destroy our unity and shatter our will to defend ourselves.

There are also American citizens, many of them in high places, who, unwittingly in most cases, are aiding and abetting the work of these agents. I do not charge these American citizens with being foreign agents. But I do charge them with doing exactly the kind of work that the dictators want done in the United States.

These people not only believe that we can save our own skins by shutting our eyes to the fate of other nations. Some of them go much further than that. They say that we can and should become the friends and even the partners of the Axis powers. Some of them even suggest that we should imitate the methods of the dictatorships. But Americans never can and never will do that.

The experience of the past two years has proven beyond doubt that no nation can appease the Nazis. No man can tame a tiger into a kitten by stroking it. There can be no appeasement with ruthlessness. There can be no reasoning with an incendiary bomb. We know now that a nation can have peace with the Nazis only at the price of total surrender.

Even the people of Italy have been forced to become accomplices of the Nazis; but at this moment they do not know how soon they will be embraced to death by their allies.

The American appeasers ignore the warning to be found in the fate of Austria, Czecho-Slovakia, Poland, Norway, Belgium, the Netherlands, Denmark and France. They tell you that the Axis powers are going to win anyway; that all of this bloodshed in the world could be saved, that the United States might just as well throw its influence into the scale of a dictated peace and get the best out of it that we can.

They call it a "negotiated peace." Nonsense! Is it a negotiated peace if a gang of outlaws surrounds your community and on threat of extermination makes you pay tribute to save your own skins?

Such a dictated peace would be no peace at all. It would be only another armistice, leading to the most gigantic armament race and the most devastating trade wars in all history. And in these contests the Americans would offer the only real resistance to the Axis powers. With all their vaunted efficiency, with all their parade of pious purpose in this war, there are still in their background the concentration camp and the servants of God in chains.

The history of recent years proves that the shooting and the chains and the concentration camps are not simply the transient tools but the very altars of modern dictatorships. They may talk of a "new order" in the world, but what they have in mind is only a revival of the oldest and worst tyranny. In that there is no liberty, no religion, no hope.

The proposed "new order" is the very opposite of a United States of

Europe or a United States of Asia. It is not a government based upon the consent of the governed. It is not a union of ordinary, self-respecting men and women to protect themselves and their freedom and their dignity from oppression. It is an unholy alliance of power and pelf to dominate and to enslave the human race.

The British people and their allies today are conducting an active war against this unholy alliance. Our own future security is greatly dependent on the outcome of that fight. Our ability to "keep out of war" is going to be affected by that outcome.

Thinking in terms of today and tomorrow, I make the direct statement to the American people that there is far less chance of the United States getting into war if we do all we can now to support the nations defending themselves against attack by the Axis than if we acquiesce in their defeat, submit tamely to an Axis victory, and wait our turn to be the object of attack in another war later on.

If we are to be completely honest with ourselves, we must admit that there is risk in any course we may take. But I deeply believe that the great majority of our people agree that the course that I advocate involves the least risk now and the greatest hope for world peace in the future.

The people of Europe who are defending themselves do not ask us to do their fighting. They ask us for the implements of war, the planes, the tanks, the guns, the freighters which will enable them to fight for their liberty and for our security. Emphatically we must get these weapons to them, get them to them in sufficient volume and quickly enough so that we and our children will be saved the agony and suffering of war which others have had to endure.

Let not the defeatists tell us that it is too late. It will never be earlier. Tomorrow will be later than today.

Certain facts are self-evident.

In a military sense Great Britain and the British Empire are today the spearhead of resistance to world conquest. And they are putting up a fight which will live forever in the story of human gallantry.

There is no demand for sending an American expeditionary force outside our own borders. There is no intention by any member of your government to send such a force. You can, therefore, nail, nail any talk about sending armies to Europe as deliberate untruth.

Our national policy is not directed toward war. Its sole purpose is to keep war away from our country and away from our people.

Democracy's fight against world conquest is being greatly aided, and must be more greatly aided, by the rearmament of the United States and by sending every ounce and every ton of munitions and supplies that we can possibly spare to help the defenders who are in the front lines. And it is no more unneutral for us to do that than it is for Sweden, Russia and other nations near Germany to send steel and ore and oil and other war materials into Germany every day in the week.

We are planning our own defense with the utmost urgency, and in its vast scale we must integrate the war needs of Britain and the other free nations which are resisting aggression.

This is not a matter of sentiment or of controversial personal opinion. It is a matter of realistic, practical military policy, based on the advice of our military experts who are in close touch with existing warfare. These military and naval experts and the members of the Congress and the Administration have a single-minded purpose—the defense of the United States.

This nation is making a great effort to produce everything that is necessary in this emergency—and with all possible speed. And this great effort requires great sacrifice.

I would ask no one to defend a democracy which in turn would not defend every one in the nation against want and privation. The strength of this nation shall not be diluted by the failure of the government to protect the economic well-being of its citizens.

If our capacity to produce is limited by machines, it must ever be remembered that these machines are operated by the skill and the stamina of the workers. As the government is determined to protect the rights of the workers, so the nation has a right to expect that the men who man the machines will discharge their full responsibilities to the urgent needs of defense.

The worker possesses the same human dignity and is entitled to the same security of position as the engineer or the manager or the owner. For the workers provide the human power that turns out the destroyers, and the planes and the tanks.

The nation expects our defense industries to continue operation without interruption by strikes or lockouts. It expects and insists that management and workers will reconcile their differences by voluntary or legal means, to continue to produce the supplies that are so sorely needed. . . .

I want to make it clear that it is the purpose of the nation to build now with all possible speed every machine, every arsenal, every factory that we need to manufacture our defense material. We have the men—the skill—the wealth —and above all, the will.

We must be the great arsenal of democracy. For us this is an emergency as serious as war itself. We must apply ourselves to our task with the same resolution, the same sense of urgency, the same spirit of patriotism and sacrifice as we would show were we at war.

We have furnished the British great material support and we will furnish far more in the future.

There will be no "bottlenecks" in our determination to aid Great Britain. No dictator, no combination of dictators, will weaken that determination by threats of how they will construe that determination.

The British have received invaluable military support from the heroic Greek Army and from the forces of all the governments in exile. Their strength is growing. It is the strength of men and women who value their freedom more highly than they value their lives.

I believe that the Axis powers are not going to win this war. I base that belief on the latest and best of information.

We have no excuse for defeatism. We have every good reason for hope —hope for peace, yes, and hope for the defense of our civilization and for the building of a better civilization in the future.

I have the profound conviction that the American people are now determined to put forth a mightier effort than they have ever yet made to increase our production of all the implements of defense, to meet the threat to our democratic faith.

As President of the United States, I call for that national effort. I call for it in the name of this nation which we love and honor and which we are privileged and proud to serve. I call upon our people with absolute confidence that our common cause will greatly succeed.

Discussion Starters

1. Evaluate President Roosevelt's statement that there could be no peace in the world until all nations would abide by set international law and universal moral standards. Who should determine those laws and codes of morality? What is meant by the concept that there are "principles of humanity" that are to govern all men?

2. How could Roosevelt pursue a policy to "quarantine" the aggressor nations and later become the "arsenal of democracy," but at the same time keep the United States out of war? Can "active" nonintervention be separated from war? If so, how effective would the former be if the United States was not prepared to back up its position by threatening the latter?

3. Assess President Roosevelt's use of the Monroe Doctrine to justify sending military supplies to Great Britain.

4. In what ways was Roosevelt's call for national unity in fact a method by which he was able to limit dissent over his policies? How valid is such a technique in the context of traditional American ideals—freedom of speech, press, association, and conscience?

Related Documents

I. What Our Position Should Be

WILLIAM E. BORAH

William E. Borah served in the United States Senate from 1907 until his death in 1940. As a key member of the Senate Foreign Relations Committee and as an avowed isolationist he worked successfully against American participation in the League of Nations. When the situation in Europe reached crisis proportions, he became one of the most vocal opponents of intervention in the Senate and in the nation.

In the following speech, how does his view of international affairs compare to Roosevelt's position that the United States could not stand idly by and watch the totalitarian nations destroy Western Europe?

MARCH 25, 1939

Ladies and gentlemen: What would happen in this country if we should permit ourselves to be drawn into a European war? It is a legitimate question to propound and about which we ought all to be thinking, for powerful influences at home and abroad are seeking by all kinds of methods to bring us to that end, to involve us in all the racial, territorial, and financial problems of Europe, and, ultimately, in war. What will happen to the American people, their homes, their children, and their liberty? What will happen to this Republic? For war, of all things on earth, is freedom's greatest enemy. We are told that we may have to go to war. Nevertheless, it is proper to ask: What will happen if we do? If we reflect sufficiently upon these matters, it will at least help us to weigh carefully—and may I say, prayerfully—the steps by which we may be led into these European controversies and into European wars.

First, what are the conditions in these days of peace, the conditions which will confront us, if war comes, for upon these conditions we will have to build for war. We now have a national debt, including obligations underwritten, of $45,000,000,000, budget of something over ten billion, a deficit somewhere around three and one-half billion. We have a tax burden so heavy that it is breaking the spirit and paralyzing the energy of millions of our people. Do these things have anything to do with preparedness for war? Do they have any bearing upon the stability or perpetuity of this Government? We also have 11,000,000 unemployed and we have the squalor and the misery, the sorrow and the discouragement, which come with such unemployment. We have one-third of our industrious, law-abiding citizens, it is estimated, men and

Vital Speeches, April 15, 1939, pp. 397–99.

women anxious to win back prosperity and a decent way of living, to rear in respect and happiness their children, living on the bare necessities of life or upon charity. Do these things have anything to do with the question of whether we should enter a war? Do not these conditions show we are wholly unprepared for war, regardless of the extent of our armaments? Do they not show that we are indeed a sick nation and that in this condition of affairs is to be found the real danger to our democracy? Are not these things which make for confusion and demoralization, socially and politically, the very things which are sapping the foundation of this Republic? Do they not create the soil from which spring the isms and systems which constitute the real menace to democracy? . . .

It is urged, especially by our friends abroad, that we as a Nation and as a people have great responsibility. We certainly have! Our first and supreme responsibility is to put our own house in order, to demonstrate that this free enterprise, this democracy of ours, is a success. At a time when doubt and challenge rest like mildew upon the faith of men and women in free government and free institutions, our first responsibility is to drive want and hunger from our midst, to give men and women an opportunity to work. Ours is an imperative responsibility to prove to the world that there is such a thing as free government with a free people—a happy, prosperous, contented, and loyal people. This would give inspiration to people everywhere who covet freedom, and above all, it would be the very best security we could have for our own peace and liberty. But, if in addition to our own tremendous task, we undertake to place all other peoples in their proper places, to designate what kind of a government they should have, to guarantee boundary lines, to cleanse and purify the inhuman creeds of other lands, I venture to say this Republic would break down in the effort and our people would be compelled to take up a load they could not possibly carry.

Twenty-two years ago we laid the conscriptive power of this Government upon the youth of our land and took them across the sea to fight and die in an effort to adjust other peoples' problems. I have no intention of reflecting upon either the wisdom or the patriotism of that sublime adventure. But has it no lesson to teach? Do we not now realize how toughly engrained and how inherently imbedded in the whole structure and civilization of Europe are the ambitions of rulers, racial antipathy, intolerance, and, most of all, the belief that only by force can such matters be dealt with. We entertained the hope then that, in the presence of the power of this Republic, these things would give way, governments would become more liberal, and liberty more secure, and, above all, the people would have a happier outlook. We returned home, leaving our dead in foreign soil, bringing with us the maimed and the insane, leaving behind a Europe poisoned and torn with bitterness and hate, the breeding ground of many wars, and saturated with more imperialistic schemes and personal ambitions than have been known since the days of the Caesars. All these things were embodied in so-called peace treaties to be preserved, fostered, and nurtured until the time should ripen them for action. Not since the Hundred Years' War was Europe so embittered and impoverished as it was the day the Versailles Treaty was signed and the great Frenchman Clemenceau truly said, in substance, "This is a continuation of the war."

About the only treasure we brought home was the story of endurance and undaunted heroism of the untrained American boy, taken from the factory or the farm and thrown almost overnight into the hell of European battlefields —a story without precedent in all the annals of war.

It is important that we discuss among ourselves and fully realize what the issue is in Europe. What is it that is threatening the world with another war? I must say that, in my opinion, it is imperialism—that is, territory, colonies, raw material, trade. These are the things which are dominating the movements of the different governments regardless of what may be said by individuals of these governments as to the issues. Let the imperialistic questions be adjusted satisfactorily to democracies and the creed of intolerance, war upon liberty, are passed over, condoned. In no official coming together to the totalitarian states and the democracies, in the discussion of differences, has the question of nazi-ism, with all its teachings, ever been brought forward, much less made an issue.

No better friend since Hitler became the master of Germany has Hitler had than the British democracy. Apparently regarding arbitrary, centralized government in Europe as the best guarantee of stability, it has built up Hitler's strength and favored his cause in every crucial situation. There is material in Europe for a crusade in behalf of morals and liberty with which a Gladstone could fire a continent, but democracies with more than half of their subjects denied such guarantees and privileges as may be found in our Bill of Rights will not make use of this material. I will say in fairness they cannot under the circumstances make use of this material or make it the issue. I will give some facts in support of my contention. . . .

During the dismemberment of Czechoslovakia no mention was ever made of the teachings and practices of nazi-ism or of the danger of enlarging its influence in Europe. Although they were turning over a vast number of people, some of whom it was too well known bore the mortal enmity of their new master, no suggestion was ever made in the settlement of territorial matters in behalf of or as to proper treatment and reasonable protection of these people. Can anyone find anything unfriendly in these proceedings, or any antipathy, to Nazi-ism, as such, during the period in which the only real republic in Europe was on the operating table? After the deed had been done and the two republics had sent the ultimatum of September 19, near midnight, to Czechoslovakia, calling for a decision within a few hours, Mr. Chamberlain made his settlement with Hitler and exhibited it to the world saying, in effect, that you can trust this man. I take up my place alongside of him. I ask for no modification of his philosophy of government. In doing so he gave greater power and greater prestige to Hitler throughout Europe than he perhaps himself ever hoped to enjoy. Nothing was said, nothing was suggested, that the individual with whom he had taken up his position was to change his creed or to modify in any respect his views, which had startled the world, and which in the near future was to enact a scene which, in its cruelty and hideousness, beggars description. . . .

For myself, I would adhere closely to the advice of Washington—no entangling alliances, express or implied. I would regard the Monroe Doctrine as a part of our national defense and a cornerstone of our foreign policy. I would send no money to European war chests, no munitions to any nation engaged in war, and, above all, no American boy to be sacrificed to the machinations of European imperialism.

II. *America for the Americans*

CHARLES E. COUGHLIN

Father Charles E. Coughlin was one of the most controversial figures of the Depression era. Using the unique approach of delivering his Sunday sermons on the radio, he built an audience that numbered into the millions by the mid-thirties. In 1932 the radio priest used his new-found popularity to campaign for Franklin Roosevelt for President. It was either "Roosevelt or Ruin" Coughlin told his audience, with "Wall Street" as the Devil breathing down the necks of Christian Americans.

But in 1934, disillusioned with Roosevelt, whom he now considered a Communist (or at best a fellow-traveler), Father Coughlin broke with the Administration and announced the formation of the National Union for Social Justice. The National Union was organized for political action and lobbied in Congress for legislation beneficial to the people of America, not the bankers of the country. By 1936 Father Coughlin claimed over a million and a half members in his National Union.

In the following sermon how did he attempt to develop his Christianity and patriotism to present an alternative to greater American involvement in world affairs? Why was he against war?

Whether you know it or not, the stage is being set for our entrance into another world war. Whether you know it or not, we are preparing to become the catspaw for saving the international bankers of the British Empire, which Empire, unfortunately, is dominated by the privately-owned and controlled Bank of England. Our formal entrance into the next war may be postponed until 1937. But today and tomorrow the manipulators of the international

Reverend Charles E. Coughlin, *A Series of Lectures on Social Justice* (Royal Oak, Mich.: Radio League of the Little Flower, 1936), pp. 14–15, 18–21.

chess board are so arranging and planning their various moves that there will be nothing left for our nation to do except sound the call to arms and duplicate the horrors which stultified and disgraced us in 1916. We are being trapped by agreeing either directly or indirectly to the iniquitous sanctions devised by the League of Nations.

How history is repeating itself! In 1916 we Americans elected Woodrow Wilson on the pledge that he would keep us out of war. A few months following his re-election the best blood of America was supplying fertilizer for the fields of France; the best brains of America became warped and frenzied when, from pulpit and press, we believed that America was saving democracy for the world whereas, in truth, it was participating in a horrible warfare of commercial greed.

I tell you this not to impugn the honor of a President but to impress upon you that Presidents' promises to keep us out of war can mean little. I would burn this thought into the substance of your soul for the purpose of arousing you to the truth that the President neither declares for war nor against war with any constitutional authority. Bear in mind that, according to the Constitution of the United States of America, section 8, article 11, we read: *"Congress shall have power to declare war . . . and makes rules concerning captures on land and water."*

Bear in mind that your Representatives and Senators, and not our President, are charged with the responsibility of keeping us out of war. . . .

As far as the National Union is concerned its forcefulness played a major part in preventing this nation from entangling the destinies of American citizens with the iniquitous World Court and its League of Nations which were organized not to protect the rights of minorities, as events prove, but to protect the dubious rights of those whose history is bloody for having desecrated the rights of minorities. The League of Nations is nothing more than a nameless, illegitimate child which was cradled in the adulterous bed of the Treaty of Versailles—a treaty that unjustly partitioned Europe and Africa. After this partitioning, the League was generated to protect an injustice. It became the false front for financial domination of the commercial world. . . .

Oh, consistency, thou art a jewel!

In 1914, when German commercial activities were almost at the point of surpassing those of the British, a world war was brewed in the courts of Europe.

In 1936, when a young and vigorous nation is rising to commercial pre-eminence, an excuse is engendered to destroy her.

Forget not England's applauding the Japanese invasion of Manchuria. Forget not England's punitive expedition into Afghanistan. And finally, be not deceived when the perpetrator of both phases of this most stupendous hypocrisy in all the lurid history of diplomatic intrigue whips the puppet peoples in the League of Nations to join with her in sanctions against Italy to endanger the peace of the world. . . .

What a tragic comedy it is to behold! England, who has shackled India and plundered South Africa, England, whose history is crimson with the blood of Ireland and small minorities, striking the pious attitude of defender of weak people!

Behold the present session of the League of Nations at Geneva! There stands England!

At the one moment she is the plaintiff, the judge and the jury as she coerces the League to do her bidding. She is so sure of the outcome that she anticipates the judgment of the League of Nations knowing full well what it will be as she marshals her soldiers and her sailors to oppose Italy.

Naturally she is vitally interested in the position which the United States will take. Thus, the old racket of propaganda is grinding out its ludicrous lies. Our papers are reprinting the same falsehoods which worked our country up to war hysteria in 1916 and 1917. In those years the Germans were pictured as barbarian huns bombing hospitals, killing nurses, firing dumdum[1] bullets and committing unspeakable atrocities.

Today the Italian army is charged with bombing Red Cross hospitals in Ethiopia when at the moment it was proven that there was not one such hospital existing in that land. The Italian troops were charged with using dumdum bullets although the only dumdum bullets found in all Ethiopia were those manufactured by England and in the possession of the Ethiopians themselves.

Why is this propaganda being centralized in the United States? The answer is simple. We must become entangled in their dirty European brawls and make the world safe for the Bank of England. We must participate either directly or indirectly in sanctions against Italy.

What has this to do with America and Americans? Only this: We must not enter either directly or indirectly into the sanctions which inevitably lead to war. And yet there is imminent danger of our doing so.

I say this because I have real reason to suspect that the United States secretly, though unofficially, has condoned the sanctions of Great Britain. Nay, I further suspect (unless the Prime Minister of Great Britain is devoid of reason) that the United States appears to have made some tentative plans to cooperate in the sanctions.

Let me read for you the astounding and startling statement made by Stanley Baldwin, the Prime Minister of England, on October 25th. He states: *"If sanctions of the severest kind are imposed that will lead inevitably to blockade . . . I would never sanction this country (England) going into a blockade unless I was sure beforehand of the attitude of the United States of America."*

Now the National Union stands for prosperity and peace—not for a false prosperity bred by war.

[1] *Editors' note:* A soft-nose bullet that upon impact expands, causing horrible wounds.

The fifteenth point of the National Union, as I developed it in former months, subscribes to these principles:

First, no entanglements with foreign nations. If that be heresy I stand condemned as a heretic with Washington. Second, no participation in sanctions against either England or Ethiopia or Italy—sanctions which do not make war upon soldiers but which make war upon women and little children by starving them to death. Bombing hospitals and shooting men with dumdum bullets is virtue compared to that kind of warfare. Third, no credit to warring nations because credit has been abused and our debts have been repudiated.

Once more I recall for you, my fellow citizens, that it is the business of Congress and not of the President to keep this nation out of war; the business of Congress to declare war and to make rules regarding captures on land and water. Shall we elect a Congress without knowing its positive position on this point?

The National Union intends to insist that this coming Congress shall make such rules that the entire American nation shall not be sacrificed because some privately owned ship will be sunk as it attempts to gain bloody profits for the munition manufacturers.

More than that, we stand for an uncompromising and permanent declaration of our neutrality. We stand for the policies advocated by the Nye committee which has made the most searching investigation ever instituted into the causes and remedies for war.

In brief, let there be no question as to the motives of the National Union when it impugns the honesty and the decency of the League of Nations. Its policy is America for the Americans. Its stand is neither for England nor Italy. And its program for this year and next year is to secure social justice for the inarticulate masses of our people whose Representatives failed to represent.

Peace and prosperity—social justice for all. If you are in accord with these principles and with the method of writing them into law, I invite your support. Let us keep America for the Americans, independent of entanglements with foreigners and rescued from the hands of domestic exploiters.

III. We Must Drop Our Isolation

HENRY L. STIMSON

President Roosevelt had the support of some influential persons in and out of government in trying to bring the American people to accept a different role in foreign affairs. One of his supporters was Henry Stimson, who had held several top governmental posts, including the position of Secretary of State in Herbert Hoover's cabinet from 1929 to 1933. Although Stimson had been involved in the various disarmament conferences in the early 1930s, by the end of the decade, after the rise of Hitler and the aggressions of Japan, he came to support a more

Vital Speeches, April 15, 1939, pp. 399–401.

active role by the United States in international affairs. In 1940 he was appointed to Roosevelt's cabinet as Secretary of War, a post he held for the duration of World War II.

How does his speech support Roosevelt's contention that the United States must accept active responsibility to maintain world peace?

APRIL 5, 1939

When your chairman honored me with this invitation to come before you, he said that the committee was to consider the general landmarks of foreign policy at the present time and particularly the Neutrality Act.

But when I came to reflect on it I realized that the problem of the present moment to which he referred is perhaps not so much a problem of normal foreign policy as a problem of national defense of the United States in a novel emergency. That's what it really is. We are not sitting down to draft peacefully and philosophically a code of behavior for normal times, but to consider how we can best make the United States safe—or as safe as possible—in a totally novel and critical situation.

When I call it a crisis I do not mean to imply that it is merely a brief emergency. It may last for many long, anxious years or even decades. But its essential characteristic is that it is novel and revolutionary as well as extremely dangerous, and so it has necessarily upset many of the standards and rules by which we have been accustomed in times past to chart our course and guide our conduct in international relations. . . .

This is the novel situation which confronts the world today and I think the mere statement of it will indicate how it has affected some of our former customs and traditions. For example, take our old attitude toward the question aggression in war which has been the basis of our attitude toward neutrality.

In the former world we had a doctrine that in considering the controversies of our neighbors across the Atlantic or the Pacific we could entirely disregard the question of aggression and treat both sides with perfect impartiality without trying to make any inquiry into the rights and wrongs of the origin of their conflict. But today the fact of systematized aggression stares us in the face and we know only too well who the aggressors are. We pick up our newspapers every morning with apprehension to read the most recent evidence of their policy. They boast of it. It is the life and breath of their principal policy to which they have applied the appropriate name of an axis. We also know only too well who their victims are, both present and potential. We only have to read about some of the occurrences to the south of us to realize that even we are within the zone of their orbit.

All this suggests another former tradition which begins to look a little shopworn in the present situation—the isolation, so-called, of the United States. Too many Americans have been brought up to think that in case of trouble in the world it wouldn't be necessary for us to do anything but sit still and let nature take its course. It looks a little differently now. The axis is moving much too rapidly and the world has become far too small and interconnected and interdependent. I have had official occasion to study the protected position of our country; its superb natural resources; its unmatched opportunity for self-containment in the maintenance of its defense. No one is more keenly alive than I am to this great advantage or to the comparative security of this country.

But the real question before us today is one of method. How shall these great advantages be most effectively used not only with regard to our own safety for this present year of our Lord, 1939, but for the future, for the protection not only of ourselves but of our children and our children's children and of the institutions of our country. Shall we be content to sit idly in this present security, which may be only momentary, or shall we use these great advantages carefully, moderately, but firmly and above all intelligently to help protect the world, which includes ourselves, from its imminent and continuing danger?

By reason of our present security we can do this more safely than can any other nation. And the fact that we are known to be ready to do so will not only tend to slow down the axis, the members of which know very well that language, but—what is even more important—will at the same time encourage their intended victims not to make surrenders which will ultimately endanger us.

For myself I agree with the President that there are methods which are "short of war but stronger and more effective than mere words." I have taken occasion to study and ponder over such possible methods.

This country is said to supply about one-third of the known raw materials of the world and to account for more than one-third of the known economic and industrial life of the globe. For the past two years we have allowed these matchless resources to be used in very large part to stimulate the activities and aggressions of our potential enemies. That, I am bound to say, does not strike me as a very intelligent behavior.

I know that it is sometimes said that an economic weapon is a dangerous one. In the case of ourselves, I have been rather inclined to doubt its truth. If it is, we are certainly in a safer position to use it than any other country in the world. And when it comes to the danger of irritating aggressor nations, why the very fact that we are a democracy irritates the axis. Economic action would do no more and it has the possibility of most effective restraint for, after all, the chief hope of today lies in the fact that each of the three members of the axis are in a notoriously vulnerable economic condition.

The foregoing is a very cursory statement of the conditions of today bearing upon our neutrality law and in the light of which it must be considered. The first act was drawn nearly four years ago, and events have traveled more rapidly during those four years than ever since the Great War. Their rapidity today is greater than ever. On its face that statute was evidently drawn under the influence and traditions of the past rather than to face conditions as they exist at present.

On its face it assumed that it would never be in our own peremptory interest to distinguish between an aggressor and its victim. On its face it assumed that it would never be in our own peremptory interest that an ill-prepared foreign nation should be able to defend its liberties by purchasing arms from us after it had been aggressively attacked. By this assumption the act violated one of the oldest traditions of the United States. On its face it was evidently designed to curb narrowly the discretionary power of the Executive in dealing with foreign conditions by making the operations of some of its chief provisions automatic and inflexible.

In all these respects it apparently assumed that the Congress in 1935 and 1937 was able to know exactly the course which the people of the United States would wish their government to follow under the conditions of 1939. Too meticulous foresight is often perilous, particularly in the drafting of unchange-able commitments. Every lawyer is familiar with the fate of a client who insists on having his will drawn as if the Lord Almighty had vested him with exact information as to what the condition of the world and his estate would be at the time of his death. And we all know that the Lord Almighty has an embarrassing habit of bringing to confusion such rigid efforts.

It is this rigidity of the act which seems to me its chief danger. I believe that in all such laws the President should have more discretion. I am a Republican and the present Administration is Democratic, but I have always tried to limit my partisanship in the zone of foreign affairs. I am a strong believer in the system of representative government, and from my observation I have come to the belief that in no sphere of government action is representa-tive action so essential, so effective or so safe from abuse as in the conduct of foreign relations.

I am not impressed with the fear that in that zone Presidential discretion is likely to be abused. It is my observation that in no sphere of political action is the sobering effect of terrific responsibility upon one man so marked as in the sphere of our country's relations with the outside world. Certainly, in the case of the two wars in which we have been involved within my lifetime the Presidency was the most cautious and conservative element in the country, clinging to every effort for peace until it was clear either that the people were determined upon war or that no other course than war would preserve our safety.

Today we find in the light of hindsight that this act has automatically placed in the hands of foreign nations, some of them possibly our future enemies, the decision as to with whom this country shall carry on some of its trade and commerce. Today we find that it compels us to treat alike the peaceful and suffering people of China and the militaristic enemies who by conquest are trying to turn China into a reservoir of potential future aggression against the rest of the world. We find that it compels us to be an effective party to this aggression on the pain of otherwise depriving China of the means for her own defense.

Recently we found that by depriving the Loyalist government of Spain of the right to buy arms for defense against the Rebels who were being supported by Mussolini and Hitler it made us a strong factor in the overthrow of the very government which the United States had recognized as legitimate. It seems entirely likely that should a general war come in Europe this Spring this Neutrality Act might put us in the position of facilitating a result of that war which would make the United States the next victim of attack.

Finally the psychological effects of such a statute may be even more widespread and disastrous than the physical results. The American people are not insensible to cruelty and aggression. Nor are they so unintelligent that under the conditions of today they cannot distinguish an aggressor nation from its victim. On the contrary, being served with the most free and enterprising press in the world, they are probably better informed of the facts necessary for such a determination than any other people. Moreover, they are not a constitutionally timid people, nor are they smitten with such an inferiority complex as to make them wish their government to avoid decisions which are really necessary to their own future interest.

Yet the form of this statute today tends to make the outside world believe each one of these fantastic falsehoods and to guide their own policy in that belief. Without going into the details of any new legislation, I believe that the greatest step to be taken and the one which would do more than anything else to give the American Government a helpful influence in preventing the threatened general war would be to make it clear beyond peradventure that these misconceptions do not represent the real present views of the American people.

IV. *What Substitute for War?*

CHARLES A. LINDBERGH

"America First" was organized in 1940 in response to President Roosevelt's developing policy of aiding the allies in the European war. The organization was a coalition of many groups and was led by such political conservatives as Chairman of the Board Robert E. Wood of Sears, Roebuck Company. The America Firsters were able to launch a highly visible propaganda campaign against intervention during 1940–41, drawing as they did on many prominent people for financial support and for active campaigners against Roosevelt's policies.

    One of the most effective speakers for America First was the world-famous aviator Charles A. Lindbergh. Lindbergh had retired from public life after the

From *The New York Times*, April 24, 1941. © 1941 by The New York Times Company. Reprinted by permission.

kidnap-murder of his infant son in 1935, but he had traveled for the United States government in the late thirties to assess the air forces of the different European nations, including Germany. His evaluation was one of gloom for the Allies, for the Germans appeared to have had a growing superiority in airplanes, crews, and production. Even so, Lindbergh was convinced that the hostilities between the nations of Europe that broke out in 1939 would not affect America because the Atlantic Ocean made it impossible for the belligerents to attack the United States—or for the United States to attack them. This concept of fortress America became the keystone of his neutrality.

In this radio address, how do his arguments for nonintervention compare with Roosevelt's arguments against America concerning herself only with America?

APRIL 23, 1941

There are many viewpoints from which the issues of this war can be argued. Some are primarily idealistic. Some are primarily practical. One should, I believe, strive for a balance of both. But, since the issues that can be covered in a single address are limited, tonight I shall discuss the war from a viewpoint which is primarily practical. It is not that I believe ideals are unimportant, even among the realities of war; but if a nation is to survive in a hostile world, its ideals must be backed by the hard logic of military practicability. If the outcome of war depended upon ideals alone, this would be a different world than it is today.

I know I will be severely criticized by the interventionists in America when I say we should not enter a war unless we have a reasonable chance of winning. That, they will claim, is far too materialistic a standpoint. They will advance again the same arguments that were used to persuade France to declare war against Germany in 1939. But I do not believe that our American ideals, and our way of life, will gain through an unsuccessful war. And I know that the United States is not prepared to wage war in Europe successfully at this time. We are no better prepared today than France was when the interventionists in Europe persuaded her to attack the Siegfried Line.

I have said before, and I will say again, that I believe it will be a tragedy to the entire world if the British Empire collapses. That is one of the main reasons why I opposed this war before it was declared, and why I have constantly advocated a negotiated peace. I did not feel that England and France had a reasonable chance of winning. France has now been defeated; and, despite the propaganda and confusion of recent months, it is now obvious that England is losing the war. I believe this is realized even by the British Government. But they have one last desperate plan remaining. They hope that they may be able to persuade us to send another American Expeditionary Force to Europe and to share with England militarily, as well as financially, the fiasco of this war.

I do not blame England for this hope, or for asking for our assistance. But we now know that she declared a war under circumstances which led to the defeat of every nation that sided with her from Poland to Greece. We know that in the desperation of war England promised to all these nations armed assistance that she could not send. We know that she misinformed them, as she has misinformed us, concerning her state of preparation, her military strength, and the progress of the war.

In time of war, truth is always replaced by propaganda. I do not believe we should be too quick to criticize the actions of a belligerent nation. There is always the question whether we, ourselves, would do better under similar circumstances. . . . It is our obligation as American citizens to look at this war objectively and to weigh our chances for success if we should enter it. I have attempted to do this, especially from the standpoint of aviation; and I have been forced to the conclusion that we cannot win this war for England, regardless of how much assistance we send.

I ask you to look at the map of Europe today and see if you can suggest any way in which we could win this war if we entered it. Suppose we had a large army in America, trained and equipped. Where would we send it to fight? The campaigns of the war show only too clearly how difficult it is to force a landing, or to maintain an army, on a hostile coast.

Suppose we took our Navy from the Pacific, and used it to convoy British shipping. That would not win the war for England. It would, at best, permit her to exist under the constant bombing of the German air fleet. Suppose we had an air force that we could send to Europe. Where could it operate? Some of our squadrons might be based in the British Isles; but it is physically impossible to base enough aircraft in the British Isles alone to equal in strength the aircraft that can be based on the Continent of Europe.

I have asked these questions on the supposition that we had in existence an Army and an air force large enough and well enough equipped to send to Europe; and that we would dare to remove our Navy from the Pacific. Even on this basis, I do not see how we could invade the Continent of Europe successfully as long as all of that Continent and most of Asia is under Axis domination. But the fact is that none of these suppositions are correct. We have only a one-ocean Navy. Our Army is still untrained and inadequately equipped for foreign war. Our air force is deplorably lacking in modern fighting planes because most of them have already been sent to Europe.

When these facts are cited, the interventionists shout that we are defeatists. . . . I charge them with being the real defeatists, for their policy has led to the defeat of every country that followed their advice since the war began. There is no better way to give comfort to the enemy than to divide the people of a nation over the issue of foreign war. There is no shorter road to defeat than by entering a war with inadequate preparation. Every nation that has adopted the interventionist policy of depending on some one else for its own defense has met with nothing but defeat and failure.

When history is written, the responsibility for the downfall of the democracies of Europe will rest squarely upon the shoulders of the interventionists who led their nations into war uninformed and unprepared. With their shouts of defeatism, and their disdain of reality, they have already sent countless thousands of young men to death in Europe. From the campaign of Poland to that of Greece, their prophecies have been false and their policies have failed. Yet these are the people who are calling us defeatists in American today. And they have led this country, too, to the verge of war.

There are many such interventionists in America, but there are more people among us of a different type. That is why you and I are assembled here tonight. There is a policy open to this nation that will lead to success—a policy that leaves us free to follow our own way of life, and to develop our own civilization. It is not a new and untried idea. It was advocated by Washington. It was incorporated in the Monroe Doctrine. Under its guidance, the United States has become the greatest nation in all the world.

It is based upon the belief that the security of a nation lies in the strength and character of its own people. It recommends the maintenance of armed forces sufficient to defend this hemisphere from attack by any combination of foreign powers. It demands faith in an independent American destiny. This is the policy of the America First Committee today. It is a policy not of isolation, but of independence; not of defeat, but of courage. It is a policy that led this nation to success during the most trying years of our history, and it is a policy that will lead us to success again.

We have weakened ourselves for many months, and still worse, we have divided our own people by this dabbling in Europe's wars. While we should have been concentrating on American defense we have been forced to argue over foreign quarrels. We must turn our eyes and our faith back to our own country before it is too late. And when we do this, a different vista opens before us. Practically every difficulty we would face in invading Europe becomes an asset to us in defending America. Our enemy, and not we, would then have the problem of transporting millions of troops across the ocean and landing them on a hostile shore. They, and not we, would have to furnish the convoys to transport guns and trucks and munitions and fuel across three thousand miles of water. Our battleships and our submarines would then be fighting close to their home bases. We would then do the bombing from the air and the torpedoing at sea. And if any part of an enemy convoy should ever pass our navy and our air force, they would still be faced with the guns of our coast artillery and behind them the divisions of our Army.

The United States is better situated from a military standpoint than any other nation in the world. Even in our present condition of unpreparedness no foreign power is in a position to invade us today. If we concentrate on our own defenses and build the strength that this nation should maintain, no foreign army will ever attempt to land on American shores.

War is not inevitable for this country. Such a claim is defeatism in the true sense. No one can make us fight abroad unless we ourselves are willing to do so. No one will attempt to fight us here if we arm ourselves as a great nation should be armed. Over a hundred million people in this nation are opposed to entering the war. If the principles of democracy mean anything at all, that is reason enough for us to stay out. If we are forced into a war against the wishes of an overwhelming majority of our people, we will have proved democracy such a failure at home that there will be little use fighting for it abroad.

The time has come when those of us who believe in an independent American destiny must band together and organize for strength. We have been led toward war by a minority of our people. This minority has power. It has influence. It has a loud voice. But it does not represent the American people. During the last several years I have traveled over this country from one end to the other. I have talked to many hundreds of men and women, and I have letters from tens of thousands more, who feel the same as you and I.

Most of these people have no influence or power. Most of them have no means of expressing their convictions, except by their vote which has always been against this war. They are the citizens who have had to work too hard at their daily jobs to organize political meetings. Hitherto, they have relied upon their vote to express their feelings; but now they find that it is hardly remembered except in the oratory of a political campaign. These people—the majority of hard-working American citizens, are with us. They are the true strength of our country. And they are beginning to realize, as you and I, that there are times when we must sacrifice our normal interests in life in order to insure the safety and the welfare of our nation.

Such a time has come. Such a crisis is here. That is why the America First Committee has been formed—to give voice to the people who have no newspaper, or newsreel, or radio station at their command, to give voice to the people who must do the paying, and the fighting, and the dying if this country enters the war.

Whether or not we do enter the war rests upon the shoulders of you in this audience, upon us here on this platform, upon meetings of this kind that are being held by Americans in every section of the United States today. It depends upon the action we take, and the courage we show at this time. If you believe in an independent destiny for America, if you believe that this country should not enter the war in Europe, we ask you to join the America First Committee in its stand. We ask you to share our faith in the ability of this nation to defend itself, to develop its own civilization, and to contribute to the progress of mankind in a more constructive and intelligent way than has yet been found by the warring nations of Europe. We need your support, and we need it now. The time to act is here. I thank you.

For Further Reading

General surveys on the origins of World War II are: Mark L. Chadwin, *The Hawks of World War II* (1968); Robert A. Divine, *The Illusion of Neutrality** (1962) and *The Reluctant Belligerent: American Entry Into World*

*Paperbound edition available.

War II* (1965); Donald Drummond, *The Passing of American Neutrality, 1937–1941* (1955); Herbert Feis, *The Road to Pearl Harbor** (1950); R. H. Ferrell, *American Diplomacy in the Great Depression* (1957); Allan Nevins, *The New Deal in World Affairs* (1950); H. L. Trefousse, *Germany and American Neutrality, 1939–1941* (1953); and John E. Wiltz, *From Isolation to War** (1968).

The disputes between those who wanted to intervene in Europe and those who believed America should "mind its own business" are examined in: Selig Adler, *The Isolationist Impulse** (1957); Wayne S. Cole, *America First: The Battle Against Intervention* (1953); Walter Johnson, *The Battle Against Isolation* (1944); and J. K. Nelson, *The Peace Prophets: American Pacifist Thought, 1919–1941* (1967).

President Franklin D. Roosevelt's role in the eventual participation by the United States in the war is considered in: William L. Langer and S. E. Gleason, *The Challenge to Isolationism, 1937–1940* (1952) and *The Undeclared War, 1940–1941* (1954); Charles A. Beard, *President Roosevelt and the Coming of the War* (1948); C. C. Tansill, *Back Door to War: The Roosevelt Foreign Policy, 1933–1941* (1952). Other personalities involved in the coming of the war are studied in: Elting Morison, *Turmoil and Tradition: A Study of the Life and Times of Henry L. Stimson* (1960); Julius W. Pratt, *Cordell Hull, 1933–1944* (1964); and Robert E. Sherwood, *Roosevelt and Hopkins** (1948).

Two specialized studies on aspects of foreign policy are Warren F. Kimball, *The Most Unsordid Act: Lend-Lease, 1939–1941* (1969), and Roberta Wohlstetter, *Pearl Harbor: Warning and Decision** (1962).

A problems book concerned with American intervention is Arnold A. Offner, ed., *America and the Origins of World War II, 1933–1941** (1971).

*Paperbound edition available.

12. Policy and Prejudice: The Relocation of Japanese Americans in World War II

It really happened: Seventy thousand American citizens were uprooted from their homes, processed through makeshift assembly centers, and eventually moved to hastily built camps behind barbed wire. There were no formal charges, no trials, no convictions. Guilt was assumed without allowing the accused a chance to prove their innocence. The action was taken by order of the President, at the insistence of the military, with the approval of Congress and the Supreme Court. Many Americans, particularly those on the West Coast, supported it enthusiastically, and across the nation practically no objections were raised. Three decades later the episode is all but forgotten except by those whose lives were touched directly by it.

The time was early 1942. The place was the West Coast. The victims were Japanese Americans, 70,000 of them American citizens and another 42,000 to whom citizenship had been denied. The incarceration of these unfortunate people was strictly a consequence of their racial identity: They shared Japanese ancestry. Within weeks after the outbreak of war between their "adopted" country and the country of their ancestors their loyalty was called into question. In the name of the war effort they were first prohibited from entering designated zones, then they were evacuated from an entire region, and finally they were interned until they were able to relocate in other areas or until the end of the war.

Even this harsh action did not satisfy the most fearful. Proposals were made by some "pro-American" organizations to revoke the citizenship of Americans of Japanese ancestry. Attempts were made, some of them successful, to deprive Japanese Americans of the right to own land. There was even talk in Congress of deporting from the United States all Japanese, citizen and alien.

World War II was total war. At great cost the United States succeeded in turning back military aggression in both the Pacific and in Europe. War costs are ordinarily measured in lives and dollars, but when the costs of World War II are considered, the sacrificing of the constitutional rights of Japanese Americans in the name of the war effort cannot be ignored. Did the military situation really require it? In retrospect it appears certain that it did not. Did the Japanese Americans really pose a danger to the national security? Again, in retrospect, it appears certain that there was no reason to question their loyalty or to assume the likelihood of subversion. Even allowing for the state of panic that prevailed and the resentment against Japan for its attack on Pearl Harbor, reasons for the actions taken against Japanese Americans can hardly be explored without starting with a look at racial prejudice in America.

The antagonism faced by Japanese Americans during the war years came as no surprise to them. The actions taken against them were the culmination of decades of racial prejudice, and they cannot be understood apart from their historical context. Interpretation of naturalization laws from the time of the first arrival of immigrant Japanese (the *Issei*) in 1869 prevented them from acquiring citizenship. A California law enacted in 1913 denied *Issei* the right of owning land in that state or of leasing it for more than three-year periods. Other states imposed similar limitations on their rights. The *Issei* were therefore forced to place title to their land in the name of their children *(Nisei),* who held citizenship by virtue of having been born in the United States. The Immigration Act of 1924 excluded completely immigration from Japan, but anti-Japanese agitation continued and hostility persisted.

The prejudice against Japanese rested in part on a stereotype white Americans had created that applied to all Orientals. In this stereotype, Orientals were seen as sneaky, unreliable, dishonest, fomenters of crime, and violators of white women. As such, they posed a "yellow peril." The prejudice also grew out of the threat of economic competition presented by Japanese Americans. Not content to continue as stoop labor, the *Issei* and *Nisei* sought diligently to be upwardly mobile—and they were successful. By 1941, for example, Japanese Americans raised forty-two percent of California's truck crops. A third source of anti-Japanese sentiment was the manner in which they stuck together, seemingly unwilling or unable to be assimilated or acculturated into the American mainstream. Considering the limitations they faced, it is not surprising that as a group they turned inward.

Core Document

Approaching an Invisible Deadline: Testimony Before the Tolan Committee

EARL WARREN

Most Americans who were alive on December 7, 1941, can still recall their shock at the news of Japan's surprise attack on Pearl Harbor. It was a day, President Roosevelt said, that would "live in infamy." In the weeks immediately following the attack Japanese Americans seemed relatively secure, but as military reverses occurred in the Pacific, sentiment developed to "do something about the Japs" on the West Coast. Fear of a surprise attack somewhere in California intensified the sentiment almost to the point of hysteria.

By February 1942, General John L. DeWitt, commanding officer of the Western Defense Command, was pressing for direct action. After differences of opinion between the Justice Department and the War Department were pushed aside, on February 19, 1942, Roosevelt issued Executive Order 9066, which authorized evacuation of areas deemed vital by the military. The order was vague as to who should be evacuated, but with General DeWitt in charge, it was certain that Japanese Americans were no longer secure.

Congress, meanwhile, was also intensifying its interest in the "Jap problem." Congressmen from western states had worked together to bring pressure for removal of Japanese Americans. On February 20, 1942, the Tolan Committee[1] opened hearings in San Francisco; its purpose was apparently to gather information that would be useful to Congress in making its contribution to solving the "Jap problem."

Among the witnesses was the Attorney General of California, Earl Warren. As the chief law enforcement officer of the state, Warren had gathered information on enemy aliens from district attorneys, sheriffs, and chiefs of police from all over the state. They overwhelmingly supported the notion that the enemy aliens posed a security problem, but that there should be differentiation by nationality in seeking a solution.[2] That they had the Japanese Americans in mind, and that they regarded the Nisei as graver threats than the Issei, is

National Defense Migration: Hearings Before the Select Committee Investigating National Defense Migration, House of Representatives (Government Printing Office, 1942), Part 29, pp. 11009–12, 11014–21.

[1] The Select Committee Investigating National Defense Migrations, chaired by Representative John Tolan of California.

[2] At a mass meeting of sheriffs and district attorneys called by Warren on February 2, 1942, a resolution had been passed urging that "all alien Japanese be forthwith evacuated to some place in the interior for the duration of the war."

apparent in their letters, submitted by Warren as exhibits supporting his testi-mony. Warren, who later served as Governor of California and as Chief Justice of the United States Supreme Court, offered the kind of testimony that was invaluable to those who favored a hard-line policy against Japanese Americans.

In studying Warren's testimony, note:

- *the emphasis placed on the threat of subversive activity.*
- *the evidence presented to support suspicion of Japanese Americans.*
- *the reasons given for believing sabotage was certain.*
- *the reasons given for fearing the* Nisei *more than the* Issei.
- *evidence of prejudgment based on race.*
- *evidence of response to political pressure.*
- *the emphasis placed on the military nature of the problem.*

FEBRUARY 21, 1942

Attorney General WARREN. Mr. Chairman, we feel in California that it is a fortuitous circumstance that this committee is here at this particular time. We believe that there has been no time in our entire crisis when the need of clarification of the alien situation is as apparent as it is today. There are some things transpiring in our State at the present moment that are rather dangerous and we believe that there is only one way that they can be prevented, and that is by a speedy solution of the alien problem. . . .

For some time I have been of the opinion that the solution of our alien enemy problem with all its ramifications, which include the descendants of aliens, is not only a Federal problem but is a military problem. We believe that all of the decisions in that regard must be made by the military command that is charged with the security of this area. I am convinced that the fifth-column activities of our enemy call for the participation of people who are in fact American citizens, and that if we are to deal realistically with the problem we must realize that we will be obliged in time of stress to deal with subversive elements of our own citizenry.

If that be true, it creates almost an impossible situation for the civil authorities because the civil authorities cannot take protective measures against people of that character. We may suspect their loyalty. We may even have some evidence or, perhaps, substantial evidence of their disloyalty. But until we have the whole pattern of the enemy plan, until we are able to go into court and beyond the exclusion of a reasonable doubt establish the guilt of those elements among our American citizens, there is no way that civil govern-ment can cope with the situation.

On the other hand, we believe that in an area, such as in California, which has been designated as a combat zone, when things have happened such as have happened here on the coast, something should be done and done immedi-ately. We believe that any delay in the adoption of the necessary protective measures is to invite disaster. It means that we, too, will have in California a Pearl Harbor incident.

I believe that up to the present and perhaps for a long time to come the greatest danger to continental United States is that from well organized sabotage and fifth-column activity.

Opportunities for Sabotage

California presents, perhaps, the most likely objective in the Nation for such activities. There are many reasons why that is true. First, the size and number of our naval and military establishments in California would make it attractive to our enemies as a field of sabotage. Our geographical position with relation to our enemy and to the war in the Pacific is also a tremendous factor. The number and the diversification of our war industries is extremely vital. The fire hazards due to our climate, our forest areas, and the type of building construction make us very susceptible to fire sabotage. Then the tremendous number of aliens that we have resident here makes it almost an impossible problem from the standpoint of law enforcement.

A wave of organized sabotage in California accompanied by an actual air raid or even by a prolonged black-out could not only be more destructive to life and property but could result in retarding the entire war effort of this Nation far more than the treacherous bombing of Pearl Harbor.

I hesitate to think what the result would be of the destruction of any of our big airplane factories in this State. It will interest you to know that some of our airplane factories in this State are entirely surrounded by Japanese land ownership or occupancy. It is a situation that is fraught with the greatest danger and under no circumstances should it ever be permitted to exist.

I have some maps here that will show the specific instances of that character. In order to advise the committee more accurately on this subject I have asked the various district attorneys throughout the State to submit maps to me showing every Japanese ownership and occupancy in the State. Those maps tell a story, a story that is not very heartening to anyone who has the responsibility of protecting life and property either in time of peace or in war.

To assume that the enemy has not planned fifth column activities for us in a wave of sabotage is simply to live in a fool's paradise. These activities, whether you call them "fifth column activities" or "sabotage" or "war behind the lines upon civilians," or whatever you may call it, are just as much an integral part of Axis warfare as any of their military and naval operations. When I say that I refer to all of the Axis powers with which we are at war.

It has developed into a science and a technique that has been used most effectively against every nation with which the Axis powers are at war. It has been developed to a degree almost beyond the belief of our American citizens. That is one of the reasons it is so difficult for our people to become aroused and appreciate the danger of such activities. Those activities are now being used actively in the war in the Pacific, in every field of operations about which I have read. They have unquestionably, gentlemen, planned such activities for

California. For us to believe to the contrary is just not realistic.

Unfortunately, however, many of our people and some of our authorities and, I am afraid, many of our people in other parts of the country are of the opinion that because we have had no sabotage and no fifth column activities in this State since the beginning of the war, that means that none have been planned for us. But I take the view that that is the most ominous sign in our whole situation. It convinces me more than perhaps any other factor that the sabotage that we are to get, the fifth column activities that we are to get, are timed just like Pearl Harbor was timed and just like the invasion of France, and of Denmark, and of Norway, and all of those other countries.

I believe that we are just being lulled into a false sense of security and that the only reason we haven't had disaster in California is because it has been timed for a different date, and that when that time comes if we don't do something about it it is going to mean disaster both to California and to our Nation. Our day of reckoning is bound to come in that regard. When, nobody knows, of course, but we are approaching an invisible deadline.

The CHAIRMAN. On that point, when that came up in our committee hearings there was not a single case of sabotage reported on the Pacific coast, we heard the heads of the Navy and the Army, and they all tell us that the Pacific coast can be attacked. The sabotage would come coincident with that attack, would it not?

Attorney General WARREN. Exactly.

The CHAIRMAN. They would be fools to tip their hands now, wouldn't they?

Attorney General WARREN. Exactly. If there were sporadic sabotage at this time or if there had been for the last 2 months, the people of California or the Federal authorities would be on the alert to such an extent that they could not possibly have any real fifth column activities when the M-day comes. And I think that that should figure very largely in our conclusions on this subject.

Approaching an invisible deadline as we do, it seems to me that no time can be wasted in making the protective measures that are essential to the security of this State. And when I say "this State" I mean all of the coast, of course. I believe that Oregon and Washington are entitled to the same sort of consideration as the zone of danger as California. Perhaps our danger is intensified by the number of our industries and the number of our aliens, but it is much the same. . . .

I want to say that the consensus of opinion among the law-enforcement officers of this State is that there is more potential danger among the group of Japanese who are born in this country than from the alien Japanese who were born in Japan. That might seem an anomaly to some people, but the fact is that, in the first place, there are twice as many of them. There are 33,000 aliens and there are 66,000 born in this country.

In the second place, most of the Japanese who were born in Japan are over

55 years of age. There has been practically no migration to this country since 1924. But in some instances the children of those people have been sent to Japan for their education, either in whole or in part, and while they are over there they are indoctrinated with the idea of Japanese imperialism. They receive their religious instruction which ties up their religion with their Emperor, and they come back here imbued with the ideas and the policies of Imperial Japan.

While I do not cast a reflection on every Japanese who is born in this country—of course we will have loyal ones—I do say that the consensus of opinion is that taking the groups by and large there is more potential danger to this State from the group that is born here than from the group that is born in Japan.

Mr. ARNOLD. Let me ask you a question at this point.

Attorney General WARREN. Yes, Congressman.

Mr. ARNOLD. Do you have any way of knowing whether any one of this group that you mention is loyal to this country or loyal to Japan?

Attorney General WARREN. Congressman, there is no way that we can establish that fact. We believe that when we are dealing with the Caucasian race we have methods that will test the loyalty of them, and we believe that we can, in dealing with the Germans and the Italians, arrive at some fairly sound conclusions because of our knowledge of the way they live in the community and have lived for many years. But when we deal with the Japanese we are in an entirely different field and we cannot form any opinion that we believe to be sound. Their method of living, their language, make for this difficulty. Many of them who show you a birth certificate stating that they were born in this State, perhaps, or born in Honolulu, can hardly speak the English language because, although they were born here, when they were 4 or 5 years of age they were sent over to Japan to be educated and they stayed over there through their adolescent period at least, and then they came back here thoroughly Japanese.

The CHAIRMAN. There are certain Japanese schools here, are there not?

Attorney General WARREN. Then we have the Japanese school system here. There is no way that we know of of determining that fact.

I had together about 10 days ago about 40 district attorneys and about 40 sheriffs in the State to discuss this alien problem. I asked all of them collectively at that time if in their experience any Japanese, whether California-born or Japan-born, had ever given them any information on subversive activities or any disloyalty to this country. The answer was unanimously that no such information had ever been given to them.

Now, that is almost unbelievable. You see, when we deal with the German aliens, when we deal with the Italian aliens, we have many informants who are most anxious to help the local authorities and the State and Federal authorities to solve this alien problem. They come in voluntarily and give us information. We get none from the other source.

Does that answer your question, Congressman?

Mr. ARNOLD. That answers it fully.

Attorney General WARREN. There is one thing that concerns us at the present time. As I say, we are very happy over the order of the President yesterday. We believe that is the thing that should be done, but that is only one-half of the problem, as we see it. It is one thing to take these people out of the area and it is another thing to do something with them after they get out. Even from the small areas that they have left up to the present time there are many, many Japanese who are now roaming around the State and roaming around the Western States in a condition that will unquestionably bring about race riots and prejudice and hysteria and excesses of all kind.

I hate to say it, but we have had some evidence of it in our State in just the last 2 or 3 days. People do not want these Japanese just loaded from one community to another, and as a practical matter it might be a very bad thing to do because we might just be transposing the danger from one place to another.

So it seems to me that the next thing the Government has to do is to find a way of handling these aliens who are removed from any vital zone.

In the county of Tulare at the present time and in the county of San Benito and in other counties there are large numbers of the Japanese moving in and sometimes the suggestion has come from the place that they leave, that they ought to go to this other community. But when they go there they find a hostile situation. We are very much afraid that it will cause trouble unless there is a very prompt solution of this problem.

Vigilantism

My own belief concerning vigilantism is that the people do not engage in vigilante activities so long as they believe that their Government through its agencies is taking care of their most serious problem. But when they get the idea that their problems are not understood, when their Government is not doing for them the things that they believe should be done, they start taking the law into their own hands.

That is one reason why we are so happy that this committee is out here today because we believe that it will help us solve this problem quickly, which is just as important as to solve it permanently.

The CHAIRMAN. We are certainly in a position to get the word right to the heads when we get back to Washington.

Attorney General WARREN. Yes, sir.

The CHAIRMAN. We can give them the facts that you are just giving us. We are the parties that can transmit them. We can get the word there anyway.

Attorney General WARREN. Yes. There has been a lot of talk of how it would disturb the agricultural situation in the State to move the Japanese. I think that is a very debatable question and I think that the records of the Department of Agriculture or the Government will show that it is not as great a problem as it is generally supposed to be. We have seen some very fantastic figures as to what part the Japanese labor plays in California agriculture. I think the facts will not support those figures, and this is one thing that I think should be borne in mind by your committee: That we have a great many large Japanese agricultural operators in this State, and when they operate on a large scale they use exactly the same kind of help that white operators use. In other words, when their crops are to be harvested they don't necessarily harvest them with Japanese. They harvest them with Filipinos and Mexicans and even white people. There is one thing this year that makes it even less desirable to have the Japanese on the land, and that is the fact that the Filipinos and the Mexicans have resolved that they will not harvest crops for Japanese. So they might have their crops on the ground and still they would not be harvested. If those people don't work for them, I have an idea that probably white people won't work for them, either.

The CHAIRMAN. We are going to have a representative from the Department of Agriculture to get those figures.

Japanese Land Ownership

Attorney General WARREN. Yes. I merely made that observation.

Now, gentlemen, I have some maps which show the character of the Japanese land ownership and possessory interests in California. I will submit them at the time I submit a formal statement on the subject. These maps show to the law enforcement officers that it is more than just accident, that many of those ownerships are located where they are. We base that assumption not only upon the fact that they are located in certain places, but also on the time when the ownership was acquired.

It seems strange to us that airplane manufacturing plants should be entirely surrounded by Japanese land occupancies. It seems to us that it is more than circumstance that after certain Government air bases were established Japanese undertook farming operations in close proximity to them. You can hardly grow a jackrabbit in some of the places where they presume to be carrying on farming operations close to an Army bombing base.

Many of our vital facilities, and most of our highways are just pocketed by Japanese ownerships that could be of untold danger to us in time of stress.

So we believe, gentlemen, that it would be wise for the military to take every protective measure that it believes is necessary to protect this State and this Nation against the possible activities of these people. . . .

Mr. ARNOLD. One thing you are sure of—it just couldn't have happened that way?

Attorney General WARREN. We don't believe that it could in all of these instances, and knowing what happened at Pearl Harbor and other places we believe that there is a pattern to these land ownerships in California and possessory interests in California.

The CHAIRMAN. In the last few years have purchases by these native-born Japanese increased in the surroundings close to these aircraft factories?

Attorney General WARREN. Yes, sir.

Mr. SPARKMAN. I was interested in your whole statement. As you were discussing it, I thought of testimony that was given before the House Military Affairs Committee, of which I am a member, by a French officer who was in the French Army prior to, and at the time of, the French capitulation. He told us of the difficulties that the French had in their own villages; that always their strategy was given away; the enemy found out about it. Their final solution to the problem was simply, when they started operating in a territory, to evacuate everybody, citizens and all. Of course, that was the field of battle.

Attorney General WARREN. Yes, sir.

Mr. SPARKMAN. Your thought is that this, too, is a possible combat area?

Attorney General Warren. Yes, sir.

Mr. SPARKMAN. And those in charge of operations should have the authority to evacuate all whom they feel should be evacuated for the defense of the area?

Attorney General WARREN. Precisely. And regardless of citizenship or alienage.

Mr. SPARKMAN. And is it your understanding that the Executive order of yesterday gave such authority to the military commander?

Attorney General WARREN. That is the way I read the newspaper report and that is the only thing that I have. The newspapers stated that specifically.

Mr. SPARKMAN. I do want to add a word to what the chairman said. I am sure you people out here know it, but your congressional delegation in both Houses of Congress has been very much on the alert in discussing and making plans for the defense of this area. A week, 10 days, or 2 weeks ago, this very recommendation was made to the President and, as I read the order, it follows out almost word for word the recommendation that was made by your congressional delegation.

I have noticed suggestions in newspaper stories. I noticed a telegram this morning with reference to the civil rights of these people. What do you have to say about that?

Attorney General WARREN. I believe, sir, that in time of war every citizen must give up some of his normal rights.

Evacuation as Military Problem

I believe that no good citizen should object to it. I do believe, however, that it should be done by proper authority and not by sporadic action on the part of agencies that do not function according to the law. That is the reason that I believe that this is a military problem and not a problem in civil government. We have had instances in this State where extra-legal action has been taken with regard to these very people, without regard to our statutes or our constitution or the Constitution of the United States. Now, I think, that is bad.

Mr. SPARKMAN. May I say there, when you say "without regard" you don't consider this as being without regard of Constitution, because isn't it true that the Constitution makes provision for just such things?

Attorney General WARREN. You mean the action the President took yesterday?

Mr. SPARKMAN. Yes.

Attorney General WARREN. I think that is entirely in keeping with it and that is why I commend it so highly. That is why I believe so sincerely in it because it does transfer the solution of this problem to the military authorities who are charged with the defense of this area and, therefore, have the right morally and legally and every other way to take any protective measures that are necessary to insure the security of the area.

The CHAIRMAN. In other words, there are two alternatives—the suspension of the writ of habeas corpus, or martial law. Is that right?

Attorney General WARREN. Yes, sir.

The CHAIRMAN. We are putting them all on the same footing. I think, like you, that it is absolutely constitutional. But if we took it direct, we would be in the courts for the duration of the war fighting that thing out. Is that not so?

Attorney General WARREN. Yes.

Authority for Exclusion of Persons From Military Areas

The CHAIRMAN. Well, we haven't the time to fight it out in the courts. That is the way we feel. Isn't that right?

Attorney General WARREN. Yes. There was a time in the Civil War— I don't have the name of the case in mind at the moment, but I have it available —where the War Department through the commander of the Army, declared certain areas to be danger zones and directed that only those who were given permits were entitled to enter and move about. Then Congress fortified that situation by declaring it in a statute to be a danger zone. When it went to the Supreme Court, the Supreme Court did not sustain the military commander but it did sustain the action of Congress in declaring it to be a zone of danger in which those things could be done by the military.

It may be in this situation that if there is any question about the right of the military to do it, Congress could draw a line so far in from the coast and say that, because of the world conditions and the things that are confronting us, that constituted an area in which the military could do certain things.

The CHAIRMAN. When you prepare your final paper, will you give us that citation? That will be very valuable to us.

Attorney General WARREN. I will be very happy to do it.

Discussion Starters

1. This is the advice Attorney General Warren received from the Chief of Police of Sacramento: "I believe all Japanese should be removed. . . . I believe all German and Italian aliens should be considered individually." What evidence is there in Warren's testimony that he concurred with this advice? How does this advice square with American judicial values?

2. Evaluate Warren's assertions concerning a sabotage plot and a land ownership conspiracy.

3. Speculate on the uses racially prejudiced Congressmen and others might have made of Warren's testimony. What might Warren have said, within the context of information he had available, to reverse the tide of racial prejudice rather than to stimulate it?

4. Compare the removal of the Japanese Americans from the West Coast with the removal of Indians from their lands wherever it occurred.

5. Respond to this statement: "Relocation of the Japanese Americans was all for their own good. It was the only way to protect them from vigilantism."

6. Under what circumstances might another attempt at mass evacuation of a feared or suspected element in the population be conceived in the future? Who might be the objects of such an attempt? Suggest guidelines that might be followed to prevent injustices from being done.

Related Documents

I. *112,000 Potential Enemies: The Army's Final Report*

JOHN L. DeWITT

As commanding officer of the Western Defense Command, Lieutenant General John L. DeWitt bore heavy responsibility for the defense of the coastal states. His apprehension concerning Japanese Americans must be understood in the light of the panic that gripped the nation, particularly the western states, in the months after Pearl Harbor. Even in this light, however, his attitude toward Japanese Americans merits attention, for it no doubt contributed to the policy of evacuation he advocated and to the steps he took to implement it. On one occasion he is reported to have testified before a congressional committee: "A Jap's a Jap. It makes no difference whether he is an American citizen or not."

Included here is a brief excerpt from General DeWitt's final report on evacuation. Note the similarities between this statement and Warren's testimony. How would one determine whether a negative attitude toward the Japa-

U.S. Army, *Final Report: Japanese Evacuation from the West Coast, 1942* (Washington, D.C.: Government Printing Office, 1943), p. 34.

nese shaped his policy or whether military necessities shaped the negative attitude?

The area lying to the west of the Cascade and Sierra Nevada Mountains in Washington, Oregon and California, is highly critical not only because the lines of communication and supply to the Pacific theater pass through it, but also because of the vital industrial production therein, particularly aircraft. In the war in which we are now engaged racial affinities are not severed by migration. The Japanese race is an enemy race and while many second and third generation Japanese born on United States soil, possessed of United States citizenship, have become "Americanized," the racial strains are undiluted. To conclude otherwise is to expect that children born of white parents on Japanese soil sever all racial affinity and become loyal Japanese subjects, ready to fight and, if necessary, to die for Japan in a war against the nation of their parents. That Japan is allied with Germany and Italy in this struggle is no ground for assuming that any Japanese, barred from assimilation by convention as he is, though born and raised in the United States, will not turn against this nation when the final test of loyalty comes. It, therefore, follows that along the vital Pacific Coast over 112,000 potential enemies, of Japanese extraction, are at large today. There are indications that these are organized and ready for concerted action at a favorable opportunity. The very fact that no sabotage has taken place to date is a disturbing and confirming indication that such action will be taken.

II. Testimony of the Mayor of San Francisco

ANGELO J. ROSSI

The first witness before the Tolan Committee at its San Francisco hearings was Mayor Angelo J. Rossi. The problem of "enemy aliens" was of great interest to him partly because of the number of foreigners in California. In fact, Italian aliens outnumbered Japanese aliens in that state by 9,000 (50,000 to 41,000). Note how he handled the problem. To what extent were his basic assumptions the same as Warren's? How can these assumptions be accounted for?

FEBRUARY 21, 1942

I am of the belief that the seriousness of having alien enemies in our midst is self-evident. Their presence might not only affect the property of our citizenry and our Government but it might also affect the very lives and welfare of all of our people. The problem is a most difficult one, but we are living in times

National Defense Migration: Hearings Before the Select Committee Investigating National Defense Migration, House of Representatives (Washington, D.C.: Government Printing Office, 1942), part 29, pp. 10966–68.

when a delicate problem must be firmly dealt with. It is true that the recent drastic measures against enemy aliens have caused great anxiety and distress among this group of people. It is true also that as a result of these measures many San Francisco families will be deprived of their livelihood. Many families will have to abandon their homes, their businesses, and their occupations; parents will have to abandon their children and go elsewhere. The great majority of noncitizens in this area is made up of elderly men and women whom I believe for the most part to be industrious, peaceful and law-abiding residents of this community. Most of them have native-born children. Many of them have sons in the armed forces and both sons and daughters engaged in defense industries and civilian defense activities. It is the well-considered opinion of many that most of these people are entirely loyal to this Nation; are in accord with its form of Government, believe in its ideals and have an affection for its traditions and that under no circumstances would they engage in any subversive activities or conduct.

It has been said that the measures which are proposed to be taken against these aliens, instead of making for national solidarity and unity of effort in this emergency may cause dissatisfaction and resentment among those of alien parentage. In my opinion all of the above-mentioned elements should be given serious consideration before any more drastic measures are taken. In my opinion the above-mentioned facts apply particularly to the German and Italian alien problems. Their problems should be considered separately from those of the Japanese.

The Japanese situation should be given immediate attention. It admits of no delay. The activities of the Japanese saboteurs and fifth columnists in Honolulu and on the battle fronts in the Pacific have forced me to the conclusion that every Japanese alien should be removed from this community. I am also strongly of the conviction that Japanese who are American citizens should be subjected to a more detailed and all-encompassing investigation. After investigation, if it is found that these citizens are not loyal to this country they, too, should be removed from the community.

The general statements I made at the outset, I repeat, pertain mainly to persons of German and Italian origin, many of whom are engaged in business, occupations pursued by them for years, the character of some of which necessarily enters into the welfare of San Francisco. The great majority of these aliens likewise have children, most of whom were born, reared, and educated in this community and are law-abiding citizens.

It must be obvious that if these alien residents about whom I have just made mention are moved from San Francisco, separated from their children and families, and deprived of the occupations in which they are now and for years have been engaged, they will be subjected to extreme hardship, mental distress, and suffering.

My opinion is that such results should be avoided, and that evacuation of Axis aliens, other than Japanese, should be avoided unless deemed imperative. If immediate removal is deemed necessary, as quickly thereafter as is conveniently practical, such aliens should be permitted to make application to resume their former places of residence (other than in prohibited areas) and their present occupations and such applications should be heard by some appropriate tribunal which could quickly and intelligently determine the same, and that in the event such applicant is found to be a person of loyalty and integrity, the desired permit be issued, subject, however, to such restrictions as might be deemed necessary.

III. A Japanese-American Citizen's Statement

MIKE M. MASAOKA

Spokesmen for Japanese Americans and supporters of their rights were also given an opportunity to be heard before the Tolan Committee, although they were substantially outnumbered by unfriendly witnesses. The chief spokesman for the Japanese Americans was Mike Masaoka, national secretary and field executive of the Japanese American Citizens League. Masaoka later became the first Nisei to volunteer for the famous 442nd Regimental Combat Team; four of his brothers also served, while their mother remained in a relocation camp. (The 442nd Infantry Regiment, composed of Japanese Americans, was activated in February 1943; it played an important role in the campaigns in Italy and Southern France and was lauded for the courage and devotion to duty that its men displayed.)

The Japanese Americans have sometimes been criticized for failing to resist the evacuation orders, and in fact they offered practically no resistance at all. Evaluate Masaoka's statement as an expression of loyalty and speculate on the response Warren might have given to it. Then respond to the criticism that Masaoka went too far in agreeing with the government's plans.

FEBRUARY 23, 1942

Our frank and reasoned opinion on the matter of evacuation revolves around certain considerations of which we feel both your committee and the general public should be apprised. With any policy of evacuation definitely arising from reasons of military necessity and national safety, we are in complete agreement. As American citizens, we cannot and should not take any other stand. But, also, as American citizens believing in the integrity of our citizenship, we feel that any evacuation enforced on grounds violating that integrity should be opposed.

If, in the judgment of military and Federal authorities, evacuation of Japanese residents from the West coast is a primary step toward assuring the

National Defense Migration: Hearings Before the Select Committee Investigating National Defense Migration, House of Representatives (Washington, D.C.: Government Printing Office, 1942), part 29, pp. 11137–38.

safety of this Nation, we will have no hesitation in complying with the necessities implicit in that judgment. But, if, on the other hand, such evacuation is primarily a measure whose surface urgency cloaks the desires of political or other pressure groups who want us to leave merely from motives of self-interest, we feel that we have every right to protest and to demand equitable judgment on our merits as American citizens.

In any case, we feel that the whole problem of evacuation, once its necessity is militarily established, should be met strictly according to that need. Only these areas, in which strategic and military considerations make the removal of Japanese residents necessary, should be evacuated. . . .

I now make an earnest plea that you seriously consider and recognize our American citizenship status which we have been taught to cherish as our most priceless heritage.

At this hearing, we Americans of Japanese descent have been accused of being disloyal to these United States. As an American citizen, I resent these accusations and deny their validity.

We American-born Japanese are fighting militarist Japan today with our total energies. Four thousand of us are with the armed forces of the United States, the remainder on the home front in the battle of production. We ask a chance to prove to the rest of the American people what we ourselves already know: That we are loyal to the country of our birth and that we will fight to the death to defend it against any and all aggressors.

We think, feel, act like Americans. We, too, remember Pearl Harbor and know that our right to live as free men in a free Nation is in peril as long as the brutal forces of enslavement walk the earth. We know that the Axis aggressors must be crushed and we are anxious to participate fully in that struggle.

The history of our group speaks for itself. It stands favorable comparison with that of any other group of second generation Americans. There is reliable authority to show that the proportion of delinquency and crime within our ranks is negligible. Throughout the long years of the depression, we have been able to stay off the relief rolls better, by far, than any other group. These are but two of the many examples which might be cited as proof of our civic responsibility and pride.

In this emergency, as in the past, we are not asking for special privileges or concessions. We ask only for the opportunity and the right of sharing the common lot of all Americans, whether it be in peace or in war.

This is the American way for which our boys are fighting.

IV. Report of the California Joint Immigration Committee

The political pressure group most responsible for maintaining anti-Japanese attitudes in California was the California Joint Immigration Committee, composed of representatives of the American Legion, the Native Sons of the Golden West, the California State Federation of Labor, and the California Grange. Their position on Japanese Americans was stated clearly in testimony and exhibits presented to the Tolan Committee.

The document given here consists of representative paragraphs from one of their exhibits. Taking into consideration the membership of their constituent organizations—Earl Warren belonged to the American Legion and the Native Sons—what conclusions might be drawn concerning anti-Japanese sentiment in California? Try to find any point in his testimony at which Warren expressed ideas inconsistent with those in this statement.

FEBRUARY 21, 1942

The 150,000 Japanese in continental United States form one of the country's most foreign-minded racial groups. The native-born among them are American citizens, but they are dominated by their ineligible alien parents, whose patriotism for Japan and its emperor, whom they worship as a god, is almost fanatical. Because of this domination and their strongly Japanese racial characteristics, these American-born Japanese are not assimilated into the social structure of this country.

Japanese immigrants have never been welcome here because of their aggressiveness, unassimilability, and low living standards. In 1892 the first unsuccessful attempt was made to keep them out of San Francisco, and soon so many coolie laborers were coming that there was much agitation for an exclusion law similar to that barring the Chinese. Congress was unsympathetic, but Japan, fearing the stigma of an exclusion law because 12,000 Japanese came in in 1 year, agreed in 1900 to keep her laborers out of continental United States. This was the first gentlemen's agreement.

In violation of this agreement, from 1901 to 1908, inclusive, 51,689 Japanese, most of whom were or became laborers, entered. California continued to protest, and in 1907 President Theodore Roosevelt, to save Japan's pride, negotiated another gentlemen's agreement, the details of which were secret, although it was announced that Japan had again agreed not to send laborers to continental United States.

This agreement was also violated, and the American courts were powerless to enforce its terms, since it was neither law nor treaty. Between 1909,

National Defense Migration: Hearings Before the Select Committee Investigating National Defense Migration, House of Representatives (Washington, D.C.: Government Printing Office, 1942), part 29, pp. 11084–87.

when it went into effect, and 1924, when the agreement was terminated, the Japanese population of continental United States increased from 76,714 to 131,357. Prolific picture brides contributed to this increase, each family averaging five children.

The Japanese quickly acquired land, not being content to work as day laborers, and frequently depleted it. Women and children worked with the men, and this sort of competition helped to drive out the Caucasian population, notably in certain communities in the Sacramento Valley. The Japanese were assertive, antagonistic, and not too honest.

Failing to get relief from Congress, California in 1913 enacted an alien land law, prohibiting aliens ineligible to citizenship from purchasing land or leasing agricultural land. The Japanese circumvented this law in a measure by operating in the names of their American children. The agricultural communities of California seemed overrun with Japanese. Feeling against them ran high, but there was little violence. The other Pacific Coast States had the same problem, in a lesser degree.

In 1924 California and her neighboring States made such a convincing presentation of their Japanese problem to Congress that the exclusion measure, barring aliens ineligible to citizenship as permanent residents, was included in the Immigration Restriction Act. The fight was a hard one, for Japan had enlisted many friends to her cause—church people, idealists, foreign traders, employers of cheap labor, and uninformed Government officials. . . .

Although no more are coming in, there are still many alien Japanese in California, living a typically Japanese life and controlling in large measure, by tremendous industry, skill and incredibly low living standards, the fruit, berry, and vegetable industry of the State. This control of much of our food supply is disquieting, as they are distrusted. . . .

But the main problem now is the second generation Japanese, or Nisei, of whom there are more than 50,000 in California. They apparently want to be part of the social structure but are not welcome because of their too evident racial characteristics. They complain constantly of racial discrimination, but their plight is the direct result of their parents forcing themselves unwanted on this country. They are splendid people in many ways, good students and workers, but they are "Americans with Japanese faces." They cannot find work except among their own kind, and while intermarriage is forbidden in California, they really do not desire it, considering it an insult to the pride and glory of the Yamato race. Even in Hawaii there is little intermarriage between the Japanese and other races, particularly the Caucasian. They must live in segregated districts, which they resent, but are accepted on equal terms into the Army, where most of them seem quite happy.

These conditions, while unfortunate, are the result of the determination of the Caucasians to keep their country and their blood white, and involves no claim of superiority. Our laws against which the Japanese protest were enacted to keep out immigrants who cannot be absorbed into the lifeblood of the country, and who form unassimilated racial blocs. The Founding Fathers of the Republic stipulated that citizenship should be granted only to free white persons. But a grave mistake was made when citizenship was granted to all born here, regardless of fitness or desire for such citizenship. Another grave mistake was the granting of citizenship to the Negroes after the Civil War. . . .

The California Joint Immigration Committee is maintained primarily to protect the exclusion measure against repeal or modification and notify the public in regard thereto. It contends that these unfortunate and highly undesirably conditions are proof of the unassimilability of the Japanese and the necessity of their exclusion as permanent residents. All Japanese, both here and in Japan, are constantly agitating for immigration quota, claiming that the number that could enter thereunder (185 annually) would be negligible. But added to that basic quota would be all those coming in under nonquota classification—visitors, students, ministers, diplomats, businessmen, and particularly alien wives for American-born Japanese (much desired). These wives would become the mothers of large, unassimilable families, and so the Japanese problem would be aggravated and perpetuated. Quota would also necessarily be extended to all other oriental countries, bringing the annual immigration from the Orient to well over 1,000. The basic principle of exclusion of those ineligible to citizenship must not be destroyed or weakened, either by grant of quota or by grant of naturalization to the colored races of Asia.

V. *"This Is a Race War"*

JOHN M. RANKIN

Racial aspects of problems relating to the Japanese American situation were apparent in congressional debates. Most outspoken against the Japanese was Representative John M. Rankin of Mississippi, whose prejudice against blacks spilled over against them. At various times on the floor of Congress he not only supported evacuation but also urged separation of sexes in the relocation centers, revocation of citizenship, and, finally, deportation.

A sample of his style and attitudes is offered in this excerpt from his remarks on the floor of the House of Representatives on February 18, 1942. His was an extreme position. Where does one draw the line between his position and Warren's? Who do you suppose was more representative of national sentiment?

FEBRUARY 18, 1942

This is a race war, as far as the Pacific side of this conflict is concerned, and we might as well understand it. The white man's civilization has come into conflict with Japanese barbarism. Christianity has come in conflict with Shint-

Congressional Record, February 18, 1942, pp. 1419–20.

oism, atheism, and infidelity. One of them must be destroyed. You cannot regenerate a Jap, convert him, change him, and make him the same as a white man any more than you can reverse the laws of nature. . . .

This is a question we have to settle now, and we might as well understand it. I am for catching every Japanese in America, Alaska, and Hawaii now and putting him in concentration camps and shipping them back to Asia as soon as possible. If they own property in this country, after the war we can pay them for it, but we must ship them back to the Orient, where they belong. Until that is done, we will never have peace on the Pacific, and we will never have any safety in Hawaii, Alaska, Oregon, Washington, or California.

Mr. BLAND. Mr. Chairman, will the gentleman yield?

Mr. RANKIN of Mississippi. I yield to the gentleman from Virginia.

Mr. BLAND. We found also that they had their own schools, in addition.

Mr. RANKIN of Mississippi. Yes, I was coming to that. The gentleman from Virginia [Mr. BLAND] was a member of that committee, and he saw what was going on. He and I discussed it at the time, along with the gentleman from North Carolina [Mr. KERR], who now sits before me. I said then that we had to get rid of those Japs or they would get rid of us. There can be no compromise.

I spoke in practically every high school in Honolulu, to practically everyone on the island of Oahu, and they told me there that just as soon as those schools were out in the afternoon the Japanese children, and children of Japanese descent, would go directly to a Japanese-language school. The distinguished gentleman from North Carolina [Mr. KERR], who was a very able member of that delegation, will vouch for that statement.

Mr. NORRELL. Mr. Chairman, will the gentleman yield?

Mr. RANKIN of Mississippi. I yield.

Mr. NORRELL. Does not the gentleman think we should have an amendment in this bill providing for the deportation of Japanese from Hawaii in place of an investigation?

Mr. RANKIN of Mississippi. Yes; that is what I want. We must get rid of the Japs in Hawaii or they will get rid of us. . . .

We are at war. We are at war with Japan, the most ruthless and damnable enemy that ever insulted this country, and I am in favor of treating it as war and stopping all this interracial nonsense by which we have been petting the Japanese for the last quarter of a century.

Mr. RANDOLPH. Mr. Chairman, will the gentleman yield?

Mr. RANKIN of Mississippi. I yield.

Mr. RANDOLPH. Mr. Chairman, I rise to vindicate the courage and the accuracy with which the gentleman from Mississippi speaks.

Mr. RANKIN of Mississippi. I thank the gentleman from West Virginia.

Mr. RANDOLPH. I should like to say that many Members of this House, including the gentleman now addressing the Committee [Mr. RANDOLPH], have suggested that the Civilian Conservation Corps camps now vacant be used to take care of the thousands and thousands of Japanese who are a menace on the west coast.

Mr. RANKIN of Mississippi. Certainly! I do not care where you put them, so long as you put them in concentration camps. I now yield to the gentleman from Washington [Mr. COFFEE].

Mr. COFFEE of Washington. I just wanted to add to what the gentleman has said about schools in Hawaii: That in the State of Washington the Japanese-Americans attend Japanese schools and study the Japanese culture daily following their attendance at the public schools. The American Legion and the Veterans of Foreign Wars have taken the same stand as the gentleman from Mississippi.

Mr. RANKIN of Mississippi. And another thing, they go to the Shinto temples and practice the Shinto religion, in which they worship the Emperor of Japan as god. Do not forget that.

Mr. COFFEE of Washington. That is correct.

Mr. RANKIN of Mississippi. Do not forget that once a Japanese always a Japanese. I say it is of vital importance that we get rid of every Japanese whether in Hawaii or on the mainland. They violate every sacred promise, every canon of honor and decency. This was evidenced in their diplomacy and in their bombing of Hawaii. These Japs who had been there for generations were making signs, if you please, guiding the Japanese planes to the objects of their iniquity in order that they might destroy our naval vessels, murder our soldiers and sailors, and blow to pieces the helpless women and children of Hawaii.

Damn them! Let us get rid of them now!

VI. *California and the Japanese*

CAREY MCWILLIAMS

An economic aspect of the evacuation of Japanese Americans was referred to by Carey McWilliams, chief of the Division of Immigration and Housing of the California Department of Industrial Relations. McWilliams was always sensitive to the situation of the Japanese Americans and other minorities and sympathetic with their plight. Note how his comments differ from Warren's. How might the difference be accounted for?

MARCH 2, 1942

People are prone to forget, in a moment of excitement, that special-interest groups have axes to grind against the Japanese. On the great wholesale produce markets in Los Angeles, the non-Japanese commission firms would, of course,

The New Republic, March 2, 1942, pp. 295–96.

like to see their Japanese competitors eliminated. "White-American" nursery-men have already organized a boycott of Japanese firms.

Quite recently the movement for the wholesale evacuation of the Japa-nese has taken an even more dangerous direction. It has been proposed, for example, that all Japanese be moved out of the coastal areas in Cali-fornia and put to work on a semi-conscription basis as farm laborers in the San Joaquin Valley "at reasonable wages." This suggestion has more than passing significance. For the first time in nearly twenty years, California agriculture in 1942 will face a close balance between the supply and the demand for farm labor. For years the interests which control California agriculture have profited by the fact of a large surplus of agricultural workers. Through the use of this surplus, they have effectively checked or-ganizational efforts on the part of the workers themselves and have been able to delay the adoption of improved labor standards. To put an army of Japanese conscript workers at the disposal of these interests—an army un-able to strike, unable even to protest over working conditions—would be to give them one of the most effective scab-labor reserves imaginable. Re-cently a modification of this proposal has appeared: to transfer all alien Japanese and all Japanese-Americans under eighteen years of age and cer-tain other groups, to the Rocky Mountain States, where "they could be used during the spring and fall when the sugar-beet farms have their peak load." The effect of such a proposal would be to displace long-resident Mexican sugar-beet workers in the same area.

Already irreparable damage has been done the Japanese population by reason of the tragic situation in which they find themselves. They will carry with them for years to come the marks of this experience. Patterns of cultural adaptation which, under more favorable circumstances and with a little more understanding, might have resulted in highly desirable conclusions, have been seriously interrupted, if not permanently disarranged. The Japanese should be encouraged to make their own contribution to the defense effort. Many of them are talented writers, radio technicians, linguists, artists. As collaborators on propaganda programs, their services would be invaluable. They all have a job to do and they should be permitted to do it. . . .

VII. *Concentration Camp: U.S. Style*

TED NAKASHIMA

A chapter on the internment of Japanese Americans would be incomplete if not one of the interned persons was represented. This article speaks for itself. How do you suppose Warren would have answered the question Nakashima asked at the end of the article?

The New Republic, June 15, 1942, pp. 822–23.

JUNE 15, 1942

Unfortunately in this land of liberty, I was born of Japanese parents; born in Seattle of a mother and father who have been in this country since 1901. Fine parents, who brought up their children in the best American way of life. My mother served with the Volunteer Red Cross Service in the last war—my father, an editor, has spoken and written Americanism for forty years.

Our family is almost typical of the other unfortunates here at the camp. The oldest son, a licensed architect, was educated at the University of Washington, has a master's degree from the Massachusetts Institute of Technology and is a scholarship graduate of the American School of Fine Arts in Fontainebleau, France. He is now in camp in Oregon with his wife and three-months-old child. He had just completed designing a much needed defense housing project at Vancouver, Washington.

The second son is an M.D. He served his interneship in a New York hospital, is married and has two fine sons. The folks banked on him, because he was the smartest of us three boys. The army took him a month after he opened his office. He is now a lieutenant in the Medical Corps, somewhere in the South.

I am the third son, the dumbest of the lot, but still smart enough to hold down a job as an architectural draftsman. I have just finished building a new home and had lived in it three weeks. My desk was just cleared of work done for the Army Engineers, another stack of 391 defense houses was waiting (a rush job), when the order came to pack up and leave for this resettlement center called "Camp Harmony."

Mary, the only girl in the family, and her year-old son, "Butch," are with our parents—interned in the stables of the Livestock Exposition Buildings in Portland.

Now that you can picture our thoroughly American background, let me describe our new home.

The resettlement center is actually a penitentiary—armed guards in towers with spotlights and deadly tommy guns, fifteen feet of barbed-wire fences, everyone confined to quarters at nine, lights out at ten o'clock. The guards are ordered to shoot anyone who approaches within twenty feet of the fences. No one is allowed to take the two-block-long hike to the latrines after nine, under any circumstances.

The apartments, as the army calls them, are two-block-long stables, with windows on one side. Floors are shiplaps on two-by-fours laid directly on the mud, which is everywhere. The stalls are about eighteen by twenty-one feet; some contain families of six or seven persons. Partitions are seven feet high, leaving a four-foot opening above. The rooms aren't too bad, almost fit to live in for a short while.

The food and sanitation problems are the worst. We have had absolutely no fresh meat, vegetables or butter since we came here. Mealtime queues extend for blocks; standing in a rainswept line, feet in the mud, waiting for the scant portions of canned wieners and boiled potatoes, hash for breakfast or canned wieners and beans for dinner. Milk only for the kids. Coffee or tea dosed with saltpeter and stale bread are the adults' staples. Dirty, unwiped dishes, greasy silver, a starch diet, no butter, no milk, bawling kids, mud, wet mud that stinks when it dries, no vegetables—a sad thing for the people who raised them in such abundance. Memories of a crisp head of lettuce with our special olive oil, vinegar, garlic and cheese dressing.

Today one of the surface sewage-disposal pipes broke and the sewage flowed down the streets. Kids play in the water. Shower baths without hot water. Stinking mud and slops everywhere.

Can this be the same America we left a few weeks ago?

As I write, I can remember our little bathroom—light coral walls. My wife painting them, and the spilled paint in her hair. The open towel shelving and the pretty shower curtains which we put up the day before we left. How sanitary and clean we left it for the airlines pilot and his young wife who are now enjoying the fruits of our labor.

It all seems so futile, struggling, trying to live our old lives under this useless, regimented life. The senselessness of all the inactive manpower. Electricians, plumbers, draftsmen, mechanics, carpenters, painters, farmers—every trade—men who are able and willing to do all they can to lick the Axis. Thousands of men and women in these camps, energetic, quick, alert, eager for hard, constructive work, waiting for the army to do something for us, an army that won't give us butter.

I can't take it! I have 391 defense houses to be drawn. I left a fine American home which we built with our own hands. I left a life, highballs with our American friends on week-ends, a carpenter, laundry-truck driver, architect, airlines pilot—good friends, friends who would swear by us. I don't have enough of that Japanese heritage "Ga-man"—a code of silent suffering and ability to stand pain.

Oddly enough I still have a bit of faith in army promises of good treatment and Mrs. Roosevelt's pledge of a future worthy of good American citizens. I'm banking another $67 of income tax on the future. Sometimes I want to spend the money I have set aside for income tax on a bit of butter or ice cream or something good that I might have smuggled through the gates, but I can't do it when I think that every dollar I can put into "the fight to lick the Japs," the sooner I will be home again. I must forget my stomach.

What really hurts most is the constant reference to us evacués as "Japs." "Japs" are the guys we are fighting. We're on this side and we want to help.

Why won't America let us?

For Further Reading

A recent scholarly account of the relocation of Japanese Americans is given by Roger Daniels in *Concentration Camps USA: Japanese Americans and World War II** (1971). A more detailed version is provided in *The Great*

*Paperbound edition available.

Betrayal: The Evacuation of Japanese-Americans During World War II (1969), by Audrie Girdner and Anne Loftis. Allan R. Bosworth's *America's Concentration Camps* (1967) is a brief, journalistic description. *Prejudice: Japanese Americans, Symbol of Racial Intolerance* (1944), by Carey McWilliams, is a firsthand account that provides good background information.

Among the first analyses of the experience of the Japanese was *Impounded People: Japanese-Americans in the Relocation Centers* (1946; reprinted in 1969), edited by Edward H. Spicer and others. Differing interpretations of the government's motives are contained in: Stetson Conn, Rose C. Engelman, and Byron Fairchild, *The United States Army in World War II: The Western Hemisphere: Guarding the United States and Its Outposts* (1964); Morton Grodzins, *Americans Betrayed: Politics and Japanese Evacuation* (1949, 1969); and Jacobus tenBroek, *et al., Prejudice, War, and the Constitution** (1954, 1968).

A biographical account of the episode has been given by Dillon Myer in *Uprooted Americans: The Japanese Americans and the War Relocation Authority During World War II (1971).*

Bill Hosokawa's *Nisei: The Quiet Americans* (1969) offers insights into the nature and character of the victims of the government's policy. A better understanding of the context in which relocation occurred can be gained from Roger Daniels' *Politics of Prejudice: The Anti-Japanese Movement in California and the Struggle for Japanese Exclusion** (1968). Racial aspects of the relocation are considered in *American Racism: Explorations of the Nature of Prejudice** (1970), by Roger Daniels and Harry H. L. Kitano.

*Paperbound edition available.

13. The Cold War: Containing Communism

The United States and the Soviet Union, despite their ideological differences and traditional suspicions, cooperated closely as allies during the Second World War. Because the cooperation grew out of military necessity rather than mutual trust, the approach of victory tempted each nation to fall back into its prewar attitudes. The two strongest nations in the world were soon standing face to face over a Europe in which—with Germany out of the picture—a vacuum of power existed, particularly in the central and eastern regions. For the defense of its western borders, the Soviet Union was determined to fill this vacuum. In turn, the United States began to look on the Soviet Union's moves in this region as overt aggression. In this atmosphere of growing mistrust over the fate of Europe and with the war still raging in Asia, the Big Three (Roosevelt, Stalin, and Churchill) met at Yalta, a Soviet city on the Black Sea, in February 1945.

At Yalta it was mutually agreed to support a new world organization (the United Nations) and to permit democratic elections in Eastern Europe. For agreeing to enter the war against Japan once Germany was defeated, Stalin was promised the Kurile Islands, southern Sakhalin Island, and a sphere of influence in Manchuria. In addition, the Soviet Union was also given the green light to annex part of eastern Poland.

Critics of the Yalta Conference have termed it a "sell-out" to the Communists, but defenders of the agreements point to President Roosevelt's determination to end the war with Japan quickly and to bring the Soviet Union into accord on the issue of structuring the postwar world. Roosevelt's bargaining position was weakened by his belief that an invasion of Japan would most probably present the Japanese with a fight-to-the-death situation and by the reality that the Red Army had already occupied much of eastern Europe. As the Soviet Union carried out what it believed to be its part of the bargain made at Yalta, the United States became increasingly alarmed over what it came to interpret as Stalin's real intentions in the world.

In July 1945 the Big Three met once again, but this time the cast of characters had changed. Roosevelt was dead and President Harry S. Truman represented the United States. Winston Churchill was replaced in the midst of the conference by Clement R. Attlee after the Labour party won the general elections in Britain. Stalin continued to represent the Soviet Union. The conference, held at Potsdam in Germany, did bring agreement among the Big Three to put the Nazi leaders on trial for "crimes against humanity," to take reparations from Germany, and to divide Germany and Berlin into zones of occupation. But the Allies could not agree on a permanent postwar settlement. Both Truman and Stalin were adamant on issues they considered vital to their nation's self-defense. The time of cooperation was ending; the United States and the Soviet Union were entering the "Cold War."

Core Document

The Sources of Soviet Conduct

GEORGE F. KENNAN

At the end of World War II, Americans were ready to return to a more normal way of life. They looked forward to a time of prosperity and peace, but they were quickly disappointed. The Soviet Union seemed bent on a policy of aggression in Eastern Europe and even threatened the survival of the nations of Western Europe. President Truman soon became convinced of the "evil" intentions of the Russians and began to search for ways to prevent the loss of all of Europe to the Communists.

One solution was offered in an article in the 1947 summer issue of Foreign Affairs. *Although signed with an "X," the authorship of the essay was soon traced to George F. Kennan of the Policy Planning Staff of the Department of*

Excerpted by permission from *Foreign Affairs*, July 1947. Copyright by the Council on Foreign Relations, Inc. New York.

State. Kennan was an old hand in questions involving Russia, having been assigned to the American embassy when it reopened in 1933 and having served as Counselor of the American Embassy in Russia during World War II. A student of Russian history, he was an invaluable resource person in Soviet-American relations after the war. In the spring of 1947 Kennan wrote a position paper for Secretary of the Navy James Forrestal. Although originally a private statement of his views on Soviet policy, Kennan passed the essay on to the Council on Foreign Relations, which published it in its journal. The "X" article, entitled "The Sources of Soviet Conduct," caused a great deal of excitement in the press, for it seemed to espouse a new doctrine of the Truman administration: the doctrine of "containment." With Kennan subsequently identified as the author, and considering his key position in the State Department, there seemed to be little doubt as to its significance. So the term "containment" came into popular usage, and with it developed a psychological attitude toward the policies of the Soviet Union.

    In reading Kennan's article identify what he believed to be:

- *basic features of Communism in 1916.*
- *reasons for the retention of a dictatorship in Russia.*
- *Soviet conceptions of capitalistic intentions toward itself.*
- *the changelessness of Soviet policy.*
- *the concept of the Kremlin's infallibility.*
- *benefits of a policy of containment.*
- *the internal political situation in Russia.*
- *the role of the United States in influencing the internal situation in the Soviet Union and other Communist nations.*
- *the need for unity in pursuing the policies of the United States.*

The political personality of Soviet power as we know it today is the product of ideology and circumstances: ideology inherited by the present Soviet leaders from the movement in which they had their political origin, and circumstances of the power which they now have exercised for nearly three decades in Russia. There can be few tasks of psychological analysis more difficult than to try to trace the interaction of these two forces and the relative role of each in the determination of official Soviet conduct. Yet the attempt must be made if that conduct is to be understood and effectively countered.

    It is difficult to summarize the set of ideological concepts with which the Soviet leaders came into power. Marxian ideology, in its Russian-Communist projection, has always been in process of subtle evolution. The materials om which it bases itself are extensive and complex. But the outstanding features of Communist thought as it existed in 1916 may perhaps be summarized as follows: (a) that the central factor in the life of man, the factor which determines the character of public life and the "physiognomy of society," is the system by which material goods are produced and exchanged; (b) that the capitalist system of production is a nefarious one which inevitably leads to the exploitation of the working class by the capital-owning class and is incapable of developing adequately the economic resources of society or of distributing fairly the material goods produced by human labor; (c) that capitalism contains the seeds of its own destruction and must, in view of the inability of the capital-owning class to adjust itself to economic change, result eventually and inescapably in a revolutionary transfer of power to the working class; and (d) that imperialism, the final phase of capitalism, leads directly to war and revolution.

The rest may be outlined in Lenin's own words: "Unevenness of economic and political development is the inflexible law of capitalism. It follows from this that the victory of Socialism may come originally in a few capitalist countries or even in a single capitalist country. The victorious proletariat of that country, having expropriated the capitalists and having organized Socialist production at home, would rise against the remaining capitalist world, drawing to itself in the process the oppressed classes of other countries." It must be noted that there was no assumption that capitalism would perish without proletarian revolution. A final push was needed from a revolutionary proletariat movement in order to tip over the tottering structure. But it was regarded as inevitable that sooner or later that push be given. . . .

Now it lies in the nature of the mental world of the Soviet leaders, as well as in the character of their ideology, that no opposition to them can be officially recognized as having any merit or justification whatsoever. Such opposition can flow, in theory, only from the hostile and incorrigible forces of dying capitalism. As long as remnants of capitalism were officially recognized as existing in Russia, it was possible to place on them, as an internal element, part of the blame for the maintenance of a dictatorial form of society. But as these remnants were liquidated, little by little, this justification fell away; and when it was indicated officially that they had been finally destroyed, it disappeared altogether. And this fact created one of the most basic of the compulsions which came to act upon the Soviet régime: since capitalism no longer existed in Russia and since it could not be admitted that there could be serious or widespread opposition to the Kremlin springing spontaneously from the liberated masses under its authority, it became necessary to justify the retention of the dictatorship by stressing the menace of capitalism abroad.

This began at an early date. In 1924 Stalin specifically defended the retention of the "organs of suppression," meaning, among others, the army and the secret police, on the ground that "as long as there is a capitalist encirclement there will be danger of intervention with all the consequences that flow from that danger." In accordance with that theory, and from that time on, all internal opposition forces in Russia have consistently been portrayed as the agents of foreign forces of reaction antagonistic to Soviet power.

By the same token, tremendous emphasis has been placed on the original Communist thesis of a basic antagonism between the capitalist and Socialist worlds. It is clear, from many indications, that this emphasis is not founded in reality. The real facts concerning it have been confused by the existence abroad of genuine resentment provoked by Soviet philosophy and tactics and occasionally by the existence of great centers of military power, notably the Nazi régime in Germany and the Japanese Government of the late 1930's, which did indeed have aggressive designs against the Soviet Union. But there is ample evidence that the stress laid in Moscow on the menace confronting Soviet society from the world outside its borders is founded not in the realities of foreign antagonism but in the necessity of explaining away the maintenance of dictatorial authority at home.

Now the maintenance of this pattern of Soviet power, namely, the pursuit of unlimited authority domestically, accompanied by the cultivation of the semi-myth of implacable foreign hostility, has gone far to shape the actual machinery of Soviet power as we know it today. Internal organs of administration which did not serve this purpose withered on the vine. Organs which did serve this purpose became vastly swollen. The security of Soviet power came to rest on the iron discipline of the Party, on the severity and ubiquity of the secret police, and on the uncompromising economic monopolism of the state. The "organs of suppression," in which the Soviet leaders had sought security from rival forces, became in large measure the masters of those whom they were designed to serve. Today the major part of the structure of Soviet power is committed to the perfection of the dictatorship and to the maintenance of the concept of Russia as in a state of siege, with the enemy lowering beyond the walls. And the millions of human beings who form that part of the structure of power must defend at all costs this concept of Russia's position, for without it they are themselves superfluous. . . .

So much for the historical background. What does it spell in terms of the political personality of Soviet power as we know it today?

Of the original ideology, nothing has been officially junked. Belief is maintained in the basic badness of capitalism, in the inevitability of its destruction, in the obligation of the proletariat to assist in that destruction and to take power into its own hands. But stress has come to be laid primarily on those concepts which relate most specifically to the Soviet régime itself: to its position as the sole truly Socialist régime in a dark and misguided world, and to the relationships of power within it.

The first of these concepts is that of the innate antagonism between capitalism and Socialism. We have seen how deeply that concept has become imbedded in foundations of Soviet power. It has profound implications for Russia's conduct as a member of international society. It means that there can never be on Moscow's side any sincere assumption of a community of aims between the Soviet Union and powers which are regarded as capitalist. It must invariably be assumed in Moscow that the aims of the capitalist world are antagonistic to the Soviet régime, and therefore to the interests of the peoples it controls. If the Soviet Government occasionally sets its signature to documents which would indicate the contrary, this is to be regarded as a tactical manœuvre permissible in dealing with the enemy (who is without honor) and should be taken in the spirit of *caveat emptor*. Basically, the antagonism remains. It is postulated. And from it flow many of the phenomena which we find disturbing in the Kremlin's conduct of foreign policy: the secretiveness, the lack of frankness, the duplicity, the wary suspiciousness, and the basic unfriendliness of purpose. These phenomena are there to stay, for the foreseeable future. There can be variations of degree and of emphasis. When there is something the Russians want from us, one or the other of these features of their policy may be thrust temporarily into the background; and when that happens there will always be Americans who will leap forward with gleeful announcements that "the Russians have changed," and some who will even try to take credit for having brought about such "changes." But we should not be misled by tactical manœuvres. These characteristics of Soviet policy, like the postulate from which they flow, are basic to the internal nature of Soviet power, and will be with us, whether in the foreground or the background, until the internal nature of Soviet power is changed.

This means that we are going to continue for a long time to find the Russians difficult to deal with. It does not mean that they should be considered as embarked upon a do-or-die program to overthrow our society by a given date. The theory of the inevitability of the eventual fall of capitalism has the fortunate connotation that there is no hurry about it. The forces of progress can take their time in preparing the final *coup de grâce*. Meanwhile, what is vital is that the "Socialist fatherland"—that oasis of power which has been already won for Socialism in the person of the Soviet Union—should be cherished and defended by all good Communists at home and abroad, its fortunes promoted, its enemies badgered and confounded. The promotion of premature, "adventuristic" revolutionary projects abroad which might embarrass Soviet power in any way would be an inexcusable, even a counter-revolutionary act. The cause of Socialism is the support and promotion of Soviet power, as defined in Moscow.

This brings us to the second of the concepts important to contemporary Soviet outlook. That is the infallibility of the Kremlin. The Soviet concept of power, which permits no focal points of organization outside the Party itself, requires that the Party leadership remain in theory the sole repository of truth. For if truth were to be found elsewhere, there would be justification for its expression in organized activity. But it is precisely that which the Kremlin cannot and will not permit.

The leadership of the Communist Party is therefore always right, and has been always right ever since in 1929 Stalin formalized his personal power by announcing that decisions of the Politburo were being taken unanimously.

On the principle of infallibility there rests the iron discipline of the Communist Party. In fact, the two concepts are mutually self-supporting. Perfect discipline requires recognition of infallibility. Infallibility requires the observance of discipline. And the two together go far to determine the behaviorism of the entire Soviet apparatus of power. But their effect cannot be understood unless a third factor be taken into account: namely, the fact that the leadership is at liberty to put forward for tactical purposes any particular thesis which it finds useful to the cause at any particular moment and to require the faithful and unquestioning acceptance of that thesis by the members of the movement as a whole. This means that truth is not a constant but is actually created, for all intents and purposes, by the Soviet leaders themselves. . . .

But we have seen that the Kremlin is under no ideological compulsion to accomplish its purposes in a hurry. Like the Church, it is dealing in ideological concepts which are of long-term validity, and it can afford to be patient. It has no right to risk the existing achievements of the revolution for the sake of vain baubles of the future. The very teachings of Lenin himself require great caution and flexibility in the pursuit of Communist purposes. Again, these precepts are fortified by the lessons of Russian history: of centuries of obscure battles between nomadic forces over the stretches of a vast unfortified plain. Here caution, circumspection, flexibility and deception are the valuable qualities; and their value finds natural appreciation in the Russian or the oriental mind. Thus the Kremlin has no compunction about retreating in the face of superior force. And being under the compulsion of no timetable, it does not get panicky under the necessity for such retreat. Its political action is a fluid stream which moves constantly, wherever it is permitted to move, toward a given goal. Its main concern is to make sure that it has filled every nook and cranny available to it in the basin of world power. But if it finds unassailable barriers in its path, it accepts these philosophically and accommodates itself to them. The main thing is that there should always be pressure, unceasing constant pressure, toward the desired goal. There is no trace of any feeling in Soviet psychology that that goal must be reached at any given time. . . .

In these circumstances it is clear that the main element of any United States policy toward the Soviet Union must be that of a long-term, patient but firm and vigilant containment of Russian expansive tendencies. It is important to note, however, that such a policy has nothing to do with outward histrionics: with threats or blustering or superfluous gestures of outward "toughness." While the Kremlin is basically flexible in its reaction to political realities, it is by no means unamenable to considerations of prestige. Like almost any other government, it can be placed by tactless and threatening gestures in a position where it cannot afford to yield even though this might be dictated by its sense of realism. The Russian leaders are keen judges of human psychology, and as such they are highly conscious that loss of temper and of self-control is never a source of strength in political affairs. They are quick to exploit such evidences of weakness. For these reasons, it is a *sine qua non* of successful dealing with Russia that the foreign government in question should remain at all times cool and collected and that its demands on Russian policy should be put forward in such a manner as to leave the way open for a compliance not too detrimental to Russian prestige.

In the light of the above, it will be clearly seen that the Soviet pressure against the free institutions of the western world is something that can be contained by the adroit and vigilant application of counter-force at a series of constantly shifting geographical and political points, corresponding to the shifts and manœuvres of Soviet policy, but which cannot be charmed or talked out of existence. The Russians look forward to a duel of infinite duration, and they see that already they have scored great successes. It must be borne in mind that there was a time when the Communist Party represented far more of a minority in the sphere of Russian national life than Soviet power today represents in the world community.

But if ideology convinces the rulers of Russia that truth is on their side and that they can therefore afford to wait, those of us on whom that ideology has no claim are free to examine objectively the validity of that premise. The Soviet thesis not only implies complete lack of control by the west over its own economic destiny, it likewise assumes Russian unity, discipline and patience over an infinite period. Let us bring this apocalyptic vision down to earth, and suppose that the western world finds the strength and resourcefulness to contain Soviet power over a period of ten to fifteen years. What does that spell for Russia itself?

The Soviet leaders, taking advantage of the contributions of modern technique to the arts of despotism, have solved the question of obedience within the confines of their power. Few challenge their authority; and even those who do are unable to make that challenge valid as against the organs of suppression of the state.

The Kremlin has also proved able to accomplish its purpose of building up in Russia, regardless of the interests of the inhabitants, an industrial foundation of heavy metallurgy, which is, to be sure, not yet complete but which is nevertheless continuing to grow and is approaching those of the other major industrial countries. All of this, however, both the maintenance of internal political security and the building of heavy industry, has been carried out at a terrible cost in human life and in human hopes and energies. . . .

To all that, the war has added its tremendous toll of destruction, death and human exhaustion. In consequence of this, we have in Russia today a population which is physically and spiritually tired. The mass of the people are disillusioned, skeptical and no longer as accessible as they once were to the magical attraction which Soviet power still radiates to its followers abroad. The avidity with which people seized upon the slight respite accorded to the Church for tactical reasons during the war was eloquent testimony to the fact that their capacity for faith and devotion found little expression in the purposes of the régime. . . .

Meanwhile, a great uncertainty hangs over the political life of the Soviet Union. That is the uncertainty involved in the transfer of power from one individual or group of individuals to others.

This is, of course, outstandingly the problem of the personal position of Stalin. We must remember that his succession to Lenin's pinnacle of preëminence in the Communist movement was the only such transfer of individual authority which the Soviet Union has experienced. That transfer took 12 years to consolidate. It cost the lives of millions of people and shook the state to its foundations. The attendant tremors were felt all through the international revolutionary movement, to the disadvantage of the Kremlin itself.

It is always possible that another transfer of preëminent power may take place quietly and inconspicuously, with no repercussions anywhere. But again, it is possible that the questions involved may unleash, to use some of Lenin's words, one of those "incredibly swift transitions" from "delicate deceit" to "wild violence" which characterize Russian history, and may shake Soviet power to its foundations. . . .

Thus the future of Soviet power may not be by any means as secure as Russian capacity for self-delusion would make it appear to the men in the Kremlin. That they can keep power themselves, they have demonstrated. That they can quietly and easily turn it over to others remains to be proved. Meanwhile, the hardships of their rule and the vicissitudes of international life have taken a heavy toll of the strength and hopes of the great people on whom their power rests. It is curious to note that the ideological power of Soviet authority is strongest today in areas beyond the frontiers of Russia, beyond the reach of its police power. This phenomenon brings to mind a comparison used by Thomas Mann in his great novel "Buddenbrooks." Observing that human institutions often show the greatest outward brilliance at a moment when inner decay is in reality farthest advanced, he compared the Buddenbrook family, in the days of its greatest glamour, to one of those stars whose light shines most brightly on this world when in reality it has long since ceased to exist. And who can say with assurance that the strong light still cast by the Kremlin on the dissatisfied peoples of the western world is not the powerful afterglow of a constellation which is in actuality on the wane? This cannot be proved. And it cannot be disproved. But the possibility remains (and in the opinion of this writer it is a strong one) that Soviet power, like the capitalist world of its conception, bears within it the seeds of its own decay, and that the sprouting of these seeds is well advanced.

It is clear that the United States cannot expect in the foreseeable future to enjoy political intimacy with the Soviet régime. It must continue to regard the Soviet Union as a rival, not a partner, in the political arena. It must continue to expect that Soviet policies will reflect no abstract love of peace and stability, no real faith in the possibility of a permanent happy coexistence of the Socialist and capitalist worlds, but rather a cautious, persistent pressure toward the disruption and weakening of all rival influence and rival power.

Balanced against this are the facts that Russia, as opposed to the western world in general, is still by far the weaker party, that Soviet policy is highly flexible, and that Soviet society may well contain deficiences which will eventually weaken its own total potential. This would of itself warrant the United States entering with reasonable confidence upon a policy of firm containment, designed to confront the Russians with unalterable counter-force at every point where they show signs of encroaching upon the interests of a peaceful and stable world.

But in actuality the possibilities for American policy are by no means limited to holding the line and hoping for the best. It is entirely possible for the United States to influence by its actions the internal developments, both within Russia and throughout the international Communist movement, by which Russian policy is largely determined. This is not only a question of the modest measure of informational activity which this government can conduct in the Soviet Union and elsewhere, although that, too, is important. It is rather a question of the degree to which the United States can create among the peoples of the world generally the impression of a country which knows what it wants, which is coping successfully with the problems of its internal life and with the responsibilities of a World Power, and which has a spiritual vitality capable of holding its own among the major ideological currents of the time. To the extent that such an impression can be created and maintained, the aims of Russian Communism must appear sterile and quixotic, the hopes and enthusiasm of Moscow's supporters must wane, and added strain must be imposed on the Kremlin's foreign policies. For the palsied decrepitude of the capitalist world is the keystone of Communist philosophy. Even the failure of the United States to experience the early economic depression which the ravens of the Red Square have been predicting with such complacent confidence since hostilities ceased would have deep and important repercussions throughout the Communist world.

By the same token, exhibitions of indecision, disunity and internal disintegration within this country have an exhilarating effect on the whole Communist movement. At each evidence of these tendencies, a thrill of hope and excitement goes through the Communist world; a new jauntiness can be noted in the Moscow tread; new groups of foreign supporters climb on to what they can only view as the band wagon of international politics; and Russian pressure increases all along the line in international affairs.

It would be an exaggeration to say that American behavior unassisted and alone could exercise a power of life and death over the Communist movement and bring about the early fall of Soviet power in Russia. But the United States has it in its power to increase enormously the strains under which Soviet policy must operate, to force upon the Kremlin a far greater degree of moderation and circumspection that it has had to observe in recent years, and in this way to promote tendencies which must eventually find their outlet in either the break-up or the gradual mellowing of Soviet power. For no mystical, Messianic movement—and particularly not that of the Kremlin—can face frustration indefinitely without eventually adjusting itself in one way or another to the logic of that state of affairs.

Thus the decision will really fall in large measure in this country itself. The issue of Soviet-American relations is in essence a test of the over-all worth of the United States as a nation among nations. To avoid destruction the

United States need only measure up to its own traditions and prove itself worthy of preservation as a great nation.

Surely, there was never a fairer test of national quality than this. In the light of these circumstances, the thoughtful observer of Russian-American relations will find no cause for complaint in the Kremlin's challenge to American society. He will rather experience a certain gratitude to a Providence which, by providing the American people with this implacable challenge, has made their entire security as a nation dependent on their pulling themselves together and accepting the responsibilities of moral and political leadership that history plainly intended them to bear.[1]

Discussion Starters

1. Identify the reasons Kennan believed were behind the Soviet leaders' perpetuating a dictatorship in Russia. What are the differences between the concentration of power in Russia under Stalin and the centralization of authority in the executive department of the United States government from 1941 to the present?

2. How does Kennan's plan for the "firm and vigilant containment of Russian expansive tendencies" commit the United States to a totally defensive foreign policy? Where is the offensive strategy in his recommendations? Evaluate the possibility that the United States would be constantly reacting to rather than anticipating Soviet moves.

3. What assumptions led Kennan to believe that the longer the struggle persisted between the United States and the Soviet government, the greater the pressure would be upon the Soviet leadership from the Russian people? Would the same be true of the U.S. leadership and the American people? Explain. What differences would there be in the demands of the Russian people and the American people on their governments?

[1] *Editors' note*: In 1967 Kennan published his memoirs covering the years 1925 to 1950. In his book he addressed himself to the concept of containment he had made popular twenty years earlier. Kennan disclaimed that he had meant containment to become a doctrine of foreign policy, but only as a principle to be followed by the United States to prevent a war between the Soviet Union and America. The principle was to cease making any more concessions to the Soviets, support resistance to their efforts, and to give the internal weaknesses of Soviet power in Russia time to modify the Kremlin's foreign ambitions. Containment was to be a temporary policy to show the Soviet leadership that America meant to resist their aggressions and that the differences between the two nations could be worked out at the conference table better than on the battlefield. As for the fear of Communism, Kennan stated that while Joseph Stalin was alive it was a monolithic structure, but with his death and with the advent of the Sino-Soviet conflict, such a view of Communism was no longer valid. Since containment was to resist Stalin and his monolithic Communism, as a foreign policy it should have ended with their demise. Therefore, Kennan stated in 1967, the policy of containment had no relevance in the 1960s to meet new challenges from the new leadership in Russia and from other areas of the world.

4. Evaluate Kennan's argument that the United States must never become disunited or indecisive in its policies because it faces the unity and decisiveness of what became known as "Monolithic Communism."

5. What evidence did Kennan give for believing that the struggle between the Soviet Union and the United States would in the end be most beneficial to the United States?

Related Documents

I. The Truman Doctrine

HARRY S. TRUMAN

In March 1947 President Truman set the United States upon the road of resistance to further expansion by the Soviet Union. The immediate problem for Truman and his advisers was the civil war in Greece. After World War II Greek Communists, supported by the Communist nations of Yugoslavia, Albania, and Bulgaria, had attacked the Greek monarchy. Great Britain, which had originally aided the monarchy, was forced to end its aid because of its own economic difficulties. This lack of aid for the monarchy seemed to spell the end of a government friendly to the West in Greece. The prospect of a Communist-controlled Greece, with its excellent ports on the Mediterranean Sea and the threat it would represent to Turkey, brought the United States into the picture.

How do Truman's reasons for aiding Greece coincide with Kennan's concept of containment?

MARCH 12, 1947

The PRESIDENT. Mr. President, Mr. Speaker, Members of the Congress of the United States, the gravity of the situation which confronts the world today necessitates my appearance before a joint session of the Congress.

The foreign policy and the national security of this country are involved.

One aspect of the present situation, which I wish to present to you at this time for your consideration and decision, concerns Greece and Turkey.

The United States has received from the Greek Government an urgent appeal for financial and economic assistance. Preliminary reports from the American economic mission now in Greece and reports from the American Ambassador in Greece corroborate the statement of the Greek Government

Congressional Record, March 12, 1947, pp. 1980–81.

that assistance is imperative if Greece is to survive as a free nation.

I do not believe that the American people and the Congress wish to turn a deaf ear to the appeal of the Greek Government.

Greece is not a rich country. Lack of sufficient natural resources has always forced the Greek people to work hard to make both ends meet. Since 1940, this industrious and peace-loving country has suffered invasion, 4 years of cruel enemy occupation, and bitter internal strife.

When forces of liberation entered Greece they found that the retreating Germans had destroyed virtually all the railways, roads, port facilities, communications, and merchant marine. More than a thousand villages had been burned. Eighty-five percent of the children were tubercular. Livestock, poultry, and draft animals had almost disappeared. Inflation had wiped out practically all savings.

As a result of these tragic conditions, a militant minority, exploiting human want and misery, was able to create political chaos which, until now, has made economic recovery impossible.

Greece is today without funds to finance the importation of those goods which are essential to bare subsistence. Under these circumstances the people of Greece cannot make progress in solving their problems of reconstruction. Greece is in desperate need of financial and economic assistance to enable it to resume purchases of food, clothing, fuel, and seeds. These are indispensable for the subsistence of its people and are obtainable only from abroad. Greece must have help to import the goods necessary to restore internal order and security so essential for economic and political recovery.

The Greek Government has also asked for the assistance of experienced American administrators, economists, and technicians to insure that the financial and other aid given to Greece shall be used effectively in creating a stable and self-sustaining economy and in improving its public administration.

The very existence of the Greek state is today threatened by the terrorist activities of several thousand armed men, led by Communists, who defy the Government's authority at a number of points, particularly along the northern boundaries. . . .

Meanwhile, the Greek Government is unable to cope with the situation. The Greek Army is small and poorly equipped. It needs supplies and equipment if it is to restore the authority of the Government throughout Greek territory.

Greece must have assistance if it is to become a self-supporting and self-respecting democracy.

The United States must supply this assistance. We have already extended to Greece certain types of relief and economic aid but these are inadequate.

There is no other country to which democratic Greece can turn.

No other nation is willing and able to provide the necessary support for a democratic Greek Government. . . .

At the present moment in world history nearly every nation must choose between alternative ways of life. The choice is too often not a free one.

One way of life is based upon the will of the majority, and is distinguished by free institutions, representative government, free elections, guaranties of individual liberty, freedom of speech and religion, and freedom from political oppression.

The second way of life is based upon the will of a minority forcibly imposed upon the majority. It relies upon terror and oppression, a controlled press and radio, fixed elections, and the suppression of personal freedoms.

I believe that it must be the policy of the United States to support free peoples who are resisting attempted subjugation by armed minorities or by outside pressures.

I believe that we must assist free peoples to work out their own destinies in their own way.

I believe that our help should be primarily through economic and financial aid, which is essential to economic stability and orderly political processes.

The world is not static and the status quo is not sacred. But we cannot allow changes in the status quo in violation of the Charter of the United Nations by such methods as coercion, or by such subterfuges as political infiltration. In helping free and independent nations to maintain their freedom, the United States will be giving effect to the principles of the Charter of the United Nations.

It is necessary only to glance at a map to realize that the survival and integrity of the Greek nation are of grave importance in a much wider situation. If Greece should fall under the control of an armed minority, the effect upon its neighbor, Turkey, would be immediate and serious. Confusion and disorder might well spread throughout the entire Middle East.

Moreover, the disappearance of Greece as an independent state would have a profound effect upon those countries in Europe whose peoples are struggling against great difficulties to maintain their freedoms and their independence while they repair the damages of war.

It would be an unspeakable tragedy if these countries, which have struggled so long against overwhelming odds, should lose that victory for which they sacrificed so much. Collapse of free institutions and loss of independence would be disastrous not only for them but for the world. Discouragement and possibly failure would quickly be the lot of neighboring peoples striving to maintain their freedom and independence.

Should we fail to aid Greece and Turkey in this fateful hour, the effect will be far reaching to the West as well as to the East.

We must take immediate and resolute action. . . .

The seeds of totalitarian regimes are nurtured by misery and want. They spread and grow in the evil soil of poverty and strife. They reach their full growth when the hope of a people for a better life has died.

We must keep that hope alive.

The free peoples of the world look to us for support in maintaining their freedoms.

If we falter in our leadership, we may endanger the peace of the world —and we shall surely endanger the welfare of our own Nation.

Great responsibilities have been placed upon us by the swift movement of events.

I am confident that the Congress will face these responsibilities squarely.

II. No Substitute for Victory

DOUGLAS MacARTHUR

In June 1950 the North Korean army invaded South Korea. Korea had been a province of Japan, and after the Second World War it was divided along the 38th parallel into a Russian-dominated northern sector and an American-dominated southern sector. Although there were to have been elections to reunify the two sectors, the controlling powers backed local governments that became the Democratic People's Republic (in the North) and the Republic of Korea (in the South). With the attack on South Korea by the Democratic People's Republic, President Truman sent United States forces into the area. Aided by a United Nations resolution to aid South Korea against the aggression of North Korea, the joint American–United Nations forces eventually stopped the North Korean advance and pushed the aggressors back across the 38th parallel and as far north as the Yalu River and the border of China.

The push to the Yalu brought the Chinese into the war, for they saw all of Manchuria threatened by what they considered to be the imperialistic forces of the United States and the United Nations. What followed was a military disaster for the United Nations forces. The Chinese troops broke the center of the United Nations line, causing the U.N. forces to retreat far below the 38th parallel. Finally they regrouped, and a rather static front was established once again along the 38th parallel.

General Douglas MacArthur had commanded the United Nation forces since the beginning of the Korean "police action." MacArthur believed that the war had to be won and to do that China had to be bombed north of the Yalu River. Such suggestions by MacArthur were rejected by President Truman, for he believed they would cause World War III. When MacArthur began to openly criticize Truman and his policies the President removed him for insubordination. MacArthur then retired from the service and returned to the United States, where he received the adulation of thousands.

On April 19, 1951, he appeared before a joint session of Congress for a farewell address. At what points does General MacArthur disagree with or show a lack of understanding of Kennan's policy of containment?

Congressional Record, April 19, 1951, pp. 4123–25.

APRIL 19, 1951

Of more direct and immediate bearing upon our national security are the changes wrought in the strategic potential of the Pacific Ocean in the course of the past war. Prior thereto, the western strategic frontier of the United States lay on the littoral line of the Americas with an exposed island salient extending out through Hawaii, Midway, and Guam to the Philippines. That salient proved not an outpost of strength but an avenue of weakness along which the enemy could and did attack. The Pacific was a potential area of advance for any predatory force intent upon striking at the bordering land areas.

All this was changed by our Pacific victory. Our strategic frontier then shifted to embrace the entire Pacific Ocean which became a vast moat to protect us as long as we hold it. Indeed, it acts as a protective shield for all of the Americas and all free lands of the Pacific Ocean area. We control it to the shores of Asia by a chain of islands extending in an arc from the Aleutians to the Mariannas held by us and our free allies.

From this island chain we can dominate with sea and air power every Asiatic port from Vladivostok to Singapore and prevent any hostile movement into the Pacific. Any predatory attack from Asia must be an amphibious effort. No amphibious force can be successful without control of the sea lanes and the air over those lanes in its avenue of advance. With naval and air supremacy and modest ground elements to defend bases, any major attack from continental Asia toward us or our friends of the Pacific would be doomed to failure. Under such conditions the Pacific no longer represents menacing avenues of approach for a prospective invader—it assumes instead the friendly aspect of a peaceful lake. Our line of defense is a natural one and can be maintained with a minimum of military effort and expense. It envisions no attack against anyone nor does it provide the bastions essential for offensive operations, but properly maintained would be an invincible defense against aggression.

The holding of this littoral defense line in the western Pacific is entirely dependent upon holding all segments thereof, for any major breach of that line by an unfriendly power would render vulnerable to determined attack every other major segment. This is a military estimate as to which I have yet to find a military leader who will take exception. [Applause.]

For that reason I have strongly recommended in the past as a matter of military urgency that under no circumstances must Formosa fall under Communist control. [Applause.] Such an eventuality would at once threaten the freedom of the Philippines and the loss of Japan, and might well force our western frontier back to the coasts of California, Oregon, and Washington. . . .

With this brief insight into the surrounding areas I now turn to the Korean conflict. While I was not consulted prior to the President's decision to intervene in support of the Republic of Korea, that decision, from a military standpoint, proved a sound one [applause] as we hurled back the invaders and decimated his forces. Our victory was complete and our objectives within reach when Red China intervened with numerically superior ground forces. This created a new war and an entirely new situation—a situation not contemplated when our forces were committed against the North Korean invaders—a situation which called for new decisions in the diplomatic sphere to permit the realistic adjustment of military strategy. Such decisions have not been forthcoming. [Applause.]

While no man in his right mind would advocate sending our ground forces into continental China and such was never given a thought, the new situation did urgently demand a drastic revision of strategic planning if our political aim was to defeat this new enemy as we had defeated the old. [Applause.]

Apart from the military need as I saw it to neutralize the sanctuary protection given the enemy north of the Yalu, I felt that military necessity in the conduct of the war made mandatory:

1. The intensification of our economic blockade against China;

2. The imposition of a naval blockade against the China coast;

3. Removal of restrictions on air reconnaissance of China's coast areas and of Manchuria [applause];

4. Removal of restrictions on the forces of the Republic of China on Formosa with logistical support to contribute to their effective operations against the common enemy. [Applause.]

For entertaining these views, all professionally designed to support our forces committed to Korea and bring hostilities to an end with the least possible delay and at a saving of countless American and Allied lives, I have been severely criticized in lay circles, principally abroad, despite my understanding that from a military standpoint the above views have been fully shared in the past by practically every military leader concerned with the Korean campaign, including our own Joint Chiefs of Staff. [Applause, the Members rising.] . . .

It has been said, in effect, that I am a warmonger. Nothing could be further from the truth. I know war as few other men now living know it, and nothing to me is more revolting. I have long advocated its complete abolition as its very destructiveness on both friend and foe has rendered it useless as a means of settling international disputes. . . .

But once war is forced upon us, there is no other alternative than to apply every available means to bring it to a swift end. War's very object is victory —not prolonged indecision. [Applause.] In war, indeed, there can be no substitute for victory. [Applause.]. . . .

I am closing my 52 years of military service. [Applause.] When I joined the Army even before the turn of the century, it was the fulfillment of all my boyish hopes and dreams. The world has turned over many times since I took the oath on the plain at West Point, and the hopes and dreams have long since vanished. But I still remember the refrain of one of the most popular barrack ballads of that day which proclaimed most proudly that—

"Old soldiers never die; they just fade away."

And like the old soldier of that ballad, I now close my military career and just fade away—an old soldier who tried to do his duty as God gave him the light to see that duty.

Good-by.

III. Policy for Security and Peace

JOHN FOSTER DULLES

When Dwight D. Eisenhower was elected President in 1952 he appointed John Foster Dulles as his Secretary of State. Dulles was a man of great experience in foreign affairs and the Republican party's principal adviser in foreign policy. It was under the leadership of Dulles that the United States and the world were introduced to the concept of "brinkmanship." The diplomacy of the United States was to be based on its nuclear capability to destroy any aggressor in the world. This policy, directed primarily at Russia and China, was intended to prevent any more brush-fire wars such as the Korean War.

In this speech before the Council on Foreign Relations, how does Dulles' reliance upon nuclear retaliation supplement or change Kennan's concept of containment?

JANUARY 12, 1954

The soviet Communists are planning for what they call "an entire historical era," and we should do the same. They seek through many types of maneuvers gradually to divide and weaken the free nations by overextending them in efforts which, as Lenin put it, are "beyond their strength, so that they come to practical bankruptcy." Then, said Lenin, "our victory is assured." Then, said Stalin, will be "the moment for the decisive blow."

In the face of such a strategy, our own measures cannot be judged adequate merely because they ward off an immediate danger. That, of course, needs to be done. But it is also essential to do this without exhausting ourselves.

And when the Eisenhower Administration applied this test, we felt that some transformations were needed.

It is not sound military strategy permanently to commit United States land forces to Asia to a degree that gives us no strategic reserves.

It is not sound economics to support permanently other countries; nor is

From *The New York Times*, January 12, 1954. © 1954 by The New York Times Company. Reprinted by permission.

it good foreign policy, for in the long run, that creates as much ill will as good. . . .

Take first the matter of national security. We need allies and we need collective security. And our purpose is to have them, but to have them on a basis which is more effective and on a basis which is less costly. How do we do this? The way to do this is to place more reliance upon community deterrent power, and less dependence upon local defensive power.

This is accepted practice so far as our local communities are concerned. We keep locks on the doors of our homes; but we do not have armed guards in every home. We rely principally on a community security system so well equipped to catch and punish any who break in and steal that, in fact, would-be aggressors are generally deterred. That is the modern way of getting maximum protection at bearable cost.

What the Eisenhower Administration seeks is a similar international security system. We want for ourselves and for others a maximum deterrent at bearable cost.

Local defense will always be important. But there is no local defense which alone will contain the mighty land power of the Communist world. Local defense must be reinforced by the further deterrent of massive retaliatory power.

A potential aggressor must know that he cannot always prescribe the battle conditions that suit him. Otherwise, for example, a potential aggressor who is glutted with manpower might be tempted to attack in confidence that resistance would be confined to manpower. He might be tempted to attack in places where his superiority was decisive.

The way to deter aggression is for the community to be willing and able to respond vigorously at places and with means of its own choosing.

Now, so long as our basic concepts in these respects were unclear, our military leaders could not be selective in building our military power. If the enemy could pick his time and his place and his method of warfare—and if our policy was to remain the traditional one of meeting aggression by direct and local opposition—then we had to be ready to fight in the Arctic and in the tropics, in Asia, in the Near East and in Europe; by sea, by land and by air; by old weapons and by new weapons.

The total cost of our secuirty efforts, at home and abroad, was over $50,000,000,000 per annum, and involved, for 1953, a projected budgetary deficit of $9,000,000,000; and for 1954 a projected deficit of $11,000,000,000.

This was on top of taxes comparable to wartime taxes and the dollar was depreciating in its effective value. And our allies were similarly weighed down. This could not be continued for long without grave budgetary, economic and social consequences.

But before military planning could be changed the President and his advisers, represented by the National Security Council, had to take some basic policy decisions. This has been done.

And the basic decision was as I indicated to depend primarily upon a great capacity to retaliate instantly by means and at places of our choosing. And now . the Department of Defense and the Joint Chiefs of Staff can shape our military establishment to fit what is our policy instead of having to try to be ready to meet the enemy's many choices. And that permits of a selection of military means instead of a multiplication of means. And as a result it is now possible to get, and to share, more security at less cost.

Now let us see how this concept has been practically applied to foreign policy, taking first the Far East. In Korea this Administration effected a major transformation. The fighting has been stopped on honorable terms.

That was possible because the aggressor, already thrown back to and behind his place of beginning, was faced with the possibility that the fighting might, to his own peril, soon spread beyond the limits and the methods which he had selected.

The cruel toll of American youth, and the non-productive expenditure of many billions has been stopped. Also our armed forces are no longer committed to the Asian mainland. We can begin to create a strategic reserve which greatly improves our defensive posture.

This change gives added authority to the warning of the members of the United Nations which fought in Korea that if the Communists renewed the aggression, the United Nations' response would not necessarily be confined to Korea.

I have said, in relation to Indo-China, that if there were open Red Chinese aggression there, that would have "grave consequences which might not be confined to Indo-China."

I expressed last month the intention of the United States to maintain its position in Okinawa. This is needed to ensure adequate striking power to implement our new collective security concept.

All this is summed up in President Eisenhower's important statement of Dec. 26. He announced the progressive reduction of the United States ground forces in Korea. And in doing so, he pointed out that United States military forces in the Far East will now feature "highly mobile naval, air and amphibious units"; and he said that in this way, despite some withdrawal of land forces, the United States will have a capacity to oppose aggression "with even greater effect than heretofore."

The bringing home of our land forces also provides a most eloquent rebuttal to the Communist charges of "Western imperialism" in Asia.

Let us turn now to Europe.

There we have readjusted the NATO collective security effort. . . .

In the first years of NATO following the aggression in Korea its members made an emergency build-up of military strength. I do not question the judgment of that time. The strength thus built has served well the cause of peace. But the pace originally set could not be maintained indefinitely.

Last April, when we went to the meeting of the NATO Council, the United States put forward a new concept which is now known as that of the "long haul." That meant a steady development of defensive strength at a rate that will preserve and not exhaust the economic strength of our allies and ourselves. This defensive strength would be reinforced by the striking power of strategic air based upon internationally agreed positions.

At this April meeting our ideas met with some skepticism. But when we went back as we did last month, December, we found that there had come about general acceptance of this "long haul" concept. . . .

In the ways I outlined we gather strength for the longterm defense of freedom.

We do not, of course, claim to have found some magic formula that insures against all forms of Communist successes. It is normal that at some times at some places there may be setbacks to the cause of freedom. What we do expect to insure is that any setbacks will only be temporary and local because they will leave unimpaired those free world assets which in the long run will prevail.

If we can deter such aggression as would mean general war, and that is our confident resolve, then we can let time and fundamentals work for us. Under these conditions we do not need self-imposed policies which sap our strength.

The fundamental, on our side, is the richness—spiritual, intellectual and material—that freedom can produce and the irresistable attraction which it then sets up. That is why we do not plan to shackle freedom to preserve freedom.

IV. Détente

JOHN F. KENNEDY

The difficulties between the Soviet Union and the United States continued in the 1950s with problems over Berlin, Indochina, the Suez, and Hungary. The United States continued to build such new alliances against Russia and China as the Southeast Asia Treaty Organization (SEATO) in 1954. In October 1957 the Soviets demonstrated their technological advances in missile capability by orbiting their first "Sputnik." The threat of Russian missiles shook American society to its very core and resulted in an intensive space program and additional governmental aid to science education to narrow the "missile gap."

In American domestic politics the presidential election of 1960 was held in the atmosphere of Soviet denunciation of the U–2 reconnaissance flights over its territory and a renewed belligerency in the Cold War. But when John Kennedy moved into the White House many hoped for a new era, a "new frontier," for America.

Public Papers of the Presidents of the United States: John F. Kennedy (Washington, D.C.: Government Printing Office, 1964), 1963, pp. 460–62, 464.

In April 1961 the new frontier was badly tarnished at the Bay of Pigs in Cuba. The Eisenhower administration had earlier agreed to help revolutionaries invade Cuba to oust the Communist-controlled government of Fidel Castro. Kennedy did not authorize the air cover the rebels needed and Castro's forces destroyed the invading forces in a few days. With the United States humiliated by the defeat of the rebels, the Soviets proceeded to use the threat of future American invasions to draw the Cubans closer to themselves.

In October 1962 the United States had hard evidence that the Soviet Union had begun to move short- and medium-range missiles into Cuba. Kennedy then appeared on television on October 22, 1962, to announce the blockade of Cuba and to demand that the Soviet Union remove the missiles already deployed. On October 27, Chairman Nikita Khrushchev of the Soviet Union agreed to remove the missiles, and the United States agreed not to invade Cuba.

President Kennedy became determined after the Cuban missile crisis to bring about an end to brinkmanship in the Cold War. In order to ease tensions he suggested to the Soviet Union that they negotiate a limited test ban treaty that would end nuclear testing in the atmosphere. Such negotiations had been going on in Geneva since 1959, but the threat of nuclear war so narrowly averted over Cuba convinced Kennedy, and, it seems, Khrushchev, that it was time to look for a way out of the cycles of crises that had enveloped their two nations since 1945. A test ban treaty would be a first step toward détente.

In what ways does Kennedy's speech abrogate the arguments and conclusions made by Kennan in his article on Soviet conduct?

JUNE 10, 1963

I have . . . chosen this time and this place to discuss a topic on which ignorance too often abounds and the truth is too rarely perceived—yet it is the most important topic on earth: world peace. . . .

Some say that it is useless to speak of world peace or world law or world disarmament—and that it will be useless until the leaders of the Soviet Union adopt a more enlightened attitude. I hope they do. I believe we can help them do it. But I also believe that we must reexamine our own attitude—as individuals and as a Nation—for our attitude is as essential as theirs. And every graduate of this school, every thoughtful citizen who despairs of war and wishes to bring peace, should begin by looking inward—by examining his own attitude toward the possibilities of peace, toward the Soviet Union, toward the course of the cold war and toward freedom and peace here at home.

First: Let us examine our attitude toward peace itself. Too many of us think it is impossible. Too many think it unreal. But that is a dangerous, defeatist belief. It leads to the conclusion that war is inevitable—that mankind is doomed—that we are gripped by forces we cannot control.

We need not accept that view. Our problems are manmade—therefore, they can be solved by man. And man can be as big as he wants. No problem of human destiny is beyond human beings. Man's reason and spirit have often solved the seemingly unsolvable—and we believe they can do it again.

I am not referring to the absolute, infinite concept of universal peace and good will of which some fantasies and fanatics dream. I do not deny the value of hopes and dreams but we merely invite discouragement and incredulity by making that our only and immediate goal.

Let us focus instead on a more practical, more attainable peace—based not on a sudden revolution in human nature but on a gradual evolution in human institutions—on a series of concrete actions and effective agreements which are in the interest of all concerned. There is no single, simple key to this peace—no grand or magic formula to be adopted by one or two powers. Genuine peace must be the product of many nations, the sum of many acts. It must be dynamic, not static, changing to meet the challenge of each new generation. For peace is a process—a way of solving problems.

With such a peace, there will still be quarrels and conflicting interests, as there are within families and nations. World peace, like community peace, does not require that each man love his neighbor—it requires only that they live together in mutual tolerance, submitting their disputes to a just and peaceful settlement. And history teaches us that enmities between nations, as between individuals, do not last forever. However fixed our likes and dislikes may seem, the tide of time and events will often bring surprising changes in the relations between nations and neighbors.

So let us persevere. Peace need not be impracticable, and war need not be inevitable. By defining our goal more clearly, by making it seem more manageable and less remote, we can help all peoples to see it, to draw hope from it, and to move irresistibly toward it.

Second: Let us reexamine our attitude toward the Soviet Union. It is discouraging to think that their leaders may actually believe what their propagandists write. It is discouraging to read a recent authoritative Soviet text on *Military Strategy* and find, on page after page, wholly baseless and incredible claims—such as the allegation that "American imperialist circles are preparing to unleash different types of wars . . . that there is a very real threat of a preventive war being unleashed by American imperialists against the Soviet Union . . . [and that] the political aims of the American imperialists are to enslave economically and politically the European and other capitalist countries . . . [and] to achieve world domination . . . by means of aggressive wars."

Truly, as it was written long ago: "The wicked flee when no man pursueth." Yet it is sad to read these Soviet statements—to realize the extent of the gulf between us. But it is also a warning—a warning to the American people not to fall into the same trap as the Soviets, not to see only a distorted and desperate view of the other side, not to see conflict as inevitable, accommodation as impossible, and communication as nothing more than an exchange of threats.

No government or social system is so evil that its people must be considered as lacking in virtue. As Americans, we find communism profoundly repugnant as a negation of personal freedom and dignity. But we can still hail the Russian people for their many achievements—in science and space, in economic and industrial growth, in culture and in acts of courage. . . .

So, let us not be blind to our differences—but let us also direct attention to our common interests and to the means by which those differences can be resolved. And if we cannot end now our differences, at least we can help make the world safe for diversity. For, in the final analysis, our most basic common link is that we all inhabit this small planet. We all breathe the same air. We all cherish our children's future. And we are all mortal.

Third: Let us reexamine our attitude toward the cold war, remembering that we are not engaged in a debate, seeking to pile up debating points. We are not here distributing blame or pointing the finger of judgment. We must deal with the world as it is, and not as it might have been had the history of the last 18 years been different.

We must, therefore, persevere in the search for peace in the hope that constructive changes within the Communist bloc might bring within reach solutions which now seem beyond us. We must conduct our affairs in such a way that it becomes in the Communists' interest to agree on a genuine peace. Above all, while defending our own vital interests, nuclear powers must avert those confrontations which bring an adversary to a choice of either a humiliating retreat or a nuclear war. To adopt that kind of course in the nuclear age would be evidence only of the bankruptcy of our policy—or of a collective death-wish for the world.

To secure these ends, America's weapons are nonprovocative, carefully controlled, designed to deter, and capable of selective use. Our military forces are committed to peace and disciplined in self-restraint. Our diplomats are instructed to avoid unnecessary irritants and purely rhetorical hostility.

For we can seek a relaxation of tensions without relaxing our guard. And, for our part, we do not need to use threats to prove that we are resolute. We do not need to jam foreign broadcasts out of fear our faith will be eroded. We are unwilling to impose our system on any unwilling people—but we are willing and able to engage in peaceful competition with any people on earth. . . .

The United States, as the world knows, will never start a war. We do not want a war. We do not now expect a war. This generation of Americans has already had enough—more than enough—of war and hate and oppression. We shall be prepared if others wish it. We shall be alert to try to stop it. But we shall also do our part to build a world of peace where the weak are safe and the strong are just. We are not helpless before that task or hopeless of its success. Confident and unafraid, we labor on—not toward a strategy of annihilation but toward a strategy of peace.

For Further Reading

General works on the origins and conduct of the Cold War include: Thomas A. Bailey, *America Faces Russia* (1950); Desmond Donnelly, *Struggle for the World: The Cold War, 1917–1965* (1965); Dana F. Fleming, *The Cold War and Its Origins,* 2 vols. (1961); Norman A. Graebner, *Cold War Diplomacy, 1945–1960* * (1962); Louis J. Halle, *The Cold War as History* * (1971); Paul Y. Hammond, *The Cold War Years* (1969); David Horowitz, *The Free World Colossus* (1965); George F. Kennan, *Russia and the West Under Lenin and Stalin* * (1969); Charles O. Lerché, *The Cold War and After* * (1965); John Lukacs, *History of the Cold War* * (1965); Robert E. Osgood, *et al., America and the World: From the Truman Doctrine to Vietnam* (1970); W. W. Rostow, *The United States in the World Arena* (1960); Paul Seabury, *The Rise and Decline of the Cold War* (1967); Marshall Shulman, *Beyond the Cold War* * (1966); John Spanier, *American Foreign Policy Since World War II* * (1965); and William A. Williams, *The Tragedy of American Diplomacy* * (1962).

East European policies are covered in Martin Herz's *Beginnings of the Cold War* (1966) and Hugh Seton-Watson's *The East European Revolution* (1956). The Cold War in Germany is described in John Gimbel's *The American Occupation of Germany* (1968) and Manuel Gottlieb's *The German Peace Settlement and the Berlin Crisis* (1960). Difficulties in Greece and the introduction of the Truman Doctrine are related in Edgar O'Ballance's *The Greek Civil War* (1966), while affairs in Cuba are examined in: Karl E. Meyer and Tad Szulc, *The Cuban Invasion: The Chronicle of Disaster* * (1962); R. F. Smith, *The United States and Cuba* (1960); and William A. Williams, *The United States, Cuba, and Castro* (1960). Books on American interests in the Far East include: Warren I. Cohen, *America's Response to China* * (1971); John K. Fairbank, *The United States and China* (1958); Akira Iriye, *Across the Pacific: An Inner History of American–East Asian Relations* * (1967); and Tang Tsou, *America's Failure in China, 1941–1950* (1963).

More specific studies on the Cold War include Cecil V. Crabb, Jr., *The Elephants and the Grass: A Study of Nonalignment* * (1965); Henry A. Kissinger's study of NATO, *The Troubled Partnership* * (1965); David Wise and T. B. Ross's *The U–2 Affair* (1962); and B. G. Bechhoefer's examination of attempts at arms control in *Postwar Negotiations for Arms Control* (1961).

There are many works by and about personalities of the era; several of the most prominent are: Dean Acheson, *Present at the Creation: My Years in the State Department* (1969); John Foster Dulles, *War or Peace* (1950); George F. Kennan, *Memoirs, 1925–1950* (1967); and Walter Millis, ed., *The Forrestal Diaries* (1951). Essays about the secretaries of state during the period are found in *An Uncertain Tradition* (1961), edited by Norman A. Graebner.

*Paperbound edition available.

Problems books concerned with the Cold War are James V. Compton, ed., *America and the Origins of the Cold War** (1972); Walter LaFeber, ed., *America and the Cold War** (1969); and Thomas G. Paterson, ed., *The Origins of the Cold War** (1970).

*Paperbound edition available.

14. McCarthyism

Some men achieve greatness or fame for what they do, others for what they symbolize. In some cases, of course, actual achievements may contribute to effective symbolization (as with Franklin D. Roosevelt), but it is possible for a person to become a symbol without scoring notable achievements. The presidency of John F. Kennedy, for example, is less important for its measurable attainments than for the new spirit it symbolized.

Following World War II domestic and international conditions worked together to create a national mood that needed a symbol to give it expression. Such a symbol emerged in the person of Senator Joseph R. McCarthy of Wisconsin. "If you sense a movement coming," says an old axiom, "lead it," and McCarthy did just that.

The movement led by McCarthy was one of fervent and at times hysterical anti-Communism. Such a movement was not new to America. Following World War I antagonism to Communism generated the Red Scare of 1919 and 1920, and through the twenties and thirties it continued to play an important part in shaping government policies. Alliance with the Soviet Union during World War II restrained expression of anti-Communist sentiments, but not long after the war anti-Communism again burst forth as a powerful movement. Between 1947 and 1954, seemingly as an almost essential ingredient of the Cold War, anti-Communist sentiment became a preoccupation, if not an obsession, with many Americans. Since then, although its strength and fervor have dissipated somewhat, anti-Communism remains a major concern of various right-wing political organizations, and the possibility of a revived anti-Communist movement continues to exist.

After a brief but controversial career as a judge, interrupted by a controversial stint in the Marine Corps, Joe McCarthy won an upset victory in the Wisconsin senatorial election of 1946. When he arrived in Washington in 1947 he was apparently in search of an issue on which to build his reputation. Several false starts left him still searching. Early in 1950 he found the issue he needed. His career as an anti-Communist was launched at Wheeling, West Virginia, on February 9, 1950, when he charged, according to the *Wheeling Intelligencer:* "I have here in my hand a list of 205 that were known to the secretary of state as being members of the Communist Party and who, nevertheless are still working and shaping the policy of the State Department." From this point on he was the spokesman, symbol, and chief congressional investigator for a national anti-Communist movement.

Critics and defenders of McCarthy can agree on several points: That although some Communists held positions in the United States government, the process of removing them had begun years before McCarthy arrived on the scene and would have continued without him. That McCarthy's investigations and exposés did not lead to the successful prosecution of a single person for disloyal or treasonous acts, yet an indeterminate number of persons were removed from their positions or left voluntarily in response to the pressures he created. And that McCarthy's yearning for the dramatic, his tendency to exaggerate, and his abrasive style caused him to cut a broad swath in which the innocent as well as the suspect were caught. In recent years, in fact, security clearances have been restored to a number of persons who had them revoked during the McCarthy era, and others whose loyalty was challenged have been vindicated.

There are also, quite naturally, points of substantial difference between the friends and foes of McCarthyism. One such point concerns the seriousness of the internal Communist menace during the McCarthy years and the extent of credit McCarthy deserves for turning it back. Another point of difference provides the focus of this chapter: It has to do with the methods used by McCarthy in his crusade against Communism, the very methods that gave rise to the term "McCarthyism." McCarthy's critics would phrase the question this way: Do good motives and desirable goals justify the use of unfair and intimidating tactics and the risk of damage to the reputations of innocent persons? McCarthy's actions have been justified by his supporters, then and since, with such expressions as, "I don't agree with his methods, but he was doing something that was necessary, and by golly, he got the job done!"

Core Documents

"The Strong Winds of Destiny Are Blowing"

BARRY GOLDWATER

Joe McCarthy generated strong feelings. A Republican, he was fiercely opposed by President Truman and most other Democrats from the very beginning of his anti-Communist activity. In time, opposition to McCarthy developed in such places as the press, in the liberal wing of the Republican party, among church leaders, and in colleges and universities. Nevertheless, because he appeared to have massive popular support, those who might have been able to curb his excesses seemed to have been intimidated. President Eisenhower was unwilling to take the lead, and Congress was slow in acting. In the summer of 1954, however, in the wake of the conflict between the senator and the Secretary of the Army, McCarthy's fellow senators were finally pushed into calling him to account for his methods. A resolution asking for his censure was introduced and a Select Committee of three Republicans and three Democrats was appointed to investigate the charges. The Select Committee, headed by Arthur Watkins of Utah, conducted scrupulously fair hearings based on rigidly enforced rules and procedures that prevented McCarthy from resorting to the very methods he had always used so successfully and for which he was under criticism. The stern manner in which Chairman Watkins insisted on "going straight down the line" prompted McCarthy at one point to charge, "I think it's the most unheard of thing I've heard of."

After nearly a month of hearings, on September 27, 1954, the Select Committee submitted its unanimous report recommending censure of Senator McCarthy on two counts: for contempt of the Senate in refusing to appear before a Senate committee investigating his activities in 1952, and for his abuse of General Ralph W. Zwicker before his own subcommittee in 1953. The report denounced McCarthy on three additional counts but declined to recommend censure. Following the November elections the Senate reluctantly took up the task of chastising one of its wayward own. Heated debate occurred on the Senate floor, and McCarthy battled there as well as in the press to prevent being discredited with his following even if censure came. In his formal statement of defense McCarthy typically charged that censure would be a victory for the Communist party, that the Communist party had "extended its tentacles" to the Senate, and that the Select Committee had been made the Party's "unwitting handmaiden."

So rough was McCarthy on Watkins and his fellow committee members

Congressional Record, November 12, 1954, pp. 16001–2, 16004–5.

*that although the Zwicker charge was dropped, it was replaced with one con-
demning him for his treatment of the committee.*

   *The strategy of the anti-McCarthy forces was to hold the debate to the
narrow issue presented by the committee's recommendations, but the wider
implications of censure were readily apparent to both sides. Before censure was
finally voted, 67–22, these implications were aired in the floor debate. Speeches
by two senators provide the core documents in this chapter. In reading the first
speech, note how Senator Barry Goldwater, Republican of Arizona:*

   • *described the larger implications of a censure of McCarthy.*
   • *interpreted the motives of those who criticized McCarthy.*
   • *explained McCarthy's purposes.*
   • *justified McCarthy's methods.*
   • *attacked the "anti-anti-Communists" who criticized McCarthy.*

NOVEMBER 12, 1954

Mr. President, let us place this debate—not merely the one we are engaged in
at the moment, but the one that has been raging for the past 4 years—in
perspective. We know that this censure move is not a disconnected happening
either in the career of Senator MCCARTHY or in America's fight against
communism. It is a part of a sequence of events. Actually, those unknown
engineers of censure hope that this will be the culminating act in the merciless
fight to destroy a United States Senator and the fight against communism
which has been crackling on a score of left-wing fronts for over 4 years. Make
no mistake about it, if this effort of theirs falls now, there will be another one.

   Why is it that this particular Senator has been singled out for this particular ordeal? In the course of the years since America has become cognizant of
the presence of communism in this country, there have been many men in
public life whose names have been just as conspicuously identified with the
fight against it, and yet it is only this Senator who has been put in the pillory
and brought before this body for censure. What has he done that has made
him such an unforgiveable figure to his strangely assorted baiters? I think that
the answer to this question will bring us very close to the real issue which we
are deciding in this special session.

   Certainly, it is difficult to believe that the junior Senator from Wisconsin
is really under attack because of the relatively trivial offenses which have been
alleged against him by the select committee. We all know that he could have
done many things even more serious, and we all know that in our memories
we can recall more drastic words having been spoken against a witness or even
having been spoken on the floor of the Senate, without the whole machinery
of the Senate having been put into motion in a special session to ask for a
particular Senator's censure.

   The reason lies somewhere else. It is buried beneath deceptive surface
appearances of this case. Our search for that reason leads us to some extremely
important men, some of them working in anonymity, who have vowed to drive

McCARTHY from a position of influence in this country. Their motives are a crisscross of spite, of fear of his political possibilities, and of the ever-present and haunting dread that his ranging investigations might lead him into certain dark places in the Washington scene which they desperately want to keep covered up.

For more than 5 years, from 1941 to 1946, this country went though a paranoiac attack of trust Stalinism. Apparently sound-minded public men during that period went on some of the most incredible pro-Russian binges. The ghosts of those wartime lunacies are buried all over Washington. When sanity returned to the Nation those who had helped Russia to cheat us out of the peace did not want the story to be told in all its unbelievable sordidness. A little of it was brought to light in one memorable year of truth telling, 1948, but most of it remained untold. There are people in this country who want it to remain that way—untold.

Here is where the Senator from Wisconsin comes in. What is it that distinguishes his attacks on the Communist and pro-Communist problem? If I may put it simply and in a single phrase, it is the fact that the Senator has never drawn back from an investigation even though he found that it was leading him to the highest sacred cows of American politics. He has not flinched from risking a finish fight with men who were powerful enough to destroy him politically when he found that, through stupidity, or through an unexplained softness toward Russia, they were making decisions which were weakening America and strengthening Moscow. I concede that this is not good politics on the Senator's part, but it is inspiring and heart-stirring Americanism.

The junior Senator from Wisconsin learned early in his career as an investigator of communism that it was not enough merely to identify the card-carrying members of the party and to immobilize them. The FBI was and is doing a magnificent job along those lines with means far superior to anything which could be commanded by an individual Senator. What the junior Senator from Wisconsin believed was important for the Congress to focus upon was the identity of the men who consciously or unconsciously were behind the Communists. He found that in every important Communist situation there invariably was some high-placed Government official who, either through inefficiency or willful tolerance of communism, had helped the Moscow tyrants. He believes that these weak links in the chain of American security constitute a threat equal to and even greater than that posed by all the adherents and disciples of communism.

In keeping with this belief, he felt that one Army official who could protect and promote a Major Peress was a far greater risk to the United States than the major himself. . . . He felt that one official of Government who could sit in Washington and issue handcuffing orders to General MacArthur and General Clark and General Van Fleet, which required them to permit the Communists to win the Korean war in which 142,000 American boys had suffered death or injury, was doing more to help Russia and to weaken America than all the Communists in America. He felt that an American Secretary of State who could declare that he "would never turn his back on Alger Hiss," even after Hiss' conviction, was not the man for that job.

It is safe to go after the minnows, but it is not so safe to challenge the marlin or the whale. Had the Senator been a mere careerist, it would have been so easy for him to have won the plaudits of some of the men who are now reviling him. All he would have had to do would have been to create an imposing record of exposing and publicizing the little men of communism, the men who, by taking on the Communist label, can actually do little to influence American events. As a watchdog against the Fosters and Flynns and Dennises and Nelsons, he could have made a great name for himself as an anti-Communist fighter without acquiring any powerful enemies capable of Washington reprisal.

But the Senator has not been overawed by the usual "don'ts" and the taboos of the Washington game. He, along with others, cannot see any logical reason for hunting out some of the Communists if, at the same time, we are going to shield and whitewash incompetents in bureaucratic offices whose costly decisions have given international communism victories at the expense of America which it could never have won on its own.

This is the basic issue with which we are faced. This is the issue on which we are actually asked to act in the Senate today. I suggest that Senator McCarthy is facing a censure vote in this body because he has put his finger fearlessly upon the men in high places who, through stupidity or muddled ideology, have stood in the way of an all-out fight against communism both in America and abroad.

Let me remind the Senate what one great American has said about this man whom we are now asked to censure:

> McCarthy is a former Marine. He was an amateur boxer. He's Irish. Combine these and you're going to have a vigorous individual who is not going to be pushed around. Certainly he is a controversial figure. But he is earnest, he is honest, and he is sincere. He has enemies. Whenever you attack subversives of any kind you're going to be the victim of the most extremely vicious criticism that can be made. I know that, sometimes, a knock is a boost. When certain elements cease their attacks on me I know I am slipping.

The man who said that was J. Edgar Hoover, and he said it in San Diego, Calif., in 1953. I might suggest to the Senate at this time that if this censure movement against the junior Senator from Wisconsin is successful, the next attack will undoubtedly be made upon this great American who has done so much for our Federal Bureau of Investigation. . . .

There is nothing new in American politics in a congressional committee which, like the Senator's committee, is vigorous, earthy, and unafraid. Such committees have been in the long and honored tradition of this body. What is new is the crybaby witness who runs to the Pentagon crying for help against the bad man McCARTHY, who had actually talked rough to him. What is new is a committee of the Senate which asks us to censure this Senator for his vigor and zeal, and not to praise him.

How flabby and how foolish have we become?

It is not easy to follow the rather involved logic of the special committee recommendations in the matter of the general. As we read them, we seem to find ourselves in a world of upside-down values. In that world, a general, and a man who tried to withhold information from the United States, appears as a hero. McCARTHY, a man who tried to turn the searchlight on the guilty parties, appears as a villain. In the Watkins report it is the men who covered up the higher ups, who were soft in their policies toward Communists, whom we are asked to vindicate. It is the challenger of communism whom we are asked to condemn. I cannot see it. I have no standard of values by which such a preposterous 2 and 2 add up to 4.

Whenever the Senate is asked to make a decision so solemn and so far reaching as this, it is important that we ask ourselves whether we have carefully thought out the steps which we are asked to take. The smear shouts and the billingsgate against McCARTHY, the man, have been so shrill that at times I am convinced we have forgotten the real inescapable issue in this whole matter, which is the fight against communism.

But certain truths stand out like an incandescent beacon in this matter. Let me briefly state them:

First. It would not be good Senate policy to condemn McCARTHY. There can be no blinking the fact that the precedent which we establish in repudiating the Senate committee chairman when he is seeking to dredge out the truth about incompetence in the executive branch is a precedent which will return to haunt us. Many Senators, for various motives, may be reluctant to go along with JOE McCARTHY in some of his anti-Communist takeoffs. None, I think, will want to take official action which will shrivel the authority of the Senate to investigate. Without that authority, this body would decline into a mere shadow of what it had once been. Without that authority vested in this body, the executive branch would achieve an immunity to checkup and legislative watchfulness which would disbalance our whole Constitution.

Woodrow Wilson recognized this truth when he wrote:

> The informing function of Congress should be preferred over the legislative function.

A censure of the chairman of the Government Operations Committee will strike all of us. And when that censure is voted, not for corruption or malfeasance, not for the breaking of any existing rules, but for excessive zeal in carrying out his proper function as an investigator for the Senate, it is doubly senseless. With such an act blazoned on the record, no future Senate investiga-

tor would feel safe to pursue his probe relentlessly when he runs into the
stormhead of executive branch displeasure and retaliation. Our committees
will find it more expedient to play safe and go along with the Executive. With
this censure as a spectacular sign that their Senate will not stand behind them
when the smut guns begin to shoot, what investigator will risk his career? We
will find ourselves in a twilight period of dead-end probes and whitewash
investigations, and Senate prestige will decay.

I ask in all sincerity, Is a scoring off of grudges against Senator
McCarthy worth this unthinkable price?

Second. It would be bad Americanism to censure McCarthy. Today, as
never before, the American people need desperately to present a united front
to overseas nations on the Communist issue. Strange and ominous forces are
at work trying to sell the poisonous doctrine of coexistence with communism
to our supposed allies. . . . Everywhere, in Europe and even in Japan, the
insidious trader is at work, trying to whittle away the determination of the free
nations to stand with the United States in an unbroken front against further
appeasement of aggressive communism.

The thing which would mean the final collapse of all that we have done
abroad since 1947 to build unconquerable defenses against the Kremlin would
be a domestic retreat of the American people from their present united stand
against communism. . . .

Do not think that this is fantastic. America's present solidarity against
communism conceals many weak and dangerous spots in our public-opinion
map. Do not think that the "trust Stalin" people of the war and Yalta period
all had a change of heart on Russia when we went into the cold war. They
adopted a protective coloration. They went into storm cellars. They put on the
anti-Communist label so that they could survive as a political or a journalistic
force. They are all ready to leap into action and set up a clamor for a new
coexistencist policy toward Russia and Red China when the psychological
moment arrives.

How can we know them? They are now almost invariably anti-Communist. Under their mask of anti-Communists, they do an "around-the-clock" job
blackguarding the dedicated men and women who do the real work of anticommunism in this country. They seek to discredit the effective "Red"
fighters in America. . . .

[At this point McCarthy interrupted Goldwater to thank him for his remarks
and to apologize for having to leave to catch a plane to attend a testimonial
dinner in Wisconsin the next evening.]

Mr. President, resuming my comments about those who pose as anti-
Communists when really they are blackguarding the efforts of the real anti-
Communists in the United States, they hurl vitriol at the American Legion,
the DAR, the Veterans of Foreign Wars, and the other great national bodies

which are holding the line against Communists and pro-Communist maneuvers in our American life.

And always and everywhere the anti-anti-Communists are against JOE MCCARTHY. They are the shock troops of the present smear drive which has led to this special censure session. Their papers and magazines, their organizations, and their forums are the incubating points for the big lies about this Senator.

This is the national background against which we meet in this session to consider the censure of JOSEPH MCCARTHY. This is the climate of opinion which is building up around us in wait for the day when America can be induced to relax its vigil against Communist aggression. . . .

I have sincere and deep respect for the six Senators who uncomplainingly executed their hard task on the Watkins committee. I know they weighed the evidence carefully, and that they voted according to their consciences, but I cannot bring myself to believe that they saw the action which they recommended against the Senator in the broader historic matrix which should have been uppermost in their thoughts. I cannot believe that they counted the staggering consequences which may flow from the ill-considered step which they have asked the Senate to take. Let us lift this decision out of the obscuring tangle of trivia into which, unfortunately, it has been placed, and let us weigh it in the broad terms of national good. Let us face the fact that a field day against Senator MCCARTHY in the Senate may well turn out to be a field day against America's global anti-Communist policy.

Over the earth today, the strong winds of destiny are blowing. They are reaching the Senate Chamber today as we make our historic decision on the pending resolution.

"The Honor of the Senate Is in Our Keeping"

SAM J. ERVIN, JR.

The following speech by Senator Sam Ervin, Democrat of North Carolina, presents a different viewpoint. Ervin, a member of the Select Committee, had been accused of bias in McCarthy's various attacks on the committee; part of his speech responds to this accusation. Note how Ervin:

- *explained his changed feelings toward McCarthy.*
- *responded to legal arguments against censure.*
- *described McCarthy's way of dealing with those who stood in his way or opposed him.*
- *explained why he found it difficult to work with McCarthy.*
- *interpreted the effect of McCarthy's methods on the Senate.*

Congressional Record, November 15, 1954, pp. 160020–22.

NOVEMBER 15, 1954

As I stated at the outset of my remarks, when I came to the Senate I had a feeling somewhat favorable to Senator MCCARTHY. I said publicly, in response to inquiries, that I did not favor expelling him from the Senate, and that I did not favor depriving him of his committee chairmanships. I am constrained to say that at this hour I am willing to admit that I have changed both of those opinions. This is true because I am wiser today in respect to Senator MC-CARTHY and his activities than I was at the time those opinions were originally given.

I do not propose at this time to urge Senator MCCARTHY'S expulsion from the Senate, but I shall make these observations upon the fantastic and foul accusations made by him against the six Senators who served on the select committee:

First, if Senator MCCARTHY made these fantastic and foul accusations against the members of the select committee without believing them to be true, he attempted to assassinate the character of these Senators and ought to be expelled from membership in the Senate for moral incapacity to perform the duties of a Senator.

Second, if Senator MCCARTHY made these fantastic and foul accusations against the six Senators who served on the select committee in the honest belief that they were true, then Senator MCCARTHY was suffering from mental delusions of gigantic proportions, and ought to be expelled from the Senate for mental incapacity to perform the duties of a Senator.

I do not propose to permit Senator MCCARTHY to try Senator WATKINS, Senator JOHNSON of Colorado, or me on the charge of partiality. I do not propose to permit Senator MCCARTHY to try the entire membership of the select committee upon his charge that they are the unwitting handmaidens or involuntary agents or attorneys-in-fact of the Communist Party.

I shall insist that the Senate try Senator MCCARTHY on the real issues. If the report of the select committee is a righteous report, what boots it if some of the members of the committee rendering the righteous report were unrighteous men in the eyes of Senator MCCARTHY?

If the report of the select committee is unsound, what boots it whether the members of the committee rendering the report were as pure as the aspirations of the angels?

The real issues now before the Senate are these: First, does the evidence taken before the select committee sustain the specific findings of fact made by the select committee?

Second, if so, do the specific findings of fact made by the select committee justify the conclusion of the select committee that Senator MCCARTHY merits censure?

If both these issues are answered in the affirmative, then Senator MCCARTHY should be censured by the Senate. If either issue is answered in the negative, then Senator MCCARTHY should not be censured by the Senate.

We have had an argument presented on the legal aspects of this matter to the effect that Senator MCCARTHY ought not to be censured, because there is no precedent whereby the Senate in times past had censured a Senator for similar conduct. We ought to thank God for the absence of any such precedent.

As I have said, the fifth section of article I of the United States Constitution provides in effect that the Senate may punish its Members for disorderly behavior.

In response to the argument that there is no precedent on this point, I wish to point out that if such an argument had been accepted as valid when the first murderer, arsonist, rapist, or burglar was brought to trial, there never would have been anybody punished for any of those offenses. We do not need a body of statutory laws to explain what the Constitution leaves to the determination of the Senate. The term disorderly behavior is very plain. The Constitution leaves that matter to the determination of the Senate. When the conduct of a Senator in his office becomes disorderly behavior, only the Senate can determine that matter, according to the Constitution.

Let us take up the first of the charges. If any charge would encompass disorderly conduct to a higher degree, I cannot imagine what it would be. What is the charge? The charge is that Senator MCCARTHY was guilty of disorderly conduct by flyblowing—that is a strong Anglo-Saxon word, but a very expressive one—and obstructing a committee of the Senate performing a task which the Senate had imposed upon that committee.

Let us consider what the evidence showed took place. The Senate had adopted a resolution which required the committee to investigate all the activities of Senator MCCARTHY after he became a Member, with a view to determining whether there was any basis for his expulsion from the Senate. Some very drastic accusations had been made. The committee went into the facts.

The evidence before the select committee showed beyond any question that Senator MCCARTHY never intended to appear before the Subcommittee on Privileges and Elections and submit himself to an examination before it on oath. For 14 months the Subcommittee on Privileges and Elections of the Senate Committee on Rules and Administration tried to get Senator MCCARTHY to appear before it, and answer certain questions with reference to the disposition of money given to him to fight communism, with reference to his action under the Corrupt Practices Act of Wisconsin, and his action with reference to whether or not he had participated in violations of the banking laws of Wisconsin.

If Senator MCCARTHY had appeared before the subcommittee, and made a complete revelation to that committee in respect to the matters in question, the whole matter would have been ended in a day or two. Instead of that, down to this good hour Senator MCCARTHY has never made an explanation with reference to those matters.

Besides not appearing before the subcommittee, what else did Senator MCCARTHY do? He first said the subcommittee had no jurisdiction to investigate the matters in question. Of course, that claim fell by the wayside when the Senate voted, 60 to 0, that the subcommittee did have jurisdiction to investigate such matters. After that happened, Senator McCARTHY said he would not appear before the subcommittee unless he was subpenaed. He said that the subcommittee did not have the power to subpena him during the session of the Senate. Of course, he knew that the subcommittee was not desirous of functioning after the Senate session adjourned.

In my time I have read many legal decisions stating how one should come to conclusions on facts. One rule, based on decision after decision, is that if a charge is made against a person which he would naturally answer or explain, and such person fails to answer that charge or offer an explanation, the finders of the facts may assume he has thereby impliedly admitted the truth of the charge.

Senator McCARTHY did not appear before the Subcommittee on Privileges and Elections. Instead of doing so, he began a systematic attack upon the character of the members of the subcommittee, similar to the attack he has made upon members of the select committee. Senator McCARTHY charged them with stealing the taxpayers' money for the partisan purpose of assisting the Democratic Party in smearing McCARTHY. Then he said, "You are aiding and abetting the Communist Party and the Communist conspiracy in their No. 1 objective, that is, getting rid of McCARTHY." Then he said, "You are dishonest, anyway. I will have nothing to do with you unless you drag me in before you by subpena."

Can any Senator, sitting as the finder of the facts, fail to arrive at the conclusion that Senator McCARTHY was guilty of contempt toward that subcommittee, and that he willfully obstructed the functioning of that subcommittee?

The second charge arose out of the General Zwicker incident. The evidence taken before the select committee indicates that General Zwicker cooperated with Senator McCARTHY and his staff prior to the hearing in giving the committee information about Maj. Irving Peress; that the McCarthy committee perhaps did not even know the name of that officer until it was given to the committee by General Zwicker; that immediately after General Zwicker got an order from the Adjutant General of the Army to discharge Major Peress, at his own request at any time within the next 90 days, he immediately furnished a member of Senator McCARTHY's staff with a copy of that order. When the hearing was held, according to the testimony, General Zwicker had a friendly conversation with Senator McCARTHY, in which he told Senator McCARTHY that he, too, was a native of Wisconsin, and he called Senator McCARTHY's attention to a Presidential order and an extract from the Army regulations which, in effect, prevented General Zwicker from testifying to any matters of a security nature. Senator McCARTHY made a statement that he was familiar with the order and regulation.

I wish to say that one thing I noticed about Senator McCARTHY is very puzzling to me. It is reflected in all his examinations. He seems to have an incapacity to distinguish between what he thinks in his head and external facts.

I do not say this in unkindness. But this characteristic makes it very difficult for one to meet him on the same mental plane.

The evidence disclosed that Senator McCARTHY jumped on General Zwicker because of the interpretation General Zwicker placed on certain press releases Senator McCARTHY had made. When we read the record, we reach the conclusion that Senator McCARTHY became angry at General Zwicker because General Zwicker was not able or willing to assume the correctness of all the statements included in the press releases made by Senator McCARTHY or under his direction. Then Senator McCARTHY abandoned a proper type of examination and began to chastise the witness. He said to the witness, as we find set forth on page 75 of the hearings:

> Anyone with the brains of a 5-year-old child can understand that question.

Mr. President, I think perhaps I understand it now; but I had to read it 4 or 5 times before I understood it.

Then Senator McCARTHY put a number of words into the mouth of the witness. Some of the things General Zwicker said seemed to anger Senator McCARTHY. Senator McCARTHY wanted General Zwicker to express his opinion that his superiors in the Pentagon acted in an outrageous manner when they issued the order for the honorable discharge of Major Peress. Well, Mr. President, anyone who expects an officer of the Army to criticize his superiors ought not be turned loose to do any questioning. I served in the Army; and I would not dare question an order that even a corporal gave me, much less question an order coming from the Pentagon.

Senator McCARTHY asked General Zwicker if he did not think that anyone who had anything to do with ordering Major Peress' honorable discharge ought to be removed from the military. General Zwicker made, in reply, about the only kind of answer any military man could have made; he said:

> I do not think he should be removed from the military.

That is all he said about that. But Senator McCARTHY put in General Zwicker's mouth some words General Zwicker never said. Here they are:

> The CHAIRMAN. Then, General, you should be removed from any command. Any man who has been given the honor of being promoted to general and who says, "I will protect another general who protected Communists," is not fit to wear that uniform, General.

Mr. President, I have searched the record in vain to find where General Zwicker ever said "I will protect another general who protected Communists."

I do not think anyone can find such a statement on the part of General Zwicker anywhere in the record.

Then Senator MCCARTHY said:

> I think it is a tremendous disgrace to the Army to have this sort of thing given to the public.
>
> I intend to give it to them. I have a duty to do that. I intend to repeat to the press exactly what you said. So you know that. You will be back here, General.

According to the undisputed testimony, Senator MCCARTHY told the general to return on Tuesday. According to Captain Woodward's testimony, Senator MCCARTHY said:

> General, you will be back on Tuesday, and at that time I am going to put you on display and let the American public see what kind of officers we have.

Then Senator MCCARTHY said, using one of his most endearing terms, that "General Zwicker was the first fifth-amendment general we have had before us."

Mr. President, Senators can claim that was legitimate cross-examination if they wish to do so; but I call it baiting and badgering and brow-beating a witness. Senator MCCARTHY gave as his excuse for his conduct in that case that General Zwicker was evasive and arrogant.

General Zwicker came before the select committee. The other day Senator JOHNSON of Colorado told the Senate what his reaction was to General Zwicker and his testimony. I think virtually all the members of the select committee at first did not even want to consider this charge we accepted as prima facie correct the position taken by Senator MCCARTHY, and we considered this charge only because all the proposed amendments to the original resolution called attention to this particular matter. I have spent a large part of one-third of a century in court rooms; and I have never seen any witness more free from arrogance than General Zwicker was when he appeared before us, and was subjected to one of the most rigorous cross-examinations I have ever witnessed.

Mr. President, Senators must not stick their heads into the sand like ostriches and thus blind themselves to the realities surrounding them. One tragic truth stands out above all the sound and fury of this sad hour: It is that Senator MCCARTHY besmirches throughout the length and breadth of this land the reputations of all Senators who dare to oppose his will or to express disapproval of his disorderly behavior in his senatorial office. As a consequence of this practice on the part of Senator MCCARTHY, every Senator sits in this Chamber under this Damoclean sword: The threat that Senator MCCARTHY will besmirch his reputation throughout the country if he does anything to incur Senator MCCARTHY's easily provoked wrath.

Mr. President, many years ago there was a custom in a section of my country, known as the South Mountains, to hold religious meetings at which the oldest members of the congregation were called upon to stand up and publicly testify to their religious experiences. On one occasion they were holding such a meeting in one of the churches; and old Uncle Ephriam Swink, a South Mountaineer whose body was all bent and distorted with arthritis, was present. All the older members of the congregation except Uncle Ephriam arose and gave testimony to their religious experiences. Uncle Ephriam kept his seat. Thereupon, the moderator said, "Brother Ephriam, suppose you tell us what has the Lord done for you."

Uncle Ephriam arose, with his bent and distorted body, and said, "Brother, he has mighty nigh ruint me."

Mr. President, that is about what Senator McCARTHY has done to the Senate. As a result of Senator McCARTHY's activities and the failure of the Senate to do anything positive about them, the monstrous idea has found lodgment in the minds of millions of loyal and thoughtful Americans that Senators are intimidated by Senator McCARTHY's threats of libel and slander, and for that reason the will of the Senate to visit upon Senator McCARTHY the senatorial discipline he so justly merits is paralyzed.

The Senate is trying this issue: Was Senator McCARTHY guilty of disorderly behavior in his senatorial office? The American people are trying another issue. The issue before the American people transcends in importance the issue before the Senate. The issue before the American people is simply this: Does the Senate of the United States have enough manhood to stand up to Senator McCARTHY?

Mr. President, the honor of the Senate is in our keeping. I pray that Senators will not soil it by permitting Senator McCARTHY to go unwhipped of senatorial justice.

Discussion Starters

1. Evaluate the reasons given by Goldwater for opposing senatorial censure of McCarthy and by Ervin for advocating it.

2. Identify the assumptions on which Goldwater and Ervin developed their arguments. Given these assumptions, where would each of the speakers have drawn the line on McCarthy's methods?

3. Goldwater's speech seems to suggest that it was impossible to oppose Communism and at the same time be critical of McCarthy and his methods. What are the risks, if any, inherent in such an attitude?

4. Ervin's speech focuses strictly on the damage done by McCarthy to the Senate. If censure was to succeed it was necessary for the charges to be as specific as possible. Nevertheless, McCarthy's accusations and attacks were by no means limited to the Senate. Respond to the assertion that the Senate, although it ultimately censured McCarthy, actually shirked its

larger responsibility to protect all whom McCarthy besmirched and that in so doing its methods, too, were open to criticism.

Related Documents

I. *McCarthy, Welch, and the Fisher Incident*

During his years as an investigator and exposer of Communism McCarthy appeared to grow increasingly bold in his charges. In a complicated series of maneuvers involving several of his staff assistants, McCarthy came into sharp conflict with the U.S. Army in late 1953. Although many issues came into play, and even more influenced his actions behind the scenes, McCarthy focused on the matter of the promotion of Major Irving Peress. As a dentist, Peress had been commissioned a captain in October 1952. Four months later it was discovered that he had refused on constitutional grounds to answer questions concerning possible activity in organizations considered to be subversive. While his case was under consideration he was routinely promoted to major in October 1953. Two months later an Army personnel board recommended that for security reasons he be separated from military service. In these unusual circumstances the simplest procedure was to grant an honorable discharge. McCarthy pressed to have the honorable discharge withheld and called for a court-martial.

When the Army ignored his demands McCarthy was infuriated, and took to task General Ralph Zwicker, commanding officer at the base where Peress was stationed. Although the Army was offended by the extremely rough treatment Zwicker received from McCarthy, it still tried to reach an understanding with him. Finally President Eisenhower stepped in, saying that he would not permit Army personnel to be browbeaten or humiliated.

As the controversy between the Army and McCarthy continued, the Army finally took the offensive. In March 1954 the controversy itself became the subject of an inquiry by McCarthy's own Government Operations subcommittee, with McCarthy temporarily stepping aside as chairman.

In addition to the issues under investigation, the televised hearings of the committee are important because they gave the nation a long look at McCarthy. The dramatic climax of the hearings came as a result of the gentle, witty, prodding of Joseph Welch, attorney for the Army. It is widely believed that the exchange of comments during Welch's cross-examination of McCarthy's aide, Roy Cohn, marked the beginning of widespread public disapproval of McCarthy.

U.S. Congress, Senate, Special Subcommittee on Investigation of Committee on Government Operations, *Special Investigation,* 83d Congress, 2d session, 1954, pp. 2426–30.

Speculate on how McCarthy's defenders (including Goldwater) and his critics (including Ervin) would differ on their interpretations of this incident.

JUNE 9, 1954

Senator MCCARTHY. . . . [I]n view of Mr. Welch's request that the information be given once we know of anyone who might be performing any work for the Communist Party, I think we should tell him that he has in his law firm a young man named Fisher whom he recommended, incidentally, to do work on this committee, who has been for a number of years a member of an organization which was named, oh, years and years ago, as the legal bulwark of the Communist Party, an organization which always swings to the defense of anyone who dares to expose Communists. I certainly assume that Mr. Welch did not know of this young man at the time he recommended him as the assistant counsel for this committee, but he has such terror and such a great desire to know where anyone is located who may be serving the Communist cause, Mr. Welch, that I thought we should just call to your attention the fact that your Mr. Fisher, who is still in your law firm today, whom you asked to have down here looking over the secret and classified material, is a member of an organization, not named by me but named by various committees, named by the Attorney General, as I recall, and I think I quote this verbatim, as "the legal bulwark of the Communist Party." He belonged to that for a sizable number of years, according to his own admission, and he belonged to it long after it had been exposed as the legal arm of the Communist Party.

Knowing that, Mr. Welch, I just felt that I had a duty to respond to your urgent request that before sundown, when we know of anyone serving the Communist cause, we let the agency know. We are now letting you know that your man did belong to this organization for either 3 or 4 years, belonged to it long after he was out of law school.

I don't think you can find anyplace, anywhere, an organization which has done more to defend Communists—I am again quoting the report—to defend Communists, to defend espionage agents, and to aid the Communist cause, than the man whom you originally wanted down here at your right hand instead of Mr. St. Clair.

I have hesitated bringing that up, but I have been rather bored with your phony requests to Mr. Cohn here that he personally get every Communist out of government before sundown. Therefore, we will give you information about the young man in your own organization.

I am not asking you at this time to explain why you tried to foist him on this committee. Whether you knew he was a member of that Communist organization or not, I don't know. I assume you did not, Mr. Welch, because I get the impression that, while you are quite an actor, you play for a laugh, I don't think you have any conception of the danger of the Communist Party. I don't think you yourself would ever knowingly aid the Communist cause. I think you are unknowingly aiding it when you try to burlesque this hearing in which we are attempting to bring out the facts, however.

Mr. WELCH. Mr. Chairman.

Senator MUNDT. Mr. Welch, the Chair should say he has no recognition or no memory of Mr. Welch's recommending either Mr. Fisher or anybody else as counsel for this committee.

I will recognize Mr. Welch.

Senator MCCARTHY. Mr. Chairman, I will give you the news story on that.

Mr. WELCH. Mr. Chairman, under these circumstances I must have something approaching a personal privilege.

Senator MUNDT. You may have it, sir. It will not be taken out of your time.

Mr. WELCH. Senator McCarthy, I did not know—Senator, sometimes you say "May I have your attention?"

Senator MCCARTHY. I am listening to you. I can listen with one ear.

Mr. WELCH. This time I want you to listen with both.

Senator MCCARTHY. Yes.

Mr. WELCH. Senator McCarthy, I think until this moment———

Senator MCCARTHY. Jim, will you get the news story to the effect that this man belonged to this Communist-front organization? Will you get the citations showing that this was the legal arm of the Communist Party, and the length of time that he belonged, and the fact that he was recommended by Mr. Welch? I think that should be in the record.

Mr. WELCH. You won't need anything in the record when I have finished telling you this.

Until this moment, Senator, I think I never really gaged your cruelty or your recklessness. Fred Fisher is a young man who went to the Harvard Law School and came into my firm and is starting what looks to be a brilliant career with us.

When I decided to work for this committee I asked Jim St. Clair, who sits on my right, to be my first assistant. I said to Jim, "Pick somebody in the firm who works under you that you would like." He chose Fred Fisher and they came down on an afternoon plane. That night, when he had taken a little stab at trying to see what the case was about, Fred Fisher and Jim St. Clair and I went to dinner together. I then said to these two young men, "Boys, I don't know anything about you except I have always liked you, but if there is anything funny in the life of either one of you that would hurt anybody in this case you speak up quick."

Fred Fisher said, "Mr. Welch, when I was in law school and for a period of months after, I belonged to the Lawyers Guild," as you have suggested, Senator. He went on to say, "I am secretary of the Young Republicans League in Newton with the son of Massachusetts' Governor, and I have the respect and admiration of my community and I am sure I have the respect and admiration of the 25 lawyers or so in Hale & Dorr."

I said, "Fred, I just don't think I am going to ask you to work on the case.

If I do, one of these days that will come out and go over national television and it will just hurt like the dickens."

So, Senator, I asked him to go back to Boston.

Little did I dream you could be so reckless and so cruel as to do an injury to that lad. It is true he is still with Hale & Dorr. It is true that he will continue to be with Hale & Dorr. It is, I regret to say, equally true that I fear he shall always bear a scar needlessly inflicted by you. If it were in my power to forgive you for your reckless cruelty, I will do so. I like to think I am a gentleman, but your forgiveness will have to come from someone other than me.

Senator McCARTHY. Mr. Chairman.

Senator MUNDT. Senator McCarthy?

Senator McCARTHY. May I say that Mr. Welch talks about this being cruel and reckless. He was just baiting; he has been baiting Mr. Cohn here for hours, requesting that Mr. Cohn, before sundown, get out of any department of Government anyone who is serving the Communist cause.

I just give this man's record and I want to say, Mr. Welch, that it has been labeled long before he became a member, as early as 1944————

Mr. WELCH. Senator, may we not drop this? We know he belonged to the Lawyers Guild, and Mr. Cohn nods his head at me. I did you, I think, no personal injury, Mr. Cohn.

Mr. COHN. No, sir.

Mr. WELCH. I meant to do you no personal injury, and if I did, I beg your pardon.

Let us not assassinate this lad further, Senator. You have done enough. Have you no sense of decency, sir, at long last? Have you left no sense of decency?

Senator McCARTHY. I know this hurts you, Mr. Welch. But I may say, Mr. Chairman, on a point of personal privilege, and I would like to finish it————

Mr. WELCH. Senator, I think it hurts you, too, sir.

Senator McCARTHY. I would like to finish this.

Mr. Welch has been filibustering this hearing, he has been talking day after day about how he wants to get anyone tainted with communism out before sundown. I know Mr. Cohn would rather not have me go into this. I intend to, however. Mr. Welch talks about any sense of decency. If I say anything which is not the truth, then I would like to know about it.

> The foremost legal bulwark of the Communist Party, its front or-
> ganizations, and controlled unions, and which, since its inception, has
> never failed to rally to the legal defense of the Communist Party, and
> individual members thereof, including known espionage agents.

Now, that is not the language of Senator McCarthy. That is the language of the Un-American Activities Committee. And I can go on with many more citations. It seems that Mr. Welch is pained so deeply he thinks it is improper for me to give the record, the Communist-front record, of the man whom he wanted to foist upon this committee. But it doesn't pain him at all—there is no pain in his chest about the unfounded charges against Mr. Frank Carr; there is no pain there about the attempt to destroy the reputation and take the jobs away from the young men who were working in my committee.

And, Mr. Welch, if I have said anything here which is untrue, then tell me. I have heard you and every one else talk so much about laying the truth upon the table that when I hear—and it is completely phony, Mr. Welch, I have listened to you for a long time—when you say "Now, before sundown, you must get these people out of Government," I want to have it very clear, very clear that you were not so serious about that when you tried to recommend this man for this committee.

And may I say, Mr. Welch, in fairness to you, I have reason to believe that you did not know about his Communist-front record at the time you recommended him. I don't think you would have recommended him to the committee if you knew that.

I think it is entirely possible you learned that after you recommended him.

Senator MUNDT. The Chair would like to say again that he does not believe that Mr. Welch recommended Mr. Fisher as counsel for this committee, because he has through his office all the recommendations that were made. He does not recall any that came from Mr. Welch, and that would include Mr. Fisher.

Senator MCCARTHY. Let me ask Mr. Welch. You brought him down, did you not, to act as your assistant?

Mr. WELCH. Mr. McCarthy, I will not discuss this with you further. You have sat within 6 feet of me, and could have asked me about Fred Fisher. You have brought it out. If there is a God in heaven, it will do neither you nor your cause any good. I will not discuss it further. I will not ask Mr. Cohn any more questions. You, Mr. Chairman, may, if you will, call the next witness.

II. Forget It's McCarthy—Remember the Constitution!

DAVID LAWRENCE

A pro-McCarthy comment on the censure proceedings was offered by David Lawrence in the U.S. News and World Report. *Using Ervin's speech as a point of reference, assess Lawrence's attempt to defend McCarthy's actions. Speculate on how it was possible for sixty-seven tradition-conscious senators to reach a conclusion different from Lawrence's.*

David Lawrence, "Forget It's McCarthy—Remember the Constitution!," *U.S. News and World Report,* October 29, 1954, p. 144. Copyright 1954, U.S. News & World Report, Inc.

OCTOBER 29, 1954

(Reprinted from *U.S. News & World Report*)

Certainly a Senator is guilty of bad manners when he denounces a witness who is evasive in testifying before a congressional committee.

Certainly a Senator is intemperate when he denounces a fellow Senator who has provoked him.

Certainly a Senator uses poor judgment when he sends bitterly worded replies to letters from a Senate committee which has invited him to testify, even if he regards its hearings as a political smear.

But—and here's the crux of the entire case—not a single statement or charge made in the report issued last week by the committee headed by Senator Watkins of Utah affords constitutional justification for punishing any United States Senator now or hereafter.

The Constitution makes no reference at all to "censure," but specifically says that each house of Congress "may punish its members for disorderly behavior."

Crimes of the mind, however, are not crimes of the hand. Censure cases in the past have primarily concerned physical acts—fist fights in the heat of Senate debate. Neither contemptuous language nor a contemptuous "manner of expression" by a Senator is legal contempt of the Senate.

Drastic treatment in cross-examination of a recalcitrant witness was vigorously defended in 1936 by Senator Hugo Black of Alabama, Democrat, then chairman of a Senate investigating committee and now a Justice of the Supreme Court of the United States. The right to excoriate fellow members off the floor of Congress has always been held to be a prerogative of members of Congress in political campaigning.

If the censure motion is approved by the Senate, the cause of freedom of speech will suffer a setback in the legislatures of the world. It will change the nature of the United States Senate. It will make of it a body in which minority rights hereafter will always be at the mercy of an intolerant majority.

The Watkins report points to an alleged act of impropriety in 1952—a refusal by the Senator in question to accept an "invitation" extended to him by a previous committee to testify on his personal finances. There's nothing in the records to justify the failure of that committee to issue a subpoena, which the same Senator repeatedly had said he would honor.

Also, the Department of Justice and the Internal Revenue Service, under the present and preceding Administrations, have not found any violations of law by the Senator in connection with his personal finances or his use of funds to fight Communism. Has it not been argued often that to ferret out violations of law is primarily an executive and not a legislative function?

The Watkins committee says, however, that an invitation by the previous committee requesting the Senator to testify should have been enough. But is that law, or is it a new code of senatorial etiquette never before proclaimed in the Senate's own rules or precedents?

Back in 1929 and 1930 a demagogue from Alabama, the late Senator Heflin, vilified the Catholic Church, the Pope and the Vatican and Americans of Catholic faith, in tirade after tirade, on the floor of the Senate. No Senator moved a vote of censure.

Likewise, in 1918 in the midst of war, the late Senator La Follette, Sr., made a speech denouncing the war and virtually inciting the populace not to allow their sons to be drafted. A Senate Committee considered censure but refused to recommend it.

Both these instances of contemptuous speech are examples of what the late Justice Oliver Wendell Holmes of the Supreme Court of the United States, a great liberal, meant when he defined the freedom of speech guaranteed in our Constitution as "freedom for the thought we hate."

That's the acid test today, too. Are we true liberals, or are we totalitarians? If we are believers in "a government of laws and not of men," the Watkins report should be rejected by the Senate.

As a substitute motion, the Senate Committee on Rules—which for many months has been taking testimony on the subject of the procedures and methods of congressional investigating committees—should be directed to bring in a report defining what is or is not permissible in examining witnesses and what is or is not the proper procedure in obtaining testimony from Senators or Representatives themselves.

Congressional history is replete with instances of a refusal by members to accept invitations to testify before investigating committees. It is regrettable that the Watkins committee declined to allow the evidence on this point to be introduced into the record.

Let's not legislate retroactively on any Senator. The Constitution says no *ex post facto* law shall be adopted. This means that no statute or rule shall punish any citizen or any member of Congress for any past action which at the time was not a prohibited offense.

Let's forget it's McCarthy, and remember the Constitution!

III. "McCarthyism Took Its Toll . . ."

DWIGHT D. EISENHOWER

President Eisenhower was frequently criticized for not condemning McCarthy's actions and disowning him as a fellow Republican. Writing nine years after the censure, Eisenhower commented on the action and on his relations with McCarthy. Assuming Eisenhower's recollection of events to be accurate, evaluate the position he took in regard to McCarthy. In the light of Goldwater's speech,

From *Mandate for Change,* pp. 330–31 by Dwight D. Eisenhower. Copyright © 1963 by Dwight D. Eisenhower. Reprinted by permission of Doubleday & Co., Inc.

what effect might more open opposition by Eisenhower have had on the Senate's deliberations?

It is doubtful that this result would have ever come about had I adopted a habit of referring to McCarthy by name in press conferences, thus making the issue one of Executive versus congressional prestige. I felt impelled, however, to express my appreciation to the man who was the hero of the episode, Senator Arthur Watkins. Accordingly I invited him to come to my office on Saturday morning, December 4 [1954], so that we might have a few words in private. He came "off the record," arriving at the East Wing and walking across through the basement of the Mansion to avoid notice, and the two of us had a pleasant conversation. Senator Watkins said his only regret was that the censure motion on McCarthy's treatment of Zwicker could not go through as originally worded.

Across the hall, outside Jim Hagerty's office, a larger crowd of newspapermen than usual had assembled. Word of Senator Watkins' visit had got out. Just as the senator was ready to leave, Jim walked in.

"The reporters would like to interview the senator on his way out," he said. "Is it O.K.?"

The senator was willing and I at once gave my approval. "Tell them," I said to Jim, "that I asked Senator Watkins to come down here so that I could tell him how much we appreciate his superb handling of a most difficult job."

Upon learning of this meeting, Senator McCarthy finally made what has been termed his "break" with me—why it was called such at that late date I could not fathom. He claimed that the administration was soft on Communism and apologized for having supported me in 1952.

But one thing was apparent. By a combination of the Senate's vote and the loss of his committee chairmanship, the senator's power was ended. Senator McCarthy died an untimely and sad—even pathetic—death in 1957, but as a political force he was finished at the end of 1954.

On the whole sorry experience I had no public comment to make but I did have an urge to go back into my memory to review the developments and to contemplate their meaning.

McCarthyism took its toll on many individuals and on the nation. No one was safe from charges recklessly made from inside the walls of congressional immunity. Teachers, government employees, and even ministers became vulnerable. Innocent people accused of Communist associations or party membership have not to this day been able to clear their names fully. For a few, of course, the cost was little—where the accused was a figure who stood high in public trust and respect, personal damage, if any, could be ignored or laughed away. But where, without proof of guilt, or because of some accidental or early-in-life association with suspected persons, a man or woman had lost a job or the confidence and trust of superiors and associates, the cost was often tragic, both emotionally and occupationally.

Not all these accusations were made by Senator McCarthy himself; but he and his cult were never known for any sense of discrimination either in their choice of targets or in determining who held the gun. The attack on General Zwicker made me furious; the innuendoes about some others, whom I knew intimately, I found ridiculous.

Measured against all the mental anguish unfairly inflicted upon people and all the bitterness occasioned by baseless charges against them, the benefits flowing from the McCarthy "investigations" do not loom large. I was told by members of the Executive departments, including the Federal Bureau of Investigation, that those discovered by the subcommittee to be, on reliable information, disloyal or unreliable were few in number. Moreover, in most of the cases, where damaging evidence was made public by them, I was informed that the truth of the matter usually had been uncovered by appropriate officials, without committee intervention.

Supporters of McCarthyism represented it as simply a dramatic effort to awaken the public to the existence of some Communist penetration into all facets of our national life and to warn everyone of the need for universal alertness. Perhaps at its beginning the movement may have had some such usefulness. But almost immediately its methods defeated its purported objectives. Un-American activity cannot be prevented or routed out by employing un-American methods; to preserve freedom we must use the tools that freedom provides.

IV. McCarthy: Wrong in Details, Right in Essentials

ROY COHN

One of McCarthy's more prominent aides was Roy Cohn, a young, ambitious attorney. Cohn's alleged attempts to blackmail the Army played an important part in bringing about the showdown between the Army and McCarthy. Cohn concluded his largely autobiographical book entitled McCarthy *with his interpretation of the senator and his methods. Respond to his concluding question.*

I was fully aware of McCarthy's faults, which were neither few nor minor. He was impatient, overly aggressive, overly dramatic. He acted on impulse. He tended to sensationalize the evidence he had—in order to draw attention to the rock-bottom seriousness of the situation. He would neglect to do important homework and consequently would, on occasion, make challengeable statements.

His impatience with detail sometimes caused minor explosions at executive sessions of the subcommittee. Much of a senatorial committee's work

Roy Cohn, *McCarthy* (New York: New American Library, 1968), pp. 275–76, 279. Copyright © 1968 by Roy Cohn. Used with permission of The Foley Agency.

consists of tedious and often uninteresting detail, so that whenever McCarthy knew that a meeting was to be devoted to ratifications of appointments, promotions, and what he called "office manager stuff" he would deputize an assistant to act for him. Once, when he could not dodge such a session, I watched him grow more and more irritated. When two senators actually quarreled over the promotion of a girl on the staff, McCarthy banged with an ashtray—he never used a gavel—and shouted: "Look, I'm trying to get my appropriation for the year so that I can get Communists out of Government. I'm not going to sit here all afternoon listening to you two arguing over whether Mary is going up to grade eleven or not. I don't want to hear about it. Fight it out later."

Ultimately, this inattention to detail, this failure to check and recheck every point he made, enabled his enemies to divert attention from the main thrust of his attack to the details—which, in too many cases, did not bear close scrutiny.

But it must be understood that in an important sense McCarthy was a salesman. He was selling the story of America's peril. He knew that he could never hope to convince anybody by delivering a dry, general-accounting-office type of presentation. In consequence, he stepped up circumstances a notch or two.

Did the urgent need to get the story across excuse a broad-bush approach? I can understand why he did it, as I can realize that his dramatizations hurt him in many quarters. I quarreled with him frequently on this score and stressed that by using this technique he sometimes placed himself in an indefensible position. But I never disagreed with the substance of his thesis. . . .

Looking back with whatever objectivity I can muster, I believe that even after all the excesses and mistakes are counted up, Senator McCarthy used the best methods available to him to fight a battle that needed to be fought. The methods were far from perfect, but they were not nearly as imperfect as uninformed critics suggest. The use of Executive sessions to protect witnesses from publicity until they had an opportunity to explain adverse evidence; the respect of the constitutional privilege; the right given each witness to have counsel beside him at all times—these compare favorably not only with methods of other investigating committees but with methods of certain prosecutors. The "methods" attack on McCarthy suffers from a credibility gap because of the double standard of many critics, particularly the press, radio, and television. To them, anything McCarthy did was wrong, but the excesses and outrageous methods of those not investigating subversion are often overlooked or excused.

He may have been wrong in details, but he was right in essentials. Certainly few can deny that the Government of the United States had in it enough Communist sympathizers and pro-Soviet advisers to twist and pervert American foreign policy for close to two decades.

He was a man of a peculiar time: the Cold War. His particular "package" would not have been deliverable in the depressed but exhilarating thirites. But he came forward at the time of Communist aggression in Korea and the triumph of Mao's revolution. The job he felt he had to do could hardly have been done by a gentle, tolerant spirit who could see all around a problem.

What is indisputable is that he was a courageous man who fought a monumental evil. He did so against opposition as determined as was his own attack—an opposition that spent far more time, money, and print seeking to expose *him* than Communism.

Since his day, Cuba has fallen to the Communists. The free world was rocked in 1967 by the Harold Philby revelation of Communist infiltration in high Government security posts. Nuclear explosions echo over China and the Soviet Union. American men are defending the borders of South Vietnam against Communist aggressors. North Korea has laid down the gauntlet to us.

Has not history already begun his vindication?

VI. The Spook

What are the main points suggested by this article from The New Republic?

AUGUST 21–28, 1971

There's a circular stone staircase in the old Capitol where you meet all sorts of strangers, and unexpected people, and ghosts. Coming down the other day I met somebody I hadn't seen in years. "Why, Joe!" I said in astonishment. He had a bulging briefcase and the same blue-black jowls, and a manner that oozed familiarity like the approach of a wet puppy that is trying to wipe its paws on you or take a bite if you turn your back.

"Why, Joe," I repeated, "it's been a long time."

"Oh, I've been here," he said easily, "you haven't seen me, but I've been around. Now I'm worried; worried about the country."

"The trip to China, you mean Joe?" I asked "It's just that the President is trying to better our relations. See Chou En-lai, and that sort of thing. Scotty Reston says Chou talks reasonably————"

The old glower came into his eyes:

"I have in my hand a list," he began. "Yes, it's *Life* magazine, June 28, 1954: the editors of *Life* call Chou 'a political thug and a professional assassin,' who 'killed men with his own hands, a ruthless intriguer, a conscienceless liar, a saber-toothed political assassin.' "

"Whew, Joe, that's strong stuff! It brings it all back, doesn't it? But *Life* magazine has changed a lot in 17 years. Why, you called some names yourself, didn't you? There was that line of yours about General of the Army Marshall: 'a man steeped in falsehood, part of a conspiracy so infamous, so immense and

TRB, "The Spook," *The New Republic,* August 21–28, 1971, p. 6. Reprinted by permission of *The New Republic.* © 1971, Harrison-Blaine of New Jersey, Inc.

an infamy so black as to dwarf any previous venture in the history of man.' "

"Those were golden days, weren't they?" said Joe grinning. "But about this trip to China, take this down for your afternoon edition and I'll have Roy telephone you a follow-up for overnight, 'The senator from Wisconsin said the China trip confirms his charges that the Democrats, ah, are the party of cowardly Communist appeasement. . . .'"

"But, Joe, it isn't the Democrats. It's *President Nixon* who's going."

There was a pause. "No?" he said. "Our Dick—going to China?" He seemed nonplussed. "Why he was one of the most patriotic ones we had!—on the UnAmerican Activities Committee; knocked off Jerry Vorhees and Helen Douglas as pinkos; you'll be telling me we're trading with Moscow next."

"Why sure, Joe; just last week the Commerce Department approved licenses for what may be a billion-dollar deal with Moscow with Mack Trucks, Inc."

He stood there weaving a minute like a pug who has taken a bad one on his jaw and is praying for the bell. "Come now," he said ingratiatingly, "I'm sure the common people are sound. They haven't turned soft. Surely they're afraid of somebody! What's my old friend J. Edgar doing?"

"He got a blow, too, Joe, last month. He had a little dandy about 'Mao's Red Shadows in America' denouncing 'pro-Peking subversion,' and offered to distribute reprints. Then suddenly he withdrew it for lack of funds. Between you and me, he got a call from the White House the day after the President announced his trip. You know Washington; he got back quick on the law-and-order track."

"Law-and-order," he said brightening. It was amazing how fast he made his recovery. "That sounds better! How's my Subversive Activities Control Board coming on, that we shoved through over Truman's veto?"

"This will please you, Joe; it's got a new lease on life. President Nixon suddenly revived it; not just against Communists anymore but against anybody the Attorney General puts on his list of subversive organizations. Mitchell nominates them and the SACB investigates them. The order's directed against 'totalitarian, fascist, Communist, subversive and other groups.' Opponents call it the new Inquisition; the new era of McCarthyism."

"No! do they really!" said Joe, rubbing his hands. "What an opportunity; what a hunting license. Not merely those who 'commit,' " he asked, almost pleadingly, "but those who 'advocate' violence, I hope?"

"Why yes," I said, surprised. "Gee, I'd forgotten how fast you are. Now I remember Dick Rovere called you 'the most gifted and successful demagogue this country has ever known.' "

"Oh, you gotta have friends," said Joe, trying to look modest. "You can't do it all yourself. I had people like Pat McCarran and Bill Jenner working with me, and that boy from Yale, what was his name?—William F. Buckley Jr., or something."

"Yes, Joe, he writes a column and edits a magazine now. He was the one who wrote, 'McCarthyism . . . is a movement around which men of good will and stern morality can close ranks.' He never repudiated you."

"You gotta have friends," repeated Joe, "You gotta be bold. Why, I accused both the Truman and Eisenhower administrations of treason. The public lapped it up! You don't have to fear the press. They'll truckle."

"Yeah, we just saw the Justice Department keep *The New York Times* from printing the Pentagon story for a fortnight. And Vice President Agnew and his friends keep the news media off balance."

"And one other thing," said Joe, "you gotta get the public concerned—scared. If they're worried enough they'll believe anything. Tell me now; this Attorney General; he's not going to double-cross us on the SACB is he?"

"Who, Mitchell? Well Joe, he's in favor of wiretapping, and protective detention, and no-knock raids, and sweep-arrests off the streets after peace demonstrations, and he claims the President has inherent power to order eavesdropping without court order."

"That's a beginning," said Joe. "But can Mitchell work 'em up, can he scare 'em?"

"He told a meeting of the Virginia Bar Association, June 11, 'Never in our history has this country been confronted with so many revolutionary elements determined to destroy by force the government and the society it stands for.' "

"That's a start," said Joe, moving off. "Well, I've got a little hearing at the State Department."

"Goodbye, Joe, Quite a start to see you!"

He looked back. "Oh, I'm never far away," he said ambiguously, and went down the staircase.

For Further Reading

Robert Griffith's *The Politics of Fear: Joseph R. McCarthy and the Senate* (1970) relates directly to the theme of this chapter.

Friendly interpretations of McCarthy and his movement have been written by William F. Buckley and L. Brent Bozell in *McCarthy and His Enemies* (1954) and by Roy M. Cohn in *McCarthy* (1968). Sharply critical interpretations are found in *McCarthy: The Man, the Senator, and the "Ism"* (1953), by Jack Anderson and Ronald W. May, and in Fred J. Cook's *The Nightmare Decade: The Life and Times of Senator Joe McCarthy* (1971). Richard Rovere's *Senator Joe McCarthy** (1959) is also unfriendly to the man and his movement.

Michael Paul Rogin's *The Intellectuals and McCarthy: The Radical Specter** (1967) is a study of the sources of McCarthy's political support.

The context in which McCarthyism developed is considered in *The Politics of Loyalty: The White House and the Communist Issue, 1946–1952* (1969), by Alan D. Harper; *The Communist Controversy in Washington: From the New*

*Paperbound edition available.

Deal to McCarthy* (1966), by Earl Latham; and in *Seeds of Repression: Harry S. Truman and the Origins of McCarthyism* (1971), by Athan Theoharis.

Arthur Watkins, the chairman of the committee that recommended censure of McCarthy, provides a retrospective look in *Enough Rope* (1969).

Joseph R. McCarthy* (1970), edited by Allen J. Matusow, contains both primary documents and interpretations.

A problems book on the subject is *The Meaning of McCarthyism** (1965), edited by Earl Latham.

**Paperbound edition available.

15. Out of Their Place: Voices of Protest in the 1960s

One wonders what the Founding Fathers had in mind when they asserted in the Preamble that one purpose of the Constitution was "to insure domestic tranquility." Were they thinking of the sort of tranquility that prevails when one element in society dominates the political and social order and others know and remain "in their place"? In such a situation, only a dispute within the dominant group can rupture the tranquility—as happened in the Civil War. Or could the Fathers possibly have been thinking of a tranquility growing out of mutual acceptance among society's various groups and full enjoyment of rights and liberties by all citizens?

It seems safe to assume, considering the setting in which they lived, that the Fathers conceived of domestic tranquility in the former terms rather than the latter. Anglo-Saxon, Protestant (at least non-Catholic and non-Jewish), white males constituted the governing establishment. As America's story unfolded, challenges to their dominance were slow in coming. Assimilation of immigrants who were not easily "anglicized" was difficult. Discrimination against Catholics and Jews faded away only gradually and some disadvantages still persist. Emancipation and suffrage and even civil rights laws did little to make blacks acceptable outside of their role as subservient citizens. Mexican Americans and Indians, too, were expected to accept without protest their exclusion from full participation in American life. More than half a century of struggle finally brought women the right to vote, but achievement of this right did not produce the improvement in their status that the suffragettes had hoped for.

Tranquility based on this sort of social order is necessarily fragile, for if the second-class groups become disaffected with their status and make known their disaffection, it is irreparably shattered. Such a shattering of domestic tranquility happened in the United States in the 1960s, and it seems inconceivable that a social order based on the original terms can ever be reconstructed. Demands of militant blacks, Indians, Mexican Americans, Japanese Americans, Chinese Americans, ethnic groups of European origin, women, the poor, and even college and high school students have called for a new social order. In the new order, tranquility, if it is ever to be achieved, will rest on open acceptance and appreciation of a wide variety of cultures and values and on extension of rights and liberties to all, regardless of their sex, racial or national origin, or religious faith.

Out of the protest, dissent, discord, and violence of the 1960s emerges this crucial question: Can the nation give birth to a new social order with a new tranquility?

Core Document

What We Want

STOKELY CARMICHAEL

Of the groups protesting against the American social order in the 1960s none was more militant or insistent than the blacks. Of the slogans raised, none evoked such fear and resentment in white America as the call for "black power." Until this call was issued, white America had adjusted, however reluctantly, to pressures from blacks. In the late fifties and early sixties, the demonstrations and marches of Martin Luther King, Jr., were tolerated largely because, no matter how strongly whites resisted his ultimate goals, they appreciated his consistent advocacy of nonviolence. Even his goals were more acceptable than the nationalism promoted by Malcolm X. As other groups mobilized, their freedom rides, sit-ins, and voter registration drives, by their directness, put white America to a test. From this test emerged a rather general acceptance of the concept—but not the practice—of integration.

Against this background, the idea of black power was jolting. White Amer-

Stokely Carmichael, *New York Review of Books*, September 22, 1966, pp. 5–6, 8. Reprinted by permission of the Student Nonviolent Coordinating Committee.

*ica might have been prepared for more insistent demands for the practice of
integration, but black power did not press for this. In fact, it rejected integration
outright. Instead, as political scientist Charles Hamilton put it, black power was
concerned with "organizing the rage of black people and with putting new, hard
questions and demands to white America." Economic power, political power,
appreciation of blackness and black culture, concern for black identity, and a
degree of racial separation were important aspects of the black power movement.
James Baldwin, the noted black writer, explained why whites were shocked:
"When a Black man, whose destiny and identity have always been controlled
by others, decides and states that he will control his own destiny and rejects the
identity given to him by others, he is talking revolution."*

*The term "black power" was popularized by Stokely Carmichael, the young
leader of the Student Nonviolent Coordinating Committee (SNCC, referred to
as Snick). Carmichael first attracted national attention when, during the famous
walk through Mississippi by James Meredith, he cried out: "The only way we
gonna stop them white men from whuppin' us is to take over. We been saying
freedom for six years and we ain't got nothin'. What we gonna start saying now
is black power." The crowds roared back: "Black Power!" and the media were
there to record and report it.*

*Whites were not alone in their concern over the slogan. Moderate black
leaders, including Martin Luther King, Jr., Roy Wilkins of the National Association for the Advancement of Colored People (NAACP), and Whitney Young of
the Urban League also denounced it, but it nevertheless gave expression to the
hopes and ideals of younger, more militant blacks.*

*In the following article Carmichael explained what he meant by black
power. In reading the article, watch for:*

- *identification of the causes of the plight of blacks.*
- *accusations against white America.*
- *reasons for stressing power rather than morality, love, and nonviolence.*
- *examples of barriers and frustrations in the way of black power.*
- *comments on the use of violence in black power efforts.*
- *suggestions concerning positive possibilities of black power for both whites
  and blacks.*
- *reasons for condemning integration.*
- *references to historical circumstances that created the desire for black
  power.*
- *references to different perspectives of whites and blacks as they view racial
  problems.*

SEPTEMBER 22, 1966

One of the tragedies of the struggle against racism is that up to now there has
been no national organization which could speak to the growing militancy of
young black people in the urban ghetto. There has been only a civil rights
movement, whose tone of voice was adapted to an audience of liberal whites.

It served as a sort of buffer zone between them and angry young blacks. None of its so-called leaders could go into a rioting community and be listened to. In a sense, I blame ourselves—together with the mass media—for what has happened in Watts, Harlem, Chicago, Cleveland, Omaha. Each time the people in those cities saw Martin Luther King get slapped, they became angry; when they saw four little black girls bombed to death, they were angrier; and when nothing happened, they were steaming. We had nothing to offer that they could see, except to go out and be beaten again. We helped to build their frustration.

For too many years, black Americans marched and had their heads broken and got shot. They were saying to the country, "Look, you guys are supposed to be nice guys and we are only going to do what we are supposed to do—why do you beat us up, why don't you give us what we ask, why don't you straighten yourselves out?" After years of this, we are at almost the same point—because we demonstrated from a position of weakness. We cannot be expected any longer to march and have our heads broken in order to say to whites: come on, you're nice guys. For you are not nice guys. We have found you out.

An organization which claims to speak for the needs of a community—as does the Student Nonviolent Coordinating Committee—must speak in the tone of that community, not as somebody else's buffer zone. This is the significance of black power as a slogan. For once, black people are going to use the words they want to use—not just the words whites want to hear. And they will do this no matter how often the press tries to stop the use of the slogan by equating it with racism or separatism.

An organization which claims to be working for the needs of a community —as SNCC does—must work to provide that community with a position of strength from which to make its voice heard. This is the significance of black power beyond the slogan.

Black power can be clearly defined for those who do not attach the fears of white America to their questions about it. We should begin with the basic fact that black Americans have two problems: they are poor and they are black. All other problems arise from this two-sided reality: lack of education, the so-called apathy of black men. Any program to end racism must address itself to that double reality.

Almost from its beginning, SNCC sought to address itself to both conditions with a program aimed at winning political power for impoverished Southern blacks. We had to begin with politics because black Americans are a propertyless people in a country where property is valued above all. We had to work for power, because this country does not function by morality, love, and nonviolence, but by power. Thus we determined to win political power, with the idea of moving on from there into activity that would have economic effects. With power, the masses could *make or participate in making* the decisions which govern their destinies, and thus create basic change in their day-to-day lives.

But if political power seemed to be the key to self-determination, it was also obvious that the key had been thrown down a deep well many years earlier. Disenfranchisement, maintained by racist terror, made it impossible to talk about organizing for political power in 1960. The right to vote had to be won, and SNCC workers devoted their energies to this from 1961 to 1965. They set up voter registration drives in the Deep South. They created pressure for the vote by holding mock elections in Mississippi in 1963 and by helping to establish the Mississippi Freedom Democratic Party (MFDP) in 1964. That struggle was eased, though not won, with the passage of the 1965 Voting Rights Act. SNCC workers could then address themselves to the question: "Who can we vote for, to have our needs met—how do we make our vote meaningful?"

SNCC had already gone to Atlantic City for recognition of the Mississippi Freedom Democratic Party by the Democratic convention and been rejected; it had gone with the MFDP to Washington for recognition by Congress and been rejected. In Arkansas, SNCC helped thirty Negroes to run for School Board elections; all but one were defeated, and there was evidence of fraud and intimidation sufficient to cause their defeat. In Atlanta, Julian Bond ran for the state legislature and was elected—twice—and unseated—twice. In several states, black farmers ran in elections for agricultural committees which make crucial decisions concerning land use, loans, etc. Although they won places on a number of committees, they never gained the majorities needed to control them.

All of the efforts were attempts to win black power. Then, in Alabama, the opportunity came to see how blacks could be organized on an independent party basis. An unusual Alabama law provides that any group of citizens can nominate candidates for county office and, if they win 20 per cent of the vote, may be recognized as a county political party. The same then applies on a state level. SNCC went to organize in several counties such as Lowndes, where black people—who form 80 per cent of the population and have an average annual income of $943—felt they could accomplish nothing within the framework of the Alabama Democratic Party because of its racism and because the qualifying fee for this year's elections was raised from $40 to $500 in order to prevent most Negroes from becoming candidates. On May 3, five new county "freedom organizations" convened and nominated candidates for the offices of sheriff, tax assessor, members of the school boards. These men and women are up for election in November—if they live until then. Their ballot symbol is the black panther: a bold, beautiful animal, representing the strength and dignity of black demands today. A man needs a black panther on his side when he and his family must endure—as hundreds of Alabamians have endured—loss of job, eviction, starvation, and sometimes death, for political activity. He may also need a gun and SNCC reaffirms the right of black men everywhere to defend themselves when threatened or attacked. As for initiating the use of violence, we hope that such programs as ours will make that unnecessary; but it is not for us to tell black communities whether they can or cannot use any particular form of action to resolve their problems. Responsibility for the use of violence by black men, whether in self-defense or initiated by them, lies with the white community.

This is the specific historical experience from which SNCC's call for "black power" emerged on the Mississippi march last July. But the concept of "black power" is not a recent or isolated phenomenon: It has grown out of the ferment of agitation and activity by different people and organizations in many black communities over the years. Our last year of work in Alabama added a new concrete possibility. In Lowndes County, for example, black power will mean that if a Negro is elected sheriff, he can end police brutality. If a black man is elected tax assessor, he can collect and channel funds for the building of better roads and schools serving black people—thus advancing the move from political power into the economic arena. In such areas as Lowndes, where black men have a majority, they will attempt to use it to exercise control. This is what they seek: control. Where Negroes lack a majority, black power means proper representation and sharing of control. It means the creation of power bases from which black people can work to change statewide or nation-wide patterns of oppression through pressure from strength—instead of weakness. Politically, black power means what it has always meant to SNCC: the coming-together of black people to elect representatives and *to force those representatives to speak to their needs*. It does not mean merely putting black faces into office. A man or woman who is black and from the slums cannot be automatically expected to speak to the needs of black people. Most of the black politicians we see around the country today are not what SNCC means by black power. The power must be that of a community, and emanate from there.

SNCC today is working in both North and South on programs of voter registration and independent political organizing. In some places, such as Alabama, Los Angeles, New York, Philadelphia, and New Jersey, independent organizing under the black panther symbol is in progress. The creation of a national "black panther party" must come about; it will take time to build, and it is much too early to predict its success. We have no infallible master plan and we make no claim to exclusive knowledge of how to end racism; different groups will work in their own different ways. SNCC cannot spell out the full logistics of self-determination but it can address itself to the problem by helping black communities define their needs, realize their strength, and go into action along a variety of lines which they must choose for themselves. Without knowing all the answers, it can address itself to the basic problem of poverty; to the fact that in Lowndes County, 86 white families own 90 per cent of the land. What are black people in that county going to do for jobs, where are they going to get money? There must be reallocation of land, of money.

Ultimately, the economic foundations of this country must be shaken if black people are to control their lives. The colonies of the United States—and this includes the black ghettoes within its borders, north and south—must be liberated. For a century, this nation has been like an octopus of exploitation, its tentacles stretching from Mississippi and Harlem to South America, the Middle East, southern Africa, and Vietnam; the form of exploitation varies from area to area but the essential result has been the same—a powerful few have been maintained and enriched at the expense of the poor and voiceless colored masses. This pattern must be broken. As its grip loosens here and there around the world, the hopes of black Americans become more realistic. For racism to die, a totally different America must be born.

This is what the white society does not wish to face; this is why that society prefers to talk about integration. But integration speaks not at all to the problem of poverty, only to the problem of blackness. Integration today means the man who "makes it," leaving his black brothers behind in the ghetto as fast as his new sports car will take him. It has no relevance to the Harlem wino or to the cottonpicker making three dollars a day. As a lady I know in Alabama once said, "the food that Ralph Bunche eats doesn't fill my stomach."

Integration, moreover, speaks to the problem of blackness in a despicable way. As a goal, it has been based on complete acceptance of the fact that *in order to have* a decent house or education, blacks must move into a white neighborhood or send their children to a white school. This reinforces, among both black and white, the idea that "white" is automatically better and "black" is by definition inferior. This is why integration is a subterfuge for the maintenance of white supremacy. It allows the nation to focus on a handful of Southern children who get into white schools, at great price, and to ignore the 94 per cent who are left behind in unimproved all-black schools. Such situations will not change until black people have power—to control their own school boards, in this case. Then Negroes become equal in a way that means something, and integration ceases to be a one-way street. Then integration doesn't mean draining skills and energies from the ghetto into white neighborhoods; then it can mean white people moving from Beverly Hills into Watts, white people joining the Lowndes County Freedom Organization. Then integration becomes relevant.

Last April, before the furor over black power, Christopher Jencks wrote in a *New Republic* article on white Mississippi's manipulation of the antipoverty program:

> The war on poverty has been predicated on the notion that there is such a thing as *a community* which can be defined geographically and mobilized for a collective effort to help the poor. This theory has no relationship to reality in the Deep South. In every Mississippi county there are *two* communities. Despite all the pious platitudes of the moderates on both sides, these two communities habitually see their interests in terms of conflict rather than cooperation. Only when the Negro community can muster enough political, economic and professional strength to compete on somewhat equal terms, will Negroes believe in the possibility of true cooperation and whites accept its necessity. En route to integration,

the Negro community needs to develop greater independence—a chance
to run its own affairs and not cave in whenever "the man" barks . . . Or
so it seems to me, and to most of the knowledgeable people with whom
I talked in Mississippi. To OEO, this judgment may sound like black
nationalism . . .

Mr. Jencks, a white reporter, perceived the reason why America's antipoverty program has been a sick farce in both North and South. In the South,
it is clearly racism which prevents the poor from running their own programs;
in the North, it more often seems to be politicking and bureaucracy. But the
results are not so different: In the North, non-whites make up 42 per cent of
all families in metropolitan "poverty areas" and only 6 per cent of families in
areas classified as not poor. SNCC has been working with local residents in
Arkansas, Alabama, and Mississippi to achieve control by the poor of the
program and its funds; it has also been working with groups in the North, and
the struggle is no less difficult. Behind it all is a federal government which cares
far more about winning the war on the Vietnamese than the war on poverty;
which has put the poverty program in the hands of self-serving politicians and
bureaucrats rather than the poor themselves; which is unwilling to curb the
misuse of white power but quick to condemn black power.

To most whites, black power seems to mean that the Mau Mau are coming
to the suburbs at night. The Mau Mau are coming, and whites must stop them.
Articles appear about plots to "get Whitey," creating an atmosphere in which
"law and order must be maintained." Once again, responsibility is shifted from
the oppressor to the oppressed. Other whites chide, "Don't forget—you're
only 10 per cent of the population; if you get too smart, we'll wipe you out."
If they are liberals, they complain, "what about me?—don't you want my help
anymore?" These are people supposedly concerned about black Americans,
but today they think first of themselves, of their feelings of rejection. Or they
admonish, "you can't get anywhere without coalitions," without considering
the problems of coalition with whom?; on what terms? (coalescing from weakness can mean absorption, betrayal); when? Or they accuse us of "polarizing
the races" by our calls for black unity, when the true responsibility for polari-
zation lies with whites who will not accept their responsibility as the majority
power for making the democratic process work.

White America will not face the problem of color, the reality of it. The
well-intended say: "We're all human, everybody is really decent, we must
forget color." But color cannot be "forgotten" until its weight is recognized
and dealt with. White America will not acknowledge that the ways in which
this country sees itself are contradicted by being black—and always have been.
Whereas most of the people who settled this country came here for freedom
or for economic opportunity, blacks were brought here to be slaves. When the
Lowndes County Freedom Organization chose the black panther as its symbol,
it was christened by the press "the Black Panther Party"—but the Alabama
Democratic Party, whose symbol is a rooster, has never been called the White

Cock Party. No one ever talked about "white power" because power in this country *is* white. All this adds up to more than merely identifying a group phenomenon by some catchy name or adjective. The furor over that black panther reveals the problems that white America has with color and sex; the furor over "black power" reveals how deep racism runs and the great fear which is attached to it.

Whites will not see that I, for example, as a person oppressed because of my blackness, have common cause with other blacks who are oppressed because of blackness. This is not to say that there are no white people who see things as I do, but that it is black people I must speak to first. It must be the oppressed to whom SNCC addresses itself primarily, not to friends from the oppressing group.

From birth, black people are told a set of lies about themselves. We are told that we are lazy—yet I drive through the Delta area of Mississippi and watch black people picking cotton in the hot sun for fourteen hours. We are told, "If you work hard, you'll succeed"—but if that were true, black people would own this country. We are oppressed because we are black—not because we are ignorant, not because we are lazy, not because we're stupid (and got good rhythm), but because we're black.

I remember that when I was a boy, I used to go to see Tarzan movies on Saturday. White Tarzan used to beat up the black natives. I would sit there yelling, "Kill the beasts, kill the savages, kill 'em!" I was saying: Kill *me*. It was as if a Jewish boy watched Nazis taking Jews off to concentration camps and cheered them on. Today, I want the chief to beat hell out of Tarzan and send him back to Europe. But it takes time to become free of the lies and their shaming effect on black minds. It takes time to reject the most important lie: that black people inherently can't do the same things white people can do, unless white people help them.

The need for psychological equality is the reason why SNCC today believes that blacks must organize in the black community. Only black people can convey the revolutionary idea that black people are able to do things themselves. Only they can help create in the community an aroused and continuing black consciousness that will provide the basis for political strength. In the past, white allies have furthered white supremacy without the whites involved realizing it—or wanting it, I think. Black people must do things for themselves; they must get poverty money they will control and spend themselves, they must conduct tutorial programs themselves so that black children can identify with black people. This is one reason Africa has such importance: The reality of black men ruling their own nations gives blacks elsewhere a sense of possibility, of power, which they do not now have.

This does not mean we don't welcome help, or friends. But we want the right to decide whether anyone is, in fact, our friend. In the past, black Americans have been almost the only people whom everybody and his momma could jump up and call their friends. We have been tokens, symbols, objects —as I was in high school to many young whites, who liked having "a Negro friend." We want to decide who is our friend, and we will not accept someone who comes to us and says: "If you do X, Y, and Z, then I'll help you." We will not be told whom we should choose as allies. We will not be isolated from any group or nation except by our own choice. We cannot have the oppressors telling the oppressed how to rid themselves of the oppressor.

I have said that most liberal whites react to "black power" with the question, What about me?, rather than saying: Tell me what you want me to do and I'll see if I can do it. There are answers to the right question. One of the most disturbing things about almost all white supporters of the movement has been that they are afraid to go into their own communities—which is where the racism exists—and work to get rid of it. They want to run from Berkeley to tell us what to do in Mississippi; let them look instead at Berkeley. They admonish blacks to be nonviolent; let them preach nonviolence in the white community. They come to teach me Negro history; let them go to the suburbs and open up freedom schools for whites. Let them work to stop America's racist foreign policy; let them press this government to cease supporting the economy of South Africa.

There is a vital job to be done among poor whites. We hope to see, eventually, a coalition between poor blacks and poor whites. That is the only coalition which seems acceptable to us, and we see such a coalition as the major internal instrument of change in American society. SNCC has tried several times to organize poor whites; we are trying again now, with an initial training program in Tennessee. It is purely academic today to talk about bringing poor blacks and whites together, but the job of creating a poor-white power bloc must be attempted. The main responsibility for it falls upon whites. Black and white can work together in the white community where possible; it is not possible, however, to go into a poor Southern town and talk about integration. Poor whites everywhere are becoming more hostile—not less—partly because they see the nation's attention focused on black poverty and nobody coming to them. Too many young middle-class Americans, like some sort of Pepsi generation, have wanted to come alive through the black community; they've wanted to be where the action is—and the action has been in the black community.

Black people do not want to "take over" this country. They don't want to "get Whitey"; they just want to get him off their backs, as the saying goes. It was for example the exploitation by Jewish landlords and merchants which first created black resentment toward Jews—not Judaism. The white man is irrelevant to blacks, except as an oppressive force. Blacks want to be in his place, yes, but not in order to terrorize and lynch and starve him. They want to be in his place because that is where a decent life can be had.

But our vision is not merely of a society in which all black men have enough to buy the good things of life. When we urge that black money go into black pockets, we mean the communal pocket. We want to see money go back into the community and used to benefit it. We want to see the cooperative concept applied in business and banking. We want to see black ghetto residents demand that an exploiting landlord or storekeeper sell them, at minimal cost, a building or a shop that they will own and improve cooperatively; they can back their demand with a rent strike, or a boycott, and a community so unified behind them that no one else will move into the building or buy at the store. The society we seek to build among black people, then, is not a capitalist one. It is a society in which the spirit of community and humanistic love prevail. The word love is suspect; black expectations of what it might produce have been betrayed too often. But those were expectations of a response from the white community, which failed us. The love we seek to encourage is within the black community, the only American community where men call each other "brother" when they meet. We can build a community of love only where we have the ability and power to do so: among blacks.

As for white America, perhaps it can stop crying out against "black supremacy," "black nationalism," "racism in reverse," and begin facing reality. The reality is that this nation, from top to bottom, is racist; that racism is not primarily a problem of "human relations" but of an exploitation maintained—either actively or through silence—by the society as a whole. Camus and Sartre have asked, can a man condemn himself? Can whites, particularly liberal whites, condemn themselves? Can they stop blaming us, and blame their own system? Are they capable of the shame which might become a revolutionary emotion?

We have found that they usually cannot condemn themselves, and so we have done it. But the rebuilding of this society, if at all possible, is basically the responsibility of whites—not blacks. We won't fight to save the present society, in Vietnam or anywhere else. We are just going to work, in the way *we* see fit, and on goals *we* define, not for civil rights but for all our human rights.

Discussion Starters

1. Identify specific points in the article that would be most disturbing to white America. Then explain why black power would mean one thing to whites and another to blacks.

2. Evaluate Carmichael's interpretation of white America's understanding of the problems faced by blacks. Evaluate also his charges concerning the responsibility of whites for the plight of blacks.

3. Why is power so essential to efforts by blacks to improve their well-being, and why does this grasping for power threaten the domestic tranquility, old style? What is the significance, if any, of the fact that Carmichael's ideas seem so much less radical today than when they were first expressed.

4. Identify in the article specific suggestions for reshaping the social order, both in terms of goals and methods. If these suggestions were implemented, what would be the possibility of creating a reasonably tranquil society?

Related Documents

I. The Red and the Black

VINE DELORIA, JR.

White America tends to think of assimilation as the answer to tensions created by cultural or racial differences. Intermittently for decades efforts have been made to assimilate American Indians into the mainstream of American life. Policies aimed at assimilation have failed, largely because of resistance by Indians. In recent years young and sometimes angry Indian leadership has emerged to challenge not only the policies but also the attitudes of white America.

A spokesman for the new Indians has been Vine Deloria, Jr., who served for several years as director of the National Congress of American Indians, which represents more than 100 tribes and their 400,000 members. In a thought-provoking book, Custer Died for Your Sins, *Deloria took white America to task for its treatment of Indians. He also dealt with the possibility of Indians and blacks working together.*

In the brief excerpt included here, he showed how the differences in origin of Indians, blacks, and whites pose problems in achieving mutual understanding. What ideas of Deloria might be drawn under the banner of black power? What might whites learn from Indians about creating a tranquil society, new style?

Time and again blacks have told me how lucky they were not to have been placed on reservations after the Civil War. I don't think they were lucky at all. I think it was absolute disaster that blacks were not given reservations.

Indian tribes have been able to deal directly with the federal government because they had a recognized status within the Constitutional scheme. Leadership falls into legal patterns on each reservation through the elective process. A tribal chairman is recognized by federal agencies, Congressional committees, and private agencies as the representative of the group. Quarrels over programs, rivalry between leaders, defense of rights, and expressions of the mood of the people are all channeled through the official governing body. Indian people have the opportunity to deal officially with the rest of the world as a corporate body.

The blacks, on the other hand, are not defined with their own community. Leadership too often depends upon newspaper coverage. Black communities do not receive the deference tribes receive, because they are agencies in the

Reprinted with permission of The Macmillan Company from *Custer Died for Your Sins*, pp. 194–96, by Vine Deloria, Jr. Copyright © 1969 by Vine Deloria, Jr.

private arena and not quasi-governmental. Law and order is something imposed brutally from without, not a housekeeping function of the group.

Above all, Indian people have the possibility of total withdrawal from American society because of their special legal status. They can, when necessary, return to a recognized homeland where time is static and the world becomes a psychic unity again.

To survive, blacks must have a homeland where they can withdraw, drop the facade of integration, and be themselves. Whites are inevitably torn because they have no roots, they do not understand the past, and they have already mortgaged their future. Unless they can renew their psychic selves and achieve a sense of historical participation as a people they will be unable to survive.

Already the cracks are showing. The berserk sniper characterizes the dilemma of the white man. Government by selective assassination is already well established as the true elective process.

All groups must come to understand themselves as their situation defines them and not as other groups see them. By accepting ourselves and defining the values within which we can be most comfortable we can find peace. In essence, we must all create social isolates which have economic bases that support creative and innovative efforts to customize values we need.

Myths must be re-examined and clarified. Where they are detrimental, sharp and necessary distinctions must be made. The fear of the unknown must be eliminated. The white mythologizes the racial minorities because of his lack of knowledge of them. These myths then create barriers for communication between the various segments of society.

What the white cannot understand he destroys lest it prove harmful. What the Indian cannot understand he withdraws from. But the black tries everything and fears nothing. He is therefore at liberty to build or destroy both what he knows and what he does not know or understand.

The red and the black must not be fooled either by themselves, by each other, or by the white man. The black has moved in a circle from *Plessy v. Ferguson,* where Separate but Equal was affirmed, to *Brown v. the Board of Education,* where it was denied by the Supreme Court, to Birmingham, Washington, Selma, and the tragedies of Memphis and Los Angeles. Now, Separate but Equal has become a battle cry of the black activists.

It makes a great deal of difference who carries this cry into battle. Is it the cry of a dying amalgam of European immigrants who are plagued by the European past? Or is it the lusty cry of a new culture impatient to be born?

The American Indian meditates on these things and waits for their solution. People fool themselves when they visualize a great coalition of the minority groups to pressure Congress for additional programs and rights. Indians will not work within an ideological basis which is foreign to them. Any cooperative movement must come to terms with tribalism in the Indian context before it will gain Indian support.

The future, therefore, as between the red, white, and black, will depend primarily upon whether white and black begin to understand Indian nationalism. Once having left the wild animal status, Indians will not revert to their old position on the totem pole. Hopefully black militancy will return to nationalistic philosophies which relate to the ongoing conception of the tribe as a nation extending in time and occupying space. If such is possible within the black community, it may be possible to bring the problems of minority groups into a more realistic focus and possible solution in the years ahead.

II. *American Indian Task Force Statement to Congress*

Despite their many rebuffs at the hands of the United States government, American Indians still hope that someday the government will understand their problems and act appropriately. In November 1969, a committee of Indian leaders from fifteen states went to Washington to express a variety of grievances felt by their tribes concerning their relations with the federal government. They met first with the vice president and then with a group of members of the House of Representatives. Their statement to Congress summarizes their position. Compare what they asked for with what Stokely Carmichael said blacks wanted. In view of the previous experience Indians have had with Congress, speculate on the judgment Carmichael might have made concerning their requests.

NOVEMBER 13, 1969

I

We, the first Americans, come to the Congress of the United States that you give us the chance to try to solve what you call the Indian problem. You have had 200 years and you have not succeeded by your standards. It is clear that you have not succeeded in ours.

On Monday, we asked the vice president of the United States to set into motion a process which would insure that our people could secure redress of grievances and could shape the government programs that affect and control their lives.

We know that a request to the executive branch—even if heeded—is not sufficient. We know that there are three branches—the executive, the legislative, and the judiciary.

We come here today to ask you to do three things:

1. To serve as watchdog on the executive branch.
2. To facilitate—and certainly, not to bar—our access to the judicial branch; and
3. To use your legislative powers to make it possible for Indians to shape their own lives and control their own destinies.

We have asked the vice president of the United States for Indian boards

Congressional Record, November 13, 1969, E9596–97.

of inquiries which would hold hearings throughout the areas where Indians live, for area conferences, for red ribbon grand juries, for circuit riders to take complaints, and for a national board of inquiry to meet and make national recommendations received on the grass roots level.

And we ask you to help us see that the process we proposed to the vice president somehow becomes a reality. We hope that he will be willing to do it on his own. But we ask you, as the representatives of the people of the United States, to serve as our representatives too—to help us see that assurances do not become empty promises. And, if necessary, to enact legislation which will create such a process where Indians can really shape government policy and control their own lives and destinies if that is not done by the executive branch.

II

We come to you with a sense of impending betrayal, at a moment when we wish to seek redress of grievances, to ask you to broaden our access to the courts to protect the rights guaranteed us by your treaties and statutes. And we find, with a sense of horror and impending doom, that instead, the Congress of the United States is on the verge of passing an amendment to the Economic Opportunity Act which would effectively diminish the slight access to the courts we have gained in recent years through the advent of the OEO [Office of Economic Opportunity] Legal Service Program. And it is an even greater irony that we find this to be the case when the governor's veto in at least one state has already killed a legal service program for Indians. What right do the governors have to interfere with what goes on on the reservation. What right do state governors have to interfere with the solemn promises made to us by the federal government in statutes and treaties which can only be enforced by resort to the courts. What right do you, or any generation of Americans, have to rip up the solemn promises of the past—promises made to us both by the Constitution and by the President of a nation which still holds and enjoys the land received in exchange for those treaties. There are none among you who would suggest that rights—and above all the right to petition one's government —can have any meaning at all without lawyers and without access to the forum where the people traditionally petition their government.

III

We come to you today to ask that you set your own house in order. We say that until the congressional committees which control nearly all Indian legislation cease to be hostile to the interests of the Indian, then we have been deprived of one of the three branches of what we have been repeatedly told is our government as well as yours.

The present committees have pushed for termination, and have fostered on Congress seemingly neutral and technical legislation, under the guise of Indian expertise, which has taken away our land, our water rights, our mineral resources, and handed them over to the white man.

You have been duped—as we have been duped. These committees have created a monstrous bureaucracy insensitive to Indians which trembles and cringes before them. The Indian suffers—and the nation pays the bill. Nothing will change so long as this unholy alliance exists between the BIA [Bureau of Indian Affairs] and these congressional committees.

On Monday we asked the vice president to seek a new arrangement within the executive branch of government—one which will bypass those channels which are hostile and insensitive to our interests. We asked him to set in motion a process by which our voices could be heard on our needs within the executive branch of government.

Today, we come to seek a new arrangement with the Congress. We have come to seek a change in the committees that deal in Indian Affairs. We ask that the committees of Congress not be dominated by interests which are hostile to our own survival. We ask that these committees act as a watchdog on federal programs which are passed especially for our benefit but which do not in fact benefit us because of the way the BIA runs them. And we ask that these committees insure that we get our fair share of general legislation passed to help all citizens—highway legislation, health legislation, education legislation, economic development legislation. We do not get our fair share of these programs now. And we do not have any means to seek redress when the very programs that are passed to help us in fact are used as means to enslave and oppress us.

We come here today to remind you that you are not just the representatives of local districts or of states. You are members of the Congress of the United States. You have national obligations. We know you are highly conscious of your national obligations when you deliberate on such problems as the war in Vietnam. We know that you have even taken those obligations seriously enough to go to Vietnam in order to personally inform yourself on how the executive carries out the commitments of the United States.

We ask that you do no less at home—for the United States has made older and more sacred national commitments to the people who have occupied these shores for 25,000 years. The United States has made national commitments in the form of treaties, legislation, and the Constitution itself, to our peoples. We ask you to come to our homes—in the cities and on the reservations. We ask that you seek with equal vigilance to determine whether national commitments have been kept to us. Guided tours by bureaucrats will only serve to hamper you in your search for truth.

You, the Congress of the United States, are being asked to come to see how we really live and to try to understand the values, the culture, and the way of life we are fighting to preserve—an American way of life. A way of life which we believe is built upon respect for differences, a tolerance of diversity.

We cannot come to Washington. We are not rich. And we cannot afford the high price of democracy.

In essence, we ask the restoration of what you claimed at the founding of your nation—the inalienable right to pursue happiness. We cannot fail worse than the experts and the bureaucrats. We do not lack for knowledge—

and we are not ashamed to hire experts and technicians. But our people do not lack for leaders, for sensitivity, for talent and ability. We ask for the right to pursue our dream—and we ask for you to respect that dream. That is the American way. We claim our birthright.

III. Viva La Raza! and Chicano Power! and Brown Power!

JOSÉ, HECTOR, ROBERTO, AND CHUCK

The following conversation between four Mexican-American youths was recorded in the book La Raza, *by Stan Steiner.* La Raza, *"the Holy Race," is a deeply evocative term, playing strongly on the idea of racial solidarity. White America has kept peace with Mexican Americans in large part by keeping* La Raza *in its place.*

If this conversation is representative of ideas held by young Mexican Americans, what predictions might be made concerning the shape of the future? Note how these young men differentiated between black power and brown power. Speculate on how a black power advocate might make the differentiation.

José: "If you have a rebellion you have to have something to rebel against. So you may become racist. Stone racist. Is 'brown power' racist? No, 'brown power' is cultural. So it doesn't have to become racist."

Hector: "I wonder. Why do militants create a lot of alienation in their communities?"

José: "Man, we're not rebelling. We're building something. We're trying to create less alienation and more community unity. A man without knowledge of his people is like a tree without a root. What we're trying to do is get people this cultural consciousness. Brown power is to know your culture."

Roberto: "I agree with him. Brown power has to be different from black power because we are not black."

Hector: "I don't agree with that. You ask a black man, What is black power? He's going to tell you, well, black power is like the black man being able to take over his institutions, running his own thing. It's black institutions run by black people for the betterment of black people. That's what he'll tell you. You know, basically, we want that."

José: "I think we have to go farther than that! Brown power has to be our cultural heritage. So we can get those values that were inherent in the Indians of ancient Mexico. And we can take those same values and same culture and use it in our lives and our movement. The way an Indian would relate to his family, to his tribe; the pride he had in his Indian nation. Brown power is first

Abridged from pp. 113–16, 119–20 in *La Raza: The Mexican Americans* by Stan Steiner. Copyright © 1969, 1970 by Stan Steiner. Reprinted by permission of Harper & Row, Publishers, Inc.

of all nationalism. But it isn't nationalism that we have to learn from reading what some intellectual says, like black people do. This is nationalism that we know existed among our people thousands of years ago. It was true then, today, and it will be true a hundred years from now."

Hector: "Our people have been saying brown power for hundreds of years —only we have been saying it in Spanish."

Chuck: "Like before anything ever started, we used to get together, some dudes where I live at, we used to drink and all that, and we used to be talking —before black power, before they had the riots and everything. Viva La Raza! and Chicano power! and Brown Power!—about things like that. So if you ask how come we copy the black people? It's just we didn't come on until later on. We didn't do all kinds of demonstrations. But we always had it. We always said it. Among ourselves." . . .

Roberto: "I don't really know what brown power is. To me it's a new feeling I have."

Hector: "Brown power means liberation to me. I don't want to be out-numbered by Anglos ten to one. I don't want to conform to what they want. Some little old lady in Pasadena is figuring out right now what us wetbacks will be doing next week. What freeway is going to run through my home. I don't go for that. I want to determine what is right for me."

Roberto: "It's not a racial thing."

José: "You see, we have some black Mexicans. We have some Mexicans with blue eyes and blond hair and white skin. He's a surfer, you would think. He's not. He's a Mexican. He can take it any way he wants. The blacks can't do that because their color is so obvious no matter what they do. What I'm saying is that brown power is not a black power sort of thing. Even though we are in the same condition, like brothers, we are not the same. I mean this is *our* motherland."

Hector: "You are using the white people's words. English, you see. English is a racist language. That's why they sound the same—brown power, black power. In Spanish we don't say a color. We say, the power of the people —La Raza." . . .

Hector: "People say the country is in a revolution. We've always been in a revolution. If burning a television store is revolution, what is it when the Ku Klux Klan burns a church?"

José: "Well, different people have different interpretations of what revolution means. John F. Kennedy, you know, talked about *his* American revolution. Man, *his* revolution wasn't ours."

Hector: "On our continent the white people are a minority. And your minority just happens to control the rest of us brown people. That's what we're fighting. Just saying self-determination isn't enough any more. See, we'll never have self-determination in this country as long as the Man runs *his* electricity into our homes, as long as he sells us *his* cars, as long as we're *his* boys. Well, you know what I'm getting at."

José: "I'm fighting as the Indian fought—for motherland."

Roberto: "If our white brothers won't accept us we'll go back to our ancestors. Our brown brothers."

José: "We're going back to our old culture. Now we don't want none of this Hispano stuff no more. The Spanish were murderers. They murdered our ancestors. It's not that we don't want to be white. We know we are part white and part Indian. It's just we have made up our minds who we want to be."

Hector: "One thing we want our people to see is America isn't a country. The United States is a country. But America is a continent. A *brown* continent."

José: "This is motherland. God put the brown man on this continent. Just like God put the black man on his continent, he put the white man on his continent, he put the Asian man on his continent. But this is motherland. I come from the part of motherland that is called Mexico—the part, it's not a country. I don't see Mexico no more as a country. I'm not talking about Mexico. I'm not talking about the United States. Now it's all just motherland to me."

IV. The Land, Our Heritage

JOSE ANGEL GUTIERREZ

Here is an expression of feeling by José Angel Gutierrez, a Mexican American. Compare his analysis of the plight of Mexican Americans with that of Carmichael concerning blacks. How do their solutions differ, and whose is more feasible?

JANUARY 11, 1968

The gringos control, they rob, and they have Texas by the throat. This machine or Establishment (as they call it) gives life to itself by its very own activity and is a symbol of gringo insanity. This insanity is called schizophrenia. When one invents a lie and then believes in his own lie or wants to make it true, one has schizophrenia.

To be part of this machine, or establishment, one has to be gringo. That's the whole scene. In order to be gringo, one has to adopt their selfish behavior. Also one has to distinguish people by the color of their skin, eyes (they love the color blue); the name (the names Garza, Martinez, or Gutierrez are worthless): and religion. One has to make himself a hypocrite. He has to think that the gringos are God's children. It is also helpful to take advantage of a Mexican or two. If one practices these rules he is a good gringo.

They protect one another. They defend themselves against all that isn't

Paul Jacobs and Saul Landau, eds., *To Serve the Devil* (New York: Random House, 1971), I, pp. 331–32. Reprinted by permission of Cyrilly Abels, Agent for the Author. Copyright © 1968 by José Angel Gutierrez.

gringo. They cover themselves with the same blanket and they believe themselves very close to the Virgin. After all this, their system is protected. The Establishment continues because they work together. There is unity among gringos.

The gringos think they are the cream of Texas society. They think they are very saintly and responsible for all people. They protect the United States as if it were their wife. All that is gringo is not naturally covered by these things. These individuals are *inferiores* according to the gringo.

Mexicans, they think, don't have anything to contribute but cheap labor. We are much lower than they. They also think that the race in general is criminal, drunk, lazy, ignorant, and irresponsible.

These are pure lies and inventions of the gringo!

This has gone on for many years. The gringo and his Establishment have exploited (robbed, killed), discriminated, and oppressed (kept down) the Mexican people since we were Mexicans from Mexico. All these lies that they tell about us are how they sap the pride of being Mexican and make us search for a means to make ourselves gringos. Mexicans also are and make themselves into gringos. Beneath this hypocrisy and the lies that we have freedom, justice, and democracy, the gringos have brought misery and ruin. What nice democracy, freedom, and justice when one lives on his knees and at the pleasure of the gringo.

Brothers, we needn't make ourselves stupid. This land was Mexican and the gringos robbed us. They have made our grandfathers, fathers, and ourselves dependent on them. They have made our way of life an ugly thing. Now they make us ashamed to bring tortillas to work if there are gringos there. The Spanish that we speak isn't permitted by gringos. Our culture (they don't have any) of many years is now important because one can make money with it. Look at the HemisFair if you don't believe it. After they have done all this to us, and have used us as floor moppers, the gringos say, " 'Los mescans' are inferior to us, they are worthless." They created this lie in order to rise. Today they believe it as if it were true! That's why I say that the gringos are nuts. Just schizophrenics.

The ugliest thing that has happened is that very few of us have the balls to admit that the gringo is using us. We want to make fools of ourselves because the truth hurts us. But we know that when one removes a backbone the pain will be gone. The same is also true with the gringo; if we get him out of here the problem will be gone. If there is unity and spirit the gringo can't take us. As they say to the blacks, "Go back to Africa!" we ought to say to them, "Dogs! Go back to England or wherever you came from. This land belongs to the Mexicans!" Viva La Raza!

V. Our Revolution Is Unique

BETTY FRIEDAN

Also seeking to be liberated from "their place" in the social order are women. Some call for a complete reordering of society; others press for less extreme goals, such as improvement of opportunity for women in professional positions, equal pay for equal work, abolition of social contrivances regarded as demeaning to women, and liberalization of abortion laws.

In their quest for change, women have naturally met with resistance from men, but they have also had to cope with apathy among women. Hence the literature of the "women's lib" movement is often two-pronged: It attacks the existing order and those responsible for it and at the same time attempts to rally more women to the cause.

Struggles for women's rights have been carried on for more than a century. The culmination of decades of efforts came in 1920 with the ratification of the women's suffrage amendment to the Constitution. The recent drive for liberation received its first big impetus in 1963 with the publication of The Feminine Mystique, *by Betty Friedan. In 1966 Friedan founded the National Organization for Women (NOW) and served as its president until 1970.*

The following paragraphs are representative of her ideas and her style. Identify the effects on American society that the liberation of women she envisions might produce. What are the similarities and dissimilarities between the black power movement and the women's liberation movement?

We new feminists have begun to define ourselves—existentially—through action. We have learned that while we had much to learn from the black civil rights movement and their revolution against economic and racial oppression, our own revolution is unique: it must define its own ideology.

We can cut no corners; we are, in effect, where the black revolution was perhaps fifty years ago; but the speed with which our revolution is moving now is our unearned historical benefit from what has happened in that revolution. Yet there can be no illusion on our part that a separatist ideology copied from black power will work for us. Our tactics and strategy and, above all, our ideology must be firmly based in the historical, biological, economic, and psychological reality of our two-sexed world, which is not the same as the black reality and different also from the reality of the first feminist wave.

Thanks to the early feminists, we who have mounted this second stage of the feminist revolution have grown up with the right to vote, little as we may have used it for our own purposes. We have grown up with the right to higher education and to employment, and with some, not all, of the legal rights of equality. Insofar as we have moved on the periphery of the mainstream of society, with the skills and the knowledge to command its paychecks, even if

Mary Lou Thompson, ed., *Voices of the New Feminism* (Boston: Beacon Press, 1970), pp. 32–34.

insufficient; and to make decisions, even if not consulted beyond housework; we begin to have a self-respecting image of ourselves, as women, not just in sexual relation to men, but as full human beings in society. We are able, at least some of us, to see men, in general or in particular, without blind rancor or hostility, and to face oppression as it reveals itself in our concrete experience with politicans, bosses, priests, or husbands. We do not need to suppress our just grievances. We now have enough courage to express them. And yet we are able to conceive the possibility of full affirmation for man. Man is not the enemy, but the fellow victim of the present half-equality. As we speak, act, demonstrate, testify, and appear on television on matters such as sex discrimination in employment, public accommodations, education, divorce-marriage reform, or abortion repeal, we hear from men who feel they can be freed to greater self-fulfillment to the degree that women are released from the binds that now constrain them.

This sense of freeing men as the other half of freeing women has always been there, even in the early writings of Mary Wollstonecraft, Elizabeth Stanton, and the rest; our action-created new awareness has confirmed this.

Another point we are conscious of in the new feminism is that we are a revolution for all, not for an exceptional few. This, above all, distinguishes us from those token spokeswomen of the period since women won the vote, the Aunt Toms who managed to get a place for themselves in society, and who were, I think, inevitably seduced into an accommodating stance, helping to keep the others quiet. We are beginning to know that no woman can achieve a real breakthrough alone, as long as sex discrimination exists in employment, under the law, in education, in mores, and in denigration of the image of women.

Even those of us who have managed to achieve a precarious success in a given field still walk as freaks in "man's world" since every profession—politics, the church, teaching—is still structured as man's world. Walking as a freak makes one continually self-conscious, apologetic, if not defiant, about being a woman. One is made to feel there are three sexes—men, other women, and myself. The successful woman may think, "I am the exception, the 'brilliant' one with the rare ability to be an anthropologist, author, actress, broker, account executive, or television commentator; but you drones out there, you watch the television set. And what better use can you make of your life than doing the dishes for your loved ones?"

We cannot say that all American women want equality, because we know that women, like all oppressed people, have accepted the traditional denigration by society. Some women have been too much hurt by denigration from others, by self-denigration, by lack of the experiences, education, and training needed to move in society as equal human beings, to have the confidence that they can so move in a competitive society. They say they don't want equality —they have to be happy, adjust to things as they are. Such women find us threatening. They find equality so frightening that they must wish the new feminists did not exist. And yet we see so clearly from younger women and students that to the degree that we push ahead and create opportunities for movement in society, in the process creating the "new women" who are *people first*, to that degree the threat will disappear.

We do not speak for every woman in America, but we speak for the *right* of every woman in America to become all she is capable of becoming—on her own and/or in partnership with a man. And we already know that we speak not for a few, not for hundreds, not for thousands, but for millions—especially for millions in the younger generation who have tasted more equality than their elders. We know this simply from the resonance, if you will, that our actions have aroused in society.

VI. *Redstockings Manifesto*

One of the militant statements on behalf of the liberation of women came from the New York Radical Feminists in their "Redstockings Manifesto." Evaluate the emphasis this manifesto places on oppression and the class struggle. Overcoming the oppressor as defined in this manifesto would mean a radical restructuring of society. To what extent might women and blacks cooperate toward that end?

JULY 7, 1969

I. After centuries of individual and preliminary political struggle, women are uniting to achieve their final liberation from male supremacy. Redstockings is dedicated to building this unity and winning our freedom.

II. Women are an oppressed class. Our oppression is total, affecting every facet of our lives. We are exploited as sex objects, breeders, domestic servants, and cheap labor. We are considered inferior beings, whose only purpose is to enhance men's lives. Our humanity is denied. Our prescribed behavior is enforced by the threat of physical violence.

Because we have lived so intimately with our oppressors, in isolation from each other, we have been kept from seeing our personal suffering as a political condition. This creates the illusion that a woman's relationship with her man is a matter of interplay between two unique personalities, and can be worked out individually. In reality, every such relationship is a *class* relationship, and the conflicts between individual men and women are *political* conflicts that can only be solved collectively.

III. We identify the agents of our oppression as men. Male supremacy is the oldest, most basic form of domination. All other forms of exploitation and oppression (racism, capitalism, imperialism, etc.) are extensions of male supremacy: men dominate women, a few men dominate the rest. All power structures throughout history have been male-dominated and male-oriented.

Mimeographed sheet, REDSTOCKINGS, July 7, 1969.

Men have controlled all political, economic and cultural institutions and backed up this control with physical force. They have used their power to keep women in an inferior position. *All men* receive economic, sexual, and psychological benefits from male supremacy. *All men* have oppressed women.

IV. Attempts have been made to shift the burden of responsibility from men to institutions or to women themselves. We condemn these arguments as evasions. Institutions alone do not oppress; they are merely tools of the oppressor. To blame institutions implies that men and women are equally victimized, obscures the fact that men benefit from the subordination of women, and gives men the excuse that they are forced to be oppressors. On the contrary, any man is free to renounce his superior position provided that he is willing to be treated like a woman by other men.

We also reject the idea that women consent to or are to blame for their own oppression. Women's submission is not the result of brainwashing, stupidity, or mental illness but of continual, daily pressure from men. We do not need to change ourselves, but to change men.

The most slanderous evasion of all is that women can oppress men. The basis for this illusion is the isolation of individual relationships from their political context and the tendency of men to see any legitimate challenge to their privileges as persecution.

V. We regard our personal experience, and our feelings about that experience, as the basis for an analysis of our common situation. We cannot rely on existing ideologies as they are all products of male supremacist culture. We question every generalization and accept none that are not confirmed by our experience.

Our chief task at present is to develop female class consciousness through sharing experience and publicly exposing the sexist foundation of all our institutions. Consciousness-raising is not "therapy," which implies the existence of individual solutions and falsely assumes that the male-female relationship is purely personal, but the only method by which we can ensure that our program for liberation is based on the concrete realities of our lives.

The first requirement for raising class consciousness is honesty, in private and in public, with ourselves and other women.

VI. We identify with all women. We define our best interest as that of the poorest, most brutally exploited woman.

We repudiate all economic, racial, educational or status privileges that divide us from other women. We are determined to recognize and eliminate any prejudices we may hold against other women.

We are committed to achieving internal democracy. We will do whatever is necessary to ensure that every woman in our movement has an equal chance to participate, assume responsibility, and develop her political potential.

VII. We call on all our sisters to unite with us in struggle.

We call on all men to give up their male privileges and support women's liberation in the interest of our humanity and their own.

In fighting for our liberation we will always take the side of women against their oppressors. We will not ask what is "revolutionary" or "reformist," only what is good for women.

The time for individual skirmishes has passed. This time we are going all the way.

VII. What the Sixties Brought Poor Folks: An Editorial

Among the disadvantaged groups to seek strength through organization in the 1960s were the poor. The National Welfare Rights Organization (NWRO) attempted to influence legislation favorable to its members and to end practices they regarded as demeaning to them. This editorial from the NWRO's Welfare Fighter *provides an interpretation of the plight and prospects of poor folks at the turn of the decade.*

Evaluate the explicit and implicit assumptions in the editorial. What positive contribution might black power ideas make to the cause of the poor?

JANUARY 1970

Do you remember what the sixties brought poor folks? Course not, the poor people have enough trouble trying to forget last night's problems without have to dredge up the nightmare of the 30's or 50's or 60's. Anyway, I'll remember for all of us and you'll say yeah, that's what happened. Maybe!

Into the political scene and into the sixties the Kennedy's became visible to poor people. First there came John F. Kennedy. This young, handsome man gave us poor folks a small glimmer of hope. Oh, he was rich but that didn't matter because he understood our problems, he heard our pleas for help. He was our Robin Hood. So what if he didn't pass any really good laws or bills in favor of helping the poor? After all, he did start the war on poverty with the establishment of the OEO (Office of Economic Opportunity). So what if the administrators of the program were the same upper middle class people who always got the big salaries for misunderstanding the "disadvantaged"? The rest of the jobs available were obviously "sell out" jobs so as usual we disadvantaged never really got any "spoils" from the "War on Poverty." We poor felt in our bones that JFK would help us, would feed us even if he had to use his own millions. In the meantime, while waiting for better, stronger, fairer bills to be passed that would eliminate some of our misery, we watched mostly middle class blacks and whites march to Washington. Some poor got to go and when they returned the report was that "it had been very nice." Eighty percent of our hope died in Dallas. JFK was gone and now nothing except maybe Robert Kennedy could help us. "Please try" we breathed! Another Robin Hood (maybe). Dr. Martin Luther King, seeing, feeling, knowing of our pain and hopelessness, started moving away from his non-violent preachings, he left the south, started a campaign in Chicago for decent, better and integrated housing for all. They spit on him, stoned and tried to kill him. He returns south to lend his support in a local garbage strike. He was assassinated. Almost all hope is gone. Ted Kennedy doesn't seem to have too much of a winning chance for President, RFK and hope died together. We hoped and we got hurt. We lost out.

Through all the marches, campaigns and killings we watched and had been hoping that the future would bring better things for our children. Our hope would be more than strong enough to keep out the diseases. The diseases of hunger, drugs, unliveable housing, unthinkable schools and the disease of forgetting all about pride and begging for desperately needed welfare checks, knowing you'd be told to "come back tomorrow."

Daring to try hope again we decided to turn more and more to the Welfare Rights Organization. We underprivileged people had heard and known about Welfare Rights for some time but didn't take that club or that group of people seriously. Poor people organized to help and in turn organized more and other poor, even and especially WELFARE CLIENTS . . . seemed impossible, in fact funny. Our organizing began to move not mountains but Congress. As a direct result of poor people organizing we got . . . cutbacks in welfare funds all across the country, clothing and furniture grants cut out completely. This is what we got for trying to help ourselves and our sisters and brothers. We marched (and we organized), we sat-in (and we organized), we slept-in, fell-in, laid in, and we organized. For our efforts we got more cuts, even worse caseworker treatment, stepped-up police brutality because we peasants were getting restless, even rebellious. We did manage to get rid of the man in the house rule (our man *can* live with us), we won the residency case (we can go to any state of our choosing to get welfare). Caseworkers, investigators, social workers cannot come into our homes (it's our right to keep them out). . . .

We organized for Bread, Justice, and Dignity. Our government gave us a spectacular TV show titled "Man Walks on Moon." We organized so that our kids would not grow up to be worse off than we are today (after all, every parent wants his kids to do BETTER, to advance much further). Our government's answer was to take them off to Vietnam to an early and heroic death. We cry "Bring Our Boys Home Stop the War." We know that if war ends NOW the Defense Department would not close down and money given to feed poor people. More bridges would be built, more urban renewal, more moon walks, anything to keep us shifty, lazy ass poor folks from their right share of this country's wealth. After all, poor people are BIG businsss. There's more money to be wrung out of the ghetto and El Barrio than in a whole town of upper middle income folks.

So we turn more to each other, with our realization that not just welfare clients but all the poor people in this country are being screwed by the same ruling class, by the same system and we know that ALL WE HAVE IS EACH

OTHER. So we'll keep organizing and we'll get more money taken from us, our families will eat even less, until finally—Welcome to 1970 Everybody, Better Known as Slower Death.

VIII. In Loco Parentis: *A Declaration of the National Student Association*

The issues raised and the demands presented by students in American colleges and universities in the 1960s showed that another group was determined to get out of "its place." The nature and role of the university—its governance, its investments, its relations with the surrounding community, its political posture (or lack of one), its government-sponsored research, ROTC, and black studies programs (or lack of them)—were among the matters of concern to student activists. From 1964, when the Free Speech Movement ruptured the tranquility of the University of California at Berkeley, to the end of the decade, turmoil and disruption visited many campuses.

One of the points of conflict between students and authorities was the doctrine in loco parentis. *According to certain nineteenth-century court decisions involving this doctrine, its purpose was to restrict universities in their dealings with students by prohibiting them from imposing restraints on students that parents could not impose on their children. As interpreted by students, however, the universities were using in* loco parentis *as the basis for establishing paternal guardianship over the moral, intellectual, and social activities of students.*

Although student activism seemed to burst upon the scene without warning in the 1960s, students had begun to express discontent with university policies and practices as early as the mid-fifties. In the following declaration, the United States National Student Association attacked in loco parentis *and attempted to create a new atmosphere of freedom for students. Compare their grievances with those cited by Carmichael (and also those by writers of other documents in this chapter). What are the implications of "student power" for the university and for the larger society?*

USNSA condemns the tradition of *in loco parentis* and the educational habits and practices it justifies.

In loco parentis doctrine permits arbitrary and extensive repression of student pursuits and thereby impairs the total significance of the university as a center for the conflict of ideas.

Equally important are the effects of *in loco parentis* doctrine on the changing student. Paternalism in any form induces or reinforces immaturity,

From the *Basic Policy Declarations* of the U.S. National Student Association, adopted in 1955.

conformity, and disinterest among those whose imagination, critical talent and capacities for integrity and growth should be encouraged and given opportunity for development.

Insofar as *in loco parentis* doctrine removes responsibility for personal decision-making from the individual student, it distorts and weakens a significant phase of the educational process. The unexamined acceptance of authority which is often appropriate to the child-parent relationship must be replaced in the universities by the encouragement of a critical and dialectical relationship between the student and his community. The range of inquiry within or beyond the classroom must not be restricted out of paternal considerations but must be opened out of educational ones.

USNSA calls on faculties and administrations to open the universities to fuller and more meaningful student participation in those university and community affairs which shape student life and development. These include the content of the curriculum, in such social disciplines as is necessary to maintain order in the classroom. The process of education does require some minimal level of order and discipline.

However, those forms of discipline which can be justified on the basis of this formula are few and scarce, and the danger is great that illegitimate paternalism will be confused with proper control. It is the responsiblity of all students to attempt to clearly delineate the equal responsibility of those academic administrators charged with the establishment of such policy to justify, individually, each attempt to impose any sort of order upon the academic community.

USNSA calls upon American students to seek not only an end to formal campus restrictions which prohibit legitimate freedoms, but also to seek the instruments with which to generate a community where men are linked by a common commitment to learning, not segregated by the atmosphere which paternalism fosters.

For Further Reading

Because of the quantity of literature available on the broad range of topics treated in this chapter, appropriate volumes are simply listed according to subject.

On blacks: John H. Bracey, August Meier, and Elliott Rudwick, eds., *Black Nationalism in America** (1970); Stokely Carmichael and Charles Hamilton, *Black Power** (1968); William M. Chace and Peter M. Collier, *The Black Man in White America** (1970); Mary L. Fisher, comp., *The Negro in America: A Bibliography* (1970; 1966 ed. comp. by Elizabeth W. Miller); Lewis M. Killian, *The Impossible Revolution?: Black Power and the American Dream** (1968); *The Autobiography of Malcolm X** (1965); Edward Peeks, *The Long Struggle for Black Power* (1971); Arnold Schuchter, *Reparations: The Black*

*Paperbound edition available.

Manifesto and Its Challenge to White America* (1970); Robert Scott and Wayne Brockreide, eds., *The Rhetoric of Black Power** (1969); Thomas Wagstaff, ed., *Black Power: The Radical Response to White America** (1969).

On Indians: William A. Brophy and Sophie D. Aberle, comps., *The Indian: America's Unfinished Business* (1966); Robert Burnett, *The Tortured Americans* (1971); Vine Deloria, Jr., *Custer Died for Your Sins** (1969) and *We Talk, You Listen: New Tribes, New Turf* (1970)—this book takes a good look at issues raised by the black power movements; Earl Shorris, *The Death of the Great Spirit: An Elegy for the American Indian* (1971); Stan Steiner, *The New Indians* (1968); Wilcomb Washburn, *Red Man's Land/White Man's Law* (1971).

On Mexican-Americans: John H. Burma, *Mexican Americans in the United States** (1970); Ernesto Gálarza, *et al., Mexican Americans in the Southwest** (1969); Richard M. Gardner, *Grito! Reies Tijerina and the New Mexico Land Grant War of 1967* (1970); Leo Grebler, Joan W. Moore, and Ralph C. Guzman, *The Mexican-American People: The Nation's Second Largest Minority* (1969); Joan W. Moore, *Mexican Americans* (1970)—a short study growing out of the previously listed work; Wayne Moquin, *A Documentary History of the Mexican Americans* (1971); Peter Nabokov, *Tijerina and the Courthouse Raid* (1969); Julian Nava, *Mexican Americans: A Brief Look at Their History** (1970); Armando Rendon, *Chicano Manifesto* (1971); Julian Samora, ed., *La Raza: Forgotten Americans** (1966); Manuel P. Servin, *The Mexican Americans: An Awakening Minority** (1970); Stan Steiner, *La Raza* (1970).

On women: Kirsten Amundsen, *The Silenced Majority* (1971); Carolyn Bird, *Born Female: The High Cost of Keeping Women Down* (1970); Cynthia Fuchs Epstein and William J. Goode, *The Other Half: Roads to Women's Equality* (1971); Betty Friedan, *The Feminine Mystique* (1963); Germaine Greer, *The Female Eunuch* (1971); Lucy Komisar, *The New Feminism* (1971); Aileen Kraditor, ed., *Up From the Pedestal: Selected Writings in the History of American Feminism* (1968); Kate Millett, *Sexual Politics* (1970); Robin Morgan, ed., *Sisterhood Is Powerful** (1970); Mary Lou Thompson, ed., *Voices of the New Feminism* (1970).

On students: Philip G. Altbach and Robert S. Laufer, eds., "Student Protest," *The Annals,* May 1971; Daniel Bell and Irving Kristol, *Confrontation: The Student Rebellion and the Universities* (1969); Peter Buckman, *The Limits of Protest* (1970); Mitchell Cohen and Dennis Hale, eds., *The New Student Left** (1966); Susan and John Erlich, *Student Power, Participation, and Revolution* (1970); James McEvoy and Abraham Miller, eds., *Black Power and Student Rebellion** (1969); Seymour Martin Lipset and Philip G. Altbach, eds., *Students in Revolt* (1969); Immanuel Wallerstein and Paul Starr, *The University Crisis Reader** 2 vols. (1971).

On the poor: Robert Coles, *Still Hungry in America* (1969); Kenneth S.

*Paperbound edition available.

Davis, *The Paradox of Poverty in America* (1969); Herman P. Miller, ed., *Poverty: American Style** (1966); Paul Jacobs, *Prelude to Riot: A View of Urban America From the Bottom* (1967).

General: Paul Jacobs and Saul Landau, eds., *To Serve the Devil: A Documentary Analysis of America's Racial History and Why It Has Been Kept Hidden** 2 vols. (1971); Wayne Moquin, ed., *Makers of America—Emergent Minorities, 1955-1970* (1971); Alfred Young, ed., *Dissent: Explorations in the History of American Radicalism** (1968); Loren Baritz, ed., *The American Left: Radical Political Thought in the Twentieth Century* (1971); Roger Daniels and Spencer C. Olin, Jr., *Racism in California: A Reader in the History of Oppression** (1972).

*Paperbound edition available.

16. The Vietnam Quagmire

The war in Vietnam has entangled the United States in a web of destruction that has seemed to have no end. Although the United States had been directly involved in affairs there since the final defeat of the French by the Vietnamese in 1954 (and indirectly before that), it was not until the mid-1960s that many Americans concluded that the war was destroying not only Vietnam, Cambodia, and Laos, but also the United States itself. These critics of the war pointed to unemployment, inflation, and moral disintegration as consequences of American participation in an Asian "civil war." Proponents of an active military presence in Southeast Asia countered by charging that the main reasons America was suffering at home was the "no win" policy of the United States government and a lack of courage on the part of many citizens. The United States had commitments, they said, to turn back Communist aggression. Devastations caused by our actions were a lesser evil than a Communist victory would surely bring. Whatever dislocations occurred on the domestic scene were, in their view, a small price to pay in a vital and noble cause.

Beginning in February 1965, when the United States escalated its war effort sharply, opposition from war critics intensified. Protest rallies and other demonstrations showed increasingly bitter dissent against the nation's war policy. Politicians, the press, and public opinion began to take sides on the issues the policy raised. Basic questions could no longer be evaded: Why was the United States in Vietnam? How could the war be ended? This chapter focuses on various answers given to these perplexing questions.

Core Document

"We Could Win the Peace"

RICHARD M. NIXON

When the defeated French withdrew from Vietnam in 1954, Richard M. Nixon, then the Vice President, supported a plan for military intervention by the United States. Instead of sending combat troops, however, President Eisenhower decided to provide only military advisers and equipment to support the government of South Vietnam. During the administrations of Presidents Kennedy and Johnson, as a private citizen Nixon supported their actions and policies in Southeast Asia. When he became the Republican party's candidate in the presidential election of 1968, Nixon asserted that he had a plan to end the war. This plan would be revealed, he said, after he was elected.

Such a plan, however, was not clearly enunciated by the new President when he took office early in 1969. The lack of progress in bringing the war to a quick end led the antiwar elements in America to organize during the summer and fall of 1969 to confront the federal government with an insistent demand to end the war. These antiwar efforts culminated in a nationwide demonstration, billed as the Vietnam Moratorium Day, on October 15, 1969. Millions across the nation, especially on college and university campuses, took part in the peaceful demonstrations against the war, but the President pointedly ignored their protest.

The Vietnam Moratorium Day was followed a month later by a mass demonstration in Washington, D.C., when a crowd of 250,000 people marched to demand an end to the war. Again the President ignored the demonstrations by keeping to his normal work schedule and, at one point, relaxing to watch a football game on television. On November 3, 1969, the President finally responded to the demonstrations in a nationally televised speech.

In reading President Nixon's speech notice:

- *the reasons given for not ordering the immediate withdrawal of American troops from South Vietnam.*
- *references to public and private contacts made with Hanoi and the results of those contacts.*
- *his reasons for believing that negotiations between the United States and North Vietnam had failed.*
- *the "Nixon Doctrine."*
- *the proposed plan to bring about the "Vietnamization" of the war.*
- *his reaction to those Americans who were against the war.*
- *his desire to "win the peace."*

NOVEMBER 3, 1969

Good evening, my fellow Americans. Tonight I want to talk to you on a subject of deep concern to all Americans and to many people in all parts of the world, the war in Vietnam.

I believe that one of the reasons for the deep division about Vietnam is that many Americans have lost confidence in what their Government has told them about our policy. The American people cannot and should not be asked to support a policy which involves the overriding issues of war and peace unless they know the truth about that policy.

Tonight, therefore, I would like to answer some of the questions that I know are on the minds of many of you listening to me.

How and why did America get involved in Vietnam in the first place?

How has this Administration changed the policy of the previous Administration?

What has really happened in the negotiations in Paris and the battlefront in Vietnam?

What choices do we have if we are to end the war?

What are the prospects for peace?

Now let me begin by describing the situation I found when I was inaugurated on Jan. 20th: The war had been going on for four years. Thirty-one thousand Americans had been killed in action. The training program for the South Vietnamese was behind schedule. Five hundred forty-thousand Americans were in Vietnam with no plans to reduce the number. No progress had been made at the negotiations in Paris and the United States had not put forth a comprehensive peace proposal.

The war was causing deep division at home and criticism from many of our friends, as well as our enemies, abroad.

In view of these circumstances, there were some who urged that I end the war at once by ordering the immediate withdrawal of all American forces. From a political standpoint, this would have been a popular and easy course to follow. After all, we became involved in the war while my predecessor was in office.

I could blame the defeat, which would be the result of my action, on him —and come out as the peacemaker.

Some put it to me quite bluntly: this was the only way to avoid allowing Johnson's war to become Nixon's war.

But I had a greater obligation than to think only of the years of my Administration, and of the next election. I had to think of the effect of peace and freedom in America, and in the world. . . .

A nation cannot remain great if it betrays its allies and lets down its friends. Our defeat and humiliation in South Vietnam without question would promote recklessness in the councils of those great powers who have not yet abandoned their goals of world conquest.

This would spark violence wherever our commitments help maintain the peace—in the Middle East, in Berlin, eventually even in the Western Hemisphere.

Ultimately, this would cost more lives. It would not bring peace. It would bring more war.

For these reasons I rejected the recommendation I should end the war by immediately withdrawing all of our forces. I chose instead to change American policy on both the negotiating front and the battle front in order to end the war on many fronts. I initiated a pursuit for peace on many fronts.

In a television speech on May 14, in a speech before the United Nations, on a number of other occasions, I set forth our peace proposals in great detail. We have offered the complete withdrawal of all outside forces within one year. We have proposed to cease fire under international supervision. We have offered free elections under international supervision with the Communists participating in the organization and conduct of the elections as an organized political force.

And the Saigon Government has pledged to accept the result of the election.

We have not put forth our proposals on a take-it-or-leave-it basis. We have indicated that we're willing to discuss the proposals that have been put forth by the other side. We have declared that anything is negotiable, except the right of the people of South Vietnam to determine their own future.

At the Paris peace conference Ambassador Lodge has demonstrated our flexibility and good faith in 40 public meetings. Hanoi has refused even to discuss our proposals. They demand our unconditional acceptance of their terms which are that we withdraw all American forces immediately and unconditionally and that we overthrow the Government of South Vietnam as we leave.

We have not limited our peace initiatives to public forums and public statements. I recognized in January that a long and bitter war like this usually cannot be settled in a public forum.

That is why in addition to the public statements and negotiations, I have explored every possible private avenue that might lead to a settlement.

Tonight, I am taking the unprecedented step of disclosing to you some of our other initiatives for peace, initiatives we undertook privately and secretly because we thought we thereby might open a door which publicly would be closed.

I did not wait for my inauguration to begin my quest for peace. Soon after my election, through an individual who was directly in contact on a personal basis with the leaders of North Vietnam, I made two private offers for a rapid, comprehensive settlement.

Hanoi's replies called in effect for our surrender before negotiations. Since the Soviet Union furnishes most of the military equipment for North Vietnam,

Secretary of State Rogers, my assistant for national security affairs, Dr. Kissinger; Ambassador Lodge and I personally have met on a number of occasions with representatives of the Soviet Government to enlist their assistance in getting meaningful negotiations started. . . .

I spoke directly in this office, where I'm now sitting, with an individual who had known Ho Chi Minh on a personal basis for 25 years. Through him I sent a letter to Ho Chi Minh. . . .

I received Ho Chi Minh's reply on Aug. 30, three days before his death. It simply reiterated the public position North Vietnam had taken at Paris and flatly rejected my initiative. The full text of both letters is being released to the press.

In addition to the public meetings that I've referred to, Ambassador Lodge has met with Vietnam's chief negotiator in Paris in 11 private sessions.

And we have taken other significant initiatives which must remain secret to keep open some channels of communications which may still prove to be productive.

But the effect of all the public, private and secret negotiations which have been undertaken since the bombing halt a year ago, and since this Administration came into office on Jan. 20, can be summed up in one sentence: No progress whatever has been made except agreement on the shape of the bargaining table.

Well, now, who's at fault? It's become clear that the obstacle in negotiating an end to the war is not the President of the United States. It is not the South Vietnamese Government. The obstacle is the other side's absolute refusal to show the least willingness to join us in seeking a just peace.

And it will not do so while it is convinced that all it has to do is to wait for our next concession, and our next concession after that one, until it gets everything it wants.

There can now be no longer any question that progress in negotiation depends only on Hanoi's deciding to negotiate—to negotiate seriously.

I realize that this report on our efforts on the diplomatic front is discouraging to the American people, but the American people are entitled to know the truth—the bad news as well as the good news—where the lives of our young men are involved.

Now let me turn, however, to a more encouraging report on another front. At the time we launched our search for peace, I recognized we might not succeed in bringing an end to the war through negotiation. I therefore put into effect another plan to bring peace—a plan which will bring the war to an end regardless of what happens on the negotiating front.

It is in line with the major shift in U. S. foreign policy which I described in my press conference at Guam on July 25.

Let me briefly explain what has been described as the Nixon Doctrine—

a policy which not only will help end the war in Vietnam but which is an essential element of our program to prevent future Vietnams. . . .

. . . I laid down in Guam three principles of guidelines for future American policy toward Asia.

First, the United States will keep all of its treaty commitments.

Second, we shall provide a shield if a nuclear power threatens the freedom of a nation allied with us, or of a nation whose survival we consider vital to our security.

Third, in cases involving other types of aggression we shall furnish military and economic assistance when requested in accordance with our treaty commitments. But we shall look to the nation directly threatened to assume the primary responsibility of providing the manpower for its defense.

After I announced this policy, I found that the leaders of the Philippines, Thailand, Vietnam, South Korea and other nations which might be threatened by Communist aggression, welcomed this new direction in American foreign policy.

The defense of freedom is everybody's business—not just America's business. And it is particularly the responsibility of the people whose freedom is threatened. In the previous Administration, we Americanized the war in Vietnam. In this Administration, we are Vietnamizing the search for peace. . . .

Let me now turn to our program for the future. We have adopted a plan which we have worked out in cooperation with the South Vietnamese for the complete withdrawal of all United States combat ground forces and their replacement by South Vietnamese forces on an orderly scheduled timetable.

This withdrawal will be made from strength and not from weakness. As South Vietnamese forces become stronger, the rate of American withdrawal can become greater.

I have not, and do not, intend to announce the timetable for our program, and there are obvious reasons for this decision which I'm sure you will understand. As I've indicated on several occasions, the rate of withdrawal will depend on developments on three fronts. One of these is the progress which can be, or might be, made in the Paris talks.

An announcement of a fixed timetable for our withdrawal would completely remove any incentive for the enemy to negotiate an agreement. They would simply wait until our forces had withdrawn and then move in.

The other two factors on which we will base our withdrawal decisions are the level of enemy activity and the progress of the training programs of the South Vietnamese forces.

And I'm glad to be able to report tonight progress on both of these fronts has been greater than we anticipated when we started the program in June for withdrawal.

As a result, our timetable for withdrawal is more optimistic now than when we made our first estimates in June.

Now this clearly demonstrates why it is not wise to be frozen in on a fixed timetable. We must retain the flexibility to base each withdrawal decision on the situation as it is at that time, rather than on estimates that are no longer valid.

Along with this optimistic estimate, I must in all candor leave one note of caution. If the level of enemy activity significantly increases, we might have to adjust our timetable accordingly. However, I want the record to be completely clear on one point. . . .

If I conclude that increased enemy action jeopardizes our remaining forces in Vietnam, I shall not hesitate to take strong and effective measures to deal with that situation.

This is not a threat. This is a statement of policy which as commander in chief of our armed forces I am making and meeting my responsibility for the protection of American fighting men wherever they may be.

My fellow Americans, I am sure you can recognize from what I have said that we really have only two choices open to us if we want to end this war.

I can order an immediate precipitate withdrawal of all Americans from Vietnam without regard to the effects of that action.

Or we can persist in our search for a just peace through a negotiated settlement, if possible, or through continued implementation of our plan for Vietnamization, if necessary. A plan in which we will withdraw all of our forces from Vietnam on a schedule in accordance with our program as the South Vietnamese become strong enough to defend their own freedom.

I have chosen this second course. It is not the easy way. It is the right way. It is a plan which will end the war and serve the cause of peace, not just in Vietnam but in the Pacific and the world. . . .

I recognize that some of my fellow Americans have reached different conclusions as to how peace should be achieved. Honest and patriotic citizens disagree with the plan for peace I have chosen. . . .

But as President of the United States, I would be untrue to my oath of office to be dictated by the minority who hold that point of view and who try to impose it on the nation by mounting demonstrations in the street. . . .

If a vocal minority, however fervent its cause, prevails over reason and the will of the majority, this nation has no future as a free society.

And now I would like to address a word, if I may, to the young people of this nation who are particularly concerned, and I understand why they are concerned about this war.

I respect your idealism. I share your concern for peace. I want peace as much as you do. There are powerful personal reasons I want to end this war. This week I will have to sign 83 letters to mothers, fathers, wives and loved ones of men who have given their lives for America in Vietnam.

It is very little satisfaction to me that this is only one-third as many letters as I signed the first week in office. There is nothing I want more than to see the day come when I do not have to write any of those letters.

I want to end the war to save the lives of those brave young men in Vietnam. I want to end it in a way which will increase the chance that their younger brothers and their sons will not have to fight in some future Vietnam some place in the world.

And I want to end the war for another reason. I want to end it so that the energy and dedication of you, our young people, now too often directed into bitter hatred against those responsible for the war, can be turned to the great challenges of peace, a better life for all Americans, a better life for all people on this earth.

I have chosen a plan for peace. I believe it will succeed. If it does not succeed, what the critics say now won't matter. Or if it does succeed, what the critics say now won't matter. If it does not succeed, anything I say then won't matter. . . .

Let historians not record that, when America was the most powerful nation in the world, we passed on the other side of the road and allowed the last hopes for peace and freedom of millions of people to be suffocated by the forces of totalitarianism.

So tonight, to you, the great silent majority of my fellow Americans, I ask for your support. I pledged in my campaign for the Presidency to end the war in a way that we could win the peace.

I have initiated a plan of action which will enable me to keep that pledge. The more support I can have from the American people, the sooner that pledge can be redeemed. For the more divided we are at home, the less likely the enemy is to negotiate in Paris.

Let us be united for peace. Let us also be united against defeat. Because let us understand—North Vietnam cannot defeat or humilitate the United States. Only Americans can do that. . . .

Tonight, I do not tell you that the war in Vietnam is the war to end wars, but I do say this:

I have initiated a plan which will end this war in a way that will bring us closer to that great goal to which Woodrow Wilson and every American President in our history has been dedicated—the goal of a just and lasting peace.

As President I hold the responsibility for choosing the best path for that goal and then leading the nation along it.

I pledge to you tonight that I shall meet this responsibility with all of the strength and wisdom I can command, in accordance with your hopes, mindful of your concerns, sustained by your prayers.

Thank you.

The War and Why We Must End It

J. WILLIAM FULBRIGHT

Senator J. William Fulbright, chairman of the Senate Foreign Relations Committee, supported the Vietnam policy of President Kennedy. For a time he also backed the continuation of that policy by President Johnson. In 1965, however, he became increasingly concerned over the future possibilities for the United States if it followed the policies as they evolved under President Johnson. By the time Johnson left the White House, Fulbright's opposition was outspoken and persistent, and his opposition continued as President Nixon gradually revealed his Vietnamization plans.

In the following speech Senator Fulbright questioned the arguments presented by President Nixon in his speech of November 3 and proposed his own solutions to the problem. In reading Fulbright's speech note:

- *his reaction to Nixon's argument that America must protect Southeast Asia from the forces of totalitarianism.*
- *why he believed America was fighting a war based on false premises.*
- *his contention that America had been on a power "trip" and how he would correct it.*
- *why he believed the massacre at Songmy (Mylai) had consequences for all Americans.*
- *why he believed the hope of "Vietnamization" was a false hope.*
- *his proposal for ending the war.*

DECEMBER 10, 1969

In his speech of November 3 President Nixon spoke of the "right of the people of South Vietnam to determine their own future" as the single American war aim which is not negotiable. "Let historians not record," declared the President, "that, when America was the most powerful nation in the world, we passed on the other side of the road and allowed the last hopes for peace and freedom of millions of people to be suffocated by the forces of totalitarianism."

The President's words are a reasonable expression of the *theory* behind our war in Vietnam. Like many theories, however, it does not tell us much about the *practice*. To remedy that omission a few additional quotes are necessary—such as the following:

> "They just marched through shooting everybody. Seems like no one said anything—they just started pulling people out and shooting them. They had them in a group standing over a ditch—just like a Nazi-type thing."

Statement by Senator J. William Fulbright, Thomas C. Hennings Memorial Lecture, Washington University, St. Louis, Missouri, December 10, 1969.

These words are probably familiar to you by now. They are an eye-witness's description of the alleged massacre at Songmy.[1] . . .

I recall to you also the now famous words of an American major after the Tet offensive in 1968: "We had to destroy Ben Tre in order to save it." This statement comes as close as any I have heard to summing up the theory and practice of America's war in Vietnam. It may stand some day as Vietnam's epitaph.

I. The Stakes

American intervention in Vietnam never has been rationalized primarily in terms of indigenous Vietnamese considerations. It was said—and is still said —to be an exemplary war—an object lesson for the makers of "wars of national liberation," and a war designed to inspire worldwide confidence in America through a demonstration of fealty to our presumed commitments. For these great purposes it has been judged necessary to make use of the Vietnamese people—or at any rate the "silent majority" of the Vietnamese people—as pawns—luckless expendables in a test of America's will.

Mr. Nixon has long subscribed to this theory of an exemplary war. Early in his campaign for the Presidency he made reference to Vietnam as "the cork in the bottle of Chinese expansion in Asia." In the spring of 1968 he asserted that the war was "not for the freedom and independence of South Vietnam alone, but to make possible the conditions of a wider and durable peace. . . ." And in his speech of November 3 the President predicted that American withdrawal from Vietnam—our "defeat and humiliation," as he chose to put it—"would spark violence wherever our commitments help maintain the peace—in the Middle East, in Berlin, eventually even in the western hemisphere."

Rooted in the analogy of Munich,[2] the idea took firm hold during the Johnson Administration that, by fighting a relatively small war in Vietnam now, we were sparing ourselves a much greater war—or a whole series of wars —later on. This notion has been reaffirmed by President Nixon. Again speaking on November 3 of the consequences of "precipitate" American withdrawal from Vietnam, the President laid it down as a flat prediction that "Ultimately, this would cost more lives. It would not bring peace. It would bring more war."

With due respect for the President's strong conviction, I submit that the theory of the exemplary war—a war to end "wars of national liberation"—is unsound.

[1] *Editors' note:* Identified in the American press as the village of Mylai.
[2] *Editors' note:* Munich Agreement, September 29, 1938. Great Britain and France agreed to German demands to annex the Sudetenland in Czechoslovakia in the belief that once appeased the Germans would not demand any more territory. This policy of appeasement of Nazi Germany was a false hope, for on September 1, 1939, Germany invaded Poland, thus starting World War II.

Expanding on the exemplary war thesis, President Nixon expressed the opinion on November 3 that calling off our war in Vietnam "would result in a collapse of confidence in American leadership not only in Asia but throughout the world." The President's own chief foreign policy adviser, Mr. Kissinger, effectively challenged this proposition in an article written shortly before he went to work in the White House. "Whatever the outcome of the war in Vietnam," he wrote, "it is clear that it has greatly diminished American willingness to become involved in this form of warfare elsewhere. Its utility as a precedent has therefore been importantly undermined."

Wedded as they have been to the idea of Chinese communism as a conspiracy for the conquest of Asia, if not of the world, our policy makers have been more than resourceful in disposing of facts that do not fit the cherished preconception. Conceding in *principle* that the world communist movement is divided, and that North Vietnam is not merely a pawn of China, our policy makers nonetheless invoke these very specters in their efforts to justify our involvement in Vietman. Mr. Rusk used to warn of a "world cut in two by Asian communism." The President's speech of November 3 was suffused with associations of this kind, including a reference to "those great powers who have not yet abandoned their goals of world conquest." For whatever their reasons —conviction, pride, or dogmatic anticommunism—our policy makers have never been willing to recognize the Vietnamese conflict for that which virtually every expert and seasoned observer has long recognized it to be: a civil conflict in which communism is and always has been secondary to the drive for national independence. . . .

Once it is clear that the war in Vietnam is neither a valid global testing of the liberation-war doctrine nor a proxy war in a grand Chinese strategy for the conquest of Asia, it follows inescapably that the United States has been fighting a war without need or justification—a war based on demonstrably false premises. My own premise of course is that our legitimate interest in southeast Asia is not ideological but strategic, having to do not with the elimination of the Vietcong or of any other indigenous communist movement but with the discouragement of overt Chinese military expansion. The prevalent view among southeast Asian specialists outside of government is that the Chinese challenge in south Asia is more political and cultural than military, that a strong independent Communist regime is a more effective barrier to Chinese power than a weak non-Communist regime, that the Hanoi government is nationalist and independent, and that, accordingly, once peace is restored— if ever it is—North Vietnam will serve as a barrier rather than as an avenue to Chinese expansion.

Assuming still that our national interest in Asia is strategic rather than ideological, it follows that the United States has no vital security interest in the preservation of South Vietnam as an independent, non-Communist state. Indeed the United States has no vital interest in whether South Vietnam is governed by Communists, non-Communists or a coalition; nor is it a matter of vital interest to the United States whether North and South Vietnam are united or divided. Our interest is in the prevalence, whatever its form, of indigenous Vietnamese nationalism; beyond that strategic interest gives way to ideological preference—if not, indeed, to ideological obsession.

On the basis of their grudging, minimal contributions to the fighting in Vietnam it would appear that our Asian and Pacific allies either do not take the ostensible threat to their own security very seriously or are content to have the United States do their fighting for them. . . .

. . . Power is a narcotic, a potent intoxicant, and America has been on a "trip." We soared for a while, gladly dispensing goods and services for the tribute which nourished our vanity. Then our unpiloted space ship came down in the swamps of Vietnam, and suddenly, instead of soaring, we found ourselves slogging in mud. The contrast could not have been greater and it has shocked and confused us. We must hope that it will also have sobered us, and that we will be able to find our way out of the swamp, not, let us hope, to take flight again, but just to get back on our feet, which is the posture that nature intended for us.

To get back on our feet we will have to shake off the lingering effects of the narcotic of power. For a start we might stop the prideful nonsense about "defeat" and "humiliation." Liquidating a mistake is neither a defeat nor a humiliation; it is a rational and mature way of accommodating to reality, and the ability to do it is something to be proud of. When President Johnson used to declare that he would not be the first American President to lose a war, and when President Nixon warns, as he did on November 3, against "this first defeat in American history," they are not talking about the national interest but about the national ego and their own standings in history. A war is not a football game which you try to win for its own sake, or in order to maintain an unblemished record of victories. A war is supposed to be fought for purposes external to itself, for substantive political purposes, not just for the glory of winning it. When its political purposes are recognized as unworthy, as they have been in Vietnam, it is rank immorality to press on for a costly, destructive and probably unattainable victory. . . .

II. The Kind of War It Is

A whole new set of questions now arises. Even if all of the rationalizations for this war were valid—even if it were containing China, preventing future "wars of national liberation," and upholding the principle of self-determination— would we have the right to do what we are doing to the people of Vietnam and to ourselves in the process?

I am not advocating an exercise in national flagellation. Quite a number of people—I among them—suggested the need for a national effort at critical self-evaluation after the murder of President Kennedy. It seemed appropriate at the time but nothing came of it. We did not look into ourselves and, instead of the cathartic reconciliation that we hoped might come of the shock we had experienced, there has occurred over the last six years a rising tide of both personal and political violence in American society. . . .

If we really want to understand the meaning of the Songmy massacre and all the other acts of indiscriminate killing in Vietnam, we are not going to do it by declaring a national day of atonement. That might satisfy other needs but it is not likely to result in the acquisition of accurate and useful information about ourselves. That can only come from an appreciation—as guiltless an appreciation as possible—of the *common* human susceptibilities with which every one of us—old and young, communist and noncommunist—is endowed by the simple virtue of being human. I stress this point to you as students because I have had the impression of a certain Puritanical stuffiness on the part of many young people, a certain reluctance to face the likelihood that deep in the soul of the most high-minded student activist are some of the same fears and longings that lurk within the soul of the most ravenous, bloodsucking, imperialist warmonger.

The really important and useful thing to know about Songmy is not the unspeakable things that certain GI's did but the unspeakable things that most human beings are capable of doing in extreme circumstances. The American soldiers who wiped out the civilian population of that Vietnamese village were not monsters but ordinary young men acting under the pressures of intense fear and anger. "You see," said one major, recounting the confession of one of his men that he had killed three children, "a half hour before, a kid had thrown a grenade that killed the guy's best buddy. So you have to understand." Another veteran of the Songmy massacre, Mr. Paul David Meadlo, who admitted on national television that he shot some thirty or forty men, women and children, is described by people in his home town of New Goshen, Indiana, as "a very nice boy," "the nicest guy you'd ever want to meet." . . .

Most of what is happening in Vietnam—the face-to-face killing of woman and children as at Songmy, the out-of-sight killing of women and children by artillery and B-52 raids in the "free-fire zones," the deliberate burning of entire villages by the so-called "Zippo squads," and the assassination of thousands of presumed Vietcong cadre under the "Phoenix" program—all these things are happening outside civilization. They are happening in a jungle of our own creation. That is the kind of war it is—a war in which civilians are indistinguishable from soldiers, a war in which mass murder is the strategy of both sides, a war which has released the furies within the human soul, a war which degrades all those whom·it does not destroy.

These atrocities in Vietnam, committed by Americans, must be taken as a warning and a symbol of what can happen to a whole society. We are, I believe, far short of the state of moral disintegration that Germany reached in the 1940's and I am all but certain that we will not descend into that abyss. It is not, however, utterly and eternally out of the question. We are susceptible to the same virus of brutalization that other societies have come to, and nothing contributes more to the moral breakdown of a society than the long continuation of an unjust and unnecessary war.

It is more nearly an inevitability than an accident that a war of this kind should make a travesty of its own nominal objectives. Finding himself in a strange, dangerous and technologically primitive place, the ordinary GI responds with something short of the perspective of a cultural anthropologist. Not only are the Vietnamese primitive by the American soldier's standard but they are also dangerous: combatants and civilians are indistinguishable; even a woman or child may throw a grenade at him. Fearing and despising the people he is suppose to be saving, the GI soon dehumanizes them, or is likely to; they are not people but "gooks" and "dinks." Again, I emphasize these are not monsters but perfectly decent Americans who are dehumanizing the Vietnamese people; they do it almost as an act of self-defense. Nonetheless, it brutalizes them. . . .

I would not want the perpetrators of the Songmy massacre let off. On the contrary, I want them tried and, if guilty, punished—not for retribution but for deterrence, not because they are different from the rest of us but because they are so much like the rest of us, because what they have done almost any of us could have done.

Vietnam has knocked us Americans off our pedestal. It has taught us that we are no better than the rest of the human race—although neither are we any worse. And that is the useful thing to be learned from all these horror stories and from the war itself. It was moral presumption—the so-called "responsibility of power" and the traditional American notion that we are better than other people—that led us into this war in which we have largely destroyed Vietnamese society while brutalizing ourselves. If out of all this we learn to respect and guard against the destructive instincts that lie within all of us, then something at least will have been retrieved from the disaster.

President Nixon said one thing in his recent speech with which I agree. He said that "North Vietnam cannot defeat or humiliate the United States. Only Americans can do that." In my opinion we have already done it, but I also think we can undo it—not with glory, because there is no glory in a charnel house, and not with "honor" in the sense in which soldiers use that term. But we can do it with dignity and we can do it with self-respect—the self-respect of human beings who have learned something about their own humanity and its terrible fallibilities. The question of course is how.

III. The Way Out

The Administration has a plan—so they tell us—for getting out of Vietnam. They won't tell us exactly what it is, or exactly how it will work, or when it will be accomplished, but they insist that they have a plan. They call it "Vietnamization."

As defined in the President's speech of November 3, "Vietnamization" means that American forces will be withdrawn gradually while the Saigon army is built up to take over a greater share of the war. How far this process will go remains unspecified. . . .

Since it is all but inconceivable that the shaky Saigon army can hope to win the victory which half a million Americans and the Saigon army besides have been unable to win, it would appear that the best possible prospect for Vietnamization—"best," that is, for Thieu and Ky and for the Nixon Administration's prestige—is a continuing war of stalemate and attrition, with a reduced number of Americans reverting to their pre-1965 "advisory" role in a semipermanent war of counterinsurgency.

For the Vietnamese people this of course would mean continuing terror and death for the indefinite future. That is the price which it is proposed to exact from them so that the Americans can withdraw with what their leaders conceive of as "honor." . . .

The weakness of the policy of "Vietnamization" is the weakness of the South Vietnamese government itself. Its claim to legitimacy is based on rigged elections and on an American-sponsored rather than an authentic Vietnamese constitution, which specifically bars all Communists from participating in the government. The electoral law barred "neutralists" as well as Communists from running for office in the supposedly free election of 1967. . . .

In his speech of November 3, President Nixon said that "we really have only two choices open to us if we want to end this war:" either "precipitate" withdrawal or, failing acceptance of our terms in the Paris peace talks, Vietnamization. The President, I think, is mistaken. There is a third and better option than either of these: the negotiation of arrangements for a new interim government in South Vietnam, for elections conducted by the interim coalition regime with or without international supervision, and for complete American withdrawal. The obstacle to such a negotiation is our continuing attachment to the Thieu-Ky government. If we could bring ourselves to deprive Saigon of its veto on American policy—as we could do without impairing either our own vital interests or, I daresay, the best interests of the South Vietnamese people —there would be no need either for the "precipitate" withdrawal which the President likes to talk about or for the condemnation of the Vietnamese people to prolonged war, which is the true meaning of "Vietnamization."

We do not have to force such a settlement on the South Vietnamese government. We need only put them on notice that these terms have become our war aims, that we hope they will join us in negotiating their realization, but that, if they are not, we shall nonetheless negotiate the conditions of American withdrawal, while they, in turn, will be at liberty to continue the war on their own, to negotiate for new alliances, or to come to their own terms with the Vietcong. If we did withdraw and the Army of the Republic of Vietnam, with its one million well-equipped soldiers, could then be inspired to defend the Saigon government, it would survive. If it could not be so inspired, then the South Vietnamese government would not survive. But we have done enough, having fought their war for over four years at the cost of over forty thousand American lives thus far. . . .

Our basic asset, which neither the Johnson nor the Nixon Administration has been willing to acknowledge, is that this war is not now and never has been essential to our interests, essential, that is, to the freedom and safety of the American people. The exact terms of peace do not, therefore, matter very much from the standpoint of American interests, but the early restoration of peace matters enormously, because every day that this war goes on the sickness of American society worsens.

Discussion Starters

1. Compare the Nixon and Fulbright views on the consequences of immediate American withdrawal from South Vietnam.

2. How might President Nixon have evaluated Fulbright's contention that the Vietnamese conflict is "a civil conflict in which communism is and always has been secondary to the drive for national independence"? What evidence could Fulbright have used to support such an argument?

3. How did Nixon and Fulbright interpret the significance of the terms "defeat" and "humiliation" when talking about the war in Vietnam? Which approach was more valid? Why?

4. Evaluate Fulbright's warning that the atrocities, committed by Americans in Vietnam, have begun to bring about the moral disintegration of American society. How might Nixon have evaluated this argument?

5. Assess Fulbright's reasons for bringing to justice the Americans who have committed atrocities in Vietnam. How should the term "atrocity" be defined? Should it refer only to the actual perpetrator of the crime or should it also include his superiors? How far up the chain of command should justice go?

6. Evaluate Nixon's plan for Vietnamization and Fulbright's proposals for ending the war. How would each assess the proposals of the other? Based on the speeches in this chapter, who would appear to have the most valid approach to end the war? Why?

Related Documents

I. Letter to President Ngo Dinh Diem

DWIGHT D. EISENHOWER

On July 21, 1954, at Geneva, Switzerland, the French agreed with representatives of the Communist and non-Communist factions of Indochina to withdraw from the war and to establish peace there. The declaration of their intentions was cosigned by Great Britain, the Soviet Union, and the People's Republic of China. For Vietnam the critical section of the document was Paragraph 7, which provided for general elections to be held in July 1956 to unify North and South Vietnam into one nation.

Although the United States attended the Geneva Conference, it refused to go along with the other major powers and sign the declaration because it feared that the Communists of the North might subvert the elections and take over the South. The loss of South Vietnam to the Communists, the United States believed, would be the first step in the realization of the "domino theory": If the Communists were permitted to gain control over one country they would then move to control its neighbors, and then their neighbors, and so on until all of Asia and possibly the world would be lost to the Communists.

President Eisenhower, who believed in the domino theory, responded to the Geneva Conference by pledging American military aid and advisers to the President of South Vietnam, Ngo Dinh Diem, to prevent the North from taking over the South. The elections provided for in the Geneva agreements were thus blocked by the United States.

How does President Eisenhower's letter to Diem compare with President Nixon's later arguments for supporting the South Vietnamese government and with Senator Fulbright's contentions that America should withdraw its support? What is the significance of the phrase "provided that your Government is prepared to give assurances as to the standards of performances it would be able to maintain in the event such aid were supplied"?

OCTOBER 23, 1954

DEAR MR. PRESIDENT: I have been following with great interest the course of developments in Viet-Nam, particularly since the conclusion of the conference at Geneva. The implications of the agreement concerning Viet-Nam have caused grave concern regarding the future of a country temporarily divided by an artificial military grouping, weakened by a long and exhausting war and

U.S. Department of State, *American Foreign Policy, 1950–1955, Basic Documents* (Washington, D.C.: Government Printing Office, 1957), II, pp. 2401–2.

faced with enemies without and by their subversive collaborators within.

Your recent requests for aid to assist in the formidable project of the movement of several hundred thousand loyal Vietnamese citizens away from areas which are passing under a *de facto* rule and political ideology which they abhor, are being fulfilled. I am glad that the United States is able to assist in this humanitarian effort.

We have been exploring ways and means to permit our aid to Viet-Nam to be more effective and to make a greater contribution to the welfare and stability of the Government of Viet-Nam. I am, accordingly, instructing the American Ambassador to Viet-Nam to examine with you in your capacity as Chief of Government, how an intelligent program of American aid given directly to your Government can serve to assist Viet-Nam in its present hour of trial, provided that your Government is prepared to give assurances as to the standards of performance it would be able to maintain in the event such aid were supplied.

The purpose of this offer is to assist the Government of Viet-Nam in developing and maintaining a strong, viable state, capable of resisting attempted subversion or aggression through military means. The Government of the United States expects that this aid will be met by performance on the part of the Government of Viet-Nam in undertaking needed reforms. It hopes that such aid, combined with your own continuing efforts, will contribute effectively toward an independent Viet-Nam endowed with a strong government. Such a government would, I hope, be so responsive to the nationalist aspirations of its people, so enlightened in purpose and effective in performance, that it will be respected both at home and abroad and discourage any who might wish to impose a foreign ideology on your free people.

II. *Why Must We Take This Painful Road?*

LYNDON B. JOHNSON

During his first eight months in office President Johnson did not significantly change the American policy of sending advisers and equipment to South Vietnam. His new policy did not begin to unfold until August 1964, when North Vietnamese torpedo boats allegedly attacked American destroyers in the Gulf of Tonkin. The crisis atmosphere that resulted from the news of the attack prompted Congress to pass a resolution authorizing the President to use American forces "to prevent further aggression." Armed with the Gulf of Tonkin Resolution, Johnson then committed combat troops to the area and the "escalation" of the Vietnamese war began. By 1968 the number of American combat

Public Papers of the Presidents of the United States: Lyndon B. Johnson (Washington, D.C.: Government Printing Office, 1966), I (1965), pp. 394–99.

troops in Indochina reached 540,000 men. But why was America there? President Johnson attempted to answer that question in the following speech delivered at John Hopkins University on April 7, 1965.

How do Johnson's reasons for American military involvement in South Vietnam compare with President Nixon's speech of November 3, 1969? In what ways could Senator Fulbright's arguments against Nixon's Vietnam policies be used to also challenge President Johnson's reasons for American involvement?

APRIL 7, 1965

Tonight Americans and Asians are dying for a world where each people may choose its own path to change.

This is the principle for which our ancestors fought in the valleys of Pennsylvania. It is the principle for which our sons fight tonight in the jungles of Viet-Nam.

Viet-Nam is far away from this quiet campus. We have no territory there, nor do we seek any. The war is dirty and brutal and difficult. And some 400 young men, born into an America that is bursting with opportunity and promise, have ended their lives on Viet-Nam's steaming soil.

Why must we take this painful road?

Why must this Nation hazard its ease, and its interest, and its power for the sake of a people so far away?

We fight because we must fight if we are to live in a world where every country can shape its own destiny. And only in such a world will our own freedom be finally secure.

This kind of world will never be built by bombs or bullets. Yet the infirmities of man are such that force must often precede reason, and the waste of war, the works of peace.

We wish that this were not so. But we must deal with the world as it is, if it is ever to be as we wish.

The Nature of the Conflict

The world as it is in Asia is not a serene or peaceful place.

The first reality is that North Viet-Nam has attacked the independent nation of South Viet-Nam. Its object is total conquest.

Of course, some of the people of South Viet-Nam are participating in attack on their own government. But trained men and supplies, orders and arms, flow in a constant stream from north to south.

This support is the heartbeat of the war.

And it is a war of unparalleled brutality. Simple farmers are the targets of assassination and kidnapping. Women and children are strangled in the night because their men are loyal to their government. And helpless villages are ravaged by sneak attacks. Large-scale raids are conducted on towns, and terror strikes in the heart of cities.

The confused nature of this conflict cannot mask the fact that it is the new face of an old enemy.

Over this war—and all Asia—is another reality: the deepening shadow of Communist China. The rulers in Hanoi are urged on by Peking. This is a regime which has destroyed freedom in Tibet, which has attacked India, and has been condemned by the United Nations for aggression in Korea. It is a nation which is helping the forces of violence in almost every continent. The contest in Viet-Nam is part of a wider pattern of aggressive purposes.

Why Are We in Viet-Nam?

Why are these realities our concern? Why are we in South Viet-Nam?

We are there because we have a promise to keep. Since 1954 every American President has offered support to the people of South Viet-Nam. We have helped to build, and we have helped to defend. Thus, over many years, we have made a national pledge to help South Viet-Nam defend its independence.

And I intend to keep that promise.

To dishonor that pledge, to abandon this small and brave nation to its enemies, and to the terror that must follow, would be an unforgivable wrong.

We are also there to strengthen world order. Around the globe, from Berlin to Thailand, are people whose well-being rests, in part, on the belief that they can count on us if they are attacked. To leave Viet-Nam to its fate would shake the confidence of all these people in the value of an American commitment and in the value of America's word. The result would be increased unrest and instability, and even wider war.

We are also there because there are great stakes in the balance. Let no one think for a moment that retreat from Viet-Nam would bring an end to conflict. The battle would be renewed in one country and then another. The central lesson of our time is that the appetite of aggression is never satisfied. To withdraw from one battlefield means only to prepare for the next. We must say in southeast Asia—as we did in Europe—in the words of the Bible: "Hitherto shalt thou come, but no further."

There are those who say that all our effort there will be futile—that China's power is such that it is bound to dominate all southeast Asia. But there is no end to that argument until all of the nations of Asia are swallowed up.

There are those who wonder why we have a responsibility there. Well, we have it there for the same reason that we have a responsibility for the defense of Europe. World War II was fought in both Europe and Asia, and when it ended we found ourselves with continued responsibility for the defense of freedom.

Our Objective in Viet-Nam

Our objective is the independence of South Viet-Nam, and its freedom from attack. We want nothing for ourselves—only that the people of South Viet-Nam be allowed to guide their own country in their own way.

We will do everything necessary to reach that objective. And we will do only what is absolutely necessary.

In recent months attacks on South Viet-Nam were stepped up. Thus, it became necessary for us to increase our response and to make attacks by air. This is not a change of purpose. It is a change in what we believe that purpose requires.

We do this in order to slow down aggression.

We do this to increase the confidence of the brave people of South Viet-Nam who have bravely borne this brutal battle for so many years with so many casualties.

And we do this to convince the leaders of North Viet-Nam—and all who seek to share their conquest—of a very simple fact:

We will not be defeated.

We will not grow tired.

We will not withdraw, either openly or under the cloak of a meaningless agreement.

We know that air attacks alone will not accomplish all of these purposes. But it is our best and prayerful judgment that they are a necessary part of the surest road to peace.

We hope that peace will come swiftly. But that is in the hands of others besides ourselves. And we must be prepared for a long continued conflict. It will require patience as well as bravery, the will to endure as well as the will to resist.

I wish it were possible to convince others with words of what we now find it necessary to say with guns and planes: Armed hostility is futile. Our resources are equal to any challenge. Because we fight for values and we fight for principles, rather than territory or colonies, our patience and our determination are unending.

Once this is clear, then it should also be clear that the only path for reasonable men is the path of peaceful settlement.

Such peace demands an independent South Viet-Nam—securely guaranteed and able to shape its own relationships to all others—free from outside interference—tied to no alliance—a military base for no other country.

These are the essentials of any final settlement.

We will never be second in the search for such a peaceful settlement in Viet-Nam.

There may be many ways to this kind of peace: in discussion or negotiation with the governments concerned; in large groups or in small ones; in the reaffirmation of old agreements or their strengthening with new ones.

We have stated this position over and over again, fifty times and more, to friend and foe alike. And we remain ready, with this purpose, for unconditional discussions.

And until that bright and necessary day of peace we will try to keep conflict from spreading. We have no desire to see thousands die in battle—Asians or Americans. We have no desire to devastate that which the people of North Viet-Nam have built with toil and sacrifice. We will use our power with restraint and with all the wisdom that we can command.

But we will use it.

This war, like most wars, is filled with terrible irony. For what do the people of North Viet-Nam want? They want what their neighbors also desire: food for their hunger; health for their bodies; a chance to learn; progress for their country; and an end to the bondage of material misery. And they would find all these things far more readily in peaceful association with others than in the endless course of battle.

A Cooperative Effort for Development

These countries of southeast Asia are homes for millions of impoverished people. Each day these people rise at dawn and struggle through until the night to wrestle existence from the soil. They are often wracked by disease, plagued by hunger, and death comes at the early age of 40.

Stability and peace do not come easily in such a land. Neither independence nor human dignity will ever be won, though, by arms alone. It also requires the work of peace. The American people have helped generously in times past in these works. Now there must be a much more massive effort to improve the life of man in that conflict-torn corner of our world. . . .

Conclusion

We often say how impressive power is. But I do not find it impressive at all. The guns and the bombs, the rockets and the warships, are all symbols of human failure. They are necessary symbols. They protect what we cherish. But they are witness to human folly. . . .

Every night before I turn out the lights to sleep I ask myself this question: Have I done everything that I can do to unite this country? Have I done everything I can to help unite the world, to try to bring peace and hope to all the peoples of the world? Have I done enough?

Ask yourselves that question in your homes—and in this hall tonight. Have we, each of us, all done all we could? Have we done enough?

We may well be living in the time foretold many years ago when it was said: "I call heaven and earth to record this day against you, that I have set before you life and death, blessing and cursing: therefore choose life, that both thou and thy seed may live."

This generation of the world must choose: destroy or build, kill or aid, hate or understand.

We can do all these things on a scale never dreamed of before.

Well, we will choose life. In so doing we will prevail over the enemies within man, and over the natural enemies of all mankind.

III. Four Points for Peace

PHAM VAN DONG

The Democratic Republic of Vietnam (North Vietnam) sent men and material into South Vietnam to try and accomplish by military means what had not been realized by the Geneva Conference of 1954. It was the North Vietnamese actions and the inability of the South Vietnamese to resist effectively them that led the United States, especially during the administration of President Johnson, to commit combat troops to the area. Early in 1965 large-scale bombing of the North was begun in an attempt to cut the flow of men and supplies to North Vietnamese units operating in the South. The bombing, which lasted almost three years, did not accomplish its objective. Some Americans argued that this was because the Hanoi-Haiphong complex was exempt as a target. Although the North Vietnamese suffered because of the bombing, instead of weakening their resolve to continue the war, it seems to have stimulated their great patriotic ardor and strengthened their resolve to carry the war to a successful conclusion no matter how long it might take.

In April 1965 Premier Pham Van Dong of North Vietnam declared the basic program of his government to be to bring about peace in all Vietnam. How do his four points compare with President Nixon's plan to restore peace in the area and with Senator Fulbright's proposal for peace?

APRIL 13, 1965

Pham Van Dong, Premier of the Democratic Republic of Vietnam, elucidated the unswerving stand of the Government of the D.R.V. on the Vietnam question in his report on Government work at the second session of the United National Assembly. The [North] Vietnamese News Agency issued the full text of the report today.

Premier Pham Van Dong said that it is the unswerving policy of the Government of the D.R.V. to strictly respect the 1954 Geneva agreements on Vietnam and to correctly implement their basic provisions as embodied in the following points:

1. Recognition of the basic national rights of the Vietnamese people—peace, independence, sovereignty, unity and territorial integrity. According to the Geneva agreements, the United States Government must withdraw from South Vietnam United States troops, military personnel and weapons of all kinds, dismantle all United States military bases there, cancel its "military alliance" with South Vietnam. It must end its policy of intervention and aggression in South Vietnam. According to the Geneva agreements, the United States Government must stop its acts of war against North Vietnam, completely cease all encroachments on the territory and sovereignty of the D.R.V.

From *The New York Times,* April 14, 1965, p. 14. © 1965 by The New York Times Company. Reprinted by permission.

2. Pending the peaceful reunification of Vietnam, while Vietnam is still temporarily divided into two zones, the military provisions of the 1954 Geneva agreements on Vietnam must be strictly respected. The two zones must refrain from joining any military alliance with foreign countries. There must be no foreign military bases, troops, or military personnel in their respective territory.

3. The internal affairs of South Vietnam must be settled by the South Vietnamese people themselves, in accordance with the program of the N.F.L.S.V. [the South Vietnam National Liberation Front, or political arm of the Vietcong] without any foreign interference.

4. The peaceful reunification of Vietnam is to be settled by the Vietnamese people in both zones, without any foreign interference.

Pham Van Dong said that the aforementioned stand of the D.R.V. Government unquestionably enjoys the approval and support of all peace and justice-loving governments and peoples in the world. The Government of the D.R.V. is of the view that the stand expounded above is the basis for the soundest political settlement of the Vietnam problem.

If this basis is recognized, favorable conditions will be created for the peaceful settlement of the Vietnam problem, and it will be possible to consider the reconvening of an international conference along the pattern of the 1954 Geneva conference on Vietnam.

The Government of the D.R.V. declares that any approach contrary to the above-mentioned stand is inappropriate. Any approach tending to secure a United Nations intervention in the Vietnam situation is also inappropriate because such approaches are basically at variance with the 1954 Geneva agreements on Vietnam.

IV. "We Should Be Out of Vietnam Now"

JOHN F. KERRY

The Vietnam Veterans Against the War was organized to bring men who had served in Vietnam into the movement to end the war in Indochina. Although the organization was small, many members went to Washington, D.C., in April 1971 to protest, along with other groups, the continuing war. Their appearance—some in wheelchairs, others on crutches, and all dressed in their old uniforms—was a distressing and depressing sight to many in and out of Congress.

The following statement was made before the Senate Foreign Relations Committee by one of their leaders, former Navy lieutenant John F. Kerry, who had served in Vietnam. What were Kerry's attitudes toward the war and how did he evaluate President Nixon's plans for "Vietnamization"?

Congressional Record, May 4, 1971, pp. E3921–23.

APRIL 22, 1971

Mr. KERRY. Thank you very much, Senator Fulbright, Senator Javits, Senator Symington, Senator Pell. I would like to say for the record, and also for the men behind me who are also wearing the uniform and their medals, that my sitting here is really symbolic. I am not here as John Kerry. I am here as one member of the group of 1,000, which is a small representation of a very much larger group of veterans in this country, and were it possible for all of them to sit at this table they would be here and have the same kind of testimony. . . .

In 1970 at West Point Vice President Agnew said "some glamorize the criminal misfits of society while our best men die in Asian rice paddies to preserve the freedom which most of those misfits abuse," and this was used as a rallying point for our effort in Vietnam.

But for us, as boys in Asia whom the country was supposed to support, his statement is a terrible distortion from which we can only draw a very deep sense of revulsion, and hence the anger of some of the men who are here in Washington today. It is a distortion because we in no way consider ourselves the best men of this country; because those he calls misfits were standing up for us in a way that nobody else in this country dared to; because so many who have died would have returned to this country to join the misfits in their efforts to ask for an immediate withdrawal from South Vietnam; because so many of those best men have returned as quadriplegics and amputees—and they lie forgotten in Veterans Administration Hospitals in this country which fly the flag which so many have chosen as their own personal symbol—and we cannot consider ourselves America's best men when we are ashamed of and hated for what we were called on to do in Southeast Asia.

In our opinion, and from our experience, there is nothing in South Vietnam which could happen that realistically threatens the United States of America. And to attempt to justify the loss of one American life in Vietnam, Cambodia or Laos by linking such loss to the preservation of freedom, which those misfits supposedly abuse, is to us the height of criminal hypocrisy, and it is that kind of hypocrisy which we feel has torn this country apart.

We are probably much more angry than that, but I don't want to go into the foreign policy aspects because I am outclassed here. I know that all of you talk about every possible alternative to getting out of Vietnam. We understand that. We know you have considered the seriousness of the aspects to the utmost level and I am not going to try to dwell on that. But I want to relate to you the feeling that many of the men who have returned to this country express because we are probably angriest about all that we were told about Vietnam and about the mystical war against communism.

We found that not only was it a civil war, an effort by a people who had for years been seeking their liberation from any colonial influence whatsoever, but also we found that the Vietnamese whom we had enthusiastically molded after our own image were hard put to take up the fight against the threat we were supposedly saving them from.

We found most people didn't even know the difference between communism and democracy. They only wanted to work in rice paddies without helicopters strafing them and bombs with napalm burning their villages and tearing their country apart. They wanted everything to do with the war, particularly with this foreign presence of the United States of America, to leave them alone in peace, and they practiced the art of survival by siding with whichever military force was present at a particular time, be it Viet Cong, North Vietnamese or American.

Each day to facilitate the process by which the United States washes her hands of Vietnam someone has to give up his life so that the United States doesn't have to admit something that the entire world already knows, so that we can't say that we have made a mistake. Someone has to die so that President Nixon won't be, and these are his words, "the first President to lose a war."

We are asking Americans to think about that because how do you ask a man to be the last man to die in Vietnam? How do you ask a man to be the last man to die for a mistake? But we are trying to do that, and we are doing it with thousands of rationalizations, and if you read carefully the President's last speech to the people of this country, you can see that he says, and says clearly, "but the issue, gentlemen, the issue, is communism, and the question is whether or not we will leave that country to the communists or whether or not we will try to give it hope to be a free people." But the point is they are not a free people now under us. They are not a free people, and we cannot fight communism all over the world. I think we should have learned that lesson by now.

But the problem of veterans goes beyond this personal problem, because you think about a poster in this country with a picture of Uncle Sam and the picture says "I want you." And a young man comes out of high school and says, "that is fine, I am going to serve my country," and he goes to Vietnam and he shoots and he kills and he does his job. Or maybe he doesn't kill. Maybe he just goes and he comes back, and when he gets back to this country he finds that he isn't really wanted, because the largest corps of unemployed in the country—it varies depending on who you get it from, the Veterans Administration says 15 percent and various other sources 22 percent—but the largest corps of unemployed in this country are veterans of this war, and of those veterans 33 percent of the unemployed are black. That means one out of every ten of the nation's unemployed is a veteran of Vietnam.

We found also that all too often American men were dying in those rice paddies for want of support from their allies. We saw first hand how monies from American taxes was used for a corrupt dictatorial regime. We saw that many people in this country had a one-sided idea of who was kept free by our flag, and blacks provided the highest percentage of casualties. We saw Vietnam ravaged equally by American bombs and search and destroy missions, as well as by Viet Cong terrorism, and yet we listened while this country tried to blame all of the havoc on the Viet Cong.

We rationalized destroying villages in order to save them. We saw America lose her sense of morality as she accepted very coolly a My Lai and refused to give up the image of American soldiers who hand out chocolate bars and chewing gum.

We learned the meaning of free fire zones, shooting anything that moves, and we watched while America placed a cheapness on the lives of orientals.

We watched the United States falsification of body counts, in fact the glorification of body counts. We listened while month after month we were told the back of the enemy was about to break. We fought using weapons against "oriental human beings." We fought using weapons against those people which I do not believe this country would dream of using were we fighting in the European theater. We watched while men charged up hills because a general said that hill has to be taken, and after losing one platoon or two platoons they marched away to leave the hill for re-occupation by the North Vietnamese. We watched pride allow the most unimportant battles to be blown into extravaganzas, because we couldn't lose, and we couldn't retreat, and because it didn't matter how many American bodies were lost to prove that point, and so there were Hamburger Hills and Khe Sahns and Hill 81s and Fire Base 6s, and so many others.

Now we are told that the men who fought there must watch quietly while American lives are lost so that we can exercise the incredible arrogance of Vietnamizing the Vietnamese.

The hospitals across the country won't, or can't meet their demands. It is not a question of not trying; they haven't got the appropriations. A man recently died after he had a tracheotomy in California, not because of the operation but because there weren't enough personnel to clean the mucus out of his tube and he suffocated to death.

Another young man just died in a New York VA Hospital the other day. A friend of mine was lying in a bed two beds away and tried to help him but he couldn't. He rang a bell and there was nobody there to service that man and so he died of convulsions.

I understand 57 percent of all those entering the VA hospitals talk about suicide. Some 27 percent have tried, and they try because they come back to this country and they have to face what they did in Vietnam, and then they come back and find the indifference of a country that doesn't really care. . . .

Americans seem to have accepted the idea that the war is winding down, at least for Americans, and they have also allowed the bodies which were once used by a President for statistics to prove that we were winning that war, to be used as evidence against a man who followed orders and who interpreted those orders no differently than hundreds of other men in Vietnam.

We veterans can only look with amazement on the fact that this country has been unable to see there is absolutely no difference between ground troops and a helicopter crew, and yet people have accepted a differentiation fed them by the administration.

No ground troops are in Laos so it is all right to kill Laotians by remote control. But believe me the helicopter crews fill the same body bags and they wreak the same kind of damage on the Vietnamese and Laotian countryside as anybody else, and the President is talking about allowing that to go on for many years to come. One can only ask if we will really be satisfied only when the troops march into Hanoi.

We are asking here in Washington for some action; action from the Congress of the United States of America which has the power to raise and maintain armies, and which by the Constitution also has the power to declare war.

We have come here, not to the President, because we believe that this body can be responsive to the will of the people, and we believe that the will of the people says that we should be out of Vietnam now. . . .

Finally, this administration has done us the ultimate dishonor. They have attempted to disown us and the sacrifices we made for this country. In their blindness and fear they have tried to deny that we are veterans or that we served in Nam. We do not need their testimony. Our own scars and stumps of limbs are witness enough for others and for ourselves.

We wish that a merciful God could wipe away our own memories of that service as easily as this administration has wiped away their memories of us. But all that they have done and all that they can do by this denial is to make more clear than ever our own determination to undertake one last mission— to search out and destroy the last vestige of this barbaric war, to pacify our own hearts, to conquer the hate and the fear that have driven this country these last ten years and more, so when 30 years from now our brothers go down the street without a leg, without an arm, or a face, and small boys ask why we will be able to say "Vietnam" and not mean a desert, not a filthy obscene memory, but mean instead the place where America finally turned and where soldiers like us helped it in the turning.

Thank you.

For Further Reading

In the past several years literally hundreds of books and articles have appeared on the Vietnam war. Among the most notable are: Dennis Bloodworth, *An Eye for the Dragon: Southeast Asia Observed, 1954–1970* (1970); Noam Chomsky, *At War with Asia** (1970); Oliver E. Clubb, *The United States and the Sino-Soviet Bloc in Southeast Asia** (1963); Committee of Concerned Asian Scholars, *The Indochina Story** (1970); Chester L. Cooper, *The Lost Crusade:*

*Paperbound edition available.

America in Vietnam (1970); Brian Crozier, *Southeast Asia in Turmoil** (1965); Theodore Draper, *Abuse of Power** (1967); Bernard B. Fall's *Reflections on a War* (1967), *Street Without Joy* (1964), and *The Two Viet-Nams** (1965); Russell H. Fifield, *Southeast Asia in United States Policy** (1963); Marvin E. Gettleman, ed., *Vietnam** (1965); Philip Geyelin, *Lyndon B. Johnson and the World* (1966); R. N. Goodwin, *Triumph or Tragedy: Reflections on Vietnam** (1966); Lyndon B. Johnson, *The Vantage Point* (1971); George Kahin and John W. Lewins, *The United States in Vietnam* (1967); Mary McCarthy, *Hanoi** (1968); Richard M. Pfeffer, ed., *No More Vietnams?** (1968); Marcus G. Raskin and Bernard B. Fall, eds., *The Vietnam Reader** (1965); Milton J. Rosenberg, *et al., Vietnam and the Silent Majority: The Dove's Guide** (1970); Arthur M. Schlesinger, Jr., *The Bitter Heritage** (1967); and Robert Shaplen, *Time Out of Hand: Revolution and Reaction in Southeast Asia* (1969) and *The Road From War: Vietnam 1965–1971** (1971).

*Paperbound edition available.

17. Cities—Are They Doomed?

Are the cities of America doomed?

In the decades of the fifties and sixties many observers, both in and out of public life, asked that question. Some even believed that there was no question involved; the cities of America were already awaiting only their burial. Whatever their judgment, those who considered the plight of the cities began to discuss it as an "urban crisis." This term referred to such things as overcrowding, traffic congestion, inadequate housing, unresponsive bureaucracy, environmental pollution, crime, and unemployment. These conditions, each on its own, would make city life difficult; when combined and seeming to increase in force and scope, they made life barely tolerable to those who could not escape.

In 1970 the population of the United States was an estimated 202.5 million people, an increase of 23.9 million over the 1960 count. Eighty percent of that increase took place in metropolitan areas, chiefly in the suburban regions outside the central cities. Growth in metropolitan areas was not, in itself, particularly significant, for this had been the pattern in America since the turn of the century. What was significant was that the central cities grew only very slowly, while the suburban growth skyrocketed, continuing a trend that had become particularly evident after World War II.

Urbanization on a massive scale naturally intensified the problems related to greater numbers of people living closer together. For example, transit systems in some cities broke down, making the old joke about "not being able to get there from here" a reality. The increasing numbers of children brought severe strains to school systems. Rising unemployment during the later 1960s affected primarily the poor people of the central cities who, for the most part, were black. In fact, blacks came to make up most of the populations of the central cities. In 1966 there were 12.1 million blacks living within the central cities; this has been projected to 20.3 million by 1985. The increase in the black population, coupled with prevailing pattern of racial prejudice and exploitation in the central cities, further heightened the tensions of city living. These tensions exploded in the mid-sixties in the riots in Los Angeles (Watts), Newark, Detroit, and Washington, D.C. Such events caused more whites to remove themselves from the central cities, thus accounting in part for the increase in suburban populations.

All of these problems have led to a torrent of articles and books on what might be done to save the cities, but none of the recommendations seem to satisfy the requirements of this monumental task. So what can be done? Maybe it is too early to know, or perhaps it is already too late. The only thing most experts agree on when talking about the plight of the cities is that the urban crisis will be a primary political issue of the 1970s.

Core Document

Why Government Cannot Solve the Urban Problem

EDWARD C. BANFIELD

Edward Banfield, a political scientist at Harvard University who has served as head of President Nixon's Task Force on Model Cities, published in 1968 a highly controversial book dealing with the urban crisis. Entitled The Unheavenly City, *the book brought favorable comment from some quarters (the "book is well informed and worth arguing with")and barbs from others (a "fundamentally mistaken book"). Banfield rejected the premise that there was an urban crisis in America, thus offending sociologists, mayors, and minority group leaders. Nevertheless, because he had stood back and assessed the American city of the present day, his conclusions make provocative reading.*

Reprinted by permission of *Daedalus,* Journal of the Academy of Arts and Sciences, Boston, Mass., Fall, 1968, *The Conscience of the City.*

In the following article, later incorporated into his book, note what Banfield believed to be:
- *the serious problems of the cities.*
- *the urban crisis.*
- *the role of government in urban problems.*
- *the nature of the problems of the cities.*
- *possible programs the government might follow to improve life in the city.*
- *the difficulties in accomplishing his suggested programs.*
- *the nature of public opinion.*
- *the American ideal of "doing good."*

The city as it exists is very largely the product of tendencies of which we have as yet little knowledge and less control.

—Robert E. Park, 1928

I shall argue, first, that all of the serious problems of the cities are largely insoluble now and will be for the foreseeable future and, second, that insofar as it is open to government (federal, state, and local) to affect the situation, it tends to behave perversely—that is, not to do the things that would make it better, but instead to do those that will make it worse. These two arguments prepare the way for the question with which I shall be mainly concerned: What is there about our politics that accounts for this perversity?

I

By the serious problems of the cities I mean those that affect, or may affect, the essential welfare (as opposed to the comfort, convenience, and business advantage) of large numbers of people or the ability of the society to maintain itself as a "going concern," to be in some sense free and democratic, and to produce desirable human types. As examples of serious problems I will cite chronic unemployment, poverty, ignorance, crime, racial and other injustice, and civil disorder. To my mind, these problems are of a different order of importance than, say, the journey to work, urban sprawl, or the decline of department store sales.

What I am calling serious problems exist mainly in the inner parts of the central cities and of the older larger suburbs. The large majority of city dwellers do not live in these places and have little or no firsthand knowledge of these problems; most city dwellers have housing, schools, transportation, and community facilities that are excellent and getting better all the time. If there is an urban crisis, it is in the inner city. The lowest-skilled, lowest-paid, and lowest-status members of the urban work force have always lived in the highest-density districts of the inner city, that being where most of the jobs for the low-skilled have always been. Improvements in transportation have in the last thirty years or so hastened a process of outward growth that has always been going on. Most of those who could afford to do so have moved from the central city to the suburbs and from inlying suburbs to outlying ones. Much manufacturing and commerce has done the same thing. The inner city still employs most of the unskilled, but the number (and proportion) that it employs is declining, and considerable numbers of the unskilled are in a sense stranded in the inner city. The presence there of large concentrations of people who have relatively little education and income accounts for—perhaps I should say constitutes—the so-called urban crisis. Most of these people are black. From an objective standpoint, this is of less importance than most people suppose: If all Negroes turned white overnight, the serious problems of the city would still exist and in about the same form and degree; it is the presence of a large lower class, not of Negroes as such, that is the real source of the trouble.

Government can change the situation that I have just described only marginally; it cannot change it fundamentally. No matter what we do, we are bound to have large concentrations of the unskilled, of the poor, and—what is by no means the same thing—of the lower class in the inner parts of the central cities and the larger older suburbs for at least another twenty years. Rich as we are, we cannot afford to throw the existing cities away and build new ones from scratch. The decentralization of industry and commerce and of residential land use is bound to continue, leaving ever larger semi-abandoned and blighted areas behind.

If government cannot change fundamentally the pattern of metropolitan growth, neither can it solve any of the serious problems associated with it. To be specific, it cannot eliminate slums, educate the slum child, train the unskilled worker, end chronic poverty, stop crime and delinquency, or prevent riots. Of course, I do not mean that it cannot eliminate a single slum, educate a single slum child, or prevent a single riot. What I mean is that it cannot put a sizable dent in the problem as a whole. These problems may all become much less serious, but if they do, it will not be because of the direct efforts of government to bring about reforms.

We cannot solve these problems or even make much headway against them by means of government action not because, as many seem to suppose, we are selfish, callous, or stupid, but rather because they are in the main not susceptible to solution. For one reason or another, solving them is beyond the bounds of possibility. In the largest class of cases, solution depends upon knowledge that we do not and perhaps cannot possess. Consider, for example, the problem of educating the lower-class child. In recent years, there has been a vast outpouring of effort on this, and a great many well-thought-out and plausible ideas have been tried, some of them, like Operation Head Start, on a very large scale. So far none of these efforts can be said to have succeeded, and most of them have clearly failed. After surveying the various efforts at compensatory education, the U.S. Commission on Civil Rights said in *Racial Isolation in the Public Schools* that "none of the programs appear to have raised significantly the achievement of participating pupils, as a group, within the period evaluated by the Commission." It is probably safe to say that if the leading educators of this country were given first call on all of the nation's resources and told that they could do whatever they liked, they would not succeed in giving what any of us would consider an adequate education to a substantial number of slum children.

The nature of some problems is such that even if we knew how to solve them, we probably could not make use of the knowledge because the cure would be worse than the disease. However attractive they may otherwise be, all "solutions" that are incompatible with the basic principles of our political system must be considered unavailable—that is, beyond the bounds of possibility. If, for example, it were found to be possible to educate the lower-class child by taking him from his family shortly after birth and in no other way, we should have to give up the idea of educating those lower-class children whose parents refused to give them up; a free society cannot even consider taking children from their parents on the mere presumption—indeed not even on the certainty—that otherwise they will grow up ignorant, dependent, lower class.

Incompatibility with the basic principles of the political system is by no means the only ground on which a "solution" may be judged worse than the disease. Consider, for example, the police "crackdown" as a method of reducing crime on the streets. I do not know how well this method really works, but suppose for the sake of argument that it works very well. Even so, it is not a solution because, rightly or wrongly, a "crackdown" would be regarded by Negroes as an affront to the race. What is accomplished if crime is reduced slightly at the cost of deepening the cleavage between the Negro and the rest of society?

It is only because we seldom pay any attention to the indirect, unintended, and unwanted consequences of government actions that we fail to see that they are often worse than the diseases that the actions are supposed to cure. The usual assumption seems to be that a desirable consequence in hand offsets two undesirable ones in the bush. This may be reasonable. But what if the bush is full of extremely undesirable consequences?

II

Although government cannot cure the serious ills of the city, it might make the patient more comfortable and enable it to lead a somewhat more useful life despite its ills. I will list what I think are the more important things that it might do to improve the situation. In general, these are not the things that one would most like to have done (those being in most cases beyond the bounds of possibility for the reasons indicated), but they are all ones that it is possible in principle for government to do and that would make a more than trivial contribution to the improvement of the situation. Some of the items on the list may strike the reader as highly implausible, but this is not the place to try to justify them.

The list is as follows:

1. Use fiscal policy to keep unemployment below 3 per cent even though this would entail undesirable inflation. (The possibility of this for more than a few years was denied by Milton Friedman in his Presidential Address to the American Economics Association in 1967. Other leading economists assert it, however, and the question must be considered unsettled.)

2. Eliminate impediments to the free working of the labor market, particularly that for low-skilled labor. This implies removing legal and other barriers to the employment of the young, the unschooled, women, and Negroes. It implies repeal of minimum wage laws and of laws that enable unions to exercise monopolistic powers. It also implies improving the information available to workers about job opportunities in other places.

3. If the second recommendation is not carried into effect, suspend immigration of the unskilled. Also, by bringing about expansion of the rural southern and Puerto Rican economies and by setting welfare allowances so as to favor rural and small-town residence, discourage migration of unskilled Americans to the large cities.

4. Pay the poor to send infants and small children to nursery and preschools. Create a competitive school system by giving vouchers for use in any private (including parochial) school to parents of children who do not go to public school. Lower the compulsory attendance age to twelve and the normal school-leaving age to fourteen (grade twelve). Give boys and girls who leave school the choice between taking a job and going into a youth corps. Make it possible for all who qualify to get higher education subject to later repayment.

5. Define poverty in terms of "hardship" (as opposed to "inconvenience" or "relative deprivation") and bring all incomes up to this nearly fixed level. With respect to those competent to manage their own affairs (that is, all but the insane, the severely retarded, the senile, and unprotected children), make the income transfer by means of a negative income tax, leaving the recipients free to spend their money as they please. Public housing, public hospital care, "rehabilitation," and other welfare services in kind rather than in cash should go only to those requiring institutional or semi-institutional care.

6. Allow police officers wider latitude to deal out "curbstone justice" to petty offenders, especially juveniles. Repeal laws against gambling and usury. Change insurance and police practices (for example, free recovery of stolen cars) so that potential victims of crime will not be deprived of incentive to take precautions to prevent loss.

7. Eliminate impediments to the free working of the housing market. Establish building codes, uniform for the whole of a metropolitan area, that will permit the widest latitude for innovation and economizing consistent with safety. Assure that some part of every suburb is zoned in a manner that does not prevent low-income occupancy.

8. Prohibit "live" television coverage of riots.

9. Avoid rhetoric tending to create demands and expectations that cannot

possibly be fulfilled or to excite alarm about nonexistent crises. Above all, stop attributing more importance to racial factors, including discrimination, than the facts warrant. Explain nothing on racial grounds that can be explained as well or better on income or class grounds.

I trust I do not need to say again that this is not a list of "consummations devoutly to be wished." Rather it is one of things that government could do and the doing of which would contribute more than trivially to the amelioration of the serious problems of the city. But even if all of these things were done, the situation would not be fundamentally changed; the improvements would be ones of degree rather than of kind.

III

Although the measures listed are possible, they are not politically feasible. It is safe to say that none of them will be tried in the near future. A politician with a heterogeneous constituency probably could not support any of them vigorously. Indeed, with respect to most of the items on the list, the politically feasible thing is the exact opposite of what has been recommended: for example, to raise the minimum wage, to raise the normal school-leaving age, to encourage immigration of the unskilled, to define poverty as relative deprivation rather than as hardship, to emphasize racial factors while denying the existence of class ones, and so on.

Why this perversity in the choice of policies? Before offering an answer to this question, I should acknowledge that its premises are questionable. Perhaps the recommendations made above are unsound; perhaps, too, the things that I said were beyond the bounds of possibility are not beyond them. Even if the recommendations are sound, the system may not be perverse in rejecting them for their opposites. It may be that "problems" arise only in those instances—which may be a very small proportion of the whole—where the system fails to select a right policy and by so doing fails to prevent a problem from arising. To explain an occasional visible failure on the grounds that the system is perverse is like explaining the presence of a few men in death row on grounds that the threat of capital punishment is not a deterrent. For all we know tens of thousands of men may *not* be in death row precisely because they *were* deterred. Space does not permit me to deal with these objections. All I can do is say that I am aware of them.

Perhaps the most palpable reason for the political infeasibility of most of the items on the list is that they would be instantly squashed by some interest group (or groups) if they were ever put forward. The founding fathers went to great pains to distribute power so widely that "factions" would check one another and prevent the growth of tyranny. This arrangement has the defects of its virtues, of course; one of the defects is that a very small group can often veto a measure that would be of great benefit to a large public. It is laughable, for example, to talk about eliminating impediments to the free working of the labor market so long as labor unions are politically powerful. New York City cannot employ unskilled laborers to repair the slum housing that they live in because to do so it would first have to get them into the building trades unions and then pay them union wages.

There are well-armed and strategically placed "veto groups" (as David Riesman calls them in *The Lonely Crowd*) for almost every item on the list. The organized teachers would veto a proposal to lower the school-leaving age. The organized social workers would veto the substitution of a negative income tax for the traditional arrangements. Civil rights organizations would veto giving policemen more latitude to deal out "curbstone justice." The television industry would veto the prohibition of "live" TV coverage of riots. And so on.

Although interest groups most often exercise their power by vetoing measures that might be injurious to them, they sometimes initiate ones that they think will benefit them. Why, it may be asked, do not the putative beneficiaries of the measures on the list above organize and apply pressure counter to that of the veto groups? The answer (as Mancur Olson has explained in *The Logic of Collective Action*) is that in most instances the benefits are in the nature of what economists call "public goods"—that is, they are such that if anyone benefits, all must benefit. This being the case, no individual has any incentive to support an organization to bring them into existence. TV stations find it to their advantage to maintain an organization that can influence the F.C.C. not to prohibit "live" coverage of riots, but the ordinary citizen, even if he were very much in favor of prohibiting it, would not pay much of anything to have his view urged upon the F.C.C. because he would be sure that his small contribution would not affect the outcome. In a certain sense, therefore, it would be irrational for him to contribute, since he would have the same chance of getting the benefit (prohibition of "live" coverage) if he kept his money in his pocket. For most of the items on the list, the logic of collective action is of this sort.

In the last analysis, however, what makes the items on the list politically infeasible is that promising them would not help anyone to get elected. To some extent this is because public opinion does not favor them. (It is not for this reason entirely, however. As Anthony Downs has explained, candidates and parties offer combinations of measures—"budgets"—that confer on voters large benefits in terms of their primary interests and, at worst, small costs in terms of their secondary and tertiary interests. Thus, in principle, a winning coalition may be built around a "budget" no single item of which is favored by more than a few voters.)

It is pertinent to inquire, therefore, why *public opinion* is perverse. An answer sometimes given is that in matters such as these it is generally dominated by the opinion of the well educated and well off. These people (so the argument runs) are indifferent or downright hostile to the interest of the less well off and the poor. In short, the "masses" are against the recommended measures because they have been misled by an elite that is looking after its own interests.

This explanation does not fit the facts. The perversity of policy does not benefit the well off; on the contrary, it injures them. The well off are not benefited by the minimum wage or by other laws and practices that price low-value labor out of the market and onto the welfare rolls. They are not benefited by laws that keep hundreds of thousands of children who cannot or will not learn anything in schools that they (the well off) must support. They are not benefited by an official rhetoric tending to persuade everyone that the society is fundamentally unjust.

I want to argue that public opinion (which I agree is decisively influenced in many matters by the opinion of the relatively well off) tends to be altruistic and that it is precisely because of its altruism that it opposes the recommendations on the list and favors instead ones that are the reverse of those recommended as well as ones that are beyond the bounds of possibility.

The American cultural ideal, which is most fully exemplified in the upper-middle and upper classes (and within those classes in people of dissenting—Protestant and Jewish—traditions), is oriented toward the future and toward progress. It sees the individual as perfectible by his own effort and society as perfectible by collective effort. Accordingly, it feels a strong obligation to engage in efforts at improvement of self and community. Americans tend to believe that all problems can be solved if only one tries hard enough, and they acknowledge a responsibility to improve not only themselves, but everything else—community, society, the whole world. Ever since the days of Cotton Mather, whose *Bonifacius* was a "how to do it" book on the doing of good, service has been our motto. I do not mean to say that our practice has corresponded to our principles. The principles, however, have always been influential and often decisive. For present purposes they can be summarized in two very simple rules: first, DON'T JUST SIT THERE. DO SOMETHING; and, second, DO GOOD.

It is the application of these two rules that produces most of the perversity that I claim characterizes our choice of policies. Believing that any problem can be solved if only we try hard enough, we do not hesitate to attempt what we do not have the least idea how to do and what may even be impossible in principle. Not recognizing any bounds to what is possible, we are not reconciled to, indeed we do not even perceive, the necessity for choosing among courses of action all of which are unsatisfactory, but some of which are less unsatisfactory than others. That some children simply cannot or will not learn anything in school and that we do not know how to change this are facts that the American mind will not entertain. Our cultural ideal demands that we give everyone a good education whether or not he wants it and whether or not he is capable of receiving it. This ideal also tells us that if at first we don't succeed, we must try, try again. To suggest lowering the normal school-leaving age is, in terms of this secular religion, out-and-out heresy.

The recommendations listed above are unacceptable—indeed, downright repellent—to public opinion because what they call for does not appear to be morally improving either to the doer or to the object of his doing. It does not appear to be improving to the child to send him to work rather than to school, especially as that is what it is to one's interest as a taxpayer to do. It does not appear to be improving to the delinquent to let the policeman "slap him around a little," especially as that accords with one's feelings of hostility toward the juvenile. It does not appear to be improving to the slum dweller to tell him that if his income is adequate and if he prefers to spend it for other things than housing, that is his affair, especially as that is in one's "selfish" interest. From the standpoint of the cultural ideal, the doing of good is not so much for the sake of those to whom the good is done as it is for that of the doers, whose moral faculties are activated and invigorated by the doing of it, and also for that of the community, the shared values of which are ritually asserted and vindicated by the doing of it. For this reason good done otherwise than by intention, especially good done in the pursuance of motives that are selfish or even "non-tuistic," is not really "good" at all. For this reason, too, actions taken from good motives count as good even when, in fact, they do harm. By far the most effective way of helping the poor is to maintain high levels of employment. This, however, is not a method that affords upper-middle- and upper-class people the chance to flex their moral muscles or the community the chance to dramatize its commitment to the values that hold it together. The way to do these things is by a War on Poverty. Even if the War should turn out to have precious little effect on the incomes of the poor—indeed, even if it should *lower* their incomes—the undertaking would be justified as a sort of secular religious revival that affords the altruistic classes opportunities to bear witness to the cultural ideal and, by so doing, to strengthen society's adherence to it. One recalls the wisecrack about the attitude of the English Puritans toward bear-baiting: that they opposed the sport not for the suffering it caused the bear, but for the pleasure that it gave the spectators. Perhaps it is not farfetched to say that the present-day outlook is similar: The reformer wants to reform the city not so much to make the poor better off materially as to make himself and the society as a whole better off morally.

There is something to be said for this attitude. The old Puritans were certainly right in thinking it worse that people should enjoy the sufferings of animals than that animals should suffer. And the reformers are certainly right in thinking it more important that society display a concern for what is right and just than that the material level of living of the poor (which is already well above the level of physical hardship) be raised somewhat higher. There are problems here however. One is to keep the impulse for doing good from gushing incontinently into mass extravaganzas (Domestic Marshall Plans, for example) in which billions are pledged for no one knows what or how; surely if it is to be morally significant, good must be done from motives that are not contrived for the individual by people with big organizations to maintain and foisted upon him by the mass media. Another is to find ways of doing good that are relatively harmless—that do not unduly injure those to whom the good is done (as, for example, children who cannot or will not learn are injured by long confinement in a school), that are not unfair to third parties (taxpayers), and that do not tend to destroy the consensual basis of the society (as headline-catching official declarations about "white racism" may).

Looking toward the future, it is impossible not to be apprehensive. The frightening fact is that vast numbers of people are being rapidly assimilated to the ethos of the altruistic classes and are coming to have incomes—time as well as money—that permit them to indulge their taste for "serving" and "doing good." Television, even more than the newspapers, tends to turn the discussion of public policy questions into a branch of the mass entertainment industry. "Doing good" is becoming—has already become—a growth industry, like other forms of mass entertainment. This is the way it is in the affluent society. How will it be in the super-affluent one? How preoccupied can a society be with reform without thereby loosening the bonds that hold it together? If there is an urban crisis, perhaps this is its real basis.

Discussion Starters

1. Evaluate Banfield's contention that it is "the presence of a large lower class, not of Negroes as such, that is the real source of the trouble" in American cities.

2. Why did Banfield believe the problems of the cities are not susceptible to solution by the government?

3. Assess the validity of the nine programs Banfield proposed to improve the conditions in the cities.

4. Evaluate Banfield's argument that public opinion is perverse, and that "serving" and "doing good" are hypocritical characteristics of affluent America.

Related Documents

I. Housing and the Urban Crisis

GEORGE ROMNEY

George Romney was appointed by President Nixon as Secretary of Housing and Urban Development in 1969. As head of HUD, Romney was responsible for creating and carrying out the federal housing programs of the Nixon administration. Although these programs were slow in achieving any real success in solving the problems of the cities, in 1969 Secretary Romney was enthusiastic and optimistic about his new position and responsibilities.

From a copyrighted interview in the *U.S. News & World Report,* July 28, 1969, pp. 48–51.

How do Romney's views compare with Banfield's interpretation of the problems of the cities?

JULY 28, 1969

Q. Mr. Secretary, how do you see prospects for solving the problems of America's big cities?

A. In the short range, we are facing some very tough difficulties—inflation and the war in Vietnam—and the picture is not particularly favorable.

From a long-range standpoint, I am more optimistic. I know President Nixon is determined to curb inflation, and I believe that he will find a way to settle the Vietnamese conflict—which, after all, has a very substantial bearing on the prospects of solving all of our other problems. Then we can give priority to the problems of cities, which the President has placed third only to the war in Vietnam and inflation.

Q. How do you plan to approach the cities' problems?

A. We are organizing a program beyond anything yet tried in the housing field. We are working to secure the cooperation of the building trades, the mayors, the Governors, the construction industry itself in a volume approach to housing production and the use of modern management and modern technology in the housing field.

This will not be at the expense of our established programs. We're going to push them as hard as we can. But from the long-range standpoint, we must take the housing industry out of the hand-built phase and into the volume-production phase if we are going to restore health to our cities.

There is no more obsolete part of the U.S. economy, in terms of methods used, than housing. This is not going to be changed in a year. It may take a couple of years, but I expect a real breakthrough in this important aspect of urban decay.

Q. Why do you see housing as the central problem of the cities?

A. I've talked with a number of people since I became Secretary of Housing and Urban Development—individuals such as Whitney Young, of the Urban League, and mayors across the country. I find that most of them, if they had to specify a No. 1 priority in dealing with the cities, would specify housing.

This is because housing has a social as well as an economic impact. Certainly from an economic standpoint, it should be our No. 1 priority, and I think it is the catalyst that can get other things moving, too.

Q. Just how serious is the housing situation?

A. Very serious. The present supply of housing is being allowed to deteriorate at a rate faster than we can build new houses as replacements. As a matter of fact, the housing shortage at present is the biggest in our history, not only because of deterioration but also because of the population explosion since World War II.

Congress has indicated the shortage to be in the area of 26 million units between now and 1978. That is the number of new or rehabilitated homes that it was estimated we would need to take care of people between now and 1978 and to replace substandard units.

I think the shortage is greater than that now because over the last five years we have fallen at least a million units behind in meeting the need for increased housing.

Q. Housing isn't the only symptom of urban decay, is it?

A. Oh, no—it is just one aspect. Other physical facilities are deteriorating, too. We have obsolete schools, obsolete recreational facilities, a lack of adequate transportation and a mounting problem of pollution.

Now, these are all elements of both progress and decay. After all, a society like ours increases its waste as it increases its production and consumption. The magnitude of our pollution is, to an extent, a measure of the affluence of our society.

But the decay is there, and not only in the environment: You have to get into the human aspect of it, too—the impact of the decay on family life, on crime and violence and on the whole society.

Q. Have cities themselves contributed to their problems?

A. Certainly in the tax aspect this is true. Confronted with the drain of resources from the core city, the response of municipalities has been to increase the property tax substantially for remaining homeowners and business firms. Furthermore, municipalities across the country have tended to assess land at a lower rate than buildings.

Together, these policies have discouraged property owners from maintaining or improving their homes: If you modernize a unit, the value goes up —and so do your taxes.

Q. Would it be practical for the Government to help cities relieve their congestion by encouraging a flow of people to outlying communities or even to "new towns"?

A. Certainly, the "new towns" are going to get a great deal of attention from this Administration. My Department has the responsibility for carrying out much of the legislation that Congress has passed so far to encourage new community development, but I think more has to be done.

"New towns" usually run into severe problems financially while getting started. But, at present, we have only the authority to underwrite their financing up to a limit of 50 million dollars for each town. We cannot ease their problem of making heavy payments on the loans we have guaranteed.

Another problem to work out is how we can help provide "new towns" with the economic payrolls they need. We've been studying the situation abroad, and in Britain we find that because of the highly centralized approach and economic controls prevailing there, they can tell firms who want to build a new plant: "You can build here, here or here." It turns out usually that "here, here or here" is where a new community is wanted.

Q. Is a "new town" the best solution to congestion in the cities?

A. It is only one of several: You can get people to move out to an existing community. Or you can even get them into a developing area within the urban center, if you can find sufficient land.

Regardless of which approach is used, I think it is time we recognized that we do not really promote our welfare or that of our country by creating isolated enclaves composed of people of the same economic and social and racial backgrounds.

Most older Americans were raised in communities where they mixed with people of all economic and social levels, and those of us who happened to be poor, as I was, knew the motivation that comes from mixing with kids of well-off people.

With business and industry having moved out of the core city to a considerable extent, it is just sound from an economic or social or moral standpoint to make it possible for people who are needed in the factories and businesses of suburbs and outlying towns to be able to live within a reasonable distance of their jobs.

Consequently, I think it is going to take both "new towns" and a new viewpoint to relieve the basic problems afflicting cities.

II. *Patterns of Civil Disorders*

NATIONAL ADVISORY COMMISSION ON CIVIL DISORDERS

In his article on urban problems Edward Banfield noted the existence of the ghettos and the disaffected people who live there. These large concentrations of people of low skill, income, and status could present a threat to law and order and possibly to the continuance of American democracy. For Banfield this was primarily a problem of poor people seeking upward mobility, while most experts in urban affairs believed the problems of the ghettos were racial, rather than class, in character.

The racial interpretation of urban problems points to a trend that began in the 1930s, when the movement of southern blacks from rural areas to northern cities quickened. This population shift led to ever-increasing concentrations of blacks in metropolitan areas, but in segregated neighborhoods. The black urban population continued to grow so that by 1966 about 70 percent of all black people in America lived in urban areas. As they moved into the central cities the whites began to move to the suburbs, hence central cities have become increasingly black. This fact, coupled with the high rate of black unemployment, has served to concentrate most of the visible poverty in America in the black ghettos of the cities. This poverty has led to an increase in crime and mass violence. In 1965 the black ghetto of Watts in Los Angeles exploded in several days of burning, looting, and bloodshed. In 1966 there were more disturbances, the most

National Advisory Commission on Civil Disorders, *Report* (Washington, D.C.: Government Printing Office, 1968), pp. 63–65.

serious in Chicago. But in the spring and summer of 1967, it seemed as if riots were becoming a way of life for the people of the cities. Particularly alarming were the riots in Newark and Detroit. Together they resulted in the deaths of 66 persons and over $30 million in property losses. One consequence of the riots was the establishment of the National Advisory Commission on Civil Disorders. The commission was charged by President Johnson with the task of answering three questions about what had taken place: What had happened? Why had it happened? What could be done to prevent similar occurrences in the future?

How do the findings of the commission and their general outlook on why riots took place compare with Banfield's assertion that the problems of the disaffected people in the cities are basically problems of rising expectations of a class, not the result of racial prejudice?

We have categorized the information now available about the 1967 disorders as follows.

• The pattern of violence over the nation: severity, location, timing, and numbers of people involved;

• The riot process in a sample of 24 disorders we have surveyed: prior events, the development of violence, the various control efforts on the part of officials and the community, and the relationship between violence and control efforts;

• The riot participants: a comparison of rioters with those who sought to limit the disorder and those who remained uninvolved;

• The setting in which the disorders occurred: social and economic conditions, local governmental structure, the scale of federal programs, and the grievance reservoir in the Negro community;

• The aftermath of disorder: the ways in which communities responded after order was restored in the streets.

Based upon information derived from our surveys, we offer the following generalizations:

1. No civil disorder was "typical" in all respects. Viewed in a national framework, the disorders of 1967 varied greatly in terms of violence and damage: while a relatively small number were major under our criteria and a somewhat larger number were serious, most of the disorders would have received little or no national attention as "riots" had the nation not been sensitized by the more serious outbreaks.

2. While the civil disorders of 1967 were racial in character, they were not *inter*racial. The 1967 disorders, as well as earlier disorders of the recent period, involved action within Negro neighborhoods against symbols of white American society—authority and property—rather than against white persons.

3. Despite extremist rhetoric, there was no attempt to subvert the social order of the United States. Instead, most of those who attacked white authority and property seemed to be demanding fuller participation in the social order

and the material benefits enjoyed by the vast majority of American citizens.

4. Disorder did not typically erupt without preexisting causes, as a result of a single "triggering" or "precipitating" incident. Instead, it developed out of an increasingly disturbed social atmosphere, in which typically a series of tension-heightening incidents over a period of weeks or months became linked in the minds of many in the Negro community with a shared reservoir of underlying grievances.

5. There was, typically, a complex relationship between the series of incidents and the underlying grievances. For example, grievances about allegedly abusive police practices, unemployment and underemployment, housing and other conditions in the ghetto, were often aggravated in the minds of many Negroes by incidents involving the police, or the inaction of municipal authorities on Negro complaints about police action, unemployment, inadequate housing or other conditions. When grievance-related incidents recurred and rising tensions were not satisfactorily resolved, a cumulative process took place in which prior incidents were readily recalled and grievances reinforced. At some point, in the mounting tension, a further incident—in itself often routine or even trivial—became the breaking point, and tension spilled over into violence.

6. Many grievances in the Negro community result from the discrimination, prejudice and powerlessness which Negroes often experience. They also result from the severely disadvantaged social and economic conditions of many Negroes as compared with those of whites in the same city and, more particularly, in the predominantly white suburbs.

7. Characteristically, the typical rioter was not a hoodlum, habitual criminal, or riffraff; nor was he a recent migrant, a member of an uneducated underclass, or a person lacking broad social and political concerns. Instead, he was a teen-ager or young adult, a lifelong resident of the city in which he rioted, a high-school drop-out—but somewhat better educated than his Negro neighbor—and almost invariably underemployed or employed in a menial job. He was proud of his race, extremely hostile to both whites and middle-class Negroes and, though informed about politics, highly distrustful of the political system and of political leaders.

8. Numerous Negro counter-rioters walked the streets urging rioters to "cool it." The typical counter-rioter resembled in many respects the majority of Negroes, who neither rioted nor took action against the rioters, that is, the non-involved. But certain differences are crucial: the counter-rioter was better educated and had higher income than either the rioter or the noninvolved.

9. Negotiations between Negroes and white officials occurred during virtually all the disorders surveyed. The negotiations often involved young, militant Negroes as well as older, established leaders. Despite a setting of chaos and disorder, negotiations in many cases involved discussion of underlying grievances as well as the handling of the disorder by control authorities.

10. The chain we have identified—discrimination, prejudice, disadvantaged conditions, intense and pervasive grievances, a series of tension-height-

ening incidents, all culminating in the eruption of disorder at the hands of youthful, politically-aware activists—must be understood as describing the central trend in the disorders, not as an explanation of all aspects of the riots or of all rioters. Some rioters, for example, may have shared neither the conditions nor the grievances of their Negro neighbors; some may have coolly and deliberately exploited the chaos created by others; some may have been drawn into the melee merely because they identified with, or wished to emulate, others. Nor do we intend to suggest that the majority of the rioters, who shared the adverse conditions and grievances, necessarily articulated in their own minds the connection between that background and their actions.

11. The background of disorder in the riot cities was typically characterized by severely disadvantaged conditions for Negroes, especially as compared with those for whites; a local government often unresponsive to these conditions; federal programs which had not yet reached a significantly large proportion of those in need; and the resulting reservoir of pervasive and deep grievance and frustration in the ghetto.

12. In the immediate aftermath of disorder, the status quo of daily life before the disorder generally was quickly restored. Yet, despite some notable public and private efforts, little basic change took place in the conditions underlying the disorder. In some cases, the result was increased distrust between blacks and whites, diminished interracial communication, and growth of Negro and white extremist groups.

III. Benign Neglect

DANIEL P. MOYNIHAN

Daniel Moynihan, one of the leading experts in urban affairs, was appointed by President Nixon as Assistant to the President on Urban Affairs in 1969 and later that same year as Counsellor to the President, a post with cabinet rank. He helped prepare the bills the Administration sent to Congress on urban mass transit, the hunger program, education, and welfare reform. In January 1971 he resigned from his governmental duties to return to teaching and writing at Harvard University.

One year earlier Moynihan wrote a secret memorandum to the President on the Administration's problems with the black population. When the memo was leaked to the press it was condemned by both the black community and the white liberals. How does Moynihan's concern for race relations in the United States and his suggestion that "benign neglect" would ease the tensions in the cities compare with Banfield's interpretation of what are the real problems of the cities?

Current, May 1970, pp. 28–29.

JANUARY 16, 1970

In quantitative terms, which are reliable, the American Negro is making extraordinary progress. In political terms, somewhat less reliable, this would also appear to be true. In each case, however, there would seem to be counter-currents that pose a serious threat to the welfare of the blacks and the stability of the society, white and black. . . .

As you have candidly acknowledged, the relation of the Administration to the black population is a problem. I think it ought also to be acknowledged that we are a long way from solving it. During the past year, intense efforts have been made by the Administration to develop programs that will be of help to the blacks. I dare say, as much or more time and attention goes into this effort in this Administration than any in history. But little has come of it. There has been a great deal of political ineptness in some departments, and you have been the loser.

I don't know what you can do about this. Perhaps nothing. But I do have four suggestions.

First: Sometime early in the year, I would gather the Administration officials who are most involved with these matters and talk out the subject a bit. There really is a need for a more coherent Administration approach to a number of issues. (Which I can list for you, if you like.)

Second: The time may have come when the issue of race could benefit from a period of "benign neglect." The subject has been too much talked about. The forum has been too much taken over to hysterics, paranoids, and boodlers on all sides. We may need a period in which Negro progress continues and racial rhetoric fades. The Administration can help bring this about by paying close attention to such progress—as we are doing—while seeking to avoid situations in which extremists of either race are given opportunities for martyrdom, heroics, histrionics or whatever. Greater attention to Indians, Mexican-Americans and Puerto Ricans would be useful. A tendency to ignore provocations from groups such as the Black Panthers might also be useful. . . .

Third: We really ought to be getting on with research on crime. We just don't know enough. It is a year now since the Administration came to office committed to doing something about crime in the streets. But frankly, in that year I don't see that we have advanced either our understanding of the problem, or that of the public at large. . . .

Fourth: There is a silent black majority as well as a white one. It is mostly working class, as against lower middle class. It is politically moderate (on issues other than racial equality) and shares most of the concerns of its white counterpart. This group has been generally ignored by the Government and the media. The more recognition we can give to it, the better off we shall all be.

IV. *America's Priorities Are Upside Down*

WILLIAM PROXMIRE

Senator William Proxmire of Wisconsin has concerned himself with the quality of American life since he was first elected to the Senate in 1957. In the following speech on the Senate floor he addressed himself to the use of federal funds to combat the problems of the cities. In what ways does Proxmire's speech seem to invalidate Banfield's contention that the federal government cannot solve the "urban crisis"?

APRIL 26, 1971

Mr. PROXMIRE. Mr. President, we are spending too much on the wrong things. America's priorities are upside down. In terms of its programs and policies, the Federal Government is making some very bad choices.

While we face the imminent collapse of our cities, the Pentagon is increasing the military budget.

While unemployment has reached the 6-percent level and while 5 million Americans who want to work are out of a job, the administration has frozen $12.7 billion of funds Congress has appropriated.

At the same time that our cities and States are starving for money to educate our children, provide health services for the sick, and care for the indigent, the administration is proposing to spend vast sums for space shuttles, the B–1 bomber, and foreign aid.

The Crisis of the Cities

That the country is facing a vast emergency was made clear again only this week. The mayor of New York City warned that unless funds were restored to the city's budget, and unless the city's taxing power increased, he would have to eliminate some 90,000 city jobs and add those 90,000 to the unemployed.

The magnitude of the crisis and the enormity of the country's misplaced priorities are clear from a few facts.

If worse comes to worst, New York City will have to close eight municipal hospitals. It will have to stop all its remedial and other special education. No freshmen will be admitted at City University for next year. Some 4,200 sanitation workers will lose their jobs; 19,700 people now in the education system will be fired or not replaced through attrition. Over 35,000 jobs in health, hospital, and welfare services will end. New York City is facing the moment when it will be unable to provide fundamental and essential public services.

Meanwhile, in the Federal budget, the administration proposes to increase our strategic weapons beyond any reasonable need, to continue the duplication

Congressional Record, April 26, 1971, pp. S5557–59.

in developing close support aircraft, to fund duplicate antisubmarine weapons with an ultimate cost of over $23 billion, and to build new tanks, ships, planes, and missiles which—if the past is any guide to the future—will cost far more than estimated, will be delivered late, and will fail to perform according to specifications.

Newark's Crisis

New York City is not alone in its crisis. Recently the mayor of Newark testified before the Joint Economic Committee on the crisis in his city.

In Newark, manufacturing industry has declined by 25 percent in the last 20 years.

Newark has the highest crime rate in the Nation.

The per capita incidence of venereal disease and infant mortality is the highest in the United States.

The unemployment rate among young people from 16 to 22 at the beginning of 1971 was 34 percent.

Thirty percent of Newark's population in January 1971 received public assistance—30 percent on welfare.

Meantime, the city is broke. The anticipated deficit of $70 million for 1971 represents 43 percent of the operating budget.

Similar situations exist throughout the major cities of the country. These are not isolated incidents.

Detroit in Trouble

This year, Detroit faces a deficit of $43 million or 11 percent of its revenues.

Unemployment in that city for 1970 averaged 11.7 percent.

Of the pitifully small number—only 828—single-family homes built in that city during the entire year of 1970, almost all of them were financed through a Federal interest rate subsidy—section 235—or were factory built; that is, they were mobile homes. Only 33 new single-family homes built in the entire city of Detroit during 1970 were valued in excess of $25,000.

From July 1969 to October 1970, there was a 42-percent increase in Detroit's welfare caseload and a 67-percent increase in welfare payments.

According to Mayor Tate, "Philadelphia will lock up 26 playgrounds this summer because we do not have the funds for the people to run them."

These are just a few examples of the magnitude of the problem of the cities.

These problems have been accentuated by the economic downturn. A major part of the gap between income and expenses is the result of the present economic condition of high unemployment and continued inflation. Mayor Lindsay testified before the Joint Economic Committee last January 22 that—

> The recession will deny us about $150 million in revenue, while inflation is driving our costs $100 million higher.

Thus the combination of inflation and recession will cost New York City one quarter of a billion dollars this year.

Unfortunately, at the national level, these terrible fiscal problems have been met by actions which are counterproductive.

While the President steadfastly refuses to initiate a general incomes policy or wage-price guidelines, the problems of inflation and unemployment are greeted by glowing statements and optimistic interpretations of the facts.

Instead of helping to meet the problem of the cities through stronger Federal fiscal policies, the administration has frozen $12.7 billion in appropriated funds. This includes $942 million in funds for public housing, $583 million for model cities, and $200 million in water and sewer grants.

City Funds Frozen—Defense Funds Boosted

Meantime, while the cities are denied $1.7 billion in desperately needed funds, the administration has increased military spending. At the beginning of fiscal year 1971, the President estimated in his budget that military spending for the Department of Defense would amount to $71.2 billion. But now that estimate has been revised upward. According to the fiscal year 1972 budget, military spending for 1971 will not be $71.2 billion, but will be $73.4 billion—or an increase of $2.2 billion.

Thus, while the executive froze $1.7 billion in desperately needed money for the cities, it boosted spending for the Pentagon by $2.2 billion. This is called reordering priorities. They reordered priorities by reordering them from the domestic economy to the military.

Other funds have been frozen as well. They include money for the economic opportunity program, salaries and expenses for the Peace Corps, REA loans, family housing, regional medical programs, higher education, facilities and equipment for the FAA, highway beautification, and farm credit, to name only a few.

Meantime, the administration is pressing for funds to begin a $9 billion space shuttle program which has no other function than as the precursor to a $100 billion manned flight to Mars. In any case, the tangible benefits of the space shuttle are almost impossible to define.

How to Meet Needs with Limited Resources

America's needs are very great. But America's resources are not unlimited. The amounts which the Federal Government can and should spend in any one year must be limited to sums which do not impose a confiscatory tax burden on the American people or promote additional inflation by continuous deficits.

How then can America's legitimate needs be met? How can we provide desperately needed funds for America's Newarks and Detroits and Milwaukees? How can we finance a jobs program to provide public service employment? Where are we to get the means to institute a broadly based health program which would lift our country to first place in the quality and quantity of medical care? Where are the funds to come from to relieve the cities and

States of the most onerous burden they must now carry, namely, the burden of welfare which would cost the Federal Government at least an additional $7 billion a year if it were to carry that burden alone?

First, Reorder Priorities

There are two fundamental means by which these purposes can be achieved. The first is through a reordering of American priorities. We must cut unneeded programs and low priority programs and transfer those resources to programs the American people need. We must cut military spending and military waste. We should deny the money for the space shuttle. We should cut back on subsidies which go to the affluent and those who need them least of all. We should chop out inefficient public works projects and programs where the return is low or where private enterprise can function better.

The funds thus saved can then be used in part to revive the cities, provide desperately needed public services, build houses, educate children, prevent disease, cure the sick, and provide for the indigent and disabled. Any adverse effects from retrenchment in space or defense spending could be more than offset by the expansionary effects of funds spent to meet America's fundamental needs.

Second, Get the Economy Moving Again

The second means of providing funds for needed services is to get the economy moving again. If unemployment were reduced to 4 percent from the present 6 percent, the economy would be producing $60 billion a year more than it now produces. Federal tax receipts would grow by about $12 billion and State and local revenues by about $3 billion with no change in existing tax rates. Millions of men and women who are now jobless or who work only part time would become taxpayers rather than the recipients of unemployment compensation or welfare payments. Business would move from red ink to black ink, profits would rise, and industry would once again pay taxes instead of absorbing losses.

There are the ways to get America moving again.

We need expansion not retrenchment.

We need schools, houses, and hospitals, not new B-1 bombers, space shuttles, and SST's.

We need to spend money for cities and cut back on subsidies and frills.

We need deeds, not words; and action in the place of rhetoric.

Were we to cut military spending, space waste, and unnecessary programs, a portion of the cuts should be channeled into job producing, economically stimulating programs, especially housing.

A Low-Income Tax Cut

A portion should also go to the hard-pressed taxpayer through cuts in his taxes. Two immediate steps should be taken. First, the increase in social security taxes now scheduled for January 1, 1972, should not be made retroactive to January 1, 1971, as the administration requests.

Second, the increases in deductions for dependents in the personal income tax now scheduled for 1972 and 1973 should be moved up into 1971.

These two actions would produce tax cuts this year of $7 billion below what taxes would otherwise be. As the cuts would go in large part to low and moderate income families, the funds would be spent. This would have a multiplier effect which would not only stimulate the economy but should increase the gross national product by about $20 billion over what it would otherwise be. That in turn would reduce unemployment, increase the revenues collected by all levels of government, help the cities and get the economy off dead center.

Conclusion

It is time to reorder priorities, put Americans back to work, and to put first things first.

It is time to choose schools over military waste, hospitals instead of space shuttles, and full employment instead of frozen funds.

We must put the needs of people on earth ahead of funds for the space shuttle.

Housing the poor must have a higher priority than billions for an excessive number of the weapons of destruction.

Cleaning the air is more important than boondoggling for the military.

Providing public transportation to get Americans to work must have a higher priority than billions for Lockheed bailouts.

Such a program is the way to provide real national security. That can only be gained by a balance between our military and our domestic needs, and by enhancing the strength of our people and the strength of our economy.

It is time to put our money where the need is.

V. A Hard Look at Our Environment

ROGERS C. B. MORTON

In the following speech at the University of Southern California, President Nixon's Secretary of the Interior Rogers Morton dealt with the complexity of the problem of environmental pollution. How does Morton's approach to pollution compare with Banfield's contention that government cannot correct any of the serious problems associated with urban growth?

In today's modern dialogue and rhetoric, the words we often hear are "environment" and "ecology." We hear discussion of the "environmental impact" of various activities. We hear the word "ecology" used in many different ways, and I think both of these words have many different meanings in the minds of different people.

Congressional Record, May 20, 1971, pp. H4162–63.

Let's ask ourselves "what is the environment?"

In short, it is everything—everything that was here before man—plus all the changes man has wrought, both directly and indirectly. In addition, and not to be overlooked, it must include man himself.

We hear speeches about the "enhancement of environment," about our desire to make it better. And again, we might ask ourselves "what are man's goals for the environment?"

I think it's fair to say that each individual has his own attitude and his own concept of environmental quality. But basically and constructively we are searching for change, for action that terminates the destruction of values of this earth necessary to support our life systems and our cultural aspirations.

Specifically, we are searching for a way to eliminate the destructive side effects of man's activities. For example:

1. The elimination of pollution of water and air from the consumption of energy and chemical reaction;

2. The elimination of the aesthetically offensive, such as litter, junk and noise.

We are searching, but perhaps less vigorously, for the elimination of waste, for a way to stretch the supply of our finite resources on which our economic and life systems depend.

We feel that there should be a larger guaranteed share for nature in the scheme of things on the planet's crust. We express this in a desire for more protected wilderness, for more forests, for more rivers, for more open spaces, for more habitat for wildlife and marine life.

But Americans are also looking for ease and comfort—for more automobiles, airplanes, air conditioners, central heat and central power, daily newspapers, paper plates and plastic spoons. We are looking for more suburban peace, for security in the home and on the street.

Our goals for a healthier environment then, are cluttered with the hopes and aspirations, the fears and the very struggle for existence of every one of us. We are caught between our personal needs and desires and the necessity of a healthy environment. Our world will not survive unless we start to sacrifice some of our personal desires.

The need today is for a realistic national commitment for a healthier environment—a national commitment fostered through the concern of millions of Americans. . . .

I don't believe as a people we have a burning desire to protect the aesthetic values of our environment. Short term economic desire has constantly overridden our patience and willingness to take the time and pay the price for beauty in the countryside and high standards of aesthetic values in design and construction.

I have observed this trend in the construction of government buildings, in the construction and design of homes, in the construction and design of libraries and university buildings, or our highways, airports, transmission lines, and all the rest. As a nation we are not beauty-conscious.

If we are to accomplish real substantive beneficial environmental impact in the area of aesthetics, I don't believe we should look primarily to government for leadership. For help, yes. But not for the genesis of those programs that will have major impact.

Here we must look to the cultural leadership of our society—to civic groups, to universities, and to the professions.

Ugliness should be a challenge to us all. Beauty is a reward worth arduous struggle. . . .

The sources of the energy we are presently using are limited. We are leaning heavily on the convenience fuels, such as oil and gas. We no longer can consider ourselves self-sufficient as far as oil is concerned.

This means that we have to look closely at our uses for energy and at our sources for fuels. In the offing is the breeder reactor, which may be a great boon to the very last years of this century and early in the next. We must look toward the technology for the use of solar energy. We must look toward an easier way to extract and a more convenient way to use the vast resources of coal with which we are blessed.

Here I believe we have to depend on government for leadership, for initiative, and for control. This does not mean that the private sector will not be the innovators of the new technology, for they will. This does not mean that government has a responsibility to work with industry and with the scientist and with the planner to assure successive generations adequate energy. It means our government must develop a national energy policy which will take into account our future needs, not just our day-to-day needs. . . .

Your generation—the most educated, talented, and gifted generation this nation has ever seen—can lead the way. You have the most to offer and the most to gain. Together we must commit ourselves to change. It will take your entire lifetime and billions of dollars, but it will be worth every minute and every dollar. For all of us, our national commitment as we lead our daily lives, must be to make every day—Earth Day.

For Further Reading

In studying the problems confronting the cities of America the student might begin by consulting the following general works: Charles Abrams, *The City Is the Frontier** (1965); Edward C. Banfield, *The Unheavenly City** (1970); Charles N. Glaab and A. Theodore Brown, *A History of Urban America* (1967); Jean Gottman, *Megalopolis* (1961); Jane Jacobs, *The Death and Life of Great American Cities** (1962); J. R. Lowe, *Cities in a Race with Time* (1967); Blake McKelvey, *The Emergence of Metropolitan America* (1968);

*Paperbound edition available.

Lewis Mumford, *The City in History* (1961); and Robert C. Weaver, *The Urban Complex** (1964).

Books concerned with the problems of the poor in the city include John C. Donovan, *The Politics of Poverty** (1967); Michael Harrington, *The Other America** (1962); and Nathan Glazer and Daniel Moynihan, *Beyond the Melting Pot: The Negroes, Puerto Ricans, Jews, Italians, and Irish of New York City* (1963).

Studies on the environmental problems found in America are Robert M. Chute's *Environmental Insight** (1971), Clark C. Havighurst's *Air Pollution Control* (1969), George Laycock's *The Diligent Destroyers* (1970), Harvey S. Perloff's *The Quality of the Urban Environment* (1969), Paul Ehrlich's *The Population Bomb** (1968) and *How To Be a Survivor** (1971), and Rachel Carson's *The Silent Spring* (1964).

A problems book on the condition of American cities is Robert L. Branyan and Lawrence H. Larsen's *Urban Crisis in Modern America** (1971). Collected readings include Jeffrey Hadden, Louis Masotti, and Calvin Larson, *Metropolis in Crisis* (1967); Irwin Isenberg, *The City in Crisis* (1968); and James Wilson, *The Metropolitan Enigma/Inquiries Into the Nature and Dimensions of America's "Urban Crisis"* (1968).

*Paperbound edition available.

72 73 74 10 9 8 7 6 5 4 3 2 1